SOUTH AFRICA:
SOCIOLOGICAL ANALYSES

SOUTH AFRICA: SOCIOLOGICAL ANALYSES

Edited by

A. PAUL HARE

GERD WIENDIECK

MAX H. VON BROEMBSEN

1979

OXFORD UNIVERSITY PRESS

CAPE TOWN

Oxford University Press

OXFORD LONDON GLASGOW
NEW YORK TORONTO MELBOURNE WELLINGTON
NAIROBI DAR ES SALAAM CAPE TOWN
KUALA LUMPUR SINGAPORE JAKARTA HONG KONG TOKYO
DELHI BOMBAY CALCUTTA MADRAS KARACHI

ISBN 0 19 570119 4

The Editors gratefully acknowledge the financial assistance of the University of Cape Town towards the publication costs of this book. Opinions expressed are those of the authors concerned and should not be attributed to the sponsor.

Set in 10 on 12 pt Times
Printed in South Africa by Citadel Press, Lansdowne, Cape
Published by Oxford University Press, Harrington House,
Barrack Street, Cape Town 8001, South Africa

Contents

Preface 7

PART 1: THEORETICAL PERSPECTIVES
Introduction – *Drew Archibald* 13
1. Introduction to Parsonian theory – *Andrew Effrat* 18
2. Marxism: Science or revolution? – *Lucio Colletti* 27
3. Toward a sociology of the absurd – *Stanford Lyman and Marvin B. Scott* 34

PART 2: CULTURE
Introduction – *Lawrence Schlemmer* 45
1. The Development of the Afrikaner's self-concept – *Hermann Giliomee* 58
2. Magic, sorcery and football among urban Zulu:A case of reinterpretation under acculturation – *Norman A. Scotch* 67
3. The rise of Black Consciousness in South Africa – *Heribert Adam* 72

PART 3: THE SOCIOLOGY OF RELIGION
Introduction – *Kenneth C. Jubber* 79
1. Religion and political involvement: A study of Black African sects – *Robert J. Janosik* 86
2. The relationship between the dogmatic teachings and attitudes towards race relations of two South African religious denominations – *Robert P. D. Buis* 99
3. A sociological perspective on religious reality – *Kenneth C. Jubber* 113

PART 4: THE FAMILY
Introduction – *Beryl Unterhalter* 123
1. Portrait of Indian South Africans – *Fatima Meer* 134
2. Impact of the city – *Allie A. Dubb* 145
3. Marriage and family life – *Marianne Brindley* 152

PART 5: EDUCATION
Introduction – *Gerd Wiendieck* 163
The dilemma of education in plural societies: The South African case – *H. F. Dickie-Clark* 168

PART 6: ECONOMY AND LABOUR
Introduction – *S. P. Cilliers* 181
1. White and Black labour relations in historical perspective – *Christopher Orpen* 188
2. Economic perspective on organised labour and socio-economic development – *Charles R. Diamond* 200

3. Industrial progress: Its social, political and economic implications – *S. P. Cilliers* 209

PART 7: LAW AND CRIME
Introduction – *Roland Graser* 221
1. Law and criminal procedure in South Africa – *Ellison Kahn* 230
2. The reformation of the South African penal system: Some possibilities – *Roland Graser* 241
3. Crime in the Coloured community – *S. P. Cilliers* 261

PART 8: SOCIAL STRATIFICATION, COLOUR AND SOUTH AFRICA: AN OVERVIEW
Introduction – *Michael Savage* 271
1. Perverse growth and income distribution in South Africa – *Sean Archer* 279
2. The emergent African middle class – *Nimrod Mkele* 285
3. Class, status and ethnicity as perceived by Johannesburg Africans – *Philip Mayer* 293
4. South African society in comparative perspective – *John Rex* 304

PART 9: POLITICAL SOCIOLOGY
Introduction – *Simon Bekker* 315
1. Decolonising South Africa – *Heribert Adam* 321
2. Democratic alternatives to the 'Westminster' model – *André du Toit* 329
3. Politics and privilege in South Africa – *F. van Zyl Slabbert* 340

PART 10: SOCIAL STRUCTURE AND SOCIAL CHANGE
Introduction – *Jonathan Wacks* 349
1. White prosperity and White supremacy in South Africa today – *Frederick A. Johnstone* 356
2. The abolition of the Masters and Servants Act – *Colin Bundy* 373

PART 11: RESEARCH: PROBLEMS AND OPPORTUNITIES
Introduction – *M. H. von Broembsen* 383
1. Social research in a divided society: The case of South Africa – *David Welsh* 385
2. Some problems in race relations research in South Africa – *Henry Lever* 399

Acknowledgements 417

Subject Index 419

Author Index 425

Preface

In this text we provide an overview of the various aspects of South African society together with selected readings to illustrate some of the patterns of social behaviour in more detail. In each of the eleven parts of the book you will find that the authors approach their analyses from various theoretical perspectives. In some cases the theoretical perspective will be explicit but in most cases it will be implicit. Taken together they represent some of the variations within the discipline of sociology. The sociologist is concerned with those aspects of human behaviour that follow from the fact that man lives in groups all his life. Some of these groups are small face-to-face groups such as a family, a small industrial work group, a riot squad, or a legislative committee. Some of the groups are of intermediate size, such as the inhabitants of a village, the members of a manufacturing firm, a national police force, or the members of the national legislature. The largest groups that tend to share common values, a common economic system, common laws, and a common political system, are the nation-states. In this text we focus on one of these nation-states, South Africa, that in common with many nation-states, presents a mixed picture of uniformity and diversity.

Although there is perhaps as much diversity as uniformity among sociologists in their analytical perspectives, some schools of thought are more prominent than others. Some of these schools are introduced in the first section of the book, on theoretical perspectives. Whatever their theoretical differences sociologists tend to share a common sociological consciousness. That is, they address themselves to the same sorts of issues and share a common understanding of themselves in relationship to the societies they study. Abraham (1973), following a British tradition, sees sociology as a science that is applied to the study of society. However, he also sees sociology as one of the humanities since it helps man understand himself in relation to society.

For Berger (1966), representing an American tradition, sociology is a form of consciousness that looks at the same phenomena as the other social sciences (namely economics, political science, psychology, anthropology, and history) but in a different way. The sociologist is one who looks behind the scenes. As he passes a house on the street he wonders what goes on inside the house as well as what goes on outside it. He is interested in aspects of society that are not ordinarily considered respectable. He takes a relative view of social behaviour, noting that a problem for one part of a social system may be a solution for another. He is cosmopolitan in that he is not caught up in the society around him, but takes a distant, and sometimes dim, view of the social behaviour of his fellow man.

Mills (1970), another American, observes that people in the present day often feel trapped in society. If they can acquire a sociological imagination he feels that they can obtain a grasp of history and of the place of their own individual biography in that history. They can come to understand the 'troubles' of the individual in the context of the 'public issues' of the social structure. Mills concludes that there are three tendencies within sociology. The first is to develop a theory of history. The second is to provide a systematic 'grand theory' to explain the nature of man in society. The third is to carry out empirical studies of contemporary social facts and problems. Each of these tendencies can be observed within the present volume.

Although an overview of the basic concepts and generalizations concerning each aspect of a society is given in each of the introductions to the sections of this text, we have not attempted to reproduce the systematic presentation of sociological concepts that one would find in the typical introductory text. We have chosen instead to emphasize the application of these concepts to South African material since the typical text that is written in America or Britain leaves the reader interested in South African society with the task of making his own application. As an example of an introductory text in the British tradition we recommend Bottomore (1972). An example of a popular American introductory text is Broom and Selznick (1975). The text by Park and Burgess (third edition, 1969) is of interest since the first edition in 1921 was one of the first textbooks in sociology. A comparison of the first edition with current texts will indicate how the science of sociology has expanded and changed over the years. Additional examples of current sociological perspectives can be found in the texts of Chinoy (1963), Cilliers and Joubert (1966), Horton and Hunt (1964), Rose (1970) and Wrong and Gracey (1967). For those who are interested in a further discussion of the nature and scope of sociology, the following references should be helpful: Friedrichs (1970), Gouldner (1971), Inkeles (1964), and Reiss (1968).

Following the first section of the text on *theoretical perspectives*, the sections of the text are presented in the approximate order that one would consider them in developing a new small group or in bringing about change in an existing society. First one considers the extent to which values concerning the basic purpose of the group and the obligations of group members are shared by the members of the group. These values are represented in general by the *culture* of the group and more specifically by *religion*. Next we look at the *family*, the principal agent for the transmission of values to new members of the society, and indeed for the creation of new members. As the child grows older, *education* shares with the family the task of providing the experience necessary for the child to eventually play an adult role in society. Once the new members of the society are ready to take their places, we turn to the area of *economy and labour* to discover how the society will provide the resources necessary for goal-attainment. Once resources are assured, we turn next to a consideration of the roles that the various members of society will play and the ways in which conflicts will be managed. Some aspects of conflict and conflict management are treated in the section on *law and crime*. The section on *stratification, class and colour*, indicates two of the ways in which roles may be allocated, on the bases of social class and colour. The section on *political sociology* includes a discussion of aspects of the political control that is necessary in a society in order to provide specific direction and goal definition by means of which solutions are found to problems that are relevant to the groups' goals. The political activity provides the coordination and leadership so that the resources available to the society can be combined with the roles played by the members, to achieve the ultimate values that form the basis of the culture. Since small groups and whole societies are continually changing, the tenth section of the text on *social structure and social change* covers some of the problems and processes of social change, especially as they have influenced the social structure of South Africa. The final section on *research and methodology* is included to give an indication of some of the problems and opportunities for research in South Africa. This section can provide some understanding of the problems faced by the social scientists who carried out the research that appears in this volume, and hopefully will encourage others to continue the work of gathering basic data about our society, which can form the basis for future analyses.

A. PAUL HARE
GERD WIENDIECK
MAX VON BROEMBSEN

REFERENCES

Abraham, J. H. 1973 – *Origins and Growth of Sociology*. Harmondsworth: Penguin.

Berger, Peter L. 1966 – *Invitation to Sociology*. Harmondsworth: Penguin.

Bottomore, T. B. 1972 – *Sociology: A Guide to Problems and Literature*. London: George Allen & Unwin, rev. edn.

Broom, Leonard and Philip Selznick 1975 – *Essentials of Sociology*. New York: Harper & Row.

Chinoy, Ely 1963 – *Society: An Introduction to Sociology*. New York: Random House.

Cilliers, S. P. and D. D. Joubert 1966 – *Sosiologie: 'n Sistematiese Inleiding*. Stellenbosch: Kosmo-Uitgewery.

Friedrichs, Robert W. 1970 – *A Sociology of Sociology*. New York: Free Press and London: Collier-Macmillan.

Gouldner, Alvin W. 1971 – *The Coming Crisis of Western Sociology*. London: Heinemann.

Horton, Paul B. and Chester L. Hunt 1964 – *Sociology*. New York: McGraw-Hill.

Inkeles, Alex 1964 – *What is Sociology? An Introduction to the Discipline and Profession*. Englewood Cliffs: Prentice-Hall.

Mills, C. Wright 1970 – *The Sociological Imagination*. Harmondsworth: Penguin.

Park, Robert E. and Ernest W. Burgess 1969 – *Introduction to the Science of Sociology*. Chicago: University of Chicago Press, 3rd rev. edn.

Reiss, Jr., Albert J. 1968 – 'Sociology: The field.' In David L. Sills (ed.) *International Encyclopedia of the Social Sciences*. Vol. 15, 1–23, New York: Macmillan and Free Press.

Rose, Peter I. (ed.) 1970 – *The Study of Society: An Integrated Anthology*. New York: Random House.

Wrong, Dennis H. and Harry L. Gracey (eds.) 1967 – *Readings in Introductory Sociology*. New York: Macmillan.

Part 1:

Theoretical Perspectives

Introduction

DREW ARCHIBALD

The nature of sociological theory is in dispute, and the readings that follow discuss or illustrate three very different kinds of theorizing in sociology today. There are, however, some things we can say that apply to all of them. Theory alters or develops our concepts and thereby changes the way we view and talk about the world. In fact it changes the world, or what the world is for us – and is there any difference between these two?

In sociology we confront the human condition, and the most important characteristic of this condition is that it *changes*. The task of sociological theory is to seek answers to the question 'Where are we and where are we going?' In my own view the best answers to date are those of the classical theorists Marx, Weber and Durkheim, and the three tendencies, schools, or perspectives illustrated in the readings are contemporary stepchildren of these three theorists; but you must make up your own minds about this.

According to the literary critic Leavis (1962:10), major novelists and poets are significant in terms of the human awareness they promote: 'awareness of the possibilities of life'. Writers who celebrate human possibility and social theorists who try to define it are doing much the same thing. We find Shelley (1948:53), claiming for poetry the modest role of 'The most unfailing herald, companion, and follower of the awakening of a great people to work a beneficial change in opinion or institution'.

I hope you will find something to stimulate your interest in the three readings that follow (or in this introduction). I cannot pretend that theory is always easy. However, most of the best of it is comprehensible to anyone with a little patience and a knowledge of the language in which it is presented (whether verbally or in print). Take the difficult parts in small doses. Come back to them after a walk or a night's sleep. Remember always that theory exists for you, not you for it, and that the duty of every speaker and especially of every writer is to suffer on your behalf in order to make his meaning as clear as possible. If after repeated efforts a passage fails to yield *any* sense the fault is more likely to be the author's than yours.

The rest of this introduction consists of a paragraph on what to read, a section on the problem of objectivity and a final section in which I allow free rein to my enthusiasm on the relationship between theory and social change, emphasizing the difficult concept 'possibility'.

What to read

Giddens (1971) is an excellent survey of the classics, despite the word 'modern' in the title; another is Aron (1965;1967). For more detail, go to Sorokin (1964). Note that 'contemporary' in this title means 1928. Every book or article you consult will lead you to many others. Two good surveys of the contemporary scene are Mennell (1974) and Zeitlin (1973).

Facts, values and objectivity

The problem of objectivity is of central importance in sociological theory and in sociology as a whole. Consider it first as it affects journalists and historians. Does a newspaper reporter 'record' or 'evaluate' events? The great editor of the *Guardian*, C. P. Scott, (1926) laid down the following rule for his profession: 'Comment is free but facts are sacred.' Commendable, no doubt; however, most thinking journalists today at least would regard as naive the implicit assumption that 'facts' can be separated from opinion, or reporting from interpretation.

The historian, like all social scientists, is also in large measure a 'reporter'. E. H. Carr (1964:21) concludes that the historian should see his main work as 'not to record but to evaluate; for, if he does not evaluate, how can he know what is worth recording?' This puts it in a nutshell. Cognition – knowing, thinking, remembering, observing – is always selective, and selection is evaluative in that it allocates priority of attention or focus.

It goes without saying that facts must be respected, but they must also be selected and ordered. They don't become facts before we look for them, or as phenomenologists might say, before we 'intend' them. Consider them as 'answers'; we must raise questions before we can get answers. Experience is an active, *selective* (discriminatory) and thus evaluative process governed by theory, that is, concepts. A railway engineer and an artist see a range of mountains differently; they see *different* ranges of mountains. Similarly a Black and a White live in different South Africas, and I live in a world different from yours, and even from my brother's. There's no viewing except from viewpoints and there's nobody here but us individuals, each with his or her unique viewpoint.

Perception and statements reporting perception always presuppose a category system or conceptual scheme. No fact is conceivable outside such a framework. Parsons (1949:41) defines a fact as an empirically verifiable statement about phenomena 'in terms of a conceptual scheme.' (Note that 'fact' is itself a concept.)

The view has recently gained ground that a fully 'value-free' social science is not attainable, and that the investigator's bias is better declared – so that its influence can be allowed for – rather than be left unstated. (Unconscious bias may only be visible to others, or may escape detection altogether.) Myrdal (1962:1064) in particular, regarding a 'disinterested social science' as impossible, advocates a methodology based on explicit value premises.

The experienced universe varies from observer to observer; reality may be conceptually dissected in many different ways, and category systems determine what an observer finds significant and even what he 'sees'. Evaluation is implicit in any conceptual scheme in terms of which facts are perceived, selected and arranged. The facts in turn influence the conceptual scheme. The processes of description and evaluation are interdependent; facts and 'interpretation' interact. Many continue to believe that it is possible to observe the world 'objectively', meaning without preconceptions, judgement or bias.

Pareto begins his well-known analysis of human conduct:

> We have no pre-conceptions, no *a priori* notions. We find certain facts before us. We describe them, classify them, determine their character . . . (1963: Para. 145, footnotes to paras. 171, 172).

It is not so simple. We do not 'find facts before us': all perception is selective. All description and classification presupposes category systems. In his next paragraph, Pareto introduces a criterion for the classification of conduct, namely its degree of correspondence with 'logico-experimental theories' (1963: para. 146). The following paragraph begins: 'Let us accordingly examine actions from the standpoint of their logico-experimental character' (1963: para. 147). The interaction of observer and observed, of facts and interpretation, is already in play.

Theory and social change: activism

Concepts change society and are in turn changed by its change. Theory transcends Marcuse's (1964) 'established universe of discourse and action.'

The history of Western thought can be viewed as the progressive weakening of the concept 'fate'. We may extrapolate here strong tendencies of long standing.

> Greek philosophy, like Greek Tragedy . . . is a struggle against fate . . . every step forward in knowledge has an exorcising effect. Knowledge restricts the power of fate, it deprives things of their frightful mystery, it makes them into mere things and subjects them to the control of the mind. In a titanic assault, carried through with great courage and brilliant clarity, Greek philosophy assails the mystery of fate and reveals it step by step with admirable power (Tillich 1955:6).

Static societies breed fatalism, and fatalism breeds static societies. No society is of course entirely static (in total stasis), but some approach it. A preliminary definition of fatalism might be: 'a belief, often implicit, that an existing order possesses necessity or essential validity'. 'Activism' is the absence of such a belief. By 'existing order' is meant for the moment primarily a social order, with emphasis on its normative aspect: values and rules of conduct.

I would suggest that a widening awareness of alternative possibilities, both individual and social, facilitates a view of social reality as contingent, i.e. as lacking necessity or 'essential validity'. A view of social reality as contingent seems to be a prerequisite of activism. As Myrdal (1962:520) expresses it: 'Man is a free agent, and there are no inevitabilities . . . History can be made. It is not necessary to receive it as mere destiny.' This conviction (that reality lacks inevitability) is likely to be associated with the belief that individual and social reality can be reshaped by conscious and purposeful action.

Fatalism is a rational attitude when the possibility of change is remote: change and the belief in its possibility are cumulatively interdependent.

Widened scientific understanding of the parameters of human life tends to reinforce a view of society as process. Change is the lesson of evolution; at a single stroke Darwin gave perspective to our situation, reinforced the growing conviction that social reality, and in particular the normative order, possesses no kind of inevitability, and taught the momentous fact and possibility of change. It makes reality no less dreadful, but relieves rational man of the crushing consciousness of its necessity.

Fatalism is an attitude of passive acceptance towards reality, both natural and social. It is strong in static or nearly static societies and also in some groups in industrial society. It accepts the inevitability of 'the way things are'. Perhaps indeed the word 'acceptance' has too active a flavour: reality is unquestioned; the question of its inevitability does not even arise. There is a lack of understanding of society as process and of the forces at work within it.

The fatalist tends to see transient states as immutable, and to have an undue respect for the way things turn out: for the momentary winner in political conflict or athletic contests or games of chance. In extreme forms fatalism seeks to propitiate the personified forces of destiny, thus reinforcing simultaneously a feeling of helplessness and a tendency to evade responsibility.

Success or failure in human action depends partly on factors beyond the actor's control. Let us define as the 'correct' course of action that which, given the actor's aggregate knowledge, appears most likely to achieve the desired end. Having done the 'correct' thing, it is irrational to repudiate it should it fail. In the opposite situation, that is, when success is achieved despite 'incorrect' action, it is equally irrational to echo the popular saying 'All's well that ends well'. Both these reactions exemplify fatalism in that they attach undue significance to chance outcomes. All is not well that ends well: it could have ended otherwise. The activist, on the other hand, 'entertains' alternatives – in this case alternative outcomes, positive or negative. Succeeding, he is nonetheless aware of the possibility that he might have failed; failing, he is aware of the possibility that he might have succeeded. For him, the real does not obscure the possible.

In activism there is a consciousness of potentiality (alternatives, possibilities) as well as of actuality. There is an awareness of the discrepancy between the real and the possible in the political sphere and everywhere else in life. Alternatives are entertained: the established universe of discourse is transcended. Recognition of reality as contingent – as a 'chance outcome' – strongly motivates the exploration of alternatives and is likely to be accompanied by a realization of the causal efficacy and historical significance of conceptual innovation, that is, theory. Static societies are characterized by conceptual poverty and rigidity.

Activism views both social and individual reality as contingent upon each other, and assumes in consequence that there is no predetermined form for society and no fixed 'innate' human nature, and that received knowledge and values do not exhaust the possibilities. Most important, it is convinced of the corrigibility (alterability) of individual and social reality. One's own weaknesses lose inevitability claims; they may persist, but they too lack the crushing authority of inevitability.

> It is never too late to give up our prejudices. No way of thinking or doing, however ancient, can be trusted without proof . . . What old people say you cannot do, you try and find that you can . . . man's capacities have never been measured; nor are we to judge of what he can do by any precedents, so little has been tried (Thoreau 1937:8–9).

The first selection in this part, by Effrat, reviews functionalism, an approach that at least until recently, dominated theoretical sociology in the United States. The review gives a good overall account of what it is that Lyman and Scott (for example) are reacting against. Central concepts for functionalists are socialization, institution, system. Colletti briefly but clearly puts the position that the scientific and political roles of theory are inseparable for a Marxist, and Lyman and Scott propose an existential phenomenology, claiming affinity with, among contemporaries, Goffman's dramaturgical approach and Garfinkel's ethnomethodology.

REFERENCES

Aron, Raymond 1965, 1967 – *Main Currents in Sociological Thought*. Harmondsworth: Penguin.

Carr, E. H. 1964 – *What is History?* Harmondsworth: Penguin.

Giddens, Anthony 1971 – *Capitalism and Modern Social Theory*. Cambridge: Cambridge University Press.

Leavis, F. R. 1962 – *The Great Tradition*. Harmondsworth: Penguin.

Marcuse, H. 1964 – *One-dimensional Man*. London: Routledge & Kegan Paul.

Mennell, Stephen 1974 – *Sociological Theory : Uses and Unities*. London: Thomas Nelson and Sons.

Myrdal, G. 1962 – *An American Dilemma*. New York: Harper & Row.

Pareto, V. 1963 – *The Mind and Society*. New York: Dover.

Parsons, T. 1949 – *The Structure of Social Action*. New York: Free Press.

Scott, C. P. 1926 – *Manchester Guardian*. May 6.

Shelley, P. B. 1948 – *A Defence of Poetry*. London: Porcupine Press.

Sorokin, P. A. 1964 – *Contemporary Sociological Theories*. New York: Harper and Row.

Thoreau, H. D. 1937 – *Walden*. New York: Random House.

Tillich, P. 1955 – *The Protestant Era*. London: Nisbet.

Zeitlin, Irving M. 1973 – *Rethinking Sociology*. Englewood Cliffs: Prentice-Hall.

1. Introduction to Parsonian Theory

ANDREW EFFRAT

(This summary of Parsonian theory first appeared as the introduction to a special issue of *Sociological Inquiry*, Volume 38, Number 2, published in the Spring of 1968 with a collection of articles on 'Applications of Parsonian Theory'. Most of the references to the articles included in the special issue have been deleted.)

Both critics and admirers of Parsons' work might claim that the cover of this issue aptly symbolizes the present state of Parsonian[1] or Action Theory. The former would no doubt point to the apparently incoherent maze of words, the lack of careful theoretical synthesis, and the Germanic passion for schematization. Those more sympathetic would emphasize, among other things, the broad range and richness of Parsons' work,[2] the ambitious effort to be *analytically* powerful and systematic, and the extent to which his theories have evolved during the past twenty years.

The cover also represents several of the principal elements that have been central in Parsons' thinking and that are included in a variety of ways in this issue. Five major themes might be pointed to by way of a preview and summary (a sixth, concerning change, will be noted later).

(1) *The Pattern Variables* first emerged in 1939 in an essay attempting to show the significance for a person's actions of role prescriptions and the institutional framework as distinct from individual motivation (Parsons 1954:34–49).[3] They were developed further in *Toward A General Theory of Action* (Parsons and Shils 1951:76–91) and *The Social System* (Parsons 1951:46–67) and were most recently revised and articulated with other aspects of his theoretical system in 1958 (Parsons 1960). The four pattern variables form two sets: the modalities of objects set – particularism-universalism and quality-performance – and the orientations to objects set – affectivity-neutrality and diffuseness-specificity. They may be seen as identifying some of the most important substantive dimensions in terms of which Parsons has characterized alternative patterns of individual choices, social relationships, and normative structures. They are also possibly the aspects of Parsonian theory with which non-Parsonians feel most comfortable and which have been most extensively used by sociologists other than Parsons.[4]

(2) *The AGIL or Four-Functions Scheme* first appeared in *Working Papers in the Theory of Action* (Parsons, Bales and Shils 1953:63–109 and 163–269), and has since gone through several versions, with the best recent summary being in *Theories of Society* (Parsons *et al.* 1961:30–79). To an important extent, the four categories of the AGIL scheme – adaptation, goal-attainment, integration, and latent pattern-maintenance and tension-management (usually, simply pattern-

maintenance) – were derived empirically from, principally, an analysis of small groups, psychotherapy, and the economic factors of production. More formally, however, they may be derived from cross-cutting two major continua of problems confronting any goal-directed action system. The first continuum concerns whether the problem is primarily *internal* to the system in question or primarily *external*. Thus, structures or processes would be classified on the basis of whether they were primarily oriented towards or specialized with respect to the former or the latter sets of problems. The second continuum concerns whether the structures or processes are primarily oriented towards *instrumental* activities or problems (such as developing, gathering, preparing or generalizing means or facilities) or towards *consummatory* ones (such as, using, applying or consuming the resources). This yields the following 2 × 2 table:

	Action direction	
	Instrumental	Consummatory
External	Adaptation	Goal-attainment
Internal	Pattern-maintenance	Integration

TABLE 1 PARADIGM OF FUNCTIONAL PROBLEMS

Thus, to quote Parsons:

> 'This paradigm analyzes *any* action *system* in terms of the following four functional categories: (1) that concerned with the maintenance of the highest "governing" or controlling patterns of the system; (2) the internal integration of the system; (3) its orientation to the attainment of goals in relation to its environment; (4) its more generalized adaptation to the broad conditions of the environment' (Parsons 1966:7).

In many respects, this scheme is the most central aspect and general framework of contemporary Parsonian theory. Increasingly, it has served as the principal conceptual structure in terms of which his and his students' work is organized. Further, in the context and development of structural-functional analysis, the AGIL scheme represented an important development. As opposed to the long lists of functional requisites that became current in the early fifties,[5] Parsons offered a set which sought to be systematic, logically exhaustive, analytically distinct, and clear about the distinctions among levels of generality of various social and psychological systems. Also, and perhaps more importantly, he sought to provide a frame of reference in terms of which a variety of different levels of organization would be comparable. Hence, in terms of this framework general similarities among cultural, social, and personality systems might become more apparent and more general theories of their structure and functioning might be formulated.

The AGIL scheme has already been applied in a number of different ways. In terms of it, Parsons has analyzed small group structure and phase movements, formal organizations, the nature and utilization of power and influence, etc. (Parsons, Bales and Shils, 1953; Parsons and Bales 1955; Parsons 1956, 1963a and 1963b). Some of the more notable applications by others are Bellah's *Tokugawa Religion* (1957), and Smelser's *Social Change in the Industrial Revolution* (1959) and his *Theory of Collective Behaviour* (Smelser 1963).[6]

(3) *The Classification of the Four Sub-systems of Action* which consists of the cultural, social, personality, and organismic levels. Although this classification is formally an application of the AGIL scheme, its development has been sufficiently distinct to be noted separately. These four levels may be seen as the four principal systems or structures of which Parsons has analyzed the processes and functional problems. He has also articulated this set with the AGIL scheme, suggesting that, for the total action system, the cultural system provides the structural anchorage – the symbolic patterns to be maintained, the organismic system provides the diffuse energy which serves as resources for action, the personality system serves as the locus of satisfaction, and the social system serves as the focus of the integration of these components in harmonious interaction. While Parsons has written extensive analyses of the cultural, social and personality levels, he has not yet done so for the organismic.[7]

(4) *The Cybernetic Hierarchy of Control* is an important way of looking at the relationships both among the functional problems and among the structural levels of an action system. Essentially, this perspective emphasizes the importance of highly generalized normative elements as the informational components that guide and control the energy components or more specific aspects of action. Thus, latent pattern-maintenance occupies the peak of the functional hierarchy as does culture of the structural set. This notion of the hierarchy of control has perhaps been most extensively and interestingly employed by Smelser in his discussion of the types and components of collective behaviour (Smelser 1963)[8].

(5) *The Generalized Media of Exchange or Interaction* have occupied much of Parsons' attention recently, although his interest could be traced back at least to *Economy and Society* (Parsons and Smelser 1956). He has written extensively on language, money, power, and influence, analyzing their nature, how they operate in social systems, some important requisites of their adequate functioning, etc.[9] Parsons' considerations on these media can be seen as some of the most important points of articulation between his work and that of Homans.[10] Both have been concerned with the importance of positive and negative sanctions in promoting compliance and learning. However, Parsons, to a much greater extent than Homans, has sought to distinguish among types and levels of generality of media, to map their operation in differentiated 'markets' and their circulation in society, and, perhaps most importantly,[11] to indicate the institutional framework which is essential for their operation.

One might see Parsons' analysis of the media as the fourth and most recent of the major phases through which his work has developed. To an important extent, the first phase, represented by *The Structure of Social Action* in 1937, involved a focus on the individual and the particular act. Although there were many institutional or macro-social elements in his analysis, the emphasis seems to have been on understanding the *units* of the system – especially how they made decisions or voluntary acts to attain goals, cooperate with others, etc. In effect, one might see this work as the effort of someone who was still very much an economist trying to develop ways of understanding individual decision processes which were not as atomistic and rationalistic as some schools of economic and sociological analysis nor as purely institutional as others. The second phase, which seemed to culminate in *The Social System* in 1951, involved an effort to develop a more patterned scheme for articulating individuals with each other and with institutions. Here the concept of role, types of role, and various patterns of interaction were central. If the first phase was a more psychological one (though a very sociologistic psychology, to be sure) the second might be seen as a more social psychological one. The AGIL scheme, then, can be seen as a breakthrough to a new level of far more 'systemic' conceptualization. The internal structures and functions characterizing the various systems and subsystems are more carefully spelled out in this phase of his work. Further, the social system level and the articulation of social institutions is more carefully delineated and more clearly conceptualized as a system autonomous from, though interpenetrating and interchanging with, culture and personality systems. Thus, a more purely sociologistic level can be said to have crystallized. Parsons' more recent work on the media of interchange and sanctions can perhaps be seen as an integration (but also partial reworking) of all these earlier emphases. That is, his analyses of sanctions and, more generally, of the interchanges among subsystems in which they are involved, seeks to specify how structures inter-relate, how systemic and subsystemic functions are fulfilled, and how processes are controlled by inputs and outputs of demands, resources, and rewards or punishments. Thus, this aspect of his work goes a long way towards articulating more carefully the various levels which Parsons has distinguished over the years.[12]

Parsons' own contribution in this issue was in direct response to a request to 'round out' the scheme by dealing with 'commitments' which is the medium presumably distinctive of the pattern-maintenance sector at the social system level (as money, power, and influence are characteristic of the adaptive, goal-attainment, and integrative sectors, respectively).

To summarize the preceding: much of Parsons' work can be seen as concerned with (1) the principal *structures* or relatively stable components of human action – particularly the four system levels (cultural, social, personality, and organismic) – and sub-structures, especially within the social system – economic, political, legal, familial, and religious – as well as with (2) their principal *functional requisites* – adaptation, goal-attainment, integration, and latent pattern-maintenance and tension-management – problems which must be solved if these structures or substructures are to operate adequately. Within both these sets, Parsons is concerned (a) with the patterns of regulation which characterize and are necessary for their operation (the hierarchy of control), (b) with the mechanisms of exerting control, of affecting others' actions, or simply of communicating (the media of exchange), and (c) with the patterns of alternative choice or operation which can characterize the structures (principally, the pattern variables).

The following table might serve as a very simplified schematic summary of some of the relationships among these categories:

	Instrumental	Consummatory
External	(1) Adaptation (2) Organismic Level (3) Money (4) Universalism, performance, neutrality, specificity	(1) Goal-attainment (2) Personality Level (3) Power (4) Particularism, performance, affectivity, specificity
Internal	(1) Pattern-maintenance (2) Cultural level (3) Commitments (4) Universalism, quality, neutrality, diffuseness	(1) Integration (2) Social system level (3) Influence (4) Particularism, quality, affectivity, diffuseness

Key: (1) the functional problem
(2) the subsystem of the total action system which is classified in this functional sector
(3) the generalized medium at the social system level classified in this sector
(4) the set of pattern variables which characterize the functional sector

Note: The hierarchy of control runs counter-clockwise from pattern-maintenance to adaptation.

This issue should also help dispel some of the criticisms of Parsonian theory which one encounters quite frequently. One is that 'There's no *action* in Action Theory.' This is based partly on a mistaken notion of the meaning of the term 'action'. Parsons employs 'action' to emphasize, with Weber, the importance of 'subjectively meaningful' aspects of activity.[13] The contrasting term is 'behavior' – activity which is not symbolically oriented or governed, such as a reflex. Thus, 'action' includes thinking, feeling, perceiving, orienting, etc., as well as overt activity. However, this criticism is often also meant to imply that Parsonian theory cannot deal with or has not dealt with dynamics or change. I would suggest that Parsonian theory can deal with change in a number of ways:

for example, the value patterns themselves can define change in general or changes of specific sorts as desirable (Parsons has brought this out in his analysis of the American emphasis on 'instrumental activism');[14] the AGIL scheme can be employed to describe and suggest stages of change (as they have been in analyses of phases of small group development) (Parsons, Bales and Shils 1953: ch. 5); inadequate solution of the major functional problems (adaptations, etc.) would also be seen as a major source of change. In addition to the above instances, Parsons has dealt extensively with the sources, patterns and consequences of change, particularly in his more recent work where he has analyzed some of the sources of structural differentiation and some of the conditions necessary for social and cultural evolution or the growth of the adaptive capacity of social systems (Parsons 1961, 1964a, 1966). However, there has never been a period in his work when he was not concerned with change. This can be traced from the very first articles he published on the nature and sources of capitalism through his work on the social conditions promoting fascism, the development of Japan, the phase movements of small groups and families, the broad scale changes leading to McCarthyism, sources of Western institutional development, the requisites and consequences of structural differentiation, changes in American medical organization and education, etc., to his current work on the evolution of societies.[15] It might also be argued that almost all the studies that try to deal with social change in relation to general and systematic analytical theory derive largely from Parsons' work.[16]

A second frequent criticism is that 'There's no *theory* in Action Theory'. This criticism seems unjustified on at least two grounds. First, I think the critics' underlying conception of theory is often rather limited and 'deflationist'. By 'theory', they seem to mean, approximately: a conceivably testable proposition (or set of propositions) stating a relationship between two or more variables. Often it is added that these must function to explain other propositions or observations. I think the bias or limitation of this notion of theory is that it tends to neglect the importance of developing and justifying generalized *frames of reference* at the expense of a concern with the more immediate 'payoffs' of specific propositions or propositional systems. The frame of reference consists in the primitive concepts, definitions, postulates, and assumptions of a theoretical system – most of which are not empirically testable. However, it is in terms of these that any theoretical system is grounded and made meaningful.[17] Much of Parsons' work is focused on developing this level of theory – a consideration which I think is seldom appreciated.

Second, I think these critics overlook much in Parsons' work which even meets their own criteria of theory. For example, one of Parsons' main sets of assertions is that particular structures, such as the economy or polity, are 'located' in particular functional sectors, such as the adaptive or goal-attainment. Critics generally regard this as 'mere classification'. However, a set of propositions are implicitly formulated when this is done: that the economy tends to specialize in performing (and contributing to the solution of) adaptive functions, that the polity tends to focus on goal-attainment functions, etc.; that insofar as these structures do not adequately perform these functions and these functions are not adequately fulfilled, the system shows signs of instability, strain, disruption, etc. The question of how these propositions might be tested – e.g., of what might be the most useful indices of 'adequate' performance and of instability – are problems of operationalization and do not negate the fact that these are propositions. A second major set of propositions concerns differentiation: that differentiation is a major historical trend, that it generally bestows significant new adaptive capacities, that roles and collectivities tend to differentiate in terms of or cluster into subsystems around the four functional dimensions, that with increasing differentiation come increasing problems of integration, that the 'creation' of generalized media of exchange help solve integrative problems, etc. There are only a few of the more general propositions that are themes in Parsons' work but they should suffice in this context.

To see our endeavor here in better perspective, one might relate it to the work of Thomas Kuhn, a historian of science and author of *The Structure of Scientific Revolutions* (Kuhn 1962) – a revolutionary book in its own right. His thesis essentially is that science has proceeded and progressed not by the simple accumulation of data and refinement of theory but rather by more 'qualitative jumps' or revolutions. A revolution essentially is a radical change in the science's existing 'paradigm' or the fundamental framework which suggests and defines the problems which are worth working on and which also indicates some model solutions. In what Kuhn calls the 'normal science' phase of the history of science, there is, by and large, a single generally accepted paradigm (for example, Newtonian mechanics or Ptolemaic astronomy) and most scientific work is oriented to solving problems in terms of this paradigm. In the pre-paradigm phase (in which sociology obviously still is), there are a number of competing schools or paradigms, each struggling to refine themselves and to demonstrate their superiority.

NOTES

1. While I have felt that Parson*s*ian is the more appropriate term (after all, one says Homan*s*ian – that is, of course, *if* one says such things), let it here be recorded that Parsons himself has indicated in a personal communication in response to my inquiry that he has 'a strong aesthetic preference for "Parso*n*ian" rather than "Parson*s*ian".' So be it.
2. In this regard, it is worth pointing out that it would be very difficult to name the subspecialty of sociology for which Parsons has not written an important seminal essay. For the most recent complete bibliography of his published works, see (1967, 539–52) Talcott Parsons *Sociological Theory and Modern Society*, New York: Free Press.
3. The pattern variables are also clearly pre-figured in his analysis of Toennies' notions of *Gemeinschaft* and *Gesellschaft*. See Talcott Parsons, (1937, 686–94) ,*The Structure of Social Action*, New York: McGraw-Hill.
4. For example, see Robert N. Bellah, 1957; *Tokugawa Religion*, Glencoe: Free Press, Lois R. Dean, 'The pattern variables: Some empirical operations,' *Amer. Soc. Rev.*, 26, February 1961, 80–90; Robert Dreeben, 'The Contribution of Schooling to the Learning of Norms,' *Harvard Educational Review*, 37, 1967, 211–237; Everett E. Hagen,

On the Theory of Social Change, Homewood, Ill.: Dorsey Press, 1962; Chalmers Johnson, *Revolutionary Change*, Boston: Little, Brown, 1966, 144–9; Seymour M. Lipset, *The First New Nation*, New York: Basic Books, 1963; Harry A. Scarr, 'Measures of Particularism', *Sociometry*, 27, December 1964, 413–32; and George A. Theodorson, 'Acceptance of Industrialization and its Attendant Consequences for the Social Patterns of Non-Western Societies,' *Amer. Soc. Rev.*, **18**, October 1963 477–84.

5. See, for example, John W. Bennett and Melvin Tumin, *Social Life*, New York: Knopf, 1948, or Marion J. Levy, Jr., *The Structure of Society*, Princeton: Princeton University Press, 1952.
6. Some other applications (which vary in their explicitness and fidelity of usage) include Karl Deutsch, *The Nerves of Government*, New York: Free Press, 1963; Shmuel N. Eisenstadt, *The Political Systems of Empires*, New York: Free Press, 1963; Amitai Etzioni, *Studies in Social Change*, New York: Holt, Rinehart Winston, 1966; William C. Mitchell, *The American Polity*, New York: Free Press, 1962; and James Olds, *The Growth and Structure of Motives*, Glencoe, Ill.: Free Press, 1956.
7. Perhaps his best summary statements are: (1) on the cultural level: Parsons *et al.* (eds.), *Theories of Society*, 963–93; (2) on the social system level: *ibid.*, 30–79; (3) on the personality system level: Talcott Parsons, 'An Approach to Psychological Theory in Terms of the Theory of Action,' in Sigmund Koch (ed.), *Psychology: A Study of A Science*, New York: McGraw-Hill, 1959, 612–711; and (4) on the organismic level: there are brief discussions in the article just cited and in his *Social Structure and Personality*, New York: Free Press, 1964, chapter 5.
8. Also see Robert N. Bellah, 'The Sociology of Religion', in David L. Sills (ed.), *International Encyclopedia of the Social Sciences*, New York: Macmillan, 1968, **13**, 406–14.
9. In addition to the works on power and influence already cited, see his 'Reflections on the Place of Force in Social Process,' 1964.
10. Homans may be seen as the leading representative of the 'social behaviourist' tradition which is generally regarded as rather antithetical to Parsonian theory.
11. Perhaps most importantly because Parsons' emphasis on the institutional framework as well as the broader market system is at or near the heart of the controversy between Parsons and Homans over reductionism. Parsons, in keeping with the Durkheimian tradition, would emphasize aspects of the broader social and cultural context, such as the values and norms governing exchange – in effect, the 'non-exchange aspects of exchange' which could be seen as a generalization of Durkheim's 'non-contractual elements in contract'.
12. I am very indebted to Enno Schwannenberg for ideas in connection with this picture of Parsons' evolution.
13. For example, see Weber's definition of 'action': 'all human behavior when and insofar as the acting individual attaches a subjective meaning to it' (Weber 1947:88).
14. See his *Social Structure and Personality*, chapter 8 and Talcott Parsons and Winston White, *American Society* (manuscript).
15. See his ' "Capitalism" in Recent German Literature: Sombart and Weber' ,*Journal of Political Economy*, **36**, December 1928, 641–61 and **37**, February 1929, 31–51; 'Some Sociological Aspects of the Fascist Movements', *Social Forces*, **21**, 1942, 138–47; 'Population and Social Structure of Japan,' in Douglas Haring (ed.), *Japan's Prospects*, Cambridge: Harvard University Press, 1946; Parsons, Bales, and Shils, op. cit.; Parsons and Bales, op. cit.; 'Social Strains in America,' in Daniel Bell (ed.), *The New American Right*, New York: Criterion Books, 1955; 'Some Reflections on the Institutional Framework of Economic Development'; *The Challenge of Development*, Jerusalem: The Hebrew University, 1958; 'Social Change and Medical Organization in the U.S.', *The Annals*, **346**, March 1963, 21–33; and *The System of Modern Societies*, Englewood-Cliffs, Prentice-Hall, forthcoming.

16. Perhaps the most outstanding examples are the works by Bellah and Smelser already cited. See also Robert N. Bellah, 'Religious Evolution', *Amer. Soc. Rev.*, **29**, June, 1964 358–74 and Marion J. Levy, Jr., *The Family Revolution in Modern China*, Cambridge: Harvard University Press, 1949.
17. For an excellent brief discussion of the nature and functions of frames of reference and their relations to theories, problem solutions, and facts, see Talcott Parsons, 'Introduction to Culture and the Social System,' in Parsons, *et al.*, 1961, 964–5. Also see Neil J. Smelser, 'Sociology and the other Social Sciences.' In Paul F. Lazarsfeld (ed.), *The Uses of Sociology*, New York: Basic Books, 1967.

REFERENCES

Bellah, Robert N. 1957 – *Tokugawa Religion.* Glencoe, Ill.: Free Press.

Kuhn, Thomas 1962 – *The Structure of Scientific Revolutions.* Chicago: University of Chicago Press.

Parsons, Talcott, 1937 – *The Structure of Social Action.* New York: McGraw-Hill.

——1951 – *The Social System.* Glencoe, Ill.: Free Press.

——1954 – 'The professions and social structure.' In Parsons T., *Essays in Sociological Theory*, Glencoe, Free Press.

——1956 – 'A sociological approach to the theory of organizations,' *Administrative Science Quarterly 1:* June,September, 63–85 and 225–39.

——1959 – 'An approach to psychological theory in terms of the Theory of Action.' In Sigmund Koch (ed.) *Psychology: A Study of a Science.* New York: McGraw-Hill.

——1960 – 'The pattern of variables revisited,' *American Sociological Review*, 25, August, 467–83.

——1961 – 'Some considerations on the theory of change,' *Rural Sociology*, 26, September, 219–39.

——1963a – 'On the concept of influence,' *Public Opinion Quarterly*, 27, Spring, 37–62.

——1963b – 'On the concept of political power,' *Proceedings of the American Philosophical Society*, 107, June, 232–62.

——1964a – 'Evolutionary universals in society,' *American Sociological Review* 29, June, 339–57.

——1964b – 'Reflections on the place of force in social process.' In H. Eckstein (ed.) *Internal War.* New York: Free Press.

——1964c – *Social Structure and Personality.* New York: Free Press.

——1966 – *Societies: Evolutionary and Comparative Perspectives.* Englewood-Cliffs: Prentice Hall.

——1967 – *Sociological Theory and Modern Society.* New York: Free Press.

Parsons, T. *et al.* (eds.) 1961 – *Theories of Society.* New York: Free Press.

Parsons, Talcott and R. F. Bales 1955 – *Family, Socialization and Interaction Process.* Glencoe: Free Press.

Parsons, Talcott, R. F. Bales and E. A. Shils 1953 – *Working Papers in the Theory of Action.* Glencoe: Free Press.

Parsons, Talcott and E. A. Shils (eds.) 1951 – *Toward a General Theory of Action.* Cambridge, Mass.: Harvard University Press.

Parsons, Talcott and N. J. Smelser 1956 – *Economy and Society.* New York: Free Press.

Smelser, Neil J. 1959 – *Social Change in the Industrial Revolution.* Chicago: University of Chicago Press.

——1963 – *Theory of Collective Behavior.* New York: Free Press.

Weber, Max 1947 – *The Theory of Social and Economic Organization.* Translated by A. M. Henderson and Talcott Parsons. Glencoe: Free Press.

2. Marxism: Science or Revolution?

LUCIO COLLETTI

Marxism as science or Marxism as revolution? There was and there still is this alternative. To resolve it is not so easy as is often thought. I shall begin with the first horn of the dilemma – Marxism as a science. The broad outlines of the argument might be presented as follows. Marxism is a theory of the *laws* of development of human society. In *Capital*, Marx has studied and analysed the laws governing the development of capitalist production, he has taken this 'mechanism' to pieces and described it as a scientific doctrine. Marxism essentially consists of the discovery of objective causal relationships. It discovers and analyses the laws which make the system work, describes the contradictions which undermine it from within and signal its destiny. But, insofar as it is a work of science and not ideology, *Capital* will not allow this analysis to be tainted with 'value judgments' or subjective choices: instead it makes only 'judgments of fact', objective judgments, affirmations which in the last analysis are universally valid. Scientific propositions are in the indicative. They do not advance 'choices' or finalities. It is impossible to deduce imperatives from the objective and impartial statements of science. This is the well-known argument developed by Hilferding in the preface to this *Finance Capital* (the argument of more or less all the orthodox Marxism of the Second International): 'Marxism is only a theory of the laws of development of society.' 'These laws which obtain their general formulation in the Marxist view of history, are applied by Marxist economics to the epoch of commodity production.' 'Marxism, which is a scientifically logical and objective doctrine, is not bound to value judgments.' The task of Marxism as a science is to 'describe causal relationships'. Though they are always being confused, 'socialism' and 'Marxism' are *not* the same thing. Socialism is an end, a goal, an objective of political will and action. Marxism on the other hand, being a science, is objective and impartial knowledge. One can accept the science without desiring the end. 'To recognize the validity of Marxism,' says Hilferding, 'does not at all mean to make value judgments, much less to point out a line of practical action. It is one thing to recognize a necessity, and quite another to put oneself at the service of that necessity.'

This view clearly allows no room for a link between *science* and *class consciousness*, between science and ideology, let alone for the 'partisanship' of science. Socio-economic development is seen as a process unfolding before the observer and the scientist like the movement of the stars. 'Economic laws' are objective laws, external to classes and independent of our wills just like the laws of nature. The 'law of value' is like the law of the fall of heavy bodies. More or less present in this conception is always a 'theory of breakdown'. The laws of the capitalist mode of production inescapably lead the system to its end. The extinction of capitalism is inevitable. It is made fatal and almost automatic by the explanation of its own laws. Nuances and slight variations apart, this was more or less the view which prevailed in the Third International too. While it existed, and above all with Stalin, all that was added was the criterion of 'partisanship' (an element anyway already latent in Lenin). But apart from the blind and sectarian way in which it was advanced, this criterion was only juxtaposed to that of naturalistic objectivism.[1] Juxtaposed, never mediated with it; i.e., united with it only by paste and string.

This 'physicalist' position, in infinitely more cultivated and refined forms, is still the dominant one among the best Marxist economists. The case of Oskar Lange is typical, and still more so is that of Maurice Dobb (who in general is a very serious scholar). Dobb sees the law of value as a law which allows us to reconstruct, unify, order and explain all the major mechanisms and movements of the system.

> Only with the work of Adam Smith, and its more rigorous systematization by Ricardo, did Political Economy create that unifying quantitative principle which enabled it to make postulates in terms of the general equilibrium of the economic system – to make deterministic statements about the general relationships which held between the major elements of the system. In Political Economy this unifying principle, or system of general statements cast in quantitative form, consisted of a theory of value.[2]

This passage stresses above all the ultimate social neutrality of the law of value. The law makes it possible to relate together the most important quantitative factors of the system, to establish certain quantifiable relationships between them – just as the law of universal gravitation does in its own field (Dobb's very example). But what does not come out here is the particular 'fetishistic' or 'alienated' nature of the quantitative factors related together by the law. For Marx, commodities and capital have not always existed, and what is more, their existence must come to an end. Apart from the relationships *within* the system, Marx analyses and criticizes the *system* itself. He discusses why the product of labour takes the form of a 'commodity'; why human labour is represented by the 'value' of 'things'; he discusses why (that is, under what conditions) capital exists and reproduces itself. Dobb, on the other hand, argues a little like Smith and Ricardo, who see the commodity as the 'natural' and inevitable form of the products of labour and the *market* as an institution which must always exist, and present the law of value as a law of permanent quantities or factors (often, in fact, confusing it with the problem of the 'measurement' of values).

There is no reason to dwell on this point here. Suffice it simply to note that for Marx too the law of value is an objective law, a law operating independently of consciousness and even 'behind the backs' of men: except that for him a quite peculiar kind of objectivity is involved. It is, so to speak, a false objectivity and one which must be abolished. The laws of the market – Marx writes – are a 'natural necessity' for men. The movements of the market are as unpredictable as earthquakes, but this is not because the market is a 'natural' phenomenon. What has taken the objective form here of *things* and interactions between things, is really nothing but the social relationships of men to each other. 'These formulae,' Marx writes, 'bear it stamped upon them in unmistakable letters that they belong to a state of society in which the process of production has the mastery over man, instead of being controlled by him.' A little earlier he had pointed out: 'The life-process of society, which is based on the process of material production, does not strip off its mystical veil until it is treated as production by freely associated men, and is consciously regulated by them in accordance with a settled plan.' And this can obviously come about only through revolution.

In the Ricardian interpretation, then, the law of value tends to be naturalized and appear as a socially natural law. The laws of nature have no class character. And by the same token, the production of commodities and the existence of a market have no class character. Hence the constant familiar speeches. The 'market' and 'profit' are not seen as the inevitable survival of bourgeois institutions in the first phase of socialist society, which is *par excellence* a *transitional* society, but as 'rational criteria or measurements of economic activity,' as something positive which must always exist. There is a 'socialist' market and there is 'socialist' profit. The revolution is not made to abolish profit, that is, to abolish exploitation. The revolution is made only for the pleasure of marching, well-drilled and cheering, past a speakers' platform.

Another basic distortion, closely related to the first, is the misinterpretation of the nature and meaning of Marx's work. For Marx, political economy is born with the extension and generalisation of commodity production. It is born with capitalism and dies with it (that is, with the progressive extinction of its surviving elements in the transitional society); which explains why all Marx's major works have the title or sub-title of the *critique* of political economy. For many Marxists today, however, the contrary is true: there must always be political economy[3] just as there will always be law, the State, and those who tell the masses what the masses themselves ought to think and believe.

I must interrupt the argument developed so far in order to look at the problem in another way and from a different angle. Open the first of Marx's really important writings, the *Critique* of *Hegel's 'Philosophy of Right'*. It has a remarkable structure. Not only does the work begin with a critique of the Hegelian *philosophy* of the State, and imperceptibly turn into a critique of the *State:* but in both cases – that is, both on the question of the way Hegel sees the State, and on the question of the State itself – the critique is developed by the use of a single model. Not only is Hegel's *representation* of the reality of the State upside down and 'standing on its head' but, Marx says, so is the actual *reality* generated by the State. 'This uncritical spirit, this mysticism,' he writes, 'is the enigma of the modern constitution . . . as well as the mystery of Hegelian philosophy.'

This point of view is undeniably abstract, but it is the abstraction of the political State as Hegel himself develops it. It is atomistic too, but it is the atomism of society itself. The point of view cannot be concrete when the object of the point of view is abstract. In general, an author criticizes another by showing him that things are not as he has described them. He criticizes him in the name of reality and on the basis of reality. But here the procedure seems to be different: the death sentence pronounced on the old philosophy at the same time applies to its *object* too. Marx does not only want to see the end of the Hegelian *philosophy* of the State: he wants to see the actual 'dissolution' of the State. This again is because he understands that not only is the philosophical representation of reality false, metaphysical, and 'standing on its head' – but so is reality itself, that is to say, the particular type of social régime which takes the form of the modern representative State or parliamentary Government.

There is an analogous situation in *Capital.* Here too Marx does not restrict himself to criticizing the 'logical mysticism' of the economists, their 'trinity formula': Land, Capital, Labour. Their 'fetishism' is explained by the fetishism of reality itself, that is of the capitalist mode of production. This is quite evident in a whole series of expressions. *Capital* contains such phrases as: 'the mystical character of commodities', or 'the whole mystery of commodities, all the magic and necromancy that surrounds the products of labour as long as they take the form of commodities'; or, finally, that the 'mystical veil' is not an invention of the bourgeois interpreters of the 'life-process of society which is based on the process of material production', but actually belongs to this process, which therefore *appears* to political economy as what it really *is.*

In fact, reality itself is upside down. It is therefore not just a question of criticizing the way in which economists and philosophers have *depicted* reality. It is necessary to overturn *reality* itself – to straighten it up and put it 'back on its feet.' 'Until now the philosophers have only interpreted the world: the point however is to change it.' In the foregoing I have looked at Marxism as a science; now I come to Marxism as revolution.

I urge the reader not to get too excited, but to keep his eyes open and use his head. In the argument I have just outlined there is a somewhat dubious and even dangerous point. An author criticizes another by appealing to *reality*, showing him that things are not as he had described and depicted them. This is the only correct kind of procedure. But Marx – with Hegel as with the economists – *seems* to be unable to do this: unable to, because the reference criterion – reality – is already itself a counterfeit standard. If this was really all, Marx would only be a prophet (which is not much), and we would be revisionists. On what basis do we say that the reality of capitalism is upside down? According to Bernstein, on the basis of the *moral ideal.* The idea of 'justice', Kant's ethics, tell me that the world should be corrected and reformed. Value and surplus value are mere words. Socialism is the product of good wishes. Change the minds of men! Abandon scientific socialism for utopian socialism. Reality is not important. 'Facts' are of no account. Reality is denied to make room for the realization of the ideal. Reason is Revolution. The contemporary Bernstein seems to lie to the left – in the petit bourgeois anarchism of Marcuse and of all those who have taken him seriously.

I must stop here a moment to put some order into the argument. Reality is certainly upside down – otherwise revolution would not be necessary. On the other hand, Marxism also needs to be a science: if not there would be no *scientific* socialism, only messianic aspirations, or religious hopes. In short, if Marx is a scientist, he has to measure his ideas and those of others against the facts, to test hypotheses experimentally against reality. In simpler and more familiar terms, this means that when Marx criticizes Hegel, the economists and all the reality of capitalism, he still has to do it in the name of reality and *on the basis of reality*. The criterion of his critique, in short, cannot be the *ideal* (which is still the ideal of just anyone). It must be a criterion drawn from and rooted in reality. If I may summarize this briefly, I would say that there are *two realities* in capitalism: the reality expressed by Marx, and the reality expressed by the authors he criticizes. I shall now try to demonstrate this as simply and quickly as possible, by examining the relationship between capital and wage labour.

I shall begin by seeing how this relationship looks from the point of view of the capitalist. The capitalist invests his money in the purchase of spindles, cotton, and labour. He finds these things on the market, that is, as commodities. He buys them as anyone might buy a whip, a horse and a carriage. After making these purchases (suppose he buys at no more than their actual value), the capitalist then puts the worker to work at the spindles to transform the cotton into thread. At this point, Marx says, 'the labour process is a process between things that the capitalist has purchased, things that have become his property. The product of this process belongs, therefore, to him, just as much as does the wine which is the product of fermentation completed in his cellar.'

The capitalist's eye, accustomed to synthesis and the overall view, does not deign to distinguish between the various things he has bought. From his point of view, wage labour is a *part* of capital, in the same way as machinery and raw materials: it is the 'variable' part of capital, the 'wages fund', as distinct from the part invested in the purchase of means of production. The fact that, besides reproducing his own value, that is the wage, the wage labourer produces surplus value, is a happy circumstance which raises no theoretical problem for the capitalists. To him, this fertility of labour appears directly as the *productivity of his own capital:* the capital of which labour is itself a part, being one of the purchases. This is, as we know, the thesis of all non-Marxist economists, what Marx calls the fetishism of political economy. It is not only labour which produces value, but capital too. Wages pay for the productivity of the former, profits pay for the latter. Land produces the harvest; capital or machinery produce profits; labour produces wages. To each his own. Then let harmony be established once and for all, and let the factors of production collaborate.

You will say that this is the 'bosses' ' point of view. But the important thing to understand is that more than a subjective point of view is involved: it is a point of view which corresponds in a certain sense to the actual course of things. The working class reproduces its own means of subsistence, and at the same time produces surplus value (that is, profit, rent, and interest); with its labour it provides the revenues of all the basic classes of society. And – *as long as it is kept down* – the working class is in fact only a cog in the mechanism of capitalism. Capital is produced by labour: labour is the cause, capital the effect: the one the origin, the other the outcome. And yet not only in the accounting of the enterprise, but in the real mechanism, the working class appears only as 'variable capital' and as the wages fund. The 'whole' has become the 'part', and the part the whole. Such is the reality 'on its head' already mentioned: the reality which Marx not only rejects as a criterion and yardstick, but which he wants to overthrow and invert.

Think of the American working class. It is only a cog of capital, a part of the capitalist mechanism. More strictly speaking, it is not even a 'class' (it does not have *consciousness* of being a class): it is an agglomeration of 'categories': car workers, chemical workers, textile workers, etc. When it reacts and goes on strike, its relationship to the whole of the social 'mechanism' is like that of a bilious irritated organ to the human body: it demands no more than a pill to make it feel better. This class (though every working class has passed through this stage, and in a certain sense remains in it until it takes power), this class is, really, a *part* of capital: although (to distinguish it from the imperialist exploitation of workers in other countries) it is also true that the thing of which it is *part* (capital), is in its turn a *part* of the value produced by the working class.

The point of view adopted by Marx is in fact the expression precisely of this other reality. Capital, of which wage labour is only the variable component, is in reality part of this its part (which is therefore the 'totality'): it is the product of 'living labour'. Without then repeating Bernstein's moralism or Marcuse's 'utopias', Marx overthrows the arguments of the economists and points to the overthrow of capitalism itself, pivoting on an aspect of *reality*. Marxism is therefore science. It is analytical reconstruction of the way in which the mechanism of capitalist production works.

On the other hand, as well as being a science, Marxism is revolutionary ideology. It is the analysis of reality from the viewpoint of the working class. This in its turn means that the working class cannot constitute itself as a *class* without taking possession of the scientific analysis of *Capital.* Without this, it disintegrates into a myriad of 'categories'. The working class (dreamers awake!) is not a given factor, it is not a product of nature. It is a destination point: the production of *historical action*, that is, not only of material conditions but also of *political* consciousness. In short, the class becomes a class when, going beyond economistic spontaneism, it develops the consciousness of being the antagonist of the whole system: the consciousness of being the protagonist of a revolution which emancipates not only the workers but the whole of society. This consciousness, through which the class constitutes itself in political organization and takes its place at the head of its allies, cannot be derived from anywhere but *Capital*. It is in this sense, I think, that Lenin said that the construction of the party also requires something 'from without'.

NOTES

1. See, for example, Stalin, *Economic Problems of Socialism in the Soviet Union.*
2. Maurice Dobb, *Studies in the Development of Capitalism*, Routledge, 1946.
3. See the *Manual of Political Economy*, USSR Academy of Sciences.

3. Toward a Sociology of the Absurd

STANFORD LYMAN AND MARVIN B. SCOTT

A new wave of thought is beginning to sweep over sociology. Aspects of the wave have been given an assortment of names – 'labeling theory', 'ethnomethodology', and 'neo-symbolic interactionism' – but these do not cover its entire range of critique and perspective. A new name must be found to cover a concept which presents not only a unique perspective on conventional sociology but is also a radical departure from the conventional.

We feel an appropriate name is *the Sociology of the Absurd.*

The term 'absurd' captures the fundamental assumption of this new wave: *The world is essentially without meaning.* In contrast to that sociology which seeks to discover the *real* meaning of action – a sociological reality, such as the *functional* meaning of social behaviour – this new sociology asserts that all systems of belief, including that of the conventional sociologists, are arbitrary. The problems previously supposed to be those of the sociologist are in fact the everyday problems of the ordinary man. It is he who must carve out meanings in a world that is meaningless. Alienation and insecurity are fundamental conditions of life – though they are experienced differently by individuals and groups – and the regular rehumanization of man is everyman's task.

The Sociology of the Absurd draws its philosophical inspiration from existentialism and phenomenology. The works of Edmund Husserl are particularly crucial to its originating ideas (Husserl 1964, 1965; Kockelmans 1967). Moreover, the interpreters of Husserl – especially Alfred Schutz (1962, 1964, 1966, 1967) and Maurice Merleau-Ponty (1963a, 1963b, 1964a, 1964b, 1964c) – are major sources of intellectual perspectives, fundamental concepts, and promising insights. On the basis of its debt to phenomenology and existentialism the Sociology of the Absurd might be called an existential phenomenology for sociology.

From existentialism the Sociology of the Absurd derives its emphases on human freedom and the life-long process of 'becoming'; on the nexus between the reality which is 'out there' and the man who is thinking, feeling, apprehending 'inside' himself; and on the broader view of man as an integral being, composed not only of *cogito*, but also of feeling, sensing, and apprehending. Finally, on the basis of existentialist thought the Sociology of the Absurd restores the individual to his rightful place as the principal agent of action, the central subject of sociology. Together with Kierkegaard, Sartre, and Jaspers, the sociologists of the new wave seek to place man at the center of study – as he already is in fact at the center of thought and action (see Tiryakian 1962:71–6).

From phenomenology, the Sociology of the Absurd derives its emphasis on certain aspects of human activity, such as intentionality, consciousness, and subjective meaning. Human intentions, contrary to the position of the Watsonian behaviorists, are definable to both social actors and their observers, not by some special technique possessed solely by experts or mystics, but rather by means of the most ordinary – but as yet not fully understood – mechanisms of perception carried on in everyday life (Husserl 1967:68–79). Human consciousness should be the principal object of study in sociology, and this has been suggested in the work of Max Weber (1947:88) and in the early formulations of Parsons' theory of action (1949:79–81, 732–733, 750–751). But methodological problems restricted research, and it has not yet excited the intellectual interest it deserves.

Phenomenology, and especially existential phenomenology, appears to have laid the basis for a solution to the methodological problem of subjective knowledge and objective existence, and in this the new sociology finds a grounding for new research. As Tiryakian has observed, existential phenomenology 'seeks to elucidate the existential nature of social structures by uncovering the surface institutional phenomena of the everyday, accepted world; by probing the subterranean, noninstitutional social depths concealed from public gaze, by interpreting the dialectic between the institutional and the non-institutional . . .' (1965:687).

Now what specifically is the nature of human action from the viewpoint of the Sociology of the Absurd? Action consists of the pursuit of ends by social actors capable of deliberating about the line of activity they undertake and of choosing among alternatives to the same end. This does not mean that men always precede action by deliberation. This is manifestly not the case. What it does mean is that men are capable of giving an account of their actions either as preactivity mental images of the action, its consequences and meanings, or as *post hoc* retrospective readings of completed acts. As images either before or after completion, these constructions emerge as statements made by the actor which give meaning to his actions. (See Anscombe 1966:1–61.) These constructions are not unintelligible to others. Most important, these statements constitute the actual meaning, though not necessarily the cause, of these actions, and thus are the basic data of the new sociology. Instead of adopting an undisguised skepticism of what humans say – a skepticism deeply rooted in the positivist and behaviorist traditions – the Sociology of the Absurd rejects the question of the truth value in face of the significance of the meaning value of these statements. In this respect the new sociology draws on yet another new intellectual strand, that introduced by the ordinary language philosophers who now contribute so much to linguistics and psychology.[1]

It follows from the emphasis on freedom and becoming in existentialist thought that human action should be considered, as Parsons once put it, 'voluntaristic' (1949:10–12). Without this idea of voluntarism, human activity would be 'mere behavior' (Devereux 1961). Instead, in concert with Parsons' early view of the theory of action[2] the sociologist of the Absurd sees activity in discernible units of action – episodes, encounters, situations – to which the actor gives meaning; meaning beyond merely the sense of a set of physical objects. Thus humans are not necessarily the creatures of social or psychological forces – class, casts, race, or deep-lying unconscious states – which *determine* their behavior in the situation. The age-old problem of freedom versus determinism is not a problem of objective philosophy but rather of the actor's construction of reality, his image of freedom and constraint. The Sociology of the Absurd conceives of man as being constructed – and of constructing – social reality in every situation. From this point of view mental illness, for instance, is a social construction, not an absolute, unambiguous disease (Szasz 1967; Foucalt 1965).

If life consists of encounters, episodes and engagements among persons pursuing goals of which they are consciously aware, or about which they can be made aware, then it appears that the fundamental structure of human action is *conflict*. This is true even if individuals are pursuing the same ends, since each is out to maximize his own interest. Thus, even two lovers in an erotic embrace, as Simmel once noted (1959:249–52), may be regarded in conflict since each may be seeking to outdo the other in demonstrating affection or providing the other with feeling. If one begins with the conception of human action as interpersonal conflict, two important implications (for theory) follow. The first concerns the kind of model of *interaction* most useful for the analysis of the social world; the second is the heuristic model of *man* most fruitful for the analysis of interaction.

Concerning the first, it seems that a *game model* is most suited for the analysis of interaction as our conception of the game model derives from the conception of man as a goal-seeking, voluntaristic, intentional actor. It follows from these characteristics that in any engagement he will employ, more or less consciously, stratagems and tactics to attain the end intended. It also follows that others participating in the engagement may be viewed as allies, opponents, or neutrals according to the goal sought and the means employed. The game model, we hold, is fruitful for the analysis of all social interactions, but it is especially so for the study of problematic statuses, such as homosexuals, paranoids, minorities and the stigmatized in general.

With regard to the second, the Sociology of the Absurd assumes a model of man in conflict – with others, with society, with nature, and even with himself. Even though much of sociology has refused to adopt this conception of man,[3] it recommends itself as the most powerful *heuristic* device for the study of man-in-society[4]. In passing it may be noted that the recent findings in animal ethology – especially the works of Konrad Lorenz (1966) – lend a curious kind of support to our conception. More significant, however, are the fruitful settings for intellectual problems provided by the adoption of this model of man. By beginning with the assumption that social life is one of conflict, it follows that every social situation is problematic for those involved. With this model the sociologist must continually search for mechanisms that permit the production – and reproduction in a continuous series of engagements – of stable, uniform and persistent interaction[5]. Thus the sociologist is induced by this model to persistently try and solve the riddle that originally set the discipline in motion: how is society possible? The sociologist must view man as the maker and remaker of social existence, as the producer and reproducer of stable engagements, as the craftsman of society and the ever-renewed social order.

The Sociology of the Absurd does not aim at building a 'social system'. Indeed system building would go against the grain. This new sociology is perhaps best characterized as a conceptual style of theoretical ideas and sensitizing concepts tied together not by logic or system, but rather by the underlying existential-phenomenological assumptions stated above. In this respect it is worth contrasting the Sociology of the Absurd with functionalism.[6]

The Sociology of the Absurd stands in opposition to functionalism on five major contentions. First, functionalism is interested in understanding human action in terms of forces unperceived by the actor. Functionalism assumes a determined world inhabited by creatures who for the most part are unaware of the forces that shape their destinies and who live by the illusion and self-deception of their own imagined freedom. The Absurd, on the contrary, holds that there is an existential continuum between freedom and determinism constructed and reconstructed by the social actors individually or in concert. Thus some men are more free than others; some are more constrained than they know. The Absurd is concerned with man's intentions and consciousness, with his 'felt' state of freedom or fatalism, and with the consequences that flow therefrom.

Second, functionalism holds that the various parts of society are non-arbitrary since they contribute to the integration of the whole. The Absurd, on the other hand, holds that all elements of society are arbitrary. These elements have no fixed, stable, and irreducible meaning. They certainly are not part of an organic system with a built-in end purpose – homeostasis. This imagery of society which functionalism inherited from Aristotle and his followers lends itself to the radical separation of events from processes, and in many cases to a peculiar sociological emphasis on processes detached from events or particular episodes (Bock 1956; Scott 1966). The Absurd emphasizes the individual and the episodic – the event – and perceives this as the factor emerging from the participants' social construction of reality.

Third, functionalism regards the social order as rooted in a basic interdependence and cooperation. As the functionalists see it, men, through the socialization process, internalize norms, and fit into roles. These roles, in turn, are meshed together to form interlocking role-sets, or institutions. Aside from our disagreement with the empirical validity of this interpretation (we believe, for example, that society in the modern complex world is better described as a collection of conflicting subcultures (Gordon 1964:132–232), which in their relations manage to maintain some pattern of stability by the employment of social mechanisms as yet imperfectly understood by sociologists), we hold that the functionalist perspective is heuristically weak because it begs the basic question for which sociology was founded. By assuming cooperation and interdependence *a priori*, by pressing society on to a teleological Procrustean bed, by conceiving of society as an organism or a mechanism, functional theory cannot make the social order problematic; it can assume that society is possible but not *discover* how it is possible.

Fourth, because functionalism sees man as a determined creature played upon by forces largely seen 'as through a glass, darkly,' it opts to study man from the point of view of the observer. Functionalism pays little attention to the perceptions made by men about their own activities. Rather it regards these as founded on ignorance of the real forces that shape human action (Matson 1964:54–101). The Absurd on the other hand rejects the *a priori* existence of a determined world discoverable by sociologists. It regards man as an actor who builds up his actions on the basis of his goals and of his continuing attempts to define and redefine the situation. Thus, the social world is studied from the point of view of the actors who construct it.

Finally, functionalism postulates a common value system in society. We hold, on the other hand, that in modern complex societies there are few if any common, binding values. Values and norms are pluralistically applicable on the basis of situations, persons, and times (Fletcher 1966). Thus what is crucial is the definition of the situation. And this definition is not simply 'given'. Rather, it is a bargain struck for the time being by the participants in the episode. For values to be employed, for norms to be operational, there must be 'negotiation' of situations and identities, and obviously the participants have significant stakes in this negotiation. Only when these interactants are agreed upon who they are and what they are do they give and receive accounts – excuses and justifications – the linguistic devices that shore up fractured social situations.

Because we cannot assume value consenses, we have a second reason for supposing the social world to be problematic. Every investigation carried out under the aegis of the Sociology of the Absurd is approached with a sense of astonishment that a social order exists. *The puzzle, the mystery of how social order somehow emerges from the chaos and conflict predicated by the inherently meaningless is the motive for the study of social phenomena.*

Much sociology has been motivated by social meliorism (Mills 1959:84–90). Although we might laud the endeavors to improve the world, and certainly recognize the multi-faceted problems in modern societies, for several reasons we cannot subscribe to the thesis that social engineering or social change is the primary objective of the Sociology of the Absurd. First, no sociological enterprise directed at healing the social ills, improving the body politic, or salvaging cultural remnants can approach the subject from the standpoint of the Sociology of the Absurd. A consciously naive but intellectual inquiry into how social order is possible supersedes questions of policy and priority in such a manner as to make the latter not only irrelevant but also a hindrance.

Second, once sociologists consciously adopt meliorism as their principal objective, they seek to influence policy-makers. Influence requires a rhetoric calculated to convince those in power that one has both the appropriate ideas and the techniques with which to make the studies that are convincing to policy makers. Thus, the policy-oriented sociologist is more likely to be inclined to low-level theorizing, quantification, axiomatic system building, and whatever other rhetorical stratagems are likely to be persuasive.[7]

Finally, sociological meliorism is a contradiction of the nature of man and society as assumed by the Sociology of the Absurd. Meliorism, were it to be the aim of sociology, assumes that sociologists are philosopher-kings, or to put it more accurately, philosophers *of* the people and advisers *to* the kings. The sociologist of the Absurd is simply an observer of the social scene and thus does not suffer from the conceit and arrogance of the social engineer who would reshape the world according to what he lays down as 'objective' ethics.

It follows from this, however, that the sociologist of the Absurd can maximize his observations and reflections in the freest of societies. Such a society is not one in which the practicing social scientist is restricted in his opportunities for observation. This does not mean a society devoid of privacy, but one in which the sociologist takes his chances to see what he can see, observing the nooks and crannies, crevices and interstices as well as the broad range of open spaces and public situations. A society marked by police regulation and extensive sumptuary legislation is unlikely to produce much good sociology, just as it is unlikely to produce much excellent art or literature.

It would be untrue, however, to say that restricted societies are unamenable to sociological inquiry. The sociologist of the Absurd must be a careful observer in any situation, and his awareness and exact description of the political, legal, social and moral restraints on the individual is part of his task. He must, insofar as possible, apprehend the exact definition the individual has of his own freedom and of the constraints upon it in every encounter, so that he can, as part of his description, locate the person precisely in the continuum between humanism and fatalism. He must uncover ideology and utopia in each man, wish and transfiguration in each situation. The sociologist of the Absurd, by his very description of society, by his everlasting unfolding and illumination of the modes and styles of social order, can summon men to build the world of their dreams, but he cannot build it for them.

Although the Sociology of the Absurd is a new wave, it grows out of contemporary issues and new ideas in other arenas of progressive thought and action. Undoubtedly one of the most important of these is the Theatre of the Absurd, a school of dramatic thought limned by such names as Beckett, Ionesco, and Genet. Indeed our definition of the Absurd derives from Ionesco's in his essay on Kafka: 'Absurd is that which is devoid of purpose . . . Cut off from his religious, metaphysical, and transcendental roots, man is lost; all his actions become senseless, absurd, useless' (Esslin 1961: 21).

If the Theatre of the Absurd illustrates the meaninglessness of the world, the Sociology of the Absurd *describes* man's constant *striving for meaning* in the face of the faceless Monolith. The Sociology of the Absurd emphasizes the episodic in man's life; it deemphasizes, though it does not discount, the predecessors and successors of contemporary man. It sees man as Simmel saw some men and Camus saw all men – as strangers. Thus Simmel wrote:

> If wandering is the liberation from every given point in space, and thus the conceptional opposite to fixation at such a point, the sociological form of the 'stranger' presents the unity, as it were, of these two characteristics . . . The stranger is thus being discussed here, not . . . as the wanderer who comes today and goes tomorrow . . . He is fixed within a particular spatial group, or within a group whose boundaries are similar to spatial boundaries. But his position in this group is determined, essentially, by the fact that he has not belonged to it from the beginning, that he imports qualities into it, which do not and cannot stem from the group itself (1950:402).

And Camus:

> A world that can be explained by reasoning, however faulty, is a familiar world. But in a universe that is suddenly deprived of illusions and of light, man feels a stranger. His is an irremediable exile, because he is deprived of memories of a lost homeland as much as he lacks the hope of a promised land to come. This divorce between man and his life, the actor and his setting, truly consitutes the feeling of Absurdity (Esslin 1961:29).

Simmel characterizes the stranger as an awe-inspiring, fearsome contributor; Camus as a victim of the irrelevant past and unpromising future. The sociologist, seeing man as the stranger, emphasizes the problematic nature of his existence. Essentially a contemporary, the stranger must struggle to establish the meaning of each new moment, even if only to get through it and be confronted by the next moment, and the next. Further he must sort out his relationships, appropriately sharing his affections between strangers and brothers, acquaintances and lovers. He is annoyed by the importunity of unwarranted fellowship; estranged by the coldness of unrequited affection; threatened by the powers of the mighty; frightened by the terror of the unknown; and doomed by the inevitability of death. And always he is confronted with life – things, events, people – which demand responses, require interpretation, cry out for meaning. Thus the Sociology of the Absurd studies existential man, the creature who strives after sense in a senseless world.

NOTES

1. For an introduction to ordinary language philosophy, see Flew (1960). Our own thinking on language and meaning has been strongly influenced by the following: Wittgenstein (1959), Austin (1961), Ryle (1949), and Shwayder (1965). Anthropologists are far ahead of sociologists in their recognition of the fundamental importance of the study of language. See Gumperz and Hymes (1964). Whatever recognition sociologists have given the study of language falls under the rubric of 'sociolinguistics'. For a sampling, see Bright (1966).

2. For an analysis of the early and more recent changes in Parsons' frame of reference, see Scott (1963).
3. Tiryakian has argued that existentialism might benefit from the sociological conception of man as interdependent. 'Sociologism, to reiterate an earlier point, does not view the relation between the individual and society as one marked by conflict, for it stresses ultimately the needs and contributions of each to the other.' See *Sociologism and Existentialism* (1962: 167). Our conception is that the conflict between individual and society, or individual and individual may not be 'marked', although sometimes it is, but it is always present, though sometimes repressed or hidden from view. Further, though men may 'ultimately' contribute to one another's needs, they act out relations which are full of conflict in the actual episodes of their lives.
4. A conflict model was employed by early sociologists derived from their awareness of the conflicts between classes, races, and states. See for example Gumplowicz (1963). A modern sociology of conflicts has been urged by Lewis Coser. See his *The Functions of Social Conflict* (1956) and *Continuities in the Study of Social Conflict* (1967).
5. Thus the value of Sigmund Freud's *Civilization and Its Discontents* is not to be found in its empirical validity, but rather in its conception of man in opposition to society and thus in a position to regard all social situations as problematic.
6. For a clear and systematic statement on functionalism, see Merton (1968:73–138).
7. We are indebted for this point to Jack Douglas.

REFERENCES

Anscombe, G. E. M. 1966 – *Intention.* Ithaca: Cornell University Press.
Austin, J. L. 1961 – *Philosophical Papers.* Oxford: Clarendon Press.
Bock, Kenneth E. 1956 – *The Acceptance of Histories.* Berkeley: University of California Press.
Bright, William (ed.) 1966 – *Sociolinguistics.* The Hague: Mouton.
Coser, Lewis 1956 – *The Functions of Social Conflict.* Glencoe: Free Press.
———1967 – *Continuities in the Study of Social Conflict.* New York: Free Press.
Devereux, Jr., Edward C. 1961 – 'Parsons' sociological theory.' In Max Black (ed.), *Social Theories of Talcott Parsons.* Englewood Cliffs: Prentice Hall.
Esslin, Martin 1961 – *The Theatre of the Absurd.* Garden City: Doubleday Anchor.
Fletcher, Joseph 1966 – *Situation Ethics.* Philadelphia: Westminster Press.
Flew, Antony 1960 – *Logic and Language*, First Series. Oxford: Basil Blackwell.
Foucalt, Michel 1965 – *Madness and Civilization.* New York: Pantheon.
Gordon, Milton M. 1964 – *Assimilation in American Life.* New York: Oxford University Press.
Gumperz, John J. and Dell Hymes (eds.) 1964 – 'The Ethnography of communications.' *American Anthropologist*, 66, December.
Gumplowicz, Ludwig 1963 – *Outlines of Sociology.* Edited by Irving L. Horowitz. New York: Paine-Whitman.
Husserl, Edmund 1964 – *The Phenomenology of Internal Time-Consciousness.* Bloomington and London: Indiana University Press.
———1965 – *Phenomenology and the Crisis of Philosophy.* New York: Harper Torchbooks.
———1967 – 'The thesis of the natural standpoint and its suspension.' In Joseph J. Kockelmans (ed.), *Phenomenology: The Philosophy of Edmund Husserl and Its Interpretation.* Garden City, Doubleday Anchor.
Kockelmans, Joseph J. (ed.) 1967 – *Phenomenology: The Philosophy of Edmund Husserl and Its Interpretation.* Garden City, Doubleday Anchor.
Lorenz, Konrad 1966 – *On Aggression.* New York: Harcourt, Brace & World.
Matson, Floyd 1964 – *The Broken Image.* New York: Braziller.
Merleau-Ponty, Maurice 1963a – *The Structure of Behavior.* Boston: Beacon.

———1963b – *In Praise of Philosophy*. Evanston: Northwestern University Press.
———1964a – *Sense and Non-Sense*. Evanston: Northwestern University Press.
———1964b – *The Primacy of Perception and Other Essays*. Evanston: Northwestern University Press.
———1964c – *Signs*. Evanston: Northwestern University Press.
Merton, Robert K. 1968 – *Social Theory and Social Structure*. New York: Free Press.
Mills, C. Wright 1959 – *The Sociological Imagination*. New York: Oxford University Press.
Parsons, Talcott 1949 – *The Structure of Social Action*. Glencoe: Free Press.
Ryle, Gilbert 1949 – *The Concept of Mind*. New York: Barnes & Noble.
Schutz, Alfred 1962, 64, 66 – *Collected Papers*.
Schutz, Alfred 1962 – *Collected Papers*. The Hague: Martinus Nijhoff.
———1964, 1966 – Three volumes. Edited by Maurice Natanson, Arvid Brodersen, and I. Schutz.
———1967 – *The Phenomenology of the Social World*. (Translated by George Walsh and Frederick Lehnert.) Evanston: Northwestern University Press.
Scott, John Finley 1963 – 'The changing foundations of the Parsonian action scheme.' *American Sociological Review*, 28, October, 716–35.
Scott, Marvin B. 1966 – 'Functional foibles and the analysis of social change.' *Inquiry* 9:205–14.
Shwayder, D. S. 1965 – *The Stratification of Behavior*. New York: Humanities Press.
Simmel, Georg 1950 – 'The Stranger.' *The Sociology of Georg Simmel*. Glencoe: Free Press.
———1959 – 'The adventure.' In Kurt H. Wolff (ed.), *Georg Simmel, 1858–1918*. Columbus: Ohio State University Press.
Szasz, Thomas 1967 – *The Myth of Mental Illness*. New York: Delta.
Tiryakian, Edward A. 1962 – *Sociologism and Existentialism*. Englewood-Cliffs: Prentice-Hall.
———1965 – 'Existential phenomenology and the sociological tradition.' *American Sociological Review*, 30, October.
Weber, Max 1947 – *The Theory of Social and Economic Organization*. New York: Oxford University Press.
Wittgenstein, Ludwig 1959 – *Philosophical Investigations*. Oxford: Basil Blackwell.

Part 2:

Culture

Introduction

LAWRENCE SCHLEMMER

I. Culture can be so defined as to include the particular characteristics of everything people in recognizable groups say, signal, do and make, as well as the values, perceptions, symbols, codes and assumptions which are the blueprints or templates for their behaviour. We will consider the definitions of culture presently, but first it is necessary to mark out some focus for a brief discussion of so large and unwieldly a topic.

Our emphasis in this volume is on South Africa and therefore this offers the obvious opportunity to impose some regional limitation on the discussion of the topic. This boundary, however, encompasses not only a multiplicity of discrete, semi-discrete, overlapping, changing and blending cultural forms but also some rather complex and elusive differences in the levels of behaviour at which culture becomes manifest. Apart from the differences in culture as conventionally understood, there are popular conceptions of culture and cultural difference; there are cultural elements in politics, but also 'culture politics' (in the sense of culture used as various kinds of justificatory schemata), as well as political cultures – hopefully the distinctions that have been drawn will become clear as we proceed. Over-arching everything is a shared culture often obscured by the more commanding conflicts of interest in South Africa. Furthermore, we cannot overlook the fact that South Africa, like any other complex urban 'mass-society' has its share of 'subcultures' and 'counter-cultures'; variants on dominant themes existing among minorities, age-segments and status groups. We will make no attempt to discuss everything systematically in a brief introduction – this essay will hopefully simply serve to highlight the major features in the rich tapestry of 'culture' in South Africa.

II. As intimated above, it is common to see culture given wide and inclusive definitions. A popular textbook refers to culture as man's 'entire social heritage, all the knowledge, beliefs, customs, and skills he acquires as a member of society' (Broom and Selznick 1963:52). Clyde Kluckhohn (1949:1951) one of the most prominent American cultural anthropologists, describes the concept of culture variously as a 'complete design for living', 'the total way of life of a people', and even as 'learned behaviour'. He states that the culture of any society is always specific; the *distinctive* but all – inclusive way of life of a people. (This view would not be a denial of the fact, however, that two or more societies can share large areas of culture, for example, Western industrial societies.) The equally prominent figure in early British social anthropology, Malinowski (1951:36, 43) adopted a similarly broad definition, referring to culture as 'obviously the integral whole, consisting of implements and consumers' goods, of constitutional charters . . ., of human ideas and crafts, beliefs and customs.' He even added the argument that the organization of people into permanent groups (social structure) must be seen as part of the configurations of culture. Raymond Firth (1951) was one of the first writers to explain the definitional superimposition of culture and social structure by saying that the two terms represented two ways of looking at the same thing.

Obviously, given a very comprehensive definition of culture, one must make certain distinctions within the concept, as, say, between material and non-material culture. It is common for sociologists to restrict the focus of attention in relation to culture to social norms and values. As is well known, Talcott Parsons (cf. 1951) made the basic distinction between three systems within which behaviour is shaped: the personality system, the social system and the cultural system; the latter referring mainly to the normative and evaluative aspects of his social paradigm, but including symbolic and ideational content as well. Equally well known are the earlier concepts of Durkheim whose analysis of religion rested heavily on the 'cultural' concepts of 'collective representations' (normative or cognitive ideas shared among members of a society), and 'collective consciousness', the patterning of ideas into a more or less coherent collective world view.

Not only from Durkheim, but, *inter alia*, from Weber as well (cf. Gerth and Mills 1958) there came the notion of culture as including systems of interrelated norms, ideas, cognitions and symbols, in part historically derived, in part emanating from or at least conditioned by structural features in society and in part following a logic of development intrinsic to group consciousness. These possibilities have led to important refinements in the definition of culture. Geertz (1973:5) introduces his discussion of culture by aligning himself with Max Weber in saying that culture is the 'webs of significance' which man has spun for himself.

Geertz questions the importance of inclusive or comprehensive definitions of culture; his concern is to narrow the focus of cultural interpretation so as to experience what, for want of a better phrase, we may describe as the essential or core elements of meaning in social interaction. His approach to culture is 'semiotic' (referring to the science of signs and symbols). He rejects, however, the rectifying view that culture is a symbolic system coherently structured by 'forces and purposes all of its own', i.e. governed only by rules intrinsic to the cultural system. He also finds unacceptable the notion that culture is the manifestation of psychological or cognitive structures and codes which guide the behaviour of individuals or groups, and predictably, questions the importance of purely subjectivist interpretations of social reality. What is important in culture, for Geertz (1973), Ricoeur (1970), and other symbolic interaction theorists, is the conceptual structures of meaning which inform social acts and social discourse. These conceptual structures, to a lesser or greater degree, relate to each other coherently, but not necessarily in the context of some super-ordinate and independent framework of symbolism; essentially in the context of human sentiment as displayed in concrete social interaction and events.

A useful analogy is to liken the interpretive analysis of (culturally informed) behaviour to literary criticism. A literary work cannot be understood by reference to some transcending universal literary code. It is an expression of style which has to be understood in the context of what the book is written about – the theme and characters, but these elements make literary sense in the light of a shared sensitivity among critics to the literary elements of metaphor, simile, ambiguity, pun, paradox, irony, hyperbole, rhythm, etc. (Geertz 1973:209). The analysis of culture, at its most telling and informative level, must be sensitive to the same sort of elements in symbol systems – metaphor-like elements present in shared social meanings.

Culture patterns, then, at least to some extent are 'extrapersonal mechanisms for the perception, understanding, judgement and manipulation of the world . . . they provide a template or blueprint for the organisation of social and psychological processes . . .' (Geertz 1973:216).

The way to discover the conceptual schemata forming behaviour is through what Geertz terms 'thick descriptions' of social events – interpretive accounts of behaviour in specific situations which attempt to fathom the meanings of social responses in particular events.

This view of culture is, for me, the most significant way of approaching the topic. Presentations of cultural symbols should not, however, become so mysteriously abstracted that the ordinary and commonplace sentiments and motivations of people, of a type which we all experience as real, have to be rejected or ignored in favour of esoteric affinities and associations, whether symbolic or cognitive, which guide men in ways they don't understand. Then again, culture described in the form of tedious (or if the society is remote, curious) descriptions of everyday living simply for the sake of recording patterns of life, is analytically rather sterile. This is simply description, not the 'thick description' which Geertz prescribes.

The difficulty about intensive interpretative accounts of specific events is that of generalization, a difficulty which Geertz fully acknowledges. How may such accounts speak to the larger issues in which we as sociologists are interested – stratification, class, power, authority, inter-group tension and the like? The reason why I have leaned so heavily on Geertz in this introduction, is precisely because he addresses his analyses to some of the larger issues like nationalism, ideology and political processes. The intensive specific analysis of the meaning-structure in a particular political event may not be able to form the basis of a social law, or allow prediction and control, but it does deepen our understanding of a much wider spectrum of political events and even of political processes. Intensive studies of varying events over time make for a more and more incisive grasp of social reality, thereby becoming the building blocks for more general statements.

III. This view of culture suggests that cultural patterns, to some degree, have an autonomous status in the configuration of social reality. How is this to be reconciled with the fairly commonly accepted view that culture – its values and forms – variously serves to 'legitimate' structural realities or, more specifically, economic or political power? 'Legitimation justifies the institutional order by giving a normative dignity to its practical imperatives' (Berger and Luckmann 1966:111). Berger and Luckmann (1966:114) argue that it is at the symbolic level that the 'reflective integration' of discrete institutional processes reaches its ultimate fulfilment. Institutional roles, in terms of the legitimating culture, 'become modes of participation in a universe that transcends *and* includes the institutional order'. These authors go on to say (126) that 'the conceptual machineries of universe maintenance are themselves products of social activity . . . and can only rarely be understood apart from the other activities of the collectivity in question. Specifically the success of particular conceptual machineries is rer lated to the power possessed by those who operate them'. The authors quote Marx: 'Die Gedanken der herrschenden Klasse sind in jeder Epoche die herrschenden Gedanken' (note, 227).

The individualistic and materialist or 'utilitarian' culture of the middle classes in the West is often taken as an example of the way in which the power of capital and the institutions of capitalism are underwritten by cultural meanings among the masses. (For a more complex discussion of this culture, see Gouldner 1970:Chapter III.) Gouldner argues that even the modern welfare state, despite its occasional claims to represent a variant of socialist values, is an *ad hoc* accommodation to group and individual egoism, and simply 'counter balances' the utilitarianism of the middle classes, and 'allows the private sector to maintain its narrow commitment to utility' (Gouldner 1970:81–2). Perhaps the most explicit exponent of the role of culture in producing orientations supportive of modern capitalism is Herbert Marcuse. 'In a specific sense advanced industrial culture is more ideological than its predecessor, in as much as today the ideology is in the process of production itself . . . the products indoctrinate and manipulate; they promote a false consciousness which is immune against its falsehood . . . as a good way of life it militates against qualitative change' (Marcuse 1964: 10–11; see also Wilensky 1964:196). Marcuse (1964:72) also concentrates his analysis on the role of today's permissive culture: 'The Pleasure Principle absorbs the Reality Principle; sexuality is liberated (or rather liberalised) in socially constructive forms (constructive for the modern capitalist system, that is). This notion implies that there are repressive modes of desublimation . . . and here, as in the desublimation of higher culture, it operates as the by-product of the social controls of technological reality, which extend liberty by intensifying domination' (Marcuse 1964:72).

O'Neill (1972) stresses the importance of what he and others, including Marcuse, see as the increasing privatization of modern consumer culture which occurs at the cost of the awareness and values of public responsibilities. Rooted in the core ethic of liberal culture, the basic concept is that the private, individual pursuit of economic welfare and happiness produces public benefits without citizens having to participate in political affairs. Furthermore, O'Neill (1972:20) argues, modern society generates 'a comfortable reality which tempts us to identify the rationality of its industrial metabolism with the whole of rationality and thus to disengage ourselves from the critical tasks of reason'.

Thus it is argued that the culture of the modern technological age produces orientations which allow monopoly capitalism and state forms and policies supportive of it to thrive in a socio-political vacuum; meaningful public participation is left to the marginal and underdog groups not incorporated within the culture spheres of privatism, utilitarianism, consumer fetishism, or the individualistic hedonism prescribed by the market.

Using much the same empirical data and observations of contemporary Western lifestyles and culture, Bell, in *The Cultural Contradictions of Capitalism* (Bell 1976) reaches a radically different conclusion. Bell observes that cultural forms which contradict the ethos of capitalism have gained a position in modern society from which the values of capitalism are being fundamentally challenged. He argues that 'modernism', emerging from diverse cultural roots, but nurtured by the individualistic liberalism of the capitalist ethic, has acquired a position of dominance in art, literature, music and the popular diversions and imagery of the masses. This cultural ethos, he claims, in a fundamental sense withdraws support from capitalism by undermining the values of success, hard work, ambition and deferred gratification. Furthermore, Bell shows how the development of policies associated with the ethic of advanced capitalism have produced a revolution of private and group material wants even in the disadvantaged levels in society; a revolution of rising 'entitlements'. An inevitable concomitant of the need for huge public expenditure and persistent wage demands is a permanent inflationary spiral in the economy. Inflation attacks the standards of living of the middle classes, discourages private savings and places the burden of capital accumulation more and more on the state, 'the investor of last resort'. The fiscal policies of the state further erode the position of the middle class, creating a danger of heightened class conflicts, not between employers and workers but between the middle and the working classes. Bell argues that these economic issues are embedded in a larger cultural question – the ethic of living in debt, and a set of economic and cultural expectations that the 'system' cannot discipline.

Broadly, Bell concludes that advanced capitalism, through the liberal cultural ethic which capitalism itself has sponsored, experiences an acute 'legitimation crisis'. The ideology of capitalism, once launched, has become autonomous and self-perpetuating. Bell notes that the capitalists themselves have lost a sense of moral conviction which would enable them to respond to the growing crisis. Caught in their own web of dependence on mass consumption, they are powerless to control the growing contradictions which, according to Bell, must finally undermine their own collective enterprise.

The issue which concerns us here, as regards our definition of culture, is that of the degree to which culture can be independent of social structure. While the conventional, perhaps crude, Marxist view is that the cultural superstructure is always dominantly a reflection and legitimation of the interests of the controlling class (until it is challenged by the symbols of legitimation of a mobilizing proletariat), this view is clearly oversimple in the light not only of analyses like that of Bell, but also of Marxist theorists dealing with the problems of what has been termed 'legitimation crisis' (see for example, Habermas 1975). It seems clear that in a complex, stratified, plural and non-totalitarian society it is futile to seek perfect consonance between cultural superstructures and dominant structural forms. The argument of those adhering to the principle of structural determinism may be reformulated, however, in the following way perhaps – society may not display perfect congruence between structure and culture, since during the processes of change in structures arising out of contradictions and conflicts, crises of cultural legitimation will arise from time to time. However, the general trend will be towards congruence of culture and structure.

In terms of this type of formulation, the legitimation crisis set out by Bell may indeed be the precursor of the collapse of one mode of capitalism to be replaced, gradually or otherwise, by another form, more able to discipline the normative and ideational character of the society. This would still be congruent with the Marxist view, since basic to that view is the notion of the emergence of new structures and social formations out of contradictions besetting the earlier forms.

This view may be unduly restrictive, however. Bell's analysis, as well as the views of Geertz and others to whom reference has already been made, suggest that culture, the more or less coherent normative orders and symbol-systems of societies and 'sub-societies', may very well be sufficiently autonomous to exert its own influence on, as well as being influenced by, the nature of social formations and political and economic structure. What is being suggested here is the notion of interaction between norms and ideas on the one hand, and social structure on the other, without according primacy to either. This seems like a fairly commonsense view, but in the light of the 'systems determinism' in a sense central to both Marxist and structural-functional theories, it is not necessarily a view which all sociologists would support.

IV. This question acquires great interest and even greater political relevance in the context of South African society. The policy of Apartheid, or Separate Development, is very frequently defended as being the only policy appropriate to a country with very diverse cultural groups. Ambassador Botha (as he was at the time), in his speech to the United Nations in October 1975, for example, declared: 'Our policy is not based on any concepts of superiority or inferiority, but on the historical fact that different peoples differ in their loyalties, cultures, outlook and modes of life and that they wish to retain them' (see also Rhoodie 1969:109–16).

The interaction of culture and political policy in South Africa has to be viewed in a number of different contexts. For example, there is the issue of ethnic group identity (especially among the politically dominant segment in South Africa –

the Afrikaners) and the ideas, beliefs and myths surrounding concepts of group identity. Hermann Giliomee (1975), a section of whose work is included as a reading at the end of this introductory essay, gives us a skilful overview and analysis of the development of political self-concepts among Afrikaners and how these relate to the policy of Separate Development. While he gives ample attention to the ideational (cultural) components of their identity, his analysis leaves us with little doubt that the strength of group identity among Afrikaners is also a function of economic and political interests. Giliomee is uncertain as to the pervasiveness and strength of essentially non-material and non-instrumental elements in Afrikaner group identity. To what extent has an idealism, nurtured in the historical struggle of Afrikaners for emancipation and political self-expression, helped to shape a self-perpetuating ideology, supported by widespread conviction, capable of conditioning political motivations among Afrikaners more or less independently of their pragmatic interests? In an empirical study of political motivations among Whites, we have found among some Afrikaners substantial evidence of a concern with identity which is unconnected with out-group denigration, with instrumental political attitudes, or with political conservatism of the conventional kind (Schlemmer 1973:50–7). We must at least consider the possibility that the ideological content of Afrikaner nationalism includes, in addition to beliefs originating in the need to justify inequality and domination, an enlightened pluralism arising out of a basic mode of political thought articulated primarily in terms of ethnic or group concepts. If this identifiable sub-theme in the Afrikaner's political belief-system exists, is it pervasive enough to be meaningful? Is it perhaps not merely superficially free of pragmatic and material content? Is the notion of power sovereignty not perhaps subtly blended in with this ideal of group self determination?

Heribert Adam (1976) argues very cogently that the ideological rhetoric of Afrikaner Nationalism is shallow and increasingly irrelevant as a means of mobilizing and shaping political attitudes and behaviour. He sees the present position as being 'a material, tactical defence with little credible spiritual rationalisation.'[1] Elsewhere I have argued that the corporate group response of Afrikaners in the political sphere (the vast majority of Afrikaners are unswerving in their support of the National Party) is not to be understood primarily in terms of any deep and pervading sense of cultural or ethnic identity, but rather in terms of mechanisms of social integration (interlocking networks) (Schlemmer 1976). These issues deserve much more attention by social scientists, however. In the realm of the analysis of culture in South Africa, the strength or weakness (in terms of pervasiveness and committed adherence by substantial proportions of people) of Afrikaner Nationalist ideology is of cardinal academic importance and political relevance.

Broadly speaking much the same questions can be posed in regard to colour prejudice and racism among Whites generally. In South Africa, as elsewhere, racial inequality and colour discrimination may be supported both by cynical and rational justifications and by myths, more or less coherent belief-systems and a variety of social taboos; the latter all essentially 'cultural' elements. In the articulation by Whites of fears regarding political change, highly emotive terms are often used, like the fear of being 'swamped', for example; the possibly extensive symbolic content underlying these terms has yet to be explored. It is fairly common to have it argued, however, that racists beliefs are either a justification of inequality and material or power interests, or more broadly, a reflection of social formations that have emerged as a consequence of the exploitation and marginalization of Blacks in South Africa. It is difficult, though, to reconcile the extreme rigidity of racial differentiation in South Africa with any simplistic assertions that out-group denigration is society's way of justifying its inequalities. The taboo-like elements in race perceptions among Whites are far too prominent to be reconciled with any simple 'prejudice as legitimation' thesis. (There are a number of specific arguments which can be adduced in qualification or criticism of this thesis but these do not really belong in a discussion of culture.) If one argues, on the other hand, that exploitation of one group by another, or the presence of material competition between groups produces certain perceptions which are pre-conditions for the development of racist culture, then the argument becomes more convincing. This view would see the structural conditions as merely providing an attitudinal climate for the acceptance of racism; the development and form of that racist culture would have to be the object of a separate and more elaborate analysis. We must consider the obvious fact that racism had very early beginnings in South African history and the passage of centuries has provided ample time for the incubation of autonomous symbolic and perceptual 'sets' in regard to race; material interests may have provided warmth for the incubation but it seems exceedingly difficult to demonstrate that these interests have shaped all the complex forms that have emerged. Lever (1976) in a review of a book by one major exponent of the materialist thesis (Johnstone 1976), reminds us of a 'reverse possibility of the emerging class structure being itself in part a product of pre-existing patterns of the racial order . . .' Clearly, much more work in this problematic area of study requires to be undertaken.

Such studies would be of particular significance now and in the near future. Pressures on South Africa to de-racialize its public order are mounting, both externally and internally. If the culture of racism and the ideological accompaniments of policy are as shallow as, say, Adam claims, then relatively facile adjustments in areas which do not involve the sacrifice by Whites of real privilege may be expected. If on the other hand, the values vested in racial or ethnic identity go deeper, one may expect, at least among a proportion of Whites, the development of what Baker (1975) terms a 'siege culture' – wherein beliefs in regard to, *inter alia*, the value of maintaining racial and ethnic integrity become more and more fervently held, dogmatic and imbued with dramatic symbolism.

In recent years a new cultural theme has emerged at the political level, carried by the 'Black Consciousness' movement. This movement emerged initially among clergy and Black students but is becoming fairly swiftly extended to more and more members of the Black middle class generally. This is not the place to discuss the entire movement as it relates to the wider society – the paper by Adam included in this chapter gives excellent coverage of this aspect. Understandably, the movement is a reaction to White racism, but it has drawn inspiration and content from Senghor, Fanon, and a host of African and Black American writers.

It is difficult to know whether the content of ideas in the Black Consciousness movement should be viewed as 'culture' in the conventional sense or not. It is certainly highly self-conscious culture at this relatively early stage, and inevitably so. Part of the central motive in the movement is to rebuild the eroded and undermined concepts of an African identity and the appreciation of indigenous culture among Blacks, i.e. to counter those aspects of culture-contact with Whites which have produced uncritical admiration of industrial culture, and also those missionary influences which have encouraged the moral rejection of indigenous heritage among Blacks. Nevertheless, Black Consciousness spokesmen are disdainful of much that is written by White ethnographers who attempt to demonstrate the uniqueness and worth of African traditional culture (Manganyi 1973), *inter alia*, because the culture to be sponsored is one which, it is felt, must transcend the conventional units of ethnographic analysis, the so-called 'tribe'.

Although certain authors in the movement seek to explore an African ontology, the symbols of identity given as examples generally tend to be more superficial and specific – names, dress, etc., and there is very little exploration of the particular nature of any authentic continental African belief-systems, values and symbols (cf. Bengu 1977). The task, it seems, is primarily to set about creating an identity in cultural opposition to (White) Western norms. It is therefore highly prescriptive. While it would be difficult, therefore, to identify the Black movement for cultural liberation in terms of a wide range of specific cultural elements of a positive kind at this stage, as the movement progresses and extends itself to wider circles and adherents, no doubt interesting elements will emerge out of the interplay between political praxis and the communication of goals and justifications for behaviour, on the one hand, and local traditional cultural forms on the other.

V. Many students of culture, whether they be ethnographers or certain social anthropologists and sociologists, will hardly recognize their field of enquiry in the subject matter I have discussed above. I make no apologies for this; South African society has become a situation of such key interest for the study of ideology, political belief-systems and racist cultures that these topics must inevitably hold centre stage. There is another reason – perhaps even more obvious, and that is the fact that I am by training and experience more at home in a 'total systems' approach than in the study of situations in micro perspective. Let me hasten to add that studies of specific African 'tribes', linguistic-cultural groupings or communities are in my view extremely important, especially if such studies are cast within a framework sensitive to major theoretical debates or to issues like the influence of colonialism, changing modes of subsistence in response to culture-contact and to the overall framework of South Africa's plural society. In this I do not refer to – indeed I plead welcome ignorance of – purely descriptive, non-interpretive ethnographic accounts of particular customs and patterns of everyday living.

In any overview of the theme of culture in South Africa, reference must be made to some of the very important interpretive works by social anthropologists. Comprehensive works like *The Bantu-speaking Peoples of Southern Africa*, edited by Hammond-Tooke (1974), are obviously essential reading in any study of culture in South Africa. The chapter by Dubb, 'Impact of the City' is an insightful overview of cultural change. Dubb points to the fact that varieties of traditional cultural forms persist in the urban areas (marriage customs, religious belief-systems, etc.) despite widespread adaptation to the pragmatic culture of industrialism. From the point of view of the earlier discussion of Black Consciousness, it is interesting to note that he finds no evidence of the emergence of a unitary urban African culture, despite similarities in traditional backgrounds and the almost uniform social encapsulation of urban Africans as a product of the system of Apartheid. Similarly informative is the comprehensive overview 'Tribalism and Detribalisation in Southern and Central Africa' by Reader (1970), who draws on a wide variety of empirical materials. Space prevents the mention of numerous other worthwhile contributions.

Rather closer to the kind of interpretation extolled by Geertz ('thick description') are the works on African cosmologies and on modern religious movements. The volume edited by Whisson and West, *Religion and Social Change in Southern Africa* (1975) is essential reading in this regard, as is a study by West (1975) of African Independent Churches in Soweto.

Perhaps the most compelling account of the impact on the values and identity of Africans exposed to the juxtaposition of pre-industrial and industrial communities in South Africa is the classical study by Mayer, *Townsmen or Tribesmen* (1961).

Specific case studies of what happens to non-Western cultural blueprints for behaviour in changing social settings are particularly important; if interpreted in depth (I refer back to Geertz) they can become the elements for systematic interpretation on a macro scale which does not lose the sensitivity and depth of the intensive approach. Although it does not have the interpretive quality that Geertz prescribes, one short reading by Scotch which perhaps begins to approximate to this requirement is included. The crisp account by Scotch of the employment of magic by soccer players is an excellent example of the synthesis of Western and non-Western cultural meanings in a competitive setting, lending itself to wider generalization.

If appeals are in order in an introduction of this nature, then it may be appropriate to suggest the importance of intensive observational studies of the meanings underlying behaviour in settings which relate directly to larger issues. Situations of race contact of various kinds, multi-ethnic employment settings[2], political policy formulation (if practical), behaviour and performance in educational settings, are examples of studies which would assist hugely in filling large lacunae in our insights into South African society.

VI. Finally it is necessary to draw attention to yet one more field of enquiry relating to culture; that of development studies. Once again, in this area of debate, there are two sharply contrasting theoretical views: the one rooted in analyses of the structural opportunities for and constraints on development – sometimes called a political economy approach, sometimes termed the theory of Dependence (e.g. Frank 1971), and the other often located in evolutionary or functional theory but almost always focussing some attention on aspects of non-Western culture as a constraining feature in development (e.g. Hoselitz 1960; and in some ways Eisenstadt 1970). It is almost unnecessary to note that the present White government authorities associated with African rural development (or even the development of manpower and labour relations) tend to stress the inappropriateness of local African culture to the tasks and challenges of development. These references almost always have a taint of stereotypy and deflect attention away from factors which would impede development whatever the orientations of the communities involved.

Although the alternative viewpoints alluded to above are usually seen as mutually incompatible, Dependency theory is very usefully supplemented by certain of the alternative approaches, particularly if they shed light on middle-range processes (the theory of Dependence provides essential insights but usually mainly at a macro level). Eisenstadt, for example, has argued that the 'cultural' incapacity of under-developed Third World populations to demonstrate the initiative or collective will to 'modernize' can often be traced to disequilibria in the development process itself. The pattern of stratification which emerges is such as to create a modernizing elite socially distant from the masses, who in turn, through lack of example, social rejection and lack of a sense of meaningful participation in development, fail to absorb the appropriate value systems.

No doubt not all problems of cultural mobilization in differing situations are to be explained in these terms, but the illustration contains a lesson. Through intensive studies of cultural constraints on development it may be possible to refute widely myths about rural African culture in South Africa. The same type of argument would perhaps apply to popular White beliefs about the inevitability of 'tribal' conflict among Africans. These are yet other ways in which the study of culture can be relevant to the most critical issues facing South African society.

NOTES

1. It is a little confusing, however, that the man described as a passé traditional Afrikaner ideologue, Dr A. P. Treurnicht, has recently gained considerable power within the National Party and I have heard his speeches listened to with great reverence in parliament.
2. The example of Hahlo (1969) needs to be extended.

REFERENCES

Adam, H. 1976 – 'Ideologies of dedication vs. blueprints of expedience.' *Social Dynamics* II, 2, 83–91.

Baker, D. G. 1975 – 'Race, power and white siege cultures.' *Social Dynamics* I, 2, 143–57.

Bell, D. 1976 – *The Cultural Contradictions of Capitalism*. London: Heinemann.

Bengu, S. M. E. 1977 – 'Cultural Liberation – Principals and Practices.' A series of lectures given at the University of Natal, April-May 1977.

Berger, P. L., and T. Luckmann 1966 – *The Social Construction of Reality*. Allen Lane: Penguin.

Broom, L., and P. Selznick 1963 – *Sociology: A Text with Adapted Readings*. Harper and Row.

Eisenstadt, S. N. 1970 – 'Social change and modernization in African societies South of the Sahara.' In J. Middleton (ed.) *Black Africa: Its Peoples and Their Cultures Today*. London: Macmillan.

Firth, R. 1951 – *Elements of Social Organization*. London and New York: New York Philosophical Library.

Frank, A. G. 1971 – *Sociology of Development and Underdevelopment of Sociology*. London: Pluto Press.

Geertz, C. 1973 – *The Interpretation of Cultures*. The Anchor Press.

Gerth, H. H., and Mills C. Wright 1958 – *From Max Weber*. London and New York: Oxford University Press.

Giliomee, H. 1975 – 'The development of the Afrikaner's self concept'. In H. W. van der Merwe (ed.) *Looking at the Afrikaner Today*. Cape Town: Tafelberg, 1–39.

Gouldner, A. W. 1970 – *The Coming Crisis of Western Sociology*. London: Heinemann.

Habermas, J. 1975 – *Legitimation Crisis*. Boston: Beacon Press.

Hahlo, K. G. 1969 – 'A European-African worker relationship in South Africa.' *Race* II, 1, 13–34.

Hammond-Tooke, W. D. (ed.) 1974 – *The Bantu-Speaking Peoples of Southern Africa*. London: Routledge and Kegan Paul.

Hoselitz, B. F. 1960 – *Sociological Factors in Economic Development*. Glencoe: The Free Press.

Johnstone, F. A. 1976 – *Class, Race and Gold*. London: Routledge and Kegan Paul.

Kluckhohn, C. 1949 – *Mirror for Man*. New York: McGraw-Hill.

——1951 – 'The study of culture.' In D. Lerner and H. D. Lasswell (eds.) *The Policy Sciences*. Stanford: Stanford University Press.

Lever, J. 1976 – Review of Johnstone: Class, Race and Gold. *Social Dynamics* II, 2, 163–4.

Malinowski, B. 1944 – *A Scientific Theory of Culture and other Essays*. New York: Chapel Hill.

Manganyi, N. C. 1973 – *Being-Black-in-the-World*. Johannesburg: Sprocas/Ravan.

Marcuse, H. 1964 – *One Dimensional Man*. London: Routledge and Kegan Paul.

Mayer, P. 1961 – *Townsmen or Tribesmen*. Cape Town: Oxford University Press.

O'Neill, J. 1972 – *Sociology as a Skin Trade*. London: Heinemann.

Parsons, Talcott 1951 – *The Social System*. London: Tavistock.

Reader, D. H. 1970 – 'Tribalism and detribalization in Southern and Central Africa.' *Zambezia*, I, 2, 55–75.

Rhoodie, N. J. 1969 – *Apartheid and Racial Partnership in Southern Africa*. Pretoria and Cape Town: Academica.

Ricoeur, P. 1970 – *Freud and Philosophy:* New Haven.

Schlemmer, L. 1973 – *Privilege, Prejudice and Parties*. Johannesburg: South African Institute of Race Relations.

——1976 – 'Theories of the plural society and change in South Africa.' Modified version of a paper read at 19th Annual Meeting of the African Studies Association. Boston, 1976.

West, M. 1975 – *Bishops and Prophets in a Black City.* African Independent Churches in Soweto, Johannesburg. Cape Town: David Philip.

Whisson, M. G., and M. West (eds.) 1975 – *Religion and Social Change in Southern Africa.* Cape Town: David Philip and London: Rex Collings.

Wilensky, H. L. 1964 – 'Mass society and mass culture: Interdependence of dependence?' *American Sociological Review*, 29, 2, 196.

1. The Development of the Afrikaner's Self-concept

HERMANN GILIOMEE

The Afrikaner's self-concepts and Apartheid (1948–1974)

In the years since 1948 much of the zeal formerly expended on formulations of Afrikaner identity, to distinguish it from that of the English, has been channelled into attempts to define the position of the White in relation to the non-Whites and to incorporate such distinctions in government policy. André du Toit (1974) points out that 'the central concern of the ideology of apartheid (is) not with the self-definition of the Afrikaner movement, which predominated in the earlier stages, but with the structuring of race and social relations in the society as a whole, thus, as it were, with its "external" relations.'

The legitimation of the apartheid policy in the decade after 1948 reflected the group concepts formed by the Whites in the preceding three centuries. Blumer's (1961) theory on the categories of attitudes and emotions of dominant groups is as applicable to the year 1800 as to 1948. The concept of the Whites as a superior and separate race remained the pivot: other groups were inferior or lower. Although leaders such as Hertzog insisted that the colour bar was based neither on colour nor on race but on profound differences in national character and civilization (Nienaber 1965: 234), debates on 'immorality' and mixed marriages made it clear that miscegenation was an 'evil' because it led to the 'degeneration' of the White race (Joubert 1974).

Genetic reasons alone were not the prime consideration; the desire for separateness and 'purity' gained impetus only in conjuction with the second component of the group concept of the Whites, i.e. that it was a group with a primary or major claim to certain privileges and benefits. The separateness and purity of the race had to be safeguarded not as ends in themselves but in order to maintain the privileged position of the racial group in an 'unadulterated' form. These two considerations were inextricably linked: without a privileged position a 'pure' and separate White race could not survive; without a 'pure' and separate White race a privileged position could not be maintained. Mr J. G. Strijdom (1949) explained the connection in the following terms (*translated*): 'If the White loses his consciousness of colour he cannot remain White' – and a 'White' is here clearly understood to be a person with a certain status and a particular socio-economic position. 'The White population of our country, which is in the minority, can remain White only if they retain their consciousness of colour . . . (and) national pride, their pride as a race . . . Sense of colour cannot be maintained on the basis of equality, that is, if there is no apartheid for daily intercourse in social affairs, politically, or in any other field . . .' He concluded by saying that 'the White race in South Africa (could) be maintained only if the Whites held the franchise in their hands'.

Parallel with the view of Afrikaner leaders that White dominance and privilege were the fulfilment of any nation's claim to self-protection and survival, there was a clear tendency to justify this view by the instrumental value it was claimed to have in South African society.[1] In the fifties Dr Verwoerd frequently expounded the view that the White man had brought civilization to this country and that everything the Bantu was now inheriting along with the White had been created by the knowledge and industry of the Whites: It was the White who was protecting the Non-white against chaos, disease and destruction; the White was the founder of the state and its prosperity, the cause [*sic*] of the growing numbers of Bantu (Pelzer 1966:112–3, 354, 474).

The third component of the group concept of the Whites was the attitude that other groups in the society were essentially different and alien. Malan took the colour line as a basic premise (*translated*): 'Difference in colour indicates a simple but highly significant fact, i.e. that Whites and Non-whites are not of the same kind. They are different.' ('Die Kleur-vraagstuk', chapter in the undated MS. *Op die Wagtoring*.) He explained it as follows: 'The difference in colour is merely the physical manifestation of the contrast between two irreconcilable ways of life, between barbarism and civilization, between heathenism and Christianity, and finally between overwhelming numerical odds on the one hand and insignificant numbers on the other.' (Kuper 1956:217). During the late 1950s this racial dichotomy became a cultural one with relativistic overtones: the Bantu were 'different', a group with its own identity and national character. Urbanization and Westernization would corrupt them; apartheid would protect them by giving the Black an opportunity to develop in his own territory according to his own nature (cf. comments cited in Du Preez 1972a).

During the sixties 'apartheid' shifted to 'separate development', with a corresponding shift in the rhetoric of justification. Firstly, the concept of superiority was replaced as the central component by a concept of 'difference'. Mr B. J. Voster (1968b) stated (*translated*) 'that the policy of separate development was conceived not because we considered ourselves better than others . . . we created the policy of separate development because we maintained that we were different from others and valued that difference, and we are not prepared to sacrifice that difference'.[2]

Secondly, the idea that the White had to rule over the whole of South Africa shifted to a concept of dominance over 'White South Africa'. As Mr B. J. Vorster (1968b) put it (*translated*), 'We have our land and we alone will have the say over that land. We have our Parliament and in that Parliament we and we alone will be represented.' This view is founded on a particular interpretation of history to the effect that the Whites and Blacks arrived simultaneously and the country was then virtually uninhabited. Arrival was followed by 'separate occupation:' the White man never used violence to deprive the Black of his land (for Verwoerd, cf. Pelzer 1966: 474; for Vorster, cf. *Die Burger* 19/9/1973).

Finally, the other group(s) are no longer seen as belonging to a different *race* but as different nations (Du Preez 1972b). On the model of the Afrikaner's nationalism and its development, the development of each nation's 'identity' and its (God-given) right to self-assertion and self-realization within its own homeland are advocated. Mr B. J. Vorster (1968a) put it as follows (*translated*): 'The Afrikaner's struggle was in its essence a struggle for the preservation of his identity . . . we therefore grant all the other nations in our country . . . the preservation of their identity and way of life.'

In the seventies the self-concept of the Afrikaners has been determined primarily by the fact that they have to share the 'White' territory with a majority of people of differing colours, *inter alia* the Coloured group, with their predominantly Afrikaans culture, who have no homeland where they can achieve 'full self-realization.' In order to escape from this dilemma Afrikaner politicians emphasize the idea that all different population groups should strive to maintain their 'identity', a term which has been much in evidence in recent years and which will probably enjoy great popularity in future. What the so-called identity comprises is seldom explained in concrete terms. If the term is analysed in the context of the foregoing study it appears not to be an ethnic identity but that of a political power group determined to control 'its affairs' in South Africa. In this sense Afrikaner identity and White identity become inter-changeable. Thus Mr Vorster could asset: Like the Voortrekkers, the people (*volk*) of South Africa (meaning the white South African nation) will not tolerate domination by anyone. The Afrikaner refuses to abandon his identity (i.e. as a group not to be dominated) and grants others their identity (*Die Burger* 17/12/1973). And on another occasion: 'I am not prepared to let my people (meaning the White "nation") be subordinate to any other people, Black or White, how well-disposed they may be' (*Rapport* 3/2/1974). Closely linked is the notion that this identity with its concomitant socio-economic privileges can only be maintained if the Whites remain a separate and 'pure' race.[3]

But what then about Afrikaner identity? Afrikanerhood has long had a connotation of colour which would make such inclusivity not such a new departure as it may seem. Yet it will have certain consequences. On the short term it will mean the disappearance of the metaphysical notions of *volksiel* and vocation which have been strongly held until recently. The long term implications are not clear. The greater degree of openness reflected by the inclusion of other Whites may pave the way for the absorption of other ethnic groups, notable the Coloured people, as well. On the other hand it is also possible that differences in colour will come to be seen as corresponding with differences in identity (cf. the argument of W. de Klerk, *Rapport* 16/3/1975) with the result that the importance of culture as a rallying point will be greatly diminished.

Afrikaner Self-*concepts and White Unity* (1961–1974)

As the Afrikaners progressed during the past decade towards seeing the people of different colours no longer as different races but as different nations (or embryo nations), there has been at the same time an increasing tendency to see themselves, in their relationship with other Whites, as members of a common race or of the (White) South African nation, rather than as a separate nation.

This trend is attributable to various factors. The founding of the Republic and the severing of ties with England have fostered consciousness of a common South African citizenship (Adam 1971). Urbanization, has ended the geographic isolation of the Afrikaner to a large extent, and simultaneously also the concept of the Afrikaners as a 'nation of farmers'. In the period 1930–1970 the economic disparity between the Afrikaner and the English was reduced considerably – in 1974 the ratio of per capita incomes was approximately 100:120 – with the result that the need for the economic mobilization of the Afrikaner has diminished. The Afrikaner has also shaken off his sense of social inferiority in respect of the English and has asserted himself on all social levels. But the prime factor has been the racial problem which has created an urgent need for White unity.

Under these circumstances Afrikaans political leaders are re-formulating traditional group concepts to embrace both Afrikaners and English-speaking persons. It is no longer the Afrikaner but the White man who 'brought civilization to South Africa.' The concept of the Afrikaner's vocation has been replaced by Dr Verwoerd's idea that the Whites were placed here to provide an anchor and a bastion for Western religion (Pelzer 1966: 193, 354).

At the same time Afrikaner political leaders are attempting to shift the focus of the Afrikaner's loyalty from the exclusive cultural group towards (White) South Africa or towards the ideological basis of the governing party, which is sometimes presented as a criterion for 'patriotism'. In 1968 Mr B. J. Vorster stated (1968a) that the issue in South Africa was (*translated*) 'no longer language . . . *The issue* (*was*) *faith in the policy of separate development*, faith in the survival of the White here in South Africa. Out of such people a nation will be built.' In 1974 he remarked that as leader of the Nationalist Party he was not speaking on behalf of the Afrikaners but on behalf of Afrikaans- and English-speaking Nationalists (*The Cape Times* 3/9/1974).

This concept of the Afrikaner, as part of a White South African nation, has drawn various responses. A number of the leading Afrikaans writers in the so-called Sestigerbeweging (Movement of the Sixties) objected to the racial connotation given to the term 'Afrikaner'. Jan Rabie (1966) maintained that the Afrikaner was someone whose mother-tongue was Afrikaans; therefore the Afrikaner nation included the Coloured people. In his view the Afrikaner was faced with the choice of being White (member of a privileged group) or being an Afrikaner (member of a multi-racial cultural group).[4]

At the other end of the spectrum there are cultural leaders who see the danger of the obliteration of the 'Afrikaner identity' in the rising white South Africanism. They see Afrikaner identity as comprising a separate White cultural group with a Calvinistic and conservative philosophy (Treurnicht 1972; Beukes 1974). More or less explicitly the idea is also propagated that the Afrikaner is a supporter of the Nationalist Party; those who are not are bad Afrikaners or no Afrikaners.

It is hard to determine to what extent Afrikaners in general accept the definitions of Afrikaner identity by cultural leaders. Phil Weber (1973), former editor of *Die Burger*, said in this regard (*translated*): 'At the Nasionale Pers . . . during the time of Fusion and in wartime, most of us saw an Afrikaner as someone whose home language was Afrikaans. Religion and political views were not qualifying factors.'

Although it is improbable that the term 'Afrikaner' has undergone a fundamental conceptual change during the past quarter of a century, the definition of the concept 'Afrikaner' by cultural leaders is significant in view of their special position in the structure of Afrikaner society. Here the principal feature is the 'encapsulation' of urban Afrikaners as a counter to denationalizing influences (Welsh 1969). Separate schools with compulsory mother-tongue education, churches, chambers of commerce, together with cultural and semi-political organizations, emphasize the identity of the Afrikaner as a separate ethnic group. Within such institutions the cultural leaders play an important rôle in the way they stress the similarity or uniqueness of this identity and through the opportunities they have for disseminating their views.

Whereas encapsulation promotes group solidarity among the Afrikaners in the urban community, contact with other life-styles and adherence especially in academic and professional circles, with universal values serve as a counter to identification with a too narrowly defined Afrikaner 'identity'. One reaction is to accept a 'broad (White) South Africanism'. Ar ecent inquiry (Pieterse 1967) shows that 50 per cent of a test sample of young Afrikaners in Pretoria saw themselves as South Africans rather than as Afrikaners or Afrikaans-speaking South Africans.

In politics this phenomenon has so far had no significant effect. The vast majority of Afrikaners follow the Nationalist Party and support the policy of homelands. It is possible, however, to see the recent conflict between 'verkramptes' (ultra-conservatives) and 'verligtes' (enlightened ones) as a conflict between those who advocate Afrikaner exclusivity as well as undisguised White domination, and those who propagate White unity and/or adjustments to the racial policies.

At this stage it is not quite clear how 'White unity' will affect the Afrikaner's self-concepts. The view of the South African people as a dual nation in which Afrikaners and English are on an equal footing is at present the official one. The political power of the Afrikaner, and particularly the view that (*translated*) 'South African nationhood (was) born in the bosom of the Afrikaans-speaking section of the population,' as Dr Malan put it (MS. *Op die Wagtoring*) creates a basis on which political and cultural leaders will endeavour more and more to see the Afrikanerdom as *the* South African nation. On the other hand tensions within Afrikaner ranks may reach such proportions that it will become more and more difficult to speak of '*the* Afrikanerdom'.

Conclusion

Over more than three centuries a pattern has unfolded, of White people deriving from different European countries and beginning to see themselves, in the particular circumstances and racial structure of the colony, as a dominant group whose position had to be entrenched economically and socially vis-á-vis the Non-whites. Simultaneously, the severing of ties with the mother country (or countries) stimulated the idea of an African nation. In the nineteenth century the British imperial element fostered the concept of a separate cultural identity in the Cape Colony and of a separate political identity in the North. At the time of Union there were enough factors present to make the Afrikaners see themselves as a unified political interest group, but disunity arose over relations with the English population group and with the British Empire. During the middle third of the twentieth century the Afrikaners came to see themselves more and more as an exclusive cultural group, and on this basis they were mobilized politically until they became the dominant class in politics.

Once he had political power in his hands the Afrikaner based his policy towards other population groups on concepts of himself which he had formed in the course of his history, i.e. (i) the view that the various White ethnic groups formed a common race whose position (White identity) in the social structure had to be entrenched and constituted a potential nation which may, like the Afrikaner himself, fuse into one nation in course of time (ii) the concept of Non-whites as different nations which should develop and preserve their own identities, as the Afrikaner has done.

The success achieved with these policies and the course of the struggle for power between Whites and Non-whites will determine the future content of the Afrikaner's self-concepts.

On the strength of the foregoing it becomes possible to distinguish four patterns of identification in the modern Afrikaner:

Firstly there are those who see the Afrikaners as a distinct White *volk*, membership of which is clearly defined. Among these two different concepts are present: (a) the concept of the Afrikaner as someone who is *born* into a *volk* which is a particular creation of God, having a definite genetic character, a cultural heritage and a characteristic outlook on life, all of which together constitute his 'identity', and (b) the view that membership of the Afrikanervolk is something which is *attained* by White persons whose home language is Afrikaans by virtue of membership of an Afrikaans church, support for a party which advocates a position of political power for the Afrikaner and an endorsement of certain social values especially with regard to public morals. Apart from a racial and cultural denominator this notion of Afrikaner identity has, moreover, components of churchliness and political power. Militating against this concept are the increasing secularization of the Afrikaners and the broadening political base of the Nationalist Party. Such a narrow definition of what it means to be an Afrikaner is unattractive to many creative artists, intellectuals and business men.

Secondly, the Afrikaner is seen as a member of a (White) population group which is becoming more and more part of the (White) South African nation together with other white ethnic groups. This *White* identity is reinforced by the privileged position the Afrikaner shares with other Whites. To entrench this position, the support of other Whites is needed, so that there is a shift from ethnic identification to racial identification. Those who refuse to identify in this way point out that it excludes another Afrikaans-speaking group, i.e. the Coloured people. It is also seen by some writers as a denial of commitment to Africa and all her peoples. For example, Breyten Breytenbach (1973) remarked (*translated*): 'We are a bastard nation with a bastard language . . . It is just that we have stepped into the trap of the bastard getting into power. In that part of our blood which came from Europe there was the curse of superiority. And to be able to do so, we had to freeze our supposed tribal identity . . .'

Thirdly there is a group, particularly of writers and academics, which seeks to rejuvenate the concept Afrikaner to make it embrace certain humanitarian values and a richer spiritual life. They wish to see the Afrikaners or Afrikaans-speaking people of all races as a *cultural group* which strives to express the full riches of modern life through its language; as a *political entity* which has a right to exist and has certain interests in the South African plural society; as a spiritual community which believes that values such as love, truth and social justice transcend communal interests. This concept is opposed by the strong racial connotations the concept Afrikaner has acquired over a period of approximately two centuries; a connotation which has been emphasized in politics over the last three of four decades by those Afrikaners who identity themselves in terms of the first two views set out above. It is to be expected that they will strongly resist attempts to give the concept Afrikaner this content. There indeed exist irreconcilable conflicts of opinion between the various groups of Afrikaners described above over the political policy of the Afrikaner and the function of art in the life of the people.

Finally, there are those who would open up Afrikaners so that an African nation might develop at the southern end of this continent,[5] one which would give priority to its basic humanity.[6] This development is not as 'unnatural' as it may appear at first glance. As Erik Erikson (1966: 235) remarked, 'man's deep-seated conviction that some providence has made his tribe and race, or class, caste or religion "naturally" superior to others . . . seems to be part of a psychosocial evolution by which he has developed into *pseudo-species.*' To this he opposes 'the fact and obligation of man's specieshood.' To promote the development away from a 'God-given' and 'fixed' national identity or racial identity, Johannes Degenaar introduced the concept 'process of identification'. In essence this means that the Afrikaner nationalist should be involved, with other citizens of the country, in a plurality of identifications and associations, among which cultural identifications would be only one of several, and especially that the cultural values of a particular ethnic group should not be employed as a primary category in politics. The advantages of this concept, according to

Degenaar 1974, a and b, would be the end of racial discrimination by the Whites and the equitable accommodation of the political aspirations of the Black population groups. But this concept is opposed by the Afrikaner's fear of Black domination and of the eventual disappearance of his language, and therefore also of the Afrikaner people.

NOTES

1. Danziger's (1971) hypotheses, that after 1948 justification of dominance was offered first in terms of intrinsic values (e.g. that the Whites were the chosen people and that the Non-whites had been condemned to servitude) and later in instrumental terms (that it ensured economic progress for all), will be hard to prove. But between, say, 1800 and 1970 there was a progression of this kind.
2. In a study of political, economic and administrative elites Adam (1971) found that the notion that the Bantu were still children in civilisation, centuries behind the White, was very firmly held.
3. For a fairly clear articulation of this, cf. the speech of Min. M. Viljoen as reported in *Rapport*, 25/8/74; also the comment on this by Gus Adams (pseudonym of a Coloured academic) in *Rapport* 1/9/74.
4. Recent surveys of opinions reveal that a remarkably high percentage of Afrikaners regard the Coloured people as 'brown Afrikaners'. This view is opposed from two quarters: by the government, which insists that the Coloured people are a separate embryo nation, and by the Coloured people themselves, who (no longer) associate themselves with the Afrikaners for political reasons and who prefer to be regarded as South Africans (cf. the speech by J. Gerwel *Rapport*, 15/9/1974).
5. The development of Afrikaner self-concepts vis-à-vis African might be summed up as follows: Not *man* of Africa (African), but *white man* of Africa (Afrikaner). Cf. Dr Verwoerd's words (translated): 'We are white, but we are in Africa' (Pelzer 1963: 319). This should be read with his view that the white man is the link between Africa and Europe. For an interesting view of the Afrikaner in the context of Africa, see Rabie 1974.
6. André P. Brink (1968) identifies himself as follows: 'I refuse to think in terms of "we", little group of Whites, against "them", the black majority. When I talk of *my people*, then I mean: every man, black, brown and white who shares my country and my loyalty to my country.'

REFERENCES

Adam, Heribert (ed.) 1971 – 'The South African power elite.' In Heribert Adam (ed.), *South Africa: Sociological Perspectives.* London: Oxford University Press, 73–102.

Beukes, D. P. M. 1974 – 'Afrikaner se plig om sy identiteit te handhaaf.' Speech published in *Die Burger*, July 12.

Blumer, Herbert 1961 – 'Race prejudice as a sense of group position.' In J. Musuoka and P. Valien (eds.), *Race Relations: Problems and Theory.* Chapel Hill: University of North Carolina Press, 217–27.

Breytenbach, B. 1973 – ''n Blik van Buite.' Lecture at Summer School, University of Cape Town.

Brink, A. P. 1968 – Answer to Smith. *Kol.* 1–3.

Danziger, Kurt 1971 – 'Modernisation and legitimation of social power.' In Heribert Adam (ed.), *South Africa: Sociological Perspectives.* London: Oxford University Press, 283–300.

Degenaar, Johannes J. 1974a – Letter to *Die Burger*, October 24.

——1974b – Philosophical Roots of Nationalism. Unpublished Paper.

Du Preez, Peter 1972a – Categories of Persons: The National Party View of Social Identity in South Africa. Unpublished Paper.

——1972b – 'The constitution of alternatives in parliamentary debate: Psychological theory and political analysis.' *South African Journal of Psychology*, 2, 23–40.

Du Toit, André B. 1974 – Ideological change, Afrikaner Nationalism and pragmatic racial domination in South Africa. Unpublished Paper.

Erikson, Erik II. 1966 – 'The concept of identity in race relations: notes and queries.' In Talcott Parsons and Kenneth B. Clark (eds.) *The Negro American*. Boston: Houghton Mifflin, 227–53.

Joubert, Dian (compiler) 1974 – *Met Iemand van 'n Ander Kleur: Beskouings en Wetgewing oor Ontug*. Cape Town: Tafelberg.

Kuper, Leo 1956 – *Passive Resistance in South Africa*. New Haven: Yale University Press.

——1970/1972 – 'Race Structure in the Social Consciousness.' In Paul Baxter and Basil Sansom (eds.) *Race and Social Difference*. Baltimore: Penguin, 77–97.

Nienaber, P. J. (Editorial Chairman) 1965 – *Gedenkboek Generaal J. B. M. Hertzog*. Johannesburg: A.P.B.

Pieterse, J. E. (ed.) 1967 – *Jeug en Kultuur*. Johannesburg: Voortrekkerpers.

Rabie, Jan 1966 – *Polemika*, 1957–1965. Cape Town: John Malherbe.

——1974 – *Minder Europa, Meer Afrika*. Ons Erfdeel 4/74.

Strijdom, J. G. 1949 – Speech in Parliament. *Hansard*, 66, col. 306–11.

Treurnicht, A. P. 1972 – 'Afrikaner Eenheid.' *Handhaaf*, 10/4/1972.

Vorster, John B. 1968a – Speech at Parow on May 17. Unpublished verbatim copy.

——1968b – Speech at Heilbron on August 16. Unpublished verbatim copy.

Weber, Phil 1973 – Republiek en Nasionale Eenheid. Gen. J. B. M. Hertzog-Memorial Lecture, May 29.

Welsh, David 1969 – 'Urbanisation and the solidarity of Afrikaner Nationalism.' *The Journal of Modern African Studies*, 7, 2: 265–76.

Newspapers and Periodicals

Die Burger, 19/9/1973, 17/12/1974.

The Cape Times, 3/9/1974.

Rapport, 25/8/1974, 1/9/1974 and 15/9/1974, 16/3/1975.

2. Magic, Sorcery and Football among Urban Zulu: A Case of Reinterpretation under Acculturation

NORMAN A. SCOTCH

In discussing beliefs in witchcraft in Africa, Gluckman (1955b) points out that native beliefs in witchcraft not only persist in the face of continuing acculturation but often expand and change to meet the exigencies of new life situations. In fact, the impact of science, and particularly the impact of modern medicine, on previously nonliterate Africans actually inhibits their traditional beliefs and practices much less than might be expected; and although it would be incorrect to assert that Africans have rejected modern medicine – rejected, say modern germ theories of disease – the fact remains that they sustain the basic structure of their traditional beliefs in spite of elemental contradictions between those beliefs and scientific explanations.

But how can opposing explanations of cause and effect be held simultaneously? According to Gluckman, concepts of science and witchcraft fulfil different functions: science explains *how* a given process occurs, as in the course of a disease, for example, whereas witchcraft explains *why* the process occurs at all, or why one man and not another contracts the disease. From the African point of view modern medicine is extremely limited in explaining total situations. It may contribute dependable probabilities, as when it predicts that ten per cent of a tribal population will die of tuberculosis, or when it prognosticates a specific disease in the individual; but it fails to explain, from the African perspective, why one particular child among ten sharing the same conditions contracts tuberculosis whereas the remaining nine do not, and it is this last explanation that witchcraft continues to provide with assurance for modern Africans. As Gluckman (1955: 101) observes: 'The difficulty of destroying beliefs in witchcraft is that they form a system which can absorb and explain many failures and apparently contradictory evidence.'

This functional aspect of witchcraft may explain, to a very great extent, its persistence in the belief system of Africans, its expansion and peculiar adaptability to industrialized Euroamerican modes of life. As Gluckman points out:

> African life nowadays is changing rapidly, and witchcraft accusations now involve circumstances arising from Africa's absorption in Western economy and polity. Conflicts between old and new social principles produces new animosities, which are not controlled by custom, and these open the way to new forms of accusation. Charges, previously excluded, as by a Zulu against

> his father, are now made. The system of witchcraft beliefs, originally tied to certain social relations, can be adapted to new situations of conflict – to competition for jobs in towns, to the rising standard of living, made possible by new goods, which breaches the previous egalitarianism, and so forth.

One example of such innovation in the application of magic and sorcery – terms which I prefer to witchcraft – to cultural change and urban living came to my attention during my recent research among the Zulu in South Africa. It illustrates not only how the changing pattern of magic is related to the changing way of life, but it does the reverse as well, and shows how innovations can only be built on previous cultural patterns. In Durban the Africans show a great enthusiasm for soccer, or, to use the local term, football. Much of the limited leisure of the native male population is devoted to watching, discussing, and participating in this game, and organized football leagues. This exemplifies the 'new situations of conflict' to which Gluckman refers. Interpersonal and intergroup hostility and aggression are much greater in an urban setting than in the more traditional rural Zulu community. Unnaturally crowded conditions and competition for scarce employment opportunities lead to more frequent accusations of sorcery in the city. Football, it may be hypothesized, serves a dual function in this context: first, it is one of the few opportunities open to the Zulu for release from the anxiety and tensions of anomic urban life; and more specifically, it allows the expression of the increased aggression and hostility that arises in the city between Africans, within the framework of a modern, acceptable form.

It is common knowledge, and not surprising, that in an effort to produce winning teams each of these football teams employs an *inyanga*, or Zulu doctor, who serves the dual purpose of strengthening his own team by magic and ritual, and of forestalling the sorcery directed at his team by rival *inyangas*. Although no *inyanga* with whom I talked would admit that he employed sorcery against opposing teams, each was convinced that this was the practice of rival *inyangas*. Actually magic in Durban football is so widespread that although in searching for players there exists at least a minimal recognition of individual talent, few players known to be the object of *umtagathi*, or sorcerers, would be considered by a team regardless of their ability; moreover, success or failure of a team is invariably attributed to the skills of the *inyangas*, as well as to the natural talent of the players. However, when a team consistently loses it is the *inyanga* who is replaced, not the players. When, on the other hand, an individual player is suspected of being the object of sorcery he may be dropped from the team for fear that the spell might generalize to include the teammates of the unfortunate victim.

That football holds a place of extreme importance to the African community is demonstrated in several ways. Players of considerable talent are much sought after and part of the work of the trainer is to scout other teams and to attempt to entice skilled players of opposing teams into joining his own. In fact, although ostensibly this is an amateur sport, players of promise are frequently paid a salary from the treasury of the team as a means of keeping them. If a skilled player has had difficulty in finding employment, it is incumbent on all members of the team to find suitable and well-paying employment for the star. So involved are the efforts of teammates to keep them happy that star players are known to pass from club to club for the 'best deal'.

Because of this, and for other reasons as well, strict discipline is maintained on the team. The trainer is in a position of supreme authority. All the normal rules of status and interpersonal relationships which have long traditions and history may be discarded in the interests of winning games. Thus, it is even possible for a trainer to strike a man older than himself – perhaps considerably older – if the trainer feels he is not doing his share. This, of course, is a gross transgression against important Zulu norms regarding seniority and status.

The supernatural is enlisted in every possible way to aid in the production of a successful football team. Thus, ritual and ceremony are used on a number of occasions, connected with football, and serve the functions of sanctioning and supporting the efforts of a team. Before the season even opens, the team slaughters a goat 'to open the doors to luck' and the season's end is marked by another slaughter.

Much of the ritual is propitiative as in the example of the slaughter cited above, but most ceremonies combine propitiation with positive attempts to combat sorcery. The following is an account, related by an educated Zulu health educator, of the ritual conducted by *inyangas* on the night preceding a match:

> All the football teams have their own *inyanga* who doctors them all for each match. The night before a match they must 'camp' together around a fire. They all sleep there together, they must stay naked and they are given *umuthi* and other medicines by the *inyanga*. Incisions are made on their knees, elbows, and joints. In the morning they are made to vomit. They must all go together on the same bus to the match, and they must enter the playing grounds together. Almost every team I know has an *inyanga* and does this – it is necessary to win. Even though players are Christians and have lived in towns for a long time, they do it, and believe in it.

Another informant gave as the reasons for this practice of camping-out the following account:

> The purpose is to avoid liquor, sexual intercourse, mixing with enemy players who might bewitch them, and mixing with other persons who might affect them with ill-luck.

The camping group is composed of the starting team and reserves, plus administrative members of the club, loyal and enthusiastic supporters, and the *inyanga*. The morning after the camping the whole group moves to the playing grounds together. A certain procedure is followed: the group keeps a very tight formation with every man touching the man in front of, behind and beside him, the pace is very slow and stylized and the group may be likened to a millipede – one organism with a million legs. Even when the group has to take a bus from one part of town to another where the football field is, they still make every effort to maintain their formation. The players themselves are placed right in the center of the group in order that they might be protected. Moving out onto the actual playing field with their stylized trotting step, the group acts very hostile to outsiders for fear that intruders will attempt to bewitch the players or in some way to weaken the 'umuthi' or the medicine of the *inyanga*.

Now, when we compare the description of the ritual magic involved in 'camping-out' with accounts by Bryant (1949:501) and Krige (1936:272) of doctoring of Zulu warriors in the time of Shaka during the early 1800's, we perceive many elements of unmistakable similarity: the circle around the fire; the medicines to endow strength and courage; the medicines on the weapons (currently, on football jerseys and shoes) to increase their potency (currently, to make them slippery); and the purificatory emetic which, in Shaka's time, was taken on the morning of the battle, and nowadays on the morning before the football match.

Further, the formation followed in reaching the playing field derives, without doubt, from historical military formations. The avoidance of sex on the eve of battles can also be traced back to earlier customs connected with warfare. These are but a few examples of the basic similarities of the ritual and ceremony used currently by football teams and formerly by army regiments.

There is an interesting parallel to be found to the above example of cultural syncretism. Sundkler (1948), in describing Zulu leadership patterns in separatist churches, has shown that the traditional roles of chief and medical specialist are carried over into the modern Christian church in much the same way as these roles are found in modern football teams.

Returning to the point made earlier – why does a belief in magic in football exist at all? As Gluckman says, because such a belief explains the inexplicable. Why does one football team win consistently and another lose? Certainly the winning team will have players who are more talented – but why, in the first place, do these teams manage to gather more talented players, and, in the second place, why are these players more talented, where does their skill come from? Why is it that the talented players avoid sorcery? These are the questions with which magic deals.

That beliefs in magic help to explain the inexplicable is illustrated by the following account:

> We health educators started a team and did very well. We made a point of not using an *inyanga*. We advertised the fact that we did not use one. We even invited a few outsiders on to our team so that they would see that we used no witchcraft, and we hoped that they would tell others about

> this. Well, we won a lot of games – and do you know what the people said? They said that because we work with European doctors we were given injections to make us strong so that we could win. We could not convince them otherwise.

By this account a number of things are made clear. Modern medicine is viewed as essentially similar to the magic of the Zulu doctor, except in this case it is the magic of the European. Formerly, Zulu avoided European doctors (except in the case of trauma) in the belief that they could only help or cure Europeans. Today, they accept the fact that an African can be helped in many cases by modern Western medicine. Nonetheless, it is still believed that there are some diseases – which they refer to as Bantu diseases – which cannot be helped by the European. Such diseases as *umfufuyana*, *chayiza* and *spoiliyana*, which are essentially psychosomatic hysterical-type personality disorders, are rarely taken to the European doctor.

On the other hand, the injections used by European doctors are viewed as being entirely magical, and Zulu who come to the European doctor for help of any kind always insist on a *jovo* – an injection – as part of any treatment. No distinction is drawn between the *jovo* of the white jacketed European doctor or the roots or herbs of the *inyanga* clad in skins. Thus, when we view the football team we clearly see how the winning of matches is almost always explained by references to magic. In usual cases it is magic of the *inyanga*, while in unusual cases, like that of the health educator team, the magic of the European doctors.

Retention by urban Zulu of magical beliefs and practices also throws some light on the persistence of conflict patterns in a changing culture. The use of sorcery practices and warfare rituals within the framework of the game of soccer introduced by Europeans illustrates the adaptations of old methods of expressing hostility to the new and highly frustrating urban situation.

REFERENCES

Bryant, A. T. 1949 – *The Zulu People*. Pietermaritzburg: Shuter & Shooter.
Gluckman, M. 1955 – *Custom and Conflict in Africa*. Oxford: Blackwell.
Krige, E. J. 1936 – *The Social System of the Zulus*. London: Routledge.
Sundkler, B. 1948 – *Bantu Prophets in South Africa* (2nd edn. 1962). London: Butterworth.

'Magic, Sorcery and Football among Urban Zulu: a case of reinterpretation under acculteration' by **N. A. Scotch** is reprinted from the *Journal of Conflict Resolution* Vol 5 (1) March 1961, pp 70–74 by permission of the Publisher, SAGE Publications.

3. The Rise of Black Consciousness in South Africa

HERIBERT ADAM

In these crucial moments – far from hypothetical since widespread strikes started in January 1973 in Durban and have continued ever since on an almost daily basis in different parts of the country, mainly Natal – the political consciousness of the participants and differing policy goals of various leaders become of decisive importance in dampening, channelling, or directing popular grievances. In this sense, the so-called 'Black Consciousness Movement' of African, Indian, and Coloured students, though not directly related to the spontaneous strikes, gains political significance beyond the esoteric students circles. It signals potentials and sparks which could perhaps overflow to those whose real power counts more than student dreams. So far, to my knowledge, no comprehensive, detached critical assessment of the Black Consciousness ideas has been attempted, apart from propagandistic descriptions or, more frequently, sweeping condemnation.

The new movement started when African students in 1968 split away from the always White-dominated liberal, though, in the South African context, often radical, 'National Union of South African Students' (NUSAS), forming their own exclusively Black group under the name of 'South African Student Organisation' (SASO). Apart from the ideological justification given, this departure from organizational multiracialism by the African opponents of apartheid had several objective reasons. It reflected the different problems and perceptions of Africans, studying since the beginning of the sixties in isolated, separate ethnic universities, which in their disciplinary code as well as exposure to outside issues differed considerably from the cosmopolitan English-language institutions with a long tradition of academic freedom.But above all, the Black students unconsciously realized an insight which sociologists have labelled 'interracial interaction disability.' This notion expresses the results of empirical research which showed that initial differences in social status in the larger society produce a similar power and prestige order in new small groups where competence at the task has no rational relationship to the state of the status characteristics. In such situations White dominance inevitably results when races interact or Blacks compare themselves to 'significant others' of the two races.

Sources and Contents

The advocates of Black Consciousness in South Africa owe much of their philosophy to the inspiration gained from its famous predecessors, the ideas of negritude and Black identity elsewhere. Although Leopold Senghor, Aimé

Cesaire or Franz Fanon are seldom acknowledged, Black Consciousness in South Africa marks their success in universalizing the experience of the colonized in different geographical settings. The accusation of plagiarizing and importing a foreign philosophy, not fitting the unique South African circumstances, therefore overlooks the common insights of a colonial existence. Many observers have wondered why the Blacks awareness in its present form has appeared so late on the South African scene. One reason would seem to be that opposition to White rule had been absorbed in other forms of African nationalism which in coalition with a few White supporters always aimed at a non-racial, common, western-type society whose values supposedly everyone would share. This old alternative of separation or integration is no longer relevant to the politically conscious new Black. His goal has changed into 'liberation' and this includes a rejection of many Western values to which the earlier Black nationalists claimed the same adherence as their White monopolizers (cf. Khoapa 1972).

In the absence of real liberation and the means to achieve it, Black Consciousness essentially represents verbal resistance. However, even in the realm of rhetoric it has to select its weapons carefully, considering the overwhelming White power structure. But more fundamental factors distinguish the South African movement from Black Power of the American version. First of all, the idea of Black Consciousness in South Africa differs from Black Power ideologies in the United States by addressing itself to a different structural and historical setting. Blacks in South Africa have no power – not the power of a gun, nor the power of a vote, or pressure groups to influence decisions affecting their lives at their urban homes or work places. The law aims at their separation in South Africa and does not support attempts for equality as in the United States. South African subordinates are at the mercy of their rulers without even the hope for an individual escape in a race-caste system which ascribes status without exception for the rich or educated. However, 83 per cent of the population in South Africa are classified African, Indian or Coloured, and this numerical majority allows for the realistic expectation of an eventual Black political and cultural system, which the 11 per cent Black people in the United States can never hope to achieve on a national level. This factor, together with the severity of disprivilege, backed by racist laws in addition to racist social practice as in the U.S., would seem to account for a much more political outlook of the movement in South Africa. There is less concern with a life-style and the cultural assertion of a different personality.

Moreover, the two situations of current racial discrimination result from different historical backgrounds of settler colonialism. The American sociologist Robert Blauner (1972:119) has suggested 'that cultural penetration is less effective and extreme when a people are colonized within their original territory.' Africans in South Africa were defeated militarily, their land was taken over by the settlers, and they were pushed back into overcrowded so-called 'tribal areas', but for the most part they were never enslaved in the sense that their American counterparts were. This historical situation of American Blacks resembles much more that of South African Coloureds. Africans, on the other hand, could fall back on cultural traditions which survived conquest and remained essentially intact. A Black Consciousness spokesman confirms that the basic tenets of Black culture have succeeded in withstanding the process of bastardisation. In South Africa there is less need to reconstruct a lost history but only to correct White distorted history books which dwell on the civilizing mission of the culturally superior Europeans. For many Black South African intellectuals, a sense of their own past is much more present than it is for their counterparts in America, although in the latter instance the specific slave culture and history have long been neglected or denied. An important difference in the two historical accounts is the not always unsuccessful resistance to White conquest, particularly by the Zulus. The unbroken memory of this dimension relates frequently to interpetations of current events. Although the migratory labour system, urbanization and industrialization would seem to have destroyed cultural tradition and its economic base in the subsistence economy for many of the urban proletariat, there exists at the same time an awareness of the alternative which is in South Africa not artificial decoration but living reality. It would seem that the Indian community in South Africa in particular has preserved facets of a traditional culture and customs which served as an immunizing shield against discrimination. In another context Amilcar Cabral (1972) stressed the 'cultural resistance of the people, who when they are subjected to political domination and economic exploitation find that their own culture acts as a bulwark in preserving their identity.' There can be little doubt that the specific Black identity in South Africa ameliorated the harshness of individual suffering and thus far has prevented extreme forms of outrage against the real source of frustration. Within the protective group membership the consequences of racial discrimination are obviously not attributed to individual failures but to the collective stigma. This decreases frustrations and the resulting aggression. In a perceptive analysis of inhibiting factors of earlier forms of African nationalism, Fatima Meer (1971:145) has pointed to a remarkable absence of violence in the face of the most dire provocation. Contrary to racist beliefs, she suggests, 'Blacks are singularly unaggressive'. The relatively unbroken cultural tradition of South African Blacks appears to have contributed to this situation, where individual frustrations are channelled into group comfort.

Black Consciousness aims above all at strengthening this group cohesion in the face of theatening anomie and White imposed fragmentation. Its slogans are solidarity and brotherhood. Central in all the statements, and almost identical with similar pronouncements in the United States, is the call for psychological liberation. Since the colonized have frequently internalized the norms and orders of their oppressors, they first of all must rid themselves of their slave 'mentality'. Inferiority feelings, distrust of themselves, and self-hate are seen as the cardinal sins and obstacles of liberation. There is almost a pathological self-assertion, rejecting what is essentially obvious and not worth-while to be negated. An American Black writer has stated a similar reservation: 'It is important to be aware of one's cultural origin, but a waste of energy to feel it necessary to disprove all White lies and to present a Black counter for everything the White world holds in esteem. My father could not give a damn if someone painted a Black Madonna. The goal of Black people should not be to attain the same level of mediocrity as White people' (Reeves 1973:28).

The adopted ridicule and deprecation of the conquereds' traditional way of life is seen as the root of continued subjugation, for which the victims are sometimes blamed more than the aggressor. Reminiscent of nineteenth century idealistic philosophers, not real liberation from material and political bondage alone, but spiritual freedom, is viewed as being able to achieve the desired state, in spite of continuing subjugation. The dehumanization of racism is countered and the violated dignity and degraded personality restored by an assertion of the 'intrinsic worth' of the Black man, a call for pride and self-reliance and a rejection of White guardianship, patronization, and paternalism in any form.

The new Blacks apply a much more realistic perspective to racism than earlier Black leaders, who basically tried to impress the White with their 'civilized' standards, appeals for justice and moral arguments. Contrary to this tactic of persuasion, the new Black generation expects that a ruling group does not give up its privileges voluntarily, unless pressured into doing so by the strength of its opponent. Racial prejudice is not to be changed by enlightenment, since racial attitudes reflect and rationalize group interests and privileges.

If this generalization is basically correct, then the Black Consciousness proponents must equally face the fact that 'self-love', 'identity', and 'cultural assertion' are not sufficient to effect real change. The crucial question remains how this cultural revolution in the minds of the subordinates can be translated into political action. It might be the first phase and necessary prerequisite for a successful mobilization – but there is also the danger that it may become an end in itself, in much the same way as cultural nationalism, the obsession with soul, and a unique life-style have frequently become a substitute for political activity among the Black people in the U.S. As Cabral (1972) has pointed out elsewhere: 'But the "return to the source" is not and cannot in itself be an act of struggle against foreign domination (colonialist and racist) and it no longer necessarily means a return to tradition.'

The strength of the apartheid ideology lies precisely in the official encouragement of an apolitical ethnic orientation as an end in itself. It is hoped that cultural revitalization, culminating in stronger ethnic ties, will weaken national unity, as it did elsewhere in Africa, given the cultural diversity of a multi-ethnic society. Unlike the nation of the 'melting pot', which so obviously has failed in the United States, the Afrikaner policy of multi-nationalism uses ethnicity maintenance as its basis (De Vos 1972).

Apartheid gambles with the strength of traditional definitions, while Black Consciousness on the other hand relies on the shared experience of oppression. The Black Consciousness proponents also want to utilize cultural revitalization, but eventually to redirect it into political mobilization. A prediction about failure or success of both strategies appears not as easy as political theorists would make us believe and earlier Panafricanists have come to learn. Increasingly, more Anglo-American social scientists, who earlier unanimously predicated continuing assimilation and acculturation, are now beginning to grapple with the very opposite of their predictions. As Blauner has observed, ethnic groups in many plural societies readily seem to seize upon their supposedly lost identity, because it provides a bulwark of identification in the face of increasing anxieties. The continued appeal of independent African churches and sects, now believed to number about 3 000 and comprising 25 per cent of all Africans, may be similarly explained.

Symbolic liberation then substitutes easily for a political programme. The rhetoric reconfirms faith and purges doubts about the ultimate success, and the meetings tend to become a cult, regenerating the spirit by confirming the pride and worth. For example, being now called Black, instead of Non-white,[1] is regarded as progress in much the same way as the liberal White feels his outlook proven by being kind to his servants, or the Nationalist feels on the left because he shifted to 'the pat on the head instead of the sjambok on the back' as Nadine Gordimer (1971:14–16) illustrates the South African way of tokenism. Among the patted, too, there are already signs of delusions and confusion over priorities.

NOTE

1. It is symptomatic for the South African domestic debate how both Whites and Blacks are preoccupied with labels at the expense of the real issues. Thus the South African Institute of Race Relations asked the public to search for a more appropriate name for the country's subordinate castes before deciding to use the term Black, as did the *Rand Daily Mail* in 1972, while the 'Progressive Party' resolved after an elaborate debate to use only the group names: African, Coloured, Indian. SASO delegates continued in the same vein by evicting journalists whose papers continued to use the term Non-white. A glance at the fate of 'Negroes' in America would have been useful.

REFERENCES

Blauner, Robert 1972 – *Racial Oppression in America*. New York: Harper & Row.

Cabral, Amilcar 1972 – 'Identity and dignity in struggle.' *Southern Africa*, 5, November, 4–8.

Devos, George 1972 – 'Social stratification and ethnic pluralism: An overview from the Perspective of Psychological Anthropology.' *Race*, 13, 4 April, 435–60.

Gordimer, Nadine 1971 – 'White proctorship and Black disinvolvement.' *Reality*, November, 14–6.

Khoapa, Bennie A. 1972 – 'Black consciousness.' *South African Outlook*, June/July, 100–2.

Meer, Fatima 1971 – 'African nationalism – some inhibiting factors.' In Heribert Adam (ed.) *South Africa: Sociological Perspectives*. London: Oxford University Press.

Reeves, Donald 1973 – *Newsweek*, 9 April, 28.

Part 3:

The Sociology of Religion

Introduction

KENNETH C. JUBBER

Whatever else religion may be, it is undeniably an integral part of society and thus qualifies for the attention of sociologists. Religion is so closely woven into the fabric of society that it is not surprising that since the founding of sociology, the sociological study of religion has received a great deal of attention. As the discipline became more firmly established, and as distinct specialities emerged, the sociology of religion came to exist as an important field of study. Simply stated, the sociology of religion is that branch of sociology primarily concerned with religious phenomena. It is a fundamental sociological truism that the elements of society exist in an interactive and reciprocal relationship. For this reason the sociological study of religion not only adds to our understanding of religious phenomena but provides important insights into other social phenomena as well.

As a branch of sociology, the sociology of religion reveals all the ideological, theoretical and methodological lines of cleavage characteristic of sociology in general. These cleavages render it inaccurate to speak of the sociology of religion as if it were a unified intellectual and academic undertaking, focusing on a well demarcated area of the social world with a specific set of analytic tools. A student entering the field of the sociology of religion would not need to travel very far to discover that he was not, in fact, traversing a single field. He would soon realize that the sociology of religion exists as a number of intersecting and overlapping fields, each with its own map and each with its own compass. In short, there is no such discipline as the sociology of religion but only sociologies of religion. This state of affairs may be extremely disconcerting on first discovery but it is not unique to the sociology of religion. The same multiplicity and confusion exists in many other branches of sociology. This state of affairs is the culmination of man's pursuit of the truth which has, paradoxically, produced what may be described as the schizophrenianization of culture. A culture lacking any certainty.

The foregoing indicates that just as religion can be studied from a number of perspectives in general, such as the theological, the scientific, and the atheistic, it can also be studied from a number of sociological perspectives. One such perspective, extensively adopted by American and British as well as South African sociologists, is known as the functionalist perspective. This perspective regards religion as an essential feature of society which serves to integrate and maintain society. According to functionalists, religion fosters the integration and maintenance of society by giving its members a common set of values and beliefs upon which to base their behaviour. Obviously, as functionalists have come to realize, the harmonization of social relationships by religion is best achieved in a situation in which all individuals subscribe to the same religion.

Conversely, integration is rendered difficult in a society where two or more incompatible or hostile religions co-exist. Under these circumstances, rather than promoting integration, religion functions as a divisive and conflict-generating factor in the overall society while still operating as an integrative factor within the bounds of the conflicting groups.

Functionalists are also concerned with the role which religion plays in the lives of individual members of society and in this concern the functionalist perspective overlaps and to some extent merges with aspects of another important sociological perspective on religion, the phenomenological approach. Both functionalists and phenomenologists are agreed that a central defining feature of religion, whether supernatural or secular, is a concern with the ultimate questions of man's existence. As a consequence they argue that religion represents mankind's most hubristic and imaginative attempt at rendering the world comprehensive. Religions constitute thought and action systems which transcend the here and now, the empirical-historical world. For this reason, and because they generally claim a reality status equal if not superior to that of the mundane world, religions possess a matchless power to help men to make sense of their lives and render their existence significant. Religion is a bulwark against the terrors of a stark, brutal and mute world. It provides individuals with a sustaining self-conception and is a source of comfort and inspiration. By answering the unanswerable and making known the unknowable, religion gives comfort in a confusing world. Religions provide believers with a firm, if not absolute, value and normative system which constitutes a blue-print for life.

Functionalist and phenomenological sociologists of religion often emphasize that they are not concerned with the truth claims of specific religions. Both claim to be concerned with religious reality and regard religion to be real in two senses. Firstly, religion is an observable feature of society and, secondly, many people take some or other religion sufficiently seriously for it to constitute an important if not paramount reality for them. Functionalists tend to stress religion as a social reality while Phenomenologists are inclined to stress it as an experiential and individual reality. In contrast to these points of view stand the Marxist sociologists of religion who constitute the third major perspective of the sociology of religion. Marxist sociologists argue that all religion is false, the result of man's ignorance of the fact that he is the author of his world. These sociologists of religion are concerned with describing the manner in which religion, as an illusory and false reality, is maintained and how it is used for political and exploitative ends by those who control society. Whereas functionalists and phenomenologists are generally tolerant of religion as a feature of society and individual consciousness, the Marxists maintain that religion is to be attacked since it is a form of false consciousness which stands in the way of the abolition of social exploitation and the fuller and truer understanding of man's world.

The particular perspective which a sociologist of religion adopts dictates to some extent the issues which will occupy his interest and even to some degree determines his results. Among the dominant issues investigated by sociologists has been the role which religious beliefs and behaviour have played in history and society. From this has stemmed an interest in tracing the effect of religious change on society as well as the effect of social change in general on religion. An important area of research among contemporary sociologists of religion is the role which religion plays in facilitating or hindering social development.

Because most modern societies are characterized by religious pluralism and because religion plays a part in determining social attitudes and social status, sociologists of religion have been concerned with investigating the ways in which religious affiliation relates to social class, political power, occupational opportunity, racial attitudes, and other important sociological variables. Religious pluralism has also stimulated an interest in the effect which this pluralism has on the religions themselves and on the faith of their adherents. Related to this concern is the issue of the notable loss of influence of religion generally in society, in culture, and in the lives of individuals. Secularization is the term used to describe the process whereby religion loses its social significance. While the general tendency during this century has been for societies to become increasingly secularized, sociologists have not failed to pay attention to the counter phenomenon of religious revivalism and renewal. The notable religious revival among the youth during the past years has been sociologically investigated, as has the increasing adoption of Eastern religions by Western people.

Sociologists have long been interested in the social and individual forces which lead to the founding of new religious movements and the part which such movements play in the lives of their adherents and in society. A number of theories have been proposed by sociologists which deal with the development and evolution as well as the demise of new religious movements. The forms of organization which religions assume have occupied the attention of sociologists for many years and this field of study has led to important insights for organizational theory in general.

The above are some of the aspects of religion which have received the attention of sociologists. Many other topics could have been mentioned but those noted should serve the purposes of this introduction. Included in the bibliography at the end of this introduction is a short list of books which deal at greater length with the above-mentioned issues. These books would serve as a good introduction to anyone interested in learning more about the sociology of religion.

The sociology of religion in South Africa

The sociology of religion as it is practised in South Africa is not very well developed. The discipline is characterized by an emphasis on certain perspectives and themes and the neglect of others. Nevertheless, despite the degree of uneven and underdevelopment, sufficient work has been done in this field for certain trends to have become noticeable and worthy of comment.

A basic sociological thesis, derived from the observation that society is an interacting whole, maintains that the overall nature of society is reflected in its parts. This seems to be the case in even so miniscule a part as the sociology of religion. Because Whites hold a monopoly over education, power and privilege, it is hardly surprising that the sociology of religion is almost exclusively their domain. Not only do White scholars study their own religions but the colonial experience of an indigenous population continues to be primarily, if not exclusively, investigated and described by Whites for the interests and purposes of Whites.

The type of sociology of religion practised and taught at the English and Afrikaans universities differs fairly considerably. What typically emerges from the Afrikaans universities is a brand of sociology best described as religious or church sociology. This is characterized by a mixed Functional-Theological perspective which focuses on one or other aspect of a particular religion, often the author's or speaker's own. Much of the sociology of religion of the Afrikaans universities reflects the Afrikaner's concern for the preservation of his culture, especially the image of the Afrikaner as a devout member of one of the Dutch Reformed Churches.

In certain respects the sociology of religion is less prominent at the English-speaking universities than at the Afrikaans-speaking universities. This reflects partly the greater religious heterogeneity of the student populations at the English speaking universities and is also probably due to the liberal humanistic atmosphere which tends to pervade these centres. There is also evidence which suggests that religion is not as vital in the lives of English-speaking South Africans generally as it is in the lives of Afrikaans speakers. The sociology of religion produced at the English language White universities in contrast to the Afrikaans language universities tends to adopt a more religiously neutral Functionalist approach and the anti-religious Marxist perspective is widely presented in the teaching of the subject.

An analysis of the works which are generally included in bibliographies on the sociology of religion in South Africa reveals that the greatest single category represented is constituted by ethnographic type descriptions of particular religions. This is not surprising. Not only has South Africa always had a great variety and richness of religions but, among the Black population there has developed a strong tendency for new religious movements to form. This latter phenomenon, the emergence and evolution of new sects, constitutes the second most widely researched and commented upon topic in the sociology of religion in South Africa. The particular brand of sociology of religion identified above as religious or church sociology forms the third most popular area of study in the sociology of religion in South Africa. This area of study includes studies of the minister or priest's role, congregational problems, and the impact which social change has had on particular religious denominations.

More general but less numerous studies in the sociology of religion in South Africa deal with such things as the relationship between religion and society, especially such factors as apartheid, voting behaviour, and race and ethnic prejudice. The impact of Christianity on indigenous African religions has received attention, as has the response of the various indigenous peoples of South Africa to attempts to Christianize them. The problems associated with evangelizing a heathen population, which received much attention in the early years of missionary activity in South Africa, are seldom dealt with any longer. A few such reports are still, however, included in bibliographies on the sociology of religion in South Africa.

Books, articles, and theses dealing with general philosophical and theoretical issues are extremely rare in the sociology of religion in South Africa. This fact reveals the under-developed nature of the discipline as well as such things as the relatively small number of individuals working in this field, the general parochial nature of their concerns, and the overall academic isolation of South African scholars. Included in the bibliography at the end of this introduction are selected examples of South African sociology of religion as well as references to comprehensive bibliographies of the sociology of religion in South Africa.

The Readings

This short section on the sociology of religion could not possibly serve to introduce the topic adequately. Religion is too vast and variegated a field and the sociological perspectives, methods and interests too numerous for anything short of a full-length book to serve as an introduction. Two of the articles selected were chosen because they focus on South Africa and deal with the interrelationship between religion and politics. They also link religion to other important sociological concerns. The third selection is included because it introduces certain contemporary theoretical issues in the sociology of religion.

The first article, Janosik's 'Religion and Political Involvement: A Study of Black African Sects', is a comparative study focused on the part religious organizations play in social change. The author is particularly interested in answering the question as to why in certain cases religious sects are politically involved in change while in others they adopt an apolitical stance. Highlighted in the article is the interplay between various sociological variables such as the nature and extent of political involvement, type of leadership, form of organization, and degree of commitment to a specific ideology, custom or ritual. The second article, by Buis, deals with the effect which religious teachings and beliefs may have on racial attitudes. The findings of his study emphasize the interrelated and interactive nature of social life. More specifically, Buis shows that what a person learns and accepts in one sector of life has implications for other sectors. Religious ideas especially, since they provide the believer with a blue-print for action, exercise an important determining influence on social behaviour. The third article presents elements of a contemporary sociological perspective applied to religion. The article argues that the sociological claim that reality is socially constructed, challenges religion's claim that the divine plays a role in the affairs of men. The article is included because it is provocative and challenges both believer and unbeliever to re-examine the grounds of their beliefs in the light of theological as well as social scientific arguments.

REFERENCES

a. General

Berger, P. L. 1967 – *The Sacred Canopy: Elements of a Sociological Theory of Religion.* New York: Doubleday.

Budd, S. 1973 – *Sociologists and Religion.* London: Collier Macmillan.

Campbell, C. 1971 – *Toward a Sociology of Irreligion.* London: Macmillan.

Hill, Michael 1973 – *A Sociology of Religion.* London: Heinemann.

O'Dear, T. F. and J. K. O'Dea 1973 – *Readings on the Sociology of Religion.* Englewood Cliffs: Prentice-Hall.

Robertson, R. 1970 – *The Sociological Interpretation of Religion.* Oxford: Blackwell.

b. South Africa

Alant, C. J. 1969 – *'n Sosiologiese studie van die beeld wat die gemeentelid in die Nederduitse Gereformeerde Kerk van die predikant het* (A sociological study of the image which the Nederduitse Gereformeerde Kerk parishioner has of the minister). Pretoria: N.G. Kerk-Boekhandel.

Barrett, D. B. 1968 – *Schism and Renewal in Africa: An Analysis of Six Thousand Contemporary Religious Movements.* Nairobi: Oxford University Press.

Cawood, L. 1964 – *The Churches and Race Relations in South Africa.* Johannesburg: South African Institute of Race Relations.

Currin, T. V. 1962 – *Indian Catholics.* Durban: University of Natal, Institute for Social Research.

Ellis, B. L. 1968 – *Religion Among the Bantu in South Africa: A List of Works Published after 1956 (bibliography).* Johannesburg: University of the Witwatersrand.

Fernandez, J. W. 1964 – 'African religious movements: types and dynamics.' *Journal of Modern African Studies* 2, 4.

——1967 – *Divinations, Confessions, Testimonies: Zulu Confrontations with the Social Structure.* Durban: University of Natal, Institute for Social Research.

Gelfand, M. 1968 – *African Crucible: An Ethico-religious Study with Special Reference to the Shona-speaking People.* Cape Town: Juta.

Hammond-Tooke, W. D. 1974 – 'World view I: a system of beliefs.' In W.D. Hammond-Tooke (ed.) *The Bantu-speaking Peoples of Southern Africa.* London: Routledge and Kegan Paul.

Higgins, E. 1971 – 'The sociology of religion in South Africa.' *Archives de Sociologie des Religions*, 32, 143–64.

——1972 – 'Predikant and priest.' *Occasional Paper*, No. 17, Institute for Social and Economic Research, Rhodes University, Grahamstown.

Jubber, K. C. 1976 – 'The Roman Catholic Church and apartheid.' *Journal of Theology for Southern Africa*, June, 15, 25–38.

Kiernan, J. (O.M.I.) 1971 – *Fragmented Priest.* Durban: Unity Press.

Lanternari, V. 1963 – *The Religions of the Oppressed: A Study of Modern Messianic Cults.* London: MacGibbon & Kee.

Mabona, M. 1971 – 'White worship and Black people.' *Pro Veritate,* May, 10, 1.

Maritz, F. A. 1959 – *Die aard en taak van die godsdienssosiologie* (The nature and task of the sociology of religion). University of Pretoria, M.A. dissertation.

Meer, F. 1969 – *Portrait of Indian South Africans.* Durban: Avon House.

Moodie, T. D. 1975 – *The Rise of Afrikanderdom: Power, Apartheid, and the Afrikaner Civil Religion.* Berkeley: University of California Press.

——1975 – 'The Dutch Reformed churches as vehicles of political legitimation in South Africa.' *Social Dynamics,* 1, 2, December, 158–66.

Oosthuizen, G. C. 1967 – *The Theology of a South African Messiah: An Analysis of the Hymnal of 'The Church of the Nazarites'.* Leiden: Brill.

——1968 – *Post-christianity in Africa: A Theological and Anthropological Study*. Stellenbosch: Wever.

Pauw, B. A. 1974 – 'The influence of Christianity.' In W. D. Hammond-Tooke (ed.), *The Bantu-speaking Peoples of Southern Africa*. London: Routledge and Kegan Paul, 415–38.

Reinders, J. E. and S. E. Welz 1972 – 'Bibliography on the sociology of religion in South Africa.' *Social Compass*, XIX, 1, 103–16.

Sundkler, B. G. M. 1961 – *Bantu Prophets in South Africa*. London: Oxford University Press, 2nd edn.

Vilakazi, A. 1962 – *Zulu Transformations: A Study of the Dynamics of Social Change*. Pietermaritzburg: University of Natal.

West, Martin 1975 – *Bishops and Prophets in a Black City. African Independent Churches in Soweto, Johannesburg*. Cape Town: David Philip.

Whisson, M. G. and M. West 1975 – *Religion and Social Change in Southern Africa*. Cape Town: David Philip and London: Rex Collings.

1. Religion and Political Involvement: A Study of Black African Sects

ROBERT J. JANOSIK

Analysts of the political situation in South Africa tend to explain the lack of visible revolutionary activity there in terms of the economic and military strength of the White regime. But strength and power are meaningless unless they are understood as relative, relational concepts. Power against whom? Strength in relation to what? The approach taken here is an effort to point up the relational aspects of this problem by examining one important sector of the black populace in South Africa – individuals involved in the numerous black sects which exist in that country.

Catalogues of the military armaments and the economic strengths of the Nationalist Party exist already. But that is not enough. Certainly, the British in Kenya exerted severe pressure, both military and economic, to squelch the nationalistic spirit which filled Blacks there in the 1940s and 1950s. Yet, in Kenya the available arsenal could not stop the growth of a revolutionary attitude among Blacks, a process which witnessed the coalescing of various sectors of African society – religious, educational, familial – and which forged a set of national symbols and a unity which finally succeeded in the struggle with White domination.

If such unity exists among Blacks in South Africa today, it does not appear that the Black religious sects so numerous there have played a significant role in developing it. At best, such sects have not helped; at worst, their attachment to local concerns and ritual to the exclusion of all else has been a barrier to unity. In sum, the goal of *apartheid* – divide and conquer – has been a success at least in the religious sphere.

Certainly this situation should be of analytical interest to the political scientist examining the causes of the South African political situation. Yet, the consideration of specifically religious organizations has been left by students of politics to other social scientists. There does seem to be some consensus among political scientists that change (development, modernization) begins with the secularization of the polity, the pluralization of the religious sphere, and a concomitant 'empiricalization' and role differentiation in government. (cf. Almond and Powell 1966:58.) It has also been recognized that voluntary associations of various types play important roles in modernization, especially in Africa and Asia. Nevertheless, churches have been little analyzed. Given the tools available to the political scientist, such religious organizations are, perhaps, more difficult to treat than organizations which are further along in the secularization process – trade unions or social clubs, for example. But as Thrupp notes (1970b:354):

> . . . the political researcher gets information of a practical character and avoids putting his nose in religious matters. If the conditions of life are changing, however, some of the facts will block out spheres of change in values.

Speaking of millenarian movements, Yonina Talmon remarks (1962:142–3):

> The revolutionary nature of millenarism makes it a very potent agent of change as it demands a fundamental transformation and not just improvement and reform . . . Millenarism is *thus* essentially a *connecting link* between pre-political and political movements.

For the political scientist, the most interesting aspect of these movements, however, is that the revolutionary disposition inherent in the constellation of values which define sects *need not* manifest itself in overt political activism. The role of such groups in bringing about the 'new millennium' is crucial, and that role may be defined by the group itself in a number of ways. Three ways religious groups may respond to secular difficulties have been isolated by Stark (1967:235): active secular political involvement (characterized by a feeling on the part of the faithful that they must act to bring about a new state of affairs); withdrawal from the oppressive society (migration and the like); or adjustment and introversion (characterized by a retreatist response to oppression and low political involvement). The adjustment option, of course, means accommodation with the larger society and a resultant hesitation to take overt action to alter the existing power structure.

It may be easier and more accurate to think not of three distinct or polar options, but rather of a continuum of political activity, ranging from active to passive, as even the accommodation option may not exclude the possibility of small-scale pressures applied by the sect on the dominant stratum. At the other end of the scale are overt acts which challenge the status quo.

Sects, too, can be dealt with in terms familiar to the student of politics. They may be dealt with as organizations in the Weberian sense, 'sects' being distinguished from 'denominations' in that the former are most frequently voluntary associations, initially characterized by the charismatic leadership and a membership defined by special personal merit which holds either a hostile or indifferent attitude toward secular society and the state. Such a definition can include the wide range of religiopolitical movements which may be messianic, prophetic, separatist, nativistic, and/or syncretic.

The approach employed here is a comparative one: the goal will be to develop some general statements and propositions concerning the involvement of sects in political activities based on a comparison of experiences within the Zulu and the Kikuyu tribes. Such an analysis should, following Przeworski and Teune (1970), take into account both the intra- and interorganizational activity of the sects. A brief model will also be sketched, based on the inquiry into these two cases. Because one of the cases selected has a low pattern of political involvement (the dependent variable), it should be possible to use the theory developed to account for what has been called the 'negative instance' (Turner 1966:282), the case in which a particular characteristic is minimal or absent in a particular historical instance.

[The author traces the rise of nationalistic and anti-colonial political activity in Kenya. He notes that from the beginning nationalistic political organizations had a close relationship with the independent sect movement. The religio-political link became stronger until, in the 1940's, both spheres were united under Jomo Kenyatta's leadership. The MAU MAU movement is cited as a typical religiopolitical organization and, it is argued, it achieved its successes because it was a religious as well as a political organization.]

The Zulu Experience: South Africa and the Independent Sects

British colonial policies in Kenya involved a scenario which has been acted out more than once on the African continent. Even in its minor details, the policy of the South African government regarding Black residents in the Republic resembles the policies which have been briefly noted in Kenya.

The South African Natives Land Act of 1913, for example, functions as did the Crown Lands Ordinances in Kenya. The Act set up a series of tribal 'reserves' to which Blacks were restricted and outside which they could not move freely. It insured vast areas for White settlement and farming. The Urban Areas Act of 1923 placed similar restrictions on the places in which Africans could work and reside. The first stirring of political activity in Kenya occurred in response to the land restrictions there; this too was the case in South Africa. The African National Congress was formed in South Africa during the period which saw early Kenyan political activism, and the A.N.C. met the same fate as did most Black political associations in Kenya. It was eventually banned by the government.

Between 1923 and 1948, the Nationalist Afrikaner party consolidated its power in the Republic, and was able at the same time to implement an increasingly burdensome set of legislative restrictions on Africans. Mention of a few such laws should serve to make the point. African trade unions are severely restricted and, for all intents and purposes, no collective bargaining mechanisms are available to non-Whites. 'Pass Laws' limit the ability of Blacks to follow the employment needs of the economy. The Group Areas Act of 1950 also establishes a pattern of migratory labor which fragments African families and restricts the amount of time a non-White employee may have to acquire tenure from a particular employer. The Bantu Education Acts prescribe separate educational facilities for non-Whites at all levels, and 'Bantu' education is financed through a set and inadequate grant of government funds which Africans must subsidize. (See, generally, International Commission of Jurists, 1960.) In toto, the social, political and economic milieu in South Africa closely parallels events in colonial Kenya.

Initially, the details of the development of independent sects in South Africa are also remarkably similar to those in Kenya. After two decades of abortive missionary activity among the Zulu, a first convert was baptized in 1864 (cf. Sundkler 1961). After this initial success, several organizations including the American Board of Missionaries and the British Wesleyans competed to provide medical and educational assistance as an inducement to conversion. But mass conversions did not occur until the 1880s, at which time Pentecostal missionaries flooded the area and touched a responsive chord in the Zulu.

The first independent sect appeared in 1884. It was founded by Nehemiah Tile among the Tembu tribesmen. Eight years later, a split in the Tembu Church resulted in the formation of the Ethiopian Church of Mangona Mokone, which Mokone designed to appeal to non-Zulu tribesmen.

Despite attempts at reconciliation by the first leaders of the early sects, Anglican and Wesleyan churchmen, like their counterparts in Kenya, felt these small sects constituted no threat to their denominations. Despite their pessimism, however, 300 such sects existed by 1925 and by 1963 the count had increased to 2 000 sects. These churches counted among their congregations more than two million adherents, about 20 percent of the total Black population of the Republic. (Cawood, 1964:139). Carstens (1971:27) estimated that in 1970, the figure had risen to 25 percent of the total Black population.

Of this total, nearly half the organizations represented are Zulu organizations by Barrett's account. These organizations can be broken down into three types: Zionist, Ethiopian and messianic. Sundkler (1961) uses such a typology and notes that the final type – messianic sects – flourished in the last decade. But this type is of little interest here as a main tenet of this type of organization is salvation from an 'otherworldly' source. As a result, the role of the members of such a congregation would be, by definition, politically passive. Such a believer merely waits for salvation and trusts that supernatural forces will hasten its occurrence.

Though Zionist and Ethiopian sects may also evidence messianic qualities, the extreme emphasis on supernatural aid by the messianic sects Sundkler discusses is less pronounced. The major initial thrust of the typical Ethiopian sect tends to be racial separatism; for the typical Zionist, on the other hand, there is generally a strong desire to integrate some particular local custom or ritual into the pattern of the parent denomination.

In both types of sects, however, the typical organizational patterns seem to derive from a number of interrelated sources. Foremost, according to Sundkler, is the Zulu ideal of leadership, an ideal which stresses a strong, centralized authority figure at the top of an organization. Moreover, unlike the Kikuyu who tends to seek corporate leadership for any group, the Zulus searches for *isithunzi*, a combination of physical size, bravery and conspicuousness in one man.

Such charismatic leaders place heavy burdens on the stability of any particular sect over time. When the founder of the sect becomes incapacitated or dies, a crisis occurs within the sect, and not infrequently, the group dissolves or splits since the congregation is unable to find one man who fills all these needs. In

Kenya, by contrast, a strong bureaucratic tendency was evidenced shortly after the founding of both the AOC and the AIPC, a tendency related both to a Kikuyu tribal tradition and a religious emphasis on lay participation in decision-making. The Kenyan pattern provides for a continuity within sects and facilitates growth to an extent which is rare in South Africa.

Some of the South African sects have attempted to solve this problem by adopting the Zulu inheritance traditions, but such a solution is not foolproof. Sundkler (1961:119) comments:

> The new device of inherited leadership in Church government in some cases has brought about a certain continuity. But nothing can guarantee that all or even the majority of the old ministers, the father's co-workers, will swear allegiance to the young man. These difficulties have, not surprisingly, given rise to a good deal of intra- and inter-sect acrimony and competition. In fact, time-consuming and extended litigations between the members of a sect is not uncommon.

Nor have the overwhelming problems generated by *apartheid* served to bridge the gaps caused by such differences. Sundkler (1961:86) points out that 'suspicion is rampant among the African ministers, with the result that quite often ministers, in their clerical collars, avoid greeting colleagues they meet in the street, who wear the same outfit.' A series of abortive conferences, held by the sects in 1924, 1937, and 1944, only served to emphasize the insurmountable differences.

Such sectarian parochialism has been heightened by tensions arising from physical isolation between the congregations, even within the same sect. The pattern is one of a multitude of sects, each with only a few adherents, scattered across various localities, clinging to unique local traditions and customs. Sundkler (1961:43) cites several instances where the leadership difficulties which have been sketched were confounded by narrow patterns of parochial loyalty. A. P. J. Mzimba, who seceded from the United Free Church of Scotland to establish the African Presbyterian Church, encountered the problem:

> The fact that Mzimba – himself of the Fingo tribe – only carried the Fingo people with him, whereas the Xhosa section of the Presbyterian church remained unmoved by his approach, throws an important light on secessionism.

The rejection of such potentially useful and powerful tribal and pantribal alliance is graphically illustrated by the Zionists, whose leaders adopt a migratory life-style for themselves and reject local, tribal ties.

> The Zionists stand out as a separate community in Zululand, as a *tertium genus*, a third race, over against both the heathen and the Christian community. Whereas in their attitude towards the white man they tend to be rather more violent than the Ethiopians, they nevertheless are not easily assimilated to the rest of the Zulu community (Sundkler 1961:95).

The political input of the South African sects has been sporadic and uneven, at best, and of comparative insignificance when placed against the Kikuyu experience in the same regard. Though in exceptional cases sect leaders have associated with groups which are frankly political like the A.N.C., little such activity exists presently. Some Ethiopian leaders were arrested for activities before and during the Zulu Rebellion of 1906, and Enoch Mgijima led his Israelite sect to face police machine guns in the hope that the bullets would turn to water (Shepperson 1968:253). But even such sporadic outbursts have diminished in number over time, and for the most part, contact with political organizations has been made only in efforts by churchmen to obtain some governmental preference for their sect.

A Tentative Theoretical Framework

What emerges, then, from this brief overview of independent African sects in the Kikuyu and Zulu tribes is an interesting contrast. Along a political activity-passivity continuum, the Kikuyu experience clearly belongs on the strongly political side of the spectrum. The history of the independence movement in that country follows and is related to the rise of nationalism which led, ultimately, to an independent Kenya in the 1960s. Overtly political acts can be noted among the leaders and congregations of the Kikuyu sects. And the impulse which sparked the formation of the Kikuyu Independent School Movement as an alternative to colonial education permitted the articulation of strong nationalist and pan-African sentiments which were exploited by Kenyatta, Mau Mau and the Kenya African Union Party. If the involvement of the various churches was not absolutely and chronologically coordinated at all points, the dominant impression is nevertheless one of cooperation among sects and other voluntary associations.

The experience among the Zulu sects, both Zionist and Ethiopian, is quite different. Along the same continuum, they would rest far to the right of the Kikuyu sects. This, despite the fact that, in most important respects, the Zulu independents sprang from a social milieu and a religious heritage comparable to that of Kenya before its independence. Among the Zulu, the picture is one of intrasect squabbling, secessionist struggles, adjustment to the rigidities of the White regime, and a distinct effort to avoid head-on clashes with White political powers. A few anomic exceptions notwithstanding, the message of the Zulu sects and churchmen has been one of political deference and quiescence. In the words of one churchman who spoke with Sundkler (1961:304):

> . . . 'I like this Nationalist government. And I tell my people, don't take any interest in this colour bar. Forget about it, forget about politics!'

The sources of these differences between Zulu and Kikuyu are likely to be found not in the societal pressures on these sects (as they were remarkably similar in both instances), nor in distinctions of a primarily theological sort, but in the structural differences between the sects.

It might be possible to develop an analysis along theological lines if the similarities were not so apparent here. Donald Smith (1970) postulates different patterns of political involvement among the major world denominations which spring from varying theological assumptions. The Catholic Church, for example, is classed as a 'historical church system' with a strong corporate identity. Smith assumes that such a pattern is likely to account for the role played by the Catholic Church in political development as distinct, say, from the Buddhist attitude in a comparable setting. But the sects we are examining all grew out of a similar tradition and despite minor cultic aberrations, exhibited strong theological likenesses. Here Smith's approach would explain away too much. It appears that even among sects coming from the same tradition, there is no predetermined conservative or revolutionary posture and hence their political impact may vary dramatically.

How, then, to account for the dependent variable here – political involvement? At the broadest level, it would seem that the key to these varying responses is bound up with a particular sect's commitment over time to retaining in a relatively pure form the original ideology and goals which first gave birth to the movement. In other words, it is suggested that the sects which, to use Worsley's phrase, 'remain locked in their original milieu,' which opt for exclusivity and ideological purity, are likely to remain small, isolated, identified with tradition and political conservatism. On the other hand, it would seem that sects whose initial doctrines become modified, which change in a broadening, nonexclusive direction are likely to become significant forces in the types of nationalistic political movements which have arisen in many parts of Africa.

Perhaps it would be useful to develop a skeletal model of the events which typically occur within a sect to clarify this position. The notion of religion as a necessarily static and inert ideological complex has been rejected from the outset. It has also been assumed that sects may be able to play an important role in the politicization of the masses in a modernizing society if their ideology does not inhibit such a role. Religious sects have been treated as voluntary associations of individuals who consider themselves 'elect' in their relationship to the supernatural. In the cases examined, the impetus for the founding of the sects seems to be related to societal stress involving conflicts between the modern and the traditional, tribal and national. The sect, then, functions to alleviate or rationalize the stresses felt by the congregation under such circumstances, to counterbalance central authority, and to integrate the members of the congregation of a particular sect. It does so by developing an ideology, a set of rituals and symbols which are means, according to Apter (1964:16), of 'relating particular actions and mundane practices within a wider set of meanings and by doing so, leading a more honourable and dignified complexion to social conduct.' That ideology is, by definition, tied to a reaction to the larger (dominant) society but it need not be either active or passive; indeed, it is often a mixture of both. Nor is that original ideological base necessarily static over time.

Furthermore, changes in the ideological content which may be noticed in some sects are in turn conditioned by a series of dilemmas which occur within the sects as they deal with the wider society. John Coleman (1968:63) neatly summarizes these 'developmental dilemmas':

> (1) at the ideological level of analysis: *Status v. Dissident values:* that is to say, the initial dissidence of the sect may be tempered upon the attainment of status within a larger section of society. Cross-pressures and increased membership (integration) insure the watering-down of the initial 'exclusive elect' ideology of any sect.
>
> (2) at the leadership level of analysis: *Charisma v. Continuity:* that is to say, charismatic leadership may be an effective unifying force within the sect at the outset, but if the sect aspires to missionary activity and involvement in secular activity . . . organization and routinization may become necessary within the sect. The prophet alone may find it difficult or impossible to carry his message beyond the bounds of his local community and to realize immediate goals and needs if he retains total, autocratic control of the sect.
>
> (3) at the membership level of analysis: *Recruitment v. Exclusivity:* that is to say, the sect which adheres to its initial ideological commitment may find that its appeal is limited within the wider community . . . with the opening of recruitment patterns, membership may rise but congregational commitment may decrease.

The resolution of these dilemmas, of course, may necessitate a redefinition of the sect's relationship to the wider society, A sect, for example, which rejects its original dissident values to some extent, which becomes bureaucratized, and which opens its membership roles, will differ significantly after such alternations in terms of its ability to cooperate with similar sorts of organizations.

This analytical approach suggests a 'conflict' theory of sect development. Such a model points out that sects face conflicts with the dominant society, the 'mother church', other congregations which draw from the same substrata of society and between leaders and congregations of the same sect. These levels of conflict correspond closely to the analytical levels in the conflict theory proposed by Kalman Silvert (1970) in *Man's Power*: value and ideology conflict, conflicts of interests among institutions, and conflicts of interest within institutions.

To the extent that a religious sect opts for values which are local rather than national, for a highly centralized authority structure, and for an exclusive and small congregation (in a word, to the extent that a sect opts for ideological purity over time), then it will not take part in the political development of a national spirit. The sect, in other words, may go on viewing itself as a dissident, not only in relation to the dominant society, but as a unique and incompatible part of the subservient society from which it springs. Such ideological purity, inhibits coalition with similar institutions and bars cooperation with more secular political groups. Coalition would imply a communality of goals which would contradict the dissident sect's view of itself as unique (McEwen and Thompson 1969:195).

When sects opt for ideological purity they insure that the major cleavage between the dominant and subservient society will be reinforced by a series of smaller, localized and 'disassociated' conflicts within the subservient society. At the end-point of such a process, a multitude of cleavages remain rather than coalescing into a few major issues which can cross tribal and local lines. Dahrendorf (1969:215) explains:

> . . . pluralism of associations is accompanied by a pluralism of fronts of conflict, none of these likely to develop the intensity of class conflicts of the Marxian type.

The member of an authoritarian, elite religious sect may then be faced with a problem of conflicting loyalties which are incompatible. He must choose between commitment to the sect, which offers him at least some potential gratification and status within his peer group, and the riskier search for that satisfaction elsewhere. Other, more secular organizations do not have the supernatural sanction available to the religious organization to influence such a choice; the sect, on the other hand, may threaten loss of salvation and impose conformity and loyalty even at a cost to the individual member's association with other secular institutions.

Given this model, a further question must be asked: Is 'commitment by the sect to ideological purity over time' truly explanatory in terms of the sect's placement along an active-passive political continuum? Or is it possible to perform a reductionist analysis and discover the causes and sources of such a commitment on the part of the sect? This operation would clarify the more general proposition and is a necessary step in the empirical testing of the general theory as the concept 'ideological purity' is difficult to handle and resistant to operationalization.

The general theory can be reframed in terms of the organizational dilemmas suggested by Coleman. The cases imply, for example, that a charismatic and authoritarian leadership pattern retained over time to preserve the original norms and ideals of the sect may inhibit political involvement. Among the Zulu, the founder of a sect frequently names an heir. Among the Kikuyu, on the other hand, sects which came to dominate the scene quickly became bureaucratic and moved away from emphasis on a single authority figure. It should be pointed out that these varying patterns can be linked to pre-existing tribal leadership customs. Among the Zulu, the common tribal leader is a single figure who retains all executive and judicial power. For the Kikuyu, however, the chief-pattern of leadership was not indigenous. The typical leadership pattern in the tribe, according to James Coleman (1954:413), was 'democratic', that is, decentralized, a fact which was reflected in the rapid bureaucratization of organizations like the AOC. And the implications for the growth of such organizations have already been treated in the model.

Membership and recruitment patterns in the Zulu case also reflect a greater concern over time for the importance of differentiating the particular sect from both white society *and* from nonelect elements of the black community. Zulu sects have, therefore, remained relatively small and numerous and have failed to cut across local and tribal distinctions. Moreover, bonds between urban and rural elements are absent for the most part within the Zulu sects. Ethiopian churches tend to be predominantly urban, and Zionists rural (Mair 1959:122).

The foregoing analysis might be crystallized into the following basic propositions about sects and their political potential:

1. The greater the commitment of a religious sect to ideological purity, the lower the level of organized political activity by that sect, and vice versa.
2. Sects with charismatic (authoritarian) leaders are more likely to stress ideological purity than bureaucratically controlled sects.
3. Sects with closed recruitment patterns are more likely to stress ideological purity than sects with open recruitment patterns.
4. Sects which place heavy emphasis on one particular issue or custom at their outset are more likely to stress ideological purity over time than sects which are born through a concern with several important issues.

This analysis has several limitations. It is unidirectional, and does not come to grips with the feedback problem – the long-range effects of political activity by a sect on its internal structure. It would not be surprising, however, to find that as political involvement increases, such activity opens up recruitment patterns at an ever faster rate. But such speculation is merely a hypothesis at this point which the cases neither confirm nor deny. Furthermore, the three variables are treated independently. It is likely, however, that open recruitment patterns within a sect ultimately stimulate further bureaucratic tendencies. But, again, such speculation cannot truly be said to be supported by the fragmentary and impressionistic data available here.

FIGURE 1

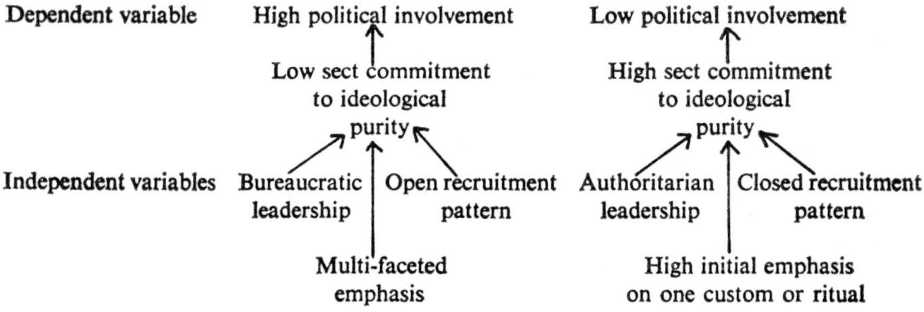

The theory suggested here, an amalgam of traditional organizational concepts developed by political scientists and political sociologists, is tentative. Based as it is on scattered observations about only two tribal experiences, it is difficult to feel entirely secure with these generalizations. Analysis in other cases would establish or disprove the propositions suggested, as would more incisive statistical data in the Kikuyu and Zulu cases.

Furthermore, even the discovery of the patterns discussed here which are often found in combination with a tendency to political involvement by a religious sect would not insure such involvement in every case. Perhaps the types of organizational interaction discovered in the Kikuyu case may be a *sine qua non* for extended political involvement by the religious sect. But without certain personality and behavioral traits and theological inputs (controlled for here in the selection of the cases), the dependent variable may still not materialize. In other words, no attempt has been made to prove that when certain organizational traits exist in combination, political involvement can *always* be predicted. Causality has been treated in the 'possibility' sense that Silvert (1970) suggests is appropriate for the social sciences.

Nevertheless, this approach may serve a number of needs. Most importantly, it permits the treatment of religiopolitical organizations with the tools which are familiar to the political scientist. Moreover, it should be possible to compare such religiopolitical institutions to other sorts of voluntary associations more traditionally of interest to the political investigator – the sorts of associations examined by Wallerstein (1964) in *The Road to Independence*.

REFERENCES

Almond, Gabriel A., and G. Bingham Powell 1966 – *Comparative Politics: A Developmental Approach*. Boston: Little, Brown.

Apter, David (ed.) 1964 – *Ideology and Discontent*. New York: Free Press.

Barnett, Donald L., and Karari Njama 1966 – *Mau Mau From Within*. London: Macgibbon & Kee.

Barrett, David B. 1968a – 'Church growth and independency as organic phenomena: An analysis of 200 African tribes.' In G. C. Baeta (ed.) *Christianity in Tropical Africa*. Oxford: Oxford University Press.

——1968b – *Schism and Renewal in Africa*. Nairobi: Oxford University Press.

Bellah, Robert N. 1964 – 'Religious evolution.' *American Sociological Review*, 3, June, 358–74.

Carstens, Kenneth N. 1971 – *Church and Race in South Africa*. New York: United Nations Unit on Apartheid, No. 23 71.

Cawood, Lesley 1964 – *The Churches and Race Relations in South Africa*. Johannesburg: South African Institute of Race Relations.

Chilver, E. M. and Vincent Harlow (eds.) 1965 – *History of East Africa*, Volume II. Oxford: Clarendon Press.

Coleman, James S. 1954 – 'Nationalism in tropical Africa.' *American Political Science Review*, 48, June, 404–26.

Coleman, John A. 1968 – 'Church-sect typology and organizational precariousness.' *Sociological Analysis*, 2 (Summer), 55–66.

Dahrendorf, Rolf 1969 – *Class and Class Conflict in Industrial Society*. Stanford: Stanford University Press.

Etzioni, Amitai (ed.) 1969 – *A Sociological Reader on Complex Organizations* (2nd edn.). New York: Holt, Rinehart and Winston.

Farson, Negley 1950 – *Last Chance in Africa*. New York: Harcourt, Brace.

Fernandez, James W. 1964 – 'African religious movements-types and dynamics.' *The Journal of Modern African Studies*, 2, 531–49.

Gluckman, Max 1963 – *Order and Rebellion in Tribal Africa*. London: Cohen and West.

Hobsbawn, E. J. 1959 – *Primitive Rebels: Studies in Archaic Forms of Social Movements*. Manchester: Manchester University Press.

Hodgkin, Thomas 1957 – *Nationalism in Colonial Africa*. New York: New York University Press.

Horrell, Muriel 1968 – *Introduction to South Africa: Basic Facts and Figures*. Johannesburg: South African Institute of Race Relations.

Hoult, Thomas Ford 1957 – 'A functional theory of religion.' *Sociology and Social Research*, 4, March, 277–80.

Hughes, Anthony J. 1969 – *East Africa: Kenya, Tanzania, Uganda* (2nd edn.). London: Penguin.

International Commission of Jurists 1960 – *South Africa and the Rule of Law*. Geneva: International Commission of Jurists.

Kenyatta, Jomo 1953 – *Facing Mount Kenya*. London: Secker and Warburg.

Kilson, Martin 1955 – 'Land and the Kikuyu: A study of the relationship between land and Kikuyu political movements.' *Journal of Negro History*, 40, April, 103–53.

Kuper, Leo 1956 – *Passive Resistance in South Africa*. New Haven: Yale University Press.

Leakey, Louis Seymour 1954 – *Defeating Mau Mau*. London: Methuen.

Mair, Lucy 1959 – 'Independent religious movements in three continents.' *Comparative Studies in Society and History*, 1, January, 113–35.

March, James G., and Herbert A. Simon 1958 – *Organizations*. New York: Wiley.

Marx, Gary T. 1967 – 'Religion: Opiate or inspiration of civil rights militancy among Negroes?' *American Sociological Review* 32, Feb., 64–72.

McEwen, William J., and James D. Thompson 1969 – 'Organizational goals and environment.' In Amitai Etzioni (ed.) *A Sociological Reader on Complex Organizations* (2nd edn.). New York: Holt, Rinehart and Winston.

Mead, Margaret 1959 – 'A comment on L. P. Mair, Independent religious movements in three continents.' *Comparative Studies in Society and History*, 1, June, 324–9.

Middleton, John 1965 – 'Kenya: Changes in African life, 1912–1945.' In E. M. Chilver and Vincent Harlow (eds.) *History of East Africa*, Volume 2. Oxford: Clarendon.

Mitchell, Robert C., and Harold Turner 1966 – *A Comprehensive Bibliography of Modern African Religious Movements*. Chicago: Northwestern University Press.

Norbeck, Edward 1961 – *Religion in Primitive Society*. New York: Harper & Row.

O'Connell, James 1965 – 'Government and politics in the Yoruba African churches: The claims of tradition and modernity.' *ODU: University of Ife Journal of African Studies*, 2, July, 92–108.

Oliver, Roland 1952 – *The Missionary Factor in East Africa*. London: Longmans.

Przeworski, Adam, and Henry Teune 1970 – *The Logic of Comparative Social Inquiry*. New York: Wiley.

Rothberg, Robert 1962 – 'The rise of African nationalism: The case of East and Central Africa.' *World Politics*, 15, Oct., 75–90.

Shepperson, G. 1954 – 'The politics of African church separatist movements in British central Africa, 1892–1916.' *Africa*, 24, 233–45.

——1968 – 'Ethiopianism: past and present.' In C. G. Baeta (ed.). *Christianity in Tropical Africa*. Oxford: Oxford University Press.

Silvert, Kalman H. 1970 – *Man's Power: A Biased Guide to Political Thought and Action:* New York: Viking.

Smith, Donald Eugene 1970 – *Religion and Political Development*. Boston: Little, Brown.

Stark, Werner 1967 – *The Sociology of Religion: A Study of Christendom*, Volume 2. New York: Fordham University Press.

Sundkler, Bengt G. M. 1961 – *Bantu Prophets in South Africa* (2nd edn.). London: Oxford University Press.

Talmon, Yonina 1962 – 'Pursuit of the millennium: The relation between religious and social change.' *Archives Europeennes de Sociologie*, 3, 125–48.

Thrupp, Sylvia L., (ed.) 1970a – *Millennial Dreams in Action*. New York: Schocken.

——1970b – 'Diachronic methods in comparative politics.' In Robert T. Holt and John E. Turner (eds.). *The Methodology of Comparative Research*. New York: Free Press.

Turner, H. W. 1963 – African prophet movements.' *Hibbert Journal*, 61, April, 112–16.

——1966 – 'A methodology for modern African religious movements.' *Comparative Studies in Society and History*, 8, April, 281–94.

Wallace, Anthony C. 1956 – 'Revitalization movements.' *American Anthropologist*, 58, April, 264–81.

Wallerstein I. 1964 – *The Road to Independence: Ghana and the Ivory Coast*. Paris: Mouton.

Weber, Max 1963 – *The Sociology of Religion*. Translated by Ephraim Fischoff. Boston: Beacon.

Welbourn, F. B. 1961 – *East African Rebels: A Study of Some Independent Churches*. London: SCM Press.

——1968 – 'A note on the types of religious society.' In C. G. Baeta (ed.). *Christianity in Tropical Africa*. Oxford: Oxford University Press.

Wilson, Bryan R. 1959 – 'An analysis of sect development.' *American Sociological Review*, 24, February, 1, 3–15

Worsley, Peter 1968 – *The Trumpet Shall Sound* (2nd edn.). New York: Schocken.

2. The Relationship between the Dogmatic Teachings and Attitudes towards Race Relations of Two South African Religious Denominations

ROBERT P. D. BUIS

Max Weber (1967) saw in social interaction a general tendency towards rationality. For Weber 'rationality' implied a deliberate and systematic adjustment of means to ends. This is directly opposed to an adjustment based on tradition or custom. Capitalism was seen by him as an example of an advanced system of rationality. Weber's definition of 'capitalism' is vague. Essentially it appears to mean the systematic and rational use of the factors of production with the criterion of success or failure being profit expressed in terms of money. In his explanation of why capitalism occurred in some countries, Weber used the concepts of 'ideas' and 'interests'. He regarded these two concepts as interdependent but was primarily concerned with the role played by 'ideas' in the origin of capitalism. He claimed that the relative independence of 'ideas' could be recognized without denying or neglecting the influence of 'interests' on 'ideas'. Bendix (1966:46) notes that it was not Weber's intention to '. . . substitute for a one-sided materialistic and equally one-sided spiritualistic causal interpretation of culture and of history'.

Weber (1967:48) claimed that only in certain Western countries was a 'capitalist spirit' found and that these countries tended to be Protestant in their religion and that only in those countries where Protestantism was dominant did a rational and systematic application of the factors of production occur. (Here Weber quotes Benjamin Franklin as an ideal example of an individual possessing a 'capitalist spirit'.)

Calvinism, a branch of Protestantism, was the faith over which the great religious struggles took place in Europe and Britain in the sixteenth and seventeenth centuries. It is important to note that Calvinism was not simply the personal views of John Calvin, but a set of religious beliefs that had been adopted by Protestants in many Western countries, for example the Huguenots in France, the Beggars in the Netherlands, the Puritans and Presbyterians in Britain and the Pilgrim Fathers in America. Calvinism has been known by other names, for instance Orthodox Reformism and Augustinism, but the same general principles were taught by most of the leaders of the Reformation with John Calvin being the first to formulate these principles into a more or less complete system. (Cross 1958:220–21) states that: 'in his revolt from Rome Calvin was more logical and systematic and a greater organizer than Luther . . .' Calvin was the most influential writer among the reformers and his Institutes were accepted with some modification by most non-Lutheran Protestant Churches.)

When constructing his 'ideal type' of Calvinism, Weber (1967:98) was referring to a set of religious ideas that had evolved among Protestants in the most highly developed countries of Europe by the end of the seventeenth century. Max Weber used the *Westminster Confession* of 1646 on which to build his 'ideal type' of seventeenth century Calvinism. (It should be noted that Weber could equally well have chosen one of the other major reform confessions, e.g. Canons of Dort, Belgic Confession on which to base his 'ideal type' of Calvinism.)

Weber points out that even in 1920 the most characteristic doctrine of Calvinism was predestination and that the great synods of the seventeenth century, especially those of Dordrecht and Westminster as well as many smaller ones raised predestination to canonical importance. Weber quotes from Chapters 3, 5, 9 and 10 of the *Westminster Confession* in his explanation of the doctrine of predestination.

This doctrine in its pure form has often been classified as 'harsh' because there was no means whatever, for those whom God had not chosen, to be saved. Neither a minister nor the Church could save an individual if he was not among the elect. Every person, at some time, must ask himself, 'Am I one of the elect?' and because 'faith' was such a vague and intangible concept, many followers sought a more concrete and visible criterion of election. 'For them (Calvinists) the "certidudo salutis" in the sense of the recognizability of the state of grace necessarily became of absolutely dominant importance' (Weber 1967:110).

It was difficult for followers of this doctrine to accept and be satisfied with the statement that true faith resulted from grace. For Calvinists the objective criterion of election became a type of human conduct which would promote the glory of God on earth. To promote His glory on earth His commandments had to be obeyed, and intense worldly activity was necessary to advance the order and well-being of the earthly community which God not only created, but predestined to be as it is. A life of good works was a sign that God was not only working through an individual but that these good works were being done by God with the individual as His instrument. Good works were not a means of attaining salvation but were indispensable as a sign of election. A life of good works consisted of diligent and successful work in a calling as well as a rational and religious home-life devoid of any lust, emotion and superstition. All these factors were signs of a true faith. Max Weber claimed that these religious beliefs led to a rational and systematic organization of the factors of production, which in turn resulted in the development of capitalism in countries where these religious beliefs were dominant.

We are not primarily interested in the economic consequences of these religious beliefs, but rather in an attitude of exclusiveness which Weber (1967:122) claims was '. . . accompanied by an attitude toward the sin of one's neighbour, not of sympathetic understanding based on consciousness of one's own weakness, but of hatred and contempt for him as an enemy of God bearing the signs of eternal damnation.' Not only did those confident of their salvation consider themselves God's chosen people but were thankful to Him for their own perfection. They felt themselves to be an aristocracy which distinguished them from the eternally damned remainder of humanity who, despite the fact that they would not be saved by God, still had to obey His commandments. All those persons who bore the signs of eternal damnation were not to be pitied or befriended but ostracized by those who were confident of their election. To summarize briefly, Max Weber claimed that seventeenth century followers of a religious doctrine known as Calvinism, developed a feeling of hatred and contempt for those people who had insufficient faith in God to be confident of their salvation.

I. D. MacCrone (1965), in discussing religious beliefs in eighteenth and nineteenth century South Africa, claimed that among the Europeans, both Dutch and French, Calvinism was the dominant creed. He stated that the term 'Christian' became synonymous not only with 'European' but also with a particular religious doctrine, i.e. Calvinism. MacCrone believed that the doctrines of Calvinism led to the development of a feeling of 'exclusiveness' and 'superiority' among Whites and an 'intolerant' and 'harsh' attitude towards outsiders. How did these religious beliefs influence race relations in South Africa in what MacCrone classifies as a 'Frontier Society' at that time? According to MacCrone (1965:129–30):

> The negative aspects of the Calvinistic creed, its doctrine of predestination, its emphasis upon the community of the elect, the exclusive twist that could be given to its teachings, were all perfectly adapted to the interracial situation of the frontier. The conclusion was readily drawn, and applied, that the heathen fell outside the scheme of salvation. Attempts to christianize them were not merely not sanctioned by, but actually contrary to, the teachings of the Bible.

MacCrone (1965:127) said of the frontier farmer:

> By virtue of his religion, he justified his right to dominate the heathen by whom he was surrounded. They fell outside the pale, and their claims, therefore, could never compete on equal terms with those of the Christian group.

An interesting fact has emerged: both Weber and MacCrone claimed that Calvinists in very different environmental conditions tended to be harsh and intolerant towards outsiders. If we look at the contemporary South African situation we find that the Whites are predominantly Protestant. This does not necessarily imply that they are Calvinists. In 1970 94% of the White population were classified as Christian, while 52% of the total White Christian population or 49% of the total White population were members of the three Dutch Reformed Churches. (There are actually three Dutch Reformed Churches in South

Africa: Nederduits-Gereformeerde Kerk, which is by far the largest of the three with almost 1,5 million White adherents; Nederduits Hervormde Kerk with almost a quarter of a million White adherents; Gereformeerde Kerk with 113 000 White adherents. These are all figures for 1970.) In the same year 1 487 million or almost 40% of the total White population in South African were members of one of the three Dutch Reformed churches, i.e. the Nederduits-Gereformeerde Kerk.

A brief look at the history of the Nederduits-Gereformeerde Kerk (N.G.K.) in South Africa reveals that it stems directly from the seventeenth-century mother church in Holland and that the history of the Church began with the arrival of Jan van Riebeeck at the Cape in 1652 (cf. Carter, nd.; Gerdener 1930; Moorrees 1937). The N.G.K. was from 1652 to 1804 under the control of the Dutch East India Company and maintained close relations with the 'Klassis' of Amsterdam. In 1804 the Church came under State control and this remained so until 1843; it was forced to break its links with Holland because of the second British occupation of the Cape in 1806. During the period 1652 to 1804 the only church recognized by the authorities was the N.G.K., but in 1774 the Lutherans were permitted to build their own Church. In 1778 the Lutherans were given additional religious rights by the Council of the Dutch East India Company but this was against the wishes of the N.G.K. in the Cape.

Between 1804 and 1843 the N.G.K. made many demands on the State for internal autonomy which was granted by Sir George Napier in the Ordinance of 1843. In 1853 the 'Trekkers' in the Transvaal broke away from the Cape N.G.K. and officially became the Nederduits Hervormde Kerk, which in 1856 was declared the State Church of the South African Republic. In February 1859 the Gereformeerde Kerk was officially established when it broke away from the Hervormde Kerk in the Transvaal; the main reasons for this split were that the Nederduits Hervormde Kerk was not sufficiently orthodox in its preaching, that the doctrinal standards of the Synod of Dordrecht were not being strictly adhered to and that non-Europeans were allowed to participate in church services with Europeans.

A report adopted by the General Synod of the Dutch Reformed Church (1966:25) states: 'In the nineteenth century the Ned. Geref. Kerk gradually changed its policy of including converts from non-white population groups in the same congregation as white members.' As a result of this policy change the Nederduits-Gereformeerde Mission Church was formed in 1881 and was granted its own constitution in 1915. In 1961 this Mission Church (N.G. Bantu Church) was given greater autonomy and changed its name to the Nederduits-Gereformeerde Kerk in Africa in May 1963. The N.G.K. policy is to provide separate churches for the different categories of people, e.g. Blacks, Coloureds and Whites in South Africa.

The Nederduitse-Gereformeerde Kerk has therefore existed in South Africa for more than three hundred years and despite the inflow of a large number of White immigrants into the country, almost 40% (1970) of the White population are members of this church. But what are the doctrinal standards and official teachings of the Dutch Reformed Church as it exists in South Africa at present? To discuss this matter and obtain a reading list, the author visited the Theological Seminary for the training for Dutch Reformed ministers at the University of Stellenbosch in the Cape.

Senior theology students, ministers and a Professor were interviewed for these purposes (cf. Kuyper 1961; Boettner 1966; Calvinist Action Committee 1951; Paton 1958; The Belgic Confession; the Heidelberg Catechism; and the Canons of Dort). The following précis is based on these discussions and the literature they recommended. In addition the summary was submitted to two D.R.C. theology Professors as well as a practising D.R.C. Minister for their criticisms and suggestions before the present manuscript was finalized.

The doctrinal standards of the Dutch Reformed Church in South Africa are the *Belgic Confession*, the *Heidelberg Catechism* and the *Canons of Dort*. The *Belgic Confession* originated in the Southern Netherlands, now known as Belgium, in 1651. Its chief author was Guido de Brès, a Reformed preacher of the Netherlands.

The *Heidelberg Catechism* originated in Heidelberg, Germany under Frederic III. 'In order that the Calvinistic Reformation might gain the ascendancy in his domain, this pious ruler charged Zacharias Ursinus, professor at the Heidelberg University, and Caspar Olevianus, the court preacher, with the preparation of a manual for catechetical instruction. The result was a new Catechism, which, after having been approved by the Elector himself and by a gathering of prominent Calvinists, was published in the beginning of the year 1563.' (Publication Committee of the Christian Reformed Church, Michigan 1959.)

The third doctrinal standard of the Dutch Reformed Church is the *Canons of Dort*, 1618–1619. These statements of doctrine we readopted by the international Synod held at Dordrecht, in the Netherlands and the twenty-seven foreign delegates as well as local representatives reaffirmed the doctrine of unconditional election, limited atonement, total depravity, irresistible grace and the perseverance of the saints. The Synod also approved and accepted the *Belgic Confession* and the *Heidelberg Catechism.*

Having dealt with the doctrinal standards of the Dutch Reformed Church in South Africa, a summary of the official dogmatic teachings of the Church based on discussions held with a Professor of Theology, the reading list he recommended, Ministers and Theology students at the Stellenbosch Theological Seminary, is presented below:

> There is only one almighty being whom we call God. He is eternal, infinite, invisible, perfectly wise and just. He created all things, the sun, the moon, the stars, the earth and all the living creatures that dwell upon it.
>
> Everything was made in accordance with His plan and is dictated by His will. Everything has a cause and a purpose and nothing happens by chance or by luck, because everything has been predestined by God. Man exists

for God and not God for man, but men should pray to God who will consider their prayers in the enactment of His will.

After God had created the earth and given it light, water, grass etc. He created man in His own image. To Adam, God gave a 'free will' and formed a covenant of 'good works' with him. God promised Adam and all his descendants eternal life, conditional upon perfect obedience, but Adam wilfully disobeyed God. Because Adam was the representative of mankind, all men are affected and depraved by 'original sin'.

God's plan includes the 'fall of man' but He is in no respect the Author of sin. God is revealed to man through the order and magnificence of the universe, through His Holy writings, the incarnation of His Son and the work of the Holy Spirit. The only writings that have been inspired by God are the Old and the New Testaments; those books often classified as the Apocrypha have not been inspired by God and should not be added to the Holy Scriptures. There is only one God, but though one in being, He reveals Himself in three distinct infinite Persons, i.e. the Father, the Son and the Holy Spirit; this is known as the Holy Trinity.

All Adam's descendants having fallen into ruin by the sin of their first parents have the mercy and justice of God revealed to them: God is merciful because He saves from this total destruction, all those whom He out of goodness and mercy and in accordance with His plan has chosen, irrespective of their good works. Good works are the result and not the cause of salvation. God is just in leaving others in the ruin and sin in which they have involved themselves. God has not revealed how many He has chosen or why He has chosen them and man should not speculate about God's plan, because it is beyond human comprehension. As the plan of God is not subject to change, those whom God has chosen are a fixed number and cannot be increased or decreased. The non-elect still have the benefits of God's common grace, e.g. health, intelligence, the sun, the rain, etc., but not eternal salvation.

Those whom God has chosen cannot be deprived of their salvation. The elect may, if they do not obey the Scriptures, be deprived of the assurance of their salvation for a limited period of time, but this is only temporary because those whom God has chosen He has also 'called' 'justified' and 'glorified'. Those people who ignore God's word and live wicked and sinful lives will suffer eternal damnation.

How does a person know that he has been saved? All those to whom God has given faith and who obey His teachings can be certain of their salvation. God has kindled a spirit of faith and obedience in those He has chosen, and although good works can never influence God or earn salvation, they are a definite sign or indication that God is working through a person and that he is among the elect. The Psalter Hymnal: Heidelberg Catechism states that good works are those works which are done from true faith and for the glory of God. '. . . and not such as are based on our own opinions

> or the precepts of men'. All that men need know about salvation is contained in the Holy Bible and God sent His only-begotten Son Jesus to die on the Cross to give eternal salvation and eternal life to those whom He has chosen.
>
> There is only one catholic or universal church. In the true Church the pure doctrine of the Gospel is preached and the pure administration of the sacraments is practised and '. . . church discipline is exercised in punishing of sin; . . .' (Psalter Hymnal: Belgic Confessions). Jesus Christ is acknowledged as the only head of the Church. God appointed the Apostles, evangelists and prophets to found the Christian Church; He also founded the offices of Ministers, Elders and Deacons. In all religious disputes the Old and the New Testaments are the final authority.
>
> On a day, determined by God but not known to man, God will pass judgement on all that have ever lived. Those who have had faith in Christ and who have proof of their salvation can look forward to this day with confidence, but those who have ignored God await this day with fear and dread.

This summary has emphasized the dogmatic aspects of the Dutch Reformed Church's teachings, which distinguish it from other Christian beliefs; those more general Christian teachings expressed in the Ten Commandments, which are common to most if not all Christian denominations, have not been included.

These dogmatic teachings are obviously very similar to those of the *Westminster Confession* discussed by Max Weber, but how do these very similar dogmatic teachings manifest themselves in the social teachings of the Dutch Reformed Church; more precisely, what is the contemporary Dutch Reformed attitude towards heathens and sinners? From a Christian point of view, one of the most spiritually backward and irreligious category of persons in South Africa are the Blacks. As recently as 1970 almost a third (31%) of the Blacks in South Africa were classified as non-Christian. The official attitude of the Dutch Reformed Church towards Blacks and other non-Whites is stated in a report adopted by the General Synod of the Dutch Reformed Church (1966) called 'Human Relations in South Africa'. The official teachings expressed in this report will be briefly summarized. In the following précis emphasis will be placed on those characteristics which distinguish these teachings from those of other major Christian denominations in South Africa.

> In this report 'race' has a biological-heriditary meaning, 'people' a cultural meaning and 'nation' a political meaning. These definitions are very vague as is the report as a whole.
>
> God created everything including the different races, peoples and nations on the earth. Had He wished to create all men the same He would have done so. 'Ethnic diversity is in agreement with God's will' (General Synod of the Dutch Reformed Church 1966). God mercifully decreed that man should have many languages and that he should be diversified and spread to

all parts of the earth. This resulted in the formation of many different races, peoples and nations, to the glory of God. God has deliberately encouraged the formation and development of different races, peoples, languages and nations. This can be seen from His anger at the sinful attempt at unity, manifest in the attempted construction of the Tower of Babel.

Every people have their own particular 'distinctiveness' and 'character' which it is the duty of the Church to maintain and preserve. This 'distinctiveness' and 'character' is threatened by the mixing of the races and peoples and is therefore sinful. Racial mixing and especially mixed marriages, for example between Blacks and Whites, cannot be permitted by the Church. If there is a situation like that which for example exists in South Africa at present, 'Then mixing must be resisted with every resource as wrong and sinful, and such a development must be opposed in principle . . . the Christian state under given circumstances would be justified in taking legislative action and prohibiting racial mixing and mixed marriages. So drastic a step would be motivated especially by a substantial danger of levelling down and intentional obliteration of lines of division if the level of civilisation and the spiritual and moral values and distinctive character of the people were endangered by the weight of numbers of "strangers", or if the distinctive existence and the maintenance of the peculiar identity of the people is threatened' (General Synod of the Dutch Reformed Church 1966:8).

This policy of no racial mixing is maintained in places of public worship where separate Churches have been built for Blacks, Coloureds and Whites. No racial mixing is permitted by the Church even if the parties concerned have the same cultural values and are all confirmed members of the Dutch Reformed Church. These people, for example Blacks who become Christianized and adopt Western cultural values, are not to be integrated into the White community but should be 'instructed' to help their own people. 'No injudicious agitation for equality should be allowed to awaken false expectations which inevitably lead to frustration; . . .' (General Synod of the Dutch Reformed Church 1966:5.)

God encouraged diversity and many different races and peoples came into being. 'As a matter of course differences in development and in level of civilisation also set in. All disruption and obscuration, however, was caused by the action of sin . . . From Deut. 32:8 – a text of which the reading is not altogether sure and the interpretation of which is also difficult – it appears that fortunes of peoples did not stand outside the will and intervention of God: on occasion He allocated each its own area, and we may assume that this process attends the providential order of God in the course of history to its end' (General Synod of the Dutch Reformed Church 1966:3–4). There is a true spiritual unity among the elect and this is the real unity in Christ which is independent of the physical unity of men on earth. Physical unity on earth does not necessarily imply a spiritual unity with Christ.

This 1966 Dutch Reformed Church report makes no comment on the many laws passed in the last twenty years which apply to non-Whites only and which in many respects can be classified as restrictive. The report does, however, mention migratory labour and implies that it is necessary but is not without injustice.

We have briefly summarized the dogmatic and certain aspects of the social teachings of the Dutch Reformed Church. How do these teachings compare with those of other major Christian denominations in South Africa? Ideally all major Christian denominations in South Africa should be compared but time and space do not permit this. One of the major Christian denominations in South Africa which differs radically from the Dutch Reformed Church is the Roman Catholic Church. Not only do these two denominations differ radically from each other but they are in fundamental disagreement on common theological issues. We shall therefore briefly summarize the dogmatic and certain aspects of the social teachings of the Roman Catholic Church in South Africa. The summary of the contemporary dogmatic teachings is based on discussions held by the author with theologians and priests of the Roman Catholic Church and on the relevant list of books they recommended (cf. Marty and Peerman 1967; McKenzie 1963; Schillebeeckx 1963; Bishops of the Netherlands 1965–1966; Bullough 1963). The theologians were members of the Dominican Order resident at Stellenbosch in the Western Cape; the Priests were Parish Priests practising in the same area. It is important to note that in the religious précis that follows, emphasis will be placed on those fundamental dogmatic teachings which distinguish the Roman Catholic Church from other Christian denominations in South Africa.

Before this summary was finalized it was submitted to two Roman Catholic theologians of the Dominican Order and two practising Parish Priests for their criticisms and suggestions.

> There is only one God and He is three persons in one Godhead; He is eternal, merciful and just. God created everything including the earth and all the things that dwell upon it. God created man in His own image with intelligence and a free will and gave man eternal life conditional upon perfect obedience to Him, but Adam disobeyed God and all Adam's descendants, i.e. man, therefore suffer from original sin. Original sin is remitted by baptism and no adult person will be condemned for original sin alone.
>
> Man will only be condemned for 'actual sin', that is, sin committed by an individual with his own consent. The covenant between God and man was broken by human sin, but each person will be judged by his own conduct and behaviour. God gave to man a free will with which he could obey or disobey God as he chose but man can obtain forgiveness for his disobedience through the visible Church on earth.
>
> God sent His only Son Jesus to die on the Cross for the redemption of man's sins. Jesus was born of the Virgin Mary, suffered and died on the Cross and rose from the dead. God wills that all men shall be saved and He

sent His Son Jesus to die for all mankind. God has absolute knowledge of all things past, present and future and He therefore knows who will accept and who will reject Him.

God is revealed to us through His creation and through the Holy Scripture; this revelation is communicated to man through the living tradition of the Church. Much of what Christ said does not appear in the Scriptures and has been handed down through the traditions of the Church. The Church and its traditions may be described as the vehicle of revelation. The Holy Scripture consists of the Old and the New Testaments and those books which are often classified as the Apocrypha. The Church, and there is only one true catholic church, i.e. the Roman Catholic Church, was founded by Christ who appointed Peter as head of the Church on earth. Christ gave to the Apostle Peter and the Popes, Cardinals, Archbishops, Bishops and Priests since His death, the authority to forgive the sins of men and lead them to eternal life.

In the true Church the Virgin Mary is recognized as the mother of God and she is exempt from original sin. As the mother of Jesus she is also mother of all who are redeemed and as such has a special intercessary role in the divine plan of salvation. Man can therefore communicate with God through her.

The true Church has not only been given the '. . . keys of the kingdom of heaven: . . .' (Matthew 16:19) but when God speaks through the head of the Church, what the Pope then says is infallible. When the Pope speaks *ex cathedra* what he says contains the truth of God's spirit and is therefore infallible. For this reason what previous Popes have said *ex cathedra* is included in the traditions of the Church.

The Church will turn no man away, regardless of how sinful he is if he confesses his sins before a Priest and asks him sincerely for forgiveness. In the true Church there are seven sacraments which were instituted by Christ and given to the Church to administer. These sacraments are Baptism, Confirmation, Mass, Penance, Extreme Unction or the Sacrament of the Sick, Marriage and Ordination of Priests and can be classified as privileged channels or vehicles of grace. The two sacraments which both Roman Catholics and most Protestants practice, i.e. Baptism and Mass or Communion, are practised differently and have different meanings in each institution. In the Mass the bread and the wine are transubstantiated by the Priest into the Body and Blood of Christ and usually only the bread is taken by the congregation. Members of the Roman Catholic Church are expected to be baptised by a Priest, to attend Mass on Sundays, to be confirmed into the Church, to confess their sins and do penance for them and to live according to the teachings of the Church. Should a Catholic decide to marry, he/she should ideally marry another Catholic in their Church. Good conduct and moral behaviour will be rewarded by only a short period of suffering in purgatory before salvation and eternal life with Christ.

Man can accept or reject the love of God and each person is responsible for his own conduct, but if a person rejects God's love and fails to obey His commandments then he will be punished. God wants to save all mankind and it is up to each individual to accept the love and mercy of Christ as revealed to man. Christ will come again at the end of time to reward the just and punish the wicked.

Having briefly explained the dogmatic teachings of the Roman Catholic Church in South African let us now look at the corresponding social teachings. We are concerned only with certain aspects of the social teachings, i.e. the official attitude of the Church towards Blacks in South Africa. This brief summary of the official teachings of the Roman Catholic Church in South Africa, towards Blacks in this country, is based on a series of statements issued by the Archbishops and Bishops of the Church between 1952 and 1966 (cf. Press Commission S.A.C.B.A., 1966).

The Roman Catholic Church does not consider skin colour a significant criterion, and the concept of race is also given very little prominence. 'It is the practice to speak of different races, but there is truly only one race, the human race' (Press Commission S.A.C.B.A. 1966:21). The Church claims that all people should communicate and mix freely with one another regardless of skin colour and that this would be to the benefit of all concerned. In Roman Catholic Churches Blacks and Whites worship together and no deliberate attempt has been made to build separate Churches for Blacks and Whites. The Church does not oppose mixed marriages for example between Blacks and Whites, and the policy of the Church is the gradual integration of all men into a Christian community regardless of skin colour. 'But the Christian duty remains of seeking to unite rather than separate, to dissolve differences rather than perpetuate them. A different colour can be no reason for separation when culture, custom, social condition and, above all, a common faith and common love of Christ impel towards unity' (Press Commission S.A.C.B.A. 1966:16).

'It is true that men gather together in groups with loyalties that arise from the bond of relationship or association, but these too must be subordinate to the great overriding fact of the human person's dignity and his unity with all fellow men' (Press Commission S.A.C.B.A., 1966:22). Man is created by God in His own image with the ability to reason and a free will; man has fallen in Adam but has been redeemed by Christ on the Cross and restored to grace; Christ died for all men and all have the same rights to eternal salvation.

The Roman Catholic Church claims that the Blacks have been deprived of many of their fundamental human rights by the White Government and that no institution or person has the right to do this. The Church feels that a common society where all persons have equal rights and obligations would

> be in the best interests of all South Africans. The Church strongly criticizes the policy of separate development and the many restrictive laws which apply only to non-Whites, because it claims that this is designed to maintain 'White supremacy'. The Roman Catholic Church tends to classify people as Catholic and non-Catholic rather than Black or White.

We have now summarized the dogmatic teachings and certain aspects of the social teachings of the Dutch Reformed and Roman Catholic Churches in South Africa. It is interesting to note that the different dogmatic teachings correspond with different social teachings; for example the Dutch Reformed and Roman Catholic Churches differ fundamentally on common theological issues and they also differ fundamentally in their attitudes towards Blacks.

If these two denominations are compared on their attitudes towards Blacks we find that the Dutch Reformed Church is opposed to racial mixing, mixed marriages and any form of integration between Blacks and Whites. The Dutch Reformed Church claims that her teachings on this subject are in accordance with the will of God as revealed in the Old and New Testaments. There also appears to be an attempt to justify the present Apartheid system in the statement which claims that God on occasions allocated to each people their own area. The formation of a separate Dutch Reformed Church for Blacks in South Africa is also consistent with the practice of separation. The attitude of the Dutch Reformed Church towards Blacks in general appears to be one of separateness combined with paternalism.

The Roman Catholic Church with its policy of integration and comparative indifference to the concept of race, reveals an attitude towards Blacks which is very different to that of the Dutch Reformed Church. Its emphasis on the unity of man and the advantages of cross-cultural integration are directly opposed to the teachings of the Dutch Reformed Church. Its policy of accepting all into a multiracial church and its opposition to the concept of an 'elect few' as well as its greater emphasis on ritual may account for the fact that the membership of the Roman Catholic Church in South African has the same racial composition as the South African population as a whole.

From the above précis it appears that a relationship exists between certain religious beliefs and attitudes towards race relations in South Africa. It may even be possible to go a little further and say that certain religious beliefs, i.e. Orthodox Reformism as officially taught by the D.R.C. in South Africa for example, opposes racial mixing of any kind and attempts to provide justification for existing race relations in South Africa.

How much influence does the Dutch Reformed Church really have in South Africa? The Whites in South Africa are comparatively religious when compared to other Western industrialized communities. Secondly, membership of the ruling White Nationalist party (in power since 1948) and the D.R.C. is highly correlated. The D.R.C. has accepted the many repressive laws passed by the White Nationalist Government as a necessary evil. Afrikaans is the language used by the D.R.C. and by the ruling White party. Consistent with Calvinistic teaching the D.R.C. has successfully opposed public entertainments on Sunday, the formation of a State lottery and the erection of gambling casinos.

Before any more conclusive statement on this relationship can be made it would be necessary to pursue further empirical research into the race attitudes of committed members of the two relevant denominations, controlling such variables as education, occupation, economic income, etc.[1]

NOTE

1. Some empirical research has in fact been carried out on a random sample of 300 church members in Somerset West (Cape) and the results were in the expected direction, i.e. the more committed N.G.K. members had less favourable attitudes towards Blacks in South Africa than did the more committed Roman Catholic respondents (to test scores significant at the 0,001 level). In addition the more committed a member of the N.G.K. was, the less favourable his attitude towards Blacks tended to be; just the opposite trend was apparent among Roman Catholic respondents (correlation coefficients significant at the 0,005 level). (cf. Buis 1975)

REFERENCES

Bendix, R. 1966 – *Max Weber: An Intellectual.* London: Methuen.

Bishops of the Netherlands 1965 – *A New Catechism*: Herder & Herder.

——1966 – Burns and Oates.

Boettner, L. 1966 – *The Reformed Doctrine of Predestination.* Philadelphia: Presbyterian and Reformed Publishing Company.

Bullough, S. 1963 – *Roman Catholicism.* London: Penguin.

Buis, R. 1975 – *Religious Beliefs and White Prejudice.* Johannesburg: Raven Press.

Calvinist Action Committee 1951 – Symposium on God Centered Living. Grand Rapids.

Carter, J. M. 19–– *The Dutch Reformed Church in South Africa.* Edinburgh: W. and C. Inglis.

Cross, F. F. (ed.) 1958 – *The Oxford Dictionary of the Christian Church.* London: Oxford University Press.

General Synod of the Dutch Reformed Church 1966 – *Human Relations in South Africa – Report of the Committee on Current Affairs.* Johannesburg: Information Bureau of the Dutch Reformed Church.

Gerdener, G. B. A. 1930 – *Boustowwe vir die Geskiedenis van die N.G.K. in die Transgariep.* Cape Town: Nasionale Pers.

Kuyper, A. 1961 – *Lectures on Calvinism.* Michigan: Wm. B. Eerdmans.

MacCrone, I. D. 1965 – *Race Attitudes in South Africa.* Johannesburg: Witwatersrand University Press.

Marty, M. E. and D. G. Peerman (eds.) 1967 – *New Theology*, No. 1 & 2. New York: Macmillan.

McKenzie, J. L. 1963 – *Myths and Realities: Studies in Biblical Theology.* London: Geoffry Chapman.

Moorrees, A. 1937 – *Die Nederduits-Gereformeerde Kerk in Suid-Afrika 1652–1873.* Cape Town: Nasionale Pers.

Paton, D. (ed.) 1958 – *Church and Race in South Africa.* London: S.C.M. Press.

Press Commission S.A.C.B.A. 1966 – *Pastoral Letters – A Report.* Southern African Bishops Conference, Pretoria.

Publication Committee of the Christian Reformed Church 1959 – *Doctrinal Standards and Liturgy of the Christian Reformed Church.* Michigan.

Schillebeeckx, E. 1963 – *Vatican II – A Struggle of Minds.* Dublin: M. H. Gill.

Weber, Max 1967 – *The Protestant Ethic and the Spirit of Capitalism.* Translated by T. Parsons. London: George Allen & Unwin.

3. A Sociological Perspective on Religious Reality

KENNETH C. JUBBER

Mary Douglas (1973:9) has asserted that 'every thinking sociologist would now agree . . . that reality is socially constructed.' But despite the ubiquitous head-nodding in the pews of the sociological cathedral which this assertion implies, Douglas is quick to suggest that some nods may be closer to a wink than a nod. She asks quite simply but pointedly of sociologists, 'But how far dare they follow it?' (10). Many contemporary sociological texts, such as that by Berger and Luckmann (1967), lead persuasively to the conclusion spoken of by Douglas; reality is socially constructed. This conclusion has become for many individuals an axiom. It offers the vision of man in control of his destiny and solely responsible for his world. This short paper sets out to examine two questions and to relate these to what passes for religious reality. The first question is one similar to that posed by Douglas, 'What are the implications of the claim that reality is socially constructed?' and the second, a question conveying some doubt, 'Is reality really socially constructed?'

Apropos the second question, it suggests that perhaps the conclusion that reality is socially constructed was too hastily reached. It would thus be fruitful to trace meticulously the route via which this conclusion was reached; in short, its validity must be retested. A pre-requisital task to this end, and an extremely difficult one, would be to spell out the meaning of the statement 'reality is socially constructed' as specifically as possible. As it stands, the statement has the allure of a cliché, it sounds full of meaning but it may actually signify very little. Taken in its most literal sense it seems to mean that the world we inhabit, the world of which we are aware, the world of our experiences, is ongoingly constructed through time by person in interaction with person and the products of this interaction. But what do the word 'reality' and the phrase 'socially constructed' actually mean? The word 'reality' remains somewhat ambiguous and obscure despite the attention it has received from writers like William James (1890), Alfred Schutz (1967), and Berger and Luckmann (1967) among a host of others. One of the things that remains unclear is what are the boundaries of reality? Broadly conceptualized, as Schutz (1967) has demonstrated, reality is composed of multiple realities and it seems possible that among these multiple realities which constitute human reality there occur certain realities or aspects thereof which are not socially constructed. The experience of extreme pain and gross insanity might be cited as possible examples. If the reality under discussion is only 'social reality' then the claim that reality is socially constructed is in danger of degenerating into a tautology.

A further problem centres on the meaning of 'social' and the reversal of the more typical forms of reductionism which it implies, i.e. that social forces are somehow independent and antecedent and that they are able to determine not only social reality but other forms of reality as well. The notion of social construction might denote to some individuals a degree of freedom in construction which is unjustified; it might lead to hope and optimism in a situation in which despair and pessimism are more appropriate. Even though these issues are of related importance, they shall not be pursued further here since to deal directly with them would detract from the main task at hand.

One of the immediate implications of the claim that reality is socially constructed when it is applied to religious reality is that it immediately challenges the veracity of that entire corpus of religious assertions pertaining to the role of the supernatural in the affairs of men and of the world. It is this challenge which has fascinated me and to which I wish to devote this paper.

Let me therefore return to the first question posed in the introductory paragraph and consider the implications of the assertion that reality is socially constructed, for religion. One of the first implications arrived at by the simple process of extrapolating from a possible meaning of the word reality, is that religious reality is a part of this encompassing reality. There is no essential discontinuity between the construction of religious reality and the construction of any other reality. In other words, sociology asserts that not only have chess, Hansel and Gretal, capitalism, the Brothers Karamazov, and Apartheid been and are ongoingly socially constructed, but also that the Bible, the Koran, the Book of Mormon, and *Das Kapital* have been and are ongoingly socially constructed. The most radical extension of this line of argument is that there is no element of human reality at any moment which has not been socially constructed. From this it follows that those who claim that God has spoken to them are either deluded or they are speaking metaphorically. God is a social construct and it is an open question whether social constructs answer prayers, heal the sick, communicate with desert hermits, or do any of the other miraculous things which have been ascribed to the supernatural. The good news is that the same applies to Satan, Hell and other such malevolent beings and places.

American and British sociology of religion is characterized in the main by an accommodative and even conciliatory attitude towards religion. This stance is supposedly justified, by those who adopt it, on sound philosophical, theoretical, methodological and (even) ethical grounds. But there is another tradition, not as easily defendable some may argue, which parades under various banners but is most accurately characterized as the anti-religious tradition. It is the general view of anti-religious sociologists of religion (what a strange animal!) that if a substantive definition of religion is adopted in preference to the accommodative anyone-may-play and everything-qualifies functional definition, there should, if we are honest in our scientific endeavours, be only one tradition in the sociology of religion, namely the anti-religious tradition (cf. Shepherd 1972).

The anti-religious tradition implying either the rejection of the ontological claims of a specific religion or the ontological claims of all religions, has a long history. If Paul Radin (1927) is correct, this history dates back almost as far as does religion. The primitive sceptic stands as the primogeniture of the anti-religious tradition and Xenophones can rightly claim to be a founding father. Has sociology advanced much beyond Xenophones who in the sixth century BC cynically remarked that if horses and cattle could sculpt they would render their deities in bovine and equestrian forms? Time and space do not permit even an outline of the anti-religious tradition but to indicate where this tradition stands two quotes from Western La Barre (1970:44) will have to suffice. La Barre has written, 'Each religion is the ghost dance of a traumatised society.' And he has proceeded to caution those who would approach religion via the social sciences with the following words:

> The dynamic study of religion is no place for the genteel mind to stray into, hoping to garner a nosegay of sublime truths by a kind of philosophical daisy-picking. He is only trying on neuroses for size. For my parallel between sacred culture and neurosis is not an idle one. A society of individuals defends its unexamined sacred culture because this sacred culture is in fact a complex of defense mechanisms, usually diffused from an identifiable charismatic individual and usually a paranoic one (50).

Attacks on religion, of which the assertion that reality is socially constructed is one, have been a persistent thorn in the side of theology. The thorn has in certain theologies bled the beast dry so that these particular theologies are now just poorly disguised sociologisms. I refer here in part to such death-of-God theologies as that propounded by Thomas Altizer (1966:154) who wrote: 'The death of God abolishes transcendence, thereby making possible a new and absolute immanence, an immanence freed from every sign of transcendence' Loosely translated this means that because God has died man must look to man for his salvation; a great deal of modern liberal theology is social science in drag. This brand of theology closely follows the lead given by the social sciences as this is one way in which theology can escape monkeytrial type embarrassments. While social science has played an important role in producing the secular theologies of advanced modern capitalistic societies, radical sociology with its volatile cargo of revolutionary rhetoric has played a part in nurturing political-revolutionary theology in third-world countries. The secular theologians according to William Garrett (1973:391) accept that 'modern society has entered a post-Christian age wherein the world – in Weber's term – has been fully disenchanted until man no longer finds need of religion at all.' To be of any value in this secular age and in order to have any chance of survival, religious functionaries must involve themselves in the world, especially the world of politics. The call of the secular theologians is a call to arms for the survival of their profession, they see the need to set out on a modern-day crusade to drive the infidel from God's proper cathedral which is the world, not the decaying structure on the corner of Fifth Avenue and 72nd Street. Of the political-revolutionary theologians it can be said that for a good cause they have performed a miraculous feat whereby they have, through some incredible cognitive and spiritual gymnastics, been able to reconcile Marxism and Christianity. For their next ecumenical liberating venture they might find it convenient to reconcile Nietzche and Christ.

The above discussion was intended to demonstrate that contrary to the opinions of some social scientists, social scientific assertions do have implications for the truth claims of religion. So much is recognized by the theologians who fall under the above rubrics and so much is recognized by the anti-religious sociologists and psychologists. The majority of social scientists, however, shielding behind their scientific aspirations, equivocate a great deal regarding the question of the truth claims of religion. By pointing to the empirical impossibility of dealing with the question of God's existence or non-existence, they then proceed to consign all the other propositions (supernatural, metaphysical, theoretical, and empirical), so widely encountered as constitutive elements of the corpus of religious beliefs, to the same untouchable category. The question of the substantive verifiability of any single religious proposition (any proposition of whatever status which is part of a recognised religious belief system) may be decided on a variety of grounds depending on the nature of the proposition. It seems a reasonable strategy that even if most religious propositions cannot be empirically verified or falsified then second, third, and even fourth order verification schemas should be resorted to. Since it is scientifically recognized that absolute verification is not possible, verification consequently becomes a matter of evidence, logic, probability, and paradigm. It is obvious that second, third, and fourth order verification schemas would produce increasingly weak probabilistic types of proof. Propositions weakly verified may have their truth claims bolstered by being directly linked via theory to other more convincingly verified empirical propositions. Science should treat theologies as scientific theories, for, after all, is this not what many theologies claim to be? Social scientists seem to be in agreement regarding the fate of a scientific theory which is not supported by the empirical facts to which it is logically bound but they are as yet not in agreement regarding the fate of a theology whose empirical claims have been falsified. In the name of social science and with its blessing, many latter-day prophets are incarcerated in asylums while in the name of these same disciplines the thoughts of similar individuals are declared out of bounds and thereby further sanctified. Truly, whatever is socially accepted as constituting religious reality is not a matter of definition, personal experience, or truth; it is a matter of politics. It is to be hoped that the day will dawn when theologians will agree with Emile-Auguste Chartier (1975:71) who wrote, 'Religion is a fairy tale which, like all fairy tales, is full of meaning. And no one ever asks if fairy tales are true.'

It is time again to return to the sociological claim that reality is socially constructed and consider a further implication of this claim. An obvious implication is that the claim must be validated, it cannot be assumed to be valid simply because it makes sense and seems to explain a variety of social phenomena. To test this claim fully it is not sufficient to test it only in terms of those elements of reality which are most amenable to sociological treatment and are professionally in vogue, the claim must also be tested in the elusive and professionally tabooed reaches of the reality under discussion. This implies among other things that sociology should look anew at the scientifically embarrassing question of the origin of religion. To speak of origins is to speak of acts of creation, acts which produce something which had previously not existed but which is, also, never something entirely new. One concern of the sociology of religion should therefore be religious creativity, and this encompasses primordial acts of religious creativity as well as those acts of creation which even to this day continue to produce new embryonic religions. Despite this rather obvious point, and one which follows as an implication of the sociological claim being examined, I have been as yet unable to find a single entry on religious creativity in the literature on human creativity in psychology. The closest I came was to an entry on hymn writing. New religious ideas and practices are continually coming into existence, yet psychology (for superstitious reasons?) does not seem to recognize such acts as creative human acts. Lest I be accused of overlooking important psychological accounts and theories dealing with the origin of religious ideas, let me hasten to add that the above reference is to that branch of modern psychology which goes under the general title 'cognitive psychology'.

To provide a satisfactory account of the origin and development of religion requires that the myriad theories which have been formulated through the centuries to explain religious phenomena in naturalistic terms must be reconsidered and synthesized into a unified theory. This is no simple task; there are within the social sciences guruistic and messianic figures and their devotees and disciples do not take kindly to attempts to synthesize the thoughts of their masters with those of less brilliant luminaries. It is a mortal sin to reconcile Jung and Freud and, judged in terms of the perfunctory treatment they receive in modern texts, it is a grave academic error to find anything worthwhile in such archaic thinkers as Tylor, Spencer, or Fraser. A grand social scientific theory of religion seems at least a possibility even if it constitutes a formidable task. The production of such a theory would be a further way in which the claim that reality is socially constructed could be further validated.

The last implication of the claim that reality is socially constructed which I wish to touch on is perhaps the most serious and one which deserves a great deal more attention than it will receive here. Mary Douglas (1973:16) has remarked of the moral order and the knowledge that sustains it (religious knowledge plays a crucial role in this), that these things are created by social convention. She goes on to say of the moral order and the knowledge forms which sustain and legitimate it, that if their 'man-made origins were not hidden they would be stripped of much of their authority. Therefore, the conventions are not merely tacit, but extremely inaccessible.' The word 'therefore' in the last sentence reveals that Douglas is reasoning functionally if not teleologically. But no matter, she has drawn attention to the important role which the denial or obscuring of the authorship of moral prescription (and by extension, religious beliefs) plays in maintaining the social order. In other words, with the good sense of a sociologist, Douglas recognizes the societal value of veiling the truth in matters moral and religious. But the sociologist's task is not only to write about the positive value which such veiling performs, the sociologist is encumbered with the additional and unhappy task of unveiling whatever is veiled, of demystifying whatever is shrouded in mystery. Peter Berger (1972:51) says of sociology that it 'carries with it a logical imperative to unmask the pretensions and propaganda by which men cloak their actions . . .' Sociologists are supposed to expose society in its true nakedness. They are urged to go to the root of the matter no matter what the consequences. The sacred cow must be shown to be high quality protein on the hoof. (As an aside, it should be noted that in the task of exposing social reality for what it is, the true nakedness of society and man always escapes detection and what stands revealed is the sociologist.)

The individual who invades the magician's stage and exposes his baffling conjurations should not expect much applause. Some solitary seeker after enlightenment may be the only genuine applauder of such an act of exposure. A few may applaud because they have now discovered the magician's secrets, all the better to use them to their own advantage by baffling others. But the majority would sit in disapproving silence or react angrily. Such behaviour in their eyes is the act of a spoilsport. For they want to be taken in, they wish to participate in the spectacle; and to be knowingly and occasionally unknowingly tricked is a small price to pay. Without deception, there could be no show.

But the magician need not fear even if he were one day exposed and his technology of deceit and cunning laid bare before the audience. For the audience will ever be ready to suspend their disbelief and he, if he be competent, will ever be able to conjure anew.

REFERENCES

Altizer, Thomas J. J. 1966 – *The Gospel of Christian Atheism*. Philadelphia: Westminster.

Berger, Peter L. Thomas Luckmann 1966 – *The Social Construction of Reality*. London: Allen Lane/Penguin.

Berger, Peter L. 1972 – *Invitation to Sociology*. Harmondsworth: Penguin.

Chartier, Emile-Auguste (pen name: Alain) 1975 – *The Gods*. (Translated by R. Pevear.) London: Chatto and Windus.

Douglas, Mary (ed.) 1973 – *Rules and Meanings*. Harmondsworth: Penguin.

Garrett, William R. 1973 – 'Politicized clergy: A sociological interpretation of the "New Breed".' *Journal for the Scientific Study of Religion*, 12, December: 383–400.

James, William 1890 – *The Principles of Psychology*. Vols I and II. New York: Henry Holt and Company.

La Barre, Weston 1970 – *The Ghost Dance: The Origins of Religion*. Garden City: Doubleday.

Radin, Paul 1927 – *Primitive Man as Philosopher*. New York: Appleton.

Schutz, Alfred 1967 – *Collected Papers I. The Problem of Reality*. (Ed: M. Natanson). The Hague: Martinus Nijhoff.

Shepherd, William C. 1972 – 'Religion and the social sciences: Conflict or reconciliation?' *Journal for the Scientific Study of Religion*, 11, September, 230–9.

Part 4:

The Family

Introduction

BERYL UNTERHALTER

Sociological definitions of the family usually include the following elements;

a. that it is a group of persons related by blood, marriage or adoption;
b. organised for the purpose of regulating reproduction and rearing children;
c. sharing a common household;
d. structured in terms of socially accepted roles and relationships. The distinction is generally made between two types of family systems . . . the nuclear family consisting of husband, wife and their non-adult children, and the extended family in which a group of related kin share a common household and co-operate in the performance of family functions. The nuclear family is a recognizable unit within the extended family and is, as Murdock (1949:1–11) points out, the key institution. Larger groupings, like the extended family, are combinations of nuclear families and their relatives.

The family has a long history dating from prehistoric times and it is even to be found in rudimentary form among many primates. Goode (1964:1–20) provides an interesting summary of the biological foundations for the family and Gough (1971) gives a useful introduction to the history of the family. From these accounts, it would appear that the human family is unique and different to that of animals because it requires advanced forms of cultural learning, an elaborate division of labour and a complex system for the control of aggressive and competitive urges to enable a creative family life, to emerge. The family in some form is recognized in all societies and it is, therefore, called the most universal and basic of the social institutions. Despite this, the sociology of the family is not a well-developed theoretical field, especially when it is compared with the volume of theory to be found in areas such as the sociology of religion, political sociology or the sociology of economic life. Goode (1965:179) complaining of this absence of basic theories of family life, says that there are numerous studies of the family, few of which advance any theory. Morgan (1975:4–5) attributes this to the high degree of involvement we all have with family life. It is usually presumed that we know the family so well because of our participation in it, that no theory is therefore necessary. A further barrier to both theory and research, is that the family is the one institution we wish to protect from enquiry and keep, as far as possible, in the realm of our private lives. It is of interest to note that none of the great theoreticians of sociology such as Weber, Durkheim, Marx or Pareto wrote of the family except tangentially and today theories of the family which criticize its disastrous effects on human personalities (Laing 1971 and Cooper 1972), are met with considerable resistance.

There are no independent theories that have come from the study of the South African family, and the descriptive studies we have are largely functionalist in orientation. They focus particularly on the relationship between modernization and family life, and because the more dramatic changes are to be seen in Black, Indian and Coloured families, most of the descriptive studies concern these ethnic groups. It is perhaps also taken for granted that the White South African family needs no further investigation because it approximates very closely to American or British middle-class families which have been extensively studied. But there are probably differences between the family life of White South Africans and that of the British or the Americans, while a further interesting field of enquiry could be possible differences between the family life of the English and the Afrikaners and their contrast in turn with the family patterns of the 'new' immigrants to South Africa in the last decade from countries such as Portugal, Germany and Italy. The readings included in this section have made use of South African source material, as can be seen from Reading 1 on the Indian family, Reading 2 on the Black family and Reading 3 on the Coloured family. The readings on the American family given in the various American introductory textbooks can be taken as applicable, with some modifications, to the White South African family.

The functionalist approach to the sociology of the family

The dominant approach to the family is to be found in the work of the functionalists, of whom Parsons (1951:24–51) is the most important. Most family sociologists adopt this functional perspective which takes as its starting point the biological imperatives which make the family functionally necessary. These include sexual relationships, the birth of children and the need to nurture the young during the prolonged period of human helplessness. Kingsley Davis (1948: 394–6), who was a pupil of Parsons, has produced a comprehensive list of the functions of the family which include:

a. the physical reproduction of new individuals;
b. their nourishment and maintenance during infancy and childhood;
c. their placement in the system of social position.

He therefore summarizes the main functions of the family as reproduction, maintenance, socialization and placement. Of these four, the last requires further discussion. By placement sociologists mean the status-conferring function of the family and this can be seen to be an important theme in family life. It is the family which confers initial status on the child, thus locating the child at a particular level in his society. This will influence the child's later life-chances, and in modern industrial society usually determines the child's health and material well-being, the number of years he will spend in high school, his chances of attending a university and whether he has a manual or non-manual occupation. This does not deny the part played by the individual's intelligence, energy or special aptitudes in influencing his life-chances, but it nevertheless accepts the role of the family in ascribing initial status and opportunities. We know, too, that the family imparts attitudes and values to the child and these are significant determinants of upward mobility. Murdock (1949:197), on the basis of a cross-cultural analysis of 250 societies, gives a slightly different list of the four functions he considers fundamental to family life. These are the sexual, economic, reproductive and the educational. According to Murdock, without the performance of these functions society and, indeed, all human life, would come to an end. Although Murdock acknowledges that other institutions could take over these functions from the family, he says that no society has devised an institution which could fulfil all these functions in the way the family does.

The changing functions of the family

The functionalist approach is not static. Parsons (Parsons Bales 1956:17) gives much attention to theories about the relationship between family change and the development of urban-industrialism. In this process the economic forces are seen as the independent variable and the family as the dependent variable. Parsons elaborates on the change in the family by referring to the pre-industrial peasant family of traditional societies. Here families were the main agencies for economic production and consumption as well as the main focus of child-rearing, education, religious experience and recreation. In such a society the family can be described as a total institution, meeting all societal needs. It is the industrial revolution or what we today call modernization, which alters this system. It transfers economic production to factories, offices and shops, thereby removing the family's economic base. The education of the young must also become the province of specialized institutions such as the school, the college and the university, as the tasks to be performed in modern industrial systems can no longer be taught by the family. Recreation also becomes part of the economy, to be bought or sold rather than enjoyed within the family circle. All these changes have led some family sociologists, like Burgess (Burgess Locke 1953:685) to conclude that the modern family has been stripped of its functions and has declined in significance. Parsons differs from Burgess in that he regards change as part of the modernization process whereby all institutions become differentiated and specialized. The family does not decline in significance, but is left rather with specialized fundamental functions. These are primarily the reproduction of the species and the socialization of the young, but to these Parsons adds the function of the 'stabilization' of adult personalities. Here he sees the family as motivating the individual to perform roles such as the economic role; providing personal satisfactions and opportunities for tension management; and thereby maintaining the social system as a whole. In this specialized family which modernization brings into existence, affectional and interactive relationships achieve a new salience and marriage is perceived increasingly in terms of love and companionship rather than in terms of benefits, property rights or status. Individuals entering such relationships expect to choose their own marriage partners on the basis of love and attraction and both partners have high expectations of marital happiness. Parsons acknowledges that many marriages end in divorce, but such failures do not imply a rejection of marriage;

they reflect the unrealized hopes that the partners had of marriage, and also their right to terminate unfulfilling relationships.

The 'fit' between urban-industrial society and the nuclear family

From an examination of the way in which economic change alters the family, it has been easy to conclude that urban-industrialism will lead to an abandonment of the extended family system in favour of the small nuclear family. This argument has been advanced by Goode (1963:10–18) who examines change in numerous societies and concludes that the relatively isolated nuclear family is well suited to the requirements of modern industrial systems. He speaks of the 'fit' or congruence between the two, as the industrial system requires individual achievement for the attainment of key roles. Obligations to kin would interfere with achievement aspirations, efficiency and rationality, all of which are essential features of modern societies. Attachments to kin would also clearly conflict with the need for geographic and social mobility necessary to modernization.

If industrialization is a sufficient cause of the small conjugal family relatively isolated from kin, we would expect that industrial societies would always be characterized by this type of family unit. This type of convergence theory (which regards all families in modernizing countries as converging towards a single model) is losing popularity today, because it is at variance with what more detailed investigations of family life reveal. For example, in Japan, one of the countries to modernize most rapidly and successfully in modern times, the extended family continues to exist, and about half of the marriages taking place are still arranged by parents and family elders (Goode 1963:321–65). In many parts of Africa, extended families have not given way to the nuclear family, despite the need for modern industrial attitudes, and it is possible that we have over-simplified the relationship between the conjugal family and industrialism. The extended family might, in fact, assist rather than impede modernization, as it acts as a support to the individual who moves into the modern sector of the economy. It can also serve as a buffer between the individual and the economic system, by maintaining the worker confronted by unemployment, illness or other hazards of industrial life, as well as providing him with warm relationships among a large group of kin . . . a compensation for the alienation of the industrial world. Reading 1 illustrates this well, providing as it does a description of the family life of Indian South Africans which remains rooted in the extended family system, despite the fact that the Indians are overwhelmingly an urban population working in industry, commerce or the professions.

Variations in family form

The functional approach should not lead to the view that the family is indispensable. Social inventiveness could produce alternatives to the family structure as we know it today. Non-kinship organizations could provide for the care of the young and members of families do not need to live in common households nor co-operate economically. This is illustrated by the Israeli kibbutz system

(Spiro 1968:68–79) which has gone much of the way in taking from the family many of the features generally considered essential. The socialization of the kibbutz child is largely in the hands of nurses and teachers; parents and children do not share common household arrangements and the economic responsibility for child care rests with the kibbutz. The Chinese commune, about which less is known in the western world, is also experimenting with communal child-rearing arrangements. Yet from what we know of these systems, neither eliminate the family entirely, and Spiro even suggests that the kibbutz itself constitutes a large extended family system. He says that the kibbutz recognizes the relationships of husbands and wives, and parents continue to play some part in the socialization of their children. Thus the indispensability of the family should be taken only to mean that the bonds of family life receive recognition in all societies, but families can and do exist in varying and attenuated forms.

It is also frequently claimed that the family is not only indispensable but universal. Statements concerning the universality of the family can be misleading if they are taken to mean that the family 'naturally' involves a legally constituted husband-wife pair and their young dependent children living in a household of their own and supported by the husband's earnings. This is a middle-class image of the family in urban-industrial societies and is of limited descriptive applicability. It leaves out of account:

a. extended families in traditional rural societies. These families retain a productive base, usually in agriculture, and are still to be found in many third world countries. They can be seen in the rural areas of South Africa among the Black population and the structure and function of such families has been well delineated in numerous anthropological studies. For the student a good introduction to these studies is to be found in Hammond-Tooke (1974:177–234). Reading 2 by Dubb illustrates the way in which the impact of the city changes the extended family system. As family members move into the modern sector of the economy the old partriarchal family unit, essentially self-sufficient and dominant in the lives of all, must undergo change.

b. the extended or quasi-extended family living in the city. Here members of a kinship network continue to live together either as an extended family in a common household, or in what may be called a quasi-extended family. In the quasi-extended family the common household cannot be shared because of limitations of living space, or because of some degree of commitment to the norms of nuclear family independence and neolocality. Yet the kinship group continues as a major unit of association. In some cases grandparents will continue to live with the nuclear family; in other cases aunts and uncles, but even if there are no additional relatives in the household, the wider kinship group continues to influence family life. Help is sought and given within the extended family and all ceremonies connected with birth, marriage and death are supervised by the kin. Authority remains in the hands of elders and children are still socialized by grandparents, aunts and uncles. Reading 2 describes this type of family situation in the urban 'townships' of South African cities and further reference to it is to be found in the work of Pauw (1963:450–62) and Hellman (1971:168–70). A change which all these authors find in the extended or quasi-extended urban family, is the new emphasis given to the matrilineage. The traditional Black family was patriarchal, patrilineal and patrilocal. Urban and industrial life has undermined traditional marriage patterns, of which lobola (bride price) was an essential element. Today, with the breakdown of marriage, many young Black women in the cities bear children out of wedlock and it is estimated that as many as half of the children born in the Black townships are illegitimate. Women may, eventually, marry the men with whom they have formed liaisons or they may marry other men, but the children of their earlier unions remain the children of *her* family. Until the young woman marries, she continues, usually, to live with her children in the home of her parents or even her grandparents, making the family matrilocal as well as matrilineal. These new family patterns and in particular the extent of illegitimacy, are deplored by Blacks as a departure from a previous proud tradition which carefully controlled sexual relationships and did not permit illegitimacy, but humane considerations keep the unmarried mother and her offspring within the family home.

c. The single parent family, consisting usually of the divorced, deserted or widowed mother and her children. In the western world with its low death rates and high rates of divorce and desertion, a father exists, but he does not reside with the family, and is peripheral to its activities. Contrary to our prejudices, one-parent families need not be deviant or distorted, and in many cases the defects of such family arrangements arise from the lack of adequate community resources to meet the special needs of such families. For many children in modern society the one-parent family is the most viable family form and adverse social judgements about it only serve to make adjustments within it, more difficult.

One-parent families in the South African context are to be found among Whites and Coloureds rather than Blacks or Indians. As already stated the Black one-parent family, is incorporated into the matrilineage, while divorce and illegitimacy are very low among the Republic's Indian population because of strict family controls. However, divorce and desertion frequently disrupt Coloured and White family life and it is women in these two groups who are subject to the many strains of rearing children without the support of the extended family.

Kinship obligations

In all family systems relatives or kin play an important role. While we know that the claims of the industrial system and the conditions of urban life, decrease kin interaction and obligations, it is doubtful if the conjugal family, even in highly urbanized societies, is entirely isolated from its kin. At first sociologists studying urban life had concluded that the city led to a family that was atomistic, individualistic and free from kinship networks (Wirth 1938). Later studies beginning in the late 1950s and continuing today, show that families who are in every way urban, retain close kinship ties. The first of these studies was carried out by Young and Willmott (1962) in the East End of London. They found a rooted attachment to relatives and a strong desire to remain in the East End because of the existence of kin networks. At first it was thought that this retention of kinship ties was characteristic of poorer families living in working class areas. Bott (1957) for example, described the strong ties which continue to unite mothers and daughters in a working-class area. Even after the daughters marry and set up independent households, their mothers continue to help them with housework and take care of young children. This enables the daughters to continue with gainful employment. When 'mom' in her turn needs support because of advancing age, help flows in the opposite direction, with daughters and even granddaughters taking over the responsibility of her care. The closeness of the relationship between mothers and daughters tends to exclude husbands, who in turn find companionship with male peer or work groups.

Further studies have shown that close kinship ties also persist among ethnic minorities in many parts of the world. Gans (1962) depicts the closeness of the kinship ties of Italian Americans in Boston, after as much as three generations of acculturation to the American way of life. The influence of the wider family group in the lives of many other immigrants is a matter for everyday observation and it seems that interaction with kin gives immigrant minorities security and mutual protection from real or imagined discrimination.

But it is not only the lower-class family or the ethnic minorities for whom the kin remain significant. Bell (1968) and Sussman and Burchinall (1969) show the same pattern among British and American middle-class families, and it has also been found that the influence of upper-class kinship networks is of considerable importance in placing young family members in good employment (Stuckert 1968). From all these accounts it is possible to conclude that the completely isolated nuclear family is an ideal type, found only among families which have been highly mobile both geographically and socially.

Family roles

Role theory has in recent years been applied to our understanding of the family. It views the family in terms of the positions and exchanges which occur within family systems and focuses on the processes of bargaining, accommodation and conflict which characterize family life. To some extent it can be seen as complementary to the functionalist approach, as clearly roles are determined by the family in terms of functional needs. But role theory does more than enlarge on a further aspect of function; it shows how each family works out a unique system of interaction. In this process the actor can interpret functional roles in a number of ways, and the role theorists have done much to draw attention to the day-to-day living experiences of the family. Turner (1970:217–21) gives a good summary of the approach of the role theorist to family interaction.

Any study of the roles of husbands, wives, parents and children in the family in modern industrial settings, must consider the conflict between family members. The functionalists tend to emphasize harmony and equilibrium and incline to the view that individual family members accept the modes of family life determined for them by society. The role theorists have given more attention to role strain between the marital pair as well as conflict situations in marriage and parent-child exchanges. They have drawn attention to some of the serious ways in which the family can be dysfunctional because of its many contradictions. Interested students should read the work of Mitchell (1971), Millett (1969), Firestone (1970), and Janeway (1971). These study women's roles, showing that the old patriarchal family was male dominated and based on a sexually discriminating system in which women are the exploited and men the exploiters. This started to change, in the western world, when modernizing forces brought women into the paid labour market, but even today there is little consensus about women's equality. This is very different from the situation in the pre-industrial family and more particularly those families which were to be found in traditional societies. In such settings husbands and wives had the same understanding of their marital roles derived from their common socialization experiences. In the modern family it is not unlikely that husbands and wives are oriented to different views of marital roles. This arises because in heterogeneous urban societies they might come from different sub-cultures or classes, or it might be due to a lack of agreement about roles in a society which changes as rapidly as ours.

Role theorists have pointed out further sources of role strain and conflict in the modern family. Disagreements and conflict easily arise in a society which places such a high value on individuality and freedom. This makes it difficult for family members to accept the disciplines and restrictions without which a family cannot exist. A further problem in the capitalist world is the emphasis on enjoyment and consumerism. This is most clearly expressed by the advertising industry and the buy now, pay later syndrome which has become widespread. It is not easy to reconcile these behaviour norms and their implicit values with the morality of self-denial and responsibility needed for the successful performance of family roles. Roles in modern industrial societies may also conflict with each other. For example the demands of the modern occupational system frequently conflict with the needs of the family. The father might be expected to work in the evenings, over week-ends, be away from home for protracted periods or even uproot the family and move to a different part of the country. In all such situations, work is expected to take precedence over the family.

A further important aspect of family interaction is the relationship between parents and children. Here, too, role strain and role conflict are inherent in the modern family situation. Most middle-class parents today accept the values of freedom and autonomy, yet they find it difficult to live in accordance with these values. There is much more violence done to children within the family than was previously recognized and for many children the ideology of the happy family is a myth (Zalba 1971; Gil 1970; and Helfer & Kempel 1968). Writers like Laing (1971) are today having considerable influence in presenting us with a picture of the family as a destructive and exploitative institution in which children are the victims (see the case of Julie in Laing 1960). While such descriptions cannot be applied to all families, his work has encouraged significant criticisms of the family and has also led to deeper insights into family interaction and the way in which this influences the development of the individual.

The family and poverty

The fulfilment of marital roles as well as parental obligations is, in many societies, seriously hampered by poverty and slum conditions, where unemployment, low income and overcrowding make it almost impossible to establish family harmony. Personal relationships are brutalized and this arises in many cases, because fathers who have jobs with the minimum of prestige and income, frequently express their rage in violent attacks on wives and children. Alcohol and drugs become ways of escape from the daily crises of life, adding in turn to the problems of family degradation. Poverty results in larger families, with poorer life chances for the children, and if we remember that it is the family which confers status on the child, it can readily be seen that in many societies, an unlovely heritage of poverty and disadvantage is passed on from generation to generation. In the Republic of South Africa many Black and Coloured families live under such conditions. Reading 3 describes such family lives in an urban Coloured community in a slum area of Johannesburg.

Conclusions

Like most institutions that have to adapt to change, the family is under siege. This arises to a large extent from the difficulty in performing the new family roles with their emphasis on egalitarianism between husbands and wives, parents and children. The many failures in marriage attest to the high proportion of people who find marriage disappointing; conflict between parents and children is endemic in the modern family, and experiments with communal child-rearing show that the small nuclear family of parents and their children might not be the most successful unit for the rearing of the young. Today the family is also fundamentally challenged by changed perceptions young people have of marriage. Contraceptive technology has made it possible to separate reproduction from sexuality and this, together with the knowledge of the extent of marital instability and an understanding of the complexities of rearing 'adjusted' children, means that for an increasing number of young people, marriage and family life are no longer considered desirable. Reluctance to enter family life can also be attributed to our information about the dangers of over-population and to the pessimism engendered by international events.

The strains and dilemmas of the contemporary family lead to speculations about its future. Such thought can be liberating if it results in a re-evaluation of old assumptions about family life. Sociologists, too, are often asked if the family is dying. The answer to this must lie in the family's ability to change. In the past the family has shown remarkable flexibility when confronted by modernizing social forces. Its ability to survive into the future will depend on still further adaptation, which might well result in an institution diverging in a number of ways, from the family as we know it today.

REFERENCES

Bell, C. 1968 – *Middle Class Families.* London: Routledge & Kegan Paul.

Bott, E. 1957 – *Family and Social Network.* London: Tavistock.

Burgess, E. W. and H. J. Locke 1953 – *The Family from Institution to Companionship.* New York: American Book.

Cooper, D. 1972 – *The Death of the Family.* London: Penguin.

Davis, Kingsley 1948 – *Human Society.* New York: Macmillan.

Firestone, S. 1970 – *The Dialectic of Sex.* New York: Free Press.

Gans, H. 1962 – *The Urban Villagers.* New York: Free Press.

Gil, David G. 1970 – *Violence Against Children: Physical Child Abuse in the United States.* Cambridge: Harvard University Press.

Goode, W. J. 1963 – *World Revolution and Family Patterns.* New York: Free Press.

——1964 – *Readings on the Family and Society.* New Jersey: Prentice Hall.

——1965 – 'The sociology of the family.' In R. K. Merton, L. Broom and L. S. Cottrell (eds.), *Sociology Today, Vol. I.* New York: Harper.

Gough, K. 1971 – 'The origins of the family.' *Journal of Marriage and the Family,* 33 (4): 760–771.

Hammond-Tooke, W. D. 1974 – *The Bantu-speaking Tribes of South Africa.* Cape Town: Oxford University Press.

Helfer, R. E. and H. C. Kempel (eds.) 1968 – *The Battered Child.* Chicago: University of Chicago Press.

Hellmann, E. 1971 – 'Social change among urban Africans.' In H. Adam (ed.) *South Africa: Sociological Perspectives.* Cape Town: Oxford University Press.

Janeway, E. 1971 – *Man's World, Woman's Place.* New York: Morrow.

Laing, R. D. 1960 – *The Divided Self.* Harmondsworth: Penguin.

——1971 – *The Politics of the Family and Other Essays.* London: Tavistock.

Millett, K. 1969 – *Sexual Politics.* New York: Doubleday.

Mitchell, J. 1971 – *Women's Estate.* Harmondsworth: Penguin.

Morgan, D. H. J. 1975 – *Social Theory and the Family.* London: Routledge and Kegan Paul.

Murdock, G. P. 1949 – *Social Structure.* New York: Macmillan.

Parsons, T. 1951 – *The Social System.* London: Routledge and Kegan Paul.

Parsons, T., R. F. Bales *et al.* 1956 – *Family Socialization and Interaction Process.* London: Routledge and Kegan Paul.

Pauw, B. A. 1965 – *The Second Generation: A Study of the Family Among Urbanized Bantu in East London.* Cape Town: Oxford University Press.

Spiro, M. E. 1968 – 'Is the family universal – the Israeli case.' In N. W. Bell and E. F. Vogel (eds.) *A Modern Introduction to the Family.* Revised edition. New York: Free Press.

Stuckert, R. P. 1968 – 'Occupational mobility and family relationships.' In N. W. Bell and E. F. Vogel (eds.) *A Modern Introduction to the Family.* New York: Free Press.

Sussman M. and L. Burchinall. 1969 – 'Kin family networks: Unheralded structure in current conceptualizations of family functioning.' In J. N. Edwards (ed.) *The family and Change.* New York: Knopf.

Turner, R. 1970 – *Family Interaction*. New York: Wiley.
Wirth, M. and P. Willmott 1938 – 'Urbanism as a way of life.' *American Journal of Sociology*, 44:1–24.
Young, M. and P. Willmott 1962 – *Family and Kinship in East London*. Harmondsworth: Penguin.
Zalba, S. R. 1971 – 'Battered children.' *Transaction* (July/August): 58–61.

1. Portrait of Indian South Africans

FATIMA MEER

Though Durban Indians are wholly integrated into the highly cosmopolitan urban economy, many of their attitudes and patterns of social life continue to be characteristically rural, and to that extent traditional. This is most conspicuous in their religious ceremonials and in the network of relations which prevail in the family. The family pattern described here is representative of the entire Indian community, holding true for the component religious and language groups. It is, however, a pattern which is subject to the effects of urbanisation and, as these intensify, modifications occur. Such modifications, however, have not up to now so changed the standard family pattern as to nullify it. Generally the economically secure groups, and in particular the Gujaratis have best succeeded in controlling the inevitable waves of change impinging on their lives, and have thereby not only averted their trauma, but have also retained much of their standard pattern. The families of professionals and semi-professionals show greatest westernization, and relations between spouses and between parents and children come close to the urban model. The poorer groups by contrast are not as well protected, and the old pattern suffers from conflict with the new. Yet it may be said of Indians that despite their great poverty, they appear to be better preserved against the disconcerting effects of abrupt changes than other similarly placed South African urban communities. This may be attributed to the inner strength of their social system, in particular to their family structure.

There is no word in any of the South African Indian languages equivalent to the English word 'family'. The nearest that come to it are *Kutum* (Gujarati, Hindustani and Urdu) and *Kudumbom* or *Kuduma* (Tamil and Tedugu respectively). These terms define a kinship system of several nuclear families hierarchically arranged by male seniority. The nuclear units may be two or more generations deep, three being the usual pattern.

The circumstances of their immigration and the attitude of the Natal Government made it difficult for Indians to realize this traditional family structure in the early years of their residence in South Africa. Most Indian immigrants were indentured male labourers who had entered into labour contracts for a specific number of years. Both the Natal Government and the planters were interested solely in their labour, and neither foresaw nor planned for the emergence of an indigenous Indian community. Hence the barrack accommodation made no provision for families. Although there were women and children in the immigrant batches of 1860, Indian marriages were not recognized until 1874, and no regulation covered the entry of women into the colony or established the right of nuclear families not to be separated.

In fact, the planters had no use for women and would have excluded them completely, had it not been for pressure on the British Government through the Colonial Land and Emigration Commission. This commission criticized the system of indenture as tantamount to slavery, and insisted that it should be modified to bear some relation to emigration by including a representative *slice* of the whole community in the indentured group. Hence it emphasized the inclusion of women, and the Natal Agreement in 1860 stipulated a minimum proportion of twenty-five per cent in each labour consignment.

Both the *coolie agent* in Natal and the planters, however, considered the women and children to be a great nuisance and ignored their presence. Many planters refused to support them with rations, or even allow them on their premises, insisting that they were the responsibility of their male workers, who at the time were employed at 10/- per month.

While there is insufficient evidence to know exactly how Indians conceived their future in the colony, interviews with some of those once indentured suggest that they were as unrealistic in their approach as the planters. Many left India in a state of adolescent irresponsibility, or peasant simplicity, lured by extravagant stories of easily gained wealth. Many, too, left without the permission of their parents, or without wives and children. It is conceivable that just as the planters felt that the Indians would leave after solving their labour problems, the labourers felt that they would return after making their fortunes.

This probably accounts for their apparent acceptance of an uninstitutionalized, *un-Indian* family pattern founded on loose unions. They very probably rationalised it as a temporary make-shift arrangement, which would be redeemed by traditional respectability once they returned home. After all, for many the very act of emigration was in itself an act of deviation, so that further deviation became relatively easy. It is sometimes thought that the smallness of their number placed a sexual premium on the Indian women. In fact, they constituted a powerless matriarchy, for too often they were held solely responsible for the children.

Gandhi, commenting on family life among indentured Indians towards the end of the 19th century, had this to say: '*I have not the space here in the present to narrate how they broke through all the restraints which religion or morality imposes, or to be more accurate, how these restraints gave way and how the very distinction between a married woman and a concubine ceased to exist among these people.*'

The *Free* or *Passenger* Indians who began to immigrate to the Colony of Natal about 1880, also came as single males or groups of males, and they sent for their families to join them much later. Up to at least the end of the 19th century, the male-female ratio throughout the South African Indian community was 3:1.

From such evidence we can deduce that an *incomplete*, or quasi-nuclear family (*quasi* because of lack of jurality), not institutionalized by any recognized form of marriage, was the typical pattern in the early years of South African Indian life. Whatever attitudes the Indians brought to the South African situation, there was at first little chance for them to establish the traditional Indian family structure.

When permanent residence in South Africa became a certainty, however, they began to reorganise affairs to fit the conventional scheme. The joint or extended family became, both by choice and economic necessity, the most common pattern, and continued to be so until as recently as twenty years ago. Though it is giving way today to the nuclear pattern, its incidence is still high, and various surveys made between 1946 and 1968 in Durban set the position to be between 29,5 per cent and approximately 50 per cent.

Whatever the proportion of the physically observable distribution of the joint family, there is no doubt that the *idea* of a joint household, or the *kutum*, as it should be called, influences Indian attitudes and sentiments to a considerable extent, and shapes relations within the community and with other South Africans. It is therefore realistic to take the extended, rather than nuclear, family as the focal point of South African Indian life.

It may be reliably stated that when the average young Indian girl marries, she expects to live with the family of her husband's parents: she is envied and considered very lucky if she becomes the wife of an independent nuclear family. For then she immediately assumes a status of independence and power without having to undergo a prolonged apprenticeship invariably fraught with conflict. A mother-in-law is to be dreaded and is often held up as a type of *bogey man* to young girls still under training for adulthood. The average young girl dreams of becoming the mistress of her own home but the longer she stays with her in-laws, the smaller the probability that she will realise this dream through factors other than the death of her mother-in-law. Hence even those families which are nuclear will pass through the joint family stage, if there are sons who marry, though the structure may persist as such, permanently.

Irrespective of the composition of his immediate household (nuclear or otherwise), the average Indian is firmly rooted to his *kutum*. His *kutum* consists of all those with whom he can trace consanguinity through a common paternal grandfather or grandfather's brother. The average size of the Indian nuclear family has been variously stated to be between 6,1 and 8,8 persons. The average size of the *kutum* is anything between 50 and 100 persons. These are the essential members who must attend all informal occasions, ranging from picnic parties to the more exclusive ceremonies which precede formal engagements, weddings and prayers. The *kutum* is a restricted kinship group tracing descent through a male head, in which the classificatory principle defines relations between members. Members of a *kutum* are in similar relation to each other as members in an immediate family, and this is reflected in the fact that aunts, uncles and cousins are not only addressed by common terms but the associated sentiment and role expectations are also extended to them in a decreasing order of intensity, depending on the closeness of blood ties. Traditionally, this included economic obligations, but with the individuation of labour in industry this is becoming increasingly, less so. Where businesses, farming or commercial, are run as family concerns, social and economic obligations continue to persist.

Parents and children, siblings and cousins, paternal uncles and their wives, nephews and nieces, all have mutual expectations, and the demands and privileges will interflow without any sense of indebtedness. Young girls visiting aunts and uncles are expected to plunge into the round of domestic chores without being asked, adults are expected to place their cars automatically at each other's disposal without asking, and to offer loans when necessary, and the more successful are expected to help the less successful to find good social positions. A person who withholds such service will be criticised, and compliance will be treated without any observable expressions of gratitude, for *kutum* members never become obligated to each other, since they merely perform their duties – *farz*. Likewise, all members of *kutum* expect to be consulted and kept informed about potential changes in status of members through proposals, engagements, marriages, property purchases, education or occupation. If these *kutum* obligations are not observed, ill-feeling is engendered, members feel that they have been ignored, '*not counted*' being the literal translation. They are keenly sensitive to any type of discrimination which implies lack of expected consideration.

The *kutum* is like an intimate *collective conscience* which socialises and controls; binds and integrates members into a closely watched system of social interaction. The average Indian finds that his *kutum* obligations so envelop him that he has little time left for any other associations. The older a person grows, the more subjected he becomes to the demands of the *kutum*. Young boys and men will have their extra-*kutum* affiliations, which may take them away on weekends to various clubs and sporting activities. They may even show open defiance or impolite exasperation in their relations to it. Yet fundamentally they are too dependent on it for emotional support to be able to do without it; hence its power.

Despite some adaptation to the individualistic nature of Western urban life, Indians continue to a large extent, to see people as members of a kin group. Where urban tradition introduces a person in terms of his individual achievement and his occupational status, Indian tradition does so in terms of his kinship link – through his father, grandfather and uncles. In marriage negotiations, to some extent, greater consideration continues to be given to the prestige of the young man's *kutum* than to that of the young man himself.

The average Indian, regardless of wealth, education or sophistication, is possibly far more conscious of the larger kin group that surrounds him than most urban people. He is at the same time less individualised from the larger group and has far less time to be introspective, egoistic, and self-centred. The *kutum* does not allow its members to isolate themselves, and applies pressures to integrate any backslider. Hence moral support in the face of any calamity, such as a mild illness, an accident, financial disaster or death, is given, almost imposed, as a duty. Likewise, there is a spontaneous thronging together of *kutum* members to share in each others, joys and sorrows, arrivals and departures. A patient in hospital is visited by streams of relatives who consider their duty to the sick too important to be distracted by the fear of embarrassing reprimands which might follow the ignoring of such official notices as, *only two persons at a time*, or, *no one is allowed to see or speak to this patient.* A student on an overseas visit, is seen off by almost a hundred relatives, and it often appears wonderful that he boards the plane at all, considering the large number of handshakes and embraces to be made.

Large wealthy *kutums* may become self-contained and, if Muslim, semi-endogamous marriage hierarchies. *Kutum* members within a town may become scattered in several suburbs, or in more than one town of a province, but they never lose their psychic unity, and on meeting, fall into an easy relationship. The fissured nuclear units, however, show a preference for residential proximity, and parents who can afford it, sensing the inevitability of fissuring due to over-crowding or conflict, will plan to build additional accommodation on adjacent plots of land.

Within the *kutum*, the closest unit is that of parents, children, daughters-in-law and paternal grandchildren. A daughter-in-law may live apart, but rarely escapes or even feels completely emancipated from the controlling influences of her mother-in-law, whose criteria of approval and disapproval continue to influence her behaviour, and she will carefully conceal from her all activities that she suspects to be in discord with her views.

One thinks of a person as a member of two families – the family into which he is born, and the family he constitutes himself through marriage. Among Indians, as among many rural communities, he is in addition a member of the family of his marriage, that is the family or *kutum* of the spouse.

Relation within one's *kutum* of birth is far more relaxed than in the *kutum* of marriage. After her marriage, a woman is expected to become integrated with the members of her husband's *kutum* and to have at least as much loyalty towards it as she has towards her own *kutum*. Her complete acceptance as a daughter, however, is rare, and this provides ground for divided loyalties and conflict. By contrast a son-in-law is never expected to integrate himself within his wife's *kutum*, and any such integration would be viewed askance. He must continue to remain a peripheral member, a visitor, whom his in-laws hold in respect and awe, and with whom they must avoid open conflict for fear of reactions on their daughter. On the other hand, a son-in-law may find himself in a favoured position in his wife's family, and if the bond with his wife is strong, which usually accompanies this situation, he may lean more and more towards his *in-law kutum*, and on conflict with his own people, become absorbed into that *kutum*. This pattern, with its 'matrilocal' in contrast to the 'patrilocal' pull, is more evident in the poorer groups.

When a child is to be born, there is wishing that it will be a son, for daughters leave home to raise children for others and parents relinquish authority over them. They visit their people at the behest of their husbands or in-laws, and parents are not free to make demands on them even in old age and illness. Neither is it considered as their right to take direct action if they believe their daughters to be ill-treated. Such concern is regarded as *interference in the households of others*. There are mothers who will adopt a martyr-like stance and say

'My blood has burnt to ash watching the agony of my child, yet my lips have remained sealed and not an "oof" or "ah" has escaped my daughter's breast.' Yet it often happens that it is to a daughter that a mother turns in old age or illness, probably due to the mutual disenchantment suffered in a mother-in-law daughter-in-law relationship in a common household.

While the foregoing sets out the theoretical position, there are deviations from it and it is not uncommon for marital discord to be blamed on interfering parents. A mother who visits her daughter too often in the joint family situation exposes herself to unnecessary suspicion and may well be accused of instigating the minor conflicts which arise between her daughter and son-in-law, or members of his family. It may be said of her, '*The prostitute locks herself up with her daughter, and they phus phus for hours and God alone knows what evil her mother puts her up to.*' It may also be imputed that the daughter-in-law sends her mother away laden with wealth which belongs to her husband and his family. A certain sign of a daughter-in-law's complete acceptance into her husband's family is her mother-in-law's boast that her daughter-in-law does not like visiting her people and has to be forced to do so.

Age and sex are important criteria for status in the *kutum.* There is tacit agreement that women are subordinate to men, the young to the old. Women do not by right make decisions or visit friends and relatives. When a wife operates as a relatively free agent it is by concession, either due to the *goodness* or *weakness* of the husband. Women, even the educated and relatively emancipated, are heard to speak with pride of their husband's authority over them. Wives have no such authority over husbands. Those who allow their movement to be questioned by their wives are considered women themselves. Husbands generally adopt an affectionately condescending attitude to their wives. They see them as minors to be protected and corrected. With the extension of higher education and gainful occupation, however, the submissive wife and daughter-in-law begins to disappear and the young woman demands power and equality within the family.

The roles of men and women are distinctive and their associations are maintained within different complexes. Even as very young children, girls and boys form separate playgroups with distinctive patterns, girls playing with dolls and at house-keeping, the boys with balls, marbles, kites, slings and crudely made carts. Each excludes members of the opposite sex and derides those who try to infiltrate. By the time they are adolescents they have completely integrated their sex defined roles and neither attempts to enter the sphere of the other.

As adults, women's work is generally confined to domestic chores: men are restrained from interfering by the threat of being derided as women. The subordinate status of women is emphasized by the identification of a large range of less valued characteristics as feminine. Hence men who gossip, nag, are over-anxious or too permissive, are said to behave like women. In daily conversations such statements as '*women carry their brains in their shoes,*' and '*women are unreliable,*' are dropped all the time by both sexes, and women rarely react to them as affronts to their sex. Men are breadwinners, and in the pursuit of this primary interest they are allowed many liberties denied or forbidden to women. Hence preference will be given to the education of boys: '*girls end up in the kitchen anyhow*,' is the oft-stated rationalisation. Hence, too, men may mix widely and freely in society, and cultivate certain *vices*, among which smoking is the most tolerated. Women must remain *virtuous*, protected within the domestic confines, and in turn, through their isolated and narrow orientation to life, protect the conventions of those confines. Thus, if there is a family scandal, an unregulated love affair, an unmarried pregnancy, the women are blamed. Popular Indian films never fail to depict heroines as virtuous, patient, suffering, and completely faithful in marriage. The wickedness of female villains never goes beyond malicious gossip or attempted, but rarely successful, seduction of heroes.

Two classes of Indian women may be considered exempt from traditionally prescribed rules relating to their status: the old and the educated. Elderly women in the more peasant and working class groups have appropriated the masculine rights to smoke and drink, and these rights are respected, as well as earned after years of service to the family. It is very probably a pattern which developed in the early years of indenture, when family life was less institutionalised and women less dominated by men. The Westernised women, through high professional qualification, may share with the men the roles of breadwinners. However, they are never excused from domestic responsibilities, and suffer feelings of guilt and inadequacy if they are unable to cope with these fully. Hence the professional Indian woman is keen to impress her domestic prowess, as if they attest to her otherwise challenged femininity.

Indian men will rarely help with housework, but some take pleasure in cooking. The best Indian professional cooks are men, and in working class families when large quantities of food have to be cooked, as on the numerous ceremonial occasions, the men take over.

Older persons expect reverence from the younger. The pattern is established early in childhood in the sibling hierarchy. Older children have their higher status made evident by the adult terms of respect with which younger children address them. Associated with the privilege is the tacit understanding of their obligation to set examples to younger siblings and cousins. The hierarchy within the sibling group has the effect of restraining sibling rivalry and hence conflicts. Children who do not constitute a common rank do not have to compete with each other. Parents do not see the need for preparing and compensating older children for the arrival of younger ones. Each child has its own age-designated position in the family and should not seek the position of another and, generally, this dictum is successfully internalised. This is not to say that children do not demand an equal distribution of material gifts. Even after marriage, a daughter will quarrel if she feels that she has been discriminated against. It is usually in families permeated by urban competitive values that serious problems of sibling rivalries arise.

Children are expected to obey their elders, and the range of elders includes elder siblings, parents, uncles, aunts, grandparents, and granduncles. This implies that behaviour should not flout or contradict their views. Most of all, they should not marry without the permission of their elders. Explicit obedience is demanded more of girls than boys. Fundamentally, girls are subjected to the full range of both masculine and feminine authority; but boys only to masculine authority. Socialisation in the *kutum* emphasizes the internalisation of discipline and respect for authority. Hence Indians do not break easily with tradition: and even the educated and professional elite, whose outer forms appear completely urban and emancipated are in effect conventional and restrained by *kutum* norms. Young people, fresh from universities, sometimes use their academic status to challenge what they consider to be the stifling effects of the *kutum*. Though their academic status will continue to be respected, their views which challenge the crystallised thought-ways of the *kutum* will be rejected. They soon learn that their comfortable and honoured position rests very much in according with behaviour which has the approval of the *kutum*, and hence find outlets for their more *liberal* or *radical* views in other associations. The *kutum* is spared, as far as possible, unnecessary tension arising from impersonal ideological differences. While the authoritarian pattern dominates relations within the *kutum*, the typical middle class urban pattern where there is a relatively equal distribution of power between husband and wife, and parents and children, also occurs, and is found particularly in the professional group.

The *kutum* is the primary community which insulates Indians in South Africa from the rigours of the larger society in which they hold a minority position. The humiliations and frustrations suffered in the external sphere through contact with White authority and members of the White public is eased in the *kutum* through talking, discussing, ridiculing, and above all, sharing. It is in the *kutum* that members are continuously reassured by the rationalizations which protect them from the frustrations of prejudice. '*The Black man's reward is in heaven*;' '*After all, the affairs of this world are only transitory*;' '*Salvation is assured exclusively to the Hindu or the Muslim, since they alone follow the correct paths set them*;' '*They, the Whites, enjoy now, but they will suffer in the hereafter.*' The technical skill of Whites is condescendingly admitted, but their social behaviour is dismissed as immoral, and their personal habits often considered unclean . . . '*They bathe in water stagnant with their own dirt and do not wash each time they relieve themselves. Their table manners are poor. They do not wait to be coaxed into eating, but accept the first offer, and actually ask for more.*' Their women are considered shameless, their men in relation to their women, spineless, and their children lacking in respect for the old. In the absence of an organized Church, both in Islam and Hinduism, the function of the *kutum* in providing emotional or *spiritual* support takes on added importance.

The urban milieu has generally proved inconducive to an extended family, let alone a kinship structure of the *kutum* dimension. While there is some evidence that Indian families are becoming increasingly nucleated, this does not necessarily indicate that there has been a weakening of *kutum* bonds, which often transcend physical nucleation.

Such nucleation occurs when an extended family grows too large and can no longer be contained within the single house, or when a son having gained professional status, finds the standards and strictures of the *kutum* unsuited to his newly acquired tastes, or when there is friction usually between women and a young wife overtly or otherwise challenges her husband to a choice between herself and her children and his extended family. The nuclear family then moves out and sets up its own establishment. Close contact, however, continues between the two families, particularly since mothers have a tendency to view their sons' homes as first and foremost their own. There is much visiting between the two households; weekends are invariably shared, and children find themselves living in two places, often sleeping with the grandparents and delighting in so doing, since there are cousins to play with, and discipline through many elders is more relaxed.

Relations between husbands and wives, and parents and children, are usually more concentrated and intimate in the nuclear family than in the extended. The husband brings a greater range of his problems to his wife, and where in the extended family he may have turned to elders and male members, in the nuclear he tends to turn to her. Children likewise learn to participate more fully in the lives of their parents: they represent them during their absences, feel greater responsibility towards their immediate family and are more conscious of its private possessions. Traditional lines of authority and distance, however, re-remain, though their magnitude decreases.

There are indications, most obvious in the reports of welfare agencies, that the Indian family is being presently threatened by many factors which may change it. There are murmurings in the younger generation which threaten the traditional balance in relations between parents and children, husbands and wives and mothers-in-law and daughters-in-law. There is a desire to grow away from the folkways of the *kutum*, a desire for individual, rather than collective, expression. The allegiance of the growing child, who in the past was prematurely pushed into adulthood without experiencing adolescence, is now being claimed by the universal cult of the teenager, effectively indoctrinated by the cinema and pop music.

The indications are that these demands of youth and of women will increasingly modify the pattern of *kutum* cohesion. Just as women and youth have until now, by their unquestioning subordination, preserved a *status quo*, so too, in the future, they may become the chief agents in changing it. Unfortunately, no experimental study indicates the precise nature of the brewing conflict, and at this stage one can only conjecture about its nature and there can be no certain prediction of the resolution.

In poorer groups, wages previously accepted as adequate for basic subsistence are now seen as bearing no relation to the newly acquired needs flashed on record covers, public hoardings and cinemas. The five rand a week at which most youths start work, is incapable of supporting a transistor, a tape recorder, a radiogram, an elegantly clad body, plus make a contribution to the family. There are youths who are unemployed because they do not consider employment worth their while on that basis. There are some who spend their entire earnings on themselves and assume standards which are glittering in comparison to the bleak surroundings in which they live. Such attempts at escape from the crippling poverty and dull, drab restrictive lives of their elders is temporary and comes to an end upon marriage.

Marriages across traditional barriers, though rare, occur among all classes, but whereas among the poorer groups they are usually preceded by clandestine affairs, among the educated, professional and student groups they occur with a sense of open defiance. Elopement is the more usual pattern under these circumstances. Generally, young people from poorer groups are more vulnerable to the hazards of such untraditional unions. Their unplanned passions lead all too frequently to unmarried pregnancies and all the complications that follow. The usual hazards of marriage are, in such cases, aggravated further by open disapproval of the elders and their very reluctant acceptance of the situation, if at all. Young people, despite their apparent air of rebelliousness, are very dependent on parental support, and when such support is withheld, or when continued criticism is directed against the one partner by the respective families, bonds, insecurely formed in the first instance, weaken and reach breaking point. Absence of adequate economic support may, in addition, drive the young wife to seek employment in a factory, and this in itself may be treated as legitimate ground for the young husband further to shirk his responsibility, for the working woman is viewed with suspicion and her position interpreted as wide open to infidelity.

There are instances where young girls elope and live with the families of their lovers for all apparent purposes as wives and daughters-in-law. Such unions are fraught with insecurity for the girls, and their lives are often made unbearable by both their 'husbands' and 'mothers-in-law', leading to suicide in extreme cases.

But for all such deviations, Indian family life has succeeded in maintaining many of its traditions, and thereby projects an image of greater integration than would be expected in a community exposed to intensive urbanization for at least three generations. There is great sensitivity to authority of elders and bonds of kin, and the attitudes which flow from such bonds as these are not confined to the family, but extended to non-kin members, resulting in informal spontaneous interaction. Hence every stranger, according to age and sex, continues to be addressed as sister, brother, uncle, aunt, mother, father. Obligations felt within the kin group are extended, with some modification, to the neighbour *padosi*, who constitutes a very important social category even when there are differences of language and religion, and thereafter, with decreasing degree of intensity, to the whole community. The Indian is committed to his community. He feels responsible to it and for it, and he expresses his commitment through his participation in the large number of voluntary associations, welfare, civic and educational, which he forms and in which he serves, and which to some large extent compensates for his exclusion from the power structure of the larger society.

In South African Indian life, the *kutum* lays the basis for group solidarity. The situation of political minority from which Indians suffer generally has led to the extension of *kutum* bonds across traditional barriers of religion, language, economics and caste, resulting in a relatively closely knit Indian community. The same situation also kindles in them desires to form links with constituent non-Indian South African communities in order to be integrated into the South African social system. The desire for integration, however, is cautioned by a simultaneous desire to retain their composite identity in the social whole. If Indian social cohesion has to some important extent been due to the type of solidarity engendered in the *kutum*, it is forseeable that serious changes in its structure can have repercussions in the general solidarity of the community, and possibly weaken the kind of reserves it has hitherto used to contend with its minority situation in South Africa.

2. Impact of the City

ALLIE A. DUBB

Among all the south-eastern Bantu-speaking people, the domestic unit was, traditionally, the patrilineally extended family rather than the nuclear family.[1] Ideally, this unit comprised a man, his wife or wives,[2] his unmarried children, his married sons and their families, and various other dependent relatives. But while this arrangement still exists, it is no longer universal even in the rural areas. In the first place, Christian missionaries tended to emphasize the nuclear family unit, while the very act of conversion led to a degree of withdrawal from the extended families to which converts belonged. In the second place, the migration of male work-seekers to European farms and towns led either to temporarily husbandless and fatherless homes in the reserves, or to the removal of wives and children to the migrants' places of employment. In the towns the traditional type of extended family is virtually non-existent. First, it is either an individual or a couple – with or without children – who migrate to town, rather than a complete extended family. In the second place, urban housing conditions would, in any case, make it extremely difficult for such a large group to establish common residence.

Pauw (1963: chapter 8) in his study of East London distinguished four types of household.[3] The first, and most common, comprises the nuclear family plus, possibly, one or two other relatives or dependants. The second type is the multi-generational male-headed household in which the nuclear family is augmented by the children of an unmarried daughter or daughters. Third, the mother-child household comprises an unattached woman (widowed, divorced, separated or an unmarried mother), and her unmarried children. In course of time, this may develop into the fourth type, the multi-generational female-headed household, in which the mother-child unit is extended to include the offspring of unmarried daughters and even grand-daughters. This type of family – which is made up of a chain of mothers and daughters without any permanently attached male, and which is becoming increasingly widespread – is especially interesting since, contrary to the traditional principle of patrilineality, the links between members of this group are entirely through females. Similarly, it is the materfamilias rather than a male, who wields authority in the household.[4]

While many female-headed households have a succession of male consorts, a relationship which is frequently encountered is known as *ukushweshwa* (Xhosa, concubinage) (see Mayer 1961:256–65; Longmore 1959:68–75). A man who has, or expects to have, a wife and children in the country will, if he is able, often also set up a fairly permanent relationship with a woman in town. They establish a common home to which the man contributes financially, and often they have children together. This is not, however, marriage, and neither has any legal rights in the other. As might be expected, some women will try to wean their lovers away from their legal wives, while on the other hand the *shweshwe* might resist the man's desire to marry her, preferring to retain her independence. Under such an arrangement, the man may form a strong attachment to the *shweshwe's* children and will assist in their support, but he has no jural rights in them nor they in him. His primary obligations are to his own heirs and successors, the children of his legal wife in the country. The *shweshwe*'s children, as any children of an unmarried woman, will be members of their maternal grandfather's lineage though, for practical purposes, this is often of little importance.

Another important aspect of the family relates to economics. In tribal society the family was the unit of production and consumption and was essentially self-sufficient. Today, probably, the larger proportion of households in rural areas rely on remittances by migrant labourers. Nevertheless even though they are no longer self-supporting, they must still produce a good deal of their own food as well as satisfy other needs by their own efforts. As the unit of production,the rural family is knit together by the mutual interdependence of its members, amongst whom those economic activities necessary for survival are divided. Most of the major roles – various types of work in the fields, house-building, tending the stock, milking, domestic chores are age - and - sex – specific. In town the family, or more precisely the domestic group, is still an important unit of consumption, but no longer of production. Here members of the household are involved in the economic life of the city as a whole, and their contribution to the household is in the form of cash rather than services. While the wife, mother or oldest daughter may, if she herself is not forced to take a job, devote her full time to serving the other members, any individual who earns money can perform most of these services himself and purchase others. The relative unimportance of a formal division of labour within the urban family makes its members less dependent on one another than in the rural setting.

This change in the economic role of the family and in economic relations between its members – together with such factors as the loosening of kinship ties and the decline of the patrilineally extended household – has had important consequences for husband-wife and parent-child relationships. Thus Hellmann (1967: 6ff.) writes that in the towns

> the family is on its own, no longer embedded in the web of kinship which was the basis of the traditional system . . . Parents are called on to accept responsibilities and functions – educational, economic and emotional – that were formerly carried out by a group of kin. In a number of families, new patterns of behaviour between husband and wife and between parents and children have developed which meet the demands of these new conditions. In such households, there is close co-operation between husband and wife, consultation about money matters, the children's education and other concerns. . . It seems to me that this pattern is regarded as the ideal to be aimed at by professional and middle class women, although by no means

> all men of the same status share this aspiration and its attainment is very infrequent. . . It is far more common to find families under strain because of the unresolved conflict between the husband's patriarchal conduct and the wife's new role as wage-earner, manager of the household budget and educator of the children. Men, including educated men, seem to resist the emancipation of women which modern conditions promote.[5]

In similar vein, a journalist, Jenny Ndale, writes in the African paper *Post* of 2 May 1965:

> Men are still bogged down in the tribal notion that taking little Enoch out for a walk is none of their business. . . The idea of sharing everything that marriage and children mean . . our African husbands just don't (accept). . . Maybe if our husbands would move up a notch into this modern age and could be persuaded to take more interest in their children, less of these would leave home for delinquency. Maybe if they paid their wives a little more attention, there'd be fewer lovers let in through the back door when they're away.

Another respect in which the urban family differs from the rural one also arises out of economic factors. Whereas in the rural areas economic activity is centred around the home and family fields, in town it takes place entirely outside of the household. In the country, then, there is always some responsible adult at hand to watch over the children whereas in the town, with its smaller nuclear family and one or both parents working, there is often no one to supervise them. With insufficient crèche andnursery school facilities, as well as a critical shortage of space in primary and secondary schools, township children roam the streets and get into all kinds of mischief. As Hellmann (1967:11–12) points out, many children 'fail to find in their homes the emotional security they need or in their parents the models with whom they will want to identify themselves. . . Parental control has weakened and youthful indiscipline has grown.' The *tsotsis* – town youths characterized by their total disrespect for authority and cynical disregard for the lives and property of others – are the bitter fruit of family breakdown in an unfavourable physical, social, economic and political environment.[6]

A final topic related to marriage and the family which we shall discuss is sexual gratification and love. Africans, generally, take a pragmatic view of sex: it is a natural urge which everyone is entitled to satisfy within socially defined limits. The limit placed on pre-marital sex by the south-eastern Bantu is, simply, that an unmarried girl should not fall pregnant. Thus among the Zulu and Xhosa, for example, an unmarried girl may indulge in sex play leading to external intercourse (*ukumetsha* in Xhosa, and *ukusoma* in Zulu), but must not permit actual penetration. To ensure observance of this rule, older women, usually grandmothers or aunts though never her mother, subject her to periodic inspection of her virginity. Although it is doubtful whether this examination has any objective validity, it appears to have the desired psychological effect.[7]

In the towns, girls who are not prepared to allow full intercourse are ridiculed, while parents do not, and did not traditionally, directly concern themselves with their children's sex instruction and supervision. Thus a girl, a mother at the age of fifteen, told Pauw (1963:112): 'My mother used to tell me that babies are bought in the market when you are grown-up. But what puzzled me is that I never saw babies on beds in the market.' Pauw points out that sexual activity in town begins around the age of eleven or twelve and that by the time a girl reaches fifteen it is almost certain that she has had intercourse. In his sample of seventy-four unmarried town-born women aged fifteen years and over, six out of ten were mothers, while of those between twenty to thirty-five years old, three-quarters had had children (Pauw 1963:118). Attitudes to pre-marital pregnancy are ambivalent: while Pauw records that some girls have even contemplated suicide (1963:119), Wilson and Mafeje (1963:43) quote the resignation of a father in Langa:

> Look at M., my own child. This is the second child she is expecting. What shall I do with her? Shall I kill her or drive her out of the house? Of what use would that be? The best thing is to let my daughter enjoy life so long as she cares for her children properly. When God wills these bad conditions in society will all be over.

But there is another aspect of pre-marital pregnancy. A young man asked by Pauw (1963:118) whether he was going to marry his girl-friend replied that he would like to but that he suspected she was barren. They had been sweethearts for some years and had been having sexual relations all that time but 'without any results.' While the custom of paying *lobolo* (bride-wealth) is still widespread, even among urbanized and Westernized people, it no longer safeguards the husband's rights to a fertile wife. In the first place, since *lobolo* is paid in money rather than cattle, it is virtually irrecoverable. Second, if the couple are married by Christian or civil rights, barrenness does not constitute a ground for divorce, while plural marriage is out of the question. A young man will, therefore, often wait until the girl has had a child before marrying her and handing over the marriage payment.

One final comment should be made: traditionally, marriage was arranged between the two sets of parents. While a young person was generally not forced to marry someone whom he or she did not like, the most important criteria of suitability were family status, wealth, probable fertility and the woman's robustness and ability to work, rather than romantic love. In the towns, however – although this was already the practice among rural Christians – choice of spouses has become a personal matter for the two young people involved, and notions of romantic love are already very common. Nevertheless, as we have seen, prospective bridegrooms are still concerned with such practicalities as child-bearing capacity, faithfulness and family background.

Kinship

Anthropologists have shown that, traditionally, kinship played a key role in organizing relationships – social, economic, political and jural – among the south-eastern Bantu-speaking peoples. Inheritance and succession, residence, marriage rules, mutual aid and hospitality, ancestor cult ritual and even proper conduct were, to a great extent, defined in terms of kinship. For most purposes it was the patrilineage – a group of kinsmen, related in the male line, who could trace descent from a common ancestor – which was of prime importance, although a person had rights and obligations within the wider group of cognates and affines as well.

Today, among conservative traditionalists, the *ideology* of kinship solidarity and amity remains although, in the day-to-day business of living, other categories may assume greater importance. Thus in the Transkei, for example, a man has no right to land in any particular area simply because his father or other agnatic (patrilineal) kinsfolk live there, nor is his only claim based on inheritance. It is as the subject of a particular headman – and whether or not they are kin is irrelevant – that he will apply for an allotment when he marries. Furthermore, since lineages are usually widely dispersed and local settlements include families belonging to several lineages and clans, non-agnates and unrelated neighbours assist each other more frequently and intensely than far-away kinsmen. (See Hammond-Tooke 1968a, 1968b.) The corporateness of the patrilineage and to a lesser degree the clan, is manifested on ritual occasions; in the expectation that members of the lineage will be informed of and invited to participate in each others' births, marriages, funerals and similar important events; and in defining preferred and prohibited marriages.

When the migrant comes to town he will, not unnaturally, seek out kinsmen or people from the same rural area both for companionship and because he can expect help from them in securing accommodation and employment (see Reader 1961a:73ff. and chapter 8). As we have already pointed out, the Red (or traditionalist) migrant tends to confine his social relationships to these *amakhaya* (home-boys) and kinsmen unless he decides deliberately to sever his rural ties and/or adopt town ways. Within the *amakhaya* group, where conversation centres on the country, its people and their affairs, traditional values are retained and reinforced. At the same time the migrant maintains direct links with the rural home through his rurally-based wife, children and other relatives, to whom he remits part of his earnings, and through his participation in ancestor cult rituals. Thus for the Red migrant, kinship plays much the same role in town as it does in the country.

The country-rooted Christian (or School) migrant also maintains strong bonds with kinsmen and *amakhaya* as well as with his rural home. However, his network is, *ab initio*, potentially wider than that of the pagan since it also includes fellow-Christians who may be neither kinsmen nor neighbours. It is clear, then, that kinship and neighbourhood may diminish in importance if Christianity becomes the primary criterion of network recruitment.

Turning now from the migrant to the townsman proper, Hellmann (1948), Pauw (1963: chapter 9) and Wilson and Mafeje (1963: chapter 4) are agreed that kinship continues to play an important role. However, as Wilson and Mafeje point out: 'kinsmen are bound by personal ties, but they do not now form defined corporate groups other than the elementary family' (1963:75). Pauw (1963: chapter 9) found that, in East London, most townsmen had locally-based kin, many being close neighbours. Kinsmen towards whom obligations were recognized and from whom help and support could be expected, were, however, selected much more on the basis of personal preference than of agnation (patrilineality) or genealogical closeness. Furthermore – as a consequence of the widespread development of the matrifocal household – maternal kin had assumed far greater importance than in the traditional system. These kin included the mother's patrilineage, other cognates related mainly through women and even the wife's parents and family. Finally, both Pauw and Wilson and Mafeje found that while clan exogamy was generally observed in town, its validity was being questioned by some. All these changes in kinship patterns were reflected in corresponding changes in terminology in which traditionally-recognized categories were now being ignored while new ones had been created (Wilson and Mafeje 1963: 86ff).

Despite these changes it is clear that townsmen include a number of kin in their social networks. In fact as they become settled and marry in town, they become involved in a gradually widening web of kinship. Given that their kinship group is not necessarily corporate or patrilineal, townsmen have, therefore, more immediate access to kinsmen than do the rurally-centered migrants (Pauw 1963: chapter 9). Kinship, then, is an important basis of social relationships for both pagan and Christian, migrant and townsman. For the townsman, however, kinship is not a *primary* basis of association as it tends to be for the migrant.

NOTES

1. The nuclear (or elementary) family is a group consisting of a man and a woman – whose union is recognized in terms of the rules of the society – and their legitimate children, own or adopted.
2. Polygamy was highly valued although, in practice, only the wealthier men were able to marry more than one wife. Among pagans polygamy still occurs, but is declining. See, for example, Hunter 1936: *passim;* and Hammond-Tooke 1962: *passim.*
3. It should be noted that although we refer to Pauw's findings, these domestic arrangements are common to all South African townships. For information on Johannesburg, see Longmore 1959: *passim.* Verster (1965: 158) gives a breakdown of types of marriage in a sample of 2 416 mothers in Soweto. She found that 2,11 per cent were living together, 9,61 per cent

had been married by civil or Christian rites, 43,32 per cent by civil or Christian as well as customary rites, 28,78 per cent by customary rites, and 16,18 per cent had never been married. Some discussion of the family in Cape Town may be found in Wilson and Mafeje 1963:76–82.

4. There is a fairly widespread belief that there is an extremely high masculinity rate among urban Africans and that this accounts for the large number of unmarried mothers. It might therefore be noted that in Johannesburg the masculinity rate was 94,1 (Verster 1965:166), in East London 108 (Reader 1961:150) and in Cape Town (Langa) 86,6. (Wilson and Mafeje 1963:4). However, masculinity is only one demographic factor which *may* contribute to the conditions described.
5. Brandel-Syrier (1971:83) points out that the wives of the Reeftown elite were important 'status symbols' as well as co-earners, and that it 'was generally agreed in Reeftown that "a wife can pull her husband up" ' (ibid., 84). At the same time she records a high degree of marital strife and instability (83) as well as noting that 'A great number, probably the majority, were known by their wives to be "unfaithful", at more or less regular intervals in extra-marital relationships' (91).
6. See Pauw 1963: *passim;* Mayer 1961: *passim;* Wilson and Mafeje 1963: *passim;* Longmore 1959: *passim.*
7. The practice still prevails among pagans in the rural areas but not among Christians, since the missionaries regarded it as a disgusting and evil custom. One of the consequences has been that, among the Xhosa at any rate, it is generally acknowledged that Christian girls have more pre-marital pregnancies than do pagan girls.

REFERENCES

Brandel-Syrier, M. 1971 – *Reeftown Elite.* London: Routledge & Kegan Paul.

Hammond-Tooke, W. D. 1962 – *Bhaca Society: A People of the Transkeian Uplands, South Africa.* Cape Town: Oxford University Press.

——1968a – 'The morphology of Mpondomise descent groups.' *Africa*, 38, 1, 26–45.

——1968b – 'Descent group scatter in a Mpondomise ward.' *African Studies*, 27, 2, 83–94.

Hellmann, Ellen 1948 – *Rooiyard: A Sociological Survey of an Urban Native Slum Yard.* Cape Town: Oxford University Press.

——1967 – 'The African family today.' Paper delivered to conference on African family life organized by Southern Transvaal Region, South African Institute of Race Relations, and the Witwatersrand Christian Council (mimeographed), Johannesburg.

Hunter, Monica 1936 – *Reaction to Conquest: Effects of Contact with Europeans on the Pondo of South Africa.* London: Oxford University Press.

Longmore, L. 1959 – *The Dispossessed: A Study of the Sex-Life of Bantu Women in Urban Areas in and around Johannesburg.* London: Jonathan Cape.

Mayer, P. 1961 – *Townsmen or Tribesmen: Conservatism and the Process of Urbanization in a South African City.* Cape Town: Oxford University Press.

Pauw, B. A. 1963 – *The Second Generation: A Study of the Family Among Urbanized Bantu in East London.* Cape Town: Oxford University Press.

Reader, D. H. 1961 – *The Black Man's Portion.* Cape Town: Oxford University Press.

Verster, J. 1965 – 'The trend and pattern of fertility in Soweto: An urban Bantu community.' *African Studies*, 24, 3–4, 131–98.

Wilson, M. and A. Mafeje 1963 – *Langa: A Study of Social Groups in an African Township.* Cape Town: Oxford University Press.

3. Marriage and Family Life

MARIANNE BRINDLEY

Workable Marriages

There are the happy, often religious marriages in Western Township such as those of Mrs de Wet who is 52 years old, has six children and was born an Anglican but changed to her husband's church, the Seventh Day Adventists, 'to keep peace.' Like many other Coloured women she accepts the church dictum that 'the man is the head but the woman is the neck' of the house. Many Coloured people summarise their household management and division of labour in similar phrases: 'The man is the head' and 'the woman is the pillar.' In practical terms this generally means that the man is responsible for finding paid employment and financing the household and the woman is responsible for caring for the children, food buying and peparation, clothing, health and housework.

In theory, most marital couples acknowledge the differentiation of duties and value of both sexes in performing their roles adequately as part of the *modus operandi* for a happy marriage and home. Although workable marital alliances are thus effected, very often such marriages tend not to evince much sharing or intimate communication. Many wives do not know what their husbands earn and husbands and wives do not discuss much: 'We are married, but he is a man and I am a woman and I do not ask him about his affairs', or 'the men drink one side, we on the other.' In such marriages one also finds a clear and distinctive philosophy concerning individual rights. The concept implies that every adult has a right to think and do what he wants within reason. Thus, though a woman vehemently disapproves of the fact that her husband is a heavy drinker, one frequently hears her say: 'Well, I tried to change him and he didn't want to listen, so that's his affair.' The equanimity with which some marital couples are prepared to accept the 'do as I like' attitude of their partners is marked, though this is never encountered with regard to flirting, sex or extra-marital affairs.

There are good marriages and it is encouraging to come across them. They are like the 'Inn of Happiness'[1] where love pervades the selfless atmosphere and the wall-hanging symbolises the lives of the people: 'God does not take sides, He takes over.'

Problems in Marriage

Where husband and wife are able to accept and fulfil the male-female role differentiation one generally finds the basis for a successful marriage, but all too often external factors impinge and introduce a tension into the individual's perception and execution of his role.

The principal sources of conflict in marriages in the Township are:

(*a*) the home is overcrowded and inadequate, or the rentals too high;

(*b*) the Coloured woman is being caught up in the same emancipating process wrought by industrialisation as her counterpart all over the world and she desires to work for paid employment of her choice;

(*c*) the woman feels dissatisfied with her husband's performance in fulfilling his role as father and husband and therefore often enters his domain as bread-winner;

(*d*) the man earns an inadequate wage because of his colour; he cannot always do the job he desires because of job reservation; he feels frustrated and humiliated at work and home, and becomes irritated and intolerant of his wife who does not understand his position and often demeans his manhood and self-esteem.

Many wives decide to go to work to supplement the family[2] income. This does not make it any easier for the man to accept his position. He feels increasingly redundant. Some men react to this situation with anger, some by being irresponsible, and others by trying to escape from it through drink.

It appears that the frustrations of the wife are closely related to the inability of her husband to provide for the family's physical needs, often linked to the changing role-expectation of women in general; whereas the problems of the husband largely derive from employment and socio-political disorientation.

The Effect of Overcrowding

It is difficult for people who have not had to experience overcrowded housing without adequate facilities to appreciate the strain this brings into everyday relations. Housing conditions are a major source of tension in the Township. In her research on working and middle-class mothers in London, Gavron (1970:58) states that: 'The quality of family life is greatly influenced by its standard of housing.' She goes on to quote the study of McGregor and Rowntree of 1962, who found that: 'Income and housing are the main indices of the quality of family environment especially when there are young children.'

Mr Haremse of the Township is frustrated beyond measure because of the overcrowding in his house. He and his wife live in three rooms with their three daughters and one son, all of whom have illegitimate infants in the house. Mr Haremse likes his privacy and needs to feel alone sometimes, 'but you cannot spend a minute without other people falling over you in this house. I have been on the waiting list for eight years to move to another, but the Rent Office just works by bribes and if ever we complain about the house, they tell us: "I'm not giving you a place for your furniture, I'm giving you a place for your family." So I say to them: You expect me to sit and eat on tomato boxes? Well I also like decent things to sit on. The walls of these houses get so wet, they don't even build airvents into them . . . I want to move to Eldorado Park on the Golden Highway, even if I have to pay R50 rent a month, but then they don't let you move where you want to.'[3]

The city environment in which the Coloured people find themselves, the pace of change and the demand for new workable attitudes also influence marriages adversely. Mr Haremse has an added problem. He is a devout Christian and a hard worker. But he walks through his home tense and aloof. Furthermore he and his wife are drifting apart because all their four teenagers are incessantly having illegitimate babies despite their orthodox religious upbringing. Mr Haremse feels smitten with guilt and rage because the grandchildren have all become *their* liability since none of the fathers will pay maintenance for them, and this has added to their overcrowding problem. His wife is 'soft' as he says, and has to wash, feed and care for them, though she suffers from a gnawing backache. Mrs Haremse runs away from home whenever her conflict between loyalty and regard for her husband and religion, and 'our children's mistake' becomes too great.

Mr and Mrs Isaacs, on the other hand, recall how they lived in the old neglected area of the Township for eight years. They had six children and the family lived in a three-roomed house. At that time Mrs Isaacs frequently became depressed and had to take sedatives: 'The cramped conditions got on my nerves.' Now they have moved to a spacious five-roomed row-house in the redeveloped area and 'This is paradise on earth. This is heavenly.' The Isaacs' maintain there has been an actual improvement in the happiness of family life with their change in living conditions.

SEXUAL INTERCOURSE

A large number of Western Township wives feel embarrassed about having sexual intercourse with their husbands because their children have to sleep in the same room. The whole situation requires caution, for as Aston and Dobson have found: 'Where the mother in the family was in some way inhibited or anxious about her sexual relationship with her husband,' she would tend to 'turn to her child for attention and satisfaction more often than did mothers who seemed to have made a better sexual adjustment to their husbands. This high degree of (mother)-child pairing probably served further to deflate the father's belief in his own value . . . thus a syndrome of disappointment appears to have been set up in these families, resulting in withdrawal on the part of the father and over-concern for the child on the part of the mother' (1972:88).

Certain parents find their way around this problem by putting all their children, except babies, in another room but 'I feel it's not right that my teenage sons and daughters sleep together and have to wash and dress together in the same room, but what can I do?' The importance of these areas of tension should not be underestimated and with such a constant exposure of children to sex and the opposite sex at vulnerable ages we should not feel surprise at rumours of incest around the Township, nor at the prevalence of promiscuity and illegitimacy.

The most common complaint about housing in the old area is the cramped conditions.[4] In most houses no more than three beds can be fitted in so the children either share a bed with one or more siblings or have to sleep lined up on newspaper on the floor of the lounge-cum-dining-room-cum-kitchen.

CHILDHOOD DEVELOPMENT

In addition to the negative consequences of crowding on parents and thus on the stability of family life, Plant (1963:510–513, 518–520) shows the detrimental effect it has on the personality development of children.

'Crowding seems very definitely to affect the self-sufficiency of children – their ability to be alone . . . It seems that persistent and constant crowding from early life destroys the sense of individuality.' Plant goes on to say: 'Our work in suburban and rural districts has convinced us that periods of being alone, or playing alone, of having the privacy of one's own room, are important fostering agents in a feeling of individuality, of self-sufficiency.'

Crowding serves to destroy the illusions which children build about other people. 'Images we build of others are the material of our dreams and goals. They are of great dynamic power – leading us to the best we can attain.' What happens in these overcrowded areas, says Plant, is that children 'do not want to follow in their fathers' footsteps,' they know them too well and they begin to distrust people.

In this respect he feels that crowding makes children become preoccupied with the sex act, rather than providing them with an understanding of coitus as a symbolic expression of a relationship, for they view the act before it has real meaning to them.

People in overcrowded conditions are subject to mental strain. They have a feeling that they 'want to get away from everybody.' 'When these periods of freedom are lacking,' Plant goes on, there is either a 'somewhat forbidding negativism, or . . . irritable outbursts of temper which belong to the phenomena of fatigue . . . One sees a constantly recurring picture of "touchy" reactions and irritability . . . When we realise that for many . . . there is never a time that they are alone, we begin to get some picture of (the effect) this tension must (have). Even the nights conspire to the same end: three to five children sleeping in the same bed means that even during the periods of relaxation and for the deeper levels of the unconscious there must always be this awareness of the imminence of others and the compromises and surrenders which this entails.'

Finally Plant has found that among people in crowded areas and families, there is what he calls 'the phenomenon of being so much in the world that there is no chance to look at it.' The ability to look objectively at oneself is of fundamental importance to the developing personality, but children and adults in these circumstances can rarely achieve more than a narrow, despondent subjectivism.

Rent and Wages: a Source of Friction

For that fifth of the Township fortunate enough to have been moved to the new area there is distinct relief at the housing improvement, even though Coloured people will take time to accustom themselves to living in flats. Unfortunately the accommodation is still not satisfactory because the rentals and electricity accounts are excessively high: one-third of the real income. Similarly Maasdorp reporting on rehousing of Africans in Durban, states: 'Although the new accommodation represents a substantial improvement on the old from the point of view of modern standards, the higher rentals involved exacerbate the already parlous economic position of the families' (1975:18).

Mr Willemse is a crane-driver. He has four children and earns a 'good' wage of R45 a week. This is his wife's budget: *Earnings* (pw) R45; *Expenditure* (pw) R64; Mrs Willemse's basic spending registers as: Rent – R15; Electricity (compulsory amount for flat dwellers) – R2; Groceries – R20; Meat (no roasts) – R8; Fruit and Vegetables – R3; and Furniture (HP) – R16. The weekly deficit is thus R19. Either the family is bedevilled by debt, or, as usually happens, Mrs Willemse has to work to make good the deficit.

I frequently met families in this zone where frictions arose over a trivial remark such as Mrs Willemse asking her husband if they could buy another chair as people always had to find a box to sit on when visiting. He flared up in anger at this suggestion and shouted: 'OK, so go and find yourself another husband if I'm not good enough for you. I can't get better money, I can't give it; go and find someone who will give it to you.'

The men in the redeveloped zone are generally earning better wages than in the old area but they are still tense and easily irritated because as husbands and fathers they cannot provide adequately. This feeling of failure, exacerbated by the wife's often tactless remarks because she battles to make ends meet and also wants some modern conveniences, is at the root of much marital discord.

In 1956 it was said that 'poverty is the chief cause of the lack of homes, and the Coloured people have, on the whole, been unable to afford to buy or build houses for themselves' (C.P.C. & A.J. Housing for Coloured People 1956:21). Professor S. P. Cilliers has stressed the same factors in broader perspective: 'The major social problems amongst Coloureds are directly related to their socio-economic position and centre around poverty and housing. It therefore concerns the provision of basic necessities of life' (1971:35).

Implications of the Working Wife

In their discussion of American family structure, Queen and Habenstein (1967: 303–4) observe that: 'Along with these changing roles have come challenges to the earlier male dominance.' Sometimes the male still makes the important decisions and has the power, in other cases the wife-mother is dominant whilst in still others there is partnership. 'All too often there is conflict and something of a power struggle. Perhaps even more often there is confusion and ambivalence, with both husband and wife uncertain as to division or sharing of labour, authority, and responsibility. These uncertainties contribute to instability in many American families.'

Some Western Township wives and mothers desire to work in paid employment because of the liberation it affords them from endless household chores. They enjoy the stimulation of a change of environment and people, can fulfil themselves in a job they like, and can buy the little luxuries that give them pleasure. But even if the wife explains that her being employed is no reflection on her husband's ability, most husbands resist this consciously or subconsciously because they know that employment out of the home makes their wives less economically and emotionally dependent on them, and because it complicates household management, often leading to a sharing of chores and blurring of traditional sex-linked behaviour patterns. . .

Over-Possessive Men

Linked with the Coloured man's general sense of insecurity and the poor communication between people in the area, is the phenomenon of hyper-possessiveness which Marsden (1973:87) also observed in a study of mothers who now live alone in Britain. 'A much more serious problem (than unfaithfulness) for about a quarter of the wives was the husband's acute sexual jealousy, which was part of his attempt to control the wife's social life' . . .'

Marsden's mothers in Northborough and Seaston (UK) had the same problems: They 'felt they lacked somebody to talk to about adult matters, sex, the neighbours' (143); and they reported somewhat prejudicial aid from the authorities who tended to discriminate against unmarried mothers (247,258–9, 283).

Distrust between Sexes

There is a good deal of distrust between husbands and wives, and acts of infidelity are not infrequent. In conversations it is noticeable how people often classify their spouses with a stereotyped image of the opposite sex and show a better understanding of and closer affinity towards members of their own sex. The Lynds found a similar pattern in their study of life in a typical small American city. In many working class families 'the necessities of shelter and food overshadow other plans; such conversation as there is may be of a bickering sort, or may lapse into apathetic silence. . . This frequent lack of community of interests, together with the ideas each sex entertains regarding the other, appears in many families in a lack of frankness between husband and wife, far-reaching in its emotional outcome' (1929:120).

Such behaviour not only prevents intimate communication and mutual sharing between the sexes on matters other than sex and organisational trivia, but it affects the children. As Lidz (1973) so rightly emphasises, the family is the dynamo of personality development and its aberrations; it is here that essential values pertaining to marriage, parenthood, male and female are formed. The problem of male violence and female back-chat is as real in Western as it is in the working-class north of England; though here the in-built safeguards of humour are perhaps not as extensively developed. However, the mutual inability to discuss things honestly and gently with a desire to understand the other's position is common to both. . .

Drink and Marriage

Alcohol is a further aggravator of marital tension. The implications of alcoholism on family life as stressed by SANCA[5] are: (*a*) the important roles of each family member may be distorted, i.e. the mother may have to compensate for the father's lack of leadership and this affects her relationship to her husband and children and the children have to adapt to a poor father-figure; (*b*) normal family behaviour becomes distorted; (*c*) values and standards held by the family seem to disintegrate; (*d*) the spouse becomes so absorbed in her partner's drinking that little energy and thought remain for the children's development; (*e*) personal difficulties with the partner are exacerbated[6] (n.d. 4–5.).

Although there are sociologists who maintain that alcohol is not a cause of marital disintegration, and although many Coloured men and some women regard drinking as a legitimate and basic form of cultural recreation, it is evident that the pattern of alcoholic drinking in the Township is a major source of family unhappiness.

Disillusionment with Marriage

There is an increasing number of people in the Township who have seen or experienced broken marriages or conjugal violence, and this has set them against marriage as a form of partnership. Not only does this have the effect of proliferating the number of fatherless children, but the mothers do not have the resources to provide for them adequately.

Patsy is about 50. Her husband is dead but gave her such a hard life beating her and refusing to talk to her that she never wants to marry again. She is contented just to live in her little house of two and a half rooms with her grandchildren and women friends who visit. Once they've had '*'n bietjie geselskap*' ('a bit of companionship') they leave again, and '*ek gee die kinders 'n bietjie kossetjie en sit hulle in die bed, dan is ek tevrede.*' ('I give the children a little food and put them to bed. Then I am satisfied.')

She has four daughters and a son. The son is in prison for 'bad company'. The daughters are not married though all have children, and the men don't want to pay maintenance. Patsy receives R80 a month from the Welfare Department to look after the four children, though she finds it too little to manage on. Her daughters don't want to marry because they say men aren't interested in marriage nor would they treat them well.

Implications for the Children

What is evident from the foregoing data is that many marriages in the Township are emotionally unstable or brittle. Not only has this kind of environment serious implications for the partners concerned but also for the socialisation and exposure of the children. The McCords (1960:108) have emphasised that: 'The general emotional tone of a family is largely governed by the nature of the relationship between parents.'

The state of human relationships as expressed in the conjugal tie in Western is a cause for concern. If, as it seems, marriage in urban settings throughout the world is becoming increasingly meaningless in the *institutional* sense (Queen and Habenstein 1967:311), then its role as a vehicle for human affection and companionship assumes greater importance. We need therefore to work at the conditions and attitudes which block effective communication and mutual pleasure between partners. Marital disruption is so real and so unresolved in the Township that the young people are rapidly losing faith in marriage as an institution specifically, and in human relations generally. Furthermore its value as a positive nurturing ground for the young is being seriously threatened, and they are receiving inadequate alternative security and affection.

NOTES

1. The name a young married couple have given to their home. House-names are rare in the Township.
2. The sample studied indicates that household composition primarily consists of the nuclear family.
3. Mr Haremse works independently as a mechanic. Houses are held back in such cases by the Department as the income is deemed 'unsteady'.
4. Two-roomed houses are normally 27,9 m^2; the largest are four-roomed units totalling 37,3 m^2.
5. The South African National Council on Alcoholism and Drug Dependence, a welfare organisation run on the basis of Alcoholics Anonymous.
6. SANCA (n.d.) *When Alcoholism Strikes – A Practical Guide for the Family.*

*Some of the case material in the original article has been omitted from this selection.

REFERENCES

Aston, P. J. and G. Dobson 1972 – 'Family interaction and social adjustment in a sample of normal school children.' *Journal of Child Psychology and Psychiatry*, 13, 2:77–89.

Cilliers, S. P. 1971 – *Appeal to Reason.* Stellenbosch: University Publishers.

Gavron, H. 1970 – *The Captive Wife: Conflicts of Housebound Mothers.* Harmondsworth: Penguin.

Lidz, T. 1973 – *Schizophrenia and the Family: The Origin and Treatment of Schizophrenic Disorders.* New York: Basic Books.

Lynd, R. S. and H. M. Lynd 1929 – *Middletown: A Study in American Culture.* London: Constable.

Maasdorp, G. and A. S. B. Humphreys (eds.) 1975 – *From Shantytown to Township: An Economic Study of African Poverty and Rehousing in a South African City.* Cape Town: Juta.

Marsden, D. 1973 – *Mothers Alone: Poverty and the Fatherless Family.* Harmondsworth: Penguin.

McCord, W. and J. McCord 1960 – *Origins of Alcoholism.* London: Tavistock.

Plant, J. S. 1963 – 'Family living space and personality development.' In N. W. Bell and E. Z. Vogel, *A Modern Introduction to the Family.* Glencoe: Free Press.

Queen, S. A. and R. W. Habenstein 1967 – *The Family in Various Cultures* (3rd edn.). New York: J. B. Lippincott.

Part 5:

Education

Introduction

GERD WIENDIECK

Education is part of the socialization process, which forms and moulds the individual into a smoothly functioning part of the complex web we call society. The connection between education and socialization is particularly clear in undifferentiated societies, where education has not been formalized and segregated, but takes place in the context of everyday activities in the family, the community, or religious groups. The learning process appears to be 'natural' since it takes place within the context for which it is geared, i.e. living and learning are one process. Learning is for life. A gap between educational objectives and the requirements for a successful and satisfying life does not emerge; this gives psychological security to the individual, but creates little social mobility and produces a stable though rather inflexible society. Social change and social progress towards particular goals are slow. Advanced industrialized societies, on the other hand, are characterized by a high degree of social differentiation and division of labour which require and depend on the formalization of education and its separation from the socialization process. The formation of a relatively independent institution specifically for the purpose of education is necessary. This necessity is the result of a shift from manual to mental labour and from low to high levels of skill (cf. Clark 1964:736). This training process is beyond the capabilities of traditional socializing agents such as the family, peer groups, and church. Advanced societies are moreover characterized by rapid scientific and technical development, which makes education within the context of everyday activities not only a difficult, but an impossible task, since skills required for tomorrow are simply not available in everyday experience of today's life. Experience in abacus calculations is of little use in computer programing and life-long experience in handling horses does not make a good motor mechanic.

The scientific study of education as a societal institution of its own has therefore two main targets, firstly the organization and dynamics of the educational institution as such, and secondly its relationship to the structure and the functioning of society of which it is a part. These could broadly be said to spring from the question: 'What are we analysing?' An additional question is: 'Why are we studying education?' This question presents us with the problem of whether we intend describing and explaining existing social realities as manifestations of social scientific laws, or constructing potential social realities as guidelines for change. This division has been symbolized by the phrase 'sociology of education *vs.* educational sociology' (Hansen 1967:21; Ashley 1969:9). The term 'educational sociology' is the older one and dates back to the early days of this century when sociologists believed that 'social science could provide the guidelines for the aims and values of education' (Ashley 1969:9). The first sociological textbook on education, entitled *Educational Sociology* (Snedden 1922) set the scene for a normative approach to these problems which was followed by many sociologists of that time (see Bolton & Corbally 1941). This approach, however, lacked a sound theoretical framework and a rigorous methodology and was 'more of an educational discipline than a sociological one' (Ashley 1969:9). The term 'sociology of education' symbolized the attempt to 'throw off this tradition of moral commitment' (Ashley 1969:9) and to utilize general sociological theories and empirical techniques for the analysis of education. This antagonism between an empirical positivistic approach and a critical normative one is by no means unique to the sociological study of education, but merely reflects the more general and still ongoing debate about the 'value-freedom' of the social sciences and the appropriateness of the natural science paradigm as opposed to the need for a unique methodology for the study of social phenomena (see Part 1:Theoretical perspectives). No scientific inquiry, however, can throw off its basic non-reducible and unprovable assumptions (axioms) without becoming anarchic, uncommunicable and incomprehensible. Neither can it throw off the normative element since the decision to study education already reflects a value commitment: 'Facts may speak for themselves, but they cannot select themselves,' as Inkeles (1964:3) vividly put it. Keeping this in mind we may say that a 'normative' educational sociology which takes no cognizance of social scientific methodologies and theories is as limited and unconvincing as is an 'empirical' sociology of education, which neglects to be aware of its underlying axioms and its implicit value judgements.

The influence of axioms, such as the basic concept of man, is particularly clear in the famous debate between Skinner and Rogers (1956) about the control of human behaviour. The decision to treat man as a free-will agent capable of shaping his own destiny, will inevitably lead to a view about meaning and purpose of educational systems which stands in sharp contrast to the one based on the assumption that man is a reactive being, who at best might be treated as a skillful observer and interpreter of his externally controlled actions. While Rogers recommends the removal of external controls as a precondition for man's growth, Skinner advocates a centrally planned system of positive reinforcement schedules as indispensible cornerstones for human and societal development.

The implicit value judgement of educational writings can most obviously be seen in a comparison of totalitarian and liberal educational goals (Lifton 1957, Dahrendorf 1975:74). The central question here is whether the individual is trained to become a 'spare part' (Dahrendorf) for specific requirements or whether all his human abilities are developed by opening them up for a variety of choices.

The paper selected for this volume argues for a liberal education. It should be noted, that the repressive and deactivating effect of an educational system is not necessarily the result of an intentional decision of a ruling elite, but that it could also stem from a consensually accepted ideological system which binds the powerful as well as the powerless by locating the causes of social reality in a realm beyond human will and control. This message tends to legitimize existing inequalities and grievances and thereby educates towards passivity and toleration.

Besides this fundamental query of 'What is (or should be) taught?' the questions of 'Who is (or should be) taught?' and 'How is it (or should it be) taught?' are revealing. Access to educational facilities and the bestowal of educational grades are not necessarily related to ability and merit but may show a closer link to group membership, political complaisance and topical needs of the economic system. A teaching process, which treats the pupil as a passive receiver of information and imbeds this communication process in an elaborate system of disciplinary norms and rules unrelated to the information content, reveals that besides the manifest function of information transmission, the school has the powerful latent function of preparing the adolescent for the role of an uncritical, loyal, and subservient citizen. Keeping these three aspects of content, context and access in mind we may classify an educational system as repressive to the extent that closed and particularistic criteria, rather than ability and human potential, determine educational goals and techniques and disruptive access to educational facilities and the bestowal of educational grades.

The paper by Dickie-Clark points to the built-in conflict and disruptive potential of segregated educational institutions in plural societies like South Africa. This disruptive potential is directly related to the central and dominant role educational systems play within industrialized societies. It is of particular interest to note that the racial unrest of 1976 was sparked off by the immediate repressiveness of the segregated South African educational system.

The centrality and dominance of the educational system can best be documented by showing its relationships to other social systems. A fundamental symbiotic link exists between the educational and the economic system in advanced industrialized societies. Education is the 'knowledge industry' (Machlup 1962) which produces the skill and brainpower necessary to maintain and develop industrial production which in turn creates surplus values as a necessary precondition for maintaining an increasing number of people inside educational institutions, i.e. outside the direct production process for longer periods of time. This interdependance of these two social systems created a hitherto unknown phenomenon: the inverse relationship between unemployment and level of education, i.e. the employability of the educated and the unemployability of the uneducated. No longer do the unskilled constitute a source of cheap labour but become an economic burden to society, especially with the spreading idea of social justice and society's obligation to guarantee minimum degrees of social security to all (Clark 1964:738). This sheds a new light on the homelands policy of the South African government, which can no longer be interpreted as an effort to create vast reservoirs of cheap unskilled migrant labour, but rather appears as an attempt to transfer social responsibility for the uneducated and hence unproductive and unemployable citizens.

A second point arises from the fact that rapid change in the occupational structure endemic to advanced industrialized societies results in skills soon becoming obsolete, necessitating retraining at all levels of skill (Clark 1964:738). The economy requires not only trained but retrainable labour, i.e. people with a rather broad educational base, which serves as a foundation for a number of different vocational programmes. A more fundamentally and broader educated labour force, however, is not only more flexible and productive, but also less controllable (Maccoby 1972:33). This may be dysfunctional to segregated societies, highly dependent on the controllability and repression of vast segments of the population. This growing mutual dependability between the educational and the economic system also has repercussions on the system of social stratification and mobility. Empirical research reveals positive correlations between education, occupation, income and social status in modern western societies (Blau & Duncan 1967, Jencks 1972). The link between the educational and the stratification system is twofold: The social stratum that one is born into determines educational achievement which in turn determines one's occupation and income, and thus social status. The first aspect points to the stabilizing effect of the relationship between education and stratification while the latter emphasizes the potential for mobility. The relevant question is whether the stabilizing or the mobilizing elements are the dominant ones. Clark (1964:741) points out: 'Family status is probably decreasing in relative importance, primarily because of the trend in modern society from ascription to achievement and the closer bond between education and economy.' So far the educational system has been characterized as central to the process of industrial development, social change and mobility, in short: education has been treated as a dynamizing social factor, but education also plays a role as a stabilizing and integrative element. This function, however, has also changed from the task of merely transmitting cultural traditions of society, its basic values, norms and behavioural patterns to the mandate of providing 'an introduction into an already dynamic society' (Mannheim 1951:248). If society is seen as a dynamic process, the crucial questions sociologists will have to ask are these: 'To what extent and by what criteria does education set the goals and the pace of this process, and to what extent is education a mere supplier for already existing demands?'

REFERENCES

Ashley, Brian J. 1969 – Harry Cohen & Roy G. Slater *An Introduction to the Sociology of Education.* London: MacMillan.

Blau, Peter & Otis Dudley Duncan 1967 – *The American Occupational Structure.* New York: John Wiley.

Bolton, Frederick E. & John E. Corbally 1941 – *Educational Sociology.* New York: American Book Company.

Clark, Burton R. 1964 – 'Sociology of education.' In R. E. L. Faris (ed.), *Handbook of Modern Sociology.* Chicago: Rand McNally.

Dahrendorf, Ralf 1975 – *The New Liberty. Survival and Justice in a Changing World.* The Reith Lectures. London: Routledge & Kegan Paul.

Hansen, Donald A. 1967 – 'The uncomfortable relation of sociology and education.' In Donald A. Hansen & Joel E. Gerstl (eds.) *On education: Sociological Perspectives.* New York: John Wiley.

Inkeles, Alex 1964 – *What is Sociology?* Englewood Cliffs: Prentice Hall.

Jencks, Christopher 1972 – *Inequality.* Harmondsworth: Penguin.

Lifton, R. J. 1957 – Thought reform of Chinese intellectuals. *Journal of Social Issues*, 13:5–20.

Maccoby, Michael 1972 – 'Introduction'. In Harold L. Sheppard and Neal Q. Herrick *Where Have All the Robots Gone?* New York: Free Press.

Machlup, F. 1962 – *The Production and Distribution of Knowledge in the United States.* Princeton: Princeton University Press.

Mannheim, Karl 1951 – *Freedom, Power, and Democratic Planning.* London: Routledge & Kegan Paul.

Rogers, Carl & B. F. Skinner 1956 – Some issues concerning the control of human behavior. *Science* 124:1057–1066.

Snedden, David 1922 – *Educational Sociology.* New York: D. Appleton Century Company.

The Dilemma of Education in Plural Societies: The South African Case

H. F. DICKIE-CLARK

It is a stock theme of sociologists that all societies, by definition, have some measure of stability, adaptability, and integration (cf. Fallding 1963). There are, however, many ways of attaining the necessary amounts of these properties, and societies differ not only in the means they use and the extent to which they use them, but also in how successfully they are used.

Some societies enlist willing support for the social order by means, among other things, of consultations, sharing in decisions, legal equality of status, and equality of opportunity for all. Other societies may rely heavily on means such as economic interdependence, material rewards, propaganda, or sheer force. Probably most societies use almost the whole range of means at their disposal at one time or another, and a major task of the social sciences is, therefore, to assess these various means and their consequences as objectively as possible so that informed and effective practical choices can be made.

There are some societies in which certain of these means are not used because they would radically change the character of the society. Among these societies are the so-called 'plural' ones which consist of two or more culturally different and socially distinct segments dominated politically by one of them. South Africa with its highly developed 'parallelism' is possibly the best modern example.[1] In a society of this kind, legal equality, universal franchise, and careers open to talent are by implication precluded.

The inability of such a society to make use of these means of achieving stability, adaptability, and integration places it in the fundamental dilemma of those who try to eat their cake and have it. For a society of this kind tries to be a single society in a political and economic sense, but at the same time insists on cultural and social differentiation.

Turning to the educational institutions in such plural societies, one can readily see that these cannot be conducted in such a way as to open all careers to talent, and so make the fullest use of their human assets, without endangering the plural character of the society. Since education is one of the chief means in modern societies of directing talents to suitable careers, this will clearly have serious consequences for the education of subordinate segments in plural societies. This chapter attempts to trace some of these consequences as they have shown themselves in the education of Africans in South Africa. It may also serve to indicate, in this one case at least, how much contradiction and conflict a society can absorb and counteract without breaking up completely. The long-foretold revolution in South Africa has not yet taken place and, now that the earlier neglect by sociologists of the positive contributions of social conflict has been redressed, perhaps the most important issue is the question of disruptive conflict and how one may judge when such conflicts are about to take place. If Coser (1956) is right, then the very limited area of normative agreement in plural societies must be a 'built-in' source of disruptive conflicts. Moreover, these societies often display the other danger signs noted by Coser, namely, deep cleavages on cultural and social lines and 'total' commitment and participation in sect-like political organizations which tend to be rigid and unresponsive to change. In fact, almost all such societies *do* have in the way of integrative factors are economic dependence and political force.

In a society of this kind, the education of the subordinate segments is likely to be torn between the need to equip them with the knowledge, skills, and attitudes they must have to play their part in the common economic and political institutions, and the need to preserve and even reinforce the cultural diversity and social segmentation on which the society rests. The thesis of this chapter is that, owing to this contradiction, not only is the education of subordinate strata in plural societies seriously impaired, but also that it serves to intensify the tensions and conflict already engendered by the plural character of the society as a whole.

Evidence for this thesis is provided by the case of African education in South Africa during the years before 1954 when it was for the most part in the hands of Christian missions. After that date, the central government, acting on the Bantu Education Act of 1953, began to take over African education with clearly very different aims. To what extent this so-called 'Bantu' education, as compared to 'mission' education, also provides support for the thesis of this chapter will be discussed later. The main evidence here presented is, however, drawn from the period of 'mission' education.

'Mission' education for Africans in South Africa has a history of over a hundred years. As time passed, the Churches received more and more financial assistance from provincial and the central governments; and these bodies gradually came to control and administer the academic side of the missionary establishments, although leaving the boarding and other domestic arrangements in religious hands. But despite this increasing help from government, African education remained as a kind of charitable good work, rather than reflecting any deliberate effort on the part of a wealthy government to uplift and make the fullest use of its people. Begun by missionaries more interested in conversion than in education for its own sake, it was tolerated rather than encouraged. It was vaguely thought to be useful to the Whites but, as yet, there was little demand for the services of educated Africans and the need for them was hardly recognized by Whites other than those actually engaged in the education and administration of Africans. Thus their education received only half-hearted official support, and was sustained chiefly by the devotion of the missionaries and the determination of the Africans themselves to get as much education as they could.

It must first be acknowledged that despite the grievous limitations of mission education, some of which are examined below, it did nevertheless achieve some measure of success. Quantitatively, this success can be gauged by the numbers of Africans who have gained various educational standards. According to figures given by the South African Institute of Race Relations (cf. Horrell 1953) one year before the central government began to take over African education, 31 per cent of Africans over ten years of age were literate and out of a population of some 10–11 millions, 167 126 had passed Standard 6 (elementary school), 38 572 had passed Standard 8 (secondary school), 8 488 had passed Standard 10 (matriculation), 1 064 were university graduates.[2] The number of Africans of school age receiving more than a very elementary education, totalling only some 3 per cent by 1953, is small indeed considering the wealth and development of the country. Nevertheless, the long years of missionary endeavour have meant that in South Africa there are a fair number of educated and professionally trained Africans.

Turning from this quantitative measure of achievement to a more qualitative assessment of mission education, it becomes readily apparent that many of its fundamental characteristics were directly determined by the plural structure of South African society. The strict segregation, the problems of which language(s) to use, the inadequacy of funds, and the fact that only about one-third of the population of school-going age ever got to a school of any sort are all features which are consequences of the subordinate position of the Africans in South African society. That these features seriously reduce the efficiency of educational institutions can hardly be gainsaid.

Two other features of the education of Africans at this time can also be traced to pluralism. First, the excessively 'bookish' curricula followed in most schools especially after the primary stage. Almost no technical or commercial subjects were taught, and often the only relief from book-work was gardening or some such lowly skill. No doubt, the more 'academic' subjects found favour in part because they were the cheapest to provide and partly because fairly early on the Africans themselves became determined to have as nearly as possible the same bookish education as the Whites received. But more important than these is the fact that careers based on technical and commercial curricula were simply not open to Africans.

Secondly, there was rigorous economic selection of pupils beyond the primary level. The costs of high school and university education were considerable and it was by no means certain that the best brains were the ones being educated. A study by the writer of matriculants at a large mission school over the years 1949–53 showed that virtually all the pupils were children of peasant farmers, teachers, clergy, and government clerks. There were almost no workers' children. Further evidence of the restricted mobility of subordinate strata in plural societies is the fact that these Africans on leaving school or university tended to follow their parents into these same callings.

A less obvious result of the Africans' position but one which also served to reduce the efficiency of African education, although in a less serious fashion, was the tendency of teachers and educational administrators 'to make allowances' for Africans in matters of standards of behaviour or scholastic achievement required. Where hardships are so obvious and the difficulties in getting an education are so great, it is a hard man, or one very confident of the worth of his own cultural values, who will not 'make allowances' but insist on the same standards for Black and White! In the domestic aspects of educational establishments it is virtually impossible not to take the disadvantaged situation of the African student into consideration. In purely academic matters there is a far more concerted and conscious effort to maintain standards and there are also more objective means of doing so. Nevertheless, while it is doubful whether anybody has ever got through an examination simply because he was an African, it is certain that many African students have not done anywhere nearly as well as they could have done simply because allowances were always being made for them and their best was never demanded.

These features of African education are, moreover, not only harmful in themselves; it could also be argued that they aggravate certain attitudes among pupils and students which further hinder their education and contribute to increased tension and potentially disruptive conflict. Certain of these attitudes would seem to be widespread among educated Africans and have been noted by other observers also (cf. Duminy *et al.* 1955; Kuper 1965). The attitudes selected for discussion here have to do with power and they are part of the larger sentiment favouring African rule and opposing continued White dominance. They express one side of the major division in South African politics which threatens the kind of fundamental cleavage along a single axis which Coser (1956) considers to be so disruptive.

The first, and perhaps most obvious of these attitudes is distrust of, and dislike for, Whites. Under the circumstances, any other attitude would be well-nigh miraculous. While it is true that an attitude of complete trust and affection would be equally dysfunctional in some human relations, there are areas, and education is surely one of them, in which excessive suspicion and dislike are especially damaging. For it leads to such distance between African students and White teachers as to make their relationships often sterile and frustrating to both. The elaborate ritual of politeness and the fear of giving offence tend to stultify contacts which should have been emotionally stimulating and fruitful for the education of the student and the teacher. No doubt sensitivity towards some issues may be sharpened precisely by suspicion and conflict, but in general an unrelieved atmosphere of distrust must serve to blunt or even block completely the reception of other ideas and insights. Where education goes beyond the imparting of information and skills to the passing on of values and attitudes, the learner must surely have some measure of confidence in the teacher's good faith and intentions. If, due to a blanket distrust of all Whites, the White teacher is seen as an agent of domination, either deluded or dishonest, then but little can come of his teaching.

Also stemming from their profound distrust of Whites is the demand of many Africans for an 'all-or-nothing', total commitment on the part of Whites offering friendship and support. This requirement for uncritical identification with the African cause is well illustrated in a book by Hopkinson (1962), sometime White editor of *Drum*. He reports an argument with Can Themba, an African reporter, in which Themba praises Father Huddleston for his whole-hearted identification with the Africans. Hopkinson attacks this abandonment of one's own judgement as wrong. But Themba replies:

> Nothing less is any good to us. We don't want someone who supports us when he thinks we're okay, but withdraws his support when we do something un-Western or ungentlemanly. We have had too much of this patronizing liberal attitude – pat us on the head when you think we're going the right way, kick us in the pants when we take a different turning.

Such a demand for total unreserved commitment to a cause or belief is, of course, a well-established characteristic of all sect-like organizations engaged in conflict. Its importance for the present thesis is that this kind of total commitment and participation in a movement or group is one means of bringing about a single disruptive cleavage and of finding, as Rex (1961:118) puts it, 'that the enemy on one front is also the enemy on others.' Segmental, conditional commitment which reduces the chance of a single basic rift is precluded by this kind of overweening loyalty.

The next cluster of attitudes to be considered is made up of African students' notions about the scope and uses of political activity.

In a country like South Africa where effective consensus about fundamentals is slight and where as a result political coercion is prominent, it is not surprising that people should come to think that there is politics in everything and that everything must be dealt with in political terms. Certainly many educated Africans accept this view and act upon it. Almost every issue, even the most trivial, seems to have political implications for them. This is probably no more than the simple truth and if that were all no great harm would be done. But this attitude often seems to go even further in that not only is everything thought to have political implications, but that this political significance is invariably considered to be *the most important aspect* of the event in all situations. Consequently, the other aspects are played down or ignored. This kind of single-minded oversimplification easily leads to the 'all-or-nothing' attitude already noted.

The practical consequences of the 'politics is all' mentality can be unfortunate in many routine activities. It sometimes entails that typically political *methods* of formal negotiations and agreements, boycotts, appeals to solidarity, and even intimidation are used in and out of season and for the slightest and most unsuitable purposes. Thus complaints or difficulties which could easily be put right by a word or action in the appropriate quarter are magnified into political issues which then necessitate meetings of the student body, petitions, formal negotiations, and all the paraphernalia of politics. When this happens the day-to-day running of an institution like a school or university, a newspaper or a hospital, becomes simply impossible.

Duminy *et al.* (1955:5–6) contains an excellent picture and diagnosis of this particular attitude, which indeed threatened totally to disrupt the College at one time. On the topic of the relationship between the Students' Representative Council and the Senate, the commissioners say:

> The humourless correspondence between these two bodies, which we have studied, reads like negotiations conducted between two 'High Contracting Parties' of equal standing in an atmosphere of cold war. The exaggerated sense of self-importance of the students as indicated in this correspondence is perhaps due to the feeling that the College must be looked upon as being in the vanguard of the political and racial struggle; but no university can run its ordinary day-by-day business on these lines, and it is very desirable that the students should learn what a Students' Representative Council is and what it is not.

The appeal to African solidarity is possibly the most notable and most frequently misused political technique in what could be relatively 'non-political' situations. This appeal to solidarity is traditionally and understandably the weapon of the powerless, but when used indiscriminately and outside its proper sphere it can only be damaging. For example, in universities devoted to objective scholarship and independence of thought it is singularly out of place.

It is obvious how such appeals for a united front contribute to a single disruptive cleavage along the single axis of colour, but the attitude is dysfunctional in the more immediate context of education as well. Anthony Ngubo of the University of California at Los Angeles, a former student of Natal University, is quoted by Leo Kuper (1965:163–4) as suggesting that it is very difficult for Africans to achieve scholarly detachment because of 'their mental energy being spent in political thinking' and because of the need to better themselves in employment and in status.[3]

Another component in the political attitudes of many educated Africans is the view of democracy as being simply majority rule. There is plenty of support for this attitude of both a practical and a theoretical kind. Successive White governments in South Africa have acted on this belief in respect of the enfranchised Whites and so have other governments elsewhere. D. V. Cowen (1961) quotes with approval Sir Carleton Allen's claim 'that on the whole' though no doubt with many exceptions, majority opinion does reach a sensible and workable solution of most practical problems of social life'. None the less, there are reasons for believing that, in a plural society, such a view of democracy as unqualified majority rule would contribute to conflict through its neglect of minority interests and rights.

The first of these reasons is that in their enthusiasm for the principle of majority rule, the qualifications and limitations set up by democratic theorists are overlooked. Thus Cowen insists on a fundamental bill of rights which would seriously hamper the majority in its attempts to achieve its aims. No doubt the desperate importance in an impoverished Africa of social and economic security makes African leaders impatient of restraint, but, as Andreski (1968) points out, this is why democracy has been so ineffective in Africa.

The second reason for holding majority rule, as understood by many educated Africans, to be disruptive in a plural society, was first set out by Georg Simmel (1922) in his note on the phenomenon of outvoting. There he showed that majority decisions have come to be invested by many of their supporters with a moral overtone. It is not merely *expedient* for the minority to submit, they are morally obliged to do so because in some mystical way the decision of the majority is taken to be the expression of a larger unity to which the minority is also considered to belong and which it is morally bound to obey. It would seem that this moral backing of majority decisions rests in turn on a consensual view of society as some kind of emergent unity over and above its component groups. It may be that where a large measure of consensus exists in a particular society, some such emergent unity can usefully be postulated and on this basis majority decisions may be justified. But where on the contrary no such measure of consensus exists, as is the case for instance in South Africa, then the attempt to give majority rule any moral backing is without doubt wholly unwarranted and can lead only to the repeated violation of the opinion and rights of minorities. In the process, the healthy criss-crossing temporary alliances of changing segments will be submerged in a single rift between a majority which is always morally right and minorities which never have a moral claim to prevail in any difference of opinion or clash of interests. If, then, in a plural society majority rule is thus invested with a moral claim on the minority, it can only increase the possibility of a single disruptive cleavage between whoever constitutes the majority and those making up the minority.

With the features listed earlier and with the attitudes just discussed, it is not surprising that mission education was in its later years racked by conflicts. For the most part, those teaching in the mission schools and colleges believed that they were educating Africans for a common, unified society which lay not too far off in the future. Hence they aimed to produce Africans who were culturally White and who would be able to fit into the common society which was thought to be evolving. Hence, also, the feature of social equality which was never able to get beyond the gates of the missionary establishments and, sometimes, not even that far. Looking back now, it is easy to see that this view underrated both the resilience of culture and the capacity of a pluralistic society to hold together despite deep cleavages and glaring inconsistencies.[4]

On the face of things, the new 'Bantu' education introduced by the Government after 1954 is quite different. In this kind of education for Africans the plural character of South African society is not only clearly recognized, but also presumed to continue indefinitely. Careers are to be open to African talents only in their own areas and there are to be no more 'Black Europeans'. In the words of the Minister of Bantu Education in Parliament, 'it is the basic principle of Bantu education in general that our aim is to keep the Bantu child a Bantu child . . . The Bantu must be so educated that they will want to remain essentially Bantu' (cf. Hansard, June 1959).

But is this lip-service to the plural character of South African society not perhaps just as superficial as was the social equality of the 'mission' kind of education? For the *content* of Bantu education remains 'Western' and it has to do so if the common economic and political structure of the plural society is to be served and to continue. The advocates of Bantu education may foster cultural diversity as much as they like and they may place their schools and universities as far out in the country as they please, but they must still reckon with and serve the common economy and political order of the plural society. Thus one may argue that Bantu education in *its* turn tends to underrate the *similarities* brought into being by the common institutions in South African society. It is possible to pretend not to *see* the similarities but it is impossible to stop the acculturation which produces them. As long as the plural character of South African society is maintained, the contradiction will remain, and the pressure of cultural similarity on the barriers maintaining social segregation must increase, even if slowly. The effect of Bantu education, no matter how segregated and controlled, must be to heighten the Africans' desire and ability to share in the common society. Thus one could expect Bantu education to produce somewhat similar attitudes and resentments on the part of its students to those produced by 'mission' education. For both kinds of education must serve the plural society in the same way – by fitting the Africans to serve the economic and political institutions common to the whole society.[5]

Therefore the conclusion suggested by these considerations is that in pluralistic societies all forms of education of subordinate groups must display features and attitudes similar to the ones discussed here. In this way the educational institutions will be reduced in efficiency and will have the latent effect of enlarging the conflicts of those societies.

However, experience shows that it is easy to overestimate the disruptive effect of such contradictions and dilemmas in a society. For it seems that they can be effectively 'contained' for long periods and perhaps even be compensated for in various ways. The case of women's inequalities and disabilities suggests that this might be so. The questions whether the effects of such gross inequalities as are found in South Africa *could* be cushioned and how this may be attempted lie outside the scope of this chapter. But perhaps two possibilities may be hinted at in conclusion. First, if the expectations of those suffering from discrimination are very low to begin with, then clearly they can be appeased by small material improvements in their lot over a considerable length of time. Secondly, the opening of even *some* careers to talent seems to be a surprisingly effective means of winning support. South African Bantustans and the whole paraphernalia of Apartheid may be far from an adequate substitute for full citizenship, but they do provide careers of a kind and, after all, the man who first effectively opened careers to talent in Europe also held that 'It is with baubles that men are led.'

In any event, it is clear that simplistic reliance on 'inherent contradictions' and incompatibilities between economic development and Apartheid or between authoritarian rule and stability will have to be revised and sharpened if future developments in Southern Africa are to be foretold with any useful degree of accuracy.

NOTES

1. The concept of a plural society used here is that based on the writings of J. S. Furnivall (1948), John Rex (1959, 1961), M. G. Smith (1960, 1961) and P. L. van den Berghe (1965, 1967). Their usage is almost the complete opposite of the term *pluralism* as it is used, for example, by Kornhauser (1959), Helge Pross (1963) and others, to describe societies in which a number of elites or interest groups have a share in making decisions and thus prevent the rise of a single ruling class.
2. *A Survey of Race Relations in South Africa* 1952–1953, 68. Not all the graduates would have come from the 'mission' university of Fort Hare since at this time the Universities of Cape Town, Natal, and the Witwatersrand admitted Africans. In 1962 figures given in the Race Relations *Survey* of that year, 183, were as follows:

Standard 6	....	295 600
Standard 8	....	75 000
Standard 10	....	15 200
University graduates	....	*c.* 2 000

3. Clearly, this line of argument, that excessive concern with the political aspects of education is detrimental to some 'educational process', conceived as politically 'impartial', is open to the charge that it is a disguised defence of the *status quo* and of White dominance. One suspects that here is an example of the kind of basic value conflict which Max Weber held to be impervious to logical or scientific solution. Either one holds that education 'at its best' has, or ought to have, some measure of autonomy; or one sees it as entirely determined by social and especially political forces. Stated more generally and in the terms of the current debate in sociology over functionalism: either one tries, as objectively as possible to set up criteria or standards on the basis of what men and societies appear from the evidence to 'need' and in this way attempts to measure existing social arrangements against them, or one becomes 'committed' to one side or the other of the prevailing political tussle and then uses this commitment as the measuring-rod.
4. John Horton (1966) seems to be suggesting that American liberals made something of the same mistake in believing that all the Negroes wanted was to become just like all the other Americans and happily compete with them for the latest model car and other outward signs of the American way of life.
5. It may be argued against this that Bantu education is designed to supply the needs of ultimately separate Bantu states. However, even if that is so, the dilemmas of a pluralistic society will only be intensified, for some Africans, Indians, and Coloureds are bound to remain in the so-called 'White' state.

REFERENCES

Andreski, S. 1968 – *The African Predicament.* London: Michael Joseph.

Coser, Lewis 1956 – *The Functions of Social Conflict.* London: Routledge and Kegan Paul.

Cowen, D. V. 1961 – *The Foundations of Freedom.* Cape Town: Oxford University Press.

Duminy, J. P., M. C. Botha and H. E. Brookes 1955 – *Report of the Fort Hare Commission.* Alice: Lovedale Press.

Fallding, Harold 1963 – 'Functional analyses in sociology.' *American Sociological Review*, 28, February, 5–13.

Furnivall, J. S. 1948 – *Colonial Policy and Practice.* London: Cambridge University Press.

Hansard 20, 17 June 1959, cols. 8318–20.

Hopkinson, Tom 1962 – *The Fiery Continent.* London: Gollancz.

Horrell, Muriel (ed.) 1953 – *A Survey of Race Relations in South Africa* 1952–1953. Johannesburg: South African Institute of Race Relations.

Horton, John 1966 – 'Commentary and debate.' *American Journal of Sociology*, 71, May, 701–21.

Kornhauser, William 1959 – *The Politics of Mass Society.* Glencoe: Free Press.

Kuper, Leo 1965 – *An African Bourgeoisie.* New Haven: Yale University Press.

Pross, Helge 1963 – 'Zum Begriff der pluralistischen Gesellschaft.' In Max Horkheimer (ed.), *Zeugnisse, Th. W. Adorno zum 60 Geburtstag.* Frankfurt: Europäische Verlagsanstalt, 439–50.

Rex, John 1959 – 'The plural society in sociological theory.' *British Journal of Sociology*, 10, June, 114–24.

——1961 – *Key Problems of Sociological Theory.* London: Routledge and Kegan Paul.

Simmel, Georg 1922 – *Soziologie* (2nd edn.). Munich and Leipzig: Duncker and Humboldt.

Smith, M. G. 1960 – 'Social and cultural pluralism.' Annals of the New York Academy of Sciences, 83, January, 763–777.

——1961 – 'The plural framework of Jamaican society.' *British Journal of Sociology*, 12, September, 249–62.

van den Berghe, P. L. 1965 – *South Africa: A Study in Conflict.* Middletown: Wesleyan University Press.

—1967 – *Race and Racism.* New York: Wiley.

Part 6:

Economy and Labour

Introduction

S. P. CILLIERS

In many circles, particularly in South Africa itself, there is a tendency to identify with the developed modern western world. Yet, viewed in its totality, South Africa is perhaps more properly to be seen as a developing country, and is, in many respects, in fact still part of the so-called underdeveloped world. In terms of Eisenstadt's (1966:53) distinction between 'old-timers' and 'newcomers' and between first and second phases of modernization, South Africa must be viewed as a newcomer to modernization, particularly to economic modernization. Up until the discovery of diamonds and gold during the last quarter of the nineteenth century, South Africa had an agricultural subsistence economy in which both the White settler population and the indigenous Black population were involved. Even these discoveries did not immediately involve South Africa in the process of economic modernization and industrialization. As elsewhere in the colonial world, it tended rather to accelerate and increase the degree of economic exploitation by the colonial power, with hardly any degree of diversification of the economy as a whole. It was only after the British Empire had been converted into a Commonwealth of Nations, during the twenties and thirties of the present century, in which each participant had gained a high degree of internal autonomy, that a slow process of economic diversification and in particular of industrial development was set in motion. (The article by Orpen in this part covers this history in some detail.)

It should therefore be noted that the modern economy of the country is of very recent origin, having emerged only during and since World War II. This modern economy is largely concentrated in and around a few major urban complexes and in certain areas of the White-occupied platteland where modernized agriculture for a market economy is being practised at a reasonably high level of efficiency. Large areas of the country, and in particular the Black homeland territories, are still in a state of economic underdevelopment and its population is being maintained through a combination of a subsistence agricultural economy and a dependency upon the proceeds of a system of migrant labour supplied to the White-dominated urban industrial and rural agricultural areas.

Since this time, the secondary and tertiary sectors of the economy have become increasingly important in achieving a high overall growth rate, with a concomitant expansion as a source of employment for the fast-growing labour force. Yet in spite of these basic changes in the structure of production, very few changes have occurred in the basic pattern of foreign trade. Agriculture, forestry, fishing and mining, producing primary products, still account for the lion's share of the export proceeds of the South African economy. Thus, as Leistner and Breytenbach have stated (1975:1):

> True, South Africa is the industrial giant of Africa . . . Yet, its economy is still heavily dependent upon the exportation of a few primary products, economic and socio-cultural life show striking contrasts between modern and traditional features; the large majority of the population are still in the process of transition from a tradition bound, rural way of life to a modern industrial society.

In economic and general social-scientific terms, such a situation is usually referred to as a dual economy. In the South African context, the complexities deriving from such duality, are, in the view of this author, compounded by the magnitude of a third type of economy, which may be termed the 'informal' economy, operating primarily in the tertiary or service sector. By this is meant that under circumstances where a large sector of the population is in the process of transition into a modern urban industrial society, particularly under circumstances which, as in South Africa, it is subjected to severe formal legal as well as informal traditional restrictions with regard to civil, political and social rights, an informal, almost clandestine socio-economic structure evolves which serves as a functional alternative to compensate for the absence of a properly developed social infrastructure. A typical example of this would be the shebeen. The economic significance of such 'informal' and often clandestine activities, and structures is, however, impossible to calculate in economic, monetary or statistical terms. Yet it should be recognized that such informal organizations and institutions produce services and goods and create job opportunities of real significance. However, in view of the informal, clandestine and often illegal nature of such activities, as well as the crude and simplistic way of accounting employed for the purposes of monitoring its economic fortunes, the magnitude of its contribution to and its significance in the total economy cannot be established. More important, it is never taken into account in the formal accounting system in terms of which the relative state of the economy as a whole is measured or assessed.

Evidence to support the thesis regarding this third type of informal interstitial economy which functions in a sense to bridge the gap between the formal modern industrial economy and the traditional subsistence economy under circumstances of rapid urbanization under severe formal disabilities imposed on those emerging from the traditional economy, is to be found, for instance, in the research reported by Gavin Maasdorp and A. S. B. Humphreys (1975:44–60). In a study of income in an urban shantytown in Natal, it was found that a 'disclosed income' deficit existed which could only be explained in terms of income derived from the informal sector of the economy of such urban areas. Undisclosed sources of supplementary income isolated by these researchers as typical of the informal sector in African cities are, for instance, illicit liquor traffic, handicrafts and artisan occupations; moneylending, borrowing and usury; gambling and sundry illegal activities.

In South Africa, economic modernization has tended to highlight the interdependence and economic integration of the various ethnic groups in the population. Yet, even in the pre-modern face of its history, the South African economy had been based on the integration of people of different ethnic and racial origins into the labour structure. Within a few years of the settlement by Van Riebeeck in 1652 a start was made with the importation of slaves and the involvement of the indigenous population in the labour force. Efforts by the relevant authorities to restrict this emerging integration were, throughout our history, overwhelmingly strongly resisted by the local settler population. Not only were such efforts resisted, but pressure was also continuously exerted on the authorities to use negative political sanctions to force the indigenous population into participating in the settler economy. Increasingly, particularly during the eighteenth and nineteenth century, successive governments had to revert to measures such as pass laws, indentured labour and the poll tax system in order to expand the supply of labour.

Thus during the whole period of history during which the economy of South Africa was basically an undifferentiated agricultural subsistence economy, market factors did not predominate in mediating the nature of labour relations in the economy. Neither was this situation significantly changed after the emergence of the mining industry during the last quarter of the previous century. After a preliminary bout of fierce competition, the mining industry soon organized itself into an effective monopsony through the creation of the Witwatersrand Native Labour Association through which Black labour for the industry was to be recruited. In this way market factors were, at least with regard to Black workers, also excluded from functioning as the effective mediating mechanism in determining the nature of labour relations in the mining industry.

While the development of the mining industry, therefore, did not have a significant impact on restructuring labour relations with regard to the Black labour force, it did introduce a significant structural change with regard to White labour. For the first time in the economic history of South Africa a significant demand for skilled labour, which could only be met by workers enticed from the Western World, arose, and wages therefore had to compete with wage rates elsewhere. A dearth of industrial skills, which has been a virtually permanent feature of the labour situation since this time, had developed. As Francis Wilson (1972:7) has put it so aptly:

> At first there were plenty of unskilled men able and willing to dig, but artisans were not so readily available. Those who were not willing to gamble their future on a lucky strike had to be enticed out of Europe by high salaries. Thus began the enormous differential between skilled and unskilled earnings. The situation was not unique but the peculiarity of the South African case was that the skilled men happened to be White and the unskilled happened to be Black. What had begun as a classical example of the free interaction of supply and demand gradually hardened into a rigid caste system.

The turn of the century and the first two decades of the present century reflect a titanic struggle by these White mine workers against their employers to retain and entrench their privileged position. This struggle was eventually effectively won by the mine workers with the institution of the Industrial Conciliation Act of 1925, the Mines and Works Amendment Act of 1926 and the civilized labour policy of the Pact government introduced during the mid-twenties. This proved, however, to be a victory not only for White mine workers, but in fact for the entrenchment of the position of White workers in general both with regard to real or potential competition from Blacks and with regard to a large differential between skilled and unskilled wage levels.

While the monopsonistic recruitment system curtailed the functioning of market factors in structuring labour relations in the mining industry, agriculture continued to pressurize government into extending negative political sanctions in order to guarantee a continued supply of Black workers for the industry. The Native Land Act of 1913, the Native (Urban Areas) Acts of 1923 and 1945, the Native Trust and Land Act of 1936, the various Native Labour Regulations and Labour Contract Acts, etc., all had the effect, albeit sometimes perhaps not consciously intended, of stabilizing farm labour and thus of curtailing the functioning of market factors in agricultural labour relations.

During the twentieth century a further factor, which was to structure the nature of industrial relations in South Africa, entered upon the scene in the form of the increasing number of unskilled Whites entering the labour force. Van der Horst (1942:157) summarized the effect of this as follows:

> In the twentieth century a cleavage of interest appeared between the European employee, on the one hand, and, on the other, the European employer and Native labourer. There were two aspects of this cleavage of interest. Some of the Native labourers began to acquire skill and to compete for work with European skilled artisans, and particularly with European miners. At the same time it became apparent that some of the Europeans who had no land were losing such means of support as were hitherto available to them. They had consequently to compete with Natives and other non-Europeans for unskilled work. In both cases Natives and Europeans became competing factors of production, and it was in the sectional interest of groups of Europeans to exclude Native competitors. The attempt of such groups to maintain or create a privileged position for themselves has been one of the dominating factors in the labour market of South Africa.

Jeffrey Lever (1974:43–60) has dealt in excellent fashion with this issue of White sectional interest and interracial labour competition, indicating that two major strategies followed by White workers are to be traced in the history of this issue thus far, viz. a '*unionist strategy*' of the rate for the job and a '*separationist strategy*' aimed at halting the process of economic integration. A study of the history of the trade union movement in South Africa will reveal the extent to which the movement vaccilated between these two strategies and remains even till today deeply divided on the very basis of this issue.

Ruling government policy and action have tended to favour the separationist strategy, but have thus far not been effective in halting the process of economic integration. At most, it has created the machinery for the protection of the interest of White workers, should the need arise, and has instituted a degree of separation in the work situation and in worker organizations.

Under these circumstances one should perhaps consider whether the realities of the present situation are still the same as those pertaining at the time when these approaches and strategies were first developed. In this connection the suggestion may be advanced that the economic and social realities of the current situation are vastly different from that of the first decades of this century, when this approach towards the relationship between White and Black in the labour situation first emerged. Firstly, however, it should be noted that the separationist approach is based upon the fallacy that economic integration between White and Black is a phenomenon of the recent past and of the present. As was shown above, right from the beginning of the formation of the South African society, the emerging economy involved the integration of Whites with Blacks in the form of slaves and increasingly also of people of indigenous descent. During this first phase of the economic history the workers consisted overwhelmingly of Blacks, i.e. of what are today termed Coloured and African workers. During this whole period labour also tended to be scarce, to such an extent that political sanctions were used in order to ensure an adequate supply of labour, and, as is known, several mass efforts to import labour were even embarked upon.

During the early part of the present century the economic roles of Whites and Blacks ceased to be only *complementary* to one another and for some Whites and Blacks, also became increasingly *competitive*. This occurred at a time when the general rate of economic expansion or growth was fairly low and when the economy experienced violent ups and downs in the business cycle. Population pressures were at the same time forcing increasing numbers of impoverished Whites and Blacks off the land and into the emerging cities. Both groups were relatively poorly equipped with the skills required by an emerging industrial economy. Hardly any social and institutional infrastructure that could provide a minimum of social and economic security had as yet been developed for any of the population groups. No formal system of industrial conciliation had as yet been instituted. Education and training for the labour needs of an industrial economy were virtually non-existent.

If we now compare this situation with current conditions, significant differences can be noted. Firstly, South Africa has made major strides in modernizing its total economy. While it is true that the mining and agricultural sectors still provide as it were the foundations of the economy in terms of the monetary value of its products, their overall importance from the point of view of providing economic opportunities for the population has diminished significantly. As late as 1946, the primary industries were still providing employment for 48,5%

of the economically active population while by 1970 this percentage had declined to 36,5%. Particularly during the immediate past, there is a clear trend for a rapid rate of increase of job opportunities in commerce and finance, transport and communication, construction and manufacturing, while the rate of increase in the primary industries tends to be relatively low. The type of labour structure which is fast emerging is one which tends to approximate that of a sophisticated, advanced, modern economy.

Secondly, it would appear that while it is true that the cyclical upswings and downturns in the economy had not yet become as effectively controllable as was thought possible a decade or so ago, extreme variations of the kind and nature which had characterized the previous era, seem to be less likely today than ever before. In other words, while the economy might not yet be totally manageable, it is no longer totally uncontrolled. More important, however, is the fact that a higher degree or social and economic security for the average worker and his family is continuously being built into the infrastructure of the socio-economic system.

Thirdly, the process of urbanization has also changed significantly over recent decades. Almost nine-tenths of the White and Asian population are already living in the towns and cities, and at present it is only the Coloured population which is still moving freely and at a high rate into the towns and cities. In the case of the African population, the population pressures for a rapid rate of urbanization are quite high, but strict measures of influx control try to ensure that over urbanization does not occur.

The spectre of real and abject poverty no longer haunts the Whites, but poverty is, of course, still very real in the case of the other population groups. As far as education and training for the needs of an industrial economy are concerned, the situation is also vastly more promising than a half-century ago. The shortages and demands for industrial skills which exist today are a function of the rapid process of industrialization and of the technological advances in an industrial age, in contrast to the total absence of any skills and the concomitant work-orientation of the twenties of this century. (See article by Diamond in this part.)

The conclusion which follows from the preceding analysis is therefore that the present situation is in reality significantly different from that which pertained at the time when the unionist and separationist strategies were devised. In fact, South Africa may very well *have moved beyond a situation of a cleavage of interest and of interracial labour competition into a new era of interracial labour complementarity.* There is virtual unanimity between all commentators in South Africa that the most important impediment to economic growth and well being in the country at present is a shortage of skilled manpower.

It may of course be argued that the interracial labour competition which gave rise to the strategies under consideration, was not only a matter of conflict over job-opportunities, but also a matter of differential wage levels. Even on this score, however, the situation today is significantly different from that pertaining at the time of the emergence of the strategies. Wages and conditions of employment are today overwhelmingly ruled by industrial agreements, and effective statutory machinery exists whereby such agreements and levels of pay could be extended to cover all categories of workers irrespective of race or colour. However, in view of the fact that a potentially large reservoir of Black labour exists, the future security of White workers may not be guaranteed.

It therefore becomes necessary to consider the prospects of a reduction of the population pressures among Africans in the homelands. While the progress obtained thus far in this connection is not spectacular, there are ample grounds for optimism that the forseeable future will witness an accelerated rate of development in these areas.

There are, however, other more impelling reasons for an appeal for a reconsideration of the wisdom of continuing to view labour relations between Whites and Blacks in terms of a cleavage of interests. It has been shown above that the South African economy has always involved an integrated labour structure. Under conditions of modernization and industrialization economic integration has developed new and impelling implications. The central question here is simply whether or not an integrated economy can be reconciled with a differential approach to the interests of the groups involved.

The paper by S. P. Cilliers (see selection in this part), deals with this subject. It shows that the social, political and broad economic implications of economic integration inevitably tie up with the nature of participation by the individual in the power system of the society. It shows that participation in the economic system cannot be divorced from the citizenship status of those involved. From this follows the conclusion that the strains in the economy and labour relations in South Africa cannot be effectively relieved without a restructuring of the political system.

REFERENCES

Eisenstadt, S. N. 1966 – *Modernization, Protest and Change.* Englewood Cliffs: Prentice-Hall.

Leistner, G. N. E. and W. J. Breytenbach 1975 – *The Black Worker of South Africa.* Pretoria: Africa Institute of South Africa.

Maasdorp, G. and A. S. B. Humphreys (eds.) 1975 – *From Shantytown to Township.* Cape Town: Juta.

Van der Horst, S. 1942 – *The Native Labour Problem of South Africa.* London: Oxford University Press.

Wilson, F. 1972 – *Labour in the South African Gold Mines 1911–1969.* Cambridge: Cambridge University Press.

1. White and Black Labour Relations in Historical Perspective

CHRISTOPHER ORPEN

(*a*) *Introduction*

It is difficult, if not impossible, to obtain a full understanding of the current labour situation without an examination of the historical forces and circumstances which led up to it. In this respect, it is important to remind ourselves of the fact, however trite it may appear, that present conditions and attitudes are not exclusively the product of current relationships in a society but are rather the result of historical developments evolved over the years and social attitudes handed down by previous generations. One of the biggest obstacles to improving labour relations in South Africa at the moment is the negative attitudes held by Whites of Black workers (and vice versa), whose origins lie in the kind of contact that the two groups have had with each other in the past in the work setting. In speaking of inter-group attitudes, the anthropologist Little (1951:167) makes the point clearly: 'Racial attitudes do not exist *in vacuo*. As they are not biological in origin, they can only be social. This means that they must be the product not only of existing circumstances but of the kind of contact which the groups concerned have had with each other in the past.' The psychologist MacCrone (1937:673), speaking specifically of inter-group attitudes in South Africa, makes the same point: 'Race attitudes have a long history so that some indication of why and how that history is to be taken into account is essential if we are to understand the way in which these attitudes operate at the present time.'

(*b*) *The Days Before the Discovery of Gold and Diamonds*

Until the second half of the nineteenth century, there were few, if any, wage-paid workers in South Africa. The majority of the population, both White and Black, were engaged in agricultural pursuits. Only a very small proportion, mainly settled in Cape Town, were involved in commerce, trade and transport. In the tribal areas, the Blacks continued their traditional subsistence farming practices in small local units, usually consisting of a few connected families. There was no wage labour because, in terms of the tribal structure, cultivation was done by members of the families according to a time-honoured division of labour. Most of the White farmers, despite popular beliefs to the contrary, were also engaged in subsistence farming. If they sold their produce, it was only a small proportion. In the Cape most of the farm labour was provided by either the Hottentots or the Coloured descendants of slaves who had been freed in 1834. Since few farmers earned any significant income in cash, cash wages were virtually non-existent, with most labourers gaining remuneration in kind, usually in the form of cattle, grazing rights or the erection of a hut. In Natal, the Orange Free State and Transvaal, most of the farm labour was done by Blacks, who lived like their counterparts in the 'tribal' lands save that, for the permission of living on the White man's farm, they had to devote some of their time to working for him. The standard of living, not only of the non-White farm labourers but also of the White frontier farmers, was very low, with few luxuries or leisure. Generally, the relationship between Whites and non-Whites was essentially that of masters to servants, improved by the fact that both were mutually dependent on each other and by the fact that often the White farmer showed a high degree of benevolent paternalism toward his non-White servants.

However, it should not be thought that the interaction between White farmers and their labourers, frozen into a master-servant kind of relationship, was not without negative attitudes on both sides. Historians seem agreed that, unlike the liberal attitudes of the seventeenth century which favoured the assimilation of those Blacks who had accepted the Christian religion, by the early nineteenth century the attitudes of the frontier farmers was already characterized by intolerance and discriminatory views, with the Whites wanting to maintain a large degree of social distance between themselves and their Black workers. In contrast to the seventeenth century, when miscegenation was fairly common and carried little stigma and when 'free Blacks' were considered a distinct social group with equal rights as Whites, by the early nineteenth century the White man who married a Hottentot was looked upon as an outcast, while the offspring of such a marriage formed a distinct social group, frequently subject to the same discriminatory laws as Blacks.

Among the frontier farmers, who formed something like 70 per cent of the White population by the 1850s, these traits of antagonism and exclusiveness seemed to have been well developed. For our present purposes, it is important to note that these early frontier farmers, being thrust against and among opposing Black groups in large numbers for the first time, were being confronted with many of the problems that exist in South Africa today. The authoritarian attitudes of in-group superiority and out-group rejection which developed should be seen in the context of the times. For instance, in many ways it is not surprising that the White farmers, who themselves (or their parents) had been successful in beating back the 'threats' from first the Bushmen, then the Hottentots and finally the Bantu, should feel superior to the latter groups. It also appears natural that in a frontier situation, marked by a bloody struggle between the farmers and the Black hordes for arable land, an attitude of tolerant acceptance should be regarded as inappropriate. Even the most 'liberal' critics have found it difficult to reconcile attitudes of kindly tolerance towards Blacks that would encourage assimilation, with the frontier situation (virtually the whole of South Africa in 1850) in which the short-term existence of the White man depended, quite literally, on the subjection of the opposing Black forces. It is difficult, in this respect, to avoid the conclusion that the attitudes of many White farmers that came to the fore at this time – a feeling of racial superiority and antagonism towards Blacks – were, in some respects, the only effective ones in terms of the situation in which they found themselves, whether they be ethically justifiable or not. Since manual labour was left entirely to the slaves and later the Coloureds and Blacks, it is not unexpected that, in addition to these attitudes of rejection, over time the frontier farmers came to regard any form of hard toil as the natural function of Blacks. During the frontier period an association developed between a white skin and certain kinds of work on the one hand and between a black skin and other kinds of work on the other hand. Moreover, the nature of the farmers' religion, with its Calvinist dichotomy of mankind into those predestined to salvation and those to damnation, provided the Whites with an ideal pattern into which to fit their inter-racial attitudes. Hence, by 1850 we find that most Whites in South Africa, especially the farmers, held an outlook which linked a white skin with Christianity and superiority and a black skin with paganism and inferiority.

The important point is that, before the discoveries of gold and diamonds in the second half of the nineteenth century, the stage was already set for the development of inter-group attitudes that have bedevilled attempts, right up to the present time, to improve the relations between Blacks and Whites in the work situation. In short, that the transformation of South Africa from a subsistence agricultural country to a fairly sophisticated industrial country occurred initially within a social psychological framework characterized by attitudes of intolerance and rejection on the part of Whites toward Blacks and attitudes of suspicion and lack of trust on the part of Blacks toward Whites, and a pattern of interaction marked by a formal master-servant kind of relationship.

(*c*) *The Beginning of Industrialization: Labour Relations on the Mines*

The discovery of diamonds in 1867 followed by the discovery of the world's greatest gold-bearing reef less than two years later, altered the economy of South Africa drastically. From our present point of view, the most important aspect of these discoveries was that they led to an almost insatiable demand for labour, as a result of which a fairly large and heterogeneous labour force came into being in South Africa for the first time. The mining industry immediately introduced a completely new element by offering hitherto unprecedented opportunities for earning cash wages. In view of the absence of local skilled labour, the mines were forced to import workers from overseas, notably from Britain and Europe. Naturally, high wages had to be paid to secure their services. To keep the wage bill within manageable proportions, the mines were thus correspondingly compelled to pay relatively low wages to the very many Black workers who, initially at least, did not possess the skills to do anything other than the simplest repetitive tasks. In the beginning the greater skills of the 'imported' White miners were, perhaps justifiably, rewarded by paying them much higher wages than the unskilled Black miners, who were nevertheless still paid much more than they were used to earning on the White-owned farms or in subsistence tribal agriculture.

The fact that they were capable of earning more on the mines resulted in an unprecedented movement of Blacks from the rural areas to the rapidly-developing mining towns. The effect of this over-supply of unskilled Black workers and the difficulty of getting White workers from overseas to do the skilled jobs was to further widen the 'natural' gap between the low wages of Blacks and the high wages of Whites on the mines. In short, it appears as if the disparity between skilled and unskilled rates was, at the beginning, mainly a reflection of the relative supply and demand situations on the mines at the time (1850–70), caused in turn by the great abundance of unskilled workers and great scarcity of skilled workers in an undeveloped country thrust hastily into an industrial era, without any period of grace. Moreover, this Black-White disparity in wages and kind of work fitted easily and rather conveniently (for the Whites) into the traditional attitudes and interaction patterns that had been established by the farmers, who formed the majority of the population before 1850, which dictated that White men should perform only supervisory, administrative and, perhaps, highly-skilled jobs, leaving the unskilled and menial tasks to be done by Blacks.

The immigrant White miners brought trade union ideas with them. In general, these ideas, which had been gaining popularity in Britain and the Continent, maintained that skilled artisans could maintain and advance their position in industrial society only by standing together and offering a united front. This was done not only negatively, by strike action, but positively, by carefully guarding their standards of training and quality of work. These 'old style' trade unions, to which many of the immigrant miners belonged, did not include unskilled workers in their ranks. They were fairly exclusive and allowed only competent workers, who had shown they possessed the necessary skills, to join the union. Given the apparent inferiority of the unskilled Black miners, these immigrant White miners, imbued with these trade union ideas, soon began, not unnaturally, to believe that their advancement as a group would be seriously impaired if they allowed Blacks to join the loose association of White miners that existed at the time. With unsophisticated illiterate Black miners as their only example of non-Whites, these White miners felt that their jealously guarded standards would be eroded if Blacks were given skilled work. However, in view of the great cultural gulf between White and Black workers, plus the large and obvious difference in their relative level of skills, the White workers did not really feel threatened by the possibility of Black advancement at this early stage.

It is difficult to establish what were the precise events which made this potential threat a reality in the minds of the White workers. De Kiewiet (1941) feels that it was the importation of Chinese workers in 1904, made necessary by the acute labour shortages after the Anglo-Boer War of 1899–1902. Unlike the Black miners, these Chinese miners, with their much higher level of skills, were regarded as a threat by the White miners to their privileged position. At any rate, shortly after the arrival of the Chinese miners, the White miners' latent fears erupted and, with the success of the trade union movement in Britain and the Continent in the forefront of their minds, they decided formally to close their ranks to protect their position as skilled workers. They were able to put pressure on the government to pass Ordinance 17 of 1907, which allowed the employment of 'non-White' immigrants (i.e. Chinese) only as unskilled labourers. As a result of political pressure (mainly from Britain) the Chinese miners were repatriated, never to return. However, the 'interlude' had the important consequence of making clear to the White miners that, with sufficient pressure, they could get the government, consisting mainly of farmers, to pass legislation effectively removing them from Black competition.

(d) The Beginning of Job Reservation

By 1911 nearly 35 per cent of the White miners had been born in South Africa. Unlike their predecessors, who were mainly immigrants, these miners had been reared on South African frontier farms where attitudes of White superiority and Black inferiority held sway. Hence, when they moved to the mining towns they naturally took these attitudes with them. These attitudes, forged in the battle for supremacy in the days of the opening-up of the interior, fitted easily into the climate of opinion that existed among the older White miners. Moreover, they enabled the latter to justify the discriminatory legislation which they had been partly instrumental in getting established. They now started stating openly that they did not want Blacks to do skilled work (e.g. blasting), because of the latter's inherent incapacity for this kind of work. Strikes by the White miners, who by now consisted mainly of South African-born men, against what they considered further inroads into their privileged position by Blacks, led to the passing of the Mines and Works Act of 1911, which prohibited Blacks from holding blasting certificates, allegedly in the interests of safety, and specified the number of Black workers a White foreman could supervise, to prevent the number of Blacks employed from outrunning the number of Whites. By this Act, the Colour Bar was legalized. From now onwards, White labour had the protection of a statute as well as that afforded by their greater skill and efficiency and the force of public opinion. The important point is that this Act, in a significant sense, was made possible by the widespread existence of a set of authoritarian attitudes of in-group supremacy and out-group inferiority which, as shown earlier, were developed initially in response to a genuinely threatening position and passed down from an earlier generation of frontier farmers. Previous legislation had been mainly concerned with increasing the supply of Black labour and making it more manageable and had been necessitated by the competition of Whites and Blacks for land and water. Now, as De Kiewiet (1941:66) so clearly puts it: 'Almost within the first year of union, an Act of Parliament (the Mines and Works Act) recognized that a new social and economic frontier had taken place of the old frontier. Where the natives were once excluded from land and ample water, now they were kept afar from skilled labour and high wages. Where once the natives had been driven from the land to labour, now men began to consider the possibility of driving them from labour back to the land.'

However, this Act did not solve South Africa's pressing labour problems.

In fact, 1911 saw the start of an intensified conflict between the three forces, represented by the government, who sought internal peace and stability, the White workers, who wanted good jobs for themselves, and the Black workers, who desired advancement to better jobs. After the First World War (1914–18) White labour, previously in great scarcity, became more abundant as depressed farming conditions caused many 'poor Whites' to leave the rural areas and drift into the cities and towns to seek work. Industry and commerce found it difficult to fit these unskilled workers into the pattern of labour relations that had been established during the preceding fifty years. Upper-level jobs were restricted to skilled Whites, entrenched behind their apprenticeships, their solidarity and high wages. Lower-level jobs were filled only by Blacks, at the mercy of the Whites by virtue of their lack of skills, their disorganized condition and their low wages. In terms of their race, the poor Whites belonged to the upper ranks. In terms of their level of skills, they could be fitted in only at the bottom ranks. In short, they were White men who, in many respects, were living like Black men. In view of the danger that by living like Blacks, sharing the same kinds of jobs and living standards as the latter, these poor Whites would (via intermarriage) become Black or at least Coloured, the government had to do something about the situation. As the historian Malherbe (1946:22) points out: 'At the time a very appreciable portion of our White population was fast sinking below the economic standard of living which was considered a White man should maintain by virtue of his white skin over against the native.'

Before the First World War various relief schemes, based on charity, had been instituted to help uplift the poor White. However, they had done little to actually increase the job opportunities open to the latter. After the war, the position of the poor Whites worsened and, with the slump in trade and revenue in the early 1920s, their plight became desperate. At the same time the mining industry, also in the midst of an economic crisis, responded by attempting to substitute a certain number of Blacks for Whites and altering the proportion of highly-paid Whites and lowly-paid Whites, in an effort to reduce costs. The White workers saw this as a direct threat and responded by arming themselves, going on strike and calling on other workers to join them. The result was the Rand Rebellion of 1922 which had to be put down by force by the government. This action, the grievances of the White workers, the poor general economic climate (for which the government was blamed) and, most important, the feeling on the part of the poor Whites that the government was not doing enough for them, led two years later to the overthrow of the government and brought the coalition government, consisting of members of the Labour Party (mainly English-speaking workers with socialist sympathies) and members of the National Party (mainly Afrikaans-speaking farmers) into power for the first time. The Labour Party was principally concerned with protecting the skilled workers in mining and industry, while the National Party were particularly moved by the plight of the unskilled Whites, who were drifting into the cities and towns in even larger numbers than before.

(e) The Civilized Labour Policy

With a clear mandate from the electorate, the government therefore embarked on a deliberate policy of protecting the position of the skilled Whites and providing work for the poor Whites. The implementation of these policies led, step by step, to the separation of the population on racial lines. With this separation went an increase in the social and cultural distance between the White rulers and their Black subjects, which was mainly responsible for breeding a remarkable ignorance about the wants and abilities of Blacks on the part of their White rulers, which has continued to the present day. In the absence of knowledge, the scope for prejudice was correspondingly increased. It was at this time that the negative views held by the White worker as regards his Black inferior really appear to have become crystallized. As can best be indicated by the kind of historical analysis presented in this chapter, these hostile attitudes should be seen simply as the outgrowth of a peculiar set of historical events and accidents, caused in turn by the existence of a small and relatively sophisticated white group amongst a very large and primitive Black population with whom there was a bloody struggle for the spoils of the land.

It appears clear that by the 1930s White industrial society had taken over the habits of mind of the White frontier society of the nineteenth century. It is not surprising that the White workers, reared in this climate and seeing Blacks only in clearly inferior positions, should forget that the latter were in these positions because of the White man's decrees and instead come to believe that the Black workers were just naturally inferior to themselves. Moreover, the increasingly superficial kind of contact that the White workers had with their Black workers allowed them to hold this belief in the innate superiority of the White man without fear of contradiction. This belief, which was supported by popular opinion in the towns and by the authority of the Bible in the country, in turn justified the Whites' determination to maintain their dominant position in South African society. In fact, it was widely believed in the 1930s that by maintaining White standards not only the Whites but also the Blacks would benefit. It was felt to be a highly responsible and not a selfish act to keep control of the instruments of power in the only hands that could use it properly, those of the White man.

The exclusion of Blacks from certain kinds of work and from the owning of land outside the African Reserves was legalized in several Acts passed by the coalition government, among them the 1926 Amendment to the earlier Mines and Works Act, which provided that positions of responsibility in the mines must beheld by White persons, the Apprenticeship Act of 1922 which, through the imposition of educational requirements for apprentices, had the effect of barring Blacks from certain skilled trades, and the Native Urban Areas Act of 1930, which gave the government the power to control the presence of Blacks in urban areas. These laws, which excluded Blacks from certain kinds of work and certain living-areas, became known as the Colour Bar Laws. Since then the term 'colour bar' has come, more generally, simply to refer to the entire complex of obstacles, some of them legal and administrative, others conventional (but no less keenly applied) which, since this time, have opposed the rise of Black workers in the industrial and commercial life of South African society.

The restriction of Black workers to jobs at the bottom end of the occupational spectrum was not only the result of the application of colour bar legislation, but was also encouraged by the fairly widespread existence of what has become known as the migratory labour system. This term refers to the system whereby a proportion of the Black labour force do not reside permanently at or near their place of work but circulate continuously between the subsistence economy of the African Reserves and the industrialized economy of the White man's cities and towns. The workers within this system merely work in the industrial areas for a period and then return to their tribal homes in the African Reserves for a time before coming back to the industrial areas again, usually to another job. This oscillation of Black workers between 'two worlds' was a feature of the South African economy from the time of the discovery of diamonds and gold, but was given extra strength by the 'civilized labour policy' of the government in the 1920s, which made it impossible for Blacks to acquire land outside the African Reserves and by the development of direct recruitment by the mines of Black workers in the Reserves themselves, usually done on a contract basis. Prevented from gaining a permanent footing outside the African Reserves and being only on contract for a specific period of time, it is not surprising that so many Black workers continued to regard the African Reserves as their home and their stay in the cities and towns of White South Africa merely as temporary visits, made necessary by the need to supplement their meagre resources in the Reserves.

By its very nature, the migrant system tended to inhibit the acquisition of those skills and abilities that were needed if the Black workers was to rise to a job above the level of unskilled labour. This suited the White workers at the time because it made the Black worker that much less of a threat. It was also a satisfactory arrangement for many industries in that it enabled them to get new recruits at a low cost each year. What was lost in efficiency and training costs was more than offset by the very low wages that could be paid. Moreover, as long as the work was of a very simple nature, the new recruit literally could not perform much worse than his experienced counterpart and the cost of training was minimal, usually consisting of little else other than telling the worker to follow the example of someone currently doing the job. The responses of White managers to the system was to establish schedules of production that capitalized upon its main features – the provision of cheap and abundant labour. As a result, starting in the 1920s factories were set up in such a way that a few highly skilled persons were called upon to supervise a large number of unskilled workers.

During the years leading up to the Second World War (1939–45) labour relations were characterized by laws and amendments and by individual action designed to draw more clearly the lines between White workers, usually skilled, on the one hand and Black workers, usually unskilled on the other. While protection of the White worker and his standard of living was the main aim and while some of the legislation and behaviour, on the part of Whites, sprang from the prejudices handed down from the frontier days, the policy and its application were not inconsistent with the genuine feeling that segregation was in the best interests of both Black and White workers. It would be a mistake to assume that it was born out of some malicious enjoyment at seeing others suffer or being oppressed.

(f) The Introduction of 'Separate Development'

The immediate post-war government was faced with a host of problems that had been hidden during the war or, in the aftermath of victory, were believed to be able to solve themselves. The cost of living soared, an acute shortage of housing developed as soldiers returned and there was a scarcity of materials. None of these problems was dealt with effectively by the government. At the same time, the White voters were becoming increasingly worried about the accelerated flow of Blacks to the towns and cities. For the first time, they felt threatened politically by the insistent demands for more rights and voting privileges (plus higher wages) made by the African National Congress, representing these Blacks, which was growing in influence and numbers as a body. There was a growing belief that in these vital matters the government did not have a clear-cut policy. Mainly for these reasons, the National Party came into power for the first time in 1948, with a mandate from the electorate to put their policy of apartheid or separate development into effect. This they did with a set of legislation designed to put into practice their belief that the choice before White South Africans was between either integration, which it was felt would amount to national suicide on the part of the Whites, or apartheid, in which Whites and Blacks would be separated into territorially distinct areas.

This so-called Apartheid Legislation covers, among others, the Industrial Conciliation Act of 1956, which made it possible for jobs, on the advice of a tribunal, to be reserved for Whites only and also outlawed racially-mixed trade unions. In 1953 the Native Labour Act was passed, which forbade strikes and lock-outs by Black workers and established Regional Labour Committees, under the direction of White appointees, to look after Black labour matters. In order to control the inflow of Blacks into the 'White' areas of South Africa, a number of so-called Pass Laws were enacted under which Black workers needed permits to enter designated urban areas. To ensure that the various races lived apart and did not mix socially, the Group Areas Act of 1950 was passed, which set aside specific living-areas for Blacks and for Whites. To prevent a 'fusion' of the White races with other races, the Immorality Amendment Act of 1950 was passed, which made sexual intercourse between persons of different races a punishable offence. Finally, the Universities Education Act of 1959 provided separate universities for Whites and Blacks. The main purpose of all this legislation was to achieve as much separation of the different racial groups as possible even at the expense of industrial and commercial efficiency. As one of the original architects of the policy described it: 'Apartheid consists in separating the heterogeneous groups from the population of the country into separate socio-economic units, inhabiting separate parts of the country and enjoying in his own area full citizenship rights, the greatest of which is the opportunity for developing such capabilities as its individual members may possess to their optimum capacity' (Eiselen 1950, 13).

The application of separate development, as the policy of apartheid has subsequently been called, was 'justified' in a number of ways, most of them derived from the belief that the White and Blacks are different 'races' and cannot live together in one political state, without either creating injustice to the Blacks or the decline of the Whites' power. Specifically, it was argued that the White race is the heir to western civilization and has the mission to protect and perpetuate this civilization. Because of this mission, the South African Whites, being in a minority, cannot allow the integration of the races because such mixing would mean the loss of the purity which is necessary for the maintenance of White civilization (Oliver 1953). It was also contended that the White man, as the guardian of the Black races, has the specific duty of ensuring that the latter develop along their own lines. This conception, in turn, is based on the view that a race can fulfil itself only if it remains true to its inner laws and processes which are radically different from those of other races. Consistent with this belief in the incompatibility of the White and Black ways of life was the idea that the best service the Whites can do is to maintain, or even reintroduce, the latter's original social forms and to provide them with living-areas in which they may preserve the customs, languages, and other aspects of their culture (Verwoerd 1955). Finally, it was contended that, by preventing the integration of non-Whites into the White industrial community, they will be spared the frustrations and bitterness that would result from their inability to compete effectively with Whites (Theron 1952).

(g) *The Current Resolution*

Since 1948 the South African economy has grown rapidly and with this growth has gone an increased demand for labour of all kinds from all races. Despite the attempt of the government to hold back the process, the proportion of Black workers in the total labour force has steadily increased. In an important sense, the 'drive to maturity' which has characterized the South African economy since 1948 has resulted in the various members of the labour force, irrespective of race, becoming inextricably more dependent on each other. In the face of apartheid legislation aimed at separating the races, they have become more integrated at work than ever before. This has even been acknowledged by some champions of separate development, who have responded by claiming that it should, nevertheless, be a main consideration of White employers to replace their Black labour in the 'white' areas of South Africa as far as possible by White workers. Some of them have argued optimistically that, by an increase in the White population and greater mechanization, planning and co-ordination, the White economy will at some time in the distant future be capable of supplying its own labour requirements.

Whether this is likely or not, most economists are agreed that the practical implementation of the separate development policy has already restricted the growth in the South African economy to a rate lower than would otherwise have been the case (Franklin 1954; Houghton 1964; Norval 1962; Brand 1972). These restrictions have been of such a magnitude that the government has been forced to grant exemptions, allowing Blacks to perform certain classes of skilled work. Even in cases where formal exemptions have not been granted, White employers who have disregarded the existing job reservation laws have often been allowed to get away with it. Hence, in practice, there exists a labour situation characterized by a large, but not complete, degree of racial separation in the interests of apartheid, along with a certain degree of integration for the sake of economic development. One of the basic problems is that, even if the government were keen to jettison the idea of racial separation, the majority of the White electorate in the mid 1970s would not support it.

This is because the negative attitudes toward Blacks held by the Whites that have grown up during the course of over 200 years still linger on today. Although it is not acknowledged as openly as previously, the average White voter still seems to hold some of these feelings of white Superiority and fears of domination that characterized his frontier farmer forbears (Orpen 1971*a*, 1971*b*; Schlemmer 1974). That this is so is due to a series of historical events, outlined in this section, which spring from the peculiar conflict situation that has existed in southern Africa for the past 200 years, in which a 'civilized' White minority has existed among a 'primitive Black majority in a balance of strength and numbers that has made it difficult for a solution to be reached. On the one hand, from the beginning the Whites have been too strong and well-entrenched to abdicate their privileged position; if there had been markedly fewer of them they could perhaps not have resisted the pressure from the Black majority, as has occurred elsewhere in Africa. On the other hand, from the beginning the Blacks have been too weak to force the Whites to abandon their privileged position; if there had been significantly more of them they could perhaps have successfully absorbed the Whites, as has occurred elsewhere in Africa. From the 'critical' proportions of Whites and Blacks that has existed in South Africa from the start, the current labour situation has emerged step-by-step, with a kind of tragic inevitability that makes a mockery of simplistic explanations that see the roots of the current situation as lying within the peculiar psychological make-up of White South Africans.

REFERENCES

Brand, S. S. 1972 – 'The socio-economic aspects of productivity improvement.' Proceedings of the National Development and Management Foundation Conference on Effective Utilization of Labour.

De Kiewiet, C. W. 1941 – *A History of South Africa; Social and Economic.* London: Oxford University Press.

Eiselen, W. M. M. 1950 – 'Is separation practicable?' *South African Journal of Racial Affairs,* 8:1–20.

Franklin, N. N. 1954 – *Economics in South Africa.* Cape Town: Oxford University Press.

Houghton, D. H. 1964 – *The South African Economy.* Cape Town: Oxford University Press.

Little, K. 1951 – 'Race and society.' In Unesco (ed.), *The Race Question in Modern Science.* Paris: United Nations Educational and Scientific Commission.

MacCrone, I. D. 1967 – *Race Attitudes in South Africa.* Johannesburg: Oxford University Press.

Malherbe, E. G. 1946 – *Race Attitudes and Education.* Johannesburg: South African Institute of Race Relations.

Norval, A. J. 1962 – *A Quarter of a Century of Industrial Progress in South Africa.* Cape Town: Juta.

Oliver, N. J. J. 1953 – 'Apartheid: A slogan or a solution?' *Journal of International Affairs,* 7:136–44.

Orpen, C. 1971a – 'Authoritarianism and racial attitudes among English-speaking South Africans.' *Journal of Social Psychology,* 84:301–2.

——1971b – 'The effect of cultural factors on the relationship between prejudice and personality.' *Journal of Psychology,* 78:73–79.

Schlemmer, L. 1974 – *Privilege, Prejudice and Parties: An Analysis of Patterns of Political Motivation Among White Voters in Durban.* Johannesburg: South African Institute of Race Relations.

Theron, P. A. 1952 – *A Psychological Approach to Separate Development.* Pretoria: South African Bureau of Racial Affairs.

Verwoerd, H. F. 1955 – 'Bantu Education: Policy for the Immediate Future.' Pretoria: Department of Native Affairs, Information Service.

2. Economic Perspective on Organised Labour and Socio-Economic Development

CHARLES R. DIAMOND

It is not an easy task to throw fresh light on the South African labour scene. I hesitate to tread on ground which has been so well covered by economists, sociologists, political scientists and, last, but decidedly not least, a heterogeneous category of non-academics. We all have our own duly weighty 'assessment' with perspectives influenced by a set of prejudices arising out of the South environment and our own more specific backgrounds. I have believed for some time that we tend to take too restricted a view of the South African labour scene. I would like to suggest a framework which is at least partially interdisciplinary and which, I think, helps to explain the limitations of some of the more conventional theories of the South African labour market.

Considerable stress is still placed on the role of the industrial colour bar. Is this justified? Is it really the most important feature of the South African labour market? As regards the migrant labour system, it is both socially and morally pernicious and economically unsound. But is South Africa unique in this regard? Educational facilities and opportunities are separate but hardly equal. Yet again, is the Republic one of the leading villains? In effect, I have always been strongly impressed by the fact that we share features with a variety of other countries, including poverty and inequality of income.

Yet here in the Republic the gap between rich and poor is particularly serious because the rich are mostly White and the poor are mostly Black. The racial income-gap has probably widened – despite the fact that real gross domestic product per capita grew on average by 3,1 per cent annually between 1961 and 1971.[1] Labour's share of the national 'cake' has risen significantly. From a little over 63 per cent in 1961, the 'remuneration of employees' accounted for nearly 70 per cent of national income by 1971.[2] Although this does not relate to the distribution of income between the different categories of labour, it does mean that employees as a group have not suffered at the expense of 'profits'.[3]

When the remuneration of employees is broken up into the different racial classifications, per capita Black salaries and wages are found to have risen only marginally slower than White salaries and wages between 1960/61 and 1970/71, while the Coloured group recorded the lowest rate of increase over the decade. These trends are shown in the table below.[4]

PER CAPITA SALARIES AND WAGES (R PER CAPITA)

	Whites	*Coloureds*	*Asiatics*	*Bantu*
1960/61	1 766	604	604	266
1970/71	3 403	998	1 123	495
Increase	+92,7%	+65,2%	+75,5%	+86,1%

PER CAPITA SALARIES AND WAGES – RATIO OF WHITES TO OTHER RACES

	Whites	*Coloureds*	*Asiatics*	*Bantu*
1960/61	1,0:1	2,9:1	2,8:1	6,6:1
1970/71	1,0:1	3,4:1	3,0:1	6,9:1

It should be stressed that the absolute differences actually widened because of the relatively low initial earnings of the non-Whites. From 6,6:1 in 1960/61, the overall White : Black gap has increased to 6,9:1. These figures even understate the racial income-gap, for all racial groups – particularly the Whites – derive income from other sources as well. Spandau (1971:182) estimated the gap for 1960 to be 15,4 to 1 between White and Black, 8,9 to 1 between White and Coloured, and 7,2 to 1 between White and Asian.

This gap is the result of a whole complex of interlocking factors which permeate the fabric of South African society. There is, however, still a great deal of disagreement about the relative importance of these factors and the nature of their interaction. There are the mono-causal interpretations which stress the overriding importance of particular factors, but inevitably lack depth. The most popular interpretation stresses the primacy of the industrial colour bar, while another stresses the economic factors of supply and demand in the labour market. Such influences are obviously important, but they should not be seen in isolation. Their importance is derived from the existence of other factors which both qualify and reinforce them, and it would be invidious to assess the relative importance of any particular factor on its own. We are concerned, not with a collection of separate entities, but with a *system* in which such entities interact.

I have found it particularly illuminating to look at the South African labour market in terms of four factors: legal, institutional, educational, and finally that variety of influences which can conveniently be summed up under that tried catchall, the 'South African way of life'. The significance of each factor will now be sketched briefly.

We may accept that in South Africa as elsewhere laws control our patterns of behaviour. Parliament has made laws or delegated authority in the form of the Industrial Conciliation Act, the Bantu Labour (Settlement of Disputes) Act, the Extension of University Education Act, the Group Areas Act, etc. These laws, in effect, comprise all the factors mentioned above, but reference is here restricted to those laws which directly prohibit the employment of any racial group. The passage of time has seen the seemingly remorseless proliferation of a whole array of laws and proclamations. Yet, although their *de jure* scope is extensive, the *de facto* application of job reservation is relatively limited, with just 3 per cent of total White employment being reserved exclusively for this racial group.

Nevertheless, one frequently hears the suggestion that this understates the effect of the industrial colour bar. Reference is made in particular to Section 77 of the Industrial Conciliation Act, 1956 (as amended), which vests wide powers in the Minister in terms of the section titled 'Prevention of Interracial Competition'. Yet, the relative ease with which 'temporary' exemptions are granted and nearly always renewed, is most remarkable. The scope and limits of the industrial colour bar can only be appreciated through a consideration of the customary colour bar. The latter preceded the former and legal enactments to restrict jobs were usually a response to the breakdown of such older customary inhibitions.

Focusing on the *institutional* aspects, it has to be stressed that South Africa has an enlightened system of industrial legislation when considering the Industrial Council system, in terms of which employers and employees settle disputes through statutory procedures. This is certainly *one* of the reasons why South Africa is so much less strike-prone than other countries. With the exception of domestic servants, farm labour, the public service, apprentices and those engaged in certain essential services, as well as African mineworkers, the various institutions established under the Industrial Conciliation Act, the Wage Act, and the Bantu Labour (Settlement of Disputes) Act (Act No. 48 of 1953), cover most workers in South Africa. Both legislation and institutions have gradually evolved as changing needs were recognised, and partially and imperfectly adapted to.

Thus, the Wage Board was initially an instrument to reinforce the 'civilised labour policy' designed as a solution to the poor-White problem of the depression years. About thirty years later, with poor-Whiteism eliminated and the poverty and unemployment of Blacks in the foreground, the Wage Board's policy is in the process of changing, with limited success (Pursell 1969:73, 81). Workers can no longer be ignored with such facility as before. The Wage Board still appears to be understaffed and with little power, and thus inherently incapable of coping with a problem of truly overwhelming dimensions.

The Wage Act created machinery for fixing wage-rates and regulating conditions of work in industries where the employers and employees were not organised. Although African trade unions both in mining and other sectors of the economy have not been officially recognised or encouraged, there has been no legislation to prevent their formation and they are not illegal. However, legal obstacles as well as more drastic measures, such as the banning of leaders, have been used to prevent African trade union organisation and strikes. The vast majority of Africans, were, furthermore, excluded from the operation of the Industrial Conciliation Act of 1924 by the definition of 'employee'.

In addition, the various Masters and Servants Acts passed in the four territories which later became the Union of South Africa, although 'ostensibly colourblind', imposed criminal sanctions for breach of a contract by a servant. Later measures further curtailed the Black man's use of the strike weapon. As Muriel Horrell has put it, from the time 'Africans first began working (for White employers) in considerable numbers, it has been well-nigh impossible for them to stage a legal strike.'[5]

These and other limitations on the African worker severely inhibited normal trade union activity and as a result they have had little scope to act collectively in order to improve their conditions of employment. After the Second World War, there was considerable agitation that the African should be granted some form of collective bargaining. The result of this pressure and the change of Government was the Bantu Labour (Settlement of Disputes) Act, finally passed in 1953, which made provision for a limited form of representation on the individual factory/establishment basis. Up to 1972 African workers have, however, scarcely bothered to establish the works committees which the Act allows. Although the Act failed to set up effective means of communication between employers and Black employees, no changes took place until 1973. In this regard it should also be remembered that the first trade unions in the mining areas were established with the primary goal of protecting White labour against the increasing use of Africans in jobs involving the same industrial skills. With a few notable exceptions, the trade union movement still pursues this discriminating policy, either directly through support for the industrial colour bar or indirectly by pleading for the substitution of the rate for the job. The final result remains much the same, i.e. the protection of employment opportunities and salary and wage levels of the White labour aristocracy against undue encroachment by Blacks.

While the rate for the job is less arbitrary than the industrial colour ban, it will only assist the advance of Black workers and narrow the racial income-gap if other conditions are favourable. Thus, not only do Black workers in South Africa suffer from the lack of institutions which they can use, but most of the existing institutions help to perpetuate Black socio-economic inferiority.

This situation is unlikely to change rapidly. According to the 'theory of expected loss', 'The failure of the individual to respond to a plea for wage restraint in the public interest may not reflect failure to appreciate the nature of the trade-off between wage price movements and unemployment in the aggregate. The representative member might be quite as sophisticated as his leader and yet pass a negative verdict on incomes policy . . . In the event of deflation . . . the probability that he will lose his job is low indeed; in fact it might be zero (Ulman and Flanagan 1971:233–34). This type of reasoning may explain the reluctance of registered unions to pursue an active policy of assistance to the non-unionised worker in South Africa. Only a small minority of Whites need to lose their jobs if economic growth is slowed down by an unwillingness to utilise labour resources fully. On the other hand the great majority would have to forego some wage increases if market forces were allowed to act freely, as can actually be illustrated by events over the last two years. With a remarkably lower growth rate non-African unemployment was at a rate of 0,5 per cent still insignificant.

I would now like to turn to the *educational* influences on the labour market. The serious lack of funds for Black education is illustrated by the following figures: 'For every R100 spent annually on the education of White pupils, roughly R28 is spent on Indians, R26 on Coloured pupils, and R6 on Africans' (Horrell 1972:496). Yet there have been distinct improvements in Black education, especially in recent years. For example expenditure on Bantu Education grew from R19,5 m in 1962/63, to R54, 4 m in 1970/71, and over R80 m in 1972. Even though the absolute amounts are hardly satisfactory, it does show that the relative share of Black educational expenditure is increasing. There has also been an increase not only in the number but also in the proportion of literate Africans. The African population 15 years and over rose by 35 per cent between the 1960 and 1970 Population Censuses but literacy, i.e. the ability both to read and write, rose by 69 per cent over the same period. Nearly half of our Black population, 15 years and over, are now literate, compared with 39,5 per cent ten years ago.

Literacy alone doesn't equip a man for the modern industrial state. Higher levels of educational attainment are required as society becomes more complex and sophisticated. In the light of this the excessive proportion of Blacks in the lower primary standards gives reason for great concern. There has also only recently been a shift toward the provision of more trade, technical and vocational training. In 1970, 68,7 per cent of total African school enrolment was in the lower primary standards, 26,54 per cent in higher primary, 4,04 per cent in lower high school, 0,32 per cent in senior high school, 0,14 per cent in Technical and Trade Schools and 0,26 per cent in Teacher Training Schools. This pattern is obviously insufficient if the African is to play his proper role in the labour market.

The migrant labour system also has important repercussions on the educational attainments of Blacks. Investment in human capital is usually only undertaken when the investor, whether employer or employee, believes he will amortise his debt as well as receive a satisfactory rate of return. Consequently investment in on-the-job training would be inhibited if the period of return were circumscribed by law. In as far as the migrant labour system inhibits investment in human capital it retards the rate of economic growth. In the literature a high correlation between investment in human capital and the rate of economic development has been revealed, but South Africa has not shown much recognition of this fact yet (cf. Harbison and Myers 1969:13–60).

The last of the four factors is the 'South African way of life', i.e. those pervasive social, economic and environmental influences which largely account for the alleged 'uniqueness' of which some South Africans are so proud. This includes the customary colour bar referred to above. In a paper emphasising the interrelationship of the legal and customary colour bars, Steenkamp argued that the customary colour bar 'would have existed in the absence of legal restrictions . . . At the first signs of . . . a threat to the living standards of the White workers, it was converted into a legal bar in mining, a wage bar in the secondary and the tertiary sectors, and an administrative bar in the public services' (Steenkamp 1971:107).

In historical perspective the colour bar grew up fairly naturally. It was not racial in character to begin with and was not to reserve jobs, but to reserve 'rights'. These 'rights' extended very far at the time, and they still do today. When colour prejudice did emerge it was not something specifically South African. The uniqueness of the South African variety of colour prejudice arises not from its existence but from its persistence and the elaborate aura of dogma which surrounds it during an era which has seen its more or less rapid eclipse throughout the rest of the world. In effect, over the years there has been a tightening-up of regulations relating to residence, trading, acquisition and occupation of land and movement of the African population. There have been constant moves to enforce and re-enforce separation.[6] And as long as we live apart, eat and drink apart and play apart, the necessary basis for a common society will be fragile and the customary colour bar will persist.

In the light of the pervasive influence of custom in South Africa, it can be asked how the situation would change, if expenditure on arms or water conservation schemes were to be diverted to Black education, or if Black trade unions were to be placed on an equal footing with their White counterparts or if the legal colour bar in all its forms were to be abolished. Black educational expenditure can serve as an example: re-allocation of funds might result in more and better-trained Blacks and thus in increased pressure to use them higher up in the job hierarchy. This suggests that the imperatives of economic development sooner or later demand measures which place a premium upon skill and not colour. These in turn may be expected to erode the colour bar.

Upon first sight it would seem that there is an equilibrium in the four factors discussed above, maintaining the dualism in the labour market. The situation described, i.e. the 'system', has survived, without undue strain, various crises till recently, the worst prognostications of those many prophets of doom whom, like the poor, we shall probably always have with us. This would seem to be confirmed by the distinguished American sociologist, Blumer, (1965:238) who has pointed out that 'half a century of industrial experience in both South Africa and the South in the United States brought no appreciable change in the position of the races in the industrial structure.' He concluded that 'industrial imperatives accommodate themselves to the racial mould and continue to operate effectively within it.'

As a result of the stability of the impeding factors, I believe one should try to pinpoint those specific policy measures, now pursued by the Government as part of its overall policy of Separate Development, which can be distinguished for their long-run potential for change. One may have different ends in mind, but one can agree on the means, although one disagrees about their possible consequences. In fact, it is my belief that one should support certain policies of the Government as they are likely to have unintentioned consequences.

In this regard I would like to emphasise the role of the current policy of decentralisation. Although there is a political rationale behind the policy, one can accept good economic reasons for decentralisation, as there certainly are in countries such as France and Italy. But the economic arguments advanced in favour of the South African brand of decentralisation have up till now not been particularly cogent and it is not primarily on economic grounds that I think we should support it. The grounds for support can be summed up in one word – leverage. Decentralisation is already providing and may further provide considerable leverage to the traditionally powerless and underprivileged majority of South Africa's population.

The policy of decentralisation, initiated in 1960, is now a cornerstone of the policy of separate development. Important concessions and financial incentives have been forthcoming and expenditure on Homeland development has increased substantially, particularly during recent years. By allowing White capital into the Homelands on an agency basis, finally an important concession was made to the exigencies of development. The activities of White entrepreneurs in the Homelands have shown that effective separation is impossible, while suspension of the application of the Wage Act and Industrial Conciliation Act have indicated the possibility for flexibility with regard to labour regulation. The training of African apprentices is now to be centred with the Homelands, with the certificates valid there only, however. Seven of the nine proposed Homeland authorities have already assumed control of education in their respective areas. Above all, improvements in the educational system are considered primary objectives of the Homeland Governments. Within the framework of the policy of separate development, it is difficult to believe that their demands in this regard will not be met. Furthermore, the Africanisation of the Homelands by the Bantu Investment Corporation and Xhosa Development Corporation cannot fail to create the basis for an African elite and an African entrepreneurial class.

These changes within the Homelands must eventually affect the 'White' areas as well, in particular the attitude of White entrepreneurs and enterprising Blacks. The necessity and desirability of migrating to the present metropolitan areas may decline as both the relative poverty of the Homelands and the attraction of the main urban areas diminish. This is, naturally, only likely to happen if the decentralisation policy is successful; so far, success has been very limited and unemployment in these areas has, in effect, continued to rise.

Decentralisation should be supported also because the development of the Homelands is long overdue. Apart from any rational economic objectives in Homeland development, the underdevelopment of these areas is a fact of life, and their vocal and articulate leaders are fast increasing pressure for more rapid development. This, in fact, is implied by 'leverage'. The Government is riding a tiger which it dubiously thinks it may be able to control. However, it is more likely that there will be a marked demonstration effect on labour patterns in the metropolitan areas. These patterns show signs of breaking up and this may be the catalyst needed. South African life cannot be compartmentalised and it is unrealistic to believe that equality of job opportunity and the performance of skilled work by Blacks in the Homelands will not have drastic repercussions on labour patterns in the rest of the country.

Support for the policy may therefore differ from that of Steenkamp, who is quoted below, but the means of achieving different objectives may at least temporarily coincide: 'The policy of separate development is a sound and an attractive one, if only for the negative reason that, by creating viable homogenous black communities, on the one hand, and maintaining a certain quantitative ethnological balance in the so-called white regions, on the other, we are likely to reduce the areas of racial conflict that bedevil our mixed society' (Steenkamp 1971:110).

I reject apartheid as both morally wrong and economically and politically unsound, but I do believe that certain aspects of the policy can be supported by those who accept that South Africa is irrevocably a multiracial society. This final evaluation can be strengthened by the conclusions of one of America's most distinguished economists, Albert Hirschman, who, stressing the 'unintended consequences of human actions,' said that 'Efforts to maintain or restore a social organisation or a way of life or a standard of living that is threatened or weakened have yielded unintended innovational changes in modern societies . . . In short, history could be viewed as the process of men in general, and the ruling classes in particular, continually outsmarting themselves in their efforts to reproduce and maintain the existing order' (Hirschman 1971:36).

NOTES

1. *Budget* 1972–73, *Statistical Survey* (W.P.B. – '72), Government Printer, Cape Town, 5.
2. Ibid., 8. National Income referred to is Net National Income at Factor Cost.
3. This term is used generally, the largest item being income from property by households (interest, divided and rent receipts by households and the profits of non-corporate business enterprises).
4. Derived from various issues of the Statistical Year Book, and Quarterly Bulletin of Statistics, Department of Statistics, Pretoria.
5. Muriel Horrell, *South African Trade Unionism*, (1961:60). The legal restrictions regarding strikes have been changed during 1973. See the final chapter.
6. The fairly recent 'Koornhof Plan', promply abandoned, to ban Africans from certain jobs in an attempt to keep races apart in offices, is a classic example; *Rand Daily Mail*, 13 April 1970.

REFERENCES

Blumer, Herbert 1965 – 'Industrialisation and race relations.' In Guy Hunter (ed.) *Industrialisation and Race Relations*. London: Oxford University Press.

Harbison, F. H. and C. A. Myers 1969 – 'Strategies of human resource development.' In M. Blaug (ed.) *Economics of Education* 2. Harmondsworth: Penguin Modern Economics Readings, 13–60.

Hirschman, Albert O. 1971 – *A Bias for Hope*. New Haven and London: Yale University Press.

Horrell, Muriel 1972 – 'Education in an apartheid society.' In N. J. Rhoodie (ed.) *South African Dialogue*. Johannesburg:McGraw-Hill.

Pursell, Donald E. 1969 – 'The impact of the South African wage board upon skilled/unskilled wage differentials.' *East African Economic Review*, June.

Spandau, A. M. K. M. 1971 – Income Distribution and Economic Growth in South Africa. Unpublished Ph.D. thesis, UNISA, vol. 1.

Steenkamp, W. F. J. 1971 – 'Labour policies for growth during the seventies in the established industrial areas.' S.A.J.E. (June).

Ulman, Lloyd and Robert J. Flanagan 1971 – *Wage Restraint: A Study of Incomes Policy in Western Europe*. Berkeley: University of California Press.

3. Industrial Progress: Its Social, Political and Economic Implications

S. P. CILLIERS

Industrial progress is both a function of social, cultural, political and broad economic forces and also, in its turn, has implications for all of these spheres of life. In this discussion, it will therefore be necessary to look at both the consequences of industrial progress and also at the extent to which social, cultural, political and economic factors will affect the rate and nature of industrial progress.

Given these parameters, this article should be seen as an attempt at the presentation of a *scenario* of the total South African society of the future, under conditions of industrial progress.

What is the diagnosis of the state of the interface in the work situation as revealed by the discussions at the Institute of Personnel Management's Interface Convention? If I have to state it in a single sentence, I would simply formulate that we have found the situation to be utterly inadequate and unsatisfactory. We have, on the one hand, as was stated in the opening address by Mr Harry Oppenheimer, chairman of Anglo American, a situation in which continued growth of the economy will create circumstances in which the political, social and industrial pressures making for change will become irresistible. Personally, I believe that they have already become irresistible! On the other hand, the papers presented have shown that we are totally unprepared for, and inadequately equipped to meet, the exigencies arising out of the need for change.

This assessment may sound unnecessarily harsh, and even negative. It is not meant to be so. But I believe that, in examining these issues, we must be honest and realistic if we are to derive any direction for future action from our discussions. My assessment simply implies that we have entered a phase in which there are bound to be severe strains in our total societal structure, and that these strains will have to be relieved if we are to maintain some form of orderly progress.

Social Structure

In trying to indicate the broad outlines of this situation, let me start by discussing the social structure of our societal setting. It has been agreed that economic growth, whether through a rapid expansion of secondary industry or a concentration on mineral development, can only be attained through the more effective involvement of all sectors of the population – Black, Brown and White – on an increasingly equal basis in the work situation, with a concommitant trend towards equalisation in the direct rewarp system.

We are, in short, faced with a situation of increasing economic integration, even though we may attain a significant degree of separate economic development in and around the Black rural and urban areas. Yet, the broad socio-political system of our country aims at attaining the maximum degree of differentiation between the various ethnic groups in the population at all levels except the economic. It uses, in social-scientific terminology, a conflict model of societal change and development, in contrast to a consensus model. It starts from the assumption that the various ethnic groups in our country do not only differ from one another physically and culturally, but that their interests are equally varied and, in effect, in direct opposition to one another. It therefore aims at creating the maximum degree of separation and the minimum degree of inter-group contact so as to eliminate points of contact, which it assumes will favour conflict.

In passing, it should be noted that these are the very type of assumptions on which Marxist ideology is based. Marx argued that capitalist society is divided into classes which have irreconcilably conflicting interests concerning control over the factors of production. It is especially the theoretical constructs of the neo-Marxists, who work with the idea of interest groups, which bears a strange similarity to the propositions of the designers of our own ideological models of societal change. It is in this sense that our purported anti-Marxist stand tends to take on rather ironical overtones.

It should be clear that a socio-cultural and political system of differentiation coupled with an economic system of integration must compound the degrees of strain and personal stress. Socio-cultural and political differentiation must of necessity be, and are in fact overtly aimed at the strengthening of group consciousness and group identities.

The interface in the work situation and economic integration, on the other hand, if they are to lead to economic effectiveness, must, as has been emphasised time and again, be based on the acceptance of common goals, on mutual trust and goodwill, on individual merit and ability. In short, they require the acceptance of personal qualities as the basis of evaluation, in contrast to ascribed group characteristics.

It should, therefore, not be surprising that we are not making satisfactory progress in realising our goal of economic effectiveness. Furthermore, it should be clear that the work situation is bound to be a primary area of strain, and that systems of industrial conciliation that will function effectively are not easily devised. Neither works committees nor liaison committees are instant solutions, and segregated unions, even if they were to be recognised in the case of Black workers, will not necessarily be unproblematic. In fact, it may not be unrealistic to expect this to be the most problematic of all. I must therefore support Mr Oppenheimer's call for a high-level investigation into industrial conciliation.

When we had the series of strikes during 1973, much attention was given to the need for industrial conciliation. Since then, the issue has virtually disappeared from the public mind. Yet, even at this time, there are work stoppages, strikes and other indications of labour unrest. These are but overt signs of the extent to which the work situation will remain an area of strain.

More equal and equitable participation in the work situation must of necessity have significant social effects. One question which arises immediately is whether the special infra-structure required to meet the needs arising out of increased economic equalisation exists, or can be created.

The simple truth is that our traditional system calls for separate social infra-structures, and that, as yet only one such system, i.e. for Whites, has been created. And since a social infra-structure consists primarily of the provision of services, its creation does not contribute directly to the raising of the level and volume of productivity of the economy. The quadruplication of such a system of social infra-structure – for that is the minimum which is implied by our ideology – requires not only a staggering capital investment, but involves also, especially during the early phases, a considerable degree of under-utilisation. It is, therefore hardly realistic to expect that such provision will be extended in accordance with the needs of the situation, and severe strains and personal frustration are bound to arise.

Considerable relief can be obtained if the existing social infra-structure, at present largely reserved for the White population, and in many respects under-utilised, is opened up for other population groups. There are, in fact,increasing instances of such extentions, especially at the level of facilities and amenities. Most promising, is the fact that such tentative steps have met with relatively little opposition. This has demonstrated what many social scientists have known for some time, namely that when confronted with real situations, people generally tend to react less extremely than one may be led to assume on the basis of expressed opinions.

The importance of the need to attend to this aspect cannot be ignored. In the past, it has often been argued that the most important way in which we, in South Africa, could ensure relative stability would be through a reasonably high economic growth rate. It has been argued that a continuation of the upgrading of the economic standing of the working classes would be the best possible guarantee against social and political unrest. It should be noted that this argument is not necessarily valid. By upgrading the economic standing of the masses, new wants are created; by promoting the assumption of greater responsibilities in the work situation through the upgrading of the interface, a greater sense of personal worth is fostered; by increased involvement in a modernised economy, greater exposure to the whole cultural world of modernity is promoted. Nowhere, not even behind the Iron Curtain, has it been possible to isolate the technological advances of modernity from the rest of its meaning.

While it is true that modernity has not yet led to the elimination of group identities, even in the most modernised societies, this does not mean that certain aspects of modernity can be embraced on the assumption that they will not have any significance for the rest of the field of human existence. What is even more important is the fact that what matters increasingly in an era of modernity is not the obligation to be totally immersed by it, but rather the freedom to choose between rejecting and embracing it.

I am, therefore, forced to the conclusion that beyond the interface in the work situation lies an even more important but inevitable field of interface at the social level. But here, as in so many respects on the level of human relations, we have a double interchange. For while it follows that successful interface in the work situation will lead to an increased need for social equalisation, it is also true that progress at this level will greatly facilitate successful interface in the work situation. It is but another confirmation of the view that change in the economic sphere cannot be viewed in isolation from the total socio-cultural and political environment in which it occurs.

The social implications are, however, unfortunately not restricted to facilities and amenities. They involve, first and foremost, adequate provision to meet elementary human needs in a modern urban setting. Of these, a physical setting in which a meaningful existence can be obtained is of primary importance. The task of providing such a setting in terms of urban layout and design, services, dwellings and the like, in view of the projected growth of our population, is indeed colossal. Yet without this, effective interface in the work situation can hardly be obtained, and insofar as it may be attained, it can only again increase the strains in the wider structure.

In a sense, the whole issue of the social implications of progress concerns the nature of the quality of life which can be attained by the individual and his family and community. If it is impossible to look towards improving the quality of life, it is equally impossible to aspire towards economic progress.

I have dealt with the social implications of ecnomic progress first, because I believe that, in a sense, this is the most important issue of all. For, in the last analysis, man's struggle in the work situation is primarily a means at trying to improve the quality of his life.

Let us now turn briefly to the broad economic picture of our industrial progress.

Economic Forces

Since the White sector of our society has made such tremendous progress in the economic and socio-cultural spheres, we tend to identify ourselves with the modern developed world. Overall, however, our position is typical of the developing world. It consists of a situation where we have a very high growth rate of the large masses of the population who are overwhelmingly still in a position of relative economic, social, cultural and political underdevelopment, and where the initiative for change rests largely with a small modernising elite.

Our situation is made more complex than that in many other developing countries, by the fact that this modernising elite consists mainly of Whites, so that the tenuous position of the elite group in such situations is complicated by the factors associated with race and colour differences. Furthermore, where modernising elites generally tend to seek to be identified with and to be accepted by the masses, in the South African situation our dominant ideology strives to ensure the retention of a separate identity for both the elite and the different sections of the broad masses of the underdeveloped.

Under such circumstances, it is indeed difficult for the modernising elitist group to legitimise their position with regard to the masses who have to be led towards modernisation. We have chosen to try to solve this problem through the creation of opportunities for separate development. Naturally, however, the White sector must play the role of the modernising elite in the non-White spheres too. Furthermore, in view of the fact that the contemporary world scene represents an era of rising expectations for the masses everywhere, there is tremendous pressure for a high rate of growth and expansion. Yet the task of creating enough opportunities for development is an immense and difficult one. We have seen, throughout the developing world since the post war era, that economic progress is not easily obtained, and our own meagre progress in the development of the homelands has confirmed this. Our experience at the turn of the seventies has, furthermore, proved to us that efforts to channel some of the impetus for development to these areas through economic decentralisation has to be very closely monitored, if it is not to stifle growth.

One is, therefore, led to the conclusion that the serious imbalance in the relative state of economic development between the major White-dominated centres and the underdeveloped areas of the country will remain for the foreseeable future, and that the pressure for opportunities to participate in these industrialised centres of growth will increase rather than decrease as population pressures and rising expectations in these areas continue to build up.

Thus, the unevenness in our economic development must continue to contribute towards the strains in our societal structure. The fact that this unevenness in the participation in our modernised sector of the economy tends to coincide with race and colour differences will naturally only compound the strains, since in a multiracial situation, cleavages which coincide with race differences tend to take on a racial character, and tend to be interpreted in such terms. For this reason, if for no other, it is imperative that greater economic equalisation, through the closing of the wage gap and the removal of racial or colour barriers to individual economic advancement, should be a first-order priority.

Like most of the developing world, we have chosen to attain progress towards economic advancement through increased industrialisation. It may yet turn out that high rates of industrialisation are not the most ideal answer to the problem and, for this reason, there may be some considerable merit in the suggestion by Prof Sadie of the University of Stellenbosch, that South Africa, at least for the interim, return to an emphasis on mineral development. It will be necessary, however, to use the opportunity created thereby to prepare ourselves more properly for a greater degree of economic diversification. This calls not only for physical planning, but also for the development of the physical infra-structure and even more importantly, for the development of the required socio-political infra-structure.

Socio-Political Design

In order to determine whether our socio-political design will be adequate to meet the exigencies of change under conditions of economic development, it is necessary to state our basic premises. These are, firstly, that in view of our population structure and growth it is imperative that a reasonably high growth rate of the economy be maintained. Secondly, that such a growth rate can be attained and maintained only by an expansion of economic opportunities, which have previously been reserved for Whites, to other sectors of the population. Thirdly, that the main thrust of this economic development will, for the foreseeable future, remain in and around the major industrial centres of the country, although decentralised development can be expected to gain momentum. Fourthly, that socio-politically, if not economically, homelands development has passed the point of no return at least for the *de facto* population of these areas. It should be noted in passing that this last assumption provides another powerful reason for the need to maintain a high growth rate. Insofar as the socio-political development of the homelands has outstripped the economic development of these areas, their increasing degree of political autonomy calls for generating the means to accelerate their economic development. The paradox which arises out of this is that, in order to validate and realise the goal of separate development for the homelands, increased economic integration in the rest of the country is inevitable.

The central question which derives from this analysis is whether our present socio-political design can be maintained under conditions of increasing economic integration. This socio-political design envisages the retention of the maximum degree of separation between the different ethnic groups and, in the case of the urban African population, even envisages its ultimate accommodation in the socio-political system of the homelands. Reflection on the nature of the relationship between the economy and the rest of the societal system will serve to convince us that, in the end, an integrated economy is simply not to be reconciled with such a socio-political design. This means that we must accept the plural character of our society and try to design a socio-political order that will make due allowances for it, without excluding individual members or categories of the population from full participation in the power system, so as to safeguard also their interests in an integrated economy.

If the central problem at the interface is that of creating ways whereby all those involved in the economy can participate in the process of decision-making with regard to the nature of their participation, it must be immediately recognised that this involves participation in the system of power – i.e. participation in the political system.

Citizenship

In the final analysis, participation in the economic system cannot be divorced from the citizenship status of those involved. For this reason a central issue in all countries in the world has been the nature of the status awarded to the individual as a citizen. The historical evolution of this status from that of a slave, servant or subject to that of citizen represents the emergence of our contemporary era of democracy. The culmination of this has been the development of the nation-state as the political organisation of modernized societies, and the development of a civil order in which all citizens, irrespective of kinship, status, ethnic affiliation, etc., participate in the same institutions. In essence, for the individual member of society, this involves the evolution of the institution of full citizenship.

As Marshall has shown in his discussion of the development of citizenship in Great Britain (Marshall 1963:67–127), there are at least three components of the status of citizenship – the civil (or legal), the political and the social. It is significant to note that the time sequence in the institutionalisation of these components, in England in particular, and generally in Western Europe, followed the order in which they are mentioned above. A definition of the content and meaning of each component will show the logical necessity for this sequence in the development of the institution of citizenship.

The civil component involves the development of elementary rights which members of the societal community enjoy. It concerns rights such as the security of the individual and of property, freedom of speech, religion, assembly and association, and both substantive and procedural equality before the law (Parsons, 1969:259). It involves, furthermore, rights such as the freedom of movement and settlement, and the right of work, i.e. to follow the occupation of one's choice, subject of course to the legitimate demands of ability. It is significant that the establishment of these civil rights was in large measure the work of the courts of law. For this reason the retention of the rule of law is the the primary guarantee for the maintenance of civil rights.

The political component involves the right to participate in the political decision-making process. Its evolution has changed the status of the individual from that of being a mere subject at the mercy of the ruler to taking part in the process of ruling himself. Its evolution did not consist of the establishment of new rights, but rather of the extension of the right to participate in the collective decision-making process, to categories of members of the societal community who had previously been excluded from this. This participation in the collective goal-attainment through the process of government has, in the modern state, found its expression in the franchise as a means of the selection of leadership, and in the influencing of policy, which is mediated through the party system and the institution of mass media.

The social component, which was to evolve largely in the present century, is aimed primarily at enabling all members of the societal community to derive the maximum benefits possible from the exercise of civil and political rights. Since civil and political rights enable the individual to utilise his abilities to the maximum in his own interests, the institution of social rights is aimed at providing him with the facilities he requires to do so. It aims, therefore, at the provision of a minimum of social and economic security to the individual. This is attained through educational provision, the institution of health and other social services, etc.

In the final analysis, the aim here is to ensure that equality between citizens which is provided for in principle through the institution of civil and political rights, shall be in practice realisable for the individual. It should be noted that this does not imply that it shall be in fact realised, but only that the individual shall have equal access to such facilities as are required for him to benefit maximally from his innate capacities. Thus, through the provision of educational facilities, and by even compelling the individual to participate in these facilities, it is ensured that he will be able to derive the maximum personal benefit from the exercise of the civil right to do the type of work that he chooses on the basis of his capacities.

It should be clear that the rapid development and extension of social rights is the major response of the capitalist countries to the challenge of the Marxist doctrine on the injustices of the inequalities of class.

In the evolution of the nation-state, which today serves as the model and ideal for the formal organisation of societal communities, *domicilium* is used as the basis for the determination of right of inclusion in the societal community. Domicile, however, relates to a territorial base, which is today expressed in terms of the recognition of boundaries within which a particular state holds sovereign authority. Citizens of the state are those who, in terms of the requirements of domicile as specified for any particular society, qualify for membership of the societal community.

It should be obvious that, in terms of the policy of separate development, not all of those who qualify for citizenship in terms of the criterion of domicile are given full citizenship rights. The reason for this is that the policy of separate development involves the utilisation of a second basis for the definition of membership of the societal community, namely a colour or racial basis.

It has been stated time and again and in very explicit terms, that the Government has as its primary concern the protection of the identity and autonomy of the Whites in South Africa. It defines the nation in South Africa as consisting of Whites only, and has recently developed the concept of multinationality with regard to the South African situation. This is logically valid with regard to the policy of separate development for the Bantu homelands, since here the principle of domicile as the basis for the determination of the right of inclusion in the societal communities may be applied. This is, however, not possible, with regard to those permanently domiciled in the White-controlled areas of our country.

It is clear that the only way in which this dilemma can be resolved would be by the rejection of the colour/racial basis for the definition of the right to membership of the societal community.

On the other hand, much of the resistance against the idea of extending the right to inclusion in the societal community arises from an oversimplified concept of the nature of the integrated society which will evolve from such a development. Integration is usually, but in fact fallaciously, equated with massive biological assimilation and with the immediate and complete disappearance of all ethnic identities. Likewise those who favour the ideal of an 'integrated society' have tended to idealise this model and to regard it as a completely friction-free system of human relations in complete equilibrium. This is wholly unrealistic. Since any system of human relations involves individuals and groups who are – thankfully – to a greater or lesser degree unique, a certain level of strain and disequilibrium is always inevitable. No society is therefore ever completely integrated, and a certain degree of cultural plurality is to be found everywhere.

When discussing the question of who should qualify for inclusion in the societal community, one must distinguish between inclusion and assimilation. All societies have a degree of cultural plurality, in the sense that not all members of the societal community form a single ethnic identity. Yet, in most of these cases, this does not preclude the inclusion of minorities in the societal community as citizens, sharing on an equal basis in all three components of citizenship.

A review of the nature of the arguments presented by those who reject the idea of extending the rights of citizenship to members of other ethnic groups, shows that no distinction is made between the process of inclusion, which is essentially a process of political modernisation, and the process of assimilation, which is essentially a socio-biological process. This failure arises because it is not fully understood that citizenship concerns the right of participation in the social institutions of society through which orderly relations are mediated, and does not concern the nature of involvement in voluntary group affiliation. Freedom of association involves the right to choose your associates.

In the end, it is the attitudes and prejudices of the politically dominant White sector of our population which stand in the way of progress towards the necessary changes in our systems. If this is true, we have for more than three centuries been using a reversed perspective in our approach to our problems. Since the times of Van Riebeeck, we have spoken of the 'Native problem', the 'Coloured problem', etc. But perhaps our problem all along has been a 'White problem'.

The fundamental requirement at this stage is to obtain clarity with regard to whether the urban African, the Coloured and the Asian peoples are to be afforded the opportunity of being included in our societal community as real citizens, or whether we want to continue to exclude them on purely racist grounds. It is my conviction that we must decide in favour of the right to inclusion, and that this conviction is being shared by an increasing sector of the White population.

Failure to recognise the urgency of the need to reconsider the present situation and to accommodate the strains in our systems, could lead to the breakdown of modernisation in South Africa and to the destruction of all that we cherish in this beloved country of ours. If you share with me this diagnosis of our situation, the time to act in accordance with our convictions has arrived and is, in fact, running out fast.

REFERENCES

Marshall, T. H. 1963 – *Sociology at the Crossroads and Other Essays*. London: Heinemann.
Parsons, Talcott 1969 – *Politics and Social Structure*. New York: Free Press.

Part 7:

Law and Crime

Introduction

ROLAND GRASER

No pretence is made in this chapter of covering the field of law in depth. That would require a full discussion of the nature and function of law in society, the specific resources of law, the various divisions of law, and the characteristic mechanisms that law sets into motion – which would cover many volumes. Furthermore, the author is not qualified to write such a comprehensive exposition of law.

In this introduction, the concept of law will be defined. The various branches of law will merely be mentioned, but criminal law will be dealt with in more detail, though by no means fully.

The intention with the selection of articles is merely to present the reader with a 'sample' from the area of criminal law, in order to arouse his interest in the field. Throughout the chapter, the focus will be on the South African situation. The issues that will be dealt with are *Law and Criminal Procedure in South Africa*, *The Reformation of the South African Penal System*, and *Crime in the Coloured Community*. This represents no more than a cursory glance at a very extensive and complicated area.

Law as a Social Control

Society consists of a complex structure of institutions, associations, organizations and groupings, which are characterized by intricate patterns of interaction. With the evolution of society, there has been a development of mechanisms which pattern, regulate, control and limit human behaviour. These social controls include customs, moral codes, law, religion, convention etiquette, familial codes and the rules and regulations of the various organizations. However, we are here concerned merely with one form of social control, namely with the legal code: the most powerful code, which is the only code that has the power of the State behind it.

Generally speaking, law is a set of rules which govern and regulate the behaviour and relationships of persons in a community. It is basically a system of control that obliges the citizens which it governs to behave in a certain way, or to refrain from particular actions. Indeed, it is the mechanism through which the State ensures compliance with its formal standards of behaviour. Thus, the legal code is prescriptive and normative; i.e. it demands compliance with certain standards of behaviour, which it ensures through threat of sanctions. In most legal systems the major sanctions brought to bear on the individual in order to ensure compliance with the law take the form of punishment, such as fines, imprisonment, corporal punishment and, in some countries, such as South Africa, the death sentence. However, it would be erroneous to see law as depending purely on coercion. While it plays an important part in a democratic society, the efficacy of law as an institution of social control depends, in the final analysis, on consensus and rationality. Philip Selznick (1968:52) points out that, 'in a developed, legal order, authority transcends coercion, accepts the restraints of reason, and contributes to a public consensus regarding the foundations of civic obligations.' In order to be effective, a legal order must be sustained by substantial public consensus and must command a sufficiently high degree of willing obedience. Although coercion is an important resource for law, education, symbolism and appeal to reason are more important resources in achieving compliance on a long-term basis.

In modern countries law is the only code which has the ultimate sanction of physical enforcement. It is the only code of conduct which is generally recognized as binding by the courts of justice, and which is applicable to the community as a whole. According to the Instrumentalists (Bentham, von Ihring, Pound), law is seen as having several functions: 'not only is it a vehicle for maintaining public order and settling disputes, but it also facilitates voluntary transactions and arrangements, confers political legitimacy, promotes education and civic participation, and helps to define social aspiration' (Selznick 1968:50). Furthermore, according to Selznick: 'The special work of law is to identify claims and obligations that merit official validation or enforcement.' He indicates that: 'This may consist of nothing more than the establishment of a public record invested with a special claim upon the community's respect as a guide to action' (1968:52).

In order to understand the role of law in society, it is necessary to be familiar with its historical background. As we know it today in the Western World, law developed from three major sources. The first was the ancient Middle East, in the form of the Codes of Hammurabi and the Mosiac Laws of the Old Testament. These are, according to archaeological evidence and historical records, the earliest formulations of rules of law.

The second source of modern law lies, firstly, in the writings of the early Greek philosophers (such as Plato and Aristotle) and in the statutes of Greek lawgivers of ancient times. It also lies, to an even greater extent, in the Twelve Tables of ancient Rome's *decemvirs*, laid down around 450 B.C. and also in the *corpus juris civilis* (Code of Civil Law) compiled by Emperor Justinian (A.D. 483–565). The Twelve Tables, drawn up nearly twenty-five centuries ago, already covered such matters as ownership, inheritance, delicts, and judicial procedure. Justinian's code was a summary of several centuries of legal developments, and established such fundamental principles as the right to a fair trial and the right to be considered innocent until proved guilty – now embodied in the legal codes of modern democratic societies.

The third source of modern legal codes is found in the development of English common law at the time of Henry I (A.D. 1100–1135). His legal code, known as the *Leges Henrici*, declared, *inter alia*, that: 'there will be certain offences against the King's peace, arson, robbery, false coinage, and crimes of violence. These we deem to be felonious' (German, Day, and Gallati 1973:17). This represented the first recognition that certain offences against a citizen of the State were also offences against the State. However, the major English contribution to modern law was the famous *Magna Carta* (1215) which grew out of the struggle between England's citizens, its nobility and its crown. It protected citizens from arbitrary arrest and tyrannical authority, and guaranteed them 'due process of law'. Every citizen was assured that he would not 'be destroyed . . . except by the legal judgment of his peers or by the law of the land.'

The major categories of law are:

Common Law, being law that is based upon or derived from custom rather than statutes enacted by legislature. Common Law is the heart of the English legal system, which, in turn, is a cornerstone of the South African legal system. It relies heavily upon tradition and the authority of the tribunal as sources of legitimacy.

Statutory Law is written law, enacted by the legislative authority in the form of ordinances, codes and laws – usually in response to situations and problems in society that require formal standards of conduct.

Constitutional Law deals with the basic concepts of government. It creates and regulates government, and takes precedence over all other law.

Case Law is established as a result of cases tried and adjudicated in courts of law. It often involves the setting of precedents.

Civil Law governs private relationships and describes the procedures for settling disputes between individuals.

Criminal Law deals with crimes and defines actions that violate the public peace, safety and welfare. Although the victim of a crime is a person or persons, the State tries the alleged perpetrator of the crime on the supposition that a crime against any of its citizens is a crime against the State. Criminal Law specifies punishments to be imposed upon violators of the law (Butler 1976).

The two major categories of law in Western societies are civil law and criminal law. In primitive societies wrongs were mainly considered as private matters – between the victim and the offender – to be dealt with by the injured party or his relatives. When there was collective intervention, it was usually to secure justice by way of arbitration or compensation, and to ensure that self-help did not get out of hand. With the establishment of central authority came increased control over the private administration of justice. Nevertheless, the reaction to offences continued to be private. While the famous early Roman jurist, Justinian, brought about major changes in the Roman legal system, most offences continued to form part of the civil law for a long time. Such offences as physical injuries and assault, robbery, damage to property, fraud and theft were generally treated as civil wrongs for which monetary penalties could be claimed. Only offences of a public nature such as, in Rome, treason, murder and desertion from the army were treated as criminal from earliest times. In England, until the nineteenth century the list of public crimes was limited, including plotting against the King's life, breaking the King's peace, perjury, adultery, and a few religious offences.

With the growth of modern industrialized societies with vast populations came increased State intervention in the form of a formal and bureaucratic law enforcement machinery. Many of the offences that were dealt with under civil law became criminal offences. Yet, to this day, the dividing line between civil and criminal wrongs remains vague, and differs from one country to another – especially where stages of industrial and socio-cultural development vary. According to William Seagle (1941:28); 'It is only when the absolute monopoly of force (of the State) has become firmly established that the act which injures the individual alone is perceived also to injure the State. It is only then, too, that vengeance can be transmuted into public punishment, transcending individual interest.'

A basic distinction between civil and criminal law is the way in which wrongs and conflicts are dealt with. In civil cases a wrong is redressed by means of awarding damages, orders for specific performance, or issuing injunctions to desist from certain actions. The emphasis lies mainly on *restitution* and *arbitration*. In criminal cases, on the other hand, the objective is mainly to *punish* the wrong-doer and to *deter* him and other potential wrong-doers from breaking the law. While there is usually no stigma attached to being involvep in a civil court case, conviction for a crime is accompanied by a certain degree of public opprobrium – depending on the nature of the crime. Civil cases generally arise from a conflict of interests between two parties, but in criminal cases a certain degree of malice or ill-will is presumed to have accompanied an offence; it is morally blameworthy.

Sir William Blackstone (1965–9: Vol. 4:20) explains this matter as follows:

> In all temporal jurisdictions an overt act or some evidence of an intended crime is necessary to demonstrate the depravity of the will, before the man is liable to punishment. And as a vicious will without a vicious act is no civil crime so, on the other hand, an unwarrantable act without a vicious will is no crime at all. So that to constitute a crime against human laws, there must be, first a vicious will and, secondly, an unlawful act consequent upon such vicious will.

The 'vicious will' and the 'unlawful act' correspond to the two essential elements in the legal concept of crime, the *mens rea* and the *actus reus*. *Mens rea* relates to the actor's intention and *actus reus* relates to the accused person's action and its legal status as distinct from his intention.

Under criminal law there is a basic distinction between, on the one hand, crimes that are considered *mala in se*, that is, behaviour which is prohibited because it is evil in its very nature, such as murder, rape, aggravated assault and arson; and, on the other hand, crimes that are considered *mala prohibita*, which involves behaviour that society regards as a violation of law because it offends against certain accepted moral codes such as codes in respect of homosexuality, prostitution, pornography, and abortion.

The criminal law has assumed an increasingly important role in the Western

World as a mechanism of social control during this century. It has taken over many of the control functions of the family, the church and other institutions. In fact, there has been an 'overreach' or 'overproliferation' of the law, to the extent where virtually every aspect of the citizen's life is governed by some law or regulation. This is causing great concern, and the sentiments expressed by Frank W. Wilson, Chief Judge, U.S. District Court, Eastern Division of Tennessee, probably reflect accurately the increasing concern among social scientists, lawyers and others:

> The law can stifle and destroy human freedom as well as nurture and protect human individual freedom and democratic institutions as excessive watering of a plant can lead to the death of that plant. I fear that we are witnessing the beginning of just that over-proliferation. Each year the number and complexity of laws and regulations are increasing at a truly amazing rate . . .
>
> Few things concern me more than the rush to pass another law or to impose another regulation to correct every ill or fancied ill in our society and then upon its passage to have a feeling of assurance that the problem is now solved. The . . . people must learn before it is too late that the true source of justice and freedom does not lie in the law nor in the courts. Rather, the true source of justice and freedom lies in the hearts and the souls of men . . .
>
> The law can grant a divorce, but it cannot put love into a marriage. The law can force a parent to support its child, but it cannot assure that child parental love and guidance. The law can punish a tresspass, but it cannot require people to be neighbourly. The law can sometimes make men do justice, but it can never make men love justice. When any morality beyond that which is legal is considered foolishness, then the State becomes the sole determiner of right and wrong and the law becomes our undoing (Wilson 1970).

The Structure of South African Courts

As the emphasis in this section is mainly on criminal law and criminal justice a brief outline of the South African courts is presented here.

SUPERIOR COURTS

1. *The Appellate Division of the Supreme Court* is the highest court in South Africa. It has no original jurisdiction but is exclusively a court of civil and criminal appeal from the provincial and local divisions of the Supreme Court, and from the Bantu Appeal Court. Decisions by the Appellate Division on questions of law are binding for all other courts in future trials.
2. *The Provincial Divisions of the Supreme Court* have original and appellate jurisdiction in civil as well as criminal matters. They act as court of appeal for the magistrates' court in their respective divisions.

Inferior courts

These consist of the two categories of magistrates' courts, namely, district courts and regional courts; children's courts, Bantu Affairs Commissioners' Courts and Courts of Bantu Chiefs.

1. *Regional Magistrates' Courts* have jurisdiction over all crimes committed in their areas, except over murder and high treason. Minimum and maximum penalties are prescribed by law. These courts may impose up to three years' imprisonment, a R600 fine, ten strokes or any two of these. However, as these powers apply to each charge, these courts can, in effect, impose heavy total sentences.
2. *District Magistrates' Courts,* being junior to regional courts, can impose lesser penalties than the latter. They have jurisdiction over all criminal cases in their respective areas, except high treason, murder and rape. District courts may impose maximum penalties of up to six months' imprisonment, or fines not exceeding R200, or a whipping of up to ten cuts.
   An Attorney General may remit a case to a magistrates' court with increased jurisdiction. In this case a maximum prison sentence of one year, or a fine of up to R400, or a whipping not exceeding ten cuts – or any two of these penalties – may be imposed.
3. *Bantu Affairs Commissioners' Courts* have jurisdiction over Africans only. As in the case of the magistrates' courts, they hear both civil and criminal cases. These courts may apply African customary law, provided that it does not conflict with the principles of public policy or natural justice. They also try cases under the vast body of control legislation which is applicable to Africans only.
4. *Courts of Bantu Chiefs.* The State may confer on any African chief or headman the authority to try and sentence Africans for certain defined (non-serious) offences in their areas, according to Bantu Law, statutory law and common law. Sentences that may be imposed are a fine of R40 or two head of cattle, or ten head of small livestock, or a whipping (on males under thirty years only).
   In addition, there are three *Bantu Appeal Courts* – in Pretoria, Johannesburg and King William's Town – which hear appeals from the Bantu Affairs Commissioners' Courts.
5. *Children's Courts* are constituted by and function under the provisions of the Children's Act No. 33 of 1960, which will not be dealt with here.

The Law and the African Population

Any discussion on law in South Africa would be incomplete without reference to the way in which it affects the minority groups (in the sense of political power) of the Republic. Of the three broad categories of minority groups – the Coloureds (Mulattos), Asians (mainly Indians) and Africans (negroid people, officially known as the 'Bantu') – the latter are most estranged from Western culture and, therefore, from the Western legal system. While the Asians and the Coloureds predominantly live in the urban areas, and have, to a large extent, accepted Western cultural values, a large proportion of the Bantu still live in the tribal areas, under traditional tribal customs. Of the Bantu living in the urban areas many are migrant labourers, who eventually return to their 'homelands'. A large proportion of the permanent residents were born and raised in the tribal areas and, to a greater or lesser degree, still hold traditional cultural values. Even those who were born in the urban areas have often not fully accepted Western values. If one keeps in mind that a person's attitudes and moral and ethical values are determined by the standards observed in his own culture, then it is obvious that a large proportion of the African population of South Africa do not identify emotionally with the Western legal norms of the dominant White population group. Consequently, the sanctions which sustain the legal system do not exercise the same inner and spontaneous control in the case of Africans as with Whites, in whose case it forms part of their cultural heritage. To be meaningful and effective a legal system must command the intellectual as well as the emotional acceptance and support of the majority of the population. Retief (1975:52) tells us that 'the Bantu people have no part in the making of the laws of White urban society. The communal needs of the group also forms no background to the social norms on which these laws are based. The ruling legal system has no emotional or ethical meaning in his personal make-up.'

It is not only the cultural background of the Africans that prevents them from identifying themselves with Western legal norms. It is also their political, social and economic position in South African society that renders the Western legal system alien to them. They have no part in making the national laws of the Republic, yet virtually every aspect of their lives is governed by these laws. Only to a limited extent do their own customs and cultural norms play a role in governing their lives. The Minister of Plural Development has the power to confer on any Bantu chief or headman the authority to try and to sentence persons for certain defined offences, according to Bantu law, statutory law and common law. However, as was pointed out in the previous section, offences of a serious nature are excluded from their jurisdiction. (See Act 38 of 1927 as amended by Act 13 of 1955.) Under the discussion of the courts of the Republic, it was indicated that Bantu Affairs Commissioners' Courts are established in areas with a large African population.

In spite of these Bantu courts, however, a large number – probably the majority – of both civil and criminal cases are being dealt with by White judicial officials, and according to the national laws of the Republic, not according to Bantu customary law. It is, therefore, understandable that the African population does not have the same degree of understanding of and emotional identification with the national law of the Republic. This is highly significant when considering the nature and extent of criminality among the African people. Also of great significance is the fact that the African population of South Africa is subject to a number of laws which apply to it only. Such laws as the Bantu Urban Areas Act and the Bantu Labour Act respectively govern the African people's movement and residence in the cities, and their employment. Their identity, education, residence, and many aspects of their lives are governed by numerous regulations and laws. Some of these will be briefly discussed below.

The Population Registration Act, No. 30 of 1950 (*as amended*) provides for the race classification of every citizen of South Africa, and for the compilation of a population register. Mixed marriages between White persons and persons of other racial groups are forbidden by law – namely by the *Prohibition of Mixed Marriages Act, No. 55 of 1949*. Sexual intercourse between Whites and persons of any other group was prohibited by the Immorality Amendment Act, No. 21 of 1950.

In terms of the *Bantu* (*Urban Areas*) *Consolidation Act No. 25 of 1945* (*as amended*), all Africans of sixteen years and over, who are citizens of South Africa, are required to carry reference books, which contain details of where the holder is permitted to be and where he is allowed to work.

This Act provides for the general regulation and control of Africans in urban areas. It states, *inter alia* that no African may acquire any right to any land in an urban area without the permission of the State President. Furthermore, the Minister of Plural Development may, after consultation with the local authority concerned, prohibit *inter alia*, the attendance by any African at any church or other religious service or church function (S.9(7)(b); the conducting by any African of any school, hospital, club or similar institution; the attendance of Africans at – schools, hospitals or clubs in restricted areas, etc.

The Act stipulates that Africans may not remain in an urban area for longer than seventy-two hours unless they have lived there continuously since birth; have worked there continuously with one employer for at least ten years, or lived there lawfully and continuously for fifteen years; are the wife, unmarried daughter or son under the age of eighteen years of an African who is legally entitled to live in the urban area concerned; or have been granted special permission to remain in the area by the local labour officer.

Another important legal provision which places major restrictions – particularly on the African population – is the *Group Areas Act No. 26 of 1965* which, for example, makes it a punishable offence for anyone to

(a) attend any place of public entertainment (theatres, public halls, public sports fields, etc.);
(b) partake of refreshments that ordinarily involve the use of seating accommodation in a licensed restraurant, refreshment or tea room;
(c) be a member or guest in any club (unless a governmental authority is the host),

in an area or building which has been allocated to persons of a racial group other than his own.

REFERENCES

Aubert, V. (ed.) 1969 – *Sociology of Law*. Harmondsworth: Penguin.

Beinart, B. 1976 – 'Crime and punishment in an historical setting.' In *Crime, Law and the Community*. Proceedings of the International Conference on Crime, Law and the Community. Cape Town: Juta.

Blackstone, Sir William 1965–9 – *Commentaries on the Laws of England*. Oxford: Clarendon Press.

Butler, A. J. 1976 – *The Law Enforcement Process*. Port Washington, New York: Alfred.

Chambliss, W. J. 1969 – *Crime and the Legal Process*. New York: McGraw-Hill.

German, A. C., F. D. Day, and R. R. J. Gallati 1973 – *Introduction to Law Enforcement and Criminal Justice*. Springfield: Charles C. Thomas.

Podgorecki, A. 1974 – *Law and Society*. International Library of Sociology. London: Routledge and Kegan Paul.

Retief, G. M. 1975 – 'Social disorganisation, crime and the urban Bantu people of South Africa.' In Midgley, J. *et al.* (eds.), *Crime and Punishment in South Africa*. Johannesburg: McGraw-Hill.

Seagle, W. 1941 – *The Quest for Law*. New York: Knopf.

Selznick, Philip 1968 – 'The sociology of law.' In David L. Sills (ed.) *International Encyclopedia of the Social Sciences*. New York: Macmillan and Free Press, Vol. 9, 50–8.

Wilson, F. W. 1970 – 'The law and the urban age.' *Federal Probation*. June.

1. Law and Criminal Procedure in South Africa

ELLISON KAHN

Formal Sources of South African Law

Two major formal authoritative sources of law may be said to exist in the Republic's legislation, consisting of the rules of conduct prescribed by Parliament or some lesser authority expressly clothed with Law-making capacity by the State; and common law, comprehending the binding rules of conduct (including those that derive from modern custom) that do not flow from legislation. Attached to both sources is the doctrine of judicial precedent, requiring a court to follow the interpretation given to a piece of legislation, or the enunciation of a rule of the common law, by a higher court or a court on the same level in the judicial hierarchy but composed of a greater number of judges.

Legislation. This is a generic word covering the instruments passed by the various legislative authorities. Any piece of legislation may be called an 'enactment' or (though this tends to be misleading) a 'law'. The word 'statute' strictly means an enactment of the highest legislative body, i.e. the legislature, which is Parliament. It may be given an extended connotation to describe also the enactments of subordinate legislative bodies that are entrusted with original as opposed to delegated legislative authority, which means that their legislation, provided it falls within the powers assigned to them, is not subject to the special tests, notably reasonableness and certainty, that delegated legislation has to satisfy. Unfortunately, consistency in the use of 'statute' is not to be found; and 'statute law' has come to be accepted as the equivalent of the totality of legislation, in contradistinction to the totality of the common law.

Parliament, which represents only the White groups, is the supreme legislative authority. In terms of the Republic of South Africa Constitution Act,[1] an Act that affects the equality of the official languages must have been passed by both Houses of Parliament (the Senate and the House of Assembly) sitting together and at the third reading by two-thirds of the total number of members of both. Whether this makes Parliament non-sovereign is a matter of debate. In every other respect, at all events, it is sovereign as regards the tests of indivisibility, originality and illimitability. In the positive sense it may make a law on any matter – there are no guaranteed rights under our Constitution; in the negative sense no other legislative body, within or outside the country, has the capacity to compete with Parliament in so far as one of its laws clashes with an applicable Act of Parliament, that law falls away; in the territorial sense it is sovereign, for it may make any of its Acts applicable beyond the borders of the Republic, and though this statute will not be law in any foreign country affected, it will be law in South Africa.

Next come the subordinate legislatures exercising original legislative powers. In each instance the draft instrument requires the approval of the Cabinet before it becomes law. The oldest are the provincial councils of the provinces of the Cape of Good Hope, Natal, the Orange Free State and the Transvaal, and the Legislative Assembly of South-West Africa,[2] all of which, like Parliament, represent only the White electorate. Their legislative powers are of a restricted character.[3]

Of much more recent origin are the legislative bodies representing various ethnic groups, created to implement the Government's policy of separate development. The first of these organs to be created was the Transkeian Legislative Assembly, and that as recently as 1963.[4] It is the oldest of the Bantu 'self-governing territories within the Republic.' Four similar self-governing territories have recently been established: Bophuthatswana, the Ciskei, Venda and Gazankulu; while three others, less advanced in constitutional status, also have legislative assemblies with original powers.[5]

Using the Transkei as an exemplar, one observes that the legislature of a self-governing territory has a more extensive legislative capacity than a provincial council; that, unlike such a council, it has a certain extraterritorial law-making power, but only over its own local citizens; and that in addition certain of its intraterritorial legislation must be confined to its citizens.

In South-West Africa similar self-governing territories have been created since 1968,[6] but it is not clear whether their legislative councils have original law-making power.

The other subordinate legislature with original legislative capacity is the Coloured Persons Representative Council.[7] Its law-making powers extend over a small range of topics and then are confined to Coloured persons: in short, they are entirely on a personality basis.

Delegated legislative power is exercised by a body or person to whom it has been lawfully assigned by Parliament, a provincial council or other competent body. Familiar examples are the by-laws and regulations framed by municipalities and other local authorities, and regulations made by the Cabinet for a Minister of State under authority conferred by an Act of Parliament. As is the case with any subordinate law-making authority, the delegated legislature must follow the prescribed procedure and exercise its powers within the limits assigned. But the test of '*intra vires*' is wider than with original legislative authority: it includes 'reasonableness', unless the parent legislation provided to the contrary. 'Unreasonableness' in this regard means (a) substantial partiality and inequality between persons, classes or races – but differentiation or separation, such as separate counters in public offices for White and other customers or applicants, is permissible, provided it does not produce this result;[8] (b) manifest injustice; (c) bad faith; and (d) oppressive or gratuitous interference with rights. Thus in general, delegated legislation would be void if it took away rights without compensation or applied retrospectivity. In addition, the *intra vires* test includes the criterion of certainty. The instrument has to indicate with reasonable clarity the act that is called for or forbidden.

Judicial precedent[9] (*including the structure of the courts*). Recognition by judges of the duty *stare decisis* – to abide by precedents – yields the prospects of confident advice to their clients by legal practitioners, of keeping members of the Bench to rational paths and of reducing legal costs by the avoidance of re-thrashing out points of law. But too strict a doctrine of judicial precedent can entail the failure of the common law to adapt itself to changing times and social outlooks, the inability of the judiciary to correct past errors and the obstruction of scientific legal development.

Our courts have garnered these advantages and skirted by these disadvantages to a commendable degree.

The Appellate Division consists of a Chief Justice and ten judges of appeal. In a case concerned with the validity of an Act of Parliament the quorum is eleven members. Otherwise the quorum is five in a civil and three in a criminal appeal; although a larger court may be assembled, this rarely occurs.

On the next level come the seven provincial divisions, with their local divisions, sharing the same judges. A local division has concurrent jurisdiction with its provincial division over a portion of the latter's area of jurisdiction. Two of these local divisions sit permanently and have a distinct title – the Witwatersrand Local Division in the Transvaal and the Durban and Coast Local Division in Natal. A third is about to be created, the South-Eastern Cape Local Division in the Eastern Cape.

The number of judges assigned to the provincial divisions varies greatly and changes from time to time. In March 1973 the Transvaal Provincial Division had 25 judges, the Natal Provincial Division 12, the Cape Provincial Division 11, the Orange Free State Provincial Division 7, the Eastern Cape Division 7, the Northern Cape Division 4 and the South-West Africa Division 2. Each provincial division's Bench is headed by its Judge President.

In general an appeal lies from a single judge's order in civil proceedings by way of motion or petition (i.e. where oral evidence is not given) to a full bench (three judges) of the appropriate provincial division, and thereafter to the Appellate Division by leave of the full bench or, if this is refused, of the Appellate Division. But the parties may agree to leapfrog the intermediate appeal. In other civil cases appeals go direct to the Appellate Division. Appeals in criminal cases are considered in the next section of this chapter.

There are a few other superior courts,[10] but they are of minor significance.[11]

The most important lower courts are those of magistrates. The country is divided into a large number of magisterial districts. (In 1971 there were 253, manned by over 600 magistrates of various grades.) In each there is at least one magistrate's court, clothed with limited civil and criminal jurisdiction.[12] A magisterial district always lies within the confines of the area of a provincial division of the Supreme Court. Since 1952 a number of magisterial regional divisions have been created, with criminal jurisdiction only, but in advance of that of a magistrate's court of a district.[13] What complicates matters is that the areas of some of the regional courts cut across those of provincial divisions.[14]

In civil suits in general an appeal lies from an order of a magistrate's court having the effect of a final judgement, to the provincial division of the Supreme Court of the area. Further appeal to the Appellate Division requires leave of the provincial division, or, if it is refused, of the Appellate Division. Criminal appeals are considered in the next section of this chapter.

For the Africans there are special lower courts called Bantu Affairs Commissioners' courts. They have jurisdiction to hear the vast majority[15] of civil actions between Africans, with no limit as to value of the subject-matter. Appeals lie to one of three Bantu Appeal Courts – the North-Eastern, Central and Southern. There are also three Bantu divorce courts to deal with civil marriages, with areas of jurisdiction corresponding to those of the Bantu appeal courts, and sitting in two or three divisions. Bantu Affairs Commissioners' courts are also vested with criminal jurisdiction in respect of offences committed by Africans, equivalent to that of a magistrate's court.[16]

The binding quality of a judicial decision lies only in the *ratio decidendi* – the principle of law it enunciates, as distinguished from any *obiter dictum*, a remark made in passing, not necessary for the decision of the case. The precise meaning of *ratio decidendi* and the process of abstracting it are matters on which there is no unanimity of views among jurists. Suffice it to say that nothing that did not contribute to the final outcome of a judgment can be part of its *ratio;* and that any pronouncement on law not in the course of reasoning producing the decision on the issue before the court is *obiter*. With multimember courts where more than one judgment is delivered, a *ratio decidendi* can emerge only where a majority of the judges who sat, and none of whom is a dissenting member of the court, agree as to the ground of the order.[17] To give an illustration: In a court composed of five judges, if all judges agree as to the order, and at least three as to a ground for it, that ground is the *ratio decidendi;* but there will be no *ratio* if only two so agree, or if each judge expresses a different ground. If four or three judges agree as to the order, and of these at least three as to a ground for it, that ground is the *ratio;* but there will be no *ratio* if only two so agree, or if each judge expresses a different ground.

There are two fundamental principles of the doctrine of judicial precedent: first, a provincial division of the Supreme Court (with its local division) is absolutely bound by the *ratio* of the decision of a higher court or a larger court on its own level, in that order, save in the most unusual case where it was given *per incuriam* (literally, through negligence, as where the other court overlooked an enactment or binding precedent) or there has been later conflicting legislation – which, of course, will have to be followed; and secondly, the Appellate Division, and a provincial (including a linked local) bench of the same size, will follow a previous decision that it rendered unless it is now satisfied it was clearly wrong. Magistrates' and other lower courts, while not creating precedents themselves, should follow the judgments of superior courts.

Save for three minor statutory provisions,[18] these rules are judge-made.

An *obiter dictum*, though it falls from a unanimous Appellate Division, need not be regarded as binding. Not only that court itself but a local division and also a magistrate's court could disregard it. But if the remark has been carefully reasoned it will almost certainly be respected. And persuasive influence may be exercised by dicta of a less exalted nature.

Even if it was not guilty of *icuria* in enunciating a previous decision, the Appellate Division will not regard itself as absolutely bound by that decision. Omniscience and infallibility of the highest tribunal was never the Roman-Dutch outlook. But our highest court will overrule itself only if it is quite clear that it was wrong, and then only in exceptional circumstances, for its earlier ruling will have been respected by other courts and relied on by legal practitioners and the public.

The Appellate Division will be particularly inclined to abide by its previous stand where to depart from it would disturb legal relationships, such as contracts and marriages, that were believed to exist on its basis. It will be more apt to overrule itself where it had incorrectly removed rights without giving rights to others: for instance, where it had wrongly deprived persons of the vote. And if on the earlier occasion there had not been full argument or deliberation, the Appellate Division might be more easily persuaded to reconsider the matter.

Naturally, that tribunal will not regard itself as bound by one of its decisions delivered per *incuriam*. This would include its having given a decision on a matter without realizing that it had already pronounced on it differently. When faced with two such conflicting judgments of its own, the court will select not the earlier or later one but the one it now considers correct.

In principle the Appellate Division is not bound by any decision or series of decisions of other superior courts. From the start it considered itself under obligation to produce uniformity in the country of the exposition of the common law, as far as possible in conformity with Roman-Dutch legal principles and rules, and uniformity in the interpretation of enactments. This might entail rejecting the views of a division or certain divisions of the Supreme Court, even at the cost of interfering with past transactions. In other circumstances, in the process of reversing or overruling a decision or decisions of lower courts that it considers to be wrong and to produce injustice, the Appellate Division will enunciate what it believes is the correct rule. If no injustice has resulted, and the expression of the true law would not work retrospectively, the highest tribunal would probably correct matters; though, as has been seen, it might not, on the ground that it is too late to disturb curial practice. Finally, as has also been shown, if reversal or overruling would entail the consequence of the disappearance of rights and obligations hitherto believed to exist, it might well hesitate to act. There is no way by which any court can confine the operation of its decision to the future or only to acts, facts, events or transactions of the future.

A provincial division (with its local satellite courts) is not bound to follow the decisions of any of its fellow tribunals. Within its own confines the two basic rules set out above are applied. To take two illustrations: a single-judge court of division X must follow a two-or three-judge decision of that division, in the absence of an overriding enactment or decision of that division of a higher court. A two-or three-judge bench will pay a single-judge decision respectful attention, and if it is in accord with a long line of precedents will be disinclined to discard it, although the bench considers it wrong. Decisions of other provincial divisions (or their local courts) are of persuasive force only. A judge sitting alone in division X may decide differently from a three-judge court of division Y. But there is some sentiment in favour of striving for uniformity in the expression of the law throughout the Republic without waiting for the Appellate Division or the legislature to enforce it, as the vagaries of litigation and the demands on Parliament's time may mean a long wait.

A magistrate ought to follow decisions of the Supreme Court in their order of priority within his area of jurisdiction. If, as a regional magistrate, he finds that this area cuts across the areas of two or more provincial divisions, he should align himself with the division of the place where he is trying the case. Where there are conflicting decisions of benches of equal size in his area, a magistrate should follow the most recent one. If there is no Supreme Court decision in his area, he should regard himself as bound by decisions of other divisions, in order of size of the court. And if two or more decisions of courts of the largest size are in conflict, he should follow the latest one. In the final resort magistrates' courts are part of a Republic-wide organization and owe a residual obedience to all divisions of the Supreme Court.

A decision of a Bantu appeal court – any one, it appears, not only the one of the area – is considered binding on Bantu Affairs Commissioners' courts. Were there to be conflicting decisions of different appeal courts, no doubt the commissioner will follow the court of his area. A Bantu appeal court takes the same attitude to its own decisions as does a provincial division of the Supreme Court: binding unless shown to be clearly wrong.

In two special instances, because of legislation, English precedents may bind lower and superior courts in the absence of an Appellate Division precedent. They fall outside the compass of this article.

Modern custom. Unlike the era before and the era of the classical Roman-Dutch law, in modern South African law, as in other advanced legal systems, custom is not an important formative source of law.

The burden is on him who alleges that a custom exists to prove that it has been long established and uniformly observed, and is reasonable and certain.

A custom may be local and of very limited range. In the leading case it was simply as to rights of fishermen between Cape Point and Fish Hoek to cast lines from beaches without permanent fishing boats. But a custom may also be ubiquitous and far-ranging. For instance, commercial usage may make a certain document a negotiable instrument, and this has very significant legal consequences.

Juridically, a trade usage is a type of custom. It is a term imported into a contract by custom, unless the parties otherwise agree.

Old authority. As was shown earlier, our common law is the Roman-Dutch law. Where the issue before a court is not governed by an enactment, binding judicial precedent or modern custom, recourse will be had to that legal system in the manner already discussed.

'*Persuasive sources*'. Reference has been made to the persuasive influence of the Anglo-American ('common-law') and certain modern Continental ('civil-law') legal systems on the declaration of unclear points of South African law by our judiciary. These are not the only types of persuasive material to which the courts have resort. There is also what the French call *la doctrine* – the writings of legal scholars.

When the Roman-Dutch writers are silent, unclear or conflicting, and recourse is had to Roman law as a subsidiary legal system, our courts are wont to consult the writings of present-day Romanists.

Then there are the authors of treatises and articles in learned journals on modern law, particularly those on South African law. A judge, normally after reference by counsel, may consult them as storehouses of scholarship from which aid may possibly be found in the formulation or fortification of conclusions as to the law; though the final decision is always that of the court itself.

The weight attached to a textbook or article will obviously depend to some extent on the scholarly standard of the author and the depth of his analysis.

Where a judge or legal practitioner is seeking persuasive material from a foreign legal system, he will naturally try to consult the writings of the leading jurists on it.

When it comes to a branch of law that is not purely local in character, and particularly where it has not been well covered by old authority, legislation or case law, the opinions of the leading jurisconsults over the entire world may assume a peculiar importance.

In general, an accused has to be tried by the court having jurisdiction over the area in which the offence was alleged to have been committed. Since 1968 the Minister has the power to decide where any offence has to be tried.

Trial by jury was abolished in 1969. A judge is entitled, if he so wishes, to summon one or two assessors to assist him. The Appellate Division has said that it is desirable for him to do so in serious cases where the death penalty may be imposed.

Issue is joined between the State and the accused when he pleads to the charge or indictment (except, of course, if he pleads to the jurisdiction). The modern tendency of preventing the vitiation of proceedings by technicalities has manifested itself in a more flexible attitude to the charge or indictment. The accused is entitled to know what he is alleged to have done; he is entitled to sufficient particularity to enable him to prepare his defence; the indictment or charge must show by its averments that he has committed an offence and it must not be so vague and contradictory as to cause him embarrassment. But sect. 179 *bis* provides that a materially defective indictment may be cured by evidence at the trial. Any number of counts for any offences whatever may be joined in the same charge. It follows that a charge of murder may now be joined with any other charge. The principle that double jeopardy has to be abjured is recognized: an accused may, of course, plead guilty or not guilty to any charge; he also has the pleas of *autrefois acquit* or *convict* available to him.

The South African law of evidence is still closely linked to that of England. In a criminal trial our law of evidence (except where otherwise laid down) is the law as it was on 30 May 1961 – on that day the courts were obliged to apply the law 'in force in criminal proceeding in the Supreme Court of Judicature in England.' As can be imagined the effect of this formula as regards the rules of precedent is somewhat of a puzzle. While English decisions made before 30 May 1961 remain authoritative, subsequent decisions are persuasive only.

Whatever the position may be as regards pre-trial procedure, the right of an accused to counsel at his trial remains completely untouched. Normally, the prosecution is required to prove its case beyond any reasonable doubt, but there have been considerable statutory inroads into this principle. Again, the normal situation is that trials have to be held in open court in the presence of the accused. The prosecution is always required first to present its case. There is no obligation on an accused to give evidence – depending always on the cogency of the case against him, he takes the risk of non-persuasion if he fails to do so – and an accused may decide, at the end of the prosecution case, to give evidence under oath (he may 'affirm' rather than take an oath if he wishes), to make an unsworn statement from the dock to close his case, with or without calling any other witnesses. At the end of the State case he is entitled to a discharge if there is no evidence on which a reasonable man might convict. Both the prosecution and the defence are entitled to address the court in argument after the evidence has been heard – the prosecution having no right of reply on the facts.

An accused has a right of appeal from an inferior court to the Supreme Court against both (or either) his conviction and sentence. This is not the position where he wishes to appeal against a decision of the Supreme Court either as a court of appeal or as a court of first instance – leave to appeal to the Appellate Division must be obtained from the court making the decision. If this leave should be refused, the Chief Justice may allow it on his being petitioned for relief.

An appeal may be brought on three grounds. An accused may, in terms of sect. 363, seek leave to appeal against his conviction and sentence. The primary consideration in granting leave is whether he has a reasonable prospect of success in law or in fact. The two other procedures are appeals on a special entry of irregularity or illegality and on a question of law that has been 'reserved' – the trial court may of its own accord, or at the instance of the accused or the prosecutor, reserve a question of law for the consideration of the appeal court.

The prosecution has more circumscribed rights. Where an accused has been convicted before an inferior court, the Attorney-General may require the magistrate to state a case for consideration by the court of appeal, and when it has been stated, the Attorney-General may appeal. Similar provisions apply when some other prosecutor wishes to challenge the decision. We have already seen that the prosecutor may request the reservation of a point of law for the provincial appeal court's decision. On leave being granted, he may appeal further to the Appellate Division. In 1968 an amendment to the Act introduced new procedures for the admission of evidence that comes to light after the conviction of an accused.

There can be little doubt that the South African criminal procedure requires consolidation. Again, there are many of its features that are felt by some to be unsatisfactory. It has been said that it is too heavily weighted in favour of accused persons; that its evidentiary rules sometimes exemplify sophistry; that the innovations in pre-trial procedure have caused an erosion of civil liberty. An inquiry into the system was warranted, and in June 1970 Mr Justice D. H. Botha of the Appellate Division was appointed as the sole member of a commission of inquiry into it. After the report of the Commissioner had been published, the controversial Criminal Procedure Bill (which also incorporated certain recommendations of the Report of the Commission of Inquiry into the Responsibility of Mentally Deranged Persons) was tabled before Parliament on 21 March 1973. The official Opposition has resisted many of its provisions and adverse criticism has also been made of some innovations by the General Council of the Bar. It would be impossible here to canvass the provisions of the Bill, but it should be noted that the following suggested changes have bred fierce controversy: the proposed modifications of the preparatory examination procedure and the introduction of a very limited and circumscribed form of pre-trial judicial interrogation; an alternation to the law relating to the admissibility of confessions, that presumes a confession that has been made to a magistrate to have been freely and voluntarily made (the presumption is rebuttable); and a provision that will enable magistrates to convict on a plea of guilty without extrinsic evidence that an offence has been committed.

A provision that is likely to be welcomed by most persons relates to preventing the Attorney-General from detaining a witness longer than 72 hours without a judicial order. Most lawyers would also agree with an abolition of an accused's right to make an unsworn statement from the dock – an anachronism from the time when an accused could not give evidence in his own defence.

Some like the official Opposition and the General Council of the Bar, may feel that these changes constitute a radical departure from accepted and good legal norms; others may feel that it is not radical enough and that the South African situation would best be served by a modified inquisitorial system. In the 1973 session the Bill passed its second reading, certain amendments having been accepted, but had not passed the committee stage when it was held over to the next session of Parliament in 1974.

NOTES

1. Act 32 of 1961 ss. 108 and 118.
2. Now governed by the South-West Africa Constitution Act 39 of 1968, replacing Act 42 of 1925.
3. For instance, the only major legislative powers of a provincial council are school education of Whites, hospitals, local institutions and roads.
4. Transkei Constitution Act 48 of 1963 (see Kahn 1963).
5. All these developments have taken place in terms of proclamations issued in terms of the Bantu Homelands Constitution Act 21 of 1971. Bophuthatswana succeeded to the area served by the Tswana Legislative Assembly since 1 May 1971: Proc. R 131 of 26 May 1972; the Ciskei to the area served by the Ciskeian Legislative Assembly since 1 June 1971: Proc. R 187 of 28 July 1972; Venda to the area served by the Venda Legislative Assembly since 1 June 1971: Proc. R 12 of 26 January 1973; and Gazankulu to the area served by the Machangana Legislative Assembly since 1 July 1971; Proc. R 15 of 26 January 1973. There remain the Lebowa, Basotho-Qwaqwa and KwaZulu Legislative Assemblies established respectively on 1 July, 1 October 1971 and 30 March 1972.
6. See the Development of Self-government for Native Nations in South-West Africa Act 54 of 1968.
7. See the Coloured Persons Representative Council Act 49 of 1964.
8. Decided in the seminal case of Minister of Posts and Telegraphs *v.* Rasool 1934 A.D. 167.
9. For a detailed discussion, see Kahn (1967).
10. (a) The special criminal court of two or three judges that may be constituted *ad hoc* to hear charges of treason, sedition, etc. The governing provision as at March 1973 was s. 112 of the Criminal Procedure Act 56 of 1955. The Criminal Procedure Bill then before Parliament retained this court. (b) A water court in each provincial division presided over by a judge of the division: Water Act 54 of 1956 ch. IV. (c) The court of the Commissioner of Patents, presided over by a Transvaal judge nominated by the Judge President of that division: Patents Act 37 of 1952 ss. 16–19. The Special Court for Income Tax Appeals, established in terms of Part III of the Income Tax Act 58 of 1962, is presided over by a judge deputed by the judge president of the provincial division of the Supreme Court of the area. But it is really only a court of revision of tax assessments and not a court in the ordinary sense (see e.g. Bailey *v.* CIR 1933 A.D. 204 at 220). Nor is the Special Court constituted under the Regulation of Monopolistic Conditions Act 24 of 1955 a true court of law, though it, too, has a judge as president.
11. The picture has now changed, as the Transkei has established its own Supreme Court in terms of the Transkei Constitution Act 1963, s. 50 of which empowers the State President to constitute a High Court for the Transkei to replace any provincial of local division of the Supreme Court and any Bantu appeal or divorce court having jurisdiction in the area, and to make the necessary regulations. The Appellate Division has the same appellate jurisdiction in respect of the High Court as it has with a provincial or local division of the Supreme Court.
12. Criminal jurisdiction does not lie with treason, murder or rape, and punishment is restricted, unless a statute specially increases it, to a prison sentence of compulsory corrective training (two to four years), otherwise six months' imprisonment or a R200 fine or both on each count or ten strokes in all, which may be additional to imprisonment: Criminal Procedure Act 56 of 1955 chap. 18; Magistrates' Courts Act 32 of 1944 ss. 89, 92. Unless the parties otherwise agree, civil jurisdiction is in general limited to a subject-matter of the value of R1 000 (R2 000 on liquid documents and contracts falling under the Hire-purchase Act 36 of 1942). Certain civil matters may not be heard by a magistrate, notably dissolution of marriage, a decree of separation, validity or interpretation of a will, status as to mental capacity (Act 32 of 1944 ss. 29, 46.)

13. It may try a case of rape, unless the accused chooses a superior court trial (Act 32 of 1944 s. 89) and its corresponding jurisdiction as to punishment is three years' imprisonment and a fine of R600 (*idem* s. 92). It may impose a compulsory indeterminate sentence (at least nine years) or imprisonment for the prevention of crime (five to eight years) or corrective training (Criminal Procedure Act 1955 ch. 18). Regional courts cover virtually the entire country, apart from the Transkei. There are some 60 regional magistrates.
14. E.g. those of the O.F.S. and Griqualand West. See Government Notices R 794 of 1964, 1651 of 1968 and 1242 of 1970.
15. The main limitations are that they may not hear cases affecting status as to mental capacity, the validity or interpretation of a will (save by consent or where the estate is under R600), nullity and dissolution of marriage, divorce or a decree of separation: s. 10 of the Bantu Administration Act 38 of 1927. There are some 400 Bantu Affairs Commissioners.
16. See Bantu Administration Act 38 of 1927; Bantu Laws Further Amendment Act 79 of 1957 s. 2. Mention may be made of the courts of Bantu chiefs and headmen, with limited civil jurisdiction in matters arising out of Bantu law and custom and limited criminal jurisdiction. There is a full appeal, involving a rehearing, to the Bantu affairs commissioner's court. Thereafter civil appeals go to the Bantu Appeal Court and criminal appeals to the provincial division of the Supreme Court.
17. Fellner *v.* Minister of the Interior 1954 (4) SA 523 (A.D.).
18. Section 385 of the Criminal Procedure Act 56 of 1955 allows the Minister of Justice to refer a doubtful criminal law decision of a superior court to the Appellate Division for a ruling for the future guidance of all courts. It is employed very infrequently – only once or twice in a decade. There is a similar provision regarding a decision of a Bantu appeal court, for the future guidance of all such courts and Bantu Affairs Commissioners' courts: s. 14 of Act 38 of 1927. Section 113 of the Magistrates' Courts Act 32 of 1944 allows the Minister to direct divergent interpretations of a provision of that Act to the Appellate Division for a final interpretation. No reported case of its employment can be found.

REFERENCES

Kahn, E. 1963 – 'Some thoughts on the competence of the Transkeian Legislative Assembly and the sovereignty of the South African parliament.' *South African Law Journal*, 80:473–82.

——1967 – 'The rules of precedent applied in South African courts.' *South African Law Journal*, 84:43–55; 175–93; 308–30.

2. The Reformation of the South African Penal System: Some Possibilities

ROLAND GRASER

Over the past few decades there has been a disturbing increase in serious crimes and delinquency in South Africa and, at the same time the Republic's prison population has grown rapidly. The Report of the South African Commissioner of Police for the year ending 30 June 1975 indicates that, during the year *i.a.* the following crimes were reported. (The figure in brackets indicates the percentage increase over a ten-year period, since 1964): 8 534 murders (43,45%), 37 896 robberies (58,95%), 263 889 assaults (31,96%), 90 842 burglaries (21,8%), and 252 037 liquor offences (115%). At the same time the South African daily average prison population has grown rapidly, from 72 627 in 1965 to 98 851 in 1975; that is, by 36% over a ten-year period. The general population increase of the Republic during that period was 27%. While South Africa had 412 persons per 100 000 population in prison in 1974, the U.S.A. had only half as many, namely 200 and the European countries all less than 100 per 100 000 in prison.

From these statistics it is clear that the South African criminal justice system has not achieved sufficient success in combating criminality. Our traditional judicial procedures are cumbersome, time-consuming, costly and largely ineffective. Let us look at the ways in which criminality is being dealt with, and consider a potentially more effective approach.

Is Imprisonment the Answer?

Nowadays it is almost universally accepted by criminologists, penologists and probably to a lesser extent, by jurists, that the traditional prison is not able to rehabilitate the majority of offenders. Basically, *rehabilitation* – insofar as it concerns the offender – means turning a person who, because of an inadequate or defective social background, a character disorder or emotional problems is unable to lead a socially acceptable life, into a useful citizen. Often it means effecting a personality change and bringing about a new way of life. Under present circumstances it is practically impossible for our penal institutions to achieve this to any meaningful degree. The extent to which our South African prisons do succeed in achieving rehabilitation can hardly be determined because the possibility of impartial, scientific investigation within our penal institutions by independent external reasearchers is severely limited.

In a paper delivered to the National Criminological Symposium on Crime Prevention (at UNISA, in August 1973), Major-General J. P. Roux, at that time Chief of the Prisons Psychological Services, posed the following question: 'Can we . . . in all honesty and fairness, claim and accept that prison is the best place to send an offender for treatment and rehabilitation?' He gave the following answer to this question: 'Despite the facilities, personnel and programmes for treatment and rehabilitation, prison is in the final analysis the most unsuitable place and environment in which to effect rehabilitation.' Continuing, he says: 'The time has come for us to seriously consider keeping the offender within the community for as long as possible, and only sending him to prison as a last resort' (Roux 1973).

Prison is not only unsuitable for rehabilitation in the true sense of the word; there are also other important considerations which make the extensive use of alternative penalties desirable. Imprisonment is extremely costly to the taxpayer in terms of the purchase of land and farms for penal institutions, the construction and maintenance of buildings, the training and remuneration of staff, the accommodation, clothing and feeding of offenders, the payment of subsistence allowances to the dependants of prisoners, etc. The total cost amounts to several million Rand each year. In social terms imprisonment is also a bad investment – seen from the point of view of the disruption of family life, the severance of the prisoner's social ties in the community, loss of employment, and the adverse effect which imprisonment often has on the character of the prisoner and on his ability to adjust himself to society after his release. On practical as well as on humanitarian grounds, therefore, large scale imprisonment of offenders is indefensible.

In the light of this, it is necessary to reconsider our present penal methods and to develop effective alternative techniques for the treatment of offenders. However, we must continually test the *effectiveness* of any measures we apply, otherwise such measures may also only be 'a shot in the dark.' It naturally presupposes that we must critically and continually review our criminal justice system. The most practical manner in which this can be effected is probably through a permanent *Law Review Committee*. In addition, the appointment of a permanent *Advisory Council on the Penal System* (such as the one that exists in England) could also be of considerable value in the development of an efficient penal system which would keep pace with the changing times.

When a new penal measure should prove to have little or no effect on the incidence of crime, but is nevertheless more human and less demanding on our resources, then it is still preferable to such destructive measures as large scale imprisonment and the application of corporal punishment.

In considering alternatives to imprisonment, the criterion should at all times be their practicability. The large scale application of community service orders (as developed in Britain) may theoretically seem attractive, but to be meaningful, a community must have sufficient facilities to enforce such a sentence. This naturally applies to all types of sentences. Nevertheless, with a certain amount of imagination and vision, viable alternative methods could, no doubt, be found and developed. The community must, obviously, also be informed about and educated in the application of community orientated sentences.

Alternatives to Imprisonment

1. Diversion from criminal procedure

A method of decreasing the prison population, which is becoming increasingly popular in various countries, is to divert certain offenders – particularly minor offenders – from the normal channels of criminal procedure. Flynn described diversion as follows:

> It refers to all mechanisms, formal and informal, that lessen the chances of criminal processing and labelling, and to organised efforts at minimising penetration into the system. Diversion programmes are essentially community-based and provide either direct assistance or referral service to a host of individuals subject to criminal sanction but who are referred to such programmes in lieu of official processing (Flynn 1973).

The burden placed on the penal system by large numbers of offenders – often minor offenders, who are rather a nuisance than a threat to the community – impedes that system in the efficient administration of justice in more serious cases. There are, undoubtedly, a large number of offenders who need not pass through the penal system in order to protect society. The channelling of such offenders as drunks, vagrants and a variety of minor offenders through the penal system generally only achieves one of the objectives of the system, namely the motive of punishment or retribution. Only to a very minor extent – if at all – does it achieve the objectives of deterrence, the protection of society and the rehabilitation of the offender. It is therefore important to consider diverting such persons from the penal system to administrative or therapeutic facilities.

The diversionary process could take place at one of the various facets of the criminal procedure – namely, arrest, trial, or commitment to prison. Here we think particularly of diversion from arrest and from the criminal trial.

Diversion of Arrest

The police are already exercising a certain amount of discretion in the arrest of offenders. The author is convinced that, when such offences as public drunkenness, vagrancy, disturbing the peace, minor assaults – particularly between members of the same family – etc. are reported to the police, they do not always result in arrest. He is of the opinion, however, that non-arrest, or rather ignoring a particular offence, frequently does not solve the problem, and that referral to suitable social welfare facilities can often have a crime preventive effect. The police in Cape Town practice a form of diversion when they occasionally bring vagrants to the night shelter operated by NICRO. However, this happens infrequently.

Misconduct is often symptomatic of serious underlying personality, psychological or social problems which require expert attention. In countries such as Switzerland and certain American cities, *i.a.* New York, social workers are attached to the police force. With the supplementary orientation, namely, the social welfare orientation, the police are in a position to keep certain cases away from the criminal procedure and to refer them to suitable treatment or social welfare facilities. In this way the number of persons subjected to the criminal procedure – and, eventually, to imprisonment – is reduced.

The British police have a procedure under which certain youthful offenders are formally cautioned, instead of being brought before the courts. During 1970 this procedure was followed in 39 % of all the cases involving youthful offenders. A prerequisite of this practice is that the offender must acknowledge his guilt and that the complainant must agree that the question of prosecution or non-prosecution be left to the discretion of the police. While there are certain dangers and problems inherent in granting discretionary powers to the police, it is preferable to the practice of large scale arrest and imprisonment, which is a serious problem in South Africa, where large numbers of petty offenders are sent to prison annually.

Diversion from Criminal Trials

In South Africa, steps have already been taken – particularly in Cape Town – to keep persons arrested for public drunkenness in the police cells overnight in order to 'dry out', after which they are discharged. The diversionary process could, however, take place even before the police go into action. If police action in the case of public drunkenness could be reduced to a large extent, or even eliminated altogether, the police would be able to devote more attention to real criminal problems.

One of the best-known programmes for diverting inadequate minor offenders from the penal system is the Vera Institute's Manhatten Bowery Project in New York. The project gives shelter to chronic drunks who are usually accommodated for a short period – on average, five days. During this period they are 'dried out' and medical services are provided. In addition they are selected for one of the twenty-five aftercare programmes which include therapeutic and rehabilitative services. A 'rescue team' consisting of a 'rescue worker', usually a rehabilitated alcoholic and a policeman in civilian clothes, patrol the Bowery District by car to collect drunks. Participation in the project is voluntary and a wide range of medical services is provided in collaboration with a local hospital. While various alcoholics are repeatedly taken up by the project and no great measure of success has been achieved in terms of permanent sobriety, fixed employment and maintenance of family and other social ties, many of the people concerned have been assisted towards leading a more constructive life and staying out of prison. In fact, the arrest of vagrant alcoholics in the Bowery District has dropped by 80 %. Police officers who were previously detailed for vagrant control, have returned to normal patrol duties.

In South Africa an attempt is made to relieve the pressure on the penal system by releasing large numbers of short-term offenders on what is erroneously called 'parole' within 24 hours of admission. In 1975, 90 729 prisoners, being 30,5% of the total number of prison admissions during the year were thus released. However, as the Republic's large prison population indicates, relatively little thought is given to the idea of diversion in this country.

2. DECRIMINALIZATION

The application of criminal sanctions on people, particularly young first offenders whose misconduct is basically due to underlying personality disturbances and emotional or psychological problems, often causes more harm than good. Increasing pressure is, therefore, being put on legislation to decriminalize certain offenders.

Edith Flynn has the following to say about decriminalization:

> Correction is characterized by an historic tendency to overload the jail with socio-medical and social welfare cases. It is clearly beyond the scope of the jails to deal effectively with the mentally ill, alcoholic and drug addicts. In fact, applying criminal sanctions simply exacerbates the problems of these individuals. Also our propensity for outlawing private behaviour because private behaviour is found to be morally objectionable, has resulted in too many laws proscribing too many kinds of behaviour. The effect has been to sidetrack the system from its mission of protecting society against really serious crime to assuming the dubious role of policing private morality. The behaviour categories involved here are 'victimless' crimes, defined as crimes without an effective complainant other than the official authority. These behaviours include gambling, homosexuality between consenting adults, prostitution, abortion, and a wide range of noncriminal activities by juveniles. The control of such actions by criminal sanctions and jailings is singularly ineffective and corrupting. The need, therefore, for substantive criminal law reform is great in order to facilitate the systematic exclusion of such problem cases from the system. Rather than ignore these problems, alternative dispositions must be developed at the local level to permit the diversion of socio-medical problem cases to other agencies and better-equipped facilities outside the criminal justice system (Flynn 1973:75–6).

One also cannot help wondering whether it is necessary for the large number of contraventions of the law committed annually in South Africa (in 1973 they amounted to nearly two million) to be referred to our criminal courts. Here we think, in particular, of contravention of the Bantu Administration Act, contravention of the Bantu (Urban Areas) Consolidated Act, registration and submission of documents by Bantus, drunkenness and other contraventions involving liquor, road traffic offences, offences under the Master and Servant's Act and Bantu Labour Regulation Act, contraventions of the Work Registration

Act, illegal possession of Bantu liquor, dog and vehicle licence offences, and contravention of ordinances and local authority regulations.

3. Reducing awaiting trial cases and acceleration of trials

According to the most recent statistical report of the Commissioner of Prisons (R.P. 47/1976), 253 797 *unconvicted persons* were admitted to our prisons during the year ending June 30 1975. Of these 65 301 were again committed to prison after trial and conviction. That is, only 25,73% of all trial-awaiting prisoners were actually sentenced to prison. From this we must conclude that it was unnecessary to detain all the 188 496 persons who, after having been tried, were not again taken up in our penal institutions. In a large number of cases, the court obviously did not consider the offence sufficiently serious to send the accused to prison (not to mention those who were found not guilty.)

Although the courts do release a large number of accused persons on bail, there are nevertheless numerous persons who are at present being detained in prison (or in police cells) who could be released on their own recognisance. This applies particularly to minor offences. Arrested persons who have a permanent address and fixed employment, and who are in possession of identification documents, can usually be released with a reasonable assurance that they would appear in court on due date. In New York it has been found that, during the first two years of a programme under which large numbers of arrested persons (a total of 36 917) who were arrested for minor offences, were released after a warrant had been issued, 5,3% failed to appear in court on the day of the trial. (This figure, however, also included those persons who were unable to attend owing to illness).

Numerous persons are being detained in our prisons because they cannot raise the amount fixed for bail. This immediately gives rise to the contention of 'a law for the poor and a law for the rich.' Where there is a possibility that a person would fail to appear for trial if he should be allowed to remain in the community, he should preferably not be granted bail, rather than fixing bail at an amount beyond his means. Ideally, bail should be adapted to the accused person's ability to pay and should be refused only in the case of serious offences, where the accused person constitutes a danger to the community, where his release constitutes a danger to himself, or where there is a real possibility that his release would defeat the ends of justice.

There is often a considerable lapse of time, sometimes lasting several months, between the date of the arrest and the conclusion of the trial. The slowness of investigating officers, prosecutors or the defence often results in court cases being dragged out for weeks or months. While one postponement follows another, the awaiting-trial prisoner is languishing in jail, frequently under circumstances which leave much to be desired. It would be preferable if separate institutions, with adequate recreational facilities, could be established for awaiting-trial prisoners who must be held in detention for valid reasons.

It is ironical that the conditions under which awaiting-trial prisoners are detained, are generally not as good as those under which convicted prisoners are detained. This also applies to South Africa, particularly as far as recreational facilities, training facilities and rehabilitation services are concerned. The situation is ironical because an awaiting-trial prisoner is theoretically innocent, and a considerable number of awaiting-trial prisoners are, indeed, found not guilty.

4. Suspended sentences

The South African courts are at present making considerable use of suspended sentences. Nevertheless a large number of first offenders and minor offenders (particularly young persons) are regularly sent to prison. It would appear, therefore, that there is a need to extend the practice of the suspended sentence – with *meaningful conditions* attached to them. If suspended sentences are imposed extensively, *without meaningful conditions and without proper expert supervision*, it would not have the desired effect in terms of safeguarding the community and in terms of the rehabilitation of offenders. People who break the law, particularly when their crimes reflect irrational behaviour, and when they include violence and dishonesty, frequently have serious emotional, psychological or social problems demanding expert attention and treatment.

5. Probation

Although the Children's Act (33 of 1960) makes provision for probation in respect of youthful offenders, there is no formal probation system for adult offenders in South Africa. It can be accepted that numerous first and youthful offenders would probably not have become hardened criminals if they had received proper diagnostic and rehabilitative treatment when first arrested. That is to say, had there been a thorough investigation into their social background, personality, criminogenic factors etc. before sentence was passed with their first appearance in court, and had they at that stage already been placed under the expert supervision of a probation officer.

In his speech on the occasion of the opening of Parliament in January 1974, the State President said: 'Because an efficient and intensive probation service is considered essential for any crime prevention and penal reform programme, the introduction of such programme is being investigated.' Several years have elapsed since the introduction of such a programme was mooted, but, by the beginning of 1977 no formal adult probation services had been established. While a probation system can be introduced in terms of para. 352 of the Criminal Procedure Act, new legislation, which accurately defined the application of probation in respect of adults, would probably be preferable.

The effective application of probation rests on two basic requirements:

(a) The judicial officer must have full, accurate and reliable information concerning the accused and his background at his disposal when he passes sentence.

(b) There must be adequate facilities for supervision and control – in other words, there must be sufficient trained personnel available to carry out effective supervision.

Sanford Bates, the well-known American penologist, made the following remark:

> No physician would undertake to prescribe treatment for a sick man unless he had a full report of his ailment and condition. In like manner a judge (and a magistrate) should not pass judgment on a defendant without a pre-sentence report even though he may be sceptical of the ability of social workers or probation officers to give him comprehensive advice and counsel. And if he does not have the staff to render this service, he should see to it that the legislature or country authorities provide it for him (Bates 1960:15).

The application of probation has a number of important *advantages*, namely:

(i) Probation enables the offender to lead a more normal and a more socially constructive life than in the case of imprisonment. The probationer can continue to work and meet his responsibilities towards his family. He can also make use of educational, cultural and recreational facilities in the community, which are inadequate or sometimes completely lacking in most penal institutions. Furthermore he is placed in a position where, under expert supervision and with the assistance and guidance of the probation officer, he must learn to shoulder normal social responsibilities.

(ii) Probation prevents the possibility of criminal contamination, that is to say, the acceptance of criminal values and anti-social behaviour patterns, which frequently results from imprisonment, particularly in the case of youthful offenders. In addition the stigma of imprisonment and its negative consequences, for the offender as well as his family, is avoided.

(iii) Probation enables the probation officer or social worker concerned to make use of the welfare and rehabilitation facilities as well as other resources within the community in the treatment of offenders.

(iv) A probation system would, in the long run, bring about a considerable saving to the taxpayer in that it would reduce the high cost of imprisonment.

6. Training centres for inadequate offenders

Social workers, psychologists and others concerned with the rehabilitation of offenders find that certain persons have a background of inadequate education and socialization and, therefore, do not have the social proficiency to function satisfactorily within the framework of a 'normal' society. In many instances such persons are a burden rather than a danger to society. It is, therefore, usually not necessary to detain them in prison in order to protect society.

The idea of establishing training centres for socially inadequate offenders – as an alternative to short-term imprisonment – originated in England fairly recently, but has not as yet been introduced in South Africa. According to Gwynn-Jones the 'Day Training Centres' function as follows:

> Selected inadequate offenders will be subject to *Probation Orders* containing a condition that they attend the centre each day for a period of sixty days – residing at home, but by the very fact of their acceptance at the Centre, they will be indoctrinated to the routine of a daily time table. The programme at the Centre will be geared to training as opposed to detention and to *social training* as opposed to vocational training. As far as possible, the programme will be adjusted to suit the needs of the individual offender. For example, an illiterate offender will be given the facilities of concentrated remedial teaching, under the guidance of an expert who will be called in to assist in this field as the need arises.
>
> One can envisage the Centre helping the trainee in simple home maintenance – elementary painting and decorating, repairing broken windows and furniture; preparing simple balanced meals from raw materials as opposed to buying pre-cooked meals at exorbitant prices; instruction in form filling; conduct at job inteviews; handling a telephone directory and a telephone; discussion groups on topical matters from world affairs to home economics – even discussions with Magistrates or Police in the maintenance of law and order; basic hygiene; bathing; dental care; chiropody (Gwynn-Jones 1974).

Like other treatment orientated alternatives to imprisonment, the offender concerned is placed under such a programme of social training *with his consent*. If it were to take place under coercion the offender may not be sufficiently motivated to give his wholehearted co-operation, and no great measure of success could be expected. It is therefore important that the court – through the probation officer or social worker concerned – should fully inform the accused, at an early stage, of the nature of the sentence and what is expected of him in this regard.

7. Community service

When an offender is detained in prison, he is removed from the relevance of his crime and he is inclined to adopt the attitude that he is 'paying' for his misconduct by being in prison and that he has no further obligations towards his victim and the community. In fact, the humiliation, deprivations and emotional suffering caused by imprisonment often lead to bitterness and self-pity, and build up an attitude of hostility towards authority and towards society in general.

Instead of sentencing the accused to detention in prison, particularly when his offence is of a minor nature, he could be ordered to render a specific service to the community. For instance, a young first offender who had robbed and assaulted an elderly person, could be ordered to serve in a home for the aged for a specified period while he is under the supervision of a *probation officer* (or some other person designated by the court). When the offender is placed in a situation where he must render a service to physically or mentally retarded persons, he may develop a feeling of sympathy towards the disabled persons and, at the same time, a sense of social responsibility. Not only may this move him to introspection but it could persuade him that he is atoning for his misconduct by rendering a meaningful and constructive service.

The idea of service to the community by certain offenders also originated in England fairly recently. According to Section 15 of the British Criminal Procedure Act of 1972, a person who is at least seventeen years of age and who is found guilty of a crime carrying a sentence of imprisonment, can be sentenced to serve the community for a period of between forty and two hundred-and-forty hours without compensation. Before the accused can receive such a sentence, the court must have obtained a presentence report on the accused and it must be satisfied that work of the nature envisaged is available for the offender; that he is capable of carrying out such work and that arrangements have been made for him to do so. However, the law also requires that the offender must agree to such a sentence. In addition, the offender must report to the probation officer in charge of the community service project; he must inform him of any change of address and must perform the work as it is assigned to him. Especially the offender who has time on his hands, and who is physically and spiritually suited for the work, but who is aimlessly frittering away his free time and channelling his energies in anti-social directions – particularly during weekends and in the evening – can benefit by this type of sentence. It is important, however, that the activity or task (namely, the community service), must be sufficiently stimulating and meaningful to satisfy the offender and to be a positive influence on his attitude of life.

As with most other diversionary techniques, the idea of community service by offenders has not been generally applied in South Africa as yet. There are, however, instances where sentencing officers have made use of imaginative alternatives that are related to the nature of the offence in a meaningful way. Mr W. A. King, a regional magistrate in Cape Town, for instance, has sentenced several offenders – particularly in offences related to negligent driving – to deliver services to the Red Cross, the St. John's Ambulance and the 'Noodhulpliga'. This involved assisting on ambulance duty over weekends and evenings for a period of about forty hours, and, occasionally, working in the casualty ward of a hospital. According to the magistrate in question, many offenders who had been sentenced in this way became members of these organizations and continued to serve them. In one instance a second offender guilty of culpable homicide, resulting from negligent driving, was sentenced to work in a morgue for several weekends. He was not sent to prison as he was the sole supporter of his children – his wife having deserted him. A condition was that he should be present if relatives came to identify a deceased next of kin. After this experience the offender apparently preferred using public transport to using his car.

When the particular magistrate sentenced an offender as indicated, it was with his consent and with the co-operation of the organization which he was to serve. He would postpone sentence for a year or so, or pass a suspended sentence with the conditioning of delivering the specified service. Not in a single case was it necessary to invoke the suspended sentence for failure to co-operate.

It would appear that other South African magistrates have not followed the example set by Mr King, but continue to sentence offenders in the conventional way – to imprisonment, a fine or a regular suspended sentence.

8. Compensation

There are probably few jurists who will not agree that the penal system should be based on the principle that it is the duty of the State to protect its citizens. This includes compensating victims of crime for damages, losses and suffering.

Under present penal system in South Africa, emphasis is laid mainly on retribution and, to a lesser (and inadequate) degree, on the prevention of crime; and then practically exclusively on secondary prevention. It can be said that plight of the victim is virtually disregarded.

There are various possible ways in which victims can be compensated, of which the most important are the following:

(i) Restitution of loss suffered, or compensation for loss by means of a civil action;
(ii) Payment of compensation as a condition of probation or release on parole.
(iii) The payment of a salary by the prison authorities for work performed and the application of part of such salary as compensation for damage or loss.
(iv) Approved tax abatements for damage or loss suffered as a result of theft, assault or fraud. This also includes medical expenses. In addition, provision could be made for tax abatements in respect of costs incurred in effecting safeguards against crime, for instance, the installation of burglar alarms.
(v) Personal insurance against damage or loss cause by a criminal act.

Although the first and last possibilities already exist in South Africa, and the application of the other possibilities would be advantageous – and would be a considerable improvement on the present system – it would not offer a complete solution to the whole problem of the victim's loss, damage and suffering. While it is considered that these possibilities should be explored and put into effect, the main solution to the problem is that the state must accept responsibility for loss and damage suffered by its citizens, and possibly also for the suffering inflicted on them as a result of crime.

There is a clear need for the establishment of a *central, state-controlled, victim compensation fund*. Such a fund must be controlled by a *national compen-*

sation board and must, as in the case of the Republic's legal aid scheme, have local offices. The establishment of a national compensation fund would, no doubt, present various practical problems. A number of questions arise, such as: How should such a fund be administered? For what crimes (assault, murder, theft, fraud, etc.) must compensation be paid? What should be the minimum and maximum amounts of compensation paid? What must be the nature of an appeal against the board's decision? Should the victim's financial circumstances be taken into consideration in determining compensation? How can malpractice and fraud be avoided in the application of a compensation scheme? All these and other questions would have to be considered if a compensation system is to be introduced.

It is obvious that it would be expected that the offender would have to contribute towards the compensation paid to his victim. If compensation is paid from a central fund, then the offender would have to pay a fixed amount – determined by the court – to the fund, if necessary by instalments. However, from the point of view of offender rehabilitation it would, wherever practicable, be preferable that he should pay compensation directly to the victim, as this would bring him into more intimate contact with the results of his negative behaviour.

9. Fines

At present, extensive use is made of fines as a penal measure, particularly in the case of minor offences. In South Africa the extent to which the courts can impose financial penalties is, however, largely restricted to fixed amounts. These amounts are often unrealistic, particularly when they are not adapted to the offender's ability to pay. While a fine of R1 000 would be of no consequence to a rich person, a poor man may find it impossible to pay a fine of R50. It would therefore be in the interests of justice if the amount of the fine could be adjusted to the offender's financial means (namely, his property, salary and other income).

There is no doubt that a large number of offenders, particularly minor offenders, land in jail because of their inability to pay their fines. It is undesirable that imprisonment should be the automatic alternative to a fine – that is, Rx or x days'/months' imprisonment in the event of non-payment of the fines. The prison population would undoubtedly be considerably less if (a) fines could be adjusted to an offender's income and assets, and (b) fines could be paid in instalments. In this regard one thinks of the *day* tariff system which operates in certain European countries, such as Austria: when an offender is given a sentence of ten day rates, it would mean that the person who earns R4 a day would pay a fine of R40, while a person earning R20 a day would pay a fine of R200. In West Germany practically all short sentences of less than six months have been eliminated and have been replaced by a system of fines, as described above. (For a comprehensive description of the Swedish system of day tariffs fine, see the report of the British Advisory Council on the Penal System, 'Non-Custodial and Semi-Custodial Penalties,' Home Office 1970: 74–6.)

10. Periodical imprisonment

One of the major problems of the South African Department of Prisons is the large number of short-term offenders that are sent to prison each year. In 1975, 296 919 offenders received sentences of imprisonment in South Africa. Of these 255 007 (85,79%) received sentences of six months and less. It is virtually impossible to institute meaningful rehabilitation programmes for such a large number of short-term prisoners, spread across the country, because of a rapid turn-over of the prison population. Furthermore, short-term imprisonment contains all the negative elements of imprisonment in general, such as potential criminal contamination through association with 'hardened' criminals, disruption of family life, loss of employment and income, and stigmatization.

With the above in mind, the legislature introduced periodical imprisonment in 1959. According to the Criminal Procedure Act (Act 56 of 1959), periodical imprisonment may be imposed in lieu of any other sentence, for a period of not less than 100 hours and not exceeding 1 000 hours. It is served in periods of not less than twenty-four hours at a time, although the head of the institution may grant exceptions to this rule. In practice such a sentence is usually served over weekends, in order to prevent disruption of family life and loss of employment, which is peculiar to continuous imprisonment.

Periodical imprisonment is usually imposed on persons who lead reasonably normal lives in society, for less serious offences such as certain traffic offences and non-payment of maintenance. As far as practicable, persons sentenced to periodical imprisonment are not allowed association with other prisoners.

While periodical imprisonment appears to be a constructive alternative to continuous imprisonment, it appears that it is applied so infrequently in South Africa that it hardly plays a role at all. According to the Report of the Commissioner of Prisons for the year ending 30 June, 1975, only 304 persons of the total 296 919 sentenced to prison received sentences of periodical imprisonment during that year – that is, a mere 0,1%!

Alternatives to Continuous Imprisonment

The attempts to reduce the prison population consist not only of alternatives to incarceration, but also the application of certain measures under which prisoners are released before the expiration of their sentences. Some examples of these measures that are applied in various countries are:

1. Temporary release

Reference has already been made to the negative consequences of isolation in prison on the ability of the prisoner (particularly the long-term prisoner) to adjust himself to society on his discharge from prison. The negative effect of this isolation is reduced by granting as many selected offenders as possible temporary release from prison, especially those who constitute no direct threat to society and who are positively motivated.

Various countries have programmes for temporary release from imprisonment. In most cases, the objective is to bridge the gap between the artificial, isolated, regimented and repressive prison community on the one hand and the dynamic and complex society on the other hand. In certain European countries as well as in Canada and the U.S.A., selected prisoners are released for periods ranging from one day to about ten days. The following quotation illustrates a programme of temporary release in California, geared to preparation for release on parole:

> The furlough program's reasoning was that, since bringing the community resources needed for the pre-release preparation into the institution had been tried without significant results, the logical alternative was to send the inmate out into the community where the resources were in the first place: to bring together in the community setting, the inmate and the resources necessary for planning his release . . . The program was designed to help inmates acquire the basic resources needed for their parole to the community, and this is what has been done. The great majority of furloughees accomplished the things they had planned: securing employment, acquiring a driver's licence, getting to know the parole agent, establishing a residence, and cementing family relationships. The program has the double advantage of not only working but of costing no more than a little extra staff time . . .
>
> The fact that all but two furloughees returned is consistent with the experience of other furlough programmes and therefore not surprising. Missisippi has operated a 'Holiday Suspension Programme' for some time. Over a twelve-year period, over three thousand inmates were sent home for ten days and only fifteen failed to return. Over a five-year period, one thousand men (between the ages of eighteen and twenty-four) were granted home leave from two Michigan camps; only three failed to return. What is surprising in the Californian programme is the amount accomplished on the prerelease furlough (Holt 1971).

2. Work release

Another method whereby the prison population can be reduced temporarily, is a work release programme. This means that prisoners spend the day working in the open community, returning at night to prison, where they also spend the weekends.

Work release has been applied for many years in a number of countries, including England, Japan, Germany, the Scandinavian Countries, the Netherlands etc. Since the late 1950's it has been applied to an increasing degree in various states in the U.S.A. The State of Wisconsin, for example, has been making use of work release for many years under its 'Huber Act' of 1913.

Generally, prisoners working within the community receive normal remuneration for their labour (that is to say, salaries and wages paid in a free economy). However, the manner in which the prisoners' wages are administered, differs from one country to another.

3. PAROLE

One of the most important and, if applied correctly, most effective methods of facilitating prisoners' adjustment in the open community and, at the same time, reducing the prison population, is the early but conditional release of prisoners under professional supervision.

By parole is meant the early release of a prisoner from a penal establishment, under specific conditions and under the supervision of a designated organization or person. The purpose of parole, in the true sense of the word, is not merely to mitigate punishment by shortening the sentence imposed by the courts; although, to a certain extent and with good reason, this is the way in which it is regarded by many officers in South Africa. Parole is a penological measure designed mainly to facilitate the prisoner's transition from the highly restricted and controlled existence in the penal establishment to the freedom of communal life.

In recent years the South African parole system has improved considerably, in that, nowadays, more emphasis is placed on the supervision of long-term prisoners who are released on parole. Measured by the standards of other countries, such as Canada, for instance, which have an advanced parole system, there is, however, considerable room for improvement in the South African system of parole. The reason for this view is discussed further on.

To be effective as far as its two main objectives are concerned, namely, to rehabilitate the offender and to protect society, the parole system must meet three important conditions:

(i) There must be intensive *prerelease preparation*. This should commence long before the prisoner's date of release, and must consist of a comprehensive programme embracing services in respect of personal problems, family and social problems, the provision of employment and housing, and so forth. Outside parties, particularly welfare organizations such as NICRO, must actively participate in this programme of preparation. The prisoner is, after all, returning to society and will be under the supervision of an organization or person within that society. Should the supervisory party not be involved in the prerelease preparation, parole would be an incoherent process without much hope of effecting the re-integration of the offender into the community to any meaningful extent.

(ii) Parolees must be released under clearly specified *conditions* which are meaningful and realistic; that is to say, these conditions must be adapted to the needs and problems of the individual offender. To be effective, however, they must be supported by suitable sanctions.

(iii) Parolees must be placed under expert *supervision*, and the supervisory officer or agency must be able to extend the necessary assistance and treatment to the parolee.

Seen as a whole, the South African parole system does not meet these conditions satisfactorily. According to the statistical report of the Commissioner of Prisons for the year ending 30 June 1975, of the 230 058 prisoners with sentences of up to and including four months who were admitted to prison during that year, 90 729 or 40% were released on parole, the majority within 24 hours.

There is no doubt that it is essential that the prison population be reduced drastically, but it is doubtful that the present system of large scale (virtually immediate) release of short-term prisoners is desirable, as this leads to loss of faith by society in the penal system. In addition an offender who is sentenced to one month or even three months' imprisonment, but is released within 24 hours, would probably also lose his respect for the law. One feels, however, that many of these offenders should never have been sent to prison in the first instance. Therefore, responsibility for this undesirable state of affairs must not be laid at the door of the prison authorities, but rests with the courts which inundate the Department of Prisons with innumerable short-term prisoners for whom there is probably insufficient accommodation, recreational facilities and rehabilitation facilities, and who often do not constitute a threat to society.

As far as release on parole of long-term prisoners is concerned, an investigation conducted by the writer in 1974 – 75 provides some insight into the position.

During the year ended 31 March 1974, NICRO had 1 415 persons under parole supervision. This figure includes persons who were placed under the supervision of NICRO during the course of the year, as well as those who were already under the parole supervision of the organization at the commencement of the year under review. A file study revealed that NICRO participated in the pre-release preparation of only 286 of the 1 415 cases – namely 20,2% of all the parolees under its supervision. In only 159 instances (11,2% of the total) did NICRO have an interview in prison with the prospective parolee.

NICRO had very limited contact with social workers or other officers of the Department of Prisons as far as preparing prospective parolees for their discharge was concerned, or preparing the families of prisoners for their return. In only 203 or 14,3% of the cases was such liaison carried out.

Of the total of 1 415 parolees who were under its supervision during the year, NICRO was advised in only 527 (37,2%) cases of the prisoners' approaching release on parole before they were actually released – in 236 (16,6%) cases by the Department of Prisons, while 291 (20,5%) cases were channelled to NICRO by one of the other State Departments concerned. This means that in nearly two-thirds of the cases NICRO was not advised of the prospective parolees' impending release. These persons simply presented themselves at NICRO's offices and indicated that they had been released.

As far as employment is concerned, arrangements were made for employment for 382 (27%) parolees before they were released. Of these, employment was arranged for 124 (8,7%) cases by the Department of Prisons; for 58 (4,2%) cases by NICRO, in 49 (10,7%) cases by relatives and friends and in 151 (10,7%)

by the prisoners themselves. NICRO assisted 634 (44,8 %) parolees in obtaining employment *after* their release.

933 (64,9 %) parolees had accommodation available to them *prior* to their release. This was provided as follows: through the Department of Prisons 83 (5,8 %) cases; through NICRO 57 (4 %) cases; through relatives and friends 478 (33,7 %) cases and through the prisoners themselves, 315 (22,2 %) cases.

The above-mentioned figures would indicate that parole, as it is applied in the Republic, does not meet the basic requirements of an efficient parole system.

Factors Mitigating Against the Development of Rational and Effective Penal Measures

(A) LEGAL LIMITATIONS

Although Section 352 of the Criminal Procedure Act (56 of 1955) makes provision for the imposition of certain sentences other than imprisonment, these alternatives are vaguely defined and are limited to fines, suspended sentences and discharge with a warning. There is no specific provision for the kind of alternative which is regarded in many countries as the basis of an enlightened penal policy, namely, probation. As it has become clear, from recidivism rates and general crime statistics, that a policy of large-scale imprisonment – as the major criminal sanction – is ineffective in controlling crime, it is important that specific provision should be made for the application of a wide range of alternative sentences under the Criminal Procedure Act. Such alternative sentences must be clearly outlined and there must be definite guidelines for their application.

Not only are there severe legal limitations in respect of effectively dealing with offenders, but the other party to the crime, the victim, is virtually ignored entirely by the criminal justice system. While there are certain possibilities of obtaining restitution through civil action, these remedies are unlikely to be successful. Firstly because of the poor financial condition and prospects of most offenders and, secondly, because offenders are often sent to prison, thus preventing them from earning money to make restitution. South Africa's criminal legislation makes no provision for compensation in respect of loss, damage and pain suffered by the victim of crime.

(B) PSYCHO-CULTURAL FACTORS

While the general public attitude towards mentally disturbed persons and alcoholics has changed drastically during the past century from a punitive and rejecting one to an acceptance that such persons can benefit from treatment and can be re-admitted to the community, the public still has a strong prejudice against criminals. This is based on irrational fears and deep-seated misconceptions, such as that all criminals are inherently evil. Furthermore, there is an almost blind faith in imprisonment as the panacea for deterring criminals and protecting society. (This attitude is reflected by the heavy reliance of the South

African courts – especially the lower courts – on imprisonment.) In general, members of the public regard offenders with hostility, fear or indifference. These attitudes impede the development of a rational and enlightened penal policy; that is to say, a policy based not so much on the nature of the crime, but rather on the person of the offender – i.e. his personality and medico-biological anomalies, his social and personal background, anticipated future behaviour and other relevant aspects.

(c) MISCONCEPTIONS ABOUT PUNISHMENT

The nature of our penal policy is to a large extent founded on certain basic misconceptions which obstruct the development of a rational penal policy. Among the most important of these misconceptions are the following:

The heavier the punishment, the greater the deterrent value

That this conception is ill-founded, is proved by the fact – to go to extremes – that although there is a death sentence which is frequently applied, a large number of murders and other crimes punishable by death are committed annually in South Africa. Persons who it is intended should be deterred by severe penalties, are frequently so inadequately socialized and are so lacking in social skills and ethical and moral values that they cannot lead a socially constructive life. Also, many offenders frequently have such deep-rooted character disorders and emotional or psychological problems that they are unable to grasp and logically consider the consequences of their misconduct.

Imprisonment Protects Society

When an offender is sentenced to imprisonment, the sentence is often justified with the statement: 'You are a threat to society; society must be protected against you.' That this conception is hardly justifiable is proved by the fact that only a very small percentage of all prisoners are detained permanently in penal institutions, and that very few people die in prison. Sooner or later the vast majority are returned to society. Of the total of 297 233 persons sentenced to imprisonment, including corporal punishment, during the year ending 30 June 1975, only 6,3% received sentences of two years and longer (including the death penalty). It is therefore clear that the imprisonment of an offender only offers society temporary protection and, in the majority of cases, for a very short period; a few weeks or a few months.

Criminals are Rehabilitated in Prison

It is impossible to determine what percentage of prisoners are rehabilitated in prison. Bearing in mind, however, that the majority are there for only short periods; that the educational and rehabilitative facilities available to the Republic's large prison population are very limited; and that the majority of discharged prisoners (usually about 60%) are recidivists, it is doubtful that prison does succeed in achieving rehabilitation to any meaningful extent. Indeed, it is unrealistic to expect the Department of Prisons, under the present circumstances, to achieve large-scale success in the rehabilitation of prisoners.

Elsewhere, reasons are given why the writer is of the opinion that, generally speaking, the traditional penal institution is not capable of rehabilitating offenders.

(D) Lack of research

The above-mentioned misconceptions are due, to a large extent, to a lack of reliable information on crime and punishment, and on their consequences.

No scientist will develop a theory or take any action before he has thoroughly examined his field and before he has gained reliable information. No normal medical practitioner would treat a patient before he has made a careful diagnosis. In the field of criminal justice, however, methods are applied which have not first been subjected to thorough scientific investigation into their desirability and their practical effectiveness.

There is little doubt that no great measure of success in the prevention of crime and the rehabilitation of offenders will be achieved unless judicial and penological approaches and methods are based (as far as is practically possible) on reliable knowledge of the crime problem – particularly on the causes, the extent and the various types of crime. There is, therefore, an urgent need for the scientific compilation of full details about the imposition of punishment by the courts, and the treatment of offenders in prison, as well as the treatment of offenders within the community. Special emphasis must be placed on the effectiveness of the various approaches and programmes.

The cost of crime and its control in South Africa is enormous, yet, relatively speaking, a negligible amount is spent on scientific research into crime, its control and prevention. In 1976 the budget of the South African Police was R171 027 000, that of the Department of Prisons was R68 622 000 and that of the Department of Justice was R37 205 000 – being a total of R276 854 000. To this must be added millions of rands of loss and damage cause by crime. That this is an unwise 'investment' is evidenced by the continuing and rapid increase in crime, and by the high recidivism rate. The amount of money spent on crime prevention programmes and on research on crime, its control and its prevention by the Human Sciences Research Council, the Universities and NICRO probably does not amount to 1% of the amount spent by the police, the courts and the prisons.

The report of the (American) Presidential Commission on law enforcement and the administration of justice puts the need for research very well. The part quoted from the report can, to a great extent, also be applied to South Africa:

> The Commission has found and discussed throughout this report many needs of law enforcement and the administration of criminal justice. *But what it has found to be the greatest need is the need to know.* America has

learned the uses of exploration and discovery and knowledge in shaping and controlling its physical environment, in protecting its health, in furthering its national security and in countless other areas. The startling advances in the physical and biological sciences are products of an intellectual revolution that substituted the painful and plodding quest for knowledge for the comforting acceptance of received notions. The Nation has invested billions of dollars and the best minds at its disposal in this quest for scientific discovery. The returns from this investment are dramatically apparent in the reduction of disease, the development of new weapons, the availability of goods, the rise in living standards and the conquest of space.

But this revolution of scientific discovery has largely by-passed the problems of crime and crime control. Few domestic social problems more seriously threaten our welfare or exact a greater toll of our resources. But society has relied primarily on traditional answers and has looked almost exclusively to common sense and hunch for needed changes . . . *There is probably no subject of comparable concern to which the nation is devoting so many resources and so much effort with so little knowledge of what it is doing* . . . (President's Commission on Law Enforcement and Administration of Justice: 1967)

REFERENCES

Bates, S. 1960 – 'When is probation not probation?' *Federal Probation*, December, 15.

Flynn, E. E. 1973 – 'Jails and criminal justice.' In L. E. Ohlin (ed.), *Prisoners in America.* Englewood Cliffs: Prentice-Hall.

Gwynn-Jones, I. 1974 – 'A new approach to inadequate offenders.' *Crime, Punishment and Reform*, 3, 1, February, 62–3.

Holt, N. 1971 – 'Temporary prison release. California's prerelease furlough program.' *Crime and Delinquency*, October.

Roux, J. P. 1973 – 'The prison: rehabilitation expectations.' *Crime, Punishment and Correction*, 2, 3, 23.

The President's Commission on Law Enforcement and Administration of Justice 1967 – *The Challenge of Crime in a Free Society.* Washington: U.S. Government Printing Office.

3. Crime in the Coloured Community

S. P. CILLIERS

Viewed in statistical terms, the Coloured population of South Africa exhibits crime rates that compare most unfavourably with those of the other population groups in the country, as may be seen in Table 1.

Statistics relating to the relative incidence of crime in different population groups should be treated with the necessary caution, especially in countries where different population groups are differentially located in the social structure of the total society. Such is the case in South Africa. Here socio-economic position, geographical distribution, age and sex structures, culture and legal and political standing all tend to vary in accordance with racial or ethnic affiliation.

Differences are, however, reflected not only in the overall crime rates, but also in the more detailed statistics of the relative incidence of various types of crimes, as may be seen in Table 2.

TABLE 1: CONVICTIONS PER 100 000 OF THE POPULATION OF 7 YEARS AND OVER, 1967–8, 1968–9[1]

Population group	1967–68	1968–69
Coloured	8 881	8 880
White	1 508	1 497
Asian	1 976	1 952
African	2 611	2 606
All groups	2 961	2 954

In comparing crime rates for the different population groups, careful note must be taken of this differential involvement in the social structure. Thus approximately one half of the African population is domiciled in tribal areas where they still maintain, to a large degree, a traditional tribal life-style and pattern. It is therefore to be expected that crime rates will be lower for the African population than for the predominantly urban Coloured population. For comparative purposes, it would therefore be more valid to compare crime rates for particular geographical regions. Unfortunately such statistical details are not readily available in published form but some of the factors contributing to high crime rates among the Coloured population may be discussed.

The Coloured population of South Africa is predominantly Western in culture, religion, life-style and economic involvement. They derive from a process of biological and cultural amalgamation and assimilation over a period of more than three centuries between slaves of a heterogeneous origin, indigenous Hottentot and other Khoisan aboriginal elements, White Europeans and the Bantu people. For the overwhelming majority of the Coloured people a distinct biological identity may be discerned, although all gradations of physical type from relatively pure Negroid on the one hand to relatively pure Caucasian on the other hand are to be found. These processes, coupled with a growing tendency towards social differentiation on the basis of colour, led to the emergence of the Coloured people as a distinct population group in the South African society; a group which at the same time, as a result of its close integration into the economic, religious and political structure of the dominant White pattern of life, gradually also assumed the social and cultural characteristics of the dominant White European society. Thus it came about that the so-called Coloured people became Westerners, though with a distinctive biological identity (at least for the overwhelming majority of the members of the category) and with a differentiated position in the economic, social and political structure of the South African society.

TABLE 2: OFFENCES – NUMBER OF CONVICTIONS PER 100 000 OF THE POPULATION OF 7 YEARS AND OVER, 1968–9[2]

Offences against or relating to	White	Coloured	Asian	African
Class A: Safety of the State and good order	111	57	148	24
Class B: Communal life	366	5 233	684	658
Class C: Personal relations	140	1 219	332	726
Class D: Property	160	1 149	205	695
Class F: Social Affairs	611	608	473	343
All other offences	109	613	110	160
Specific crimes:				
Drunkenness	286	4 644	208	388
Assault	109	684	263	373
Aggravated Assault	17	501	59	324
Theft	149	1 029	182	654

The process of total westernization has been remarkably complete when one considers the many different cultural origins of the people that today comprise the Coloured population. The Dutch settlement at the Cape which was begun in 1652, soon developed into a centre of permanent colonization in which stock farming became the standard activity. This meant rapid expansion, with the result that the colony soon extended into the territory frequented by the nomadic aboriginal Hottentot and Bushman tribes. Although few withstood the pressure of White expansion, the majority were gradually absorbed into the economic structure of the dominant community. As was common practice then, slaves were imported, chiefly from the Dutch East Indies and West Africa to meet the need for personal service and labour. The aboriginal peoples were reluctant and generally regarded as unsuitable for this type of activity. A degree of biological assimilation took place between the White and the slave elements. The female population of the settlement was small and in spite of a prohibition on intermarriage that was based more on grounds of religion than colour, a large proportion of the children born to slave mothers in the early years of the colony were of White fathers. Although there were contacts between Whites and aboriginal Khoisan, these were sporadic, since the Europeans regarded the Hottentots with great contempt. Mixing between slaves and the growing numbers of mulattos and the aboriginal Hottentots was, however, common. The forces of cultural assimilation were much more significant, so that by the turn of the 19th century when the British assumed control of the Cape, the cultural and linguistic origins of the Khoisan, the slaves and the other non-European peoples who had settled at the Cape, were far less recognisable.

With the advent of British rule and under the influence of Victorian philanthropy represented chiefly by the missionaries, the position of the Coloured people, especially after the abolition of slavery, improved considerably. But this was rejected by large sections of the established population which was, by then, committed to segregation. A long struggle between those who favoured a liberal point of view and those who desired total segregation ensued. In the Republics which were established after this, the Coloured people were accorded no status. More recent developments have seen a reversal of the rights enjoyed by the Coloured people in the Cape in which the patterns of differentiation of the northern areas have been extended to the country as a whole. Political, social and even economic differentiation has been legalized and maintained by statute.

Numerically, the Coloured people comprise approximately one-tenth of the total South African population, but are largely concentrated in the Cape Province, and more specifically in the Western Cape. Virtually three-tenths of the total Coloured population of the country are concentrated in the Cape Peninsula itself, on which the city of Cape Town is situated. While not yet as urbanized as the White population, the Coloured people are at present experiencing a very high rate of urbanization. This is illustrated by the fact that one third of the increase in the Coloured population in the metropolitan area of Cape Town during the last decade was due to the immigration of people from outside this area. Demographic details are provided in Table 3.

As a population group, the Coloured people exhibit all the demographic characteristics of an industrial and agricultural working class, such as a high birth rate, a high death rate, a relatively low though growing life expectancy at birth and so on. They are experiencing a relatively high rate of natural increase although there are indications of a decline in the birth rate as the result of a spread in the acceptance of family planning and contraception (Cilliers 1960: ch. 2).

Socio-economically, the Coloured people of today overlap with the unskilled African labouring class on the one hand, and with the White middle-class on the other (Cilliers 1960: ch. 4). Though not subject to the same stringent legal and civil restrictions as Africans, they are in many respects treated on a par with other 'non-White' population groups.

TABLE 3: COLOURED POPULATION OF SOUTH AFRICA: URBAN-RURAL AND GEOGRAPHIC DISTRIBUTION[3] 1970

Province	Urban	Rural	All provinces
Cape	1 260 696	490 850	1 751 546
Other	233 794	33 113	226 907
All provinces	1 494 490	523 963	2 018 453

Under these circumstances, it is to be expected that significant differences will exist in both the incidence and nature of crime between the various population groups. In the case of the Coloured people, drunkenness is by far the most frequent cause for convictions, followed by assault (both serious and common) and the various forms of theft.

The very high rate of conviction for drunkenness must be viewed in terms of the drinking habits and pattern of a large section of the Coloured community, the particular nature of the South African liquor laws and the location of liquor outlets. During the era of the Dutch East India Company at the Cape in the seventeenth and eighteenth centuries, liquor was an important item in the barter trade with the indigenous Hottentot tribes which formed one of the important elements in the formation of the present Coloured population. The slave population of that era, which formed the second important original component of the Coloured people, were equally closely involved in the use (and abuse) of liquor, since the development of the wine industry at the Cape was largely accomplished through the use of slave labour. Thus the descendants of these people, very much like the peasantry of the wine-producing areas of southern and central Europe, developed a pattern and style of life which involved a strong tendency towards a heavy consumption of liquor. It is therefore not surprising that it is today still the Coloured farm labourer who is most often convicted for drunkenness.

The system for the commercial distribution of liquor which developed in South Africa was largely modelled on the British system of strictly controlled licensing for both 'on-and-off-premises' consumption of liquor. Outlets for the consumption of liquor evolved mostly in the form of bars associated with hotels located in and around the White-controlled central business districts of towns and cities as 'on-premises' consumption outlets, together with off-sales liquor stores. It is only since the beginning of the sixties that, as a result of a revision of the liquor laws of the country, there has been a new development which favours the combined consumption of liquor and food, with more people moving away from the traditional 'stand-up' bar.

At present, however, there is still a concentration of licensed premises where alcoholic liquor may be consumed or bought in the White-controlled central business districts of most towns and cities. As may be expected, these areas are policed more effectively than most other areas, so that persons who have over-indulged in liquor are more likely to be apprehended in such areas than elsewhere. Since these business districts serve all sectors of the population, there is a strong influx of both Coloured and White shoppers into these areas, especially on Fridays and Saturdays. Under these circumstances intensive policing and strict action against boisterous, rowdy or drunken behaviour is inevitable.

A large proportion of the Coloured people is inadequately housed. A survey conducted towards the end of 1972 in the Greater Cape Town area, where more than a third of the total Coloured population of South Africa is located, showed that 41,01 % of the Coloured population of the region were in need of housing (Cilliers 1972). Under these circumstances, overcrowding and squatting occurs very frequently. Furthermore, public housing provision tends to be at the level of minimum standard, especially in the case of sub-economic and economic housing in which a large proportion of the city's Coloured population is housed. The result is that housing standards are such that the home is very seldom used for recreational and social activities, and much of this has to occur out of doors and in public. In view of the fact that the consumption of liquor in public constitutes a criminal offence in South African law, there is a tendency for quick consumption of large quantities of liquor in public places, leading to a high incidence of drunkenness.

One further factor in the system for the control of the distribution of alcoholic beverages tends to promote unhealthy drinking patterns among Coloured people. Only licensed distributors may sell alcoholic beverages, and licences are strictly controlled. The result is that licensed premises are not easily accessible, especially in the case of Coloured farm workers. The buying pattern is therefore that of weekly acquisitioning, when a week's supply of liquor is purchased. For large numbers of simple working class people the judicious consumption of a ready supply of liquor, spread over a whole week, cannot be realised. While a week's supply of liquor is therefore bought on one occasion, this invariably leads to heavy consumption over a relatively short period of time.

The above should suffice to indicate that many facets of the life circumstances and heritage of the Coloured people, as well as certain aspects of the legal system for the control over the distribution of alcoholic beverages, results in behaviour patterns which favour heavy drinking under circumstances which in turn favour chances of arrest for drunkenness for a large sector of the Coloured population. The very high rate of drunkenness convictions among Coloured people is shown in Table 4.

In more general terms the socio-psychological, economic, cultural and political position of the Coloured people in South African society, in terms of the bearing that these factors have on crime, very largely explains the high incidence of crime in this community. A large proportion of the Coloured population lives either in overpopulated urban slums or have recently been moved into low-cost housing schemes where the physical setting is amenable to crime through the absence of effective policing, the inadequacy of street lighting, social services, transport services, public amenities and schooling facilities.

Coloured homes, even in the new housing schemes, are mostly overcrowded due to both the housing shortage and a very high birth rate. Incomes are generally at a relatively low level and, on an average, only about one-fifth to one-quarter of that of the average White family. All these, and other characteristics of the living conditions of a large sector of this population group, are typical of conditions which have been found all over the world to be the breeding ground of drunkenness, violence and crime.

TABLE 4: CONVICTION RATE BY TYPE OF OFFENCE – PERCENTAGE DISTRIBUTION, 1968–69[4]

Type of Offence	White	Coloured	Asian	African
Drunkenness	19,1	52,3	10,6	14,9
Assault	8,5	13,4	16,5	26,8
Theft	9,2	11,4	9,0	24,6
Gambling	0,4	0,7	13,5	1,9
Dagga	2,4	4,3	8,9	6,5
Road Traffic	40,8	6,8	24,2	13,1
Income Tax	6,5	0,2	6,5	—
Other	13,1	10,9	10,8	12,2

There are also other factors which are of equal importance. An analysis of crime statistics will show that drunkenness, disorderly behaviour and acts of violence such as assaults make up the bulk of the crimes other than technical offences among Coloured persons. Next to these, theft is the most important type of offence. These crimes are all of a nature which are indicative of a low level of sensitivity to feelings of human worth and dignity. It seems only too obvious that this is related to the general position according to the man of colour in South African society. It relates, therefore, to the marginality of his position in the wider society of which he forms part, and derives ultimately from the attitudes and actions of that sector of society which not only wields all power, but sets the tone and pattern of normative behaviour. This is the White sector of the population of South African society.

If the preceding argument is accepted, it follows that the direction for action aimed at combating such high crime rates should proceed along the following lines:

> A high rate of economic growth should be attained and maintained so that poverty can be dealt with more effectively;
> educational provision should be extended so as to provide at least a minimum schooling for all children. Educational services should be expanded to include adequate child guidance services for all children;
> housing and township development should be expanded in order to eliminate slum conditions and to provide adequate housing;
> the provision of basic public amenities and services such as adequate street lighting, street paving, public transport and police protection in all residential communities;
> the strengthening of family and community life through the expansion of family and community organization services;
> the development of a social and political order in which it will be possible for all members of the society, irrespective of colour and race, to develop a sense of human worth and dignity.

This last point is of fundamental significance since, in the final analysis, the ultimate reward for conforming to normative order – the reward for maintaining the rules of behaviour – lies in being accorded status and the recognition and respect of fellow citizens. If a man is denied recognition as a fellow human being, a fellow citizen and a fellow member of the community, he will have no stake in maintaining normative order and will be coerced to conform only through a fear of punishment.

NOTES

Cilliers, S. P. 1960 – *The Coloureds of South Africa.* Cape Town: Banier.

——1972 – 'Facing the crisis in housing for the Coloured people.' Unpublished paper read before the Cape Chamber of Commerce, 21 November.

South Africa, Department of Statistics 1972 – *Population of Cities, Towns and Rural Areas.* Report No. 02–05–01. Population Census of 6 May. Pretoria.

——1971 – *South African Statistics,* 1970. Pretoria.

REFERENCES

1. South Africa, Department of Statistics: *South African Statistics,* 1970. (1971) G.6.
2. South Africa, Department of Statistics: *South African Statistics,* 1970. (1971) G.6.
3. South Africa, Department of Statistics: Population Census of 6 May, 1970: *Population of Cities, Towns and Rural Areas.* Report No. 02–05–01. (1972) 21.
4. South Africa, Department of Statistics: *South African Statistics,* 1970. (1971) G.2.

Part 8:

Social Stratification, Colour and South Africa: An Overview

Introduction

MICHAEL SAVAGE

All studies of stratification in one way or another are concerned with a central question: Who gets what, why, how, when, where and to what effect? Implicitly this question indicates that the field of social stratification is concerned with the 'distributive process' that is at work in any society whereby access is regulated to the 'goods' of that society, those goods being both material and tangible (such as land, machinery or income) as well as non-material (such as social and occupational positions or political power). Each society in distributing these 'goods' creates some pattern of socially structured inequalities and it is the study of these socially structured inequalities, and of how they originate and are maintained, and with what effect, that is of particular concern to the student of social stratification.

To put this bluntly: one can say that analysts of social stratification are primarily involved in examining those inequalities in a society which are manmade and in studying how these inequalities are legitimized, how they persist over time and are built into the institutional structure of a society. Each society's system of stratification is conditioned both by the particular historical past of that society and by the cumulative effect of its recent decisions concerning the distribution of its resources and opportunities. Over time, relatively stable patterns of ranking individuals and families into strata, sharing unequally in their access to the 'goods' of a society, are built up. Such ranking can be illustrated in a variety of ways. The study of medicine has shown us that health is a purchasable commodity and that generally a community can purchase as much, or as little, of this commodity as it either sees fit or can afford. It can channel its resources into one direction and its death rate ascends, it can turn its resources in another direction and can increase the life expectancies of particular individuals and groups within it. Similarly each society's historical past together with its recent decisions influence how its income, education or housing is distributed over its population. Furthermore, over time the particular access that particular individuals or groups have to such goals produce different forms of stratification systems and different means of justifying the rankings produced by the distributive process. In brief: all such phenomena are concerns within the field of stratification. More formally one can define social stratification as the study of the institutionalization of power arrangements that perpetuate economic, political and social inequality among individuals and social groups within a society.

Most analysts agree that there are two fundamental and opposite approaches to the study of social stratification, the functionalist (or evolutionary) liberal approach and the conflict (or structural) approach. The functional approach views systems of stratification as emerging as a natural consequence of the mobility of individuals who are biologically and socially most deserving and 'fit'. The conflict approach on the other hand views stratification emerging as a conscious result of economic, political and social arrangements to create and maintain inequalities in a society. The differences between these two positions are stark: the functional perspective sees social stratification as being inevitable and natural; as being essentially a phenomenon emerging from individual differences in I.Q., talent, skill, and training. It also views stratification systems as being basically just and as ensuring, through social mobility, that every member of a society gets his due. The conflict or structural perspective on the other hand, views systems of stratification as being consciously created, founded on coercive forms of group differentiation and as producing inequalities which are unjust.

As Ossowski (1963) has pointed out these differences are not only theoretical but they suggest 'different practical policies'. Crudely expressed, within the South African context the functional perspective would suggest that the viable strategy to begin to address the massive array of interrelated social disabilities that Blacks suffer under would be the opening up of the individual opportunity structure to ensure that talent rises to the top irrespective of the skin colour surrounding it. The conflict perspective would suggest a different starting point involving the redistribution of power between the different groups within the society and the necessity of reallocating existing economic resources. This overly simplistic illustration of the practical consequences flowing from the two fundamental perspectives indicates that the differences between them are not merely the topic of an academic game but involve serious clashes of intellectual frameworks, theoretical positions, research methods and interpretation of 'evidence'. The theoretical starting-point in any study of stratification is consequently of the utmost significance.

The dominant theoretical starting point of most western sociologists is the functionalist model; classically the work of Max Weber and more pointedly the arguments of Davis and Moore (1945) exemplify this perspective. Davis and Moore's arguments are a particularly important point of reference and have produced a wide ranging debate (see Pease *et al* 1970). Davis and Moore argue that stratification is functionally necessary as each society must have some mechanisms for inducing its most talented members to undergo training and make the sacrifices of time and leisure that are necessary if they are to occupy the important positions in a society. The differential way in which class and status rewards are distributed ensures that 'the most important positions are conscientiously filled by the most qualified persons' (Davis & Moore: 1945:243). Consequently, they argue that stratification is essential, positive, just and rational, and that it ensures that the most able individuals rise to the top while the least able occupy lower positions.

Not only the work of Marx but also the writings of such alphabetically illustrative persons as Althusser (1970), Bottomore (1965) and Cox (1959) exemplify the position of the conflict school. This means that the conflict perspective must not be viewed as being a purely Marxist one, although the Marxist perspective forms the most provocative statement of this position. No one article can be taken to exemplify the conflict perspective and thus the reader is referred to the bibliography of Shaw (1974) and to Zeitlin (1972). For Marx the key and critical concept in an analysis of stratification is 'class'. The development of class relations in production undermines the existing legal relations and poses the possibility of a class – the proletariat – overthrowing them. As is well known, classes, for Marx, are dynamic elements and agents of historical change that are deeply rooted in the basic social realities of production. Marx sees the whole of history not merely as a succession of modes of production but as a series of conflicts between classes concerning the direction of social development. These crude pointers to Marxist thought are illustrative of the view held by conflict theorists that the study of stratification cannot be compartmentalized into a narrow specialism within the overall study of any social formation but, rather, that the study of any social formation must be rooted and initiated in the examination of its stratification system.

Up till this point the general term 'stratification' has been used and little mention has been made of the existence of distincts forms of stratification systems. Four distinct major types of such systems can be identified – slavery, estate, caste, and class systems and some argue that a possible fifth form of system is emerging, or has emerged, in the state socialist nations of the contemporary world. Exactly how to define each such system is a matter of considerable theoretical and empirical controversy. For purposes of this introductory essay it is sufficient to point toward the historical and geographical location of these systems. The slave system has existed in diverse types of society, for instance in Ancient Greece and Rome and more recently in the United States, particularly in its Deep South. The estate system is traditionally identified with feudal societies, while the caste system is identified with Indian society. It is more complex to locate historically or geographically the class system, for the very definition and approach to the concept of class that a particular analyst has, conditions the view adopted as to when and where such a system has manifested itself. In short *how* one defines a class system will help determine *where* one will see it – as the debate amongst students of South African society has illustrated (Wright 1977). To oversimplify for the sake of brevity, generally class systems are seen as emerging out of feudal societies and as being located in capitalist societies.

This necessarily succinct overview has thus far indicated some of the concerns in the field of social stratification, the major approaches to the field, a few of the implications of such approaches, and has pointed to the existence of different forms of stratification systems. It must immediately be emphasized that the warp and woof of stratification studies have not been touched upon for neither description nor analyses of a complex variety of theoretical positions, of different methodical approaches, of the economic, political and social correlates of stratification systems, nor particularized empirical studies, have been examined.

Instead, as in the following section of this essay, merely a selection of the important landmarks in the study of stratification have been pointed to and discussed.

Stratification, Colour and South Africa

'Classes coexisting at any given time bear the marks of different centuries on their brow' wrote Schumpeter (1955:111). Schumpeter's point that it is important to view the present in its historical context is a vital observation when approaching the study of South African society. The existing South African system of stratification has been profoundly shaped by the historical past and by the particular types of relationships that emerged between groups during the development of South African capitalism, relationships that emerged first in the agricultural and subsequently in the industrial setting.

Despite what could be seen as some tentative claims to the contrary the present South African system of stratification did not descend from heaven. It was shaped in the crucible of economic, political and human experiences over different epochs. The form that stratification has taken has varied widely over the course of South African economic development. Thus, for instance, at one stage a system of slavery was coexisting with class, colour and ethnic cleavages. However, the slave society of the seventeenth century in South Africa was restricted in terms of the numbers of people it encapsulated and as an institution slavery at the Cape was legally abolished in 1834, prior to its abolition in the United States. A further form of stratification system could also be argued to have been manifested in the Voortrekker Republics in that these Republics had distinctly feudal elements within their structures and patterns of relationships between groups that were in many ways reminiscent of those found within the classical estate system of feudal Europe. Simply put, no unitary system of stratification has existed continuously over the years and neither did the current South African system emerge Phoenix-like from any one important political moment in the twentieth century. The present stratification pattern must be seen rather as evolving slowly out of an extraordinary complex past.

There is considerable difficulty in knowing into which sociological pigeon-hole to classify South Africa's existing social structure for as Simons (1970) has argued, none of the terms usually employed to describe social strata quite cover the South African situation. There are classes, in both the Weberian and Marxist sense, but enforced segregation inhibits the full development of these classes. The class segments existing in South Africa consequently terminate at the boundaries of each colour group, thus reinforcing ethnic exclusiveness at the expense of a true class solidarity. As a result, some social scientists think that caste, rather than class, is the more appropriate term by which to describe and label South African society.

But there is a considerable debate over the issue of whether or not caste can be used to denote the form of organization of the major strata in the society. Such people as Warner (1936) in the United States and West (1971) in South

Africa, analyse colour-divided societies by reference to broad colour-based castes, within which there are 'class' divisions. In using the caste concept the similarities between colour-divided societies and the Indian caste system are stressed, similarities such as the taboos on intermarriage, as well as other forms of intimate association, the hierarchical features associated with the ranking of whole groups one to another and the restraints on social mobility. Cox (1959) provides a devastating attack on those who use the caste framework in analysis of colour hierarchies and shows that there are several crucial dissimilarites between inter-caste and inter-colour group relations by indicating the very different roles that such things as religion, statutory sanctions and individual assent to social inequalities all play in a caste form of society as contrasted to a 'class' form of society. Put minimally it seems dubious to hypothesize that South Africa's colour-orientated system of stratification is a caste-based system and indeed studies by Watson (1970), Rex (1970) and others point to the falsity of such a hypothesis.

The mere taxonomic approach to stratification in South Africa has little intrinsic significance; any significance that it has derives from the important debate that gives rise to classificatory concerns, that is the debate about the adequacy of the sociological concepts of class, caste and ethnicity in analysing colour-divided societies.[1] Ultimately, this debate feeds into a simple question, raising complex issues about the very nature of the South African stratification system. Briefly, this question is: Although it may not be generally possible to lean more toward the one than the other, which factor is more crucial in accounting for the existing shape of the South African system of stratification – colour or class?

Such a question has stimulated a continuing controversy, a controversy that is perpetually sidetracked by those writers, from all viewpoints, who exhibit in their approach to the question 'the fetish of a single cause' and put forward monocausal explanations of the origins of inequalities in South Africa. If caste is an unacceptable concept to use in the South African context then, as the question indicates, the problem arises as to whether the cleavages in the society initially can best be understood through a class frame of reference or a frame of reference that is more 'culture-based' and concerned with the problems of colour and ethnicity. Those favouring the latter approach do so for a variety of reasons but chiefly because they see distinct groups, irrespective of whether they share a similar class position, as remaining 'permanently aloof' from one another. In Furnivall's words 'they mix but do not combine. Each group holds by its own religion, its own culture, its own ideas and ways. As individuals they meet, but only in the market place, in buying and selling' (Cohen 1972:233). In relegating any class framework to a secondary place in an analysis of colour-divided societies, a frame of reference is drawn upon which stresses the concepts of 'cultural pluralism' and 'differential incorporation'. Such a framework is discussed and its concepts spelled out by Kuper and Smith (1969), examining pluralism in Africa.

A variety of difficulties and ambiguities surround the utilization of class concepts in the study of South African, and other African, stratification systems. Many of these difficulties are examined in a provocative article by Cohen (1972) who argues that most of the difficulties are connected to the fact that power, class and ethnicity intersect with each other and can be treated separately only for analytical purposes. Cohen sees ethnic stratification and class differentiation as being intimately inter-related to each other and to the concentration and distribution of political power. Such interconnections may be conceptualized as comprising four variants: (a) situations where ranking along both class and ethnic lines is coincident, (b) situations where there is a conflict between class and ethnic membership but where ethnicity predominates, (c) situations where there is a conflict between class and ethnicity but where class identity predominates, and (d) situations where the conflict between class and ethnicity is unresolved or could go either way depending on particular circumstances. Cohen's typology highlights the fact that class and ethnicity must be considered together and be viewed in connection with the distribution of political power. The task of doing this, and consequently of using a class framework, is riddled with challenging problems.

As in the previous section no detailed studies of South Africa stratification have been discussed – provocative and valuable as many of these are – instead the focus has been on raising the problems of what type of stratification system exists in Southern Africa and identifying some of the different departing points for examining this system of stratification. The different readings, however, give some indication of the variety of studies of South African stratification.

The Readings

The selected readings have a specific South African focus: students wishing to read further in the general area of social stratification are referred to the readings in the books edited by Heller (1969) and Bendix and Lipset (1966). The readings that follow not only illustrate several theoretical viewpoints but also give some limited historical dimension to the South African system of stratification. Readers are referred to Wilson and Thompson (1969) for a fuller range of historical evidence dealing with colour and stratification in South Africa. Such evidence is important in showing that at the start of White settlement in South Africa there was no rigid dividing line between Black and White; instead a multi-tiered system of stratification emerged. Only slowly did a formal dividing-line between Black and White come into being as the nature of the relationship between colour and power altered to produce White dominance.

The first article examines the sorely understudied aspect of South Africa's current system of stratification, namely its pattern of income distribution. In this article Archer assesses evidence to show a gross skewness in the distribution of income, for in 1970/71 the richest 10% of the income recipients in South Africa received some 58% of personal income. Archer shows further that this pattern of income distribution places South Africa in the ranks of those Latin American countries which are notorious for their income inequalities. The absence of any adequate South African figures dealing with property or wealth distribution means that Archer's income data forms one of the few national *measures* of South African inequalities.

Mkele, in a controversial and pioneering article written in 1960, examines the emergence of an African middle class in South Africa. Mkele argues that government policy has effectively meant that only an embryonic middle class has been able to form yet, and although this class is small, its political significance is out of proportion to its size. What is controversial in Mkele's analysis is his definition of this embryonic middle class and his brief statements about its possible political role.

Next, Mayer examines how Black townspeople in Soweto, South Africa's largest Black urban complex, view and interpret the social universe in which they live. Mayer, on the basis of his fieldwork, shows how Soweto Blacks view White dominance and examines the differences between the class and ethnic 'models' of stratification held in Soweto.

In the final reading a clear clash of viewpoints emerges. Rex argues that to employ a class framework, in particular a Marxist one, in the study of South African stratification results in the complexities and intricacies of stratification in a colour-obsessed society, being obscured. He believes class analysis to be one amongst several starting points necessary in approaching the study of South African stratification. In contrast to Rex, such sociologists as Wolpe (1976), Legassick (1974), and Davies (1973) argue that racial divisions are primarily the outcome of class struggles between capital and labour and thus the analysis of these class struggles is an essential point of departure for the understanding of the South African stratification system. Such writers make a compelling case for distinguishing between the manifestations – economic, political, and cultural – of colour divisions and the economic and historical origins of these divisions.

The clash between such positions is ultimately an ideological clash and in ending the readings on this note, attention is hopefully drawn to an important and continuing ideological debate pervading most contemporary writings about, and analyses of, South African society. This debate revolves around the 'liberal' and 'radical' interpretations of South African racial policy and economic development and is a debate reflected in other readings in this book, and further is one that should deeply influence each student's approaches to the problems of reaching an understanding of the South African system of social stratification.[2]

NOTES

1. See Glazer and Moynihan (1975) for a discussion of ethnicity. As is shown in this work the term ethnic refers to a social group which consciously shares some aspects of a common culture and is defined primarily by descent.

2. Some of the contours of this debate are sketched out in a controversial book by Wright (1977); the bibliography of this book is particularly valuable.

REFERENCES

Althusser, L. 1970 – *Reading Capital.* London: New Left Books.

Bendix, R. and S. M. Lipset (eds.) 1966 – *Class, Status and Power.* New York: Free Press.

Bottomore, T. B. 1965 – *Classes in Modern Society.* London: Allen and Unwin.

Cohen, R. 1972 – 'Class in Africa: Analytical problems and perspectives,' In R. Miliband and J. Saville (eds.), *The Socialist Register*, London: 231–55.

Cox, O. C. 1959 – *Caste, Class and Race.* New York: Modern Reader.

Davies, R. 1973 – 'The white working class in South Africa.' New Left Review, 82, November-December.

Davis, K. and W. E. Moore 1945 – 'Some principles of stratification.' *American Sociological Review*, 10, April, 242–9.

Glazer, N. and D. P. Moynihan 1975 – *Ethnicity: Theory and Experience.* Boston: Harvard University Press.

Heller, Celia (ed.) 1969 – *Structured Social Inequality.* London: Collier Macmillan.

Kuper, L. and M. G. Smith 1969 – *Pluralism in Africa.* Berkeley: University of California Press.

Legassick, M. 1974 – 'Legislation, ideology and economy in post-1948 South Africa.' *Journal of Southern African Studies*, 1, October, 5–35.

Ossowski, Stanislaw 1963 – *Class Structure in the Social Consciousness.* New York: Free Press.

Pease, John, W. H. Form and J. H. Rytina 1970 – 'Ideological currents in American stratification literature.' *American Sociologist*, 5, May, 127–37.

Rex, John 1970 – *Race Relations in Sociological Theory.* London: Weidenfeld and Nicholson.

Shaw, Martin 1974 – *Marxism versus Sociology: A Guide to Reading.* London: Pluto Press.

Schumpeter, Joseph 1955 – *Imperialism and Social Classes.* New York: Meridan.

Simons, H. J. 1970 – 'Preface' to G. Watson, *Passing for White.* London: Tavistock, vii–xi.

Warner, W. Lloyd 1936 – 'American class and caste.' *American Journal of Sociology*, 42, 234–7.

Watson, Graham 1970 – *Passing for White.* London: Tavistock.

West, Martin E. 1971 – *Divided Community.* Cape Town: Balkema.

Wilson, Monica and L. M. Thompson (eds.) 1969 – *The Oxford History of South Africa* (2 volumes), London: Oxford University Press.

Wolpe, M. 1976 – 'The "White working class" in South Africa.' Economy and Society, 5, 2 May, 195–240.

Wright, Harrison M. 1977 – *The Burden of the Present: Liberal-Radical Controversy over South African History.* Cape Town: David Philip.

Zeitlin, Irving M. 1972 – *Capitalism and Imperialism: An Introduction to Neo-Marxian Concepts.* Chicago: Markham.

1. Perverse Growth and Income Distribution in South Africa

SEAN ARCHER

. . . It is not deemed necessary to demonstrate the intrinsic interest of size and race inequalities of income in South Africa. But, having said that, some hard questions pertaining to categories remain unanswered. Our conception of the most meaningful form for income and wealth distributions has to be dictated by our analytical framework, and it is here that the greatest unclarity exists. Orthodox economics, concerned with the operation of markets and the explanation of relative prices, ignores the *intrinsic* significance of the structure of personal incomes. Indeed, hard neoclassicals like von Hayek explicitly deny such significance exists once the rules of an order of economic freedom are accepted. This is a consistent position. Division of the product is then one aspect of the pricing process in a free market system such that exchange and technological relations govern, as a by-product, who gets what and how much. Hence the focus within such a theoretical framework upon the 'functional' distribution of income.

In the South African case this will certainly not do; a strict neoclassical schema is not only inadequate, it is misleading. We need the concepts of appropriation, class formation, coercion and power to examine the determination of income differentials and shares, and therefore to inform our categories of data collection. Regrettably, work along these lines has barely begun, and to say anything about the concentration of income and wealth at the present time in South Africa one must perforce take information as it presents itself. In the present paper my interest in the data of inequality is instrumental rather than intrinsic, a concern with the effects of the structure of income more than with its causes and mechanisms of perpetuation. But this does not lessen the importance of appropriate form for such empirical material.

There are no satisfactory macro-statistics of the personal distribution of income in South Africa. The usual sources of such information in other countries are (i) special field surveys of personal income and expenditure, capital transactions and wealth; (ii) population censuses; (iii) compilation of data from income tax records, and (iv) combinations of these and of particular aspects of income distribution. These sources exist in South Africa, but they reflect the peculiar institution of race divisions in the data, so that, for instance, even the ten-yearly census takings do *not* ask Africans about their incomes.[1] That this should be so in a country by wide consensus and by self-definition not 'less developed' or 'developing' is surprising, particularly as published national accounts, balance of payments and industrial statistics by and large do reflect the latest international conventions.[2] Whatever the reason be, there is a remarkable paucity of systematic data by income interval, occupation, industrial activity, region or even race group itself, and therefore no direct method of identifying change or the absence of it in the structure of income historically.

What little information exists is either highly aggregated in the functional categories of national accounting and in estimates of race group shares; or pertains to earnings in single industrial sectors, mainly mining and manufacturing. Yet enough is available to demonstrate that the South African distribution exhibits such a gross skewness that, even after allowance for error and aggravation, we are faced with a unique degree of inequality within one economy.

In tables 1 and 2 I have set out the data on race group shares and per capita differentials by race. Table 1 summarizes the relevant proportions though without reference-dates for the income totals.

A number of observations need to be made about this information. First, while the various calculations span fifty years they cannot be used for tracing trends in race shares of real income over time. There is variation in the income concept, methodology and in certain key assumptions, e.g. concerning the racial division of property income accruing to government and the public corporations. Second, data of this kind, strictly, should not be interpreted as telling us about the spread of welfare amongst households and individuals.[3] Taxes and transfer payments have variable effects upon disposable incomes, both by race and size. As a *measured* flow of goods and services the income concepts used ignore components of welfare which are, arguably, more important in South Africa than elsewhere. These are: length of journeys to work and travelling time; constraints upon choice and upon equalising differences between jobs; access to leisure facilities; quality of public services and collective consumption; proportions economically active per household; differentiated price structures and monopoly rents, e.g. the 'poor pay more' phenomenon documented for Black ghettoes in the United States; and numerous others. All are tangible constituents of welfare or levels of living which escape the usual statistical net. But in South Africa their differential incidence by race is a direct function of the system of social organization and *this is likely, on balance, to bias the distribution towards even greater inequality*.

TABLE 1

SOUTH AFRICAN POPULATION INCOME SHARES AND RATIOS BY RACE
SUMMARY OF ESTIMATES

Source Date	*Income Base*	*White*		*African*		*Asian*		*Coloured*		*Income per Head: Ratios by Race*			
		%P	%Y	%P	%Y	%P	%Y	%P	%Y	W:Af	W:As	W:C	W:AAC
(a) 1917–18	Net domestic product	21,6	78,0	67,9	–	2,4	–	8,2	–	–	–	–	13.4:1
(b) 1924–25	Gross domestic product	21,5	75,2	68,2	17,9	2,4	1,6	7,9	5,3	13.2:1	5:1	5.2:1	11:1
(c) 1936	Net national income	20,9	74,5	68,8	19,7	2,3	1,7	8,0	4,1	12.4:1	4.7:1	6.9:1	11:1
(d) 1939–40	Net national income	20,9	68,9	68,9	–	2,3	–	8,0	–	–	–	–	8.5:1
(e) 1946–47	Net national income	20,7	73,8	68,5	20,1	2,5	1,9	8,2	4,2	12.1:1	4,7:1	6.9:1	10.8:1
(f) 1956–57	Net national income	19,9	74,0	68,0	19,0	2,9	2,1	9,1	4,9	13.3:1	5.3:1	6.9:1	11.4:1
(adjusted)		19,9	72,5	68,0	20,6	2,9	2,0	9,1	4,8	12:1	5.3:1	6.9:1	10.6:1
(g) 1960	Gross domestic product	19,3	76,5	68,3	17,7	3,0	1,6	9,4	4,2	15.4:1	7.2:1	8.8:1	13.6:1
(h) 1962	Claimed personal income	18,8	71,9	68,7	20,6	3,0	2,0	9,5	5,5	12.7:1	5,6:1	6.6:1	11:1
1967		18,2	73,4	69,4	18,8	2,9	2,4	9,5	5,4	14.9:1	4.8:1	7.0:1	12.5:1
(i) 1964	Employee income	–	64,3	–	27,2	–	1,9	–	6,5	–	–	–	–
1966		–	64,3	–	27,0	–	2,0	–	6,6	–	–	–	–
(j) 1970–71	Private consumption expenditure	17,8	73,7	70,0	19,1	2,9	2,1	9,4	5,2	15.2:1	5.7:1	7.5:1	12.9:1

(*Note:* The full text identifies the primary sources from which these figures are drawn.
%P = percentage of total South African population
%Y = percentage of total income as defined in each source – *Eds.*)

TABLE 2

Aggregate Income Distribution in South Africa

Summary by (a) estimated race-group share:
(b) race differential:
(c) by richest decide.

(a) Percentage range:	*Population share*	*Income share*
White	17,8 – 21,6%	69 – 78%
African	67,9 – 70%	17,7 – 20,6%
Asian	2,3 – 2,9%	1,6 – 2,1%
Coloured	7,9 – 9,4%	4,1 – 5,5%

(b) Ratios of income per head:	
White/African	: 12.1/1 – 15.4/1
White/Asian	: 4.7/1 – 7.2/1
White/Coloured	: 5.2/1 – 8.8/1
White/Black	: 8.5/1 – 13.6/1

(c) Percentage share of highest ordinal group:		
All race population		*Share of total income, 1971*
Richest 10%	:	58% or more

So, our basic data raises a number of doubts, both of accuracy and interpretation. However, looking at Table 1 the inter-estimate variation in income shares is remarkably small. The arithmetic differences in the White share calculations for example, between 69 and 78%, are not excessive by size distribution standards elsewhere in the world, even in advanced countries. But the cardinal question in the South African case is whether *all* such exercises are subject to systematic bias leading to common over or under estimation; that is, whether proportionate shares for one particular race-group are either all too big or all too small. This cannot be decided *a priori*, and I have not yet sufficient familiarity with certain of the sources to attempt a uniform appraisal. Consistent error in these figures is thus a singular possibility.

TABLE 3

*Income shares by richest decide, selected countries**

Date	*Percentage*	*Source*
Israel, 1957	22,4	Adelman & Morris (1971)
Denmark, 1966	25,8	Dich (1970)
Australia, 1954/5	27,9	Weiskopf (1972)
United States, 1968	28,0	Budd (1970)
Japan, 1962	29,8	Yamamura (1967)
Pakistan, 1963/4	30,0	Bergan (1967)
United Kingdom, 1959	31,0	Meade (1964)
Chile, 1968	33,5	Adelman & Morris (1971)
Ceylon, 1963	36,8	Adelman & Morris (1971)
Argentina, 1963	37,0	Sutcliffe (1971)
1961	39,1	Adelman & Morris (1971)
India, 1960/1	38,5	Mukherjee (1969)
1955/6	34,0	Lydall (1960)
1953/4	28,0	Reserve Bank of India (1962)
Mexico, 1963/4	41,0	Sutcliffe (1971)
Colombia, 1961	42,0	Bird (1970)
Brazil, 1970	50,2	Fishlow (1972)
(Northeast) 1970	45,3	Langoni (1972)
1960	58,0	Cline (1971)
South Africa, 1970/1	58,0	*In text*
El Salvador, 1968	61,4	Adelman & Morris (1971)

Because the subject of South African income distribution is so sensitive, domestically and abroad, I have been at some pains here and in the Appendix [to the full paper – eds.] to stress the tentative nature of every measurement of race and personal income structure. Such caution applies with equal force to fine comparisons, cross-national and over time. Table 2 show the percentage share of income accruing to the top 10% of recipient units in various countries at different dates. In part these are purposely selected to make the South African figure comparable in a more meaningful way, notably the Latin American examples. But mostly the choice is random and reflects ease of access to decile calculations. I have not tried to check the commensurability of recipient units, income concepts, averaging procedures on the fitting of functions for extension or interpolation. This is a well nigh impossible task, and certainly in the absence of so doing the weight one is entitled to place on the comparison is limited. But clearly it requires large margins of error to upset the conclusion that there are few countries indeed which, *in terms of this measure*, have a more skewed distribution than South Africa. And, with the possible exception of Brazil, no other which has this skewness coupled to the advanced structural characteristics of the economic system found in South Africa. . .

NOTES

*Extract from an unpublished seminar paper (1973) presented to the Institute of Development Studies, University of Sussex.

1. *United Nations* (1969), Statistical Commission: National Practices in Statistics of the Distribution of Income, Expenditure and Wealth: E/CN. 3/399, p. 4. This lists South African practices in a comparative way, but fails to indicate their racial dichotomy and partial coverage.
2. In the Yearbook of National Accounts Statistics, *United Nations* (1972), South Africa is one of the few countries to adopt the 1968 SNA which, incidentally, makes international comparability of the most recent figures difficult.
3. J. L. Nicholson 'Redistribution of income-notes on some problems and puzzles,' *Review of Income and Wealth*, 16, 3, 1970, provides a useful list of the conceptual and econometric puzzles to be faced in measuring the inequality of *income* in an extended sense.

*For Chile, 9,3 % of recipient units; for Brazil, 1970 it is 9,1 %. Some ascriptions are not to the primary source for the calculation quoted.

2. The Emergent African Middle Class

NIMROD MKELE

Emergence of classes among Africans

. . . Social stratification, a term used by social scientists to mean 'formalized inequality of rank' (Packard 1959:9), was known in African society before the coming of the White man. Unlike Indo-European and similar exploitive societies, however, its basis – at least in the groups south of the equator – was political rather than economic. It served to maintain the cohesion of social groups by giving them a single political head (who combined religious functions) through whom the groups realized their common identity and interests . . .

The reason African societies did not have the kind of class system to which Europeans are accustomed was that there was no private ownership of the means of production. Land, the major unit of production, was available to all on a usufructuary basis. The economics of these societies produced goods for consumption and not for profit. There were no markets, and thus no exchange, except for a system of barter. Specialization of functions, except in the very limited areas of chieftaincy, medicine and smithing, formed hardly any part of the system. Classes, in the Western sense, could not, therefore, exist in such societies.

It was the coming of the White man that changed the character of African society. As the African became increasingly drawn into the White man's society, his own tribal structure tended to disintegrate in the process. White policies then, as now, were designed to ensure that the African entered the White man's service. As de Kiewiet says of Shepstone's policy '. . . he believed that the Natives held too much land, which was an encouragement to idleness, that they held it in too large areas, which made them a military menace. The need of Native policy, in his view, was a reduction in the amount of land held by the Natives and a system of taxation calculated to force them more freely into the labour market' (de Kiewiet 1937:31). In the beginning, the African became a farm labourer. Later, when the diamond mines at Kimberley and the gold mines on the Witwatersrand opened, he found himself working on these mines. The process of economic differentiation had begun.

The process, however, went further. The missionaries needed teachers and ministers to evangelize the African effectively. They opened schools, and introduced the African to the literary mysteries of the West. The first two Africans in the Cape to go through the process naturally enough became ministers of religion. Then, as now, voices were not lacking which predicted the dangers of educating the Africans for a condition of life which they would not be permitted to enjoy. In 1891, Dr Dale,[1] who was then Superintendent General of Education in the Cape, sounded one of the first warnings. He felt that the social, political and economic implications of educating thousands of Africans and uprooting them from their tribal system would have to be answered. Labour, especially agricultural, was needed by the Whites, but would the educated African be willing to take it up? 'If not,' he said, 'the crowding together of educated Natives, living without a trade or regular habits of daily employment, must tend to mischief and social disturbance . . . Knowledge is power even to them but it may be a power for ill.' He was satisfied, however, that 'while the present cautious system is pursued, no social inconvenience or practical danger can result.' Dr Dale's views are of special interest today, because they have come to form the basis of what is known as Bantu Education – a system of education specially tailored to suit what are conceived to be the needs of the African. Unlike the advocates of Bantu education, Dr Dale did not consider it necessary to change the content of African education, since, in his view, the *festina lente* policy, which his department had pursued for 33 years, was safe, 'unobtrusive, but slowly progressive.'

For a long time afterwards, the only distinction was between 'educated' and 'uneducated' Africans, and the only jobs to which an educated African could aspire were teaching, preaching and clerking. After Union, a handful of Africans went overseas to take up medicine and law. In fact, teaching became a noble profession, and the teacher was honoured. Then two things happened. The Second World War gave an impetus to the growth of secondary industry in South Africa, and the African migrated in large numbers to the industrial centres to take up the jobs that were offering. Secondly, as a result of this growth of an African urban population, educational opportunities widened. There was a growth in primary school attendances, secondary education made rapid strides, and university training increased. Employment opportunities widened and with them economic differentiation. The African thus became a member of an urban industrial society. Today, a third of the African population is in the urban areas compared with an eighth in 1921.

The working classes

What form did this differentiation take? First, we have the mass of African labourers on White men's farms, who, to all intents and purposes, are still at the pre-industrial stage of the South African revolution. Secondly, we have the Africans in the reserves, the majority of whom still cling to an outmoded and attenuated tribal system. Economically, they are no different from farm labourers, and form a reservoir of labour for the mines. Thirdly, we have the urban African who exemplifies most strikingly, the resolution that has taken place in African society. It is to the urban African that we have to look for the emergence of classes on the European model and for evidence of a middle class.

African urban society falls into three groups. A working class, white collar workers and an independent group of self-employed Africans. There is a large industrial proletariat, most of it unskilled, although there is an increasing proportion entering the semi-skilled and skilled occupations. There is no doubt that if our laws did not confine the African to unskilled occupations, the proportion in skilled occupations would be much higher. Furthermore, our policies ensure that African wages remain low in order to subsidize the higher wages of the Whites. Higher wages for the African would, in fact, increase the process of differentiation, and induction into skilled occupations, the pace of adaptation to a Western technological culture. It is for these reasons that the African is denied access to skilled jobs and to higher wages. The argument that higher wages must be preceded by increased productivity is merely another way of maintaining the *status quo*. It is not used with Whites who automatically qualify for higher wages irrespective of their level of productivity. Can anyone say that the White lift operator, who is replacing the African under the new job reservation dispensation and at a higher rate of pay, is any more productive than the African whose place he is taking?

The lower rungs of the occupational hierarchy do not comprise only an industrial proletariat, but there is a whole army of Africans employed in commerce and domestic service whose position does not differ in any significant way from that of the industrial workers.

The second group comprises those who are employed in intellectual occupations – the white collar workers. White collar workers, particularly those in teaching, the ministry and nursing, enjoy a high status in the African community because of their education. This is understandable in a literate society where education is equated with success, and, more particularly, when it is realized that to the mass of the African people education represents something worth striving for. This group has increased greatly as a result of urbanization. Today (1960), there are 25 000 teachers, 7 000 nurses, 200 laboratory assistants, 70 postmasters, 70 librarians and an unknown number of clerks and interpreters, salesmen, social workers and ministers of religion. These have arisen to serve the various community needs of the African people. Policemen, although not wearing white collars, fall into this group. Today there are about 12 000 of them.

This group, too, is not without its problems, for South African policy has the effect of retarding its emergence. The main instrument that is being used is Bantu education, whose purpose, as stated by the Minister of Native Affairs [the current President], is that the African is not to be educated above certain levels. Thus, the content of African education is being altered to keep it in line with government policy. There is instruction in African languages, which tends to limit the horizons of Africans, because the African vernaculars are not sufficiently developed to cope with the concepts of a technological culture. The status of teachers has been reduced to that of labourers. They have no security of tenure in their jobs, and their training standards are being lowered – and this at a time when all provincial departments which had been responsible for African education before the Bantu education take-over had started raising them. *Apartheid* has been introduced into the nursing profession, and even here one can expect a lowering of standards. The extension of Bantu education to university level must inevitably produce 'Kaffir' graduates, no matter what the Government says to the contrary. By harnessing African education to the chariot of *apartheid*, the Government is reducing education to the status of a handmaiden to political expediency.

The middle class

A white collar is, however, not necessarily synonymous with middle-class status. To be middle class, certain conditions must be fulfilled, and the only groups of Africans that can be said to meet these conditions in any way are those who work on their own. But even these groups do not fulfil these conditions in all respects. Perhaps the best way of looking at what is meant by the term 'middle class' is to examine middle classes elsewhere to see what gave them the particular character which stamps them as middle class.

Middle classes are a product of the European Renaissance. Their rise is bound up with the growth of commerce and the emergence of modern economic society at about the beginning of the sixteenth century. What defined the middle class from other classes in the emergent capitalist system was the fact that they were men with capital, which may be defined as property in flexible form. They invested this first in commerce and later on in industry. This capital generated profits on which these groups lived. They were, therefore, men of independent means who exercised political influence to further their claims.

The growth of vast industrial corporations and cartels has had profound effects on the class structure of Western societies. We still have the upper classes consisting of the landed gentry and aristocratic families in England and of the moguls of our industrial and financial empires. To the middle classes has been added a serving middle class, comprising an army of highly salaried managers and technicians who are needed to run the affairs of these bureaucratic structures. But these are middle class in outlook only, for, however highly paid they may be, they still remain employees. For the factor differentiating the middle classes from the ranks of labour is that they are men of independent means, and are not subject to the whims of employers.

Now let us take a look at what is called the African middle class and see if it comes up to these specifications. The African is all but excluded from profit, rent and interest which form the three main pillars of our modern capitalist economy. A fourth pillar should be added – and that is skills which can be converted to capital. It is not surprising that there are only 16 000 African business men, 100 doctors and about 50 lawyers in the country today, in spite of the phenomenal development of industry over the past two decades. There are no Africans in finance, banking, industry and many other investment fields, for the country's policy restricts African participation in our economic life. Having said this, let us see what classes of Africans can be regarded as middle class, the factors that have favoured their emergence, and those that have operated to retard such emergence.

The African middle class is drawn from four areas – property owners, merchants, professionals and artists. [Hereafter follows a brief examination of each of these groupings – Ed.] . . .

Political role of middle class

Several implications follow from this (examination of middle-class groups), which must now be discussed. The first of these is that European policies here, as elsewhere in Africa, have retarded the emergence of social classes among Africans to a considerable extent, and have thus tended to blur class distinctions among Africans. While distinctions in wealth and education have become real among Africans and exert a powerful influence, 'there is no sharp cleavage between classes . . . The cleavage between Bantu and European . . . overshadows economic differences within the Bantu community itself' (Hunter 1936). Thus Africans, suffering as they do, from disabilities common to *all* classes, translate their struggle for status and personal recognition, not into class terms which would cut across colour lines, but into a struggle for the recognition of all Africans (Simons 1949). They see their struggle as a struggle against White domination.

What happens then, to the middle class that is expected to 'make for future social order and act as a go-between linking the European and the mass of the Bantu people?' (Longmore 1959:20). Can it exert the moderating influence that is regarded as one of its claims to usefulness in our society? The answer to these questions appears to be in the negative. The Whites refuse to extend the normal conventions of commerce and industry to Africans, and deny them access to the values of Western society. It is this limited participation in, and access to, Western culture that has resulted in a narrowing of vision as to the role that an African middle class can play in the evolution of our multi-racial society.

Furthermore, unlike their White counterparts in this country and elsewhere, the African middle class cannot form political pressure groups to secure for themselves specifically middle-class advantages. In fact, political activity of any kind is hazardous. As Lewin (1958) has pointed out, 'indeed it is the political implications of the precarious position held by the African middle class that have become important in late years. In all other except communist countries, the middle class has long contributed a solid conservative element in politics – for obvious reasons. The men of property, with the proverbial stake in the country, are the last to support wildly radical social changes.'

In the Union, however, as elsewhere in colonial Africa before the 'wind of change' started sweeping away colonialism, the emergence of an African middle class is in conflict with the policy of *apartheid*, and obstacles are placed in the way of its development. While it is true that the majority of African businessmen eschew political activity, many of them have joined hands with the professionals and working class in their demands for a radical transformation of South African society. Herein lies the reason for the adoption of radical policies by the African

National Congress and the even more extreme Pan-Africanist Congress. The African middle class has no stake in the country, and sees its salvation in making common cause with the masses with whom it shares common disabilities. In such a situation there can be no compromise for the Whites, on their side, refuse to give in one iota – 'to abdicate', as the Nationalists are always saying – and the Africans, on their own side, want nothing short of full and unfettered participation in our economic and political life, which is what they mean by equality.

To counteract the growing influence of radical African leaders, the Government is engaged in building up the chiefs by way of Bantu Authorities as the real leaders of the people. Tribal 'ambassadors' have already been appointed in some urban areas to act as a link with the Bantu Authorities. But there is a flaw in this scheme. The traditional authorities ceased to be a significant political factor when the tribal system, which gave them meaning, was destroyed by the White man's economy. The White man further destroyed their influence when he incorporated them into the authoritarian structure which he built to control the African. As recent events show, the implementation of the Bantu Authorities Act is seriously undermining the already untenable position of the chiefs who are now regarded even by their own people, no longer as leaders, but as Government stooges – 'Policemen-chiefs', as the Africans call them. Posterity may yet be grateful to the Nationalists for finally breaking down the hold of the chiefs on the people at a time when they thought they were strengthening it. The 'reserve' African will come to look more and more to his urban brother for leadership. As for the urban African, the pathetic efforts being made to revive tribalism and loyalty to chiefs would be laughable if they were not so tragic. Africans will look increasingly to their educated élite and their middle class for leadership rather than to the traditional élite.

Future of the middle class

It has been shown that an African middle class has emerged in South Africa because the demands of an expanding economy have led to large concentrations of the African population in the urban areas, which needed the services that such a middle class could provide. The development of this class has, however, been hampered by policies which limit African participation in our economy and restrict opportunities for the acquisition of capital and for its investment. While this class is small at present, its political significance is out of all proportion to its size. Thus, the degree to which African participation in our economy is hindered or facilitated will determine the fate of the middle class and the kind of leadership it will provide for the African masses.

There is no doubt, however, that the middle class has come to stay. This much is conceded even by the Nationalists. The only point of difference is on what conditions it will stay. The Nationalists envisage increasing opportunities for African economic development in what they call the 'Bantu homelands', which are better known as Reserves. Some of their leading spokesmen have painted a glowing picture of the possibilities for Africans in these areas. Towns will be be developed and Africans will find employment in them as business men, industrialists, engineers, doctors, teachers and so on. A Bantu Development Corporation has already been launched with a capital of £500 000 to assist Africans who want to go into these areas. That figure must be regarded as little more than a gesture when seen against the astronomical sums that would be required to develop these areas.

The Bantu University Colleges, which started operations at the beginning of this year, and the Medical School in Durban are expected to produce the kind of personnel such developments will require. For the moment, however, only the Medical School can be said to be producing anything like the sort of people who would fulfil that role. The other three have no facilities for the training of such people, nor are they likely to have them for quite a while. What, however, is likely to happen is that, if and when these institutions do provide such training, it will be inferior, and their products will have limited horizons. But it is one thing to produce such people and quite another to keep them satisfied with their position. And, so long as they have been introduced to the value of Western culture, to whatever limited an extent, it is problematic that they will remain contented with policies that could be interpreted as holding back their development.

A complementary aspect of this policy is that Africans in the present urban areas – 'White' areas, as the Government calls them – are there on sufference, and can never expect to get unlimited opportunities for development there. There are indications that attempts will be made to reduce opportunities for the growth of middle classes in these areas. In fact, the Minister of Bantu Administration and Development, the Hon. M. C. de Wet Nel, has stated it as the policy of his Department that the African business man in the urban areas is temporary, and is only allowed to remain in them '. . . to build up capital and gain experience . . . When a Bantu trader in a location has sufficient capital to establish a large business, he must move his business to a Bantu area . . .' The Minister added, however, that African business men would be compelled to move to Bantu areas only when 'comparable towns, markets and opportunities' were available to them.[2] That, of course, is the crux of the problem: whether these 'Bantustans' will ever materialize.

In the meantime, the African urban population continues to grow. Even the Tomlinson Commission working on the assumption that the government policy of diverting the African urban population to the Bantu areas would be implemented, predicts its continued growth (Hobart Houghton 1959:22). Provision will have to be made for these people, and such provision envisages, among other things, a middle class. Thus, increasing urbanization of the African may well counteract the policy of restricting the evolution of an African middle class.

NOTES

1. *Report of the Inter-Departmental Committee on Native Education*, 1935–36, U.G. No. 29/ 1936, para. 26.
2. M. C. de Wet Nel: Reports in *The Star* dated October 23, 26 and 28, 1959.

REFERENCES

de Kiewiet, C. W. 1937 – *The Imperial Factor in South Africa*. London: Cambridge.

Hobart Houghton, D. 1959 – 'The Tomlinson Report – Summary of Findings and Recommendations.' Johannesburg: S.A. Institute of Race Relations.

Hunter, Monica 1936 – *Reaction to Conquest*. London: Oxford University Press.

Lewin, Julius 1958 – 'The dice are loaded against the African trader.' *Contact*, August 9.

Longmore, Laura 1959 : *The Dispossessed*. London: Jonathan Cape.

Packard, Vance, 1959 – *The Status Seekers*. London: Longmans.

Simons, H. J. 1949 – 'Trade unions.' In Ek Hellman (ed.), *Handbook on Race Relations in South Africa*. London: Oxford University Press.

3. Class, Status and Ethnicity as Perceived by Johannesburg Africans

PHILIP MAYER

In common with other Black town populations in South Africa, the people of Soweto are (as of 1973) becoming increasingly diversified by income and occupation, but unlike most others, they are polyglot, drawn from many different Black ethnic groups.[1] Two themes interweave from a Black viewpoint – the theme of White domination and that of class versus ethnicity. Where Whites tend to lean on the idea of multiple Black ethnicities, which is supportive to White domination, it appears that most urban Blacks would for most purposes place those ethnicities second to class or status considerations, or they would substitute a single Black ethnicity.

Perceptions of class within the Black community are basically perceptions of status groups with varying degrees of prestige and honor. Class perceptions are sometimes extended to the field of Black-White relations too but 'class' in a more Marxian sense – workers ranged against employers. Class perceptions have to compete in this context (Black-White) with the 'race' concept of status ascribed by color, and the latter has more emotive power.

Some Blacks perceive themselves as being linked by common or complementary interests with some Whites, across the basic color cleavage. Some are aware of the interests that divide them from other Blacks. This combination of crosscutting links and internal oppositions provides some kind of brake on the dynamics of total Black-White confrontation. Indeed, there is not yet among urban Blacks a general sense of irreconcilable color conflict. However, the braking power is also rather uncertain. Many notions are 'open-ended' – they can equally well serve a sense of cross-linkage or a sense of cleavage. For instance, the people say that most inhabitants of the townships are committed to a 'Western' way of life. This commitment can be cited in support of co-operation with Whites, and rejection of a plural model, or as the basis for an anti-White Black unity.

So far, at least in the South African context, topics like race, class, and ethnicity have been discussed without systematic attention being paid to the subjective angle, the people's own perceptions. It seems a major omission,[2] as Peter Lloyd (1973:15) points out: 'To understand behaviour of members of any one society, it is not our models . . ., based on our pre-conceived ideas of what is significant, which is important, but theirs.'[3] Their own interpretation of social reality is the one which will determine their choice of action, notably between peaceful accommodation or violent protest.

Degrees of 'Unfreedom' of Labour[4]

There are four categories of residents of Soweto that represent different degrees of unfreedom of labor or of differential incorporation in the city in which they work.

(a) Foreign migrant workers: these are largely engaged in mining and live without families in compounds.
(b) South African migrant workers: some of these work in the mines, some in industries: the latter live in the townships for the duration of their contract (usually one year), after which they are repatriated. Most are in lower paid and less attractive jobs,[5] and live without families in Soweto's 'single quarters.'
(c) The illegal residents: lodging in the houses of legal residents, illegal residents are liable to be fined and 'endorsed out' when caught. They represent the main body of people prosecuted for pass offences (Horrell:161).[6] They live by their wits, often forced to accept cut wages from unscrupulous employers.
(d) Legal residents: to qualify as a legal resident under section 10 of the Bantu (Urban Areas) Consolidation Act, a Black has either to have been born in Johannesburg or to have worked there for one employer for ten years consecutively or for more than one employer for fifteen years. This is the only category of Blacks legally entitled to have their family staying with them. They are not liable to be 'endorsed out' if they merely change jobs, or fall out of work for a time, but only if they fall foul of the authorities. They hold the better paid jobs and benefit most from the recent improvements in the job structure and pay.[7]

This chapter focuses specifically on the last category.

Even these permanent residents remain unfree labor. They have no right of collective bargaining; they lack mobility; they have limited access to skilled work; the wage gap for comparable work by Whites is wide; and they are still stigmatized as 'temporary sojourners' in the cities. Nevertheless, a sharp dichotomy between the migrants and the residents has replaced former gradual transition between them.[8] The migrants today remain a rural-oriented population by necessity. Most have no future in town and probably little inducement to participate in its social life.[9] Nearly all remit money to their families at home and keep up the links with their rural home, even with homeland politics. They have low status but could be prominent in conflict situations, since they have least to lose and many are not entirely dependent on wages. They were prominently represented among the strikers in 1973 and 1974. Those who 'wait for the revolution' will put some of their money on them and on illegal residents, but as the army rather than the leadership.

The residents are the most significant category from the point of view of gradual social change, though they may also provide leadership for violent protest. They are the urban rooted core element who are evolving the norms of a new Black industrially committed society. Differentiation of occupation has progressed furthest among them and has resulted in an elaborate status system in which the other categories are only marginally involved. The normality of the age-sex profile of the Soweto population, with its broad base of children and slight preponderance of females, indicates that residents are also the numerically predominant element.[10]

There are various types among the residents. 'Ordinary working people' are mostly children or grandchildren of economically struggling rural born immigrants. They may have had four to eight years in primary school (standards 2 to 6) leaving because their parents could not afford more, or could not control them, or because of pregnancy, and seeing the small minority who went on to secondary or high school as 'different', from themselves. After a period of street life, they join the ranks of the unskilled or semiskilled workers in industry or commerce, or domestic service. They speak of themselves as 'poor', but also as 'medium' or 'middle people', because they have steady jobs and feel they can cope economically. These self-styled 'middle' people then are far removed from the sociological concept of the 'middle' class.

Second, there are the 'better-off'. These include semiskilled factory workers, drivers, policemen, teachers, sales representatives or clerks, up to professionals and businessmen. They share a general life-style – one with more Western urban middle-class amenities. In local language this is called being more 'civilized'. They own sitting room or bedroom suites; they can afford a more varied diet, some entertainment, sometimes a car. 'Better educated' coincides largely, but not entirely, with being 'better-off'.

Third, there are 'top' people – the bourgeoisie, the elite, or the upper stratus (as they are called respectively by Kuper, Brandel-Syrier, and Nyquist).[11]Those are a fairly small number, many of whom are concentrated in the prestigious section of Dube township. Except, where they are specifically singled out, they are included in the category of the 'better-off'.

BLACK AND WHITE: SOWETO PEOPLE'S IMAGES OF THE WIDER SOCIETY

The images our Soweto respondents had of their overall place in the wider South African society were framed in terms of their relations with Whites – a stark perception of Whites being at the top and Blacks at the bottom. But this was viewed in two alternative ways. Sometimes it was put in terms of power or racial domination, sometimes in terms of capitalists versus workers. The 'class' model occurred mostly among ordinary working people; the better educated respondents tended to by-pass the class model and put their answers straight into racial or power terms.

Blacks as Pariahs

The term 'pariah model', is a more expressive name for the race domination or caste model (Mayer 1972:5ff). It seems to convey better the sense of total deprivation experienced by people who see their Black identity as a stigmatized identity, and themselves as being despised, and effectively confined to the lowest kind of work. We are using 'pariah' in a sociological sense given to it by Max Weber.[12] Weber explained the development of pariah status as often rising from the historical process of invasion and conquest, whereby conquered tribes become a guest or pariah people in the land of their birth, producing for or serving the dominant population.

A sense of Black people having been treacherously conquered by White people seemed well engraved in our respondents' consciousness. 'We are oppressed in our own land and have to bow down to the will of the conqueror.' As Black people see it, pariah status is made inescapable by being tied to the ascriptive criterion of colour. The fact that government policy today is supposedly based on the concepts of nation or culture, rather than race, has failed to affect the reality of their experience. 'The Whites are oppressing me simply because I am Black'; 'a Black man is a slave whose function is to enrich the Whites.'

When ordinary working people spoke along these lines, it was in moving but general terms of being denied human status, not a mere abstract concept, but the vital core of their everyday experience. Better educated respondents would list and comment on the more important institutional forms of discrimination – pass laws, job reservation, inability to own land, 'petty apartheid' (which they regard as far from trivial), and lack of political expression. They used certain stock expressions that seem to be in general use in other South African towns as well. (Two illustrations out of many: Soweto, 1965: 'We are keen to have a say and not be thought for.' Mdantsane, 1971: 'I can't think. The government is doing the thinking for me.')

Distinguishing between White ethnic groups, our respondents saw Afrikaners as the main human agents of their relegation to a pariah role. They combined two generalizations: Afrikaners are the government, and Afrikaners hate Blacks. 'They took over the government, not because they are wise but because they are rough.' 'Because Chaka killed their people, they still hate all Africans.' 'They are the police: they arrest everybody.' A more positive image of Afrikaners was confined to a very few respondents drawn from the top elite. Perhaps some have 'manipulated' the 'system' and have found Afrikaner officials straightforward and predictable. 'Afrikaners can be very helpful friends, though only as long as the relationship is clearly defined.' Some of them contrasted Afrikaner directness with English 'hypocrisy.'[13] Only a few isolated individuals seemed aware of a change in the Afrikaner, or drew a distinction between the better behaved 'educated' Afrikaner and the 'rough types.' 'Some of them today will say "sorry" when they bumped into you, whereas before they used to call us "bloody Kaffirs".'[14]

Blacks as a lower class

In this, the alternative model, Black people are tracing their plight to economics, not conquest. 'The reason why we are the lowest is that we don't own anything and depend on working for others.' The idea of the ownership of capital and 'firms' as the decisive factor in class status was carried through quite logically. Thus Coloreds were sometimes said to be no better than Africans, because they too do not 'own firms' and 'have to work for the Whites.' Conversely, 'There are some Africans who are above the Coloreds, especially those who have their own shops.' Occasionally we even heard it argued that Africans rank above Afrikaners, because some Africans have shops whereas 'I have never yet seen an Afrikaner with a shop.' A very few informants took this to its furthest limits in claiming the employer-employee opposition as the essential criterion cutting even across color lines; they ranked 'non-White business people' next to 'European business people' and above 'European skilled workers.'

White ethnic groups were distinguished on similar lines. 'The top people are the Jews. They have money; they have businesses all over the country. The next are the English. They have experience in management and manufacturing.' 'The English bring us business here in South Africa'; 'the Jews provide us with money and work,' sometimes followed by the statement 'and we must be grateful to them.' The Afrikaners come last, because 'they have not so much experience in business and don't own factories.' Indeed some Black working people saw Afrikaners as fellow working people: 'They are not so rich and not so educated. They are quite like us Black people, but all they think about is how to ill-treat us.' Only a few, more educated informants were more realistic: 'Afrikaners are a growing force in commerce and industries. They have made great strides in recent years.'

These informants were not querying capitalist premises, not asking whether workers should be at the mercy of the owners of businesses and factories. They accepted that as legitimate. On the one hand, English and Jews were commended for their humane attitudes as employers. 'English treat the African well, and we in turn respect them' (even if it was sometimes added, 'they are very diplomatic in dealings with Africans'). Afrikaners, on the other hand, were often spoken of as the unilateral authority figures, whose actions are resented. 'The Afrikaners work for the English and Jews as supervisors, and all they have to do is to make the African work harder.' This picture of the supervisor links up with that of the Afrikaner policeman, and even the farmer, into a picture of brutal physical control. 'They are cruel from nature.'

Keeping the Class and Pariah Models Apart

All in all then, Black working people tended to contrapose cruel Afrikaners against 'good' English. In the race domination or pariah model the Afrikaners were shown as the central villains; in the economic class model they were seen as minor villains, with the 'good' English or Jew occupying the center of the scene. The crux of the matter is that the 'cruel' roles of the Afrikaners are emphatically denied legitimacy, whereas the employer role of the English and Jews is not. This distinction seems to have played a critical part in preventing total

Black-White polarization, for it seems to serve as a barrier against a fusion of the class and the pariah models.

While acutely aware both of their low wages (presumably paid by English and Jews) and of their pariah status in the other system (dominated by Afrikaners), somehow Black working people do not blame their low wages on the wider system and the way it loads things in the employer's favour. Rather than query the discrepancy between White and Black wages, they would speak of their particular boss being 'hard' compared with others who pay more. Many attributed their failure to obtain or to hold a reasonably paid job to their own shortcomings. Such 'intrapunitive' statements are in fact made in comparison with fellow Africans, who have done better than themselves, a perception of economic failure in terms of status in the townships.

In Marxist terms it would be argued that these Black workers lack proper class consciousness. If class can be seen as an 'event' (Thompson 1964), it has not quite arrived as far as they are concerned. In the language of everyday politics they could be said to lack political awareness or even political sense.[15] They seem willing to see themselves in the role of a 'normal' working class in a capitalist system and to ignore their 'abnormal' position as unfree labor.

For the men and women in Soweto with steady jobs, or with residence qualifications that allow them to choose between jobs, the working life in town can have many positive, reassuring aspects. The harrowing incidents of pariah status are likely to be more sporadic and to be felt elsewhere, either at home in the townships or out in the city streets. Thus they can remain existentially separable from the everyday working life. The working life and the township life can remain, in Schütz' (1967:207) language, two related 'sub-universes of reality.'

As against the workers who have forgone the development of 'worker consciousness' by distinguishing English, Jews, and Afrikaners, there were those who saw Blacks and Whites in uncompromising terms of 'us' versus 'them', insisting that they cannot distinguish between different categories of Whites. For them all Whites are rich and all Blacks are poor. This view seems to prevail where wages are very low and reasonable jobs difficult to get, as was the case in East London-Mdantsane in 1971. There the fusion of the two sources of indignation had become widespread. 'We Blacks are made poor by the laws of South Africa.' 'We are oppressed by those many laws which are made just to keep us subservient.' 'They want me as a laborer, but don't want to give me the rights of a citizen.' The fusion between political and economic dissatisfaction was more common in East London than in Grahamstown, although employment was worse in Grahamstown. There was more political awareness among the rank-and-file workers in Port Elizabeth and East London than among similar groups in provincial towns like Grahamstown or on the Rand (Carter 1972). During the Durban strikes in 1973 and in Johannesburg in 1974, it appears Africans were operating mainly within an economic model.

The better-off element in Soweto spoke less about Whites as the employer class and more about Whites as the dominant class. Since it was here that they saw the basic clash of interests, they did not identify with the working masses (except for a few politically motivated intellectuals). They visualized White discrimination as an instrument of competition rather than of 'exploitation', dwelling on the better jobs and better pay received by Europeans with no higher qualifications than their own. 'We (i.e., the better educated Blacks) do the same type of work as the Whites and are in a position to compare salaries.' Some Black businessmen wanted to be large-scale capitalists themselves. And there were the highly educated, who unlike the ordinary people, felt qualified for decision-making positions and aspired to them. Both these groups stand to gain more directly from a change in the 'system' than the working population.

Social Stratification Within Township Society

We found in Soweto a prevalence of rather 'advanced' models in which recognized social stratifications are seen as overriding 'tribal' affiliations. It would be inappropriate to say of Soweto, as is said of other towns in Africa, 'that kinship and other kinds of *Gemeinschaft* relationships are predominant while social class has little meaning' (Himmelstrand 1971). Nor is 'status crystallization' in Soweto limited to the higher strata of professionals and businessmen as in West Africa. In Soweto we are dealing with the most highly industrialised Black population in Africa. A high percentage of the ordinary workers claim to be 'following Western culture'; residents of all kinds, poor and well-to-do, illiterate and well educated, share a consensus of values concerning social superiority and inferiority in township society that would seem to fit a functional theory of class.

The complex play of status differentiation is entirely acted out behind the impenetrable curtain of social segregation and separation of Blacks and Whites. It has not been South African policy to lift the curtain even for the highly educated Black elites in the cities. And yet the models of status differentiation that have taken hold in the townships are not without a bearing on social change in the wider South African arena. There are even some discernible lines of potential class opposition.

Successful business men who take active parts in community life, within the given framework, are accused of being stooges ultimately motivated by their material interests. The highly educated are accused of withholding their full share in community activities. Many admit to doing so, because, they say, they can perceive the futility of it all. The highly educated professionals are depicted less as leaders than as 'idols' of the townships; they are symbols of Black achievement. The secondary educated are seen as incapacitating themselves by their low self-esteem and introverted bitterness, and their use of 'manners' and English as distancing mechanisms to separate themselves from the ordinary people.

Calculating the cost

We have noted that ordinary working people had developed ways of 'insulating' the race or pariah model (which referred to their experience of discrimination) from the 'class' model (belonging to their everyday experience as workers). To the discriminatory political aspects of the system they accorded at the most a pragmatic acceptance, i.e., they denied their legitimacy, but perceived no realistic alternative. To the 'class' or economic dimension of the system on the other hand they might virtually accord normative acceptance. Many seemed to have internalized the legitimating concept that success comes to those who deserve it through 'hard work' and ability. Thus, their acceptance of the status structure of location society with its middle-class aspirations shaded into a readiness to accept the economic inequalities between employers and workers, even if they recognized those inequalities as being aggravated by racial discrimination. There is then no coherent philosophy uniting the two models and pointing to total rejection of White dominance, uniting the two models in consciousness of Blacks. A similar 'schizophrenic' picture has been noted among the working classes in Britain and the United States (Free and Cantril 1967), but with this important difference. Whereas workers in Western countries have been observed to hold 'rather confused values with surprisingly conservative bias' at the political level, largely it would seem owing to school indoctrination (Mann 1970). Black workers in Soweto tend to hold conforming values in the economic sphere and to withhold value consensus in the political field.

It is this difference that makes social cohesion more fragile in South Africa than in liberal Western democracies. The grudging pragmatic acceptance of political domination is no match emotionally or ideologically for the painful pariah experience of racial discrimination, which remains therefore (at least potentially) a dynamic force toward major change. Seen at the receiving end, the stigmata of racial discrimination go even deeper than those of class; the ascribed inferiority is the more basic indignity. Moreover, the class (worker-employer) model was stressed only among working people, whereas the pariah model was found among all sorts of residents, as well as the illegal residents and migrants who are the categories most severely affected by discriminatory regimentation. The present data then lends little support to the orthodox Marxist view on the priority of the class conflict.[16]

It seems to follow that economic concessions would not easily 'buy' long-term political support, though they might further legitimize, in their own eyes, Africans' participation in the capitalist *status quo*. Second, only a fusion between the pariah and the class model would be needed to lead to bitter confrontation. So far most African trade union leaders as well as the striking workers of 1973 and 1974 have seen their business first and foremost as a struggle for bread. The government, however, regards fully fledged African trade unions as a major political risk, greater, it seems, than the risk of mediation in labor disputes by homeland officials, whereas Mr Oppenheimer thinks industrial disputes 'are best settled within industry itself, and any system which makes intervention by the political leaders of independent or semi-independent states inevitable and indeed necessary is likely to prove at once inefficient and dangerous.'[17]

Soweto residents have been assessing their scope for manoeuvre rationally and realistically. Our material illustrates this on the verbal level; the recent strikes show it in action. If urban residents are to continue seeing cohesion of the South African social system as worthwhile, their stake in the system will have to be increased. They would accord legitimacy only to a system in which they have a meaningful share in the decision-making. This is a price the ruling White party is not yet prepared to pay. To this extent, change in the direction of a 'democratic plural society' seems not yet to have become practical policy.

The alternative is a short-term policy, an attempt to buy time by concessions that do not affect the differential access to central political institutions: rights to own houses, scaling down of petty apartheid, endowing township boards with executive powers, giving more substance to the homeland affiliation of urban residents, and so on. It could mean the Black urban resident, while still seeing himself as 'unfree', would feel significantly better off materially, compared with the homelanders who, though 'free' are poverty-stricken in the country and heavily regimented in town.

Black townspeople might continue to prefer this as a *modus vivendi* compared with the trouble and agony entailed by political protest. This seems to be the basis for the hopes of most White 'verligtes'.

Indeed, in this sense a political moratorium for urban Blacks could 'work'. An upward tendency in their real income would be a *sine qua non* for its success. But we would still be left with the unanswerable question: how long the euphoria of raised material well-being could be expected to last? Only as long as it lasted would the doors remain open for peaceful 'fundamental' change. And it could be abruptly ended by anything that seriously threatened the military or economic stability of the present regime.

NOTES

1. According to figures supplied by the West Rand Bantu Administration Board the distribution in 1973 of ethnic groups (National Units) in Soweto and Eastern Bantu townships was as follows:

Nguni speakers	Zulu	167 309
47 percent	Xhosa	56 119
	Swazi	38 452
Sotho speakers	Tswana	90 759
40 percent	South Sotho	79 702
	North Sotho	55 422
Others	Tsonga	40 509
13 percent	Venda	24 523
	Others	8 048

2. As an attempt to picture the interplay of class, status, ethnicity, and race through Black South African eyes, this chapter has had little previous work to draw upon. The nearest comparable material would be in the three monographs so far available on Black South African élites: L. Kuper, *An African Bourgeoisie*, New Haven, 1965; M. Brandel-Syrier, *Reeftown Elite*, London, 1971; T. Nyquist, *Toward a Theory of the African Upper Stratum*

in South Africa, Athens, Ohio, 1972. E. Hellman has published several excellent short studies of social change in Soweto. *See* 'Social Change Among Urban Africans,' in H. Adam, (ed.), *South Africa: Sociological Perspectives*, Oxford, 1971, 158–76. *See also* her *Soweto;* and E. Hellman and D. Goldblatt 'Soweto,' in *Optima*, 23, 1 (March 1973): 16–21. M. Edelstein, *What Do Young Africans Think?* (Johannesburg, 1972) contains an attitude survey of African matric pupils in Soweto.

3. *See also* L. Kuper, 'Theories of Revolution and Race Relations,' *Comparative Studies in Society and History*, 13, January 1971, 87–107.
4. Rex (1970) stresses the key importance of 'unfree labor.'
5. It appears that there are at present no figures available to substantiate this assumption. Through the call-in card system, employers are able to use migrants also for jobs that require steady incumbents; so far these would seem to be a small minority.
6. In 1971 to 1972 615 000 Blacks were prosecuted for such offences.
7. Far too little is known about the relative size of the four categories; their change in size relative to one another in recent years; their economic characteristics; their respective contributions to the high rate of crime and acts of violence in Soweto; or about their social relations with each other. One reason for our ignorance is that the contract labor system (with automatic repatriation at the end) is relatively new. *See* Republic of South Africa, Bantu Labour Relations (Bantustan, Government Notice No. R 74, *Government Gazette Extraordinary*, No. 2029, 29 February 1968.
8. On the element of choice as it existed previously, *see* P. and I. Mayer, *Townsmen or Tribesmen*, Oxford, 1974.
9. This is brought out by G. Sack, 'Black Railwaymen in a Durban Compound,' M.A. Thesis, Rhodes University, which deals with railway single quarters near Durban.
10. Or at least have been until fairly recently. For population profiles (referring to 1965), *see* Lewis, *A City' Within a City*, 49–50. F. Wilson, *Migrant Labour: Report to the South African Council of Churches*, Johannesburg, 1972, estimates the percentage of migrants in single quarters as over 40 percent of the total population of Black Migrants.
11. *See* n. 2.
12. For a brief exposition of Weber's view of 'pariah', *see* R. Bendix, *Max Weber*, New York, 1962, 150.
13. On 'hypocrisy' as part of the stereotype of the English-speaking South African, *see* Kuper, *African Bourgeoisie*, 397 and appendix C; for Brandel-Syrier's comments on Kuper's view, *see Reeftown Elite*, 315.
14. Brandel-Syrier is alone in finding among Johannesburg Blacks a greater preference (42 percent) for Afrikaners than for English (12 percent). Two comments may help to show that there is no real contradiction: her figures represent the views of fifty-five members of the elite, of whom about thirty-nine were government or municipal employees, and none were engaged in business; it is precisely from this kind of elite element that our Soweto material produced a favorable view of Afrikaners.
15. Similar phenomena have been noted elsewhere. W. Runciman, writing of English workers, noted that 'appeals to explicit principles of overall comparison, remained as infrequent as ever . . . The relation of grievance to hardship remained anomalous.' *See Relative Deprivation and Social Justice*, London, 1966, 91. And M. Abrams has recently pointed to 'the apparent paradox' in Britain that people are satisfied on one level, while at the same time showing disquiet about many aspects of their lives, feeling that they were entitled to a better deal and that the quality of their lives had declined. *See Social Trends*, 4, London, 1973.
16. For a critique of the orthodox Marxist view, *see* Kuper, 'Theories of Revolution,' 87 f; *see also* review article by L. Kuper and of H. and R. Simons, *Class and Color in South Africa*, 1850–1950, Harmondsworth, 1969 in *Race*, 12, 4, 1971, 495–500; Rex, *Race Relations*; J. Rex, *Race, Colonialism, and the City*, London 1971.
17. As reported in *Daily Dispatch*, East London, 30 July 1974.

REFERENCES

Carter, D. 1972 – 'The defiance campaign: A comparative analysis of the organisation, leadership and participation in the eastern Cape and the Transvaal.' In the University of London, Institute of Commonwealth Studies, *Collected Papers on the Societies of Southern Africa*, 2, London.

Free, L. and H. Cantril 1967 – *The Political Beliefs of Americans*. New Brunswick: Rutgers University Press.

Himmelstrand 1971 – 'Rank Equilibrium.' In R. Melson and H. Wolpe (eds.) *Nigeria: Modernization and the Politics of Communalism*. East Lansing: Michigan State University Press.

Horrell, M. (ed.) 1972 – *Race Relations 1972*. Johannesburg: S.A. Institute of Race Relations.

Lloyd, P. C. 1973 – *Classes, Crises and Coups*. London: MacGibbon and Kee.

Mann, M. 1970 – 'The social cohesion of liberal democracy.' *American Sociological Review*, 35, 3, June, 435.

Mayer, P. 1972 – *Urban Africans and the Bantustans*. Hoernle Memorial Lecture, Johannesburg.

Rex, J. 1970 – *Race Relations in Sociological Theory*. London: Weidenfeld and Nicolson.

Schütz, A. 1967 – *The Problem of Social Reality*. Collected Papers I. The Hague: Nijhoff.

Thompson, E. 1964 – *The Making of the English Working Classes*. London: Gollanz.

4. South African Society In Comparative Perspective

JOHN REX

It is very difficult to adopt a detached and objective sociological approach to South African society. Indeed, few people attempt to do so. Usually what is discussed is the simple and straightforward question of how far South Africa deviates from the ideal type (using that notion to refer to what is ideal in the commonsense use of the term, as well as to a Weberian methodological device) of a democratic society. Such discussion is, of course, important, but it draws attention away from the primary question which should be faced by students of South African society: what sort of society is it, and to what laws of development is it likely to conform?

When this question is faced, it becomes clear that the conceptual tools which we have for dealing with it are inadequate. What has happened too often is the simple application to South Africa of models derived from the political sociology of European society, without any recognition that this might be a new sociological type which, if it is not compounded of entirely new elements, at least combines the old ones in entirely new ways.

I have not been concerned in my own recent research with the study of South Africa. What has concerned me, however, may be relevant, for I have been trying on a more general international and comparative scale to see what it is which distinguishes race relations situations, structures and problems from other categories of situation, structure and problem in sociology (Rex 1970). I hope, therefore, that what I am doing will throw light on the problems of a society whose members define their major preoccupations as racial ones.

At the risk of oversimplifying grossly, I would suggest that the major areas of argument in the comparative study of race relations boil down to two. The first concerns the kinds of social structure which are present when there is thought to be a conflict of a racial kind. The second is about the relationship between ideas and theories on the one hand, and social structures on the other.

Under the first heading of structural studies there are two kinds of argument. One is that race relations problems may be reduced to problems of social *stratification*, albeit of a special kind. The other is that concepts derived from stratification theory do not adequately cover crucial cases of race relations and that a different set of concepts, namely, that derived from the theory of *pluralism*, has to be introduced.

As a starting-point for the consideration of stratification theory, we may take the functional theory advanced in a simple form by Davis and Moore in 1945 and, in a much more sophisticated form, by Talcott Parsons (1954). What is common to these theories is the view that stratification follows from the existence in a society of a common value system. Given that values are shared, certain qualities and performances of individuals are likely to be rewarded in order to encourage such qualities and performances in the future.

Quite clearly this theory of stratification is not dealing with the same sort of sociological material as Marxist theory is or, when he talks about 'class', the sort of structure Weber (1967) discusses. It will be important, therefore, to return to their type of theory later. What is of immediate importance, however, is that theories of stratification of the functionalist kind break down when applied to Black-White relations in the United States.

Lloyd Warner (1936) suggested dealing with the problem by his theory of class and caste. According to this view there was an upper, middle, and lower class in the Negro as well as the White community, but a caste-like barrier marked by taboos on interracial eating and marrying. As more Negroes entered the higher social classes the caste-line would swing round from a horizontal to something nearer a vertical position. But it would not, as Warner saw it, break down. According to this view, it should be noted there is still thought to be a value-system common to Whites and Negroes in terms of which each community ranks its own members. Its main deviation from functionalist theory is simply its inclusion of the notion of a caste-barrier cutting across the status-stratification system. The exact nature of this caste-barrier remains unclear and its origin is unexplained.

We shall have to deal in a moment with criticisms of the notion of a common value system in colonial societies, but before we do so we must notice the Marxist criticism by Cox (1959) of the notion of the caste-barrier . Cox argues that the barrier between Black and White bears no relationship at all to, say, the Indian caste system (which, curiously, Cox represents in a somewhat un-Marxist way as being based upon a shared value system and the consent of the lower castes). Rather it is seen as being simply the line between contending classes brought into being by colonial capitalism. The difficulty with this theory, however, is to explain why the white working-class does not fall on the same side of the line as its negro equivalent. For my own part, I find valuable insights in all three of the types of theory mentioned. I would not, of course, want to accept an oversimplistic functionalist or Marxist view of the nature of the colour-line. What I would suggest, however, is a formulation somewhat as follows.

Advanced industrial societies in the capitalist world do not have a simple and unitary value system. Rather they are historical products, which have arisen from the attempt by a ruling group to impose values and institutions which accord with its own interests on the population at large. In opposition to this set of values and institutions, those who are most conscious of exploitation in the society have created their own defensive institutions and values. In so far as the society stabilizes itself, however, these two sets of values have been able to coexist, and members of all classes have come to value the state of stability itself.

This is what Lipset (1959) seems to be getting at when he talks of advanced capitalist societies having solved their political problems.

All of this occurs within a population which shares a common history, language and culture. But members of such a population also enter into economic relations with outside groups and these relations may be of a less peaceful kind and lead to the establishment of economic institutions quite different from those which exist within the first-mentioned population. Hence, if one looks at the total social system which includes a metropolitan society and its colonies or its colonial immigrants, one finds an absence of a shared value system and not one class struggle, but two. In the case of the 'colonial' class struggle, at first there may be less overt conflict than there is in the metropolitan one, simply because the colonial people are lacking in power. But in the long run the colonial people might be active in their resistance at the very time that the metropolitan working class are becoming 'incorporated.'

The failure of both functionalist and Marxist theories to explain the differences of value and interest between differing colour and ethnic groups, however, has led to the exploration of an alternative theory, namely that of the *plural* society. As Furnivall (1948:304), the first author of this concept, described what it meant:

> probably the first thing that strikes the visitor is the medley of peoples – European, Chinese, Indian and native. It is in the strictest sense a medley, for they mix but do not combine. Each group holds by its own religion, its own culture, its own ideas and ways. As individuals they meet but only in the market place, in buying and selling . . . There is a plural society, with different sections of the community living side by side, but separately within the same political unit. Even in the economic sphere there is a division of labour on racial lines:

Smith (1965:82), has elaborated the concept and applied it to the Caribbean; he argues that plural societies are marked by the fact that institutional systems including 'kinship, education, religion, property and economy, recreation and certain sodalities' are not shared. Instead each segment of the society has its own institutional set. The sole factor holding the segments together is political power:

> Given the fundamental differences of belief, value and organization that connote pluralism, the monopoly of power by one cultural section is the essential precondition for the maintenance of the total society in its current form (86).

Finally, the concept of stratification has to be thought of as applying within the segments rather than between them. It will be noticed that, relatively speaking, pluralist theory seems to accept a certain looseness in the relationship of one segment to another while at the same time attaching a crucial significance to cultural differences. By contrast, functionalist and Marxist stratification theories both seem to point to a much closer involvement of one group with another. Functionalism emphasizes the ultimate value system, Marxism the activity within the social relations of production as the central issue in men's lives. Pluralist theory seems to imply that involvement in the polity and in production is less important for men, as a central life-interest, than is the culture which governs their relations outside of their working lives.

For myself, I would certainly want to criticize Smith for his failure to see that one cannot, in the former slave society of the Caribbean, speak of each 'segment' as having its own institutions relating to 'property and economy', and that the dynamics of the society turn upon the involvement of men of differing ethnic backgrounds in the same social institution, viz., the slave plantation. But, for all this, the emphasis of pluralist theory does draw attention to some central features of colonial social structure, which Marxism, for instance, does not.

Marxism, of course, points out that all societies with capitalist institutions must become internally differentiated and that, in the more advanced stage of their development, the revolutionary working class will move from being a class-in-itself to being a class-for-itself. This change in the consciousness of the working class seems to imply the development of structures, organizations and programmes of action, if not institutions in the sense in which Smith uses the term. For the Marxist there is a certain state of organization and awareness which constitutes true consciousness, and, in the long run, economic events are likely to sweep away any form of false consciousness. But one such form of false consciousness would be the feeling of the plantation worker in Guyana that before being a worker he was an East Indian. The Marxist theory would appear to imply that such segmentary culture consciousness must give way to true working-class consciousness.

One of the difficulties of Marxist theory in European contexts has been to show that the working-class does become a class-for-itself, does become, that is, a collective actor in history. In fact, in the hundred post-Marxian years, working men have given their loyalty to many groups other than merely revolutionary classes. How much more likely is it then that colonial workers who already have the capacity of collective actions through their ethnic organizations will prefer these organizations to the classes and parties which seek to recruit them.

This is not, however, merely a matter of ideas and culture, of consciousness and ideology. For the groups of men who feel themselves to be united in colonial contexts are in fact united by their history and their destiny. They are not groups which were differentiated from one another by developing economic institutions. They are the descendants of distinct groups, who were compelled to live together and operate the same economic institutions together, by that group which possessed the necessary military force. Hence what we are witnessing is not simply the class struggle engendered by capitalist development, but the 'race war' engendered by colonial conquest. This is why normal stratification models do not appear to apply, and why colonial societies seem so recalcitrantly plural in character.

There remains the question of the influence of ideology. For Cox this is purely a question of the 'superstructure'. Racial conflict is less acute in Brazil than in the USA, not because of its Catholic religion, but because of its relative backwardness of economic development (Catholicism is merely another consequence of its backwardness). On the other hand others have suggested that, along with Catholicism, there went the shaping of a wholly different set of legal and economic institutions than that which was to be found in the United States or, for that matter, in South Africa (Cox 959).

I am not sure of my own position on this, since I am insufficiently expert in the evaluation of the historical data. I am inclined to feel, however, that the Catholic countries of Latin America had, at the turn of the century, a set of institutions of a semi-feudal kind, which made their social structures sharply different from that of the USA, most crucially, of course, in that graduations of colour were recognized rather than an absolute division into White and Coloured, or White, Coloured and Black. These differences were so great that I do not believe that any amount of industrialization is going to cause Brazilian society to converge with the social system of the USA or South Africa.

Rather unsystematically I would like also to mention three other variable elements in these colonial situations before I turn to South Africa.

1. The extent to which the subjugated colonial people retain the culture of their ancestors in the pre-conquest period.
2. The relative differentiation of a mixed-race group and the nature of its cultural affiliation (i.e. to the ruling or the subjugated group's culture).
3. The extent to which status differentiation develops within subjugated groups and to which the upper strata within these groups affiliate culturally with the ruling group.

With this background we are now perhaps in a better situation to see what the major problems are in delineating the South African social type. Obviously I do not propose to solve these problems in a few paragraphs, but hope that what I have to say may stimulate further thought and research.

In the first place South Africa is an advanced capitalist country whose religion is basically Protestant. That is to say that there is no ideological obstacle to development of the institutions of an advanced capitalist society, and the country has now passed beyond the stage of economic take-off and generates capital for its own economic development. It is of some interest, perhaps, to note that the purest form of Calvinism was located in the rural areas and in white working-class areas in the towns, and that it was associated with what some might see as pre-capitalist institutions, whereas business enterprise was the work of other Protestant and Jewish entrepreneurs. However, there was always the world of difference between the economic life of the Afrikaner farmer and that of the

Portuguese settler in Brazil, and in the last twenty years the various Dutch Reformed Church and Afrikaner nationalist organizations have helped to put the Afrikaner into business. Given the importance of this variable from a sociological point of view, the study of changes in ideology amongst Afrikaner nationalists becomes a crucial area of research.

It would be wrong, however, to approach South African society and its economic institutions purely in terms of ideologies. The fact is that its economic development was able to take the course which it did, because of the fact of the military conquest of the Bantu peoples and their availability as a reservoir of cheap and rightless labour. Rhodes's taxes, the Glen Grey Act and the activities of the labour-recruiting companies laid the foundations of a kind of socio-economic structure quite unlike those of other advanced capitalist countries. Yet, just as it is worth noticing that, whereas Max Weber sees slavery as incompatible with pure capitalism, Elkins speaks of the American plantations as operating according to the logic of unopposed capitalism, so in the South African case the military situation post-conquest makes possible the use of unfree labour as part of an efficient capitalist system of production. There is a central need in the sociological study of South Africa for a study of migrant and compound labour, not in its effect on tribal life, but as one of the possible types of labour organizations and exploitation. The problem would be to investigate the fit between this type of labour and the other institutions of a capitalist society.

Given that South Africa is an advanced capitalist society, the question arises as to how far it can be understood in terms of Marxist models intelligently applied. I say 'intelligently applied' because I do not believe that we can get very far by insisting that the important 'class' difference in South Africa is between those who own and those who don't own the means of production, whereas the difference between Black and White workers is only a difference between strata. Surely the point is that there are a number of different relationships to the means of production more subtle than can be comprehended in terms of a distinction between owners and non-owners and that each of these gives rise to a specific class-situation, or, as Marxists might say, to distinct classes-in-themselves.

The basic distinction which has to be made and which makes it necessary to distinguish South African society from, say, Australian society, is that between free and unionized labour on the one hand and labour which is subject to a variety of restrictions on the other. Further, there is the distinction between compound and other forms of unfree labour and the distinction between labour in mining and manufacture on the one hand, and farm labour, domestic service and subsistence farming on the other.

Some might argue that to extend the Marxist notion of 'class-in-itself' to cover all these cases is to rob it of its distinctiveness. Perhaps this is so, but in the opinion of the author, the notion of a whole range of class situations such as we have mentioned here is an illuminating one. There might be some case for speaking of 'estates', since the group concerned is affected by the degree to which it has or lacks political rights. But if that term or the term caste is taken to imply consent to the overall pattern of apportionment of rights, its use would be misleading.

The next question which arises is the capacity of the free and unfree workers (including one or more of the groups mentioned above) to become classes-for-themselves, i.e. to achieve a degree of autonomy in their culture, their organization and capacity for collective action in pursuit of their interests. Here we would have to see the class-for-itself possibility as only one of several possibilities. The others are the control of the organizations and culture of the working-class group by the ruling or property-owning class, the 'incorporation' of the working-class groups through the development of shared goals between labour and capital, and, thirdly, tribalism and nationalism in which ethnic rather than class identity is given precedence.

The free unionized White working class has, of course, like the working classes of the advanced capitalist societies of Europe, been largely 'incorporated', and though the history of White labour's relations with capital is a bitter and even a bloody one, the free White worker today enjoys rights and privileges in the economic sphere which, together with his political and social privileges, put him firmly on the opposite side to his fellow-workers. This is not to say that South African White workers, particularly poor-Whites, do not experience class bitterness and hostility. This is, of course, an underlying theme in all nationalist politics. But it is to say that on balance reformist rather than revolutionary ideologies prevail.

So far as the African workers are concerned, the possibility of incorporation in this sense is not even open. What the government's labour legislation has done is to seek to establish *control* by government officials and to prevent any spontaneous organization of a class-for-itself kind. In the nature of the case it is unlikely that there will be much research into this question to show whether or not the possibility of control has been successful. What is, perhaps, more interesting, is the fact that the group structure and consciousness on which resistance to control is based might have nationalistic or even a tribal form.

It is interesting to compare the situation of the North American slave with that of the South African worker in this respect. The slave had his own culture completely destroyed, and his master saw to it that he was both deprived of the possibility of any cultural or political autonomy and educated to accept his servile status. The African worker in South Africa can look to his own culture and social organization as a base for the establishment of a measure of autonomy.

This situation, however, has much greater complexity than has been suggested hitherto. From the point of view taken here, the distinction made by Mayer (1963) between 'red' and 'school' people is of considerable significance. The 'reds' provide the African worker with a 'reference-group' which seems to offer autonomy, if not the capacity to pursue economic interests more effectively. The 'school-people' on the other hand offer a number of alternative social strategies ranging from complete acceptance of White authority and White values to political and trade union-based resistance to those values. Here, however, we are forced to pass beyond a narrow focus on the social relations of production as the basis for our studies of South Africa. For cross-cutting any distinction between groups of workers possessing varying degrees of freedom is the distinction between individuals according to the degree in which they accept 'white' or 'western' values. Clearly the proportion of the African population who become 'detribalized' increases every year. What the policy of 'apartheid' has meant here is a dual policy of restricting the rate of inflow into the detribalized sectors, and ensuring that those who do make the transition do so on the Europeans' own terms. Bantu education implies a unitary value system but one which consigns even those Africans who accept it to a position of inferiority.

On another level, too, a narrow Marxist approach must break down. In what we have said so far we have spoken as though there was some kind of ruling class marked by its control of the means of production. It would be gravely misleading, however, to sketch any outline of a sociology of South Africa which did not draw attention to the implications of the separation of political and economic power. The incorporation of the White working class takes place, not through trade union bargaining, but through White control of political power, which means control of that power by privileged White workers and farmers. Thus, instead of a welfare and trade union bargain such as forms the basis of a political contract in Western Europe, the bargain sought and won by the White voters is a guarantee of privilege in the labour market for workers and in the market for labour by farmers. This bargain may, of course, be more precarious than that between labour and capital in Europe, but it has held since Smuts's pro-capitalist policies were defeated in the twenties.

Finally we must give some consideration to three other groups, the 'African middle class', the Cape Coloureds, and the Indians. How far can one detect in South Africa what may be called the tipping of the Lloyd Warner caste line? If one can, should this be interpreted simply as the growth of a service-group within African society, or should it be seen as the basis on which an African élite or class will emerge either to change or to stabilize South African society. For myself I do not see this group as playing any role independent of a wider African nationalist movement, though it might, it is true, affect the goals of that movement. However, apartheid, by depriving the African community of the advantages and disadvantages of being serviced by Indian, Chinese and other traders, certainly increases the numbers of this group and the Nationalist party hopefully looks to it as a source of potential allies, while others see in it the seeds of political change: All one can really say at the moment, therefore, is that we need more studies of such strata, élite or classes.

The Cape Coloureds represent a different kind of problem. They are non-Whites who have a variant of White culture. Moreover they are recognized politically, culturally and socially as a distinct group. There is no equivalent group in the United States, though there does seem to be, on the social and cultural level, in the Latin American countries. What are the implications for the stability of the system of this group in South Africa being placed at an intermediate point on the scale of rightlessness, and what views, in the long run, are to be found amongst Cape Coloureds as to their ultimate affiliation? Clearly in recent years the ambiguity of their political status has been resolved in the direction of their being separated from the Europeans, but is it not possible that in the long run political power will be shared with them? Much will depend on how far the racism of the South African Whites has taken on a life of its own. In so far as this is a factor which is related to economic self-interest, the likelihood would seem to be that the White group (opposed of course by those poor-White factory workers and artisans who are in competition with the Coloureds) will eventually want the Cape Coloured allies more than it wants to preserve its racial purity.

So far as the Indians are concerned, it would seem at first that apartheid, pressed to its logical conclusion, might endanger the fabric of South African society. For the Indians are both a pariah group (i.e. a group of outsiders who perform essential roles, such as those of traders in African areas, which are beneath the dignity of White society) and a scapegoat group (who are blamed for the manifest evils in the society). To remove them from their organic relation with the multi-racial society as a whole would seem to raise the question of how their role as pariahs and scapegoats will be fulfilled.

REFERENCES

Cox, O. C. 1959 – *Castle, Class and Race: A Study in Social Dynamics*. New York: Monthly Review Press.

Davis, K. and W. E. Moore 1945 – 'Some principles of stratification.' *American Sociological Review* 5: 242-249.

Furnivall, J. S. 1948 – *Colonial Policy and Practice*. London: Cambridge University Press.

Mayer, P. 1963 – *Townsmen or Tribesmen: Conservation and the Process of Urbanization in a South African City*. Cape Town: Oxford University Press.

Parsons, T. 1954 – *Essays in Sociological Theory*. New York: Free Press.

Rex, J. 1970 – *Race Relations in Sociological Theory*. London: Weidenfeld and Nicolson.

Smith, M. G. 1965 – *The Plural Society in the British West Indies*. Los Angeles: University of California Press.

Warner, L. 1936 – 'American class and caste.' *American Journal of Sociology* 42: 234-237.

Weber, M. 1967 – 'Class, status and party.' In R. Bendix and S. M. Lipset (eds.), *Class, Status and Power: Social Stratification in Comparative Perspective*. London: Routledge and Kegan Paul.

Part 9:

Political Sociology

Introduction

SIMON BEKKER

> 'If a South African were asked to classify his party system, his answer would probably depend upon his prescribed status in South African society. An Afrikaner would probably label it to a two-party system . . . An English-speaking white South African would be inclined to state (that) in reality South Africa has become a one-party state . . . a non-white South African would probably say that South Africa is an authoritarian state, ruled by a government responsible to an ethnic oligarchy . . . There is some truth in each statement.' (Thompson 1966:150–51)

To make the subject of politics in South Africa seem even more complex, it is worth pointing out that the Republic has been classified in many ways: a pigmentocracy, a racial oligarchy, a divided plural society, a settler society. It is imperative, then, that some common ground about the subject of politics be found. Only then can agreement be reached about what questions should be asked. Differing answers under these conditions may well lead to fruitful argument.

One classical approach to political sociology begins with the problem of order. It can be stated as follows: Most men desire some kind of order in their and others' lives most of the time. They will not, in general, accept any order for its own sake but they do have a stake in what is sometimes called the *status quo*. In a society, men in groups, or alone, conceive of this *status quo* in different ways. In addition, there are some, and, under certain conditions, many who desire a change in the *status quo*. The fact, therefore, that there exists peaceful coexistence between people and the groups they belong to in a society at any one time, requires sociological explanation (cf. Bekker 1974).

This problem of order can be discussed by defining a political system as a set of interactions which structure generalized conflict over scarce goods, services and values. This is the definition used in the selection by Du Toit, included as a reading in this chapter. Two interrelated problems now emerge: On the one hand, men compete with each other, individually or in groups, over scarce items such as land, prestige, wealth and power. On the other, they desire some type of order in their society. They want to avoid disruption or revolutions.

In a modern society characterized by a complex division of labour and differentiation of roles, specialized institutions are developed to regulate this conflict over scarce items and to legitimate people's search for societal order. In order to regulate this endemic conflict, these institutions have recourse to certain means of coercion: influence is brought to bear on people, threats are made, and if necessary, violence is used. The object is to structure and contain, to regulate the generalized conflict in society.

If those involved in the conflict – the competitors – accept such regulation as legitimate, it is clear that the object can be achieved more easily. This is why such institutions continually attempt to give normative justifications for their policies and actions. Applications of legitimate coercion are usually more effective and can be more easily repeated than applications of nonjustified coercion or violence. In short, these specialized institutions regulate conflict in society by means of coercion and by attempting to legitimate this coercion in the eyes of the competitors. Such institutions can be called political institutions.

The most powerful political institution of a modern society is the state. As Weber (1946:78) defined it, the state is 'a human community that successfully claims the monopoly of the legitimate use of force within a given territory.' This definition is worth some reflection. Weber argues that the monopoly refers to the legitimate use of force, i.e. legitimate coercion. He thereby excludes other types of coercion (such as a rebellion, for instance) even though they may well be effective coercive forces. Examples of legitimate coercive means are the law courts, the police force and the military. In practice, however, the legitimacy of any one of these can be, and has been, questioned by a section of a society. This is the reason why Weber argues that state officials – the human community referred to – *claim* to have this monopoly. It is probable that a section of a society will question this claim even if they do nothing about it. They may well acquiesce to threats of coercion without accepting the legitimacy thereof. Finally Weber argues that this claim is successful. If it were not, the state would not be in a position to regulate conflict by using its monopoly. Another group in the society would make a similar claim and the stronger of the two claimants would presumably force through their claim by using superior force. This situation can be called a revolutionary situation. It is probable that each claimant will have an ideology and that both will claim to have, in evaluative terms, the superior ideology.

Three related questions emerge from this discussion:

Which group has effective control over the political institutions (and the state) in South Africa?

How does this group attempt to maintain and legitimate this control?

How effectively does this group maintain and legitimate this control?

The rest of this chapter including the readings can be seen as a discussion of these three questions.

A comparison of the Union Constitution of 1909 – The South Africa Act – and the Republic Constitution of 1961 reveals a surprising similarity in content. Apart from severing South Africa's link with the British Crown, the Republic Constitution does not include the entrenched clause guaranteeing the franchise for a small section of Blacks who qualified under previous legislation. All members of the Republic's central parliament are required to be White South African citizens, answerable to a White South African electorate. Otherwise, the heritage of a two-party Westminster type of government, as is argued in the chosen excerpt from *South Africa's Political Alternatives*, is continued by this Constitution. The cabinet, vested with supreme executive power, is chosen by the Prime Minister who is simultaneously leader of the majority party. The ruling party holds a majority of elected seats in the House of Assembly and thereby gains a majority of seats in the Senate. Each elected seat represents a geographic constituency.

This system of government, which was developed and refined in Britain and then exported by her, is one attempt at attaining democratic conflict-regulation in society. The central premise of this system is that responsible members of the society (aged eighteen or over, for example) participate, through the vote, in choosing governing representatives. In this way, responsible members of a society exert a continuing influence on political decision-making and thereby legitimate the decisions which their representatives take.

This system, when measured against Slabbert's principle of 'the desirability for accountable government'[1] suffers from two critical shortcomings in South Africa today. In the first place, in practice, this system creates a situation in which 'the winner takes all.' The party that gains a majority of seats at a general election forms a government on its own. If the electorate is divided into two or more groups by factors deemed important by the voters, such as language, class or culture, then a majority group which votes as a group may well remain the permanent winner and thereby exacerbate the differences in the society. It is common knowledge, substantiated by Schlemmer's survey in Durban (1973) that White politics in South Africa can be interpreted in this way.

Secondly and of more import, over eighty percent of South Africans are voteless in this system. Furthermore, when the deep language, class and cultural differences of the various groups in South Africa are taken into consideration, it is improbable that a simple extension of the vote to the unfranchised within the present Westminster system has a chance of creating a stable democratic form of government.

These two shortcomings in the present system of central government in South Africa are of obvious concern to the rulers: successful conflict-regulation necessitates legitimacy. This legitimacy is embodied in the ruling party's ideology of separate development. In the government's terminology of 1976, separate development has as objective a plural democracy guaranteeing separate freedoms for the different ethnic groups of South Africa. However, 1976 also produced irrefutable proof that a substantial group of South Africans in the urban Black townships rejects this ideology. Furthermore, through far-reaching and sudden structural changes in the Republic's immediate northern neighbours, increased pressure from without and within has been brought to bear on these rulers. South Africa's internal political situation has become internationalized as never before.

This beleaguered ruling elite, the National Party, is forced to search for more effective means of coercion and legitimation in order to cope with external threats, attempts at internal insurgency and restive supporters increasingly critical of their ideology. This search can be analysed in a number of ways. We shall look at four of these.

Afrikaner nationalism as the main origin of the ideology of separate development, has been at one and the same time the key to entrenching the ruling elite in their positions of power, and the legitimation for those positions. Under stress, it may be argued, different components of this ideology will be emphasized. It has been argued, on the one hand, that the ruling elite will broaden the scope of its ideological legitimacy to include all Whites, will mobilize this larger group on the basis of the values embodied in 'western civilization', and will form a laager to combat external and internal attempts at structural change (cf. Baker 1975). Here the racial, and to a lesser degree, cultural components of the ideology are emphasized. By implication, less attention will be paid to a similar legitimating ideology for Blacks and purer means of coercion will be devised to cope with opponents. Adam's (1971 and 1976) well-known argument, on the other hand, points to the pragmatic nature of the ideology. As a growing group of Afrikaners came to share the privileges and rewards of the upper class in post-Second World War South Africa, the ruling elite tended to relax the more overt racial and cultural restrictions in its policies. Legitimation and coercion, the carrot and the stick, are increasingly fashioned by, and serve, the growing material interests of established wealth and privilege. South Africa is slowly changing from a racially stratified to a class stratified society.

Afrikaner nationalism and the policy of separate development can also be seen in institutional terms. It has been argued that the National Party is the centre of a network of interlocking bureaucracies and thereby draws its strength simultaneously from often disparate cultural, economic, professional and political institutions (cf. Slabbert 1975). Furthermore, the result of its policy of separate development has been the proliferation of a series of tiered state institutions designed to multiply the state apparatus serving White South Africa. The Coloured Persons Representative Council coupled with Coloured Consultative and Management Committees form an example of such a tier. One implication of this argument is that the National Party is clearly different from, and more than, a political party in a Westminster-type system and will in all probability survive intact a change in that system. Furthermore, the institutional infrastructure it has created during the last quarter-century may well serve as a basis for the new political system. For instance, these series of tiered institutions may form the nucleus of a federal form of government of the proposed Turnhalle type (in South West Africa) in regions where sovereign independence is rejected by the groups concerned. An example of such an argument may be found in the selection by Du Toit. This argument, however, is predicated on the assumption that both the ruling political elite and the elite serving in these institutions are prepared to negotiate a new political system. Alternatively, the ruling elite may institute a more dictatorial form of government, and, without negotiation with any of their political opponents, force through changes which they feel are required.

The existence of such an institutional basis is a prerequisite for any negotiated alternative form of democratic government. The receptivity and conciliatory attitudes of the White and Black political elites is another salient factor. It has been argued that conflict-regulation is promoted if such elites are secure in their leadership positions *vis à vis* the non-elites to whom they are answerable, and if they share conflict-regulating motives. Nordlinger (1972:18) notes that: 'More specifically, one or more of four motivations must be present to make regulatory efforts: the strong desire to ward off pressure from external states, to maintain or increase a level of economic well being, to acquire or retain governmental offices and power, or to avoid bloodshed among the leaders' own segment.' Since the banning and virtual obliteration of African Nationalist movements in the sixties, South Africa and particularly its urban areas have not produced a Black institutionalized leadership cadre which is in a position to, let alone prepared to, negotiate with the White ruling elite. In fact, the attempted insurgency of 1976 and the government reaction to it, manifested few regulatory attempts on the part of the White elite and little institutionalized leadership on the part of the urban Blacks.

Finally, the government's changes in ideology and policy can be analysed within the political economy. One relatively new argument holds that the ideology of separate development, in its effects, dovetails with, and promotes, capital interests in South Africa. Though overt disagreement between the government and private enterprise has continually been taking place over the last quarter-century, their true interests coincide to produce an underlying dynamic of change. Black urban and rural workers, unorganized in both the sphere of labour and of national politics, are exploited by large capitalist conglomerates. The effects of the policy of separate development exacerbate this exploitation, for Bantu Homelands can best be understood as areas in which large under-employed masses of workers may most advantageously be recruited for capitalist development without threatening White domination. This Marxist argument[2] is a direct attack on the liberal Durkheimian theory that the demands of a free market economy dissolve irrational prejudices and attitudes. Adherents of the latter theory hold that increased opportunities and upward mobility inherent in a free market economy will all but dictate a movement away from racially discriminatory policies (cf. O'Dowd 1974:29–43). It is clear that both arguments emphasize changes in the economic structure and that they point to processes of some considerable historical depth. They both hold that the present government elite has little control, in the long run, over its ideology and policies. The economy is given primacy over the polity.

In conclusion, this short introduction attempts to pose salient questions about contemporary South Africa from the point of view of a political sociologist. It claims to be neither comprehensive nor non-partisan. Together with the chosen readings to which reference has already been made, it hopes to stimulate debate about a number of important arguments in the field.

NOTES

1. This is the criterion Slabbert uses in his article included in this Part.
2. For an overview *see* Yudelman (1975).

REFERENCES

Adam, H. 1971 – *Modernizing Racial Domination.* Berkeley: University of California Press.

——1976 – 'Ideologies of dedication vs. blueprints of expedience.' *Social Dynamics*, 2, December, 83–91.

Baker, D. G. 1975 – 'Race, power and White siege cultures.' *Social Dynamics*, 1, December, 143–57.

Bekker, S. B. 1974 – *The Plural Society and the Problem of Order.* Unpublished Ph.D. thesis, University of Cape Town.

Nordlinger, E. A. 1972 – 'Conflict regulation in divided societies.' Occasional Papers in *International Affairs*, No. 29. Harvard University Press.

O'Dowd, M. 1974 – 'South Africa in the light of the stages of economic growth.' In A. Leftwich (ed.), *South Africa: Economic Growth and Political Change.* London: Allison and Busky.

Schlemmer, Lawrence 1973 – *Privilege, Prejudice and Parties.* Johannesburg: South African Institute of Race Relations.

Slabbert, F. van Zyl 1975 – 'Afrikaner nationalism, White politics, and political change in South Africa.' In L. Thompson and J. Butler (eds.), *Change in Contemporary South Africa.* Berkeley: University of California Press.

Thompson, L. M. 1966 – *Politics in the Republic of South Africa.* Boston: Little, Brown and Co.

Weber, M. 1946 – 'Politics as a vocation.' In H. H. Gerth and C. Wright Mills (eds.), *From Max Weber.* Oxford: Oxford University Press.

Yudelman, D. 1975 – 'Industrialization, race relations and change in South Africa.' *African Affairs*, 74, January, 82–96.

1. De-colonising South Africa

HERIBERT ADAM

The de-colonisation of the Portuguese colonies has fostered speculations about hastened similar developments in the South African metropole. Ali Mazrui (1974), for instance, maintains: 'Once violence breaks out on a sufficient scale it begins to put strains on the cohesion of the dominant group within itself. A Black military challenge in South Africa will first bring Whites closer together – but will later begin to turn White man against White man.' It is an interesting hypothesis that, contrary to popular psychology, increased pressure will lessen rather than strengthen group cohesion.

More than the time dimension which Mazrui suggests, it seems that the dependent variable in such an event is whether the group under pressure has any realistic options, short of full surrender to the demands of the opponent. If these options do not exist and the threat is perceived as one of survival rather than concessions, then increased group solidarity is likely. This is usually the case in sectarian, religiously perceived conflicts. There is no bargaining over principles, and only one truth can prevail. The other side is the embodiment of evil, a threat to the fundamentals of an ideological existence, called 'identity', 'character' or 'mission.' In a polarisation, defeat and total surrender, the triumph of one or two mutually exclusive principles in a contested area, is the goal of the contenders. A modified co-existence under a new inclusive formula, which would try to accommodate both views, is precluded by definition. The refusal of Israel to bow to Arab demands for a secularised state, which would be incompatible with the religiously defined Jewish character of such a state, is a typical example. The antagonisms in Northern Ireland feature a similar absolutism, at least in the perception of the militants in both camps, though the underlying issues of political and economic privilege at the cost of the ethnically defined enemy is always at the heart of such conflicts.

There was also little room for manoeuvre on the question of political de-colonisation in Africa. Liberation from foreign domination, however phony the newly gained political independence was (in light of continued neo-colonial foreign control), represented a quasi-religious principle over which a compromise was neither possible nor necessary. Our argument, however, will be that the analogy between South Africa and events in the rest of the continent is misleading and that de-colonisation in the White South will take different forms.

In the traditional de-colonisation process the colonial administrators had to make way for an indigenous bourgeoisie if the growing Black elites were to have any chance to reap the same rewards in profit and status as their former masters. Continued dependency was ensured anyway through the vast economic gap, the terms of trade determined by the metropole and the Black elite's socialisation in the same Western – Capitalist – Christian tradition. Above all, equal or better investment opportunities in the booming postwar economies of Western Europe and North America made it feasible to follow the dominant public opinion in the cold war competition and to adhere to the rhetoric of self-determination. This dispossessed White group had the option of returning home if they did not wish to adjust to the new arrangement locally. Where this European local colony was numerically strong, as in Algeria and Kenya, they acceded only after a military struggle, in which the metropolitan interests and not the indigenous insurgents ensured their final defeat. This is an important factor to remember when assessing the chances of liberation movements in South Africa, where metropolitan interests weigh more heavily in favour of the settlers.

In other areas with relatively strong European groups, such as Katanga and Rhodesia, secession was tried but clearly against the dominant political powers in Brussels and London who preferred the neocolonial solution to the crude traditional rule of their distant kith and kin.[1]

The exception to this process of de-colonisation in Africa was Portugal, which, however, followed the same pattern, albeit with a fifteen-year time lag. This delay was due to the impoverished position of Portugal at the margin of the capitalist centre but also due to the absence of a free anti-colonial public opinion in the fifty year long dictatorship of Salazar. Under these conditions the weak 'neo-colonial lobby' in the army and business families could only come to the fore after the colonial wars became too costly in terms of life, redirected resources and harmful isolation from the European Common Market in the metropole itself.

It will be argued that South Africa represents a qualitatively different case from the conflicts sketched above for three main reasons:

(a) The Whites have no homeland to which they can return, they have become indigenous to the area and this has been accepted by their Black counterparts.[2] The early political independence of South Africa under White rule gives this state additional legitimacy and excludes direct intervention through a metropole in the conflict between settlers and the indigenous peoples.

(b) The numerical strength of South African Whites and, above all, the resources which they control in their country together with its advanced level of industrialisation makes this settler society largely self-sufficient, and not comparable with the outside dependency of deviant settlers in other parts of Africa, including Rhodesia.

(c) Because of her strong socio-economic position in neocapitalist terms, South Africa has now been directly incorporated, economically, politically and strategically, as an essential part into the overall network of Western global interests. This process has taken place in both directions: not only has outside investment in South Africa increased considerably, but South African based companies have acquired substantial interests abroad as well. At the political level the South African state and public corporations have, for instance, been given extended opportunities for loan raising at European money markets and there are preferential tariff terms for many South African goods, not available to competitors.

It is the major thesis of this article that the above outlined trends have decreased the chances of any socialist type change in South Africa, unless one adheres to the unrealistic belief of an imminent collapse of the total capitalist system. But at the same time, the extended incorporation of South Africa into the global neocapitalist system has greatly increased the outside pressures for socio-political reforms away from traditional racism towards a more acceptable system of social stratification and political decision, making the line with the colour blind global etiquette at the elite level.

It would seem that the perspectives and policies of the present leading decision makers in South Africa are realistically oriented towards this framework of pressures and opportunities, rather than being determined by an Afrikaner national character of unbending intransigence. As a regional metropole, their policies since Verwoerd are basically an imitation of the previous European colonial powers: i.e. the use of geographical partition and ethno-cultural and rural – urban fragmentation together with the meaningless political independence to continue to dominate in a different form. However, this pragmatic adjustment towards neo-colonial policies different from traditional racial discrimination encounters resistance within the ruling White group. There is frequent doubt in the academic writing on South Africa whether, and if so, the ingrained racism of this society can be overcome, even if a few pragmatists wished to make adjustments. These issues are often raised in a wider theoretical framework which therefore will be briefly discussed.

There is no place here to recall the elaborate Marxist debate on the dialectical relationship between superstructure and objective economic conditions, but this classical theoretical question is highly significant for an assessment and prediction of South African racism. Paradoxically, there are often Marxist scholars or those selectively using Marxist concepts who argue the unbending, inevitable dominance of ingrained racist ideology even in the face of fast changing economic circumstances. With an extraordinary blindness that simply refuses to acknowledge the far-reaching manoeuvres of the 'pragmatic oligarchy' (cf. Adam 1971) in South Africa, so-called revolutionaries argue against 'reformists' that essentially nothing has changed in the fascist South African police state, except its increasing oppressiveness, with the inevitable day of reckoning and White doom (cf. Maud 1974; Asheron (pseudonym for Maud) 1969).

The possibility that history in Southern Africa does not necessarily constitute the linear progress towards the liberation of African mankind, but represents a complex interaction of permanently changing power bases and their fluid perceptions of the main factors is not conceded. Because, it is argued, the weight of South Africa's 'historical legacies' has permeated the total society and its political culture so fundamentally, no change of parts of the whole is conceivable or even possible. In a typical vulgarisation of dialectical concepts it is said in this context: 'the reformist thesis reveals the paucity of its theoretical perspectives in its ignorance of the vital sociological insight into the manner in which the whole (society) dominates the parts (individuals) in that society' (Maud 1974: 291). Quite contrary is the case. The whole in the Marxist tradition represents above all the historical form in which people reproduce their specific life styles. This is not a process in which all parts are involved in the same uniform fashion, dictated by the same interests. Certain parts often break loose from a traditional mode of production, which has been superseded by more adequate forms, including institutional and ideological arrangements. Fredrickson (1974) notes that there is no need to dent that racism 'when it also functions as a ruling class ideology . . . takes on a life of its own.' While the often quoted Thomas statement that 'if men define situations as real they become real in their consequences' is indeed relevant, there are many competing definitions as well as permanently changing situations of different interests.

Of course, in South Africa as elsewhere many 'historical legacies' exist which 'are crucial for any attempt to explore the country's future,' as has been stressed. The 'cultural lag' in White South African society is obvious, but it is not a static phenomenon. Its content, in terms of specific ideologies and attitudes, is permanently changing, though painstakingly slowly, in response to new structural needs and events inside and outside South Africa. Racism has developed as a 'legitimising rationale' for specific group privileges. As such it is of a qualitatively different nature than a natural law, quasi-religious doctrine or biblical text. At times men may believe in pseudo-scientific theories of biological determinism with the same sacred awe as they adhere to divine revelations but such attitudes will soon be abandoned when they no longer fulfil their initial psycho-political functions. To consider historically developed racist ideologies as static – forever imprisoning 'historical legacies' until they are smashed by revolutionary change – reveals an ahistorical perspective and amounts to a reification of the superstructure.

Such a view would not deny that frequently in history the ideological weapon has taken over. Internalised belief systems have dominated the actions of their proponents regardless of their survival interests. In a Marxian perspective that is, indeed, an important contributing factor to the final revolution. A ruling group, relying on an outdated mode of production was unable to change to a more efficient production system and to adapt its institutions to the new found necessities. The landholding feudal aristocracy in its incapability to adjust to the new requirements of an industrially based, market orientated production is the prime historical example in this respect. The final fate of capitalism may well emerge in a similar inability to solve its ever increasing internal contradictions, as Marxists have always argued. But the ultimate reason for the collapse of a ruling class in this sense is never its stupidity, its adherence to false perceptions of reality, but the structural inability to resolve economic, not ideological, contradictions in a given system of societal reproduction.

The same applies to the facism of Nazi Germany. In short, Hitler's, or for that matter Japan's, inevitable defeat came about not as a result of extreme irrationality but was in the last analysis due to the hardly resistable need of a conflict ridden, colonially deprived and yet economically growing country to seek geographical expansion in military adventures and market competitions which soon threatened the core of the system of which it was initially a subdued part.

To concede that 'belief systems often become a "material force" as significant as any economic variable in determining human behaviour' (Maud 1974:292) does not explain much. Rulers may indeed find themselves prisoners of their myth but it depends on the nature of the myth and its specific socio-economic function whether and how long this is the case. It is foremost an empirical question to measure and assess the persistence and depth of such an outlook rather than to assume its importance on the basis of a numerical ratio or political rhetoric. On the other hand, what has been called the 'politics of fear' in South Africa represents an attitude which embodies in itself a rational quest for a modified coexistence. Both antagonists do not deny each others' right to the same country but only differ about its form of government, essentially the share or control of the country's wealth. Black opposition to White dominance, so far at least, centres around a nationalistic, not a socialist – revolutionary challenge to exclusive White control. In turn, what Whites have emotionally labelled 'die swart gevaar' (the black peril) boils down now to sharing or giving up certain traditional privileges, not necessarily abandoning a whole way of life, as it is often portrayed. This is qualitatively different from a 'siege mentality', which feels its entire existence threatened.

In other words, there are now options to the simple Hobbesian type dichotomy of 'dominate or be dominated'. Again, it is not suggested here that Whites will voluntarily give up traditional domination because of a sudden change of heart. What is likely is that the majority of Whites will gradually bow to a reduction of traditional dominance under increasing Black bargaining power which becomes somewhat more accommodated with each new challenge. This mutual measuring of strength in permanent conflicts takes place at various levels and in numerous forms, not only in strike situations. But because it is bargaining over goals where concessions are possible and in the material interest of both antagonists, this process never reaches the threshold of a final confrontation or indiscriminate, widespread violence. Where the level of open violence has come close to this all-out warfare, such as in Rhodesia since December 1972, the regional representatives of the overall system (South Africa and Zambia) were ready to step in and force their respective clients to substantial concessions and to a truce.

On the part of South Africa the two salient factors accounting for the unusual pressure it put on Rhodesian Prime Minister Smith was (a) the realisation that, as an Afrikaans paper has put it, 'an old-fashioned military victory is impossible in the particular circumstances[3] and (b) that, the continuing international illegality of Rhodesia provided a vehicle for an attack on her South African backers and thereby increased the vulnerability of the centre. On the part of Zambia, the advantages of restoring the economic links with the South became obvious in light of the dismal economic situation. Therefore, many African politicians have now come to accept the White overtures of which they themselves will be the first beneficiaries. In the prevailing conditions of scarcity in Africa, economic dominance, not ideological principles, will be the determining factors, regardless of the rhetoric of historical legacies which are readily changed on both sides to fit more fundamental interests in common. For South Africa, the need to establish or extend new outside markets for her commodities is of decisive importance, as long as her domestic market is so underdeveloped through the skewed income distribution.

It can also be safely assumed that the international corporations with major interests in both camps, such as Lonrho and Anglo-American, have contributed their share to defusing the lingering confrontation. For our argument what is decisive is the empirical evidence that the political representative of Black and White did assess the conflict quite outside racial considerations, that they could ignore the historical relics and come to a rational rather than ideological calculation of their interests and mutual strength as parts of the same system.

There is a clear intention to solve the South West Africa (Namibia) dispute as well. A staunch Nationalist newspaper,[4] for instance, lists South Africa's former mandate over the German colony together with the Portuguese territories and Britain's nominal hold on Rhodesia as 'the last remains of colonialism' in Africa, an era which the paper states 'is now finally at an end.'

The secret Nationalist formula for Namibia, however, encounters considerable resistance among the political activists of the largest ethnic group in the area, the Ovambos, comprising almost half of the total population of Namibia. By aiming at a secession and independence of traditional Ovambo territory in the north along the Angolan border, Pretoria intends to block this group's potential leading role in the country at large, since the remaining ethnic groups are culturally diverse and politically splintered, with a long history of mutual hostility among each other and towards the Ovambo group. Based on this ethnic fragmentation, an independent South West Africa without the Ovambos, or perhaps partitioned even further into 'traditional homelands' would be as little a threat to the economic and military might of the South African metropole as the other client states.

The likely reduction in the size of the new motherland would strengthen the lone decisive centre and remove the sole internationally exploitable legal cause for an attack. With the Rhodesian constitutional outcast settled and the now chronic South West African issue 'resolved', South Africa would have shed her two most vulnerable cases for external critique and emerged with shorter and far more legitimate boundaries. Unless the United Nations are prepared to redefine its most disastrous and abused principle, that *internal* national matters and injustices fall outside of its concern, South Africa then has a strengthened credibility in replying: 'mind your own business.' On the basis of their own domestic policies there is indeed little justification for most UN members to self-righteously point the finger of moral criticism at others. With a few exceptions, political repression of government critics is now the rule in most countries, particularly in the Third World. Not one African state, at present, has an independent press, free of government control. Civil liberties exist on paper only. Politics is essentially an elite matter, and the game among the equally corrupt competitors is 'access to wealth,' as a recent penetrating study has again convincingly demonstrated (cf. Bretton 1973).

Stanislav Andreski (1971:29) has perceptively argued that 'the true explanation of the world-wide unanimity against apartheid has little to do with internal injustice – which, to repeat, is common enough among the signatories of the Charter of Human Rights – but stems from the incompatability of the South African system of stratification with the requirements of polite intercourse between the governments and elites of the world.'

It is doubtful that the remaining structural racism of White dominance will prove any longer an insulting obstacle, once the symbols of White supremacy are further eliminated from the social contact of Black and White elite members. Since Verwoerd for the first time shook hands with a Black Prime Minister in 1966, the South African rulers have pursued this strategy of non-racial formality among equals, combined with continued separatism towards the African masses at home.

In other words, racism proves as irrelevant among the competing bourgeoisies as their different accents. Unlike religiously perceived conflicts racism has become negotiable. It is not intractable. Legalised, manifest colour stratification is so vulnerable now that even its former advocates are embarrassed as the shift to cultural rather than biological criteria of segregation signals. After all, the apartheid ideology in all its manifestations has been the outgrowth of specific historical conditions and group interests. South African Whites are not giving up their so-called identity, security or basic dominant position by abandoning an outdated ideology and racial practice in favour of more acceptable class and cultural differentiations.

NOTES

1. This has been most convincingly argued by Arghiri Emmanuel (1972). For a thorough discussion of the concept 'settler-society' and its implications see Leo Kuper (1969). The inevitability of revolutionary change is argued in Kenneth Good (1974). Good relies on the Rhodesian case which is only partially comparable with South Africa, as will be argued.
2. See the much neglected Lusaka Manifesto of 1960. The essential difference between the perception of Afrikaners and traditional colonisers with a metropole abroad is summed up in an election speech by a cabinet minister: 'We cannot experiment with our one and only fatherland. We are not prepared to leave this country. We are not Europeans. We are White Africans and out future lies in this continent.' (C. P. Mulder, as quoted in *The Star* WE, 30 March 1974, 6.)
3. *Beeld*, 9 December 1974. There is the same realisation that this applies to the South African domestic situation as well. The Afrikaans papers are now busy to preach through the

description of incidents where Black dignity has been insulted by White officials. *Die Vaderland*, (9 October 1974) concludes: '. . . and heaven knows, if human relations within our borders deteriorate, the bullet in the sten-gun on our borders will not help us.'

4. *Die Vaderland*, 4 December 1974.

REFERENCES

Adam, Heribert 1971 – Modernizing Racial Domination. Berkeley: University of California Press.

Andreski, Stanislav 1971 – 'Reflections on the South African order from a comparative viewpoint.' In Heribert Adam (ed.), *South Africa: Sociological Perspectives.* London: Oxford University Press.

Asheron, Andrew (pseudonym for Ruan Maud) 1969 – 'Race and politics in South Africa.' *New Left Review*, January/February, 55–68.

Bretton, Henry L. 1973 – *Power and Politics in Africa.* London: Longman.

Emmanuel, Arghiri 1972 – 'White-settler colonialism and the myth of investment imperialism.' *New Left Review* 73 May/June, 35–57.

Fredrickson, George M. 1974 – 'Will South Africa explode?' *The New York Review of Books*, 21, 17, October, 33.

Good, Kenneth 1974 – 'Settler colonial societies.' Paper for Sociological Association Conference, Armindale.

Kuper, Leo 1969 – 'Political change in White settler societies: The possibility of peaceful democratization.' In Leo Kuper and M. G. Smith (eds.), *Pluralism in Africa.* Berkeley: University of California Press, 169–93.

Maud, Ruan 1974 – 'The future of an illusion: The myth of White meliorism in South Africa.' In Adrian Leftwich (ed.), *South Africa. Economic Growth and Political Change.* London: Allison and Busby, 287–318.

Mazrui, Ali 1974 – *Africanus*, 4, 2, September, 11.

2. Democratic Alternatives to the 'Westminster' Model

ANDRÉ DU TOIT

i) *Alternative Electoral Systems: Social and Political Consequences and Conditions*

If a purely constitutional approach along the classical liberal lines of extending the franchise on a common roll, however admirable in itself, is not feasible in the conditions of a divided plural society, then perhaps we should look to alternative political and electoral systems. It is surprising to what extent the 'Westminister' model (i.e. parliamentary government with election by relative majority in single member constituencies resulting usually in a two-party system) is unquestioningly assumed as the natural framework in most South African political thinking, including that of the present government. The official policy of separate development could even be summarised as proposing not one Westminister-type government for the whole country, but series of them in the various homelands. Thus the architects and the critics of separate development have, in a sense, a common regard for Westminster-type government; the only difference between them, at least insofar as the representational system is concerned, relates to the areas and the populations for whom it is to be established. In this way, at least, our political tradition continues to show a surprising attachment to the institutional heritage of our initial British tutelage.

Despite its deserved pre-eminence in the Anglo-Saxon world, the Westminster model is not the only successful system of democratic institutions which has been devised. Leaving aside the controversial examples of the socialist democracies and the one-party systems of the developing countries, and restricting ourselves to western democracies, the predominant pattern is somewhat different from what is usually expected. In the English-speaking world, and certainly in this country, all thought about democratic systems has been so dominated by the 'two-party' models of Britain and the United States that they are assumed to be the standard which all other democracies seek to emulate or from which they deviate. Yet a recent comparative survey of western democracies has shown that two-party systems are in fact a substantial minority compared with the prevalent multi-party systems and are, moreover, limited almost exclusively to the English-speaking world. Robert Dahl concludes that among Western democracies the Westminster model would appear to be the deviant case rather than the norm: 'In sum, it might be reasonable to consider multi-party systems as the natural way for government and oppositions to manage their conflicts in democracies, while two-party systems, whether resembling the British pattern or the American, are the deviant cases. It is conceivable, of course, that the deviant cases represent superior forms; yet multi-party systems exist in Denmark, Norway, Sweden, the Netherlands, and Switzerland, countries widely thought to have handled their political, social and economic problems with at least as much skill, justice, and social peace as any other democracies' (Dahl 1966).

What are the main alternatives to our familiar electoral system? A detailed comparative survey would show that there are many alternative electoral devices and arrangements, sometimes designed expressly to cope with the political problems of heterogeneous populations and minority groups. Examples are *proportional representation* (PR), *multi-member districts*, *multiple-ballots*, various kinds of *list systems*, the *single* and the *multiple transferable* vote. They may be found in many combinations with each other, as well as with components of the Westminster system. This is, of course, a large and extremely complex subject, and we cannot hope to deal with it at all adequately in the present context. For that we must refer to the specialised literature. For example Douglas Rae (1971) has carefully identified a number of major variables both of the electoral law and of party systems, and submitted the empirical evidence bearing on their interaction to a rigorous analysis. From this certain patterns and tendencies emerge. The popular association of proportional representation with multi-party systems does have a sound basis in the facts, though the evidence does not warrant a causal explanation or, as Duverger (1954) thought, a 'true sociological law.' On Rae's analysis the single-member constituency emerges as a basic factor favouring two-party systems, with the absence or presence of strong local minorities accounting for deviations from the rule. In practice, of course, single-member districts are nearly always associated with majority rather than proportional electoral formulae, though this need not necessarily be so. In general, ignoring technical details and allowing for exceptions such as the Austrian case and hybrids such as the West German one, multi-party PR electoral systems may thus be contrasted with two-party majority single-member district systems.

This contrast corresponds to different theoretical perspectives. On the one hand, an electoral system may be expected to provide an outcome giving a 'true' reflection of actual voting preferences. This axiom usually underlines the case for the theoretical superiority of PR systems, as in Enid Lakeman's (1970) survey *How Democracies Vote* . In fact, all electoral systems 'distort' to a certain extent and generally favour larger parties at the expense of smaller ones, but PR systems less so, and considerable ingenuity has been devoted to devising technical formulae which may further minimise the 'distortion' (cf. Rae 1971 and Lakeman 1970). On the other hand, an electoral system may be required to settle effectively the issue of who is to govern under the majority-rule. Only in a strict two-party system will one party necessarily obtain an absolute majority of the popular vote, but in many other cases the electoral system can and does transform a relative majority or even a minority of the votes into a parliamentary majority of seats. In Rae's words, 'electoral laws may create majorities where none are created by the voters.' This is precisely the sort of distortion that PR systems aim to counteract, but the concomitant of this aim now appears as a fractionalisation of the party system, often necessitating coalition government and generally obscuring the link between the outcome of the election and the process of government and legislation. In certain circumstances this may lead to parliamentary deadlock inhibiting legislative action and resulting in the disruption of stable government. It has been argued, for example, that PR and multi-party systems contributed largely to the fall of the mid-European democracies in the 'twenties and 'thirties (cf. Newman 1970). But such evaluations of cases where a system is successfully operating, or where it has been tried and failed, are complicated by many other factors in the local political climate and history. Rather than pursue an increasingly abstract discussion on the debatable democratic merits of electoral systems stressing proportionality as against the virtues of 'majority' government we must widen the scope of our discussion to the general social and political consequences of, and conditions for, these different systems.

In considering alternatives to the 'Westminster' model it may be useful to turn to a vigorous defence of the classical two-party system of majority government on the grounds of its general social and political consequences, by the political sociologist S. M. Lipset. Lipset (1963) argued that in a competitive two-party system both parties will aim at securing an over-all majority, they will accordingly seek the broadest possible base of support in elections, and they will thus tend to stress the common interests of divergent groups. All of these trends he takes to be conducive to maintaining democratic stability and the general consensus upon which the polity rests.' Lipset maintains that the two-party system also encourages compromise and reduces ideological conflict, and this again is assumed to favour democratic stability. Elsewhere (Lipset and Rokkan 1967:4) he also argues that, in contrast to a monolithic polity or one-party state where the regime is easily equated with the state and national loyalties become identified with support for particular leaders and their policies, a system of alternating temporary regimes and competitive parties encourages the citizen to distinguish clearly between the state and the current office-holders, thus favouring a continuing commitment to the overall system which transcends party-political conflicts.

In a multi-party system, on the other hand, Lipset argues that parties do not aim at an overall majority, or at least have little chance of attaining this, and hence settle for the very different goal of the greatest possible electoral support from a limited group or section. Party politics will thus tend to stress the interests and cleavages dividing that group from other groups in society. This is further heightened by proportional representation which in fact substitutes an interest or ideological group for the territorial unit as the basis of representation, eliminating any possible effect of cross-cutting regional solidarity. Moreover the system also tends in some ways to alienate the ordinary voters from the political elite. Thus there is a basic tension between the party's function as a representative of a group (and its) function of integrating the group in the body politic' (Lipset 1963). At the electoral level it lessens the need for compromise and enhances the ideological content of the conflict; in short, it encourages divisiveness, while at the elite level the necessity of coalitions increases the need for co-operation and compromise. Added to the general lack of a clear link between election outcomes and government action, the divorce between the party's symbols in the electoral arena and its actions as a partner in coalition governments may lead to a pervading cynicism towards the conduct of politics and may even, Lipset believes, become a source of irresponsibility and manipulation.

The general trend of these comparisons will be clear. Even if we should qualify the overall picture somewhat by pointing out, as Dahl does, that PR systems also tend to decrease the concentration and distinctiveness of opposition, and that at the level of government they also increase the rewards of co-operation and bargaining strategies, there could still be little doubt as to which set of electoral institutions would, on this analysis, be more favourable to social cohesiveness and democratic stability, and conversely, which one would encourage divisiveness and disruptiveness. In a divided society with major problems of containing political conflict there could thus, on the grounds of social and political consequences, hardly be any doubt of the superiority of the Westminster model.

This argument is radically reversed, however, if we look at the conditions necessary for the success of a two-party system, and thus at the source of these consequences. In Lipset's words: 'There are, however, conditions under which a two-party system is less conducive to the preservation of democratic order than a multi-party system. The two-party system works best where it is based on an elaborate, cross-cutting solidarity structure, in which men and groups are pulled in different directions by their diverse roles and interests. Wherever the solidarity structure is polarised by class, race, or religion, and the political lines follow those of social cleavage, a two-party system may intensify internal conflict rather than help integrate the society. In general, where the class struggle is superimposed upon a conflict between religion and irreligion, or between different ethnic groups, a two-party system is more destructive of political stability than one in which centre parties can mediate between extreme opponents' (Lipset 1963: 107; Lipset and Rokkan 1967:32). So the Westminster model may better maintain democratic stability and a general consensus only within an open pluralistic society. In a divided plural society, or where the question of political alternatives centres, as in South Africa, on the transition to a more open pluralistic society and to a more democratic polity, these advantages fall away.

But does it follow, if the Westminster model will not produce these results here, that multi-party PR systems will? Clearly not. The features of such systems which encourage divisiveness and fragmentation will do so, perhaps to an even greater extent, in a divided plural society. If there are advantages to alternative systems in these conditions then they must be due to features other than the logic of the electoral institutions themselves. We might, for example, think of the shift to political co-operation and bargaining at a leadership level. Or we might argue that the consequences of the fragmentation of the political system in a multi-party state tends to prevent both effective domination and concentrated opposition. In short, we must shift our focus of attention from the electoral system as such, its consequences and conditions, to a wider view of alternative political systems as different ways of regulating and structuring political conflict.

ii) *Social Conflict and Politics: Bargainability and Polarisation*

Different political systems may be seen as alternative ways of structuring generalised conflict over scarce goods, resources and values in a society. In this sense politics is itself a form of conflict and it also presupposes the existence of generalised social conflict. A political system has been defined as that set of interactions through which authoritative allocations (or binding decisions) are made and implemented for a society (Easton 1953). The 'authority' of such binding decisions by any individual or institution may be derived either from its access to coercive force or from popular support for its legitimacy. In Weber's (1947) classic definition the state is accordingly defined as that institution which has the monopoly of the legitimate use of coercive force.

In practice, if perhaps not in constitutional theory, a breakdown of the state's 'authority' is certainly a distinct possibility: its decisions may fail to bind because of lack of support for their legitimacy, or because of a failure to exact compliance through coercive force. In conditions of discord or anarchy the conflict is likely to continue by other, more direct and even violent means. Writing on the strife in Northern Ireland, Richard Rose says that 'as war is the continuation of diplomacy by another method, so disagreement escalating to demonstration and rebellion is the continuation of politics by another form of bargaining. The fact that the bargaining encounter takes place in the streets, rather than around a conference table, does not mean that politics has ceased. People who have turned to extra-legal acts are still pursuing the same goal and still confronting the same opponents' (Rose 1971:31). Obviously this does not mean that there is no difference between violent disorder and orderly government and politics. Even if both involve a form of bargaining, the means in the one case is destructive force, not easily susceptible to rational control. The basic question for civil government and politics is precisely whether it can develop stable and effective institutions and procedures for the rational conduct of disputes, the peaceful management of conflicts, and the non-violent pursuit of social reform. In this way conflict would not be eliminated; but it would be contained within and structured in terms of the institutions of government and the law in the widest sense. Whether this will happen depends both on the intensity of the conflict and on the resilience of the political system concerned.

There is thus a highly complex interaction between social conflict and politics. Generalised social conflicts may provide the very stuff of politics, but they are in turn affected by the political system. There are two crucial questions: what is the potential for political discord in any given set of social conflicts, and how will a specific political system cope with them. In the next section we will consider the latter, and ask to what extent the different procedures by which men manage disputes and discord may increase or decrease conflict. First, however, we must turn to the substantive issues which are the occasion of conflict, which cannot be made to disappear by recourse to constitutional engineering, and which may largely determine the nature and intensity of the conflict (Rose 1971:397).

What are the most important social differences that can lead to political conflict? Of course most differences within a society rarely become political issues and are settled in other ways: privately, by economic competition, and so on. The political system primarily concerns those conflicts which in some way affect society as a whole. Are there specific kinds of social differences which tend to be the occasion of such generalised political conflict? On the basis of comparative studies Lipset and Rokkan have emphasised a four-fold typology of such social differences, viz. social differences concerned with 'centre-periphery' relations (including the relations between the dominant national elite and subordinate regional or cultural groups), religion, urban, rural and industrial class differences (see also Rose 1971:40). The typology does not help us much to assess the impact of such differences on various political systems. The crucial questions are whether any particular type of issue, or a specific configuration or juxtaposition of different sets of issues, is likely to engender more intractable or explosive political conflicts and thus place greater demands on the political system which has to contain or structure them. Let us briefly deal with each of these questions in turn.

The first question, concerning the kind and intensity of conflict which a particular type of issue is likely to engender, might perhaps best be put in terms of the extent to which such issues are *bargainable*, in a very general sense of this word. There are issues which from the nature of things are more amenable to rational negotiation, and others which tend to lead to an all-or-nothing conflict. Richard Rose (1971:397–8) has provided a useful summary of the main considerations here: 'Peaceful bargaining is possible, if the matter in dispute permits negotiations that can lead to an outcome acceptable to all. An issue is not bargainable if there is no way in which all concerned can be sufficiently satisfied to accept the outcome. Whether or not an issue is bargainable is reflected by three characteristics: whether it involves a zero-sum conflict (i.e. the sum of what one group can gain equals the sum of what other groups would thereby lose); whether it involves private or collective goods (i.e. goods that must be available to all or none), and whether competing claims are stated as absolute values or advanced as demands for more or less of something. Demands that concern absolutely valued collective goods that can only be distributed in zero-sum ways will cause greatest discord. By contrast, demands for relative adjustments in private goods that can be distributed without anyone being worse off are least likely to create political discord.'

Viewed in this light appreciable differences begin to appear between the various types of issues, in particular between 'interest-specific' and ideological oppositions. Thus economic issues, despite their dominant role in theories of class conflict, are to a considerable extent bargainable. Usually they can to a large extent be expressed in monetary terms and thus allow a settlement in incremental ways; under conditions of economic prosperity industrial disputes can be settled by a non-zero outcome in which both parties benefit; and economic benefits are not collective goods which must in every case be granted to all or none. Urban-rural differences are less bargainable in so far as they involve contrasts between different life-styles; and religious differences often raise issues based upon non-bargainable absolute values, though they need not be about collective goods, as the conflicts between the dominant national elites and subordinate regional or cultural groups usually are. Rose concludes that non-bargainable differences about religion and nationality have the greatest disruptive strength.

The implications for the conflict potential of divided plural societies will be obvious: once ethnic and racial differences become salient they readily provide non-bargainable issues par excellence. What is more, they can easily become impacted with the inherently more bargainable economic differences and thus complicate the chances of rational negotiation on these issues as well. As our earlier chapters have demonstrated, the South African political economy is a paradigm example of this, as seen in the strong pressures for entrenchment of the colour bar, the major obstacles preventing an appreciable closing of the wage gap, and the virtual exclusion of organised African labour from corporate bargaining.

It will clearly be very important whether a political system will permit, or even encourage, the translation of such non-bargainable issues into political conflict, or whether it will tend to avoid and restrain them.

The second major question is whether a specific configuration or juxtaposition of different sets of issues is likely to have a high conflict potential. To the extent that the different sets of social differences coincide and thus reinforce each other, with a consequent convergence of the potential lines of conflict, this will be very likely indeed. A specific conflict on one set of issues will be easily generalised to other spheres as well and occasion a polarisation of whole sections of the society seemingly quite disproportionate to the immediate issue . . . the high conflict potential of divided plural societies is due not to the racial or ethnic differences as such, but to the superimposition of these cleavages on the other major social differences. The structure of a divided plural society is thought by some to necessitate its coercive regulation, usually by a dominant minority and the transition to a more open pluralistic society is 'likely to be abrupt, revolutionary and violent' (Kuper 1971). We must look more closely at this association between polarised social conflict and political domination and violence.

In an essay on the ideologies of violence in plural societies Leo Kuper has argued that the conception of polarised groups plays an important and even necessary role both in the revolutionary call to violence of subordinate groups and in the ruler's justification of their resort to coercive force. According to Kuper: 'The ideology of violence includes a characterisation of the plural society. The main component of this characterisation is a polarised conception, which directs violence unambiguously against the enemy. The complex patterns of pluralism are reduced to the simple dichotomy of a dialectical opposition. There can be no sharing of power. An irreconcilable conflict, an absolute opposition of interests, separates the parties. In a world of radically opposed and irreconcilable interests, there can be no evolutionary change toward a shared society. Being convinced of the absolute incompatibility of different sections of the plural society, and therefore of the impossibility of social synthesis, they perceive the alternatives as either to rule or be ruled. There is thus an almost exact correspondence between the ideologies of revolution and of counter-revolution' (Rose 1971:156–7, 161). Kuper comments that in a divided plural society this ideological picture of extreme polarisation and inevitable violence or domination may have some factual basis, but is not always borne out by the empirical evidence. Thus decolonisation in divided societies, for example, has not always been a violent phenomenon; and the argument only establishes the need for great pressure to bring about political change and does not prove that violence is the only efficient means for change at all. In particular the extent of social polarisation is rarely so extreme, and it is usually offset by social and economic interdependence and common interests. In short, 'few plural societies show the polar structure ascribed to them in ideologies of violence. There is generally tension between the ideological image and the social reality' (Rose 1971:163). It is crucially important in a society approximating the structure of a divided plural society whether the dominant ideologies and the dolitical system itself tend to encourage or reduce the polarisation of social and political conflict.

Our brief discussion of the substantive issues and patterns of social conflict points to at least two major requirements for a political system able to contain or cope with conflict in conditions with a high potential for political discord: (i) it should minimise as far as possible the emergence of non-bargainable issues as the occasion of political conflict; (ii) it should prevent the generalisation and polarisation of social and political conflict as far as possible. To what extent can these requirements be met by the Westminster model or by other alternative political systems?

Alternative political systems and South Africa: the problems of transition

In South Africa there is a considerable variety of political alternatives, in both the limited sense of different electoral and party systems, and also the wider sense of different ways of structuring political conflict through, for example, the consociational alternative or corporate national bargaining. In the second place our analysis of the complex interaction between generalised social conflict and politics has helped to clarify the requirements for a democratic system that might be able to structure and contain the high conflict potential of polarised and unequal societies.

It would serve little purpose to continue an exhaustive survey of all possible political systems, or to give an abstract assessment of their appropriateness for this or that set of conditions, in order to come up with some theoretically 'best' solution. If we are to get to grips with the problem of political alternatives confronting us, then we have to relate the different political systems and their requirements as directly and concretely as possible to our South African situation, including our present political system. In this way we might then see what the crucial issues and the major options are.

We have seen that where there is a high conflict potential, as in our own unequal and polarised apartheid society, there are serious objections to a two-party system of representative government, particularly if this is coupled with a strong executive in a centralised and unified state. In any effective contestation for the control of the government such a system would tend to increase the intensity of political conflict greatly, given the very high stakes, the concentration of the opponents, and the relative decisiveness of a single major site. If it did not succeed in containing such intense conflict the result would be severe civil discord if not civil war, or alternatively coercive government and sectional domination. On the whole this has so far been borne out by the South African case. To the extent that a democratic system does exist here, it has a competitive and centralised structure, although the majority of the population is excluded from access to it and thus from the means of constitutionally and effectively contesting the control of government. This is no doubt the main reason for the relative stability of this restricted system of representative government. The South African political system as a whole is by and large one of coercive government and domination. It follows that we are unlikely to arrive at a stable and democratic polity in South Africa merely by extending the franchise and so making the existing centralised and competitive system more inclusive. We can now see more clearly that there should also be basic structural changes in the political system if it is to structure and contain the heightened political conflict. But what are to be the starting points and the mechanisms for such changes if our present political system is indeed such an unfortunate compound of competitive party-politics and coercive government? Are there perhaps other features which might offset these?

It may be appropriate here to bring out more explicitly a somewhat unexpected result of our basic analysis of alternative political systems. We began by emphasising the central significance of the Westminster model for most political thinking in South Africa. In a sense this is merely a reflection of the present system – at least if we confine ourselves to the electoral and party system. If, however, we look carefully at the evolving South African political system in the wider sense, i.e. as a way of structuring and containing conflict, we can also recognise, apart from the predominant role of various kinds of coercion and regulation, a number of structural elements which would tend to decrease the intensity of conflict and improve the conditions for rational negotiation in ways not provided for by the Westminster model. There is, for example, the growing pattern of granting a measure of local autonomy to various groups, the creation of sub-systems of representative government on a non-competitive basis, the restriction of direct popular involvement and the growing emphasis on consultation and even contestation between established representative leaders. Much of this is still in embryonic form and co-exists with extensive centralised government regulation, but it is not peripheral to our present political system. It may therefore be unwarranted and misleading to think of this evolving political system solely in terms of the Westminster model. It may be more fruitful to investigate the potential of these other features as starting points for bringing about further structural changes, as part of a development towards political justice.

It should be emphasised, however, that the mere presence of some of these elements by no means guarantees an acceptable or democratic political system. On the contrary, in terms of the policy of Separate Development, i.e. on the basis of homeland separatism and independence, these very elements would largely contribute towards a more sophisticated strategy of continued White domination. It must accordingly be a major objective to attempt to spell out the conditions in which, for example the decentralisation and devolution of powers would really begin to contribute towards a more just and democratic society; to extrapolate the kind of political system this would require; and to envisage the ways and means by which such a system could evolve from the present one. In this way the question of alternative political systems would be approached not merely as an abstract theoretical exercise but with the focus squarely on the many concrete problems of transition.

NOTE

According to Rae the electoral system did not in any of the elections covered by his study create an *artificial minority*, i.e. allocated a minority of seats to a party with an absolute majority of the vote, though this is theoretically possible. This of course happened in the 1948 elections in South Africa.

REFERENCES

Dahl, R. (ed.) 1966 – *Political Opposition in Western Democracies.* New Haven: Yale University Press.

Duverger, M. 1954 – *Political Parties.* London: Methuen.

Easton, D. 1953 – *The Political System: An Inquiry into the State of Political Science.* New York: Knopf.

Kuper, Leo 1971 – 'Plural societies: perspectives and problems.' In L. Kuper and M. G. Smith (eds.), *Pluralism in Africa*. Berkeley: California University Press.

——1971 – 'Conflict and the plural society: Ideologies of violence among subordinate groups.' In L. Kuper and M. G. Smith (eds.), *Pluralism in Africa*. Berkeley: California University Press.

Lakeman, E. 1970 – *How Democracies Vote*. London: Garber.

Lipset, S. M. 1963 – 'Party systems and the representation of groups.' In S. M. Lipset (eds.), *The First New Nation*. New York: Basic Books; also in R. Dahl and D. E. Neubauer (eds.), *Readings in Modern Political Analysis*. Englewood Cliffs: Prentice-Hall.

Lipset, S. M. and S. Rokkan 1967 – 'Cleavage structures, party systems, and voter alignments: An introduction.' In *Party Systems and Voter Alignments: Cross-National Perspectives*. New York: Free Press.

Newman, K. J. 1970 – *European Democracies Between the Wars*. Translated by K. Morgan. London: Allen and Unwin.

Rae, Douglas W. 1971 – *The Political Consequences of Electoral Laws*. New Haven: Yale University Press.

Rose, Richard 1971 – *Governing Without Consensus*. London: Farber and Farber.

Weber, Max – 1947 – 'Politics as a vocation.' In *From Max Weber*. Translated by H. H. Gerth and C. Wright Mills. London: Routledge and Kegan Paul.

3. Politics and Privilege in South Africa

F. VAN ZYL SLABBERT

Introduction

A popular misconception about the nature of politics is that it only has to do with political parties competing for seats in an assembly of some sort by the occasional eliciting of support from voters. If this was all that politics was about then many countries where you do not have electoral politics of this nature would not have politics at all. This would be absurd, i.e. a society without politics. Yet in our society the majority of adult Whites usually think that their 'political activity' is confined to by-elections and general elections for central and local government. You make a cross on a piece of paper and having done so your 'political activity' ends. However, the fundamental point is that the cross made on the paper forms part of a basic process in our society which has to do with one thing only: *the acquisition, distribution and use of power.*

The word power causes a great deal of confusion in many minds. Some think of force, violence or coercion; others think of particular personal qualities such as strong character, divine inspiration or charisma; still others think of positions of status or the ownership of property and wealth. These are all valid examples related to power. However, the defining characteristic of power is that it has to do with the *ability to influence the decisions that people make whatever the basis might be on which this ability rests.* This ability is present in the most simple and most complex relationship in society. A man with a gun can influence the decisions of another man; a father influences his son; a teacher his pupil, etc. The point about *political power*, of course, is that this ability is used to influence the decisions of all the members of a society.

If we think back to the definition of politics given earlier it is apparent that this ability is present and used in every society which has existed throughout time: and yet there have been important differences amongst societies in this respect. The most important difference refers to the *manner* in which a person or a group has *gained* the ability to influence the decisions of all the members of a society. Basically there are three typical ways in which power is gained in a society, through force, e.g. a dictatorship; through tradition, e.g. a monarchy, and through the vote, e.g. a democracy. There may, of course, be mixed cases in actual fact but they would simply be a combination of these possibilities. The fundamental importance of the vote is that by means of it the ordinary man has a say in who eventually attains the ability to influence the decisions of all the members of society. This is a relatively new phenomenon in societal politics and its occurrence is one of the most striking characteristics of the 20th century. We live in an era in which the desirability for accountable government predominates and this accountability is made possible through the participation of the ordinary man in electoral politics. Perhaps it is vitally important to keep in mind that the next time you vote for a candidate in any type of election you are voluntarily giving another man the ability and the right to influence the types of decisions *you* are allowed to make, i.e. you are giving him power.

However, it was said that politics not only concerns the *acquisition* of power but also its *distribution* and *use*. By the distribution of power is meant the organizations and departments created by those in government and within which power is effectively used. By the use of power is simply meant the decisions taken by those in power and which concern the lives of all the members of a society.

In our society it is obvious that although White people are intimately linked with the process by which others acquire power, they do not have the same direct involvement in the distribution and use of power. In a sense those who distribute and use power have been given a mandate by the voters to distribute and use power as they see fit until the next time when they have to appeal to the voters again for such a mandate. On what basis can those in power lodge such an appeal? In the last analysis only on the basis that their use of power has effectively contributed towards maintaining or improving the life chances of those who support them by means of the vote. By life chances is simply meant the chance one has during a lifetime of enjoying the rewards and facilities that your society has to offer. These chances refer to one's position of privilege in society. At this stage I do not think it is any longer necessary to belabour the point that those who wield political power in society have direct influence in the distribution of privilege in society. Politics in this sense has to do with who gets what, when and how. Thus if Parliament should decide that for the next budget the R300 million earmarked for defence should be allocated to African Education this would have a significant impact on the life changes of many more Black people than the roughly R60 million which was used for this purpose last year. Of course, it is very unlikely that Parliament would take such a decision because at the next election the government would have to give account of how they had used their power to maintain or improve the life chances of those people who supported them and these people are White, not Black.

This curious, and of course, hypothetical example provides an appropriate starting point for discussing politics and privilege in South Africa.

THE STRUCTURE OF POLITICAL PARTICIPATION IN SOUTH AFRICA

South Africa consists of roughly 20 million people of which 3½ million have the potential to vote for a government which takes decisions that affect the lives of 20 million people. We may justify, explain away or reject this occurrence but that it is *the* basic fact of the nature of political participation cannot be denied. That is why the analysis of political participation in South Africa must distinguish between the voters and the voteless.

(a) The Voter

It is common knowledge that in South Africa only White persons above the age of eighteen years have the vote. They elect people to distribute and use power for the structuring of privilege for all the inhabitants of South Africa. It would however be a mistake to think of the White voters as a homogeneous group with a high degree of consensus. The most important difference between voters is a cultural one represented by the fact that we have two official languages in South Africa. Generally speaking, this cultural difference is also manifested in an institutional cleavage in the sense that you have Afrikaans schools, churches, business organizations, newspapers, clubs and to a certain extent residential areas with English counterparts. This cleavage introduces an extra dimension into White entrenched democratic politics. White politics is not only concerned with how one party can provide a better deal for White voters than another, but also with the problem of whether one White group, the Afrikaners, can compete effectively with the rest of the voters in the pursuit of the rewards and facilities that South Africa has to offer, and ultimately of course, how political power can be used to influence the nature of this competition. The Afrikaner is at present in power and for himself and for many others it is difficult to conceive of him in opposition after 25 years in government. More important, it is highly questionable whether he can maintain the type of cultural unity he has forged for himself during this time without the control and use of political power. The politics of privilege has become part and parcel of the Afrikaner's present cultural identity. When government ministers and government supporting editors warn against the danger of voting for any opposition parties they are not only warning, as they conceive of it, against the future of the White man in South Africa but in a very real sense, against the future of the Afrikaner as an influential force in White politics in this country, should an opposition party ever come to power.

The English, on the other hand, have never had the same collective ethos in terms of which they could mobilize political support. The most prevalent attitude towards political involvement was one of *laissez faire* rationality with an underlying optimism in the therapeutic powers of economic development to look after the major societal problems. Unlike achievement-oriented Afrikaners, politics is seldom considered a worthwhile full time career but rather as a worthy pastime after one has established oneself financially and socially. As part of the opposition their only hope of gaining political power is to erode the degree of Afrikaner political ethnocentrism by pitching their appeal to *common conditions* shared by all Whites.

These common social conditions transcend the internal differences amongst White voters and are immediately linked to a position of racial privilege. To put it differently: In terms of the principle of relative deprivation (relative to Blacks and to their own level of living); the vast majority of Whites have grown accustomed to material comfort and the promise of prosperity. At the grassroots level of political support, a switch of political allegiance can only be expected if a sufficient number of voters feel that through the maladministration of the government these conditions of comfort and prosperity are effectively threatened and that an opposition party promises to give them a better deal.

These are some of the reasons why electioneering politics in South Africa are fought on issues which seem somehow completely unrelated to the major political problems of South Africa, for example, a packet full of sand to farmers in Caledon; the necessity to give due respect to both official languages in White hotels, etc. The major political problems of the country focus of course on the relationship between the voters and the voteless.

(b) The Voteless

Despite the fact that there are various representative bodies for which Black people can vote it is analytically appropriate to view them as voteless insofar as their votes are not effectively related to the central institutions of political decision making at present. This is another way of saying that the people they elect cannot be held accountable for the major political decisions taken in the country because those elected simply do not take these decisions. This also means that the elected Blacks are given power that cannot be used directly in a politically effective sense.

The constitution of the voteless also displays internal differences of a cultural or ethnic nature. In addition, there is also a marked urban-rural difference which is reflected in different life-styles and tempo of living. It would be shortsighted to argue that the words Xhosa, Zulu, Tswana, etc. refer to figments of a government ideologue's imagination.

Again, however, it has to be argued that these internal differences are of secondary political importance in the present situation. The primary important factors relate to the common characteristics of the voteless which increasingly transcend these internal differences. Only a few of these characteristics need to be mentioned to emphasize this fact:

1. Since Union the voteless have been exposed to a White democratic form of government without participating in its functioning. From this Government numerous decisions have flowed that have affected the lives of the voteless without them being able to make those responsible for these decisions account for them. The Westminister model of parliamentary democracy has been such an accepted feature of government in South Africa that, although academically speaking, some federal or decentralized system of government would be far more effective in coping with the political problems of South Africa, it is questionable whether both Black and Whites would not feel their interests undermined if they had to participate in a governmental system other than a parliament with a two-party system.

2. The process of industrialization has drawn millions of the voteless people into an economic structure which emphasizes achievement and performance and exposed them to consumer products which can be acquired as a reward for such

efforts. This process more than anything else has eroded tribal ethnocentrism and made a readjustment to a pastoral subsistence economy almost impossible.
3. Mass education, mass communication and urbanization have led to new aspirations and value orientations. Rather than the problem of cultural lag we are increasingly experiencing a discrepancy between the expectations of a mass urban culture and the technological conditions for realizing these expectations.

The most important consequence of these common characteristics of the voteless in South Africa is that they reflect the fact that both Black and White people in this country participate in the same reward structure, or to put it differently, they have to compete within the same framework to improve their life chances. The position of the voteless *vis-à-vis* the voters is exactly this: that they cannot use political power to manipulate privilege and so improve their life chances.

POLITICS AND THE DISTRIBUTION OF PRIVILEGE IN SOUTH AFRICA

When one makes even a cursory analysis of how political power has been used over the last few decades in South Africa it is abundantly clear how directly it has improved the life chances of White people generally. A few examples should suffice to illustrate this fact:

1. The vast majority of employees in state departments, civil service and semi-state organizations are Afrikaners. The occupational opportunities opened up by the Afrikaner's control of political power contributed more than anything else towards coping with the so-called 'poor White' problem.
2. Through the implementation of the Group Areas Act many Whites have been able to buy cheaper homes than would otherwise have been possible. For example, from Rondebosch to Simonstown homes have become available in ways which have very little to do with the impersonal economic forces of supply and demand.
3. The Bantu Education Act of 1953 among others had as an important consequence the advantage that White children could study in relatively uncrowded conditions for their future careers.
4. The Separate Amenities Act of 1953 provides a host of privileges for Whites of a more leisurely nature, such as uncrowded beaches, theatres, public facilities, etc.

It might be argued that these acts were not intended to be used in this way; that much more lofty and worthy sentiments motivated their coming into being. Be that as it may, the net consequences of their implementation has simply underlined in a very real day-to-day way, the fact that it is much more comfortable to be White in our society. In fact, it is a privilege ensured by the use of political power.

The relation of the voteless to privilege in South Africa can also be spelled out but this would simply be belabouring the obvious. Their conditions of employment, residence, freedom of movement etc. are all directly linked to acts of parliament that are the consequences of lengthily motivated and laboriously argued political decisions. The point is, of course, that if Blacks had the vote many of these Acts would not have been passed. This is a ridiculously obvious sort of statement to make but its elaboration highlights the central political problem in South Africa.

THE CRUX OF THE POLITICAL MATTER IN SOUTH AFRICA

The crux of the problem in South Africa is not as some would have it, the easing of race discrimination, nor the disappearance of ethnocentric irrationalities; nor the gradual improvement of economic opportunities; nor, to put it in vague humanistic terms, the treating of every person with 'respect and human dignity.' All these are obviously eminently desirable and worthy. However, even if they should all come about, and they do so without the extension of effective political participation the relative conditions of privilege would remain very much the same between the voter and the voteless. *The crux of the problem is therefore the devolution of effective political power to the voteless.*

This is a major problem simply for the following reasons:

1. No one can realistically expect that after 62 years of White parliamentary rule in South Africa the leaders of the Black communities have not got a keen awareness of how political decisions have affected the lives and life chances of the voteless. There is consequently an increasing demand for participation in the making of effective political decisions on the part of the Blacks.
2. However, the extension of political participation to the voteless in whatever effective manner, and assuming that it would take place constitutionally and therefore relatively peacefully, is dependent on the White voter putting political leaders into power, that can create the constitutional machinery for the devolution of power. This is an extraordinarily difficult thing to introduce into electoral politics for in effect it demands of the White voter that he expects of those in power to use such power to make political decision-makers in future accountable to a much wider group of people than has ever been the case in the political history of South Africa. This is another way of saying that political decision-makers will no longer only be accountable to White voters for the structuring of privilege for all in South Africa. The peaceful devolution of power introduces voluntary sacrifice of privilege into electoral politics, and sacrifice is a very difficult political commodity to sell.
3. The devolution of power is also a problem in yet another sense. In the absence of such devolution the political decision-makers are confronted with contradictory sets of demands, one electoral and the other outside electoral politics. The extent to which a White government has to cope with the social and economic problems of the Blacks, it has had to justify to the Whites on the grounds that

it does not effect the material welfare of the Whites too drastically. If this justification cannot be given satisfactorily, reactionary opposition groups can accuse the government of not 'looking after the interests of the White man' or 'doing too much for the Blacks.' This accusation can take a number of forms: 'The government ignores the farmer', 'lower income Whites cannot buy houses', 'there are not enough telephones', 'the cost of living is too high', etc.

Given the problematical nature of the devolution of political power in South Africa, to argue to the contrary of its necessity would be to consider alternatives of even greater complexity. It would mean in effect that one would argue that political stability can be maintained with indefinite White minority rule in South Africa despite all the demographic; social; economic and political changes taking place which affect the majority of people in this country and who are are excluded from effective political power.

Conclusion

This has been a very general analysis of present political conditions in South Africa. Very little attention has been paid to how this has come about or why these conditions are considered justifiable. To a large degree this has been a deliberate omission born of the conviction that a voter is neither a historian nor a full-fledged ideologue. By this I do not mean that he is an amateur sociologist but simply that one of the major assumptions of a sociological analysis of political life is that present forces contribute greatly to political action and that the understanding of these forces helps one to identify major problems in society. We can end this more or less where we started by saying that the major political problems of South Africa focus on the act of making a cross on a piece of paper and that this cross symbolizes the acquisition, distribution and use of power for the pursuit of privilege.

Part 10:

Social Structure and Social Change

Introduction

JONATHAN WACKS

This introduction is divided into two parts. The first attempts a brief outline of a particular social theory that provides a framework for the analysis of social structure and social change. Little more is attempted here than the explication of some of the key concepts of what may be termed a Marxist structuralist approach. This approach is based directly on Althusser's (1969 and 1971) and Althusser and Balibar's (1970) reading of the major Marxist texts, in particular Marx's *Capital.* It also draws on the work of Althusser's most faithful disciple Nicos Poulantzas (1973a, 1973b and 1975). It must be stressed that without a study of the actual texts (Marx's and Althusser's in particular) most of the depth and comprehensiveness of the theory will be missed. My aim is to stimulate (or confuse) the reader toward that end.

The second part addresses itself to the articles included in this chapter and tries to raise some critical questions on the basis of the theory outlined. The emphasis throughout the introduction is on social structure rather than social change. This is not because the latter concept is considered less important or less problematic, but rather because questions relating to social change are more transparently the subject matter of the selected readings, while a coherent conception of social structure is largely absent.

I.

To make sense out of changes taking place in the society it is essential to specify these changes with respect to the various *levels* of the social structure.[1] Each of these *levels* (economic, political, ideological, theoretical) is the site of a distinct *practice* (economics, politics, ideology, theory). These practices present themselves as a specific combination of the following *elements:* (a) raw material, (b) human labour, (c) means of production, and (d) product. Although the different practices are *formally* similar in that they each entail a process of *transformation* (cf. Althusser 1969) of a raw material into a product (that is effected by human labour employing a means of production), in their *content* they are distinct, i.e. in that they apply to different kinds of raw material, employ different kinds of labour, means of production and produce a different type of product.

Economic practice, for example, involves putting to work labour power and means of (material) production (e.g. machinery), while *theoretical* practice employs 'thought power' and means of (theoretical) production ('the concepts of a theory and its methods') to produce: 'socially useful products' in the first case and 'knowledges' in the second (cf. Geras 1972). The raw material of economic practice is 'natural or already worked up material', while that of theoretical production comprises the 'raw' notions, concepts, information, and intuitions that constitute a 'conventional wisdom.'

Not only do the various practices differ in *content*, but as a result of the uneven nature of historical development, each level of the structure tends to develop at a different rate and rhythm and consequently displays a *relative autonomy* (cf. Poulantzas 1973 (b):255–321). In South Africa, for example, the ideological level, despite the fundamental political and economic functions that it performs, has achieved a certain measure of independence, relative autonomy. A consequence of this development is that in certain instances ideological practices have been in contradiction with certain economic practices (in particular).[2] To identify the specificity of each level, the quality of its effects (practices) and the rhythm of its own development, careful study of the concrete conditions of the society must be undertaken.

Having raised the question of the relative autonomy of the levels of the structure it is important to indicate how these levels combine to form a complex totality. The totality is *complex* because the various levels do not simply interact with one another but the combination of levels articulate the *contradictions*[3] that each of their practices entail. The contradictions in each practice determine and are determined by the other practices in a process that Althusser has called '*overdetermination.*' But the totality may also be considered complex, because it does not constitute a nice, balanced symmetrical whole, but a so-called '*structure in dominance.*'

It is difficult in this short space to provide more than a definition of this difficult concept. To grasp its meaning the reader should turn to Althusser's texts. Here, we may briefly note that the totality is a complex combination in which one of the levels is dominant; which level is the dominant one is determined 'in the last instance'[4] by the economy. The economy may determine itself or any other level as the dominant one but there is always a dominant level. The dominant level is not however fixed for all time but shifts in response to the 'overdetermination' of the contradictions which fluctuate with the actual historical development of the society (i.e. development of productive forces, the nature of class alliances and conflicts, ideology, etc.). In very broad terms we can say (echoing Marx's discussion) that in 'feudal society' the ideological level was dominant while in 'capitalist society' the economic level dominates. Again it must be stressed that only close historical research into the conditions and circumstances peculiar to the society being studied will reveal its 'index of dominance', i.e. the particular form of articulation maintained by the levels of the structure.

It was pointed out earlier that each level of the structure is the site of a distinct practice. The articulated combination of levels is reflected in what are termed *social relations* (the ensemble of political, economic and ideological practices). The generality of this term is transformed by conceptualizing it in terms of *class relations*. Paraphrasing Poulantzas (1973(b):67–8) we may say that *social class* is a concept which indicates the effect of the social structure (and its index of dominance) on the agents which constitute its supports: this concept reveals the effect of the social structure in the field of social relations. It follows easily from this that social classes are not simply determined by the economic level (as is often erroneously assumed) but by *all* the levels of the structure such that a social class is defined 'by its place in the ensemble of (social) practices, i.e. by the ensemble of the division of labour which includes political and ideological relations.'[5]

Before proceding to the second part of this introduction it might be useful to cast in some of the lines that have been thrown, at least to the extent of listing the terminology that defines the key concepts of this theoretical approach and that in all likelihood is new to the reader, at least in its usage in this discourse: social structure, levels, practices, elements, transformation, relative autonomy, contradiction, overdetermination, determination-in-the-last-instance, structure-in-dominance, social relations, social class. These concepts are the building blocks of a theory that is complex and often needlessly abstruse[6] but one that appears to me to be the most fecund currently available in the social sciences: to grasp this theory fully requires a preparedness to learn a new discourse, to leave one discourse for another – a prerequisite for any intellectual endeavour that attempts to go beyond the 'obviousness' of immediate reality.

II.

The publication in 1970 of Johnstone's much celebrated article[7] injected a new clarity into both academic and popular discussion of contemporary South African society. Alongside the writings of a handful of scholars[8] working mainly in England, Johnstone's paper stands out as an example of well-reasoned argumentation. The aim of his article is explained as 'a broad and integrated overview which might suggest further directions for research.' Since its publication a fair measure of progress has been made both at the level of theorizing and historical research – a welcome advance on the naive empiricism of the so-called 'prevailing thesis' that Johnstone sets out to criticize.[9]

An enduring irony of the academic 'debate' stimulated by the writings of of Johnstone and others is that it is the 'liberal' pundits of the 'prevailing thesis', arguing that economic development is destroying the prevailing politico-ideological superstructures of apartheid, that have mindlessly slipped into the 'economic determinist' position usually associated with Marxism. In the meantime contemporary Marxist theory (as I tried to illustrate above) has begun to articulate a theoretical approach capable of specifying the levels (economic, political, ideological, theoretical) of the social structure and their forms of combination in a rigorous and coherent way, leaving the crude simplicity of an earlier economic determinism way behind. While the full potential of this approach has still to be exploited by South Africanist scholars, a beginning has been made (cf. Johnstone 1976).

A measure of both the merit and deficiency of Johnstone's essay is its enduring relevance Its merit lies in the fundamentally correct argument that the economy reinforcing and reinforced by the dominant political and ideological practices is located in a social structure that effectively reproduces class relations along racial lines. Although not expressed by Johnstone in quite this way, who prefers to talk rather vaguely of the 'power structure of White supremacy (being) continually strengthened by its own material output . . . in a circular process,' the argument is substantively the same. But it is precisely this looseness of terminology that would seem to be responsible for its continuing relevance. Repeatedly in this article categories are employed that are so vague as to escape the possibility of falsification.

To take an example. The assertion that 'employers have been in conflict with the government over the geographical and occupational labour control' (Johnstone 1976:130) while useful as a first approximation, to be at all rigorous should then be refined by giving attention to at least the following three problems:

(i) the sectoral breakdown of the economy as the basis for the examination of the interests of particular 'fractions' of the capitalist class. In this way, the elementary notion 'employers' may be more accurately specified and various 'fractional interests' analysed.

(ii) the nature of State *power* the specificity (relative autonomy) of and the relationship between the various branches of the state *apparatus* including its administrative (civil service), repressive (police, military) and ideological (schools, mass-media, etc.) functions need to be illucidated. In this way the loosely descriptive term 'government' can be located with respect to the political and ideological levels of the social structure. The term 'government' is clearly not identical with that of the State apparatus but 'covers a political power centre by denoting a particular functioning of the State apparatus.'[10] Moreover, the posing of the question of government control as part of the analysis of the *State* power, leads to the specification of the various forms of State control. Johnstone manages to smother completely these distinctions. For example, by reducing 'White supremacy' to the 'labour structure of White supremacy' the specific forms of *ideological* control entailed by this notion are smuggled away.

(iii) the particular historical time-scales that characterize the development of each level of the structure must be clarified. Part of the meaning of 'relative autonomy' is that each level possesses a time-sequence specific to its own (relatively autonomous) history. The articulated combination of the time-sequences of all the levels of the structure constitute an historical *stage* in the development of the society. This is the problem of *periodization* of which Johnstone is completely oblivious.[11] In our example the phrase 'have been in conflict' although in itself seemingly innocent, points to the absence of any concept of historical development. Even in his assumption of a simple (linear) chronology of events, Johnstone fails to identify rigorously specific historical periods in which to locate his discussion of class

> conflict and racial discrimination.[12] The problem that this absence in the article poses is far too complicated to be dealt with here, but does point to serious weakness in the argument that leaves it floating in an historical vacuum. (This weakness continues to manifest itself in subsequent studies of South Africa particularly with respect to the analysis of 'ideology' and its patterns of development.)

Despite some of its failings Johnstone's article can still be read with profit and stands out as undoubtedly the most coherent introduction to the study of social change in South Africa.

The second article included in this chapter is a brief discussion by Colin Bundy of the recent (1974) repeal by Parliament of the so-called Masters and Servants Acts. Apart from the intrinsic importance of the subject matter of the article, it is also a useful analysis of the relationship between a particular event – the scrapping of the Masters and Servants Act – and the conditions and circumstances in which it occurred. To that extent it is a valuable (although partial) illustration of how the study of social change might proceed.

I say 'partial' because Bundy does not manage to go much further than to refer to relevent 'backup' legislation (e.g. the Bantu Laws Amendment Act (67 of 1964)) that situates the 'change' in question but only in relation to the 'juridico-political'[13] level of the structure. A more comprehensive analysis would attempt to locate this change with respect to the (overdetermined) practices that constitute the social structure. To analyse social change in this way is not to reduce all change to structural change but to establish the theoretical framework in which to discover the significance or particular events that often appear to herald social transformation. We should not mistake the winds of change for change itself.

NOTES

1. It should be made clear at the outset, that the concepts that are being introduced here and the texts referred to require close attention and the reader unfamiliar with this discourse should be prepared to struggle at first to come to grips with a language that is often very taxing.
2. For example, the demand for skilled labour during the recent period of economic expansion was contradicted by the dominant (racist) ideology which had for specific historical reasons constructed a comprehensive industrial colour-bar effectively preventing Black workers from being trained and employed in skilled occupations (cf. Johnstone's article included in the readings.)
3. Each level of the society expresses specific contradictions. At the economic level the general contradiction between the forces and relations of production (cf. Althusser, 1970:317) entail a multiplicity of other contradictions: for example, the contradiction between 'ownership' and 'non-ownership' of the means of production (in the capitalist mode of production) is part of the general contradiction mentioned and itself entails a variety of contradictions between different 'fractions' of the 'owning' or capitalist class as well as within the non-owning class (proletariat), etc. It is, incidentally, these agents of production

(conceptualized as *social classes*) that are the 'supports' or 'bearers' of the social structure and their ongoing conflicts, alliances, struggles and levels of consciousness that make up the field of *social relations* or what is sometime called social interaction (cf. Poulantzas 1973(a)).

4. This formulation avoids the problem of 'economic determinism' by recognizing that the contradictions that constitute the economic level are 'never simple but always specified by the historically concrete forms in which it is exercised.' In other words, a pure Economy asserting itself against a passive politico-ideological superstructure is ruled out, precisely because the economic level is overdetermined by the other levels in an irreducibly complex totality. However, although the economy is embedded within this complex structure, it is nevertheless attributed a determining role 'in the last instance.' While Althusser assures us that the 'lonely hour of "the last instance" never comes,' this is only to reassert the special sense in which 'determination' is employed in his discourse. Given the centrality of this concept it is surprising that its meaning is never satisfactorily explicated. In the last analysis it must be assumed that the concept simply rephrases a theoretical *assertion* based on Marx's historical research.

   'It is always the direct relationship of the owners of the conditions of production to the direct producers . . . which reveals the innermost secret, the hidden basis of the entire social structure . . .' (Karl Marx, *Capital*, Vol. III, Lawrence and Wishart, London, 1974, 791).

5. In that *social relations* are the reflection or effect of the social structure, the character (or 'index of dominance') of which is determined ('in the last instance') by the economic level, it follows that the *principal* role in the determination of *social classes* is played ('in the last instance') by the economic level (cf. Poulantzas 1973(a):27–28 and 1973(b):57–70).

6. For those who plough through the texts of Althusser and Poulantzas the following words of Karl Popper may at times seem pertinent, they are ultimately self-satisfying:

   I suggest that in some of the more ambitious social sciences and philosophies . . . the traditional game which has largely become the unconscious and unquestioned standard, is to state the utmost trivialities in high-sounding language (Karl Popper 1976).

7. The article 'White prosperity and White supremacy in South Africa today' is included in the readings.

8. See especially: Legassick 1974(a), 1974(b), 1974(c) and Wolpe 1970, 1972 and 1976. A much more trivialized discussion of the same topic by Simson (1975), that some of the concepts outlined above are employed for the first time in the literature on South Africa, albeit in a confused state. See also Trapido (1971:309–20). See also the Collected Seminar papers on the Societies of Southern Africa in the 19th and 20th Centuries (University of London Institute of Commonwealth Studies).

9. For a summary of the 'prevailing thesis' see Johnstone's article. References to the writings of those who argue the 'prevailing thesis' are footnoted in Johnstone's article.

10. Poulantzas (1973b) goes further by identifying a distinction between the legislative and executive aspects. This he does as a basis for distinguishing between forms of state.

11. To the extent that any serious discussion of this problem emerged only after the publication of Johnstone's article it is unlikely that Johnstone would have been aware of the problem. However I make the point to assist in a critical reading of the article and obviously not as a comment on Johnstone's abilities.

12. For a clear example of *simple* historical chronology cf. Legassick (1974) where he identifies the following periods: (i) the mercantile era of colonialism (1652–1875); (ii) the mining era (1875–1924), the period of secondary industrialization. For a discussion of *complex*, uneven periodization cf. Althusser and Balibar (1970).

13. 'Juridico-political' is really a shorthand for the 'juridicial level of the political level of the structure'. It should be apparent that each of the *levels* of the social structure is itself structured by different levels.

REFERENCES

Althusser, Louis 1969 – *For Marx*. London. Allen Lane: Penguin.

——1971 – *Lenin and Philosophy and Other Essays*. London: New Left Books.

Althusser, Louis and Etienne Baubar 1970 – *Reading Capital*. London: New Left Books.

Geras, Norman 1972 – 'Althussers Marxism: An account and assessment.' *New Left Review*, 71.

Johnstone, F. A. 1976 – *Class, Race and Gold: A Study of Class Relations and Race Discrimination in South Africa*. London: Routledge and Kegan Paul.

Legassick, Martin 1974a – 'South Africa: Capital accumulation and violence.' *Economy and Society*, 3, 3, August, 253–91.

——1974b – 'South Africa forced labour, industrialisation and racial discrimination.' In R. Harris (ed.), *The Political Economy of Africa*. Shenkman.

——1974c – 'Legislation, ideology and economy in post 1948 South Africa.' *Journal of South African Studies*, 1, 1, October, 5–35.

Popper, Karl 1976 – 'Reason or revolution?' In T. W. Adorno *et al.*, *The Positivist Dispute in German Sociology*. London: Heinemann.

Poulantzas, Nicos 1973a – 'On social classes.' *New Left Review*, 78.

——1973b *Political Power and Social Classes*. London: New Left Books.

——1975 – *Class in Contemporary Capitalism*. London: New Left Books.

Simson, N. 1975 – 'The myth of the White working class in South Africa.' *African Review*, 4, 2.

Trapido, G. 1971 – 'South Africa in a comparative study of industrialisation.' *Journal of Development Studies*, 7, 3, April, 309–20.

Wolpe, Harold 1970 – 'Industrialism and race in South Africa.' In S. Zubaida (ed.), *Race and Racialism*. London: Tavistock.

——1972 – 'Capitalism and cheap labour power in South Africa: From segregation to apartheid.' *Economy and Society*, 1, 4, November, 425–56.

——1976 – 'The White working class in South Africa.' *Economy and Society*, 5, 2, May.

1. White Prosperity and White Supremacy in South Africa Today

FREDERICK A. JOHNSTONE

In the past decade, extensive economic development has taken place in South Africa, and the visitor to that country quickly becomes aware of the affluence of the Whites, who enjoy one of the highest material standards of living in the world.[1] But the political significance of this economic expansion is less obvious and the subject of growing debate.

It is the view of many observers that this economic development is undermining the government's racial policies of apartheid and the system of White supremacy, or that it is likely to do so in the not too distant future. For while the official goal of apartheid is increasing racial segregation and 'separate development,' economic expansion is seen to mean continued racial integration and inter-dependence at the economic level, which is seen to be subversive to apartheid policies. The desire of the Whites for both prosperity and apartheid is thus seen to be basically contradictory, and their determined quest for the former and apparent failures of the latter are thought to be undermining White supremacy.[2]

It would appear, however, that this prevailing thesis has serious limitations. The purpose of this study is to assess the relations between economic development, apartheid labour policies and White supremacy in South Africa today, and to develop a critique of this thesis. It is not a detailed examination of any particular aspect of the subject, but rather an attempt at a broad and integrated over-view, which might suggest directions for further research.

At the outset, two important distinctions which underlie the whole analysis need to be made. First of all, 'apartheid' must be distinguished from 'White supremacy.' 'Apartheid' refers to the South African government's racial policies and ideology, while 'White supremacy' refers to the overall power structure in South Africa, which is partly maintained by apartheid policies. The blurred use of the terms together, however, often seems to imply that the power structure of White supremacy is the product of apartheid policies alone, which it is not. The second distinction is between two levels of apartheid – that of actual policies, and that of justificatory ideology. "Apartheid ideology refers to the official goals and doctrines in terms of which the actual racial policies of the South African government are justified; while "actual apartheid" refers to the racial policies actually being pursued and implemented by the government."[3]

The article falls into three parts, first examining the limitations of the prevailing thesis in relation to apartheid labour policies, and then in relation to the persistence of the basic labour structure of White supremacy, and concluding with a brief critique of this thesis in the light of the evidence and conclusion of the earlier sections.

Economic development and apartheid labour policies

The basic goal of apartheid ideology is the increasing and eventually total segregation and separate development of the different racial groups. But certain economic developments – in the spheres of geographical and occupational labour mobility – have been moving in the opposite direction to this official ideology. The growing movement of African workers into the 'White' urban areas, and their increasing employment in semi-skilled work, have furthered the economic integration of the two major racial groups (Africans and Whites), which is seen to contradict apartheid.

The movement of Africans into the urban areas has continued steadily. Between 1911 and 1960, while the total urban population multiplied by 2,75, the urban African population multiplied by 7.[4] Between 1951 and 1960, the number of Africans in urban areas rose by nearly 50 per cent, from 2,4 million to 3,4 million, and it was estimated to be about 4,3 million in 1968.[5] Today the non-Whites outnumber the Whites in all of South Africa's major cities, forming 64 per cent, 62 per cent and 71 per cent of the populations of Johannesburg, Cape Town and Durban respectively (Horrell 1968b:2).

African labour underpins the whole South African economy, with Africans providing about 70 per cent of the country's economically active population, and with the majority of them engaged in essential labour for the whole population (Malherbe 1969:1, 3, 4, 35). But the movement of Africans to the urban areas reflects their growing importance in the industrial labour force. In manufacturing, their numbers rose by about 200 000 between 1960 and 1966. The non-White proportion of the manufacturing labour force rose from 70 per cent in 1961 to 75 per cent in 1966, and it is estimated that it will reach 80 per cent in 1971.[6]

This has been accompanied by a degree of upward occupational mobility. For some time South Africa has been suffering from an acute shortage of skilled labour, which has exerted pressure on the traditional job colour bar reserving all skilled work for Whites, and implemented as a government policy.[7] A growing number of non-Whites are being employed in semi-skilled and operative jobs.

It is these features of the situation on which the prevailing theory focuses its attention. The mobility of non-White labour in these spheres is seen to be basically at variance with apartheid policy. But is this in fact the case?

The prevailing theory could mean two things. Either these developments are contradicting apartheid because the government is sincerely attempting to implement the official ideology of total separate development, which in these cases appears to be contradicted; or the government is not implementing this ideology, and is just drifting along without a comprehensive policy and gradually succumbing to the pressure of these developments. But this perspective ignores a third possibility, which is in fact the reality – that these developments are not contradicting apartheid because the government is not literally pursuing the official ideology, but does have a comprehensive policy, which far from being in conflict with these developments, has encouraged them and is secured by them.

In fact, in relation to apartheid labour policies, the prevailing thesis is invalid for two basic reasons. The incompatibility which it claims to see in these spheres is not in fact present, because of the nature of actual apartheid. Secondly, the absence of such incompatibility between the imperatives of economic development and apartheid policies in other areas of greater importance to White supremacy is also ignored. Both these points will now be examined more closely.

In the first place, it is a mistake to believe that the continued and increasing use of African labour in 'White' industry is a contradiction of apartheid. For the government is not in fact attempting literally to implement its official ideology of total separate development. The actual goal of apartheid policies is the pragmatic development of an economically powerful White supremacy. The Whites want continued prosperity and continued supremacy, and the government is seeking to secure both of these goals together. The true rationale of apartheid policies is thus to maximise economic development both for the sake of White prosperity and for the material protection of White supremacy. The function of the official ideology is to justify the increasing denial of rights to, and servile status of, non-Whites in the 'White' areas in the name of future rights and opportunities for them in 'their own' areas.

The nature of actual apartheid is evident in many ways, some of which will be examined now and others in the following sections. Here we are concerned to see how this rationale expresses itself in relation to those economic developments (non-White labour mobility in the 'White' areas) which are supposed to contradict apartheid. It is clearly apparent in the actual policies being pursued by the government in this regard: the reduction of Africans in the 'White' areas to an *essential minimum* (but their continued extensive presence in these areas rather than the total separation forseen by official ideology); the reduction of the status of those Africans still in 'White' areas to that of *rightless migrants* (but the continued large scale use of their labour in these areas, and the absence of work and thus of meaningful rights for Africans in the Reserves); the diversion of industrial development to the border areas near the Reserves (rather than the industrial development of the Reserves); and a flexible policy towards the job colour bar (rather than its rigid ideological implementation).

The removal of 'inessential' Africans has taken two basic forms: the removal of whole African settlements from rural areas designated as 'White', and the removal of individual Africans by 'endorsing them out' under various movement controls. Up to the beginning of 1968, 193 African communities – a total of 73 000 people – had been removed from their rural settlements, and 276 more were scheduled for removal.[8] Each year thousands of Africans are endorsed out of the urban areas to the Reserves.[9] The government has made it clear that it intends to expel economically inactive Africans from the 'White' areas.[10]

The migrant and rightless status of Africans working in the 'White' areas is secured by a complex system of labour and movements controls which severely restricts the rights of these Africans.[11] The government has been extending the migrant status of these workers, notably by the Bantu Laws Amendment Act of 1964, the Bantu Labour Act of 1964, and the Bantu Labour Regulations of 1965 and 1968.[12] Under these Regulations, no African may leave the Reserves unless he has obtained a contract of employment through a government labour bureau, and no such contract may be valid for more than a year, though it may be renewed. Through these labour bureaux, the government wields very wide powers over African workers. The rights of Africans to stay in 'White' areas because of certain qualifications such as birth, long residence or continuous employment in them, have been whittled away. Commenting on the 1968 Regulations, a government minister declared that through them 'we now give judicial recognisance of our expressed policy of *building our economy on contract labour*.'[13]

The Whites want the continued use of African labour without the continued residential presence of African people in the 'White' areas. Thus non-essential Africans are removed, while essential African workers are shuttled about, deprived of rights in the places where they live and work, and without jobs in the 'homelands' where they are told to exercise their rights. Through this migrant labour system the Whites secure their supposedly contradictory goals of prosperity and White supremacy and racial separation, at the expense of the Africans, on whom it inflicts permanent instability, the destruction of family life, and other serious disabilities.

Another response of actual apartheid to the movement of African labour into 'White' industry is the border industry policy, which seeks to divert industrial development to the borders of the African Reserves. These are to function as reservoirs of cheap labour within easy access of industry rather than to become the economically developed regions pictured in apartheid ideology. Through such measures as the Physical Planning and Utilisation of Resources Act of 1967 the government is encouraging the establishment of new industries and the relocation of urban industries in the border areas.[14]

Among the incentives offered by the government to companies to move into these areas has been the authorization of African wage rates lower than those in the cities.[15] Government Wage Determinations for industries in these areas have tended to recommend wages lower than elsewhere, and often lower than those actually being paid in them at the time.[16] Between 1960 and 1968 over £150 million had been invested in these border industries, creating employment by 1969 for about 109 000 Africans and 36 000 others (Horrell 1969:97). While at the moment this is of only marginal significance relative to the size and importance of urban industry, it must be contrasted with the almost total neglect of industrial development in the Reserves, where between 1960 and 1966 only 35 new industries were established, employing 945 Africans.[17]

The pragmatic and flexible nature of actual apartheid is also apparent in the government's policy towards non-White occupational mobility. The job colour bar is extensively prescribed in legislation, and up to 1968, 24 job reservation determinations had been made under the Industrial Conciliation Act, which gives the government wide powers to make such discrimination. The job colour bar is also secured by various other means. But these determinations affected only about three per cent of the labour force, and up to June 1967, out of 891 applications from employers for exemptions, only 74 were refused.[18] Early in 1969, Mr B. Schoeman, the Minister of Transport, announced that thousands of Africans were being employed by the government in semi-skilled work on the railways, and would continue to be as long as their labour was required. The government has thus encouraged a certain flexibility in the job colour bar for the sake of continued economic expansion, and as long as the basic master-servant relationship between White and non-White workers is maintained.

This policy reflects the changing disposition of many White workers. Prosperity and the labour shortage have relaxed the traditional rigidity of their attitude towards job reservation. The White workers have been prepared to make 'deals' with employers, whereby they receive better wages and job security in certain occupations in exchange for allowing certain other jobs to be 'diluted' into operative work to be performed by non-White labour at low wages.[19]

The conventional claims about the contradiction of apartheid in these spheres of geographical and occupational mobility thus turn out to be unfounded, in the light of the actual nature of apartheid policies in these areas. Only certain aspects of apartheid ideology are contradicted, but this is of little significance since in these spheres actual apartheid is not concerned with the literal implementation of ideology but with the pragmatic realisation of White South Africa's dual goals of continuing prosperity and continuing supremacy. Thus the government is not essentially opposed to the continuing movement of African labour into the 'White' economy; it is simply opposed to this process of *labour* mobility, which is necessary to continued economic development, becoming at the same time a process of *residential* and *political* mobility, which is not indispensable to economic growth and which is effectively being restricted through the system of labour controls.

It is true that employers have been in conflict with the government over the geographical and occupational labour controls. But it would be wrong to interpret this as a rejection of all apartheid labour policies and as a sign of a fundamental incompatibility of interests between employers and the government. Rather it is a conflict over the distribution of benifits.

Because of the high degree of consensus among the Whites in favour of White supremacy, which reflects the material interests of the different White groups in its structure, conflict among the Whites is concerned essentially with the form that White supremacy should take, and with the manner in which the benefits accruing to the Whites as a whole from it should be shared among the different White groups, notably the capitalist employers, the White workers and the Afrikaner nationalists. These different groups all seek to maximise their own particular interests, and this may sometimes lead to a certain degree of conflict. But their common commitment to an economically prosperous White supremacy obviously implies certain constraints on the pursuit of these specific interests. The function of actual apartheid is to regulate these different constraints in such a way as to permit the maximisation of different White interests in the two goal areas of prosperity and White supremacy without jeopardising the essential security of either.

Not only are the conventional claims about contradiction in these spheres of economic development and apartheid invalid; the significant fact is ignored that in relation to other important apartheid labour policies – in the spheres of African labour organisation and wages – there is a marked absence of conflict between capitalist development and apartheid. The denial of trade union rights to African workers and the maintenance of low African wages have been cardinal elements of apartheid labour policy both ideologically and in practice. While employers have attacked the job and geographical colour bars, they have not been known seriously to oppose the trade union and wage colour bars, which on the contrary they have on the whole tended to exploit and perpetuate.

This compatibility is all the more significant in view of the basic importance of labour discrimination in these spheres to the power structure of both capitalism and White supremacy in South Africa. For the most important labour controls are those which most essentially deprive Africans of access to and control of economic power (trade union, educational and income colour bars) rather than the job and movement colour bars. The latter can be – and are being – administered flexibly without endangering the White power structure. But this cannot be said of the others, certainly not of the trade union colour bar for instance. Powerful African unions with the right to strike could force higher wages, cripple the South African economy and serve as bases for political action. It is significant that in this more important area of labour discrimination, employer and government policies have not been in conflict. The strong persistence of these other colour bars, which will be referred to as the 'core structure' of labour discrimination, will now be examined.

Economic development and White supremacy

Not only are the limitations of the prevailing thesis evident in relation to apartheid labour policies. They are further indicated by the fact that economic development has not been undermining the core labour structure of White supremacy. Moreover, the persistence of this structure testifies to more than just the weakness of the conventional theory; it points also to the collaborative nature of the relations between the economic system and White supremacy. For it would be a mistake to imagine that this structure is the product of apartheid policies alone; it is also extensively determined by the controllers of private economic power (and by the White workers) who benefit so greatly from it.

The economic position of Africans in South Africa must be examined in the light of three important questions. What is the nature of the economic relationship between Whites and Africans? Has the essential structure of this relationship been significantly undermined by recent economic development? And if not, what light does this throw upon the relations between the capitalist system and White supremacy in South Africa? But first some basic distinctions and facts need to be made clear.

Assessments of the economic status of Africans in South Africa commonly adhere to one or more of four justificatory standards: a subsistence standard, comparisons between different countries, comparisons in time, and comparisons of access to the means of power within one system. Justifications of the economic position of Africans by supporters of the regime in South Africa tend to adhere to the first three of these, taking one of three forms: the 'basic needs of the Africans are satisfied' argument, the Naples Slum Analogy ('there's worse poverty in Naples'), and the 'things are better than they were before' argument.

It must first be pointed out – without accepting the validity of the subsistence standard – that, even by this minimal standard, the position of Africans in South Africa is far from adequate. Recent surveys have found that the average income of Africans is so low that the majority of them actually live below the poverty datum line.[20] In Johannesburg, the incomes of nearly 70 per cent of African families were found to fall below the minimum subsistence level for healthy living.[21] The majority of Africans suffer from malnutrition, which accounts for an exceptionally high African child mortality rate. The average annual death rate of 1–4 year old African children is estimated to be about 45 per 1 000 live births (compared with 2 per 1 000 for White children in this age group) (Richardson 1968).[22] Research has found that in one African Reserve, at least 50 per cent of all children die before the age of five (Leary and Lewis 1965).

But in fact, of the four commonly used standards, only the last can be accepted as morally valid. What sort of access do the Africans in South Africa have to the means of economic power, and what is their share in the distribution of wealth? These are the vital questions in terms of which economic development in South Africa must be assessed, and in answering them, the first three standards are invalid.

The economic structure of White supremacy is maintained by various forms and measures of racial discrimination, which are too extensive to be fully described here. But the core of these measures consists of those which most basically restrict the access of Africans to the means and possession of economic power, namely the denial of labour organisation and education to Africans, and the unequal distribution of income which reflects and further consolidates this distribution of power.

Probably the most important of all the measures of labour discrimination barring African access to economic power are those which prohibit African labour organisation. African trade unions are excluded from legal recognition (under the Industrial Conciliation Act), and strikes by African workers are illegal (under the Bantu Labour (Settlement of Disputes) Act). Under this latter Act, the interests of African workers are supposed to be represented by government officials. Other laws, such as the General Law Amendment Act and the Suppression of Communism Act, also seriously restrict the rights of African workers to organise and strike.[23] It is measures like these which indicate, in the view of the United Nations Economic and Social Council, that 'the international standards relating to trade union freedoms are being seriously and persistently violated by South African legislation and by administrative and penal measures.'[24]

The African workers are thus deprived of the most elementary rights of labour organisation and are unable to assert their interests freely and legally. The African trade union movement has been virtually hounded out of existence by the government. As a result, today only about half a per cent of the economically active African population is organised, and there have been no major strikes by African workers in the last decade.[25] Out of an African industrial labour force of well over a million, the number of African workers officially listed as having been on strike was a mere 10 050 in 1956, and fell to 5 500 in 1960 and to 3 531 in 1967.[26]

A good example of these conditions is provided by a recent strike of Africans in Durban. In April 1968 about 2 000 African dockworkers struck in support of a demand for higher wages. Government and police officials were called in, and the Africans were given the choice of returning to work under existing conditions or being dismissed. About 1 500 of them were then dismissed, and given four hours to leave Durban. New dockworkers were obtained from African labour in and about Durban.[27] As the South African Institute of Race Relations commented:

> 'The whole episode . . . points to the helplessness of African workers, in the midst of a burgeoning national economy, in overcoming the obstacles facing them. They have no power to negotiate on their own behalf for better pay and working conditions.'[28]

African access to the means of economic power is also severely restricted by educational discrimination. The administration of African education is tightly controlled by the goverment under the Bantu Education Act of 1953, which also pegged government expenditure on African education at a fixed annual amount. While the proportion of state expenditure on education as a whole remained fairly constant between 1950 and 1963, the proportion of it devoted to African education has fallen from 0,57 per cent in 1953 to 0,396 per cent in 1966.[29] Per capita government expenditure on African education has also been declining, falling from R17,08 in 1953/54 to R11,50 in 1962/63, and remaining at about R12 for the rest of the 1960s. Real per capita expenditure on African education today is considerably less than it was twenty years ago (Horrell 1968a: 38–9).

African enrolment in primary schools has increased, but this is deceptive, owing to the high drop out rate and the concentration of pupils in the very lowest classes. Thus in 1962, 44 per cent of Africans in school were in the two lowest classes of primary school, while only 2,9 per cent were in any of the five forms of secondary school (Horrell 1965). In 1967, 71 per cent of all Africans in school were in the four lowest primary classes.[30] The proportion of school age Africans in secondary school has not been growing, it was 3,4 per cent in 1953 and 3,43 per cent in 1966.[31]

The conditions in African schools are inadequate in every respect. Whereas schooling is free and legally compulsory for Whites, it is neither for Africans. A high pupil-teacher ratio reflects the shortage of teachers, who are badly paid and on the whole poorly qualified. Because of the serious shortage of African schools, those that exist have to work double sessions. It is officially estimated that Soweto, Johannesburg's African town complex, is short of about 60 schools.[32] And the content of African education is closely determined by the government, which fixes the syllabus and aims to condition Africans into an acceptance of an inferior position in society.[33]

Conditions in higher education are no different. In 1968 the non-Whites, who make up four-fifths of South Africa's population, furnished less than 12 per cent of its university students.[34] Since 1959 all universities in South Africa have been segregated, and the facilities and opportunities in the non-White colleges are far inferior to those in the White Universities. In the academic year 1968–9, 10 740 degrees and diplomas of higher education were awarded to Whites, and 277 to Africans.[35] While the number of Whites attending vocational and technical schools has approached 100 000, the number of Africans in such schools remains a few thousand.[36]

This denial of trade union and educational rights and opportunities is reflected in the pattern of income distribution in South Africa. It is estimated that in 1969, the Africans – who form about 68 per cent of the population, received 18,8 per cent of South Africa's personal cash income, while the Whites – who make up only 19,2 per cent of the population, received about 74 per cent of it.[37] The average per capita income of Africans in 1969 is estimated to have been about eight per cent of that of Whites – an average of R7 per month compared to a White average of R95 per month.[38] The racial distribution of income in South Africa is thus characterised by a very high degree of inequality. This varies between different sectors of the economy: in manufacturing Whites earn about six times as much as Africans, while in mining they earn eighteen times as much – R304 per month compared to R17 per month for Africans (who receive however some payment in kind).[39] Even in manufacturing, it takes the average African worker a week to earn what the average White worker earns in a day.

The recent economic boom has fostered the idea that this income inequality has diminished. But in fact the reverse seems true. Between 1957 and 1967 the difference between the average monthly wages of Whites and Africans in the manufacturing industry rose from R120 to R194, and it was calculated that just to stop this difference from increasing, the percentage of future pay increases for Africans would have to be five and a half times greater than that of White pay increases (Hepple 1969:54). Between 1962 and 1967, White earnings in the manufacturing industry rose from 440 per cent to 485 per cent of those of non-Whites.[40] In the gold mining industry the gap has widened steadily. In 1911 the average cash earnings of White workers were 11,5 times those of non-White workers; in 1951 they were 14,5 times, and in 1966 17,5 times the African rate. It has been calculated that the real wages of African workers in South Africa's gold mines today are no higher and are possibly even lower than in 1911 (Wilson 1968). As one observer comments:

> 'It is true that Bantu wages have been increased in recent years . . . But if one takes into account the accompanying rises in the cost of living figures, one is struck by the ever-widening gap between White and non-White wages' (Malherbe 1969:34).

Thus simple statements about increases in African money wages have very little significance, because of inflation, because of far greater increases in White wages, and because of their arbitrary nature, since African workers are deprived of collective bargaining power. And it should be noted that the inequality of total assets in South Africa is much greater than the income disparity portrayed here.

All of the major White interest groups share responsibility for these conditions; they are not the product of apartheid policies alone. The employers, who in the prevailing thesis are pictured to be basically in conflict with White supremacy, in fact play an important role in determining African wage rates. The very low wages of African workers, and their negligible share in the distribution of income, indicate what the response of employers to the rightlessness of African workers has tended to be. They have sought, and obtained, cheap labour. The fact that the White workers also play a part in determining African Wages does not negate this responsibility of the employers. While the majority of real African wages have remained around or below the poverty line, productivity and profits have expanded enormously. By the beginning of 1967 the total net profits of over 200 South African companies had increased by R71,7 million in just four years.[41]

Economic development has thus not been undermining the basic labour structure of White supremacy in South Africa. Access by Africans to the essential means of economic power remains severely restricted and controlled, the distribution of income remains grossly unequal, and the general coercive powers of the government over African labour have been growing rather than diminishing. The core structure of labour discrimination remains strongly entrenched.

These conditions indicate the exploitative nature of the economic relationship between the Whites and the Africans. It is a master-servant relationship in all spheres, enforced through a variety of effective controls and sanctions. It is a system in which the Africans are forced to work for the Whites at bare subsistence wages, deprived of all basic rights to assert their interests freely and legally, and subject to some of the most draconian and tyrannical labour controls ever developed in modern history. The enormous power and prosperity of the Whites in South Africa is based on this systematic exploitation of African labour.

The strong persistence over time of this discriminatory labour structure testifies to the collaboration of the different White interest groups in perpetuating it. Capitalist business, far from being incompatible with the system, secures high profits through very cheap, unorganised and rightless labour; White nationalists and White workers obtain prosperity and the material strengthening of White supremacy.

In fact, far from undermining White supremacy, economic development is constantly reinforcing it. Its power structure is continually strengthened by its own material output. In a circular process, the African workers produce the wealth and power which enable the Whites to go on strengthening this structure of production which goes on producing the power which goes on strengthening the structure and so on. It is precisely the function of actual apartheid to render this process as effective as possible.

Concluding critique of the conventional wisdom

In attempting to shed more light on the relations between economic development, apartheid policies and White supremacy in South Africa, this analysis has simultaneously been developing a critique of the prevailing theory on this subject. It is proposed now to conclude this critique in a more unified and theoretical form, on the basis of the empirical analysis of the preceding sections.

It may be useful to set out briefly the essential tenets of the prevailing thesis, which are that:

1) the relations between economic development and the system of White supremacy are essentially conflicting and contradictory;

2) this is an expression both of the liberalising and integrative nature of the capitalist economy and/or of industrialisation, and of the rigidly ideological and segregative nature of apartheid policies and the system of White supremacy;

3) this conflict is apparent in the spheres of non-Whites geographical and occupational mobility, where developments are taking place which contradict apartheid and which are demonstrating its absurdity and impracticability;

4) the advantage in this conflict tends to lie with the forces of the market economy and industrial development, which tend towards integrated and rational functioning, because South Africa is seen as being incapable of tolerating for long the serious dysfunctions and inefficiencies that stem from the incompatibility of the imperatives of economic expansion and White supremacy. Over time, the already evident contradiction between these two imperatives will increase, at the expense of apartheid and White supremacy.

The great bulk of writing and comment on this issue, from academic work to the mass media, implicitly or explicitly adheres to parts or all of this interpretation. It constitutes the conventional wisdom on the subject. Thus one economic historian sees modern South African history as essentially the unfolding of a basic conflict between the free enterprise economy and the 'political factor', led by Afrikaner nationalism and controlling the government since 1948 (Horwitz 1967:1–7). Another sees the whole question in terms of a fundamental conflict between the 'liberating' forces of the capitalist economy and the 'subjugating' force of 'government interventionism,' concluding that 'the dissolution' of colour injustice has been continuously assisted by competitive capitalism (Hutt 1964:180). Countless articles in the mass media report and comment on the issues in terms of this general thesis.[42]

The basic weakness of this thesis lies in the assumptions which it makes about the imperatives of economic development and White supremacy, and about the relations between them. Capitalist development and industrialisation are assumed to be necessarily liberalising in their nature and effects. White supremacy on the other hand is assumed to be a quite distinct and separate phenomenon, and essentially the product of apartheid policies, which are seen to be the basic source of discrimination. The relations between the two are assumed to be fundamentally conflicting.

That these assumptions are not supported by the empirical evidence has been suggested earlier on. But there is in fact no logical *a priori* reason why they should hold true. The thesis that industrialisation and the market economy tend necessarily to liberalise inegalitarian structures of group relations is untenable, as Herbert Blumer (1965) has shown for instance in his useful paper 'Industrialisation and Race Relations.' Nor, when one considers the likely interests of capitalism and White colonialism in each other, should the assumption that they are basically incompatible seem at all logically necessary. But the actual compatibility between them, and its empirical manifestation, are not considered by the conventional thesis, which instead begins with this unwarranted polarisation of the situation into 'economic' and 'political' spheres that are somehow quite separate and incompatible.

Given these invalid assumptions, it is not surprising that the perspective in which the thesis goes on to define and investigate the issues is highly misleading. Attention focuses on the constraining effects of the system of White supremacy on aspects of capitalist development, which are taken to be the manifestation of the alleged incompatability (thus diverting critical investigation away from the points of real compatibility). The 'problems' of business in its 'conflict' with government policies, and the economic inefficiencies resulting from these policies, are emphasized. The central importance of the occupational and geographical colour bars as obstacles to further economic expansion is an invariable conclusion.

The following passage offers a good specific example of this interpretation. After commenting on the widening gap between White and non-White wages, a recent research paper goes on to say:

> 'Merely raising non-White wages by itself is not the solution . . . What is needed rather is to create a much larger national cake in which case fairer slices could be distributed on the basis of higher contributions. To sum up, this implies simply the more productive use of non-White labour and the related requirements of education . . . accompanied by geographical and vertical mobility. Herein however lies the conflict between the worship of a myth and the country's economic development' (Malherbe 1969:34).

This contains within a short space most of the key tenets of the thesis: the assumptions – that the real conflict is between 'the worship of a myth' and 'the country's economic development,' and that the solution lies in greater economic expansion *per se:* and the conclusions – that this solution is secured through the more productive employment of non-White labour, which means that the most important economic colour bars are those which tend to prevent this – the occupational and geographical ones. This overlooks the significant facts – which need to be explained – that the 'national cake' *has* expanded rapidly within the framework of White supremacy, and that this has not produced a more equitable distribution of wealth and power, and that the colour bars in question are being administered flexibly anyway.

The serious limitations of this theory, and the nature of the empirical evidence, as set out in the earlier sections, give rise to the thesis developed in this analysis. Its essential tenets are that:

1) the relations between capitalist development, apartheid policies and the core structure of White supremacy are essentially collaborative, and conflicts which do take place between them are only over the marginal distribution of class benefits and constraints;

2) this is an expression both of the extensive compatibility of capitalist interests with the relations of production maintained by actual apartheid and embodied in the power structure of White supremacy, and of the pragmatic nature of actual apartheid in its pursuit of an economically powerful White supremacy;

3) this is apparent in – (a) the absence of significant contradiction between economic development and apartheid policies where it is alleged to exist, (b) the absence of such contradiction in other spheres that are also of greater importance to both capitalism and White supremacy, and (c) the strong persistence over time of the core structure of labour discrimination;

4) in fact, quite contrary to the prevailing thesis, White supremacy is continually being re-inforced by economic development.

Proponents of the prevailing theory tend to assert that 'development cannot be separated,' but ignore the fact that it *is* being separated fairly effectively in South Africa, and that the ways in which it is not are of only marginal importance to the power structure of White colonialism and the aims of actual apartheid. To say that 'apartheid is never going to be realised,' is to misunderstand the nature of actual apartheid, and to ignore the fact that its real goal of an economically powerful White supremacy is already being extensively realised. The future mode of 'separate development' in South Africa is thus not some vague mystery, but very likely to be essentially an extension and refinement of the particular structure of White supremacy currently being developed by actual apartheid.

Another common assumption is that somehow prosperity is mellowing the commitment of Whites to White domination. This is not confirmed by the evidence however. The trend of election voting in the last twenty years has moved steadily to the right. Most of the Whites are grateful to the Nationalist government for the way in which it has secured prosperity and strengthened White supremacy at the same time. The norms of acquisitive individualism and those of White colonialism are co-existing harmoniously together, with the former tending to dominate material life style, and the latter continuing to dominate political perceptions and behaviour. Until there is substantial evidence to the contrary, there is every reason to believe that this will continue to be the case.

With all its attention on economic inefficiencies and alleged incompatibilities, the conventional thesis tends very largely to ignore the considerable measure of success of actual apartheid in realising its dual goals. Explaining the extent of this success would mean analysing its structural causes, which in turn would mean recognising the collaborative nature of the relations between private economic power, apartheid and White colonialism. Emphasizing the 'failures' of the system has provided a diversion from having to analyse these underlying causes of its continuity and success. As one writer comments:

> 'To assert that the system is going to disintegrate is wishful thinking. It is the liberal conscience which refuses to see that power is exercised precisely because of the mediation of these 'dysfunctions' . . . In other words, to believe (for it is indeed a belief) that the machine will break down is to spare oneself from explaining why it does not, and has no *internal* reason for doing so – if one but considers the dynamism which it has expressed for years.'

An accurate understanding of what is really happening in South Africa, and of the true nature of the relations between the economic system, actual apartheid and White supremacy, is thus precluded by the assumptions and analytical framework of the prevailing thesis. The ideological significance of this is perhaps worth pointing out, in view of a not infrequent tendency in some quarters to dismiss radically different theses as being invalid because they are alleged to be 'ideological'. For this predominant thesis – whether its adherents are aware of this or not – serves an ideological function, in diverting critical attention away from the extensive collaboration of the capitalist system – both in South Africa and internationally – in the economic operation of White supremacy.

The conventional wisdom concerning economic development in South Africa is thus not only of limited analytical value, but also has a certain ideological significance. It is hoped that this study may contribute to the development of a useful alternative framework for the continuing analysis of these various aspects of White supremacy in South Africa.

NOTES

1. For more information on the South African economy and its development, see D. H. Houghton, *The South African Economy*, Cape Town: Oxford University Press, 1967, 2nd edn. Between 1962 and 1966 South Africa had the second highest real growth rate in the world (nearly seven per cent per annum surpassed only by Japan's nine per cent) (*Financial Mail*, Johannesburg, 6 September 1968, 833).
2. The tenets of this thesis will be set out more fully in the third section.
3. In this study, attention to the non-Whites is concentrated essentially on the Africans, since they form such a large percentage both of the total population (nearly 70 per cent) and of the non-White population (about 85 per cent), because the disabilities of the Indians and Coloureds, while severe, are less so and less uniform than those of the Africans, and because the Africans form the bottom part of the power pyramid.
4. South African Bureau of Statistics, *Urban and Rural Population of South Africa*, 1904 to 1960, Report 02–02–01 Pretoria, 1968, Table 1.5, 5.
5. Ibid. The 1968 estimate is that of Market Research Africa, *The Times, Supplement on South Africa*, 27 October 1969, 7.
6. Trade Union Council of South Africa (TUCSA), *Labour in South Africa: A Statistical Analysis of the Changing face of the South African Manufacturing Labour Force* (Johannesburg, 1967), 1–2.
7. The five year development plans of the South African Department of Planning estimate that even with an annual immigration of 30 000 Whites, the demand for skilled workers in the early 1970s will exceed the supply by tens of thousands (TUCSA, *Labour Research in South Africa* Johannesburg, 1967 5–6; *The Times Supplement* 1969, 13).
8. International Labour Office, *Fifth Special Report of the Director General on the Application of the Declaration concerning the Policy of 'Apartheid' of the Republic of South Africa* Geneva, 1969, 8. It was one such removal, to a place called Limehill in January 1969, in which about 2 000 Africans were taken away from their homes in trucks and left in fields without housing, sanitation, running water or firewood, that became a public scandal. (See press reports, and South African Institute of Race Relations, *A Survey of Race Relations in South Africa*, 1968 Johannesburg, 1969, 126 *et seq.*)
9. Between November 1967 and April 1968 an average of about 1 400 Africans were endorsed out of Johannesburg every month. (*House of Assembly Debates*, 7 May 1969, col. 4 766).
10. E.g. speech by G. F. van L. Froneman, Deputy Chairman of the Bantu Affairs Commission, May 1968, cited in *Survey of Race Relations 1968*, 166–7.
11. The best detailed analysis of the whole complex of discriminatory labour controls in South Africa is to be found in the reports of the International Labour Office. I.L.O., *Declaration concerning the Policy of 'Apartheid' and I.L.O. Programme for the Elimination of 'Apartheid' in Labour Matters in the Republic of South Africa* Geneva 1964; and annual *Special Reports of the Director-General on the Application of the Declaration concerning the Policy of 'Apartheid' of the Republic of South Africa*, Geneva 1965–9.
12. For details of the contents of these and other relevant measures, see I.L.O. *Programme* and *Reports*. The government is seeking to extend its powers over African labour in the 'White' areas through the present Bantu Laws Amendment Bill, which would give the government more sweeping control over the employment and residential rights of Africans. See, e.g., speech of Deputy Minister of Bantu Administration and Education, *House of Assembly Debates*, 18 June 1969.

13. Quoted in the *Financial Mail*, 19 July 1968, 198 (author's italics).
14. This Act provides that government permission is necessary for most forms of industrial development (zoning of new industrial land, establishment of new industrial townships and expansion of a factory – including any increase in the African labour force) in proclaimed areas. In January 1968 all the main industrial areas of South Africa except Natal's were declared proclaimed under this Act.
15. TUCSA, *The Industrial Development of the Border Areas of South Africa*, Johannesburg, 1966, 8, 41.
16. Ibid., 43–4. For example Wage Determination No. 235 (Soap, Candles, Edible Oils and Fats Industry); No. 240 (Labourers' Wages in Estcourt); No. 244 (Ladies' Stocking Industry in East London). In the last case, the median wage for a labourer was R9,75 per week, and the newly prescribed wage rate was R6,00.
17. *House of Assembly Debates*, 20 February 1968, col. 851.
18. *House of Assembly Debates*, 9 June 1967, cols. 7481–4.
19. For example, by the industrial agreement reached between the employers and White trade unions in the steel and engineering industry in 1968, the employers and White workers secured benefits (dilution of some jobs, job reservation in others, higher wages and benefits at the expense of the African workers, who received negligible wage increases for higher graded and previously higher paying jobs). *Financial Mail*, 15 and 29 March 1968, and *Survey of Race Relations*, 1968, 88–9.
20. Various cost of living studies, cited by the Director of the Institute of Race Relations, *Race Relations News*, Johannesburg, May 1969, 5.
21. Horrell 1968b:35; *Financial Mail*, 18 April 1969, 169. The poverty datum line was R53 per month.
22. See also J. F. Potgieter, 'Incidence of Nutritional Deficiency Diseases Among the Bantu and Coloured Populations in South Africa,' ibid., 18 June 1966, 505.
23. E.g. section 21 of the General Law Amendment Act defines *sabotage* in very sweeping terms, including the putting out of action of a large number of essential services and facilities, or encouragement to do so, with a *minimum* penalty of five years' imprisonment, and liability for the death penalty for any such action. This would apply for instance to any strike by African workers which, *inter alia*, had the effect of injuring, obstructing or putting out of action the supply and distribution of light, power, water, fuel or foodstuffs, or the postal, telegraph and telephone services, or the free movement of traffic, or the property of any person or of the State. See ILO *Programme*, 35–6. At the beginning of 1969, nearly 1 000 Africans were detained in prison under the General Law Amendment Act, the Suppression of Communism Act, the Unlawful Organisations Act, and the Terrorism Act. *House of Assembly Debates*, 30 May 1969, col. 6948.
24. United Nations Economic and Social Council (ECOSOC), *Allegations regarding the Infringement of Trade Union Rights in the Republic of South Africa*, UN Document E/4459, Geneva, 1968, 87.
25. United Nations, ECOSOC, *A Study of Apartheid and Racial Discrimination in Southern Africa*, UN Document E/CN.4/949, Geneva 1967, 119; M. Horrell, 'The Non-White Workers in South Africa,' *Race Relations News*, September 1969, 2; TUCSA, *Labour Research in South Africa*, 12–13.
26. South African Bureau of Statistics, *South African Statistics 1968*, Pretoria, 1968, H–58.
27. *Race Relations News*, May 1969, 1.
28. Ibid. For more information on the comprehensive barriers against African labour organisation, see ILO *Programme* and *Reports*, and the ECOSOC report, *Allegations regarding Infringements of Trade Union Rights*, 1968.
29. United Nations, ECOSOC, *Study of Apartheid*, 149.
30. Horrell, 1968a 51–2. South African government statistics in general, and on education for example, must be treated with caution, for they are sometimes deliberately misleading. Thus for instance a recent survey compares relative school attendance in South Africa with

several other countries, and then claims that South Africa has with New Zealand 'the distinction of having the highest percentage of its population at primary and secondary schools amongst all the countries referred to,' when in fact all the Table does is divide the *White* population *only* by the number of Whites at school (*South African Statistics 1968*, Table 5, 77).

31. United Nations, ECOSOC, *Study of Apartheid*, 154.
32. Report of the Bantu Education Department to the Johannesburg City Council. *The Star*, Johannesburg, weekly edn., 17 May 1969.
33. For more information on the content of African education in South Africa, see UNESCO, *The Effects of Apartheid on Education, Science, Culture and Information* (Paris, 1968).
34. *Survey of Race Relations* 1968, 254; *Cape Argus*, Cape Town, 16 April 1969.
35. *House of Assembly Debates*, 13 May 1969, col. 5834.
36. United Nations, ECOSOC, *Study of Apartheid*, 157.
37. *Financial Mail*, 18 April 1969, 169, reporting on research of Market Research Africa.
38. Ibid.
39. Ibid.
40. *Financial Mail*, 6 September, 1968, 833.
41. *Financial Mail*, 2 February 1968. Between 1960 and 1964 the total profits of manufacturing firms in South Africa rose from R236 million to R406 million, and between 1956 and 1966 the dividends declared by mining companies rose from R108 million to R237 million (*South African Statistics* 1968, M-44, L-5).
42. For instance articles in the *Financial Mail*, and in *The Times Supplement on South Africa*, 27 October 1969, and *The Economist Supplement on South Africa*, 29 June 1968.
43. S. Thion, *Le Pouvoir Pale, ou Le Racisme Sud-Africain*, Paris, 1969, 103. Translation: This does not mean that the system is not threatened, both internally and externally, but that it is not threatened in the way it is conventionally alleged to be. For a most important contribution to the analysis of Southern Africa and the critique of the conventional wisdom, see the writings of G. Arrighi (*The Political Economy of Rhodesia* (The Hague, 1967), and various articles).

REFERENCES

Blumer, H. 1965 – 'Industrialisation and race relations.' In G. Hunter (ed.) *Industrialisation and Race Relations*. London:Oxford University Press.

Hepple, A. 1969 – *South Africa: Workers under Apartheid*. London: Christian Action Publications.

Horrell, M. 1965 – 'Some educational statistics,' S.A. Institute of Race Relations research paper, Johannesburg, 6.

——1968a – *Bantu Education up to 1968* Johannesburg: SAIRR.

——1968b – *Introduction to South Africa: Basic Facts and Figures*. Johannesburg: SAIRR.

——1969 – *Survey of Race Relations* – Johannesburg: SAIRR 1970.

Horwitz, R. 1967 – *The Political Economy of South Africa*. London: Weidenfeld and Nicolson.

Hutt, W. H. 1964 – *The Economics of the Colour Bar*. London: Institute of Economic Affairs.

Leary, P. M. and Lewis, J. E. S. 1965 – 'Some observations on the state of nutrition of infants and toddlers in Sekhukhuniland' *South African Medical Journal, Nutrition Supplement*, 18 December, 1157.

Malherbe, E. G. 1969 – *Bantu Manpower and Education*. Johannesburg: SAIRR.

Richardson, B. D. 1968 – 'Mortality rates in preschool children,' *South African Medical Journal, Nutrition Supplement*, 21, September, 964.

Thion, S. 1969 – *Le Pouvoir Pale, ou le Racisme Sud-Africain*, Paris: Du Seuil.

Wilson, D. F. 1968 – 'Gold wage inquiry a must.' Based on Ph.D. research. *Financial Mai* 10 May.

2. The Abolition of the Masters and Servants Act

COLIN BUNDY

Commentators in the South African press hailed with hearty satisfaction last October's (1974) announcement that the Masters and Servants laws were to be abolished. It was 'one of the most enlightened legislative moves in years': it represented a 'new deal' for agricultural and domestic employees; such 'a wise decision' was 'excellent news for South Africa'; and, more generally, the step was applauded as further instance of the less dogmatic, more flexible, and increasingly 'modern' approach of the Vorster regime.

These reactions fall some way short of an adequate or accurate response to the abolition of the Masters and Servants legislation. Certain other questions arise. Why did South Africa retain these laws a century after Britain repealed essentially the same statutes? Is there any similarity between their repeal in Britain in 1875 and in South Africa in 1974? Why did the laws exist in the first place; in whose interests did they chiefly operate; and have they ceased to do so now?

The Historic Context

Viewed historically in the context of class relations between (predominantly White) employers and (pre-dominantly Black) employees, certain obvious features of the legislation's past strike one immediately. The first is that the laws were originally enacted when the overwhelming number of employers were farmers; secondly, that they have remained most relevant and most frequently applied in agricultural labour relations. In the wider social context, the Masters and Servants legislation was conspicuously clumsy and ineffective, and came to be replaced by other more specific, more complex measures to control the labour force. Finally, that by the time of their repeal, the laws were of very slight overall significance in disciplining Black labourers in South Africa, and cost White employers very little.

The legal emancipation of slaves in the Cape was enacted in Westminster in 1834. The buying and selling of servants, as well as the total restraints on slave mobility, were ended; but many features of the Master/Slave relationship continued to be reproduced in the system of 'free' labour that succeeded it. Certain of these features were actually buttressed by legislation – the Masters and Servants laws exemplified such legislative efforts. Particularly on farms, relations between employer and employee resembled in important aspects owner/ slave relations: the payment of workers at a subsistence level, the degree of physical discipline administered by the farmer, and the ambivalent interdependence between farmer and farm-workers, living on – and off – the same land, jointly experiencing, in tragically opposite ways, the ties of dominance and bondage.

Legal emancipation was not accompanied by social emancipation: without education, without political rights, without a base of economic independence, ex-slaves could not withhold their labour even at the low wage levels being offered. At the same time that slave labour was replaced by cheap labour, there began the process of transforming tribesmen into low-paid agricultural workers, not only through the dispossession of the African tribesman's lands, but also through his involvement in a system of rents, taxes, and fees, and his integration into exchange economy (cf. Bundy 1972).

The Cape Masters and Servants Act

In the Cape, the Master and Servant laws of 1841, and especially the law of 1856, were ostensibly colour blind, and were also 'fair' in that they spelled out obligations of both masters and servants. But since almost all masters were white, and almost all browns were servants, an apparently race-free law consolidated rather than weakened race domination. The main effect of the law was to entrench the class rather than the colour aspect of racial domination – to strengthen Whites at the expense of Blacks – within the framework of a law that was tilted in favour of masters at the expense of their servants.

The 1856 law made the registration of contracts compulsory, and made the breach of contract by master *or* servant illegal. The range of offences constituting breach of contract by a servant, as well as the severity of the penalties thus incurred, made the law harsher than its predecessor. Breach of contract by a servant was defined to include insubordination, neglect, insulting behaviour, and desertion. Breaches were punishable by fines and/or imprisonment.

The main author of the 1856 act was J. C. Molteno, the most prominent spokesman of the Cape farmers. Farmers in the Cape then, as throughout the nineteenth century, complained bitterly of a 'labour shortage' – they complained, that is, that at the wages they were offering, an insufficient stream of brown or black labour was forthcoming. (The several commissions appointed to gnaw away at this perennial problem all contained abundant evidence that African farm labour *was available* where higher wages were paid; but that African peasants, preferred to wring a living off their own land, or off white-owned land that they occupied on a quasifeudal basis, rather than working for low wages.) To these farmers, the Act represented the enrolment of the force of the State on their behalf: the controls and discipline which the farmer had hitherto exercised haphazardly, on a private and individual basis, the court-based administrative machinery could now exercise systematically, publicly, and on a large scale.

The extent to which the statutes were an attempt to bind the farm worker to his employer through coercion and discipline rather than through the 'laws of supply and demand', dear to the political economists of the nineteenth century, was made very clear in the Cape by an amendment of 1873. This discriminated against farm servants, making them liable to a particularly harsh penalty – imprisonment with hard labour, spare diet, and solitary confinement. In Natal, the law of 1850 relied heavily on intimidation and discipline: it included a flogging clause (Natal earned the grim soubriquet of the 'lashing colony' in the late nineteenth century) that qualified minor infringements of the 'proper' behaviour of servants for severe corporal punishment.

Master and Servant statutes were also passed in the Boer republics (Transvaal 1880, Orange Free State 1904) and all Master and Servants legislation continued to operate with minor amendments in the Union and then the Republic of South Africa.

The Act during the Twentieth Century

The legislation came in the twentieth century to be applied almost exclusively to Africans in agricultural and domestic service. An important amendment of 1930 saw the laws extended to cover labour tenants (as well as wage labourers) on White farms, an application that had been held invalid in a 1921 court case. This was significant inasmuch as labour tenancy long remained, in South Africa's rural areas, preferable in the eyes of Black labourers to complete proletarianization.

Prosecutions under the Masters and Servants laws showed a gradual, steady decline in the twentieth century: in 1928, there were some 43 000 prosecutions; in 1955 28 500 prosecutions; in 1968 just 23 000, while for the year ended 30th June 1973, there were 16 477 cases in terms of Masters and Servants laws *and* the Bantu Labour Registration Act. This decline – quite evident in absolute terms – is even more striking when viewed in relation to prosecutions under other legislation. Other laws that directly affected the mobility and 'obedience' of African workers, like the pass laws, trespass and vagrancy laws were applied with an enormously accelerated frequency: in 1928 there were 44 000 pass law prosecutions and 10 000 for trespass; in 1960 the respective totals were 670 000 and 166 000 prosecutions. In short, the use of Master and Servant laws to bring offending employees to book declined quite sharply at the same time that other statutory controls over Black South Africans were being greatly extended and intensified. The reason for this will become clear below: Before making them explicit, it may be instructive to examine the operation of the British Masters and Servants law in the nineteenth century, and see what grounds there exist for comparison between metropolis and colonies.

The British Act

In Britain, the early 1820s was a period of sharp conflict between capitalist employers and the 'combinations'(as the infant trade unions were known). In 1824, under intense pressure from Westminster Radicals, the House of Commons repealed all the statutes that made combinations illegal. In the following year, the Ministers 'came to the conclusion that they had been guilty of a serious blunder' (cf. Halévy 1961) in this blanket repeal. An Act was passed which sharply restricted the forms that combinations might take; a step, comments the great liberal historian Halévy, that appeared to discover a method 'by which disorder among the working class could be suppressed' even while conferring upon the proletarian the right to organize (cf. Halévy 1961).

During this same phase of acute class conflict, the Masters and Servants Act of 1823 was passed. At its heart were provisions that discriminated against the servant: the master who broke his contract was liable to *civil* action for damages or the recovery of the wages due, while the defaulting servant was punished for a *criminal* act, and liable to hard labour for three months. Breach of contract by a servant was widely defined: not only failure to enter in service, or absence from service, but also any 'neglect' or 'misdemeanour or misconduct' in the execution of contracted service.

A Remnant of Earlier Legislation

This law drew on earlier legislation – especially the lengthy Tudor statute of 1563 – and indeed possessed a lineage that extended back to the fourteenth century. At that time, wage labour was making its first general appearance in England, mainly in the form of commodity production based on domestic industries; and legislators devised contractual relationships that nestled within the prevalent unfree labour relations of the late feudal period. In essence, the Masters and Servants laws were not part of the general law of contract, but the tail end of the penal labour laws essential to the early growth of the capitalist system in Western Europe. By the nineteenth century, the law of 1823 was 'the last remnant of extra-economic compulsion to labour' (cf. Simon n.d.).

The number of prosecutions in England under the 1823 Act, according to a detailed study of the operation of the law, declined relative to the number of employees: between 1858 and 1875 (for which years statistics are available) an average of 10 000 cases a year were prosecuted in England and Wales. The source of these prosecutions in terms of which employers used the law – is emphasized in Simon's study: essentially, the law was the recourse of the small employer. In the textile, coal and iron industries, prosecutions were initiated by 'small and backward undertakings' (Simon n.d.).

In addition to this pattern in the industries mentioned, the Act was also commonly used in agriculture. Simons writes that where 'old yearly hirings still survived, as they did very extensively in agriculture, prosecutions were apt to be frequent'; she adds later that in agriculture 'prosecutions were certainly very common.' A member of Parliament testified in 1865 that

> 'when the spring of the year came round and labour bore a high price . . . a great number of agricultural labourers found themselves in consequence the inmates of a gaol because they . . . attempted to break their contracts with their masters.' (Simon n.d.).

In other words, Simon illustrates very clearly that in the British instance, the Masters and Servants Act was relied on by employers who found it hard to keep labourers in the face of competition from larger and more successful capitalists. The repeal of the legislation in 1875 came after years of militant trade union pressure, at a time when the law 'was no longer worth preserving' as far as the most wealthy and influential part of the capitalist class was concerned. In the same way that mid-Victorian entrepreneurs jettisoned protection for free trade, relying on the operation of the market to secure their profits, so they embraced the mobility of a free proletariat instead of having labourers inhibited by the workings of a law harking back to a much earlier stage of capital accumulation.

Implications for the South African Case

Simon's study has significant implications for the South African case. We have already seen that the nineteenth century statutes in South Africa were urged by farming interests, and also that their use became almost exclusively restricted to agricultural and domestic service in the twentieth century. As in Britain, 'small and backward' employers were the beneficiaries of the law. In contrast to nineteenth century Britain, however, the electoral and representative power of agrarian capital remained far more powerful. Any suggestion of repealing the Masters and Servants legislation before – say – 1960 would have encountered stern resistance from a sizeable farming interest.

Other Legislative Controls

The policy of the Nationalist government has operated, in several respects, to make the Masters and Servants laws increasingly anachronistic. First, the barrage of laws that controls, directs, and disciplines the black labour force has been rationalized, centralized and strengthened. In particular, the Bantu Laws Amendment Act (67 of 1964) is a legislative keystone, with the registration of black workers at labour bureaux and the subsequent directives – or endorsements; while the huge administrative structure of surveillance/arrest/punishment that rests on the Pass Laws makes state control over labour as pervasive and potent as it is. It will be readily appreciated how cumbersome are the workings of the Masters and Servants laws – with the need for the employer to be involved in a court case for each offender – compared with the sweeping bureaucratic vigilance and ubiquity. And how irrelevant and blunt a penalty is a few months imprisonment when compared with the abilities of Bantu Affairs officials to correlate, canalise, and centralise the 'labour units' – to dictate, that is, the lives of workers involved in a migrant system that takes on more and more of the characteristics of bureaucratically ordered forced labour.

Destruction of Labour Tenant System

Even the farmers, for so long the twentieth century beneficiaries of laws that even in the nineteenth century were retrogressive, have recently found the Masters and Servants code less necessary to secure the labour of underpaid, rightless workers, less essential to punish labour tenants who retained distinct rights, however limited, on White-owned lands. The success of the government in reducing labour tenants to the status of wage labourers has greatly exceeded the success of all previous efforts in pursuit of a long-standing policy. The Bantu Law Amendment Act of 1964 gave the labour authorities far greater control over labour tenants, and the number of registered tenants fell from 163 000 in 1964 to 27 585 by 1970, until in 1973 it was announced that there were no longer any labour tenants in the Cape, Free State or Transvaal, and only 16 000 in Natal. (House of Assembly Debates 13/6/73.)

Influx Control

Parallel with the destruction of the labour tenant and squatting systems on South African farms, and their replacement with full time wage labour, has been the greatly increased influx control of urban Africans. The fears of White South African farmers – fears that have matured for 150 years – that African labour will be attracted away from the farms into the cities have been greatly soothed. A single quotation demonstrates eloquently enough the advantages of centralized labour control laws over the Master and Servant statutes:

> A record of every registered Bantu farm labourer is kept in a central register in Pretoria, and the position is that the labourer cannot be employed in the urban areas, because as soon as his service contract must be registered, it will be established that he is a farm labourer, and then he cannot legally be taken into service (Vosloo 1968).

Conclusion

In conclusion, the Masters and Servants laws in South Africa, as in Britain, served to benefit the most backward employers in a capitalist economy; as that economy became more industrialized, they played an increasingly insignificant and ineffectual role in coercing and controlling labourers, and were largely replaced by more effective because more specific and more highly centralized measures.

Even so, they were retained long, long after their abolition would have been tolerated with equanimity by South Africa's larger, least backward, employers: they were retained because they were still of some use, specifically to those farmers who relied on indentured workers and labour tenants. In Britain their repeal came about through a combination of trade union opposition and a willingness on the part of the industrial capitalists to abolish an archaic law. In South Africa, the colonial setting and the historical suppression of Black workers' organizations precluded effective union pressure against the laws.

When pressure did come, it did so partly in the form of a generalized movement by Black workers for better conditions, and partly in the form of specific pressure from an external group of workers. Dockworkers and miners in Mobile, Alabama, refused to discharge South African coal from a ship, citing a clause in the 1930 tariff that prohibited importations of goods produced under forced labour. The repeal of the penal provisions of the Masters and Servants code seems to have removed the grounds for the court action pressed for by the United Mineworkers Union in Alabama to prevent the importing of South African coal.

Gracefully enough, the South African government announced its intention to repeal the laws that had attracted such pointed critical attention. It could conduct the repeal with something of a flourish secure in the knowledge that even the (politically so influential) 'small and backward' agricultural employers were sufficiently equipped with other means to acquiesce in the employers' consensus that the Masters and Servants legislation was not only anachronistic but also obsolete.

REFERENCES

1. Bundy, C. 1972 – 'The emergence and decline of a South African peasantry.' *African Affairs*, October.
2. Halévy, E. 1961 – *History of the English People in the* 19*th Century*, Vol. 2. Benn.
3. Ibid., 210.
4. D. Simon: 'Masters and servants.' In J. Saville (ed.) *Labour and Democracy.*
5. Ibid.
6. Quoted in Simon, op. cit.
7. House of Assembly, Debates, 13/6/73.
8. A. H. Vosloo, Deputy Minister of Bantu Development, opening an agricultural show at Middleburg 25/4/68. (University of Cape Town Wages Commission: Report on Farm Labour.)

Part 11:

Research: Problems and Opportunities

Introduction

M. H. VON BROEMBSEN

The first reading in this section gives a good history of the development of social research in South Africa, and covers a number of problems that the social researcher might encounter while conducting research. The second reading deals with the problems of conducting race relations research, a topic of central interest in South Africa. The article also provides the reader with an idea of what has been done in this area of research, and suggests many avenues for future research. Both readings are abbreviated versions of the originals.

The readings are also chosen for both the thought and debate which they might stimulate. For example, Welsh, in the first article, states that some scholars believe that the Human Sciences Research Council (HSRC), a government-sponsored research and funding organization, prefers to allocate funds for non-controversial research. In the following reading Lever notes that the HSRC, which is in a position to discourage research in the controversial field of race relations, does not do so.

Another point raised by Welsh provides stimulation for thought concerning academic freedom to conduct research and the ethics of research. Welsh notes that the research conducted by E. G. Malherbe in the 1930s into the extent of bilingualism amongst Whites evoked comment from the Church and an attack in Parliament. Welsh seems to be illustrating the point that certain types of research may be of such a sensitive nature that it eventually comes under the close scrutiny of the Church and Parliament, and raises a question of academic freedom. He notes that in this case Malherbe 'questioned children, without the parents' consent, on a variety of household affairs.'

When one considers the question of ethics of research, which includes the principle of informed consent and voluntary participation, this incident must be viewed in a different light. Should individual rights to privacy be infringed upon, the question of academic freedom should be subordinate to the question of ethics. This case should have become a controversial issue, not for the reasons cited, but rather on the grounds that the households being studied were not afforded the opportunity of refusing to participate – i.e. information was being gathered through a third party, the children.

It is worth noting that as a result of experiments being conducted on prisoners in the United States without their knowledge, severe restrictions have been placed on researchers dealing with human subjects in that country. These restrictions are designed to protect the individual rights of subjects. For a good overview of the subject of ethics of social research the reader may wish to consult Babbie (1973: Ch. 19). For an interesting example of how one researcher dealt with the moral and ethical problems of research, see Wallis (1977), and the comment on Wallis' observations by Gaiman (1977). These two articles point out some ethical problems that researchers must face, and how researcher and subject may interpret data and evidence in different ways.

Although the readings are informative and may stimulate thought on issues of research (and I have mentioned only two issues above), and Welsh does point to the practical problems of obtaining permits to enter certain areas and the mistrust that may arise, there are also other problems which have not been addressed. Even if the problems of obtaining funds and permits are overcome, the social researcher must still overcome the problems of sampling and gathering the required information. Standard sampling techniques, as described in Babbie (1973) and a host of other texts on methodology, may be used. However, survey techniques such as mail questionnaires and telephone interviews which are currently popular in the developed countries, obviously must be used with caution in South Africa. High mobility of the population, illiteracy and a low proportion of households with access to telephones make mail questionnaires and telephone interviews impractical techniques in many cases. The researcher is thus often required to indulge in what Welsh terms 'the art of the impossible.'

While the above by no means covers the whole field of problems and opportunities for research, and indeed only scratches the surface of the topic, the serious student is encouraged to consult other books and articles. For example, Wiendieck (1975) points to the need for the careful operationalization of concepts and scales in the study of ethnic attitudes. This article stimulated an exchange of views between Lever (1976) and Wiendieck (1976) which highlight the problems of the reliability and validity of research.

REFERENCES

Babbie, E. R. 1970 – *Survey Research Methods*. Belmont, California: Wadsworth.

Gaiman, David 1977 – 'A Scientologist's Comment.' In C. Bell and H. Newby (eds.). *Doing Sociological Research*. George Allen and Unwin: London.

Lever, H. 1975 – 'Some problems of race relations research in South Africa.' *Social Dynamics*, 1, 1, 31–44.

——1976 – 'A critical note on Wiendieck's views on attitude measurement.' *Social Dynamics*, 2, 1, 60–2.

Wallis, Roy 1977 – 'The moral career of a research project.' In C. Bell and H. Newby (eds.). *Doing Sociological Research*. George Allen and Unwin: London.

Welsh, D. 1975 – 'Social research in a divided society: The case of South Africa.' *Social Dynamics* ,1, 1, 19–30.

Wiendieck, G. 1975 – 'The behavioural relevance of ethnic attitude studies.' *Social Dynamics*, 1, 2, 125–42.

——1976 – 'A further note on the problem of measuring ethnic attitudes.' *Social Dynamics*, 2, 1, 63–5.

1. Social Research in a Divided Society: The Case of South Africa

DAVID WELSH

Social research in South African universities, at least on any sizeable scale, is a comparatively recent phenomenon. The major emphasis in research has traditionally been in the physical and natural sciences. Writing in 1932 an American observer, Robert Herndon Fife, explained this emphasis in terms of South Africa's 'newness' as a country which made conditions difficult for maintaining European standards of life. Research was viewed in instrumental or utilitarian terms which meant that universities allocated much the greater proportion of their funds and energies to the physical and natural sciences, whose 'pay-off' in these terms is greater than those of the humanities or social sciences (Fife 1932).

Substantially the same analysis holds good today. In 1971 a total of approximately R45 million was spent on research and development, of which about R29 million was spent by the state and the remainder by industry. Of this little over one per cent was allocated to the social sciences.

Official reports published in 1938, 1939, and 1940 showed conclusively that university institutions were conducting only limited research, in all fields. They were understaffed, starved of funds for research, and handicapped by inadequate libraries. Although there were varying degrees of emphasis on its centrality in a university's role, the universities and university colleges were favourably disposed to the sponsoring of research. The constraints, however, forced them to remain substantially in the high-school mould as primarily teaching and examining institutions.

The major source of research funds was the state. A Research Grant Board established in 1918 provided paltry sums for university research. The National Bureau of Educational and Social Research was established in 1929 to serve all those state departments which dealt with educational and social welfare: by 1939 the government was spending about £6 000 p.a. on the Bureau, compared with £200 000 p.a. spent on agricultural research. To be sure, these limited funds were augmented by generous grants from the Carnegie Corporation of New York, which funded the first major sociological investigation into the poor White problem.

In 1937 the Bureau invited applications for research grants from funds given by the Carnegie Corporation. The response from the universities, however, was largely disappointing. In attempting to ascertain why this was so the Bureau elicited from the universities an acknowledgement that insufficient research work was being conducted in the educational and social fields. Apart from the general constraining factors cited above, the universities singled out further handicaps that were peculiar to educational and social research. First, these areas were relatively new as fields of scholarly investigation; secondly, there was a shortage of trained investigators who could train others in the techniques of social research; thirdly, there was a serious deficiency of public statistics relating to such issues as unemployment, housing, income distribution and, especially, the vital and social statistics of the African and Coloured populations.

Significantly, nearly all the universities stressed the need for research into the problems arising out of the racial issue. One of the projects funded was a study of the origins and incidence of miscegenation in South Africa during the seventeenth and eighteenth centuries. A more controversial topic in the South African context can hardly be imagined! It appears, however, never to have emerged as a published study.

Politicians, university administrators and academics themselves expressed wholehearted support for the idea that scholars involve themselves in research into the pressing political, racial and social problems of the day. In an address to the South African Association for the Advancement of Science in 1921 Professor J. E. Duerden (a zoologist!) urged that scientific studies be made of South Africa's diverse peoples:

> Much of the study calls for that personal detachment and freedom which we hold to be one of the prerogatives of the man of science. Though it may not be usual to regard these problems as subjects of scientific enquiry (there is) urgent need for the methods which science can apply, and . . . it is fitting that questions of this nature should receive the attention of the Association. We do not encroach upon the stormy preserves of the politician. We assist by the elaboration of facts and principles for him to apply in practice, among the varied and often divergent interests of the whole population; and at the same time may help in the building up of correct ideals for the public (Duerden 1922).

In his presidential address to the Association in the same year C. T. Loram (a prominent figure in African education) endorsed these sentiments, and suggested a list of highly contentious topics in the field of race relations for scholarly investigation. According to Loram 'those engaged in the administration of Native Affairs want your help. Our neglect of a scientific treatment of the Native question has not only become a reproach but is now a positive danger' (Loram 1922).

In 1929 a young Stellenbosch academic, Dr H. F. Verwoerd, expressed a strong plea for a closer connection between the activities of the state and those of the universities. He cited examples of fields such as the administration of the railways and gaols, where scholars and students could become practically involved in research to the mutual benefit of themselves and the state. In this way the state would get:

> honest and enlightened investigation, which was at present almost impossible, owing to the fact of the political party, in power for the time being, fearing that the discoveries of defective or antiquated methods, could be used as a weapon by the other political party.

Verwoerd (1930) urged that the universities be accorded greater liberty to discuss the big problems that faced South Africa. Intellectuals, he said, should be encouraged to approach these problems on the basis of their knowledge and mental outlook.

It was partly with a view to the 'solution' of the racial problem that a 'School of African Life and Languages' (the forerunner of the present school of African Studies) was established at the University of Cape Town in 1921. In 1919 an official committee recommended to the government that it should immediately establish:

> a school of such strength as will show a real and adequate interest on the part of South Africa in problems whose solution is necessary for the future safe development of a country in which White and Black are to live side by side.

The government accepted the recommendation and allocated a sum of £3 000 for the purpose in 1920–1. This amount was slashed by half even before the School was established and seriously jeopardised its early expansion. If the official view was that scientific studies of changing African Societies and of race relations were highly desirable, official practice showed a disinclination to pay overmuch regard to the research findings of academics. The *Native Economic Commission*, 1930–1932 grappled with some of the thorniest issues facing South Africa, but it did not include among its members a single academic who was professionally concerned with African affairs. The commission noted the interest which the universities showed in 'the Scientific study of the Natives' and recommended that greater encouragement be given to such work.

General Smuts repeated this call in a speech at the University of Cape Town in 1938 when he urged the universities to tackle South Africa's most fundamental problem: 'as world peace is today the greatest of all human interests, we in South Africa could at least make a beginning by stabilising racial and social peace within our own borders and this University should even be in the forefront of that noble cause' (*The Star*, 8 March 1938).

But what did the academics achieve? The experiences of W. M. Macmillan, the historian, suggest that conclusions that ran counter to official predispositions were coolly, even hostilely, received. In his pioneering historical works Macmillan did much to undermine the orthodox White view of South African history. As a pamphleteer and as author of *Complex South Africa* (Macmillan, 1930) he brought a keenly critical focus to bear upon contemporary problems. For these activities Macmillan incurred the Hertzog government's hostility to his conclusions and recommendations in the field of official policy.

A leading social anthropologist, Isaac Schapera, acidly criticised policy makers in 1939 for ignoring academic findings. The practical use of anthropology was obvious but 'in few other countries with similar problems has the influence of the anthropologist been so small.' The anthropologist himself was partly to blame 'but the Government and the public at large cannot be absolved from indifference and even wilful neglect' (Schapera 1939).

The truth was that White South Africans (of both linguistic groups) were highly sensitive to criticism of their way of life and the racial policies associated with it. This sensitivity applied not only to academic investigators, but to creative writers as well as their writings probing into the basis of White attitudes. In his introduction to the Hogarth edition of William Plomer's novel *Turbott Wolfe*, Laurens van der Post gives a vivid description of white South African reaction to the novel which had explored the theme of sexual attraction across the colour line. It caused an 'intellectual riot'. It reminded van der Post of the way in which baboons reacted to seeing their reflections in a mirror – they looked frantically behind the mirror but always from the front there was 'an authentic baboon-person staring back at them. They could never accept reality and finally they would smash the mirror to pieces.'

In his autobiography Plomer says that *Turbott Wolfe* 'had particularly stung the Whites in that part of their psychological being where guilt and fear and self-deception in regard to the Natives . . . had been wrapped away from the light of reason.' Similar sensitivity to sharply critical writing about South African attitudes led to the early demise of the journal *Voorslag* with which Roy Cambell, Plomer and Van der Post were associated.

Fieldwork in African communities in this inter-war period was not especially difficult. In conducting the research for her classic study *Reaction to conquest* in 1931–3 Monica Hunter found African and official informants in Pondoland co-operative. By using personal contacts she was able to move around easily. In the urban part of the research (in East London) her work was facilitated by a meeting with the trade union leader Kadalie, who used his influence to facilitate her access to the African community. Possibly because of this contact she was subject to a measure of police surveillance. There were more difficulties in obtaining information about conditions on White-owned farms, especially those of the poorer farmers. There was resistance to probing of labour conditions, but, again, use of personal contacts overcame some of the problems.

E. G. Malherbe encountered problems, however, in conducting research in the late 1930s into the extent of bilingualism among Whites. He wrote (Malherbe 1939): 'Social thinking in South Africa is at the present time so shot-through with racial and political suspicion and prejudice, that it becomes very difficult to conduct scientific investigations of an objective nature into social and cultural phenomena . . .' His research required an investigation of the home background. His probings evoked bitter comment from a church magazine which considered his research a violation of parental sovereignty because he asked children, without the parents' knowledge, a variety of questions about household affairs. He was, moreover, attacked in Parliament because the questions would allegedly heighten ethnic consciousness among the young respondents. Another member attacked the survey as 'an attempt to collect ammunition' in order to carry out the policy of bilingual education, i.e. teaching Afrikaans and English-speaking children in the same classrooms in both languages. Bilingual education was a hotly-contested political issue. The study, when it was published, evoked much heated controversy which might have daunted a scholar who was less sturdy than Malherbe (1946).

A consideration of the problems arising out of the climate for social research was the subject of a large conference held in Durban in 1954 (University of Natal, 1954). Much attention was paid to the problems caused by racial polarization and by the possible reluctance of government agencies to foster research that questioned, even if only by implication, the fundamental postulates of policies. Research workers reported that difficulties were being encountered in the African reserves; permits were being refused and resistance to research was emanating from the people themselves. Two of the civil servants present, Dr P. A. W. Cook of the Native Affairs Department and Dr P. J. Olckers, Director of Public Service Training, expressed willingness to co-operate and explicitly welcomed research by academics. Cook said that research on race relations had never been the monopoly of his department and it was prepared to assist individuals and teams from universities to conduct research.

The African academics at the conference pointed out some of the reasons behind African suspicions of research. Z. K. Matthews said that Africans in urban and rural areas would co-operate with investigators provided they were convinced that their motives were genuine and that they were not subtle conveyors of propaganda. Selby Ngcobo outlined in detail the difficulties. A researcher would be watched from both sides of the colour line; if he were seen often in company with or was too friendly towards White officials African suspicions would be aroused; conversely a too friendly relationship with Black officials would evoke the suspicions of the officials. The officials expected research activities not to disturb the existing system of discipline and control; while the Africans who constituted the subject of the research expected or hoped that it would contribute to an amelioration of their position. Ngcobo, drawing upon his experience as research assistant in the Economics Department of the University of Natal, said that educated Africans, African trade unionists and leaders of other organizations tended not to draw distinctions between research conducted by independent scholars and that undertaken by various governmental bodies:

> Just as they doubted the impartiality of the latter so they were sceptical of the value to them of the former; they often argued that the powers-that-be would either ignore any findings in their favour or only make use of those facts which were in line with their policy.

A second line of criticism from Africans was that some of the research had been conceived in purely instrumental terms and was aimed at making Africans slot more easily into the limited range of occupational roles that were open to them.

The issues that were raised at this conference cover fairly fully the range of problems experienced by academic social researchers in South Africa. The dominant White group has created for itself a social charter, justifying that dominance. Many of the elements for the social charter, concern the group's history, its beliefs about its own characteristics and those of the groups whom it dominates. Academic research into an or all of the elements of the charter could, in the nature of things, have explosive results by demonstrating the mythical or false bases of beliefs. The government, naturally, has a strong vested interest in perpetuating the charter as a means of legitimating its authority. It follows that insofar as the government is a major pump primer of reseaich or allocator of research funds its interest will be primarily in fostering research of a 'problem-solving' or utilitarian natuie; it will be less interested in or, perhaps even hostile to research that examines the dominant group's sacred cows (in whatever fields they may graze).

A further factor, related to what I have said, is the growing authoritarianism of the State. The range of permissible views and opinions has been contracted by laws that place untrammelled powers in the hand of the executive. Over a wide area of political, economic and social life increasing powers of official discretion have been established. Now, free scientific inquiry has what Reinhard Bendix (1970:95) has called 'an inherent radicalism.' It is the social sciences primarily that provide the challenge to authority in all spheres, because their focus is upon human affairs and the problems of social interaction. The more authoritarian the society the more likely it is that free inquiry in the social sciences will be circumscribed. Louis Wirth (1936:17) has written:

> That there is an area of 'dangerous thought' in every society is . . . scarcely debatable. While we recognize that what it is dangerous to think about may differ from country to country and from epoch to epoch, on the whole subjects marked with the danger signal are those which the society or the controlling elements in it believe to be so vital and hence so sacred that they will not tolerate their profanation by discussion. But what is not so easily recognized is the fact that thought, even in the absence of official censorship, is disturbing, and, under certain conditions, dangerous and subversive. For thought is a catalytic agent that is capable of unsettling routines, disorganizing habits, breaking up habits, undermining faiths, and generating scepticism.

Of course, it should not be inferred that the State is the only agency that shapes the climate for research. While its importance in this respect is undoubted, religious groups, group loyalties and pre- and anti-scientific *weltanschauungen* can all contribute to resistance of free inquiry (Hobson 1926:39). All of these factors operate in South Africa and reinforce the areas of 'dangerous thought' with an extra patina. But the decisive factor is the structural position of the dominant group as a numerical minority which perceived itself as being in danger of its grip on the society. Its authoritarianism flows from this, and decisively affects the conditions for social research.

In 1965 Dr S. Biesheuvel noted that there was a discernible trend to expect the scientist, especially the social scientist 'to operate within the framework of government policy, not to question but to provide support.' He decided that it was 'only one step to the production of acceptable information.' He alluded also to an increasing tendency for the research function of the universities to be taken over by the State, by State-sponsored organizations or by large industrial laboratories (Biesheuvel 1965:13).

In quantitive terms the amount of social research conducted by universities and by autonomous bodies exceeds the amount conducted by State-sponsored bodies such as the Human Sciences Research Council or the National Institute for Personnel Research. The former body was created by statute in 1968 and is governed by a Council appointed by the Minister of National Education. It contains under its umbrella ten research institutes which actually conduct or promote research in the respective divisions; and it disburses also research and publication grants and bursaries to individual scholars or to academic departments (a total of R325 000 was disbursed on research grants in 1970–1).

According to its first annual report (1969–1970) the H.S.R.C.'s attitude is that:

> social sciences research is not a dogma super-imposed from above as an instrument of national policy; and the aim of the Human Sciences Research Council is to encourage and stimulate research in the social sciences by free and independent scholars whose labours it is hoped, will lead to the fuller satisfaction of the needs and aspirations of the various peoples in our country.

It is also stipulated that the members of the Council, who are appointed for two-year periods must have distinguished themselves in the field of human sciences or possess special qualifications in respect of some or other aspects of the Council's activities.

The recommendations for the funding of research projects emanate from a series of advisory committees in the different broad fields of the social sciences. Most of these committees (whose memberships are detailed in the Council's third annual report, 1971–1972) are numerically dominated by academics from conservative institutions. No Blacks serve on any of the committees, and nor, indeed, are the Black universities represented. (This presumably follows from the Council's operating under the aegis of the Ministry for National Education which is concerned with White education only.)

From a review of the annual reports and publications of the H.S.R.C. it is clear that its own research workers 'operate within the framework of government policy' and provide useful information for policy makers. What is less clear are the considerations that govern its allocative function. It is believed by some scholars that the H.S.R.C. accords preferential treatment to those research projects that do not impinge upon controversial areas, It is not possible to confirm or deny the validity of this feeling because the projects and scholars who are refused research grants are not listed in the Council's annual reports. Those who make this assertion, however, do so emphatically and cite examples of refusals in support. It is alleged also that some scholars, having regard to this belief about the H.S.R.C., simply do not apply to it for funds in the first place.

The allegations cited in the preceding paragraph do not rest on hard evidence: indeed it is most of the hearsay variety. It should also be noted that the allegations are vigorously denied by the H.S.R.C.

A major area of government control of social research is the requirement that scholars wishing to conduct research in the African reserves or homelands first obtain a permit from the Department of Bantu Administration and Development. It is not possible to say precisely how many scholars are granted or refused permits. The Minister declined to answer a parliamentary question seeking to elicit this information on grounds that the categories of applicants' occupations were not kept. What is known is that a significant number of applications from academics have been refused. It is also true that the processing of applications can take as long as six months or even longer.

Officially the Department's attitude is to treat each application on its merits. It appears that South African citizens tend to receive preferential treatment over foreigners who, it seems, are automatically viewed with greater suspicion. This is not to say, however, that no foreigner is granted a permit. Once granted, the permit may be withdrawn at any time, without reasons being given. It stipulates also that permit-holders may not lodge with Africans – which means that a social anthropologist cannot live in a hut in a village. Mostly, it appears that the permits do not allow persons to be in a reserve at night time. This means that important after-dark ritual activities cannot be observed at first-hand. A further departmental requirement is that permit-holders must show the drafts of the writings to the Department prior to publication. It is clear that this may lend itself to a form of pre-publication censorship either by officials or by the investigator himself as he may well think that his future applications may be jeopardised if the Department takes a poor view of his findings. One academic told me that he had a permit which he could not afford to have withdrawn as he was in the middle of a large project: he applied self-censorship in his other writings and in what he said.

Most, but not all, of the applicants who have been refused permits are from the English-medium universities. Permits have also been refused on occasions to members of the South African Institute of Race Relations, which is a liberal though highly-respected and sober organisation. The situation in regard to permits is viewed so seriously in the English-medium universities that two departments of social anthropology have now abandoned hope of conducting research (either by staff or by graduate students) in the reserves.

Permits were also required from local authorities to conduct research in urban African townships. Far fewer problems about getting permits have been encountered with local authorities than with the central government. It is feared, however, that the takeover of urban African administration by administration boards under the aegis of the central government will lead to the same problems as encountered in other areas. As far as I know, only one permit has been refused to a student by a local authority. In this case the proposed study was a survey of African political attitudes. Local authorities tend to be reluctant to allow research workers into the townships after dark, out of concern for their physical safety. Nor can a social anthropologist live with the community he is studying, as he would do in normal fieldwork conditions. As with the central government permits issued by the local authority can be withdrawn at any time without reasons having to be given.

To a greater or lesser extent the social investigator, as in every country, will be dependent in each case on the co-operation of the authorities for statistical and other information about the subject being investigated. Such co-operation can have an important bearing on the quality and richness of the material assembled by the scholar. It is evident that the political complexion of the scholar has bearing on the amenability of officials. It is unlikely that a radical opponent of official policies would be granted permission to enter a reserve in the first place, but assuming he were, and his views were known, it is unlikely that officials would be as frank and co-operative with him as they might well be with a scholar who accepted the basic framework of the policy. Of course much depends upon the individual officials and scholars concerned, but social scientists, critical of official policies, and especially those from the universities with liberal traditions, believe that they receive differential treatment from government departments.

Bureaucracies tend by nature to be secretive; in South Africa the tensions of society and growing authoritarianism give an added dimension to this fundamental predisposition. Opposition members of Parliament report that over the past twelve years it has become steadily more difficult to extract information from the executive by way of parliamentary questions. In some cases the requested information is refused on the ground that 'it is not in the public interest' that it be made known; in other cases a minister will plead that the business of his officials does not permit the time to be expended in gathering information, or that the information is not kept, or that it is not filed according to the categories required by the questioner. More and more questions relating to Bantu affairs have been refused answers on grounds that the desired information is kept by the homelands government. To some extent an analogous situation applies in respect of Coloured affairs.

Similar problems are encountered in connection with the official census. At the 1954 Durban conference on social research several participants complained about the inadequacy of official statistics. E. G. Malherbe explained that the permissible questions on census forms were determined by the Statistical Council and 'obviously this body tended to be conservative in its views.' The conference passed a resolution emphasizing 'that the Census of the Union of South Africa asks fewer questions and thus makes less total data available than any other member of the British Commonwealth of Nations.'

A major objection to the Census today is the incredible length of time taken for the data to be published. There are also curious breaks in continuity (i.e. data furnished in previous censuses not being furnished again) which in one case, at least, appears to be because the trend revealed was politically embarrassing. A further serious problem about census-taking has been the resistance of Blacks. 'The enumerators . . . are often regarded as agents of the administration, even detectives. They are to be avoided or confused as much as possible particularly by the many who are illegally within the urban area.' Such attitudes can seriously hinder the research worker whose questions may lead subjects to suppose that he is a census official. In one case the result was the boycott of a study.

Resistance to investigation has increased with the growing polarization of the society. The more authoritarian the political system becomes the more nervous subjects are about imparting information. Difficulties are encountered especially by scholars investigating 'total' (i.e. multi-racial) communities. Concerning his study of Port Nolloth, Martin West (1971:117) reported that his close contact with Black people in the town prevented his doing any serious work among the Whites:

> Whites were suspicious of my presence in the town (some believing me to have political motives) and disapproved strongly of my relationship with non-Whites. It was therefore impossible to establish any rapport with the White population as a whole, and most information was gained from casual meeting and observations, particularly in the hotel and bar.

Similar problems were encountered by Pierre L. van den Berghe, an American sociologist who studied race relations in Natal in the early 1960s. He made no secret of his value orientations and determined that even in a highly colour-conscious society he would remain 'colour-blind.'

He reported:

> On both sides of the colour bar, attempts were made to explain or rather re-interpret my unconventional behavior in terms of existing roles. For Whites I was a Communist agitator or more frequently an odd foreigner who has not yet learned how to 'handle the Natives.' Amusement at my social 'ineptness' was a more common reaction than anger or even annoyance. Often, Whites predicted that I would soon become converted to their way of thinking and acting. It was probably on the part of westernized Indians that my role was most readily accepted at face value, and that

> initial suspicion, amusement, or hostility was most completely absent. Politically militant and educated Africans often tried to fit me into the role either of a police informer or an *agent provocateur*, or of a missionary-type 'do-gooder' or paternalist. Traditional or older Africans, on the other hand, whether through caution or through inability to shed suddenly the force of habit, often continued to behave in the submissive manner that most Whites expected. Needless to say, this imbalance in the relationship made for much awkwardness (Van den Berghe 1967:189–90).

In as politically tense a society as South Africa it is not surprising that the outsider investigating a community is often assumed to be engaged in political activity – by a process analogous to that of witchcraft. In his study of a Cape Coloured reserve W. P. Carstens found his informants generally cooperative, but in one locality his fieldwork was blighted when a White church official accused him of subversive political activity within a few hours of his arrival. In other areas he found that barriers were occasionally raised when he was eliciting information about those aspects of religious belief which would not be acceptable to the missionary (Carstens 1966: 10).

Several cases have occurred where security police have tailed research workers and subsequently questioned informants. This is naturally intimidating both to the investigator and to the investigated, the former fearing that the information he has obtained could land his informants in trouble, and the latter fearing that their information could be prised out of the investigator. Gwendolen M. Carter and her associates reported several incidents involving security police surveillance and interference, including 'a mysterious disappearance and reappearance in a police station of a briefcase in a locked hotel room.' In another episode an African opposition member of the Transkei Legislative Assembly was rudely ejected from a hotel room by the manager on grounds that the hotel was for Whites only and subsequently questioned by the security police. Two members of Professor Carter's team were searched by the security police on leaving the country (Carter, Karis and Stultz 1967: 13–14).

Anthropological studies of Black communities in recent years have tended to mute or avoid altogether examination of political attitudes and activities. It is largely absent in Philip Mayer's study of Xhosa in East London. Mayer reports that

> in a present-day South African town the role of a White newcomer closely questioning Black informants about their private affairs can never be a grateful one, and that he may risk being given incomplete or misleading information because of his colour (Mayer 1961:297).

In their study of Langa, Monica Wilson and Archie Mafeje elected not to investigate political organizations or trade unions. They say:

> Questions were not asked about them early in the investigation because that would have aroused suspicion, and during the course of the study the two main political organizations, the African National Congress and the Pan African Congress, were banned. Furthermore, two cases occurred in which journalists were imprisoned for refusing to reveal to the police their sources of information on political matters (Wilson and Mafeje 1963:11–12).

It can, in other words, be dangerous for the informant and for the investigator personally to be in possession of 'hot' material. As far as I am aware, however, no scholar has been detained by the authorities for interrogation about information obtained in the course of his investigations. But the very existence of such a possibility is probably a deterrent to embarking in the first place upon investigations that may uncover explosive material.

It should not be inferred from the cases cited above that *all* investigation into political attitudes has become impossible. In Henry Lever's study of the South African voter the refusal rate among respondents was only about two per cent, even though many searching questions probing political attitudes were asked. Other studies of voting behaviour have also been made, and opinion polls on highly contentious issues are regularly published in the Press. Nearly all of the latter are undertaken by reputable survey organisations. Furthermore, studies have been made of African political attitudes.

Several social scientists have encountered resistance from the groups being investigated on the ground that such investigation willy-nilly highlights their difference. Thus Hilda Kuper found some Indians who felt their position in the country was 'so insecure that some of them expressed anxiety at a book which discussed their way of life as being in any way different from that of White South Africans' (Kuper 1960). A similar reaction was encountered by an African fieldworker investigating African community life in Johannesburg. Apart from the suspicion that the fieldworker was an informer or a municipal official, there was ambivalence among some educated respondents who felt that any attempt to study Africans was a means of providing justification for separate development 'which aims at giving Africans no contact with the broad stream of world culture.' According to the leader of this project refusal rates were as high as 50 to 60 per cent.

An unknown factor in research into sensitive areas in the 'lie factor'. Several scholars report that they were given deliberately misleading information, or that they strongly suspected that it was misleading. For example, with the rigorous application of urban influx controls it has become increasingly difficult to extract reliable information from Africans about their job histories, length of sojourn in the urban area, rural land rights, and related questions. This is especially so where the data required is directly related to the right to remain within the prescribed urban area.

The rise of Black consciousness – itself an index of racial polarisation – is also making its effect felt upon academic research. African organisations that were willing to be studied only two years ago have become much more 'secretive' and resistant to probing. The new mood marks a rejection of all things White, including social research. As the racial line is more firmly drawn the different categories of Whites are lumped together as representing a cohesive bloc; and heightened racial pride increasingly takes on the form of resentment that any non-Black should take an interest in, or have any empathy with, Black society.

So far much of the discussion has focused upon the problem of Whites conducting (or sponsoring) research into Black communities.

But it is also apparent that the tensions of society and the high degree of group conflict make social research within the White groups difficult in some respects as well. Two interestingly parallel case studies may be cited as examples. Dr C. J. Alant's sociological study of the way in which members of the *Nederduitse Gereformeerde Kerk* relate to the Church ran into serious difficulties because of objections by elements within the church to the questionnaire which respondents were asked to complete. Particular objection was made to two questions: 'It is a sin to vote for a political party which does not specifically maintain the Afrikaans language and traditions'; 'and it is a sin for a White to marry a non-White even if this were not against the law of the land.' The objections were aired in the Press and the publicity adversely affected the return on completed questionnaires.

The second case is Mr J. Polley's investigation of a large Protestant Church's response to separate development. The survey sought to examine the question at all levels within the Church. The proposed project encountered hostility from the university department to which Polley was attached, presumably because it was 'too controversial'. He then transferred to another department which took a more kindly view of the project. But then he encountered resistance from elements within the Church itself. Synods refused to allow the questionnaire to be distributed on the ostensible ground that this would interfere with synod business. Polley was then forced to send out the questionnaires by post and involve himself in substantial costs that could have been avoided if the official channels of the Church had been made available to him.

In both of these cases it seems clear that the Churches concerned did not want the hard and steady light of academic investigations to shine upon their inner essence. In both cases the investigations *could* have produced embarrassing findings, such as that rank and file members, clergy or other office-holders did not share fully the official views of the Church on highly-charged issues. Both bodies, therefore, proved resistant to probing.

Conclusion

This paper has sought to isolate the problems which social research encounters in South Africa. Much evidence could be cited to show, however, that these problems are by no means unique to South Africa. Nor do the findings alter my views that South Africa's complexity makes it one of the most interesting societies in the world and a richly rewarding laboratory for social research. There are ways around most, if not all, of the problems; but the investigator's ingenuity and resourcefulness may often be taxed to the limit. Social research, it seems to me, is the art of the impossible: it can be done even in the most hostile of environments.

REFERENCES

Bendix, R. 1970 – *Embattled Reason – Essays in Social Knowledge*. New York: Oxford University Press.

Biesheuvel, S. 1965 – *The Changing Function of the Universities*. Durban: University of Natal.

Carstens, W. P. 1966 – *The Social Structure of a Cape Coloured Reserve*. Cape Town: Oxford University Press.

Carter, Gwendolen M., Thomas Karis & Newell M. Stultz 1967 – *South Africa's Transkei*. London:Heinemann.

Duerden, J. E. 1922 – 'Social anthropology in South Africa: problems of race and nationality.' *South African Journal of Science*, 18, 8–30.

Fife, R. H. 1932 – *Report on Tendencies in Education in East and South Africa*. New York: Carnegie Corporation.

Hobson, J. A. 1936 – *Freedom and the Social Sciences*. London: Constable.

Loram, J. A. 1922 – 'The claim of the native question upon scientists.' *South African Journal of Sciences*, 18, 99–109.

Macmillan, W. M. 1930 – *Complex South Africa*. London: Faber & Faber.

Malherbe, E. G. 1939 – *Educational and Social Research in South Africa*. Pretoria: South African Council for Educational and Social Research.

——1946 *The Bilingual School*. London: Longmans, Green.

Mayer, P. 1961 – *Townsmen or Tribesmen*. Cape Town: Oxford University Press.

Pauw, S. 1964 – 'South Africa.' In Joseph S. Roucek (ed.) *Contemporary Sociology*. London: Peter Owen, 1095–99.

Pollak, H. 1968 – *Sociology Post Graduates of South African Universities*. Durban: Joint University Committee on Sociology and Social Work.

University of Natal 1954 – *Research Needs and Priorities in the Social Sciences*. Durban: mimeo.

Van den Berghe, Pierre L. 1967 – 'Research in South Africa – The story of my experiences with tyranny.' In Gideon Sjoberg (ed.) *Ethics, Politics, and Social Research*. Cambridge: Schenkman, 183–97.

West, Martin E. 1971 – *Divided Community*. Cape Town: A. A. Balkema.

Wilson, Monica & Archie Mafeje. 1963 – *Langa*. Cape Town: Oxford University Press.

Wirth, Louis. 1936 – 'Introduction.' In Karl Mannheim, *Ideology and Utopia*. London: Routledge & Kegan Paul.

Znaniecki, Florian 1968 – *The Social Role of the Man of Knowledge*. New York: Harper Torchbooks.

2. Some Problems in Race Relations Research in South Africa

HENRY LEVER

Explanation

The problems concerning research on race relations in South Africa can be considered from a number of different perspectives. The level at which problems within the ambit of sociology present themselves varies a great deal from the broad issues of a political and quasi-political nature to the minutiae of research design and technology. It will be necessary, therefore, for the discussion to fluctuate between these levels.

This paper has a four-fold purpose, namely: (1) to provide a number of focal points for debate, (2) to be controversial with a view to provoking activity (of a sociological kind), (3) to indicate areas in which research is needed and (4) to comment on some aspects of research design and methods relevant to the field of enquiry.

This paper, of course, does not provide an exhaustive list of the problems in research on race relations.

The Need for Research

There is wide-spread support for the view that South Africa's gravest problems lie in the field of race relations. Elections are won or lost on race policies, parliamentary debates focus on these policies, legislation bears the stamp of ideology on race relations, the electorate acknowledges it as the most important problem confronting the country (Lever 1972a: chapters 4 and 14), discussion amongst ordinary South Africans usually turns at some stage or another to problems of race and millions of lives are regulated and determined by efforts purporting to deal with the country's race problems. South African sociologists have made very few concerted efforts to develop the study of race relations. Comparatively few sociologists regard race relations as their field of primary interest; no qualifying courses in race relations are taught at the under-graduate level in South African universities; there is only one Professor of Race Relations in the country (who is the head of a research institute); proportionately few papers on race are presented at scientific conferences; and most of the new research instituted does not lie within the field of race relations. Wilson (1961) maintains that creative writers have been more effective than social scientists in portraying race relations in South Africa.

An analysis of recently instituted research in Sociology as presented in the Bulletins of the Human Sciences Research Council is illuminating. The Bulletins published in 1972 showed that of the 99 new research projects initiated within the field of sociology only 10 were concerned with race relations. A reader of the Bulletins would conclude that South Africa's most important problems were concerned with church attendance, worker productivity, worker absenteeism, broken homes and drug addiction. One can only marvel at the work-shyness of South African sociologists in the field of race relations!

There is another school of thought which maintains that sociologists are devoting too much attention to research on race relations. In the past few years this point of view has been espoused particularly by the younger sociologists. They argue that too much attention has been devoted to descriptive studies (this part of the argument does not appear justified in any event) and too little attention to bringing about meaningful change. The younger sociologists are concerned with the restrictions on activities and with the inequalities in education, health services, welfare services, housing and income which characterise South African society. To them, decisions on whether to use logarithmic or semi-logarithmic co-ordinates when confronted with inequalities and human suffering is tantamout to fiddling while Rome burns. There is much merit in this argument. Unfortunately, all too frequently, it is presented in its extreme form in which (*a*) all descriptive studies are dismissed as 'irrelevant' and (*b*) an almost total pre-occupation with social change is insisted upon. This is, at least, the form which it has taken at the University of the Witwatersrand. Yet, quite clearly, enthusiasm and good-will are no substitutes for knowledge. Becker and Horowitz (1972:641) who have espoused the viewpoint of radical sociology, point out that the work of radical sociologists does not differ markedly from that of non-radicals and that 'ideologically "correct" analyses are no substitute for empirically verifiable observations.'

In spite of the deficiencies in their arguments the younger sociologists have adopted a valuable standpoint. They have placed the problem of values in such a position in the sociological arena where it can no longer be avoided. The vexed problem of values has been referred to in a Presidential address to this Association [for Sociologists in Southern Africa] (Cilliers 1972), in an invited address to the same body (Loubser 1972), and in two recent inaugural lectures (Lever 1972b; Watts 1972). None of the occasions for the addresses, however, have provided a suitable opportunity for discussion or for the full exploration of the problem and its implications. A full exposition of the problem of values requires more time than is available here. I should, at least, attempt to state my standpoint. I do not believe that sociology can or should be value-free. The problem seems to be to harness values in such a way that they will maximise the scientific endeavour and lead to the most productive efforts. A value-free sociology is apt to become a value-less sociology. Gray (1973:355) asserts that only when values have been accorded their proper place 'will a worthy and important discipline replace a large amount of well-verified irrelevance with a body of relevant knowledge truly worth communicating to a receptive and appreciative audience.' Within the field of race relations, I believe that sociologists can justify efforts to reduce prejudice, discrimination and human suffering either in terms of the values intrinsic in the scientific method (Lever 1972b:20), or in terms of humanistic values (Loubser 1972), or in terms of the benefits to society as a whole. The problem of values becomes acute when there is a clash of values, each of which is commendable in itself. This is a problem which South African sociologists have not had occasion to debate yet.

Political and Quasi-Political Issues

Since 1948 the policy of apartheid, has dominated the political scene in South Africa. There are a number of assumptions underlying the policy of apartheid which need to be tested empirically. For example, the advocates of apartheid have claimed that social contact between members of different ethnic groups leads to conflict. Critics of the policy have maintained that social contact has the opposite effect. The indications are that in South Africa, social contact can become an important means of dispelling false generalizations (Lever 1967; Russell 1961). However, it must be acknowledged that there are situations in which contact can lead to friction (Saenger 1953: 219). It may, therefore, be expedient for sociologists to ascertain the conditions under which social contact leads to friction or to harmony. The answer may already have been indicated in the 'Robbers Cave experiment' reported by the Sherifs (1954; 1956).

The question of whether segregation with equal facilities is tantamount to discrimination is a crucial one for the policy of apartheid. It is doubtful whether segregation with equal facilities is ever provided and hence it is difficult to test the proposition. There are good reasons for believing that even under conditions of equal facilities, segregation is tantamount to discrimination. It has been argued that segregation causes psychological harm to members of minority groups. Segregation (non-voluntary, that is) signifies to the minority member that he is less worthy than the segregating group or that he is repugnant to them in some respect. Segregation in South Africa is enforced at the instance of the White group and domination is implicit in such action with the phrase 'equal facilities' constituting the sugar coating of the bitter pill. Voluntary separation, on the other hand, may imply an entirely different set of propositions. The overwhelming majority of social scientists in America who have gained recognition from their research in race relations believe that segregation with equal facilities has harmful effects for the segregating group as well as for the segregated group (Deutscher and Chein, 1948). A very small proportion feel that it has no harmful effects. A great deal of the impetus for further research in the United States was lost when the courts upheld the view that segregation with equal facilities amounted to discrimination. The research programme outlined by Chein (1949), has accordingly not been pursued further. Nor has any social scientist appeared eager to test the proposition that segregation has beneficial results for minority members or that it does not have harmful consequences. Since the issue remains unresolved in South Africa it is useful to consider some of the hypothese suggested by Chein. Chein maintains that minority members may be expected to be characterised by feelings of inferiority and insecurity, self-doubt, self-ambivalence, feelings of isolation and not belonging, cynicism, loss of initiative and efficiency, diminished sense of personal behaviour, ideas of persecution, displaced aggression, anti-social behaviour and disturbances in the sense of reality. Members of the segregating group, he feels are likely to be characterised by guilt-feelings, dissociation of moral values and disturbances in the sense of reality. The Separation of Amenities Act precludes judicial officers from considering the reasonableness or adequacy of separate facilities provided for the different racial groups. Nonetheless, it is important to undertake research in this area particularly as the beneficence underlying segregation is continually emphasised and the virtues of segregation continually extolled. In view of the paucity of data in South Africa it may be helpful to refer, very briefly, to two exploratory studies undertaken by Honours students in the University of the Witwatersrand. The one study is based on interviews undertaken with a quota sample of 120 Chinese residents in Johannesburg (Luk Sun 1965). A set of open ended questions dealing with experiences of discrimination drafted by the present writer was included in the interview schedule. Respondents were asked whether they were able to recall from their own experiences any incident in which they had been discriminated against or unfairly treated by virtue of their being Chinese. If they replied in the affirmative, they were asked to describe the incident and certain selected features pertaining to the incident. The set of questions was asked three times allowing a maximum number of 360 incidents of discrimination to be reported. In fact, 270 such incidents were reported by the 120 respondents with a disproportionate number being reported by the Chinese males. A number of incidents referred purely and simply to segregation. The segregation referred to took place mainly in queues or in offices. Incidentally, the majority of situations involving incidents of discrimination were not suffered at the hands of government officials but were instigated by private organisations and individuals. The government is made the whipping-horse far too frequently.

The second study was based on questionnaires administered to African pupils attending a night school at the University of the Witwatersrand (Jacobs 1965). They were asked to report their emotional state when they entered a post office which had been partitioned into an area for Whites and an area for non-Whites. The majority reported that they approved of the situation and that they felt comfortable with the arrangement. The evidence from the two studies is conflicting but, nevertheless, interesting and should give rise to further investigation.

It is sometimes suggested that restrictions are placed in the way of the scientific study of race relations in South Africa (van den Berghe 1962). It should be pointed out in this connection that the National Council for Social Research (now the Human Sciences Research Council) was and is in a position to discourage this kind of research had it so wished, but it has not done so. Perhaps the one study which might have caused the most embarrassment to the government was Russell's (1961) study of an interracial neighbourhood which was supported by a grant from the N.C.S.R. The N.C.S.R. and its successor, the H.S.R.C. have provided grants and scholarships for a number of projects within the field of race relations without specifying any conditions, requirements or qualifications or limiting the studies in any way. If the government wished to discourage research it could easily have done so through the N.C.S.R. There appears to be no valid reason why research which generates more light than heat will not continue to be so sponsored.

There are two restrictions which do hamper free enquiry. One is the prohibition of entry into African residential areas which Nationalist as well as United Party City Councils and government officials have enforced. Entry into the residential areas of Coloured and Indians is permitted without special permission being required. Even in the case of African residential areas the prohibition can be circumvented by procuring the services of an African research worker who is entitled to enter the area. The second restriction concerns the banning or impounding of books which are deemed to be 'undesirable publications.' Dollard's book, *Caste and Class in a Southern Town* (1939), which should be prescribed reading for every student in the social sciences if only as an object lesson on the need to be aware of and to continually re-assess the research worker's own value judgements, is not freely available in South Africa. No apologies are made for the following value-judgement: the banning of Dollard's *Class and Caste in a Southern Town* is an act of sheer stupidity comparable with the banning of *Black Beauty*, Voltair's *Candide* and the use of the peace emblem on T-shirts. Dollard's books does not contain a single reference to South Africa. Possibly the principal reason why the book evoked the wrath of the authorities was its discussion of sexual contacts across the colourline. Many South Africans react with revulsion at the thought that they are sexually attracted to Blacks. It is this very revulsion ostensibly concealing a love – guilt – hate relationship which gives rise to the curiosity of the social scientist and suggests that it may be an important ingredient in racial attitudes in South Africa.

In spite of the above, the impediments to social research in South Africa are not very great. South African sociologists are far freer to pose controversial questions than their colleagues in communist and most African countries and have fewer restrictions placed on their choice of topics or on the manner in which they are discussed.

Some Suggested Areas for Research

There is hardly an area of investigation which cannot be regarded as virgin territory. Such a situation does make social research an exciting process, since wherever we stand we are on the boundaries of knowledge. A certain measure of responsibility is also implied.

Obviously it is not possible to draft an exhaustive list of topics for research. Mention will merely be made of some topics which come readily to mind. Some suggestions for research have already been made.

There is a need for an adequately documented study of internal disturbances in South Africa. Such a study could be of a descriptive kind and might be modelled on Sorokin's study of internal disturbances (Sorokin 1937–41); that is, listing dates, numbers of deaths, numbers injured, costs, etc. It may be possible to go further and investigate the precipitants and underlying causes of such disturbances. It is difficult to anticipate what the results of such an analysis would be. It may be that there is a cyclical pattern to such disturbances or that the presence or absence of an external factor might be a principal cause. Sociologists in South Africa have not devoted much attention to the study of riots, protests, boycotts, etc., and have not made any effort to have a sociological perspective presented. Judicial commissions are generally established to investigate the major disturbances. It is hoped that no further occasions of a similar kind will present themselves in the future; but if they do, representations should be made to have a sociologist appointed to such commissions. The sociologist's knowledge of social conditions and collective behaviour should prove to be a useful supplement to the knowledge of the judge who must perforce, be less skilled in these respects. If, at times, it is difficult to investigate the precipitants and causes of disturbances, an attempt could at least be made to ascertain how the public reacts to these incidents. Orpen (1972) has set a praiseworthy example by including a question on the Gelvandale (Port Elizabeth) riot in a questionnaire administered to Coloured clerical workers in Cape Town. He found that 70 per cent of the respondents expressed approval for the rioters. He points out that there is less approval for Negro rioters in the United States.

Many observers of the South African scene have been puzzled by the absence of a major conflagration involving the races. Warnings of riots and bloodshed have continually been made over the years. More than 50 years ago, Jabavu (1920:2) warned that: 'It will not be very long before the whole White community must deal with a situation overwhelmingly beyond their control.' He pointed out that there was a need to be familiar with the causes of unrest in order to assist in arriving at a solution 'that will save the country from what will, if not arrested in time, surely come up sooner or later as an anarchist disruption of this land' (Jabavu 1920:17). The 'revolution' which so many have anticipated has not occurred. Possibly it may occur within the next 50 or 100 years and it will then be possible to say: 'I told you so.' But this is hardly worthy of being termed a prediction. In general, the South African scene has been characterised, if not by peace, then at least by quiescence. The racial disturbances which have occurred have been at infrequent intervals and on a modest scale. In relation to the data on Europe presented by Sorokin, the disturbances in South Africa can best be described as 'skirmishes'. The quiescence in which South Africa finds itself suggests that those who have warned against a major conflagration have omitted an important ingredient from their analysis. Why hasn't 'the revolution' occurred? Some critics maintain that a brutal police force and an effective system of informers are responsible for maintaining a facade of peace. Contrary to beliefs held in some countries, our police do not patrol the townships in armoured cars machine-gunning Africans on the streets. In fact, many township residents complain at the absence of police and maintain that regular police patrols of the townships should be undertaken in order to protect life and property and to curtail the activities of the tsotsis. In any event, revolutions have succeeded where the oppression has been more intense than it is in South Africa. The lack of organisation amongst Africans has limited effective political activity. However, the Alexandra bus boycott (Luthuli 1962) of the late 1950s and the Durban strikes early in 1973 have demonstrated that determined Africans can succeed in protests notwithstanding the lack of an official organisation and the pressures of the government (as far as Alexandra was concerned). An explanation for the absence of 'the revolution' must be sought elsewhere.

The relative submissiveness of Africans may be explicable in terms of a theory which involves an extension of the principle of relative deprivation. To an outside observer a group of people may appear deprived, although the members of the group concerned do not regard themselves in those terms. Similarly, an outside observer may regard a group as not being deprived, whereas the members of that group regard themselves as deprived. The frame of reference in which the individual chooses to assess his position is crucial (Stouffer *et al.* 1949). If the African assesses his status, income, educational opportunities, houses, facilities and life chances by comparison with those of Whites, he will feel deprived. However, if he chooses another point of reference or comparison there may not be a feeling of deprivation. It is suggested that the African does not compare his position with that of the White. He compares his position with that which he held in the past, either in the urban areas or in the tribal lands. If he uses this as his point of reference, then he will conclude that he has made progress and there is a certain measure of satisfaction with his lot. The surveys of the household goods of Africans conducted by the Bureau for Market Research of the University of South Africa (Bureau of Market Research, undated reports no. 6 and 2; see also Langschmidt 1962) indicate that there has been an improvement in the standard of living of Africans. Other indicies such as declining infant mortality rates and increases in life expectancy testify to the general improvement of social conditions. Progress has also been made in housing and in education, albeit far less than may be desired. It is not suggested that the life of the African is one of perfect bliss. He cannot help but be aware of the harassments and exploitation to which he is subject. There is also a measure of bitterness and resentment in the African. But this crucial factor is that there is a measure of satisfaction and it is this measure of satisfaction which has tipped the scales in favour of quiescence rather than revolution. It is suggested that the absence of a major confrontation between the races in South Africa is not due so much to the omnipotence of the police, but rather to a lack of motivation to actively oppose the system. There is no reason for Africans to feel deprived simply because sociologists (or anyone else) tell them that they are deprived. Although my own contacts are admittedly limited, I cannot help gaining the impression that White liberals appear to be more frustrated with the South African social system than the bulk of Africans.

The measure of satisfaction which Africans have of the social system is reinforced by a number of processes including the following:

(1) The limited intellectual horizons of Africans due to their restricted education.
(2) The stability of the social system where the pattern of race relations has become institutionalised.
(3) The tendency of dominated groups to lower their levels of aspiration as a means of warding off further frustrations (Simpson and Yinger 1965:139; Rosen 1959).
(4) The prominent part which the process of acculturation and the transition from tribal to urban life, with its attendant stresses and strains, plays in the lives of most Africans.

Those Africans who are the most educated the most urbanised and who pursue professional careers are likely to feel the most frustrated or deprived.

The views expressed above are presented as hypotheses for further research. Conditions may, of course, change as a result of which the 'measure of satisfaction' will take second place to 'the measure of bitterness and hostility.' However, in the short term at any rate, the possibility of a major confrontation between the races seems remote.

One of the areas in which research is most needed concerns the attitudes and beliefs of Africans and their reactions to discrimination. A number of studies have been undertaken in this area but they tend to be deficient in one or more respects. They should be regarded as exploratory studies. The definitive study has yet to be undertaken. Some of the research problems are immense and need to be recognised. Firstly, there is the very real difficulty of persuading Africans to talk freely about their hardships, resentments and the manner in which they perceive race relations in South Africa. There are difficulties even when rapport has been built up over a long period of time. The excellent psycho-analysis of an African witch-doctor undertaken by Sachs (1937) is instructive. There is also the temptation on the part of research workers to seek out African respondents who are better educated. Most surveys on African attitudes and beliefs are not based on representative samples, for example van den Berghe (1962). The reliability of many samples is also questionable. The shortage of suitably-trained African sociologists and interviewers is a further handicap. There are difficulties in communication with African respondents and in the drafting of questionnaires arising from differences in customs, interpretation, manner of speech, etc. Amongst the best studies in recent times are those reported by Edelstein (1972) and Schlemmer (1971). An excellent study of an earlier period has been reported by Biesheuvel (1957).

The classification of reactions to discrimination in terms of avoidance, aggression and acceptance, does not seem to be adequate (Simpson and Yinger 1965: Ch. 7). The study of the Chinese in Johannesburg referred to earlier showed that some respondents ignored the situation, others reported the incident to a higher authority, some refused to obey the injunction and a number of people reacted by displaying friendliness towards the offender. The nature of the minority member's response also needs to be related to the type of discrimination encountered. For example, Chinese tended to withdraw from the field when discrimination was encountered in private institutions, but were apt to comply when the incident took place in government or public offices (Luk Sun 1965:79). Social discrimination and name calling tended to be ignored. Likewise the emotions aroused by the incident were related to the kind of discrimination encountered. Anger was evoked by name-calling, discrimination on public transport, in privately-owned institutions, public offices and in the sphere of recreation. Embarrassment was likely to be encountered in discrimination on public transport or in recreation. Anxiety was characteristic in the face of political discrimination. A sense of depression was aroused by discrimination encountered in employment, education or in the failure to obtain trading or firearm licences. Residential discrimination gave rise to a sense of frustration. A feeling of being unfairly treated was evinced as a result of discrimination in employment, the political sphere and the failure to procure the requisite business or firearm licences (Luk Sun, 1965:69).

Attention needs to be devoted to the psychological, social and economic consequences of discrimination. In discussing the self-evaluation of low-status Whites, Schlemmer asks: 'If lower-status Whites feel relatively demoralised and inadequate, how demoralised and inadequate must Blacks not feel? (Schlemmer 1972:24). This is a legitimate question. Low self-esteem often leads to self-hatred (Simpson and Yinger 1965:147), traces of which are evident in the African population. American studies have shown that a stable and happy family life can act as a buffer against a hostile environment (Pettigrew 1964:15ff). It is doubtful whether the fragmented African family, brought about by the migratory labour system, can fulfil this role.

A number of authorities maintain that members of minority groups are likely to be characterised by a lack of patriotism and an ambivalent attitude towards the law (Simpson and Yinger 1965:141). The costs of discrimination to the nation as a whole also needs to be assessed.

The Myrdal hypothesis relating the fears of Whites to the aspirations of Blacks may well be applicable to South Africa. The hypothesis is that the fears of Whites are inversely related to the aspirations of Blacks (Killian and Grigg 1961).[1] For example, Whites are most fearful of inter-marriage, a matter which is of little concern to Blacks and comes lowest in their list of aspirations. Blacks are most concerned with better jobs and good homes which are amongst the least important of the fears of Whites.

Very little research has been done on the cognitive dimension of prejudice since MacCrone's (1937) early work on stereotypes. There is also a need to study the manner in which stereotypes have changed in response to altered circumstances. Many years ago, Klineberg (1964:Ch.4) suggested that there was a 'kernel of truth' in most stereotypes. He expressed the view that the examination of the 'kernel of truth' was a suitable field of enquiry. Unfortunately, his suggestion does not seem to have given rise to further enquiry. Why are certain characteristics of groups regarded as important? Does the attitude condition the stereotype? How many members of the group need to share the characteristic before it is incorporated into the stereotype? Klineberg also draws attention to the tendency of some people to act in accordance with the stereotype. He refers to a French colleague, placid by nature, who felt impelled to display his Latin temperament at international gatherings because he felt that that was what was expected of him. There is a need to study the relationship between the cognitive and affective dimensions of prejudice. The only South African study undertaken on this relationship (Viljoen 1972) has drawn a conclusion contrary to the data. Nor does the author appear to be aware of the studies which have been undertaken elsewhere, particularly the important study reported by Saenger and Flowerman (1954).

There is a need for developmental studies of race attitudes. Such studies should not only focus on the years in which race awareness manifest itself and race attitudes are formed, but should also study the mechanisms by which attitudes are transmitted. Quinn's (1954) article may be helpful to research workers who wish to initiate studies on this topic in South Africa.

Myths and rationalisations form an essential ingredient of the White cultural ethos. Every society sustains itself, to a certain extent, by means of myths. South Africa is not alone in this respect. An analysis of myths and rationalisations could well be rewarding.

A few final topics might be mentioned as miscellaneous items.

(1) The study of humour in inter-ethnic relations (Burna 1946), which should be entertaining as well as instructive.
(2) The assessment of the extent of 'passing' from the Coloured group into the White group and from the African group into the Coloured group (Eckard 1947).
(3) The relationship between covert attitudes and overt behaviour.
(4) Some tests of the symbolic theories of prejudice (Rose 1957; MacCrone 1957).
(5) The study of regional differences in race attitudes.
(6) An enumeration of the cultural differences between groups which lead to friction and misunderstandings.
(7) The assessment of the extent to which apartheid is leading to 'unity' among the non-White groups.

Research Design and Methods

Perhaps the most urgent need is for a community study of a South African 'Middletown' to be undertaken. Van den Berghe's study of 'Caneville' (van den Berghe 1964; van den Berghe and Miller 1961) is unsatisfactory in a number of respects. 'Caneville' is about as a-typical a town as it is possible to find in South Africa. It is a town which is dominated by a single industry and the sugar industry at that! As it is a perfect example of a 'company town' (van den Berghe 1964:6) it is accordingly unlike most South African towns. The population distribution in Caneville differs very markedly from the distribution in the country as a whole and from most South African towns. It is probably only on the Natal north coast that there are towns in which Indians constitute nearly 70 per cent of the population. The absence of Coloureds and the small proportion of Whites are further limiting conditions. It is apparent from a reading of the book that van den Berghe antagonised the White community, the only group in which he could effectively function as a participant observer. Dollard's work in 'Southerntown' was of a far superior kind. Dollard was able to retain his ethnical standpoint without annoying people. Van den Berghe (1964:9) concedes that he was unable to communicate effectively with the African community. He does, however, claim that he was readily accepted by the Indian community. It is hoped that the future study of a South African 'Middletown' will avoid repeating van den Berghe's mistakes.

There is a need for the more extensive use of experimentation in the study of race relations. Comparatively few sociological experiments of any kind have been carried out in South Africa. It is important to exploit the many advantages which experimentation offers. Laboratory experiments facilitate replication, enable variations to be introduced systematically and permit of the observation of behaviour under controlled conditions. Laboratory experiments may be most suitable for studying the conditions under which change can be induced and in analysing a number of variables which have a bearing on face-to-face contacts. Use should be made of the natural experiment in those cases where it is difficult to bring certain types of behaviour into the laboratory. There are a number of natural experiments of the before-after variety which are fairly easy to undertake. For example, the effect of lifting the prohibition on Africans purchasing 'hard liquor' on the incidence of drunkenness can be ascertained fairly easily. Contrary to the fears of some parliamentarians, there appears to have been a decline in the incidence of drunkenness. A slightly more complicated experiment would be to determine the effect of Mr M. C. Botha's plea for more White babies to celebrate the establishment of the Republic. He claims that his plea had the desired effect.

There is another type of natural experiment which does not fit neatly into the categories of 'before-after' or 'ex post facto.' This has been labelled the 'conversion experiment.' The conversion experiment enables the effect of an important event to be studied by making modifications to a research design which has been prepared for the study of another, albeit related, issue. The study of the effect of the Johannesburg Station explosion is an example (Lever 1969). The conversion experiment is similar to the before-after experiment in that a measurement of the dependent variable is made both before and after the event. In the before-after experiment the important event is anticipated and planned for; in the conversion experiment it is not. Unlike the before-after experiment, the 'before' and 'after' measures in the conversion experiment are not comparable without undertaking modification to the research design. The modification can usually be made by matching respondents either by precision control of frequency distribution control. The conversion experiment makes it possible to study the effect of an event which occurs during the course of a social survey. A crucial event may also occur after a survey has been concluded. Taft (1967) has shown that this type of incident can be studied by undertaking subsequent interviews with a sample of the respondents which had been previously interviewed. The effect of the six-day war on Melbourne Jewry could accordingly be ascertained with a fair degree of precision.

Content analysis of newspapers and magazines can be a fairly inexpensive method of obtaining valuable information. By analysing newspapers Shrieke (1936) was able to study the changing stereotype of the Chinese in America. It is likely that the stereotype of Indians and of other immigrant groups have undergone marked changes from the time of their first entry into South Africa. The study of such changes, particularly when they are linked with economic, social and political changes, will serve to illuminate the sources of intergroup tension in South Africa.

Insufficient use has been made of observations for the study of race relations. Such observations as have been undertaken have been of a casual kind. In order to be most effective, observations need to be undertaken in a systematic manner.

There are a number of difficulties pertaining to the measurement of attitudes. It is often necessary for a number of pilot studies to be undertaken before finalising questionnaires designed for administration to Africans. Biesheuvel's technique for measuring the attitudes of educated Africans (Biesheuvel 1953) needs to be used more extensively. Schlemmer (1971) has used the technique in modified form. A large number of attitude scales have been administered, particularly to Whites, in South Africa. Very often the nature of the research problem has necessitated the construction of a new attitude scale. The use of a variety of attitude scales has made it difficult to compare findings for different regions, different groups and different times. In order to ensure comparability and enhance the contribution to knowledge of attitude studies, it is suggested that such studies be confined, largely, to the use of three attitude scales. If it is necessary to construct a new attitude scale for a particular research problem, it may be prudent to use such a scale in conjunction with at least one of the three attitude scales. It is suggested that the three most suitable attitude scales are MacCrone's scale of attitude towards the Native (or its revision),[2] the Bogardus (1925) social distance test and Hartley and Mintz's (1946) study of the racial saturation point. MacCrone's scale is of the equal-appearing interval type and permits of a detailed study and analysis of the finer gradations of attitude towards Africans. The advantages of the Bogardus social distance test have been pointed out by the present writer (Lever 1972c). In brief, the merits of the scale lie in its validity, reliability, scalability, ease of administration, ease of analysis, and the vast quantities of information which can be gained in a comparatively short time. Furthermore: 'It is the most frequently used of all attitude scales and is probably the only attitude test that permits cross-national comparison' (Lever 1972:204). There have been a number of modifications to the social distance test. Some have been undertaken by Bogardus (1933; 1958) and some have been undertaken by other workers, for example, Dodd 1935:194–204; MacCrone 1957: Ch. 10; Hartley 1944. The early version of the scale (Bogardus 1925; 1928) still appears to be the best (Campbell 1952). The test of the racial saturation point does not appear to have been used in South Africa as yet. It consists of taking a category of social distance, e.g. 'would allow into my school or university' and ascertaining how many members of a racial or ethnic group would be allowed into that category before a 'saturation point' is reached. The 'saturation point' refers to the number or proportion of minority members who will be tolerated or accepted in a particular situation. If a fourth attitude scale is needed it might be based on Thurstone's paired-comparison method (MacCrone 1938). It sometimes becomes desirable to relate the prejudice expressed by a majority group to the prejudice as perceived by a minority group. In such an event, use could be made of Siegel and Greer's (1956) variation of the Bogardus social distance test as a measure of perceived prejudice. In this variation the usual categories of social distance are used but are prefaced by a statement in the form of: 'Do you think English-speaking South Africans willingly admit Africans to . . .'

In studying stereotypes it may be desirable, for a while, to make use of open-ended questions before proceeding to a more structured investigation.

Many studies have floundered because inadequate attention has been paid to sampling. The final *caveat*, therefore, is for the principles of good sampling to be observed.

Conclusion

What is the reason for the inadequate state of our knowledge of race relations in South Africa? The funds available for social research in South Africa are admittedly far more modest than those made available in Britain and America. The lack of a sufficient number of adequately trained research workers is a further aggravating factor. The study of race relations has suffered through neglect. It is submitted that the primary responsibility for the inadequate state of our knowledge rests with South African sociologists. There are many aspects of race relations which are of interest to our colleagues in the various social sciences. But the study of the relations between groups is essentially a problem for sociologists who should have been in the vanguard and not in the rear of those seeking knowledge. South Africans have often been accused of desiring to avoid issues and burying their heads in the sand in ostrich-like fashion. This tendency is discernable in South African sociologists (the 'kernel of truth' in the stereotype?). It is regarded as more convenient, less troublesome and less contentious not to become involved in matters concerning race relations. Mr Harry Oppenheimer (1973) has recently pointed out that the objective study of race relations is apt to be regarded as contentious in South Africa. The study of race relations does necessitate the raising of awkward questions. Yet no scientist worth his salt has ever baulked at this prospect. Sociologists face a difficult future. They need to realise that there can be no progress for sociology in South Africa unless progress is made in the study of race relations. Race relations loom so large on the South African scene that it is not possible to understand South African society without understanding the dynamics of race relations. It will require the concerted efforts of a great many sociologists before we will be able to make a significant contribution to the study of South Africa's most important problem. Sociologists need to bestir themselves.

NOTES:

1. The only South African study is Melamed (1970). The best American studies are Warner and Dennis (1970), Linn (1965), De Fleur and Westie (1958), Kohn and Williams (1956) and of course, the classic Lapiere (1934).
2. The earliest form of the scale was set out in MacCrone (1932). The refined scale (which should be used) is set forth in MacCrone (1957); the revision is by the present writer (Lever, forthcoming).

REFERENCES

Adam, H. 1971a – *Modernising Racial Domination.* University of California Press.
——1971b – *South Africa: Sociological Perspectives.* London: Oxford University Press.
Becker, H. S. and Horowitz, I. L. 1972 – 'Radical politics and sociological research.' *American Journal of Sociology*, 78, 641.
Biesheuvel, S. 1953 – 'A technique for measuring attitudes of educated Africans.' Proceedings of the South African Psychological Association, 4:13–20.
——1957 – 'The influence of social circumstances on the attitudes of educated Africans.' *South African Journal of Science*, 53, 309–14.
Bogardus, E. S. 1925 – 'Measuring social distances.' *Journal of Applied Sociology*, 9:299–308.
——1928 – *Immigration and Race Attitudes.* Boston: Heath.
——1933 – 'A social distance scale.' *Sociology and Social Research*, 17, 265–71.
——1958 – 'Racial distance changes in the United States during the past 30 Years.' *Sociology and Social Research*, 43, 127–35.
Bureau of Market Research, University of South Africa – 'Income and expenditure patterns of non-White urban households.' Research Reports No. 6 and 27.
Campbell, D. T. 1952 – 'The Bogardus social distance scale.' *Sociology and Social Research*, 36, 322–6.
Chein, I. 1949 – 'What are the psychological effects of segregation under conditions of equal facilities?' *International Journal of Opinion and Attitude Research*, 3, 229–34.
Cilliers, S. P. 1972 – 'Some remarks on the State of sociology.' Presidential Address to the Third Congress of Sociologists of Southern Africa.
De Fleur, M. L. and Westie, F. R. 1958 – 'Verbal attitudes and overt acts.' *American Sociological Review*, 23, 667–73.
Deutscher, M. and Chein, I. 1948 – 'The psychological effects of enforced segregation: A survey of social science opinion.' *Journal of Psychology*, 26, 259–87.

Dodd, S. C. 1935 – 'A social distance test in the near East.' *American Journal of Sociology*, 41, 194–204.

Dollard, J. 1939 – *Caste and Class in a Southern Town.* New Haven: Yale University Press.

Edelstein, M. 1972 – *What do Young Africans Think?* Johannesburg: S.A. Institute of Race Relations.

Gray, D. J. 1973 – 'Value-free sociology: A doctrine of hypocrisy and irresponsibility.' In R. Cochrane (ed.), *Advances in Social Research.* London: Constable.

Hartley, E. L. 1944 – *Problems in Prejudice.* New York: Kings Crown Press.

Hartley, E. L. and Mintz, A. 1946 – 'A technique for the study of the dynamics of the racial saturation point.' *Sociometry*, 9, 14–20.

Hellman, E. (ed.) 1949 – *Handbook on Race Relations in South Africa.* Cape Town: Oxford University Press.

Jacobs, S. 1965 – 'Reactions to minority groups status by a group of urban Africans in South Africa.' Honours dissertation, University of the Witwatersrand.

Jabavu, D. D. T. 1920 – *The Black Problem.* Lovedale Press.

Klineberg, O. 1964 – *The Human Dimension in International Relations.* New York: Holt.

Koffka, K. 1935 – *Principles of Gestalt Psychology.* London: Routledge and Kegan Paul.

Kohn, M. L. and Williams, R. M. 1956 – 'Situational patterning in intergroup relations.' *American Sociological Review*, 21, 164–74.

Kuper, L. 1963 – 'Racialism and integration in South African society.' *Race*, 4.

Langschmidt, W. 1962 and 1967 – *An African Day.* Johannesburg: M.R.A.

Lapiere, R. T. 1934 – 'Attitudes vs. actions.' *Social Forces*, 13, 230–7.

Lever, H. 1967 – 'Reducing social distances in South Africa.' *Sociology and Social Research*, 51, 494–502.

——1969 – 'The Johannesburg station explosion and ethnic attitudes.' *Public Opinion Quarterly*, 33, 180–9.

——1972a – *The South African Voter.* Cape Town: Juta.

——1972b – *Applied Sociology.* Johannesburg: Witwatersrand University Press.

——1972c – 'Changes in Ethnic attitudes in South Africa.' Sociology and Social Research, 56:202–10.

——A revision of MacCrone's scale of attitude to the native.

Loubser, J. J. 1972 – 'The values problem and the role of the sociologist in society: Towards a humanistic sociology.' Paper presented to the Third Congress of Sociologists of Southern Africa.

Luk Sun, G. 1965 – 'Some aspects of prejudice and discrimination affecting the Chinese in Johannesburg.' Honours dissertation, University of the Witwatersrand.

Linn, L. S. 1965 – 'Verbal attitudes and overt behaviour: A study of racial discrimination.' *Social Forces*, 43, 353–64.

Luthuli, A. 1962 – *Let My People Go.* New York: McGraw-Hill.

MacCrone, I. D. 1932 – 'An experimental scale for measuring the attitudes of Whites to the Native.' *South African Journal of Science*, 29, 826–30.

——1937 – 'A quantitative study of race stereotypes.' *South African Journal of Science*, 33, 1104–11.

——1938 – 'A comparative study of European and non-European differences in race preferences.' *South African Journal of Science*, 35, 412–16.

——1957 – *Race Attitudes in South Africa.* Johannesburg: Witwatersrand University Press, ch. 14.

Malherbe, E. G. in Holleman, J. F. *et al.* (eds.) – *Problems of Transition.* Pietermaritzburg: Natal University Press. No date supplied.

Melamed, L. 1970 – 'The relationship between actions and attitudes in a South African setting.' *South African Journal of Psychology*, 1, 19–23.

Morse, S. and Orpen, C. – *Contemporary South Africa: A Social Psychological Perspective.* Oxford University Press.

Oppenheimer, H. 1973 – Opening Address to the 43rd Annual Council Meeting of the South African Institute of Race Relations.

Orpen, C. 1972 – 'Internal-external control and brown militancy: The case of a South African minority group.' *Sociology and Social Research*, 56, 466–70.

Pettigrew, T. F. 1964 – *A Profile of the Negro America*. Princeton: Van Nostrand.

Pollak, H. 1968 – *Sociology Post-Graduates of South African Universities*. Durban: Joint University Committee on Sociology and Social Work.

Quinn, O. W. 1954 – 'The transmission of racial attitudes among white Southerners.' *Social Forces*, 33, 41–7.

Rose, A. M. 1957 – 'The causes of prejudice.' In M. L. Barron (ed.) *American Minorities*. New York: Knopf, 76–93.

Rosen, B. C. 1959 – 'Race, ethnicity, and the achievement syndrome.' *American Sociological Review*, 24, 47–60.

Russell, M. 1961 – 'A study of a South African interracial neighbourhood.' Master's dissertation, University of Natal.

Sachs, W. 1937 – *Black Hamlet*. London: Bles.

Saenger, G. 1953 – *The Social Psychology of Prejudice*. New York: Harper.

Saenger, G. and Flowerman, S. 1954 – 'Stereotypes and prejudical attitudes.' *Human Relations*, 7, 217–38.

Schlemmer, L. 1971 – 'City or rural "homeland": A study of patterns of identification among Africans in Durban.' Paper presented to the Second Annual Conference of Sociologists of Southern Africa.

——1972 – 'Social status, perceptions of personal adequacy, and morale: A neglected field of enquiry.' Paper presented to the Third Annual Conference of Sociologists of Southern Africa.

Shaw, Bernard 1932 – *The Apple Cart*. London: Constable.

Sherif, M. and Sherif, C. W. 1956 – *An Outline of Social Psychology*. New York: Harper, 301–28.

Sherif, M. *et al.* 1954 – *Experimental Study of Positive and Negative Intergroup Attitudes Between Experimentally Produced Groups. Robbers Cave Study*. Norman: University of Oklahoma.

Shrieke, B. 1936 – *Alien Americans*. New York: Viking.

Siegel, A. I. and Greer, F. L. 1956 – 'A variation of the Bogardus technique as a measure of perceived prejudice.' *Journal of Social Psychology*, 43, 275–81.

Simpson, G. E. and Yinger, J. M. 1965 – *Racial and Cultural Minorities*. New York: Harper.

Sorokin, P. A. 1937–41 – *Social and Cultural Dynamics*. New York: American Book Co., 4 vols.

Stone, J. 1973 – *Colonist or Uitlander?* London: Oxford University Press.

Stouffer, S. *et al.* 1949 – *The American Soldier*. Princeton: University Press, vol. 1.

Taft, R. 1967 – 'The impact of the Middle East crisis of June 1967 on Melbourne Jewry.' *Jewish Journal of Sociology*, 9, 243–62.

Tiryakian, E. A. 1960 – 'Apartheid and politics in South Africa.' *Journal of Politics*, 22, 682–97.

Van den Berghe, P. L. 1962 – 'Race attitudes in Durban, South Africa.' *Journal of Social Psychology*, 57, 55–72.

——1962 – 'Some trends in unpublished social science research in South Africa.' *International Social Science Journal*, 14, 723.

——1964 – *Caneville, The Social Structure of a South African Town*. Middletown: Wesleyan University Press.

Van den Berghe, P. L. and Miller, E. 1961 – 'Some factors affecting Social relations in a Natal north coast community.' *Race Relations Journal*, 28, 24–31.

Viljoen, H. G. 1972 – 'Nasionale stereotipes en sosiale afstand van 'n groep Afrikaanssprekende studente.' *South African Journal of Sociology*, 4, 61–7.

Warner, L. G. and Dennis, R. M. 1970 – 'Prejudice versus discrimination: An empirical example and theoretical extension.' *Social Forces*, 48, 473–84.

Watts, H. L. 1972 – 'Sociology, the university, and the community.' Pietermaritzburg: University of Natal Press.

Wertheimer, M. 1945 – *Productive Thinking*. New York: Harper.

Williamson, R. C. 1954 – 'Race relations in South Africa.' *Sociology and Social Research*, 39, 165–71.

Wilson, M. 1961 – 'Recent research in race relations in South Africa.' *International Social Science Journal*, 13, 225–44.

Acknowledgements

Acknowledgements and thanks are due to:

The Institute for Race Relations for 'The rise of Black consciousness in South Africa' by **Heribert Adam** from *Race* 15 2(1973) pp 152–7; Donald G. Baker, editor of *Politics of Race* (England: D. C. Heath) for Africa' by **Heribert Adam.**

Sean Archer for 'Perverse growth and income distribution in South Africa' – previously unpublished seminar paper.

The Ravan Press, Johannesburg for 'Marriage and family life' by **Marianne Brindley** from *Western Coloured Township – problems of an Urban Slum* (1976), pp 40–50.

Robert D. Buis for 'The relationship between the dogmatic teachings and attitudes towards race relations of two South African religious denominations' from *Paper* (1975) presented at the 6th annual congress of the Association for Sociology in Southern Africa, Kwaluseni, Swaziland.

The South African Labour Bulletin 2 (1) 1975 for 'The Abolition of the Masters and Servants Act' pp 37–46 by **Colin Bundy.**

People and Profits (published by the Institute of Personnel Management South Africa) for 'Industrial Progress: Its social, political and economic implications' by **S. P. Cilliers.**

S. P. Cilliers for 'Crime in the Coloured Community' from *Crime and Punishment in South Africa* (1975) pp 39–45 J. Midgley, J. H. Steyn and R. Graser (eds) Johannesburg: McGraw-Hill.

New Left Books for 'Marxism: Science or Revolution?' from *From Rousseau to Lenin* (1973 London) by **Lucio Colletti.**

David Philip Publisher (Cape Town) and Wolfgang H. Thomas (ed) for 'Economic Perspective on organised labour and socio-economic development' by **Charles R. Diamond** from *Labour Perspectives on South Africa* (1974) pp 43–60.

Heribert Adam for 'The dilemma of education in plural societies: the South African case' by **H. F. Dickie Clark** from *South Africa: Sociological Perspectives* (1971) Heribert Adam (ed) © Oxford University Press pp 214–227.

Routledge and Kegan Paul Ltd. for 'The impact of the City' by **Allie Dubb** from *The Bantu-speaking Peoples of South Africa* W. D. Hammond-Tooke (ed) pp 456–462.

The Ravan Press, Johannesburg for 'Democratic alternatives to the Westminster Model' by **Andre du Toit** from *South Africa's Political Alternatives* (1973) P. Randall (ed) pp 144–153, 169–171.

Andrew Effrat for 'Introduction to Parsonian Theory' from *Introduction 1968 – Parsonian issue.*

Hermann Giliomee for 'The development of the Afrikaner's self-concept' from *A Look at the Afrikaner Today* (1975) H. W. van der Merwe (ed) Cape Town: Tafelberg pp 25–34.

Roland Graser for 'Ther eformation of the South African penal system: some possibilities.' – previously unpublished paper.

The Society for the Scientific Study of Religion Inc., St John's University Jamaica, New York for 'Religion and Political involvement: A study of Black African sects' by **Robert J. Janosik.**

Kenneth C. Jubber for 'A sociological perspective on religious reality' – previously unpublished paper.

Frederick A. Johnstone and *The Royal African Society, Vol. 69* for 'White prosperity and White supremacy in South Africa.'

Ellison Kahn for 'Law and criminal procedure' from *Crime and Punishment in South Africa* (1975) pp 99–125 J. Midgley, J. H. Steyn and R. Graser (eds), Johannesburg: McGraw-Hill.

Social Dynamics 1975 1 (1) pp 31–4 (Department of Sociology, University of Cape Town) for 'Some problems in race relations research in South Africa' by **Henry Lever.**

Stanford Lyman and Marvin B. Scott for 'Toward a Sociology of the Absurd' from *A Sociology of the Absurd* Appleton Century Crofts 1970 pp 1–12.

The Regents of the University of California, reprinted by permission of the University of California Press for 'Class, status, and ethnicity as perceived by Johannesburg Africans' by **Philip Mayer** from *Change in Contemporary South Africa* Thomson and Butler (eds) pp 138–167.

Fatima Meer for 'Portrait of Indian South Africans' from *Portrait of Indian South Africans* (1969) Durban: Avon House pp 64–73.

Optima for 'The emergent African middle class' by **Nimrod Mkele.**

Christopher Orpen and Juta and Company (Cape Town) for 'White and Black labour relations in historical perspective' from *Productivity and Black Workers in South Africa* (1976) pp 4–14.

Routledge and Kegan Paul for 'South African Society in comparative perspective' by **John Rex** from *Race, Colonialism and the City* (1973).

F. van Zyl Slabbert for 'Politics and Privilege in South Africa' from *South African Society: Its Central Perspectives* (University of Cape Town, Department of Extra-Mural Studies).

Social Dynamics (1975) Sociology Department, University of Cape Town 1 (1) pp 19–30 for 'Social research in a divided society: the case of South Africa' by **David Welsh** and for 'Some problems in race relations research in South Africa' by **Henry Lever.**

Subject Index

Acculturation: 67, 76, 129, 406
Action
- Theory: 18
- individual: 35
Activity/Activism: 15-17
- Political: 86-96
Adaptation: 18-19, 22
Afrikaner
- identity: 58-65
- four patterns of Afrikaner identity: 63-65
- Nationalism: 318
- vis-à-vis English: 61
Alienation: 34
Anomie: 74
apartheid (separate development): 58-59, 196, 206, 231, 287, 356, 360, 397, 402
arbitration: 224
assimilation: 76
- biological: 217, 263
- cultural: 263
- of Black labour: 189
attitudes
- in education: 171-2
- labour: 189
- of White entrepreneurs: 206
- racial: 188, 192
- through family: 124

behaviour
- patterns: 157
- control of: 221
Black Consciousness
- in South Africa: 72-76
Black
- middle class: 285-291
- movement: 52
bureaucracy
- -tization of sects: 93, 95

Calvinism
- and Capitalism: 99
- and race relations: 99-111
capitalism
- Weber's explanation of: 99
caste: 274
category systems: 14
causal relationships: 27
citizenship: 215
coercion
- through law: 221, 316
clans: 149
class: 32, 143, 273, 350
- African entrepreneurial: 206
- African middle-class: 285-291
- and ethnicity/race: 274, 293-301, 352
- consciousness: 27, 32
- dominant class: 63
- working class: 286
collective
- bargaining: 203
- conscience: 137
colonial
- neo, power: 322/3
commodity
- production: 29→
community
- Black: 207
comparative
- perspective on South Africa: 304-312
conceptual scheme: 14
conflict: 36
- and politics: 333-336
- approach to stratification: 272
- in plural society: 175, 207, 210
- in the family: 130
- theory of sect development: 93
control: 164
- law as social control: 221
crime: 246-253
- inal association: 253
- distribution: 266
- in the Coloured community: 261-267
- prevention of: 267
- (Criminal) Procedure Act: 253
culture: 45
- and political policy: 50
- Black: 74→, 227
- change: 68→
- counter-: 45
- differentiation: 168
- leaders: 62
- material/non-material: 46, 48
- nationalism: 75
- of the technological age: 49
- pluralism: 275
- revitilization: 76
- system, Black: 73

– 'thick descriptions of': 47
– vis-à-vis social structure: 49/50
– White: 74→
customs
– and sects: 90
– in law: 235-6
cybernetic
– hierarchy of control: 20

decentralization: 206, 213
de-colonizing
– in S.A.: 321-327
democracy
– systems: 337
– White: 343
determinism
– vs. freedom: 36
differential
– wage levels: 186
discrimination
– against Black labour: 189
drunkenness: 265-6
dysfunction
– in segregated society: 166, 171, 173
– in the family: 130

economy/ic
– development: 212
– differentiation: 286
– growth rate: 214
– implications of Industrial progress: 209-217
– integration: 210
– sector, informal: 182
– subsistence: 183
education: 163
– African: 169→, 204, 364
– and law: 222
– in plural society: 168→
elite
– African: 206, 321
– modernizing: 212
ethnic
– groups: 50/1, 183, 210
– identity: 51
– orientation: 75
ethnography
– ic descriptions of religion: 82
ethnomethodology: 34→
existential
– phenomenology: 34

facts: 14
family: 123→
– and poverty: 131
– conjugal: 126
– extended and nuclear: 126-7, 136, 145
– Indian: 134-144
– lower-class: 129
– matrilocal/matrilineal: 128
– nuclear: 135
– one-parent: 128
– roles: 129-30
– traditional/rural: 127, 147
– urban: 147
fatalism: 15-6
Four-Functions Scheme: 18
franchise: 342-3
Functional/ism: 37, 38
– approach to stratification: 271
– requisites: 21
– vis-à-vis the family: 124
– vis-à-vis religion: 79, 82
function/s
– of the family: 124-5
– of law: 221

game model: 36
goal/s: 210
– attainment: 18-19, 22, 215
group/s
– Areas Act: 228
– ascribed characteristics of: 210
– consciousness: 210
– differentiation: 272
– dominant: 390-1
– ethnic: 210
– identity: 210
– in-group/out-group: 189, 192

housing:
– Coloured: 265

ideal type
– of Calvinism: 100
ideology: 209-217, 336, 352/3
– ical purity in sects: 94
– of kinship solidarity: 149
imprisonment alternatives: 253-257
income
– distribution of: 277, 279-284
– inequality of: 200
industrial
– conciliation (Act): 210, 184, 206
– progress: 209-217
industrialization
– and rural society: 182
– and the family: 125

– and voters: 343
– vis-à-vis Black culture: 74
inequality
– of income: 200
– socially structured: 271
institution: 123, 125, 169, 225
– aspects of industry/labour: 202
– of citizenship: 215
– phenomena: 35
integration: 18-19, 22, 80, 168
– cross-cultural: 110
– economic: 210
– in Indian community: 143
Interactionism
– neo-symbolic: 34→
– social: 36

kinship
– groups: 136-143, 149

Labelling theory: 34→, 243
labour
– and economy: 181→
– and religion: 190
– differentiated: 183
– division of: 188
– laws: 194, 374-5
– organized: 200-207, 364, 375
– patterns: 206-7
– policy: 184, 194
– relations, White and Black: 188→, 286, 357
– structure: 186
– supply and demand: 201
– unrest: 211
law/s
– and crime: 221→
– and Criminal Procedure: 230-238
– definition of: 221-228
– of the market: 29
– Modern S. African: 235
legislation: 230
legitimation crisis: 50

majority rule: 173-4
marginality: 266
marriage
– and family life: 152-159
– problems: 152
Marxism: 27-33
– and Black workers: 298
– and Race Relations: 305
– and Religion: 80
– and Structure/Change: 349-353
– as a science: 27-30
– as revolution: 30-33
Masters and Servants Act
– abolishment of: 373
miscegenation: 58, 189
mobility: 125
– occupational: 357
– social: 166
mode of production
– capitalist: 30
modernization
– and family life: 124→
– economic: 181
moral ideal: 30
Movement
– Millenarian: 87
– Political: 87

nation state: 215/6
national/ism
– compensation board: 252
– multi-n.: 75, 216
– symbols: 86
naturalistic objectivism: 28
norms: 37, 141, 227
nucleation: 142

objectivity: 14
– existence: 35
opportunity, job: 193, 213
organization
– al activity of sects: 87
– of education: 163
– of factors of production: 99, 100
– of trade unions: 202
– political: 86-96
– religious: 86-96

pattern maintenance: 18-19, 22
pattern variables: 18
phenomenological approach to religion: 80
physical types: 262
placement: 124
plural, society and education: 168→
pluralism of associations: 94
polarization, politically: 335-6
politics/al
– alternative systems and SA.: 336
– and privilege: 340–346
– implications of Industrial progress: 209-217
– institutions: 316
– introduction: 315-319
– system: 315

– theology: 115
population: 187
– groups: 60-65, 262
– Registration Act: 228
– vis-à-vis religious attitudes: 102
power: 341
– structure and Millenarian movements: 87
poverty: 131, 186, 200
process, social: 16, 406
– distributive: 271
– of identification: 64
– of men: 207
– of production: 29
– labour: 31
– learning: 163
– life: 29/30
– middle-range: 55
production
– factors of: systematic application: 99, 100
productivity of labour: 31
Protestantism and Capitalism: 99→
punitive measures: 246-257
– misconceptions about: 258

race
– and class: 352, 374
– caste system: 73
– interracial interaction disability: 72
– multi-racialism: 72
– prejudice: 75, 205, 388
– racial dichotomy: 59
– racial separatism: 89
–relations: 58, 207, 408-412
– White race: 58/9
reality: 29, 30
– social construction of: 113, 114
rehabilitation: 241
religion: 79-83
– and race relations attitudes: 99-111, 297
– and social change: 86-96
– and social class: 81
– anti-religion tradition: 114
– Marxist approach to: 80
– origin of: 117
– phenomenological approach to: 80
– religious pluralism: 81
reproduction: 131
research
– and bureaucracy: 393
– and race relations: 399-412, 401
– design and methods: 408
– H.S.R.C. (Human Sciences Research Council): 391, 403
– in a divided society: 385-398
– permits: 392
– problems, opportunities: 383→
– suggested areas: 403
restitution: 224
revolution: 27-33
– ary attitudes: 86
– ary theology: 115
– ideology: 32
ritual: 69, 92, 149
roles: 37, 70, 123, 124/5, 129/30, 146, 156
– economic: 185
– marital: 130
– strain: 130
– through education: 165

sects: 82, 86-96, 172
– and nationalistic political organizations: 88
– independent African: 86-96
– organized activity of: 87
secularization
– of the polity: 86
self-concept
– The Afrikaners': 58-65
social
– change: 15, 22-24, 209-217, 300/1, 349→
– change and religion: 81
– controls: 163
– differentiations: 163, 168
– implications of Industrial Progress: 209-217
– infrastructure: 211, 213/4
– institution: 123, 163
– meliorism: 38
– order: 37/8, 118
– reality: 36
– stratification: 166
– structure: 209 (and change: 349→)
– training: 249
socialism: 27
socialization: 127, 159, 163
society
– and religion: 82
– cross-cultural analysis of: 125
– South African: comparative perspective: 304-312
– static: 15, 16
structure: 209

- subsistence: 188
socio-economics
- of the Coloured population: 264
sociology
- of religion (introduction): 79-84
- of the Absurd: 34-40
- theory: 13
State
- dissolution of the: 30
- philosophy of the: 30
- the economic: 29→
- the political: 30→
solidarity: 144
- kinship: 149
status: 124, 263
- and ethnicity/class: 293-301, 407
- in sects: 94
- quo and challenging sects: 87→
- quo and order: 315
strain, in social structure: 209-217
stratification (social)
- and colour: 271→, 323
- in townships: 299
- Readings on: 276
structure
- al theory: 349-353
- and change: Marxist analysis: 349-353
- of S.A. courts: 225
Structural Functionalism: 18-24
- of education: 163
subculture: 37, 45
subjective
- knowledge: 35
- meaning: 34-35
sub-systems of Action: 20
system: 201
- caste: 183
- electoral: 329-333
- kinship: 134
- of family: 128
- of Protestant beliefs: 99
- of rewards: 209
- of stratification: 271, 273
- multi-party: 329
- penal: 241-260
- social: 165
- socio-cultural: 210

tautology: 113
theology
- revolutionary: 115
- secular: 115
theory
- of Dependence: 55
two-party system: 331-3

urban/ization
- and the family: 134
- influx control:
- Urban areas (Bantu) Consolidation Act: 228
- vis-à-vis Black S.A. family: 145

validity/validation: 117
value/s: 14, 124, 130-1, 227, 305
- change in: 87
- criminal: 248
- in education: 171
- in research: 400
- judgements: 27, 164
- surplus: 31
- systems: 38, 305
- the law of: 28
victim compensation fund: 251
voluntary associations: 86, 144

wage/s
- Act: 206
- Black: 364
- White: 365
westernization: 262
'Westminster' model: 329
White
- prosperity and supremacy: 356-370
witchcraft: 67-71
workers
- white collar: 287

Author Index

Abraham, J. H.: 7, 9
Abrams M.: 302
Adam H.: 51, 56, 61, 65, 318, 320, 323 328, 412
Adams G.: 65, 66
Alant C. J.: 84
Almond G. A.: 86, 96
Althusser L.: 272, 278, 349, 353, 354, 355
Altizer T.: 115, 118
Andreski S.: 174, 177, 327, 328
Anscombe G. E. M.: 35, 41
Apter D.: 92, 96
Aron R.: 13, 17
Asheron A.: 323, 328
Ashley B. J.: 163, 164, 166
Aston P. J.: 154, 159
Aubert V.: 229
Austin J. L.: 40, 41

Babbie E. R.: 383, 384
Baker D. G.: 52, 56, 318, 320
Bales R. F.: 18, 20, 23, 25, 26, 125, 132
Balibar E.: 349, 354, 355
Barnett D. L.: 96
Barrett D. B.: 84
Bates S.: 248, 260
Becker H. S.: 400
Beinart B.: 229
Bekker S. B.: 315, 320
Bell C.: 129, 132
Bell D.: 49, 56
Bellah R. N.: 20, 25, 26, 96
Bendix R.: 99, 111, 276, 278, 302, 390, 398
Bengu S. M. E.: 53, 56
Bennett J. W.: 25
Berger P. L.: 7, 9, 48, 56, 84, 113, 118
Beukes D. P. M.: 61, 65
Biesheuvel S.: 391, 398, 406, 410, 412
Blackstone Sir W.: 224, 229
Blau P.: 166
Blauner R.: 73, 76
Blumer H.: 58, 65, 205, 207, 367, 372
Bock K. E.: 37, 41
Boettner L.: 103, 113
Bogardus E. S.: 410, 411, 412
Bolton F. G.: 164, 166
Botha M. C.: 171, 173, 177
Bott E.: 129, 132
Bottomore T. B.: 8, 9, 272, 278
Brand S. S.: 198
Brandel-Syrier M.: 151, 302
Bretton H. L.: 327, 328
Breytenbach B.: 64, 65
Breytenbach W. J.: 181
Bright W.: 40, 41
Brink A. P.: 65
Brookes H. E.: 171, 173, 177
Broom L.: 8, 9, 45, 56
Bryant A. T.: 70, 71
Budd S.: 84
Bullough S.: 107, 111
Bundy C.: 374, 379
Burchinall L.: 129
Burgess E. W.: 8, 9, 125, 132
Burna M.: 408
Butler A. J.: 223, 229

Cabral A.: 74, 75, 76
Campbell C.: 84
Campbell D. T.: 411, 412
Cantril H.: 300, 303
Carr E. H.: 14, 17
Carter D.: 298, 303
Carter G. M.: 395, 398
Carstens K. N.: 89, 96
Carstens W. P.: 395, 398
Carter J. M.: 102, 111
Cawood L.: 84, 89, 96
Chartier E. A.: 116, 118
Chein I.: 401, 412
Chilver E. M.: 96
Chinoy E.: 8, 9
Cilliers S. P.: 8, 9, 156, 157, 264, 265, 267, 400, 412
Clark B. R.: 163, 165, 166
Cohen R.: 275, 276, 278
Coleman J.: 94, 96
Coleman J. A.: 93, 96
Cooper D.: 123, 132
Corbally J. E.: 164, 166
Coser L.: 41, 169, 177
Cowen D. V.: 173, 177
Cox O. C.: 272, 275, 278, 305, 308, 312
Cross F. F.: 99, 111
Currin T. V.: 84

Dahl R.: 330, 338
Dahrendorf R.: 94, 97, 164, 167

Dale Dr.: 285
Danziger K.: 65
Davies R.: 277, 278
Davis K.: 124, 132, 312
Davis R.: 272, 278, 304
Day F. D.: 222
Dean L. R.: 24, 25
De Fleur M. L.: 412
Degenaar J.: 65, 66
De Kiewiet C. W.: 191, 192, 199, 285, 292
De Klerk W: 60, 66
Dennis R. M.: 412, 414
Deutsche K.: 25
Deutscher M.: 401, 412
Devereaux Jr. E. C.: 35, 41
De Vos G.: 75, 76
de Wet Nel M. C.: 292
Dobb M.: 28, 33
Dobson G.: 154, 159
Dodd S. C.: 411, 413
Dollard J.: 403, 413
Douglas M.: 113, 117, 118
Dreeben R.: 24, 25
Deurden J. E.: 386, 398
Duminy J. P.: 171, 173, 177
Duncan O. D.: 166
du Preez P.: 59, 60, 66
du Toit A. B.: 58, 66
Duverger M.: 330, 338

Easton D.: 333, 338
Eckard M.: 408
Edelstein M.: 302, 406, 413
Eiselen W. M. M.: 197, 199
Eisenstadt S. N.: 25, 55, 56, 181, 187
Ellis B. L.: 84
Emmanuel A.: 327, 328
Erikson E.: 64, 66
Esslin M.: 39, 40, 41
Etzioni A.: 26, 97

Fallding H.: 168, 177
Farson N.: 97
Fernandez J. W.: 84, 97
Fife R. H.: 385, 398
Firestone S.: 130, 132
Firth R.: 46, 56
Flanagan R. J.: 203, 208
Fletcher J.: 38, 41
Flew A.: 40, 41
Flowerman S.: 408, 414
Flynn E. E.: 243, 245, 260
Form W. H.: 278
Fouchalt M.: 36, 41
Frank A. G.: 55, 56
Franklin N. N.: 198, 199
Fredrickson G. M.: 324, 328
Free L.: 300, 303
Friedrichs R. W.: 8, 9
Froneman G. F. van L.: 370
Furnivall J. S.: 176, 177, 306, 312

Gaiman D.: 383, 384
Gallati R. R. J.: 222
Gans H.: 129, 132
Garrett W. R.: 115, 118
Gavron H.: 153, 159
Geertz C.: 46, 47, 54, 56
Gelfand M.: 84
Geras N.: 349, 355
Gerdener G. B. A.: 102, 111
German A.: 222, 229
Gerwel J.: 65, 66
Giddens A.: 13, 17
Gil D. G.: 131, 132
Giliomee H.: 51, 56
Glazer N.: 277, 278
Gluckman M.: 67, 68, 71, 97
Goldblatt D.: 302
Good K.: 327, 328
Goode W. J.: 123, 126, 132
Gordimer N.: 76
Gordon M. M.: 37, 41
Gouch K.: 123, 132
Gouldner A. W.: 8, 9, 48, 56
Gracey H. L.: 8, 9
Gray D. J.: 400, 413
Greer F. L.: 411, 414
Grigg M.: 407
Gumperz J. J.: 40 41
Gumplowicz L.: 41
Gwynn-Jones I.: 249, 260

Habenstein R. W.: 156 159, 160
Habermas J.: 50, 56
Hagen E. E.: 24, 25
Hahlo K. G.: 55, 56
Halevy E.: 376, 379
Hammond-Tooke W. D.: 54, 56, 84, 127, 132, 149, 150, 151
Hansard M.: 175, 177
Hansen D. A.: 163, 167
Harbison F. H.: 204, 208
Harmondsworth: 302
Hartley E. L.: 410, 411, 413
Helfer R. E.: 131, 132

Heller C.: 276, 278
Hellman E.: 128, 132, 146, 147, 150, 151, 302
Hepple A.: 265, 372
Herbert S. A.: 97
Higgins E.: 84
Hilferding: 27
Hill M.: 84
Himmelstrand U.: 299, 303
Hirschman A.: 207, 208
Hobart Houghton D.: 291, 292
Hobsbawn E. J.: 97
Hobson J. A.: 390, 398
Hodgkin T.: 97
Holt N.: 254, 260
Hopkinson T.: 172, 177
Horowitz I. L.: 400
Horrell M.: 97, 170, 177, 204, 207, 208, 294, 303, 357, 359, 364, 371, 372
Horton J.: 176, 177
Horton P. B.: 8, 9
Horwitz R.: 367, 372
Hoselitz B. F.: 55, 56
Houghton D. H.: 198, 199, 370
Hoult T. F.: 97
Hughes A. J.: 97
Humphreys A. S. B.: 156, 159
Humphries A. S. B.: 182, 187
Hunt C. L.: 8, 9
Hunter M.: 150, 151, 289, 292
Husserl E.: 34, 35, 41
Hutt W. H.: 367, 372
Hymes D.: 40, 41

Inkeles A.: 8, 9, 164, 167

Jabavu D. D. T.: 404, 413
Jacobs S.: 402, 413
James W.: 113, 118
Janeway E.: 130, 132
Jencks C.: 166, 167
Johnson C.: 24 or 25
Johnstone F. A.: 52, 56, 351, 355
Joubert D.: 58, 66
Joubert D. D.: 8, 9
Jubber K. C.: 84

Kahn E.: 239, 240
Karari N.: 96
Karis T.: 395
Kempel H. C.: 131, 132
Kenyatta J.: 97
Khoapa B. A.: 73, 76
Kiernan: 84
Killian: 407
Kilson M.: 97
Klineberg O.: 407, 413
Kluckhohn C.: 45, 56
Kockelman J. J.: 34, 41
Kohn M. L.: 412, 413
Kornhauser W.: 176, 177
Krige E. J.: 70, 71
Kuhn T.: 26
Kuper H.: 396
Kuper L.: 59, 66, 97, 171, 173, 177, 275 278, 302, 327, 328, 335, 339
Kuyper A.: 103, 111

La Barre Weston: 115, 118
Laing R. D.: 123, 131, 132
Lakeman E.: 330, 339
Langschmidt W.: 405, 413
Lanternari V.: 84
Lapiere, T. R.: 412, 413
Laubser J. J.: 400, 413
Leakey L. S.: 97
Leary P. M.: 362, 372
Leavis F. R.: 13, 17
Legassick M.: 277, 278, 354, 355
Leistner G. N. E.: 181, 187
Lever H.: 384, 399, 400, 401, 409, 411, 412, 413
Lever J.: 52, 56, 184
Levy M. J.: 25, 26 or 27
Lewin J.: 289, 292
Lewis . . .: 302
Lewis J. E. S.: 362, 372
Lidz T.: 157, 159
Lifton R. J.: 164, 167
Linn L. S.: 412, 413
Lipset S. M.: 24, 25, 276, 278, 331, 332, 339
Little K.: 188, 199
Lloydd P. C.: 293, 303
Locke H. J.: 125, 132
Longmore L.: 145, 150, 151, 289, 292
Loram C. T.: 386
Lorenz K.: 36, 41
Loubser J. J.: 401, 413
Luckmann T.: 48, 113, 118
Luk Sun G.: 402, 407, 413
Luthuli A.: 405, 413
Lund H. M.: 157, 159
Lynd R. S.: 157, 159

Maasdorp G.: 156, 159, 182, 187
Mabona M.: 84

Maccoby M.: 166, 167
Mac Crone I. D.: 101, 111, 188, 199, 407, 411, 412, 413
Machlup F.: 165, 167
Macmillan W. M.: 387, 398
Mafeje A.: 148, 150, 151 396, 398
Mair L.: 95, 97
Malherbe E. G.: 193, 199, 357, 365, 368, 372, 388, 389, 398, 413
Malinowski B.: 46, 56
Manganyi N. C.: 53, 56
Mann M.: 300, 303
Mannhein K.: 166, 167
March J. C.: 97
Marcuse H.: 15, 17, 48, 56
Maritz F. A.: 84
Marsden D.: 157, 159
Marshall T. H.: 215, 218
Marty M. E.: 107, 111
Marx G.: 97
Marx K.: 27, 33, 349, 354
Matson F.: 38, 41
Maud R.: 323, 324, 325, 328
Mayer: 310
Mayer I.: 302
Mayer P.: 54, 56, 145, 151, 295, 302, 303, 312, 395, 398
Mazrui A.: 321, 328
McCord W.: 159, 160
McEwen W. J.: 94, 97
McKenzie J. L.: 107, 111
Mead M.: 97
Meer F.: 74, 84
Melamed L.: 412, 413
Mennell S.: 14, 17
Merleau-Ponty M.: 34, 41, 42
Merton R. K.: 41
Middleton, J.: 97
Miller E.: 408, 414
Millett K.: 130, 132
Mills C. W.: 7, 9, 38, 46, 56
Mintz A.: 410, 413
Mitchell J.: 130, 132
Mitchell R. C.: 97
Mitchell W. C.: 25
Moddie T. D.: 84
Moore W. E.: 272, 278, 304, 312
Moorrees A.: 102, 111
Morgan D. H. J.: 123, 132
Morse S.: 413
Moynihan D. P.: 277, 278
Mulder C. P.: 327
Murdock G. P.: 123, 125, 132
Myers C. A.: 204, 208
Myrdal G.: 14, 15, 17

Newman K. J.: 331, 339
Ngcobo: 389
Nicholson J. L.: 284
Nienaber P. J: 58, 66
Norbeck E.: 97
Nordlinger E. A.: 319, 320
Norval A. J.: 198, 199
Nyquist T.: 301

O'Connell J.: 97
O'Dea: 84
O'Dear T. F.: 84
O'Dowd M.: 319, 320
Oliver N. J. J.: 197, 199
Oliver R.: 97
O'Neill J.: 48, 49, 56
Oosthuizen G. C.: 84
Oppenheimer H.: 411, 414
Orpen C.: 198, 199, 404, 413, 414
Ossowksi S. 272, 278

Packard V.: 285, 292
Pareto V.: 15, 17
Park R. E.: 8, 9
Parsons T.: 14, 17 18, 19, 20, 23, 24, 25, 26, 35, 42, 46, 56, 124, 125, 132, 215, 218, 305, 312
Paton D.: 103, 111
Pauw B. A.: 85, 128, 132, 145, 148, 150, 151.
Pauw S.: 398
Pease J.: 278
Peerman D. G.: 107, 111
Pelzer: 59, 61, 65
Pettigrew T. F.: 407, 414
Pieterse J. E.: 62, 66
Plant J. S.: 155, 160
Pollak H.: 398
Popper K.: 354, 355
Potgieter J. F.: 371
Poulantzas N.: 349, 350, 354, 355
Powell G.: 86, 96
Pross H.: 176, 177
Przeworski A.: 87, 97
Pursell D. E.: 202, 208

Queen S. A.: 156, 159, 160
Quinn O. W.: 408, 414

Rabie J.: 61, 65, 66
Radin P. 115, 119

Rae D. W.: 330, 339
Reader D. H.: 54, 56, 149, 151
Reeves D.: 75, 76
Reinders, J. E.: 85
Reiss Jr. A. J.: 8, 9
Retief G. M: 227, 229
Rex J.: 172, 176, 177, 275, 278, 302, 303 304, 312
Rhoodie N. J.: 50, 56
Richardson B. D.: 362, 372
Ricoeur P.: 46, 56
Robertson R.: 84
Rogers C.: 164, 167
Rokkan S.: 331, 332, 339
Rose A. M.: 408, 414
Rose P. I.: 8, 9
Rose R.: 333, 334, 339
Rosen B. C.: 406, 414
Rothberg R.: 97
Roux J. P.: 242, 260
Runciman W.: 302
Russel M.: 401, 402, 414
Ryle G.: 40, 42
Rytina: 278

Sachs W.: 406, 414
Sack G.: 302
Saenger G.: 401, 408, 414
Scarr H. A.: 25
Schapera I.: 388
Schillebeeckx E.: 107, 112
Schlemmer L.: 51, 56, 198, 199, 317, 406, 407, 410, 414
Schumpeter J.: 274, 278
Schutz A.: 34, 42, 113, 119, 298, 303
Scott C. P.: 14, 17
Scott J. F.: 41, 42
Scott M. B.: 37
Selznick P.: 8, 9, 45, 56, 222, 224, 229
Shaw B.: 414
Shaw M.: 273, 278
Shelley P. B.: 13, 17
Shepherd W. C.: 114, 119
Shepperson G.: 91, 97
Sherif C.: 414
Sherif M.: 401, 414
Shils E. A.: 18, 20, 23, 25, 26
Shrieke B.: 410, 414
Shwayder D. S.: 40, 42
Siegel A. I.: 411, 414
Silvert K. H.: 93, 96, 97
Simmel G.: 36, 40, 42, 174, 177
Simon D.: 376, 779
Simons H.: 302
Simons H. J.: 274, 278, 289, 292
Simons R.: 302
Simpson G. E.: 406, 407, 414
Simson N.: 354, 355
Skinner B. F.: 164, 167
Slabbert F. van Zyl: 318, 320
Smelser N. J.: 20, 26
Smith: 306
Smith D.: 92, 98
Smith M. G.: 176, 177, 275, 278, 312
Sneddon D.: 164, 167
Sorokin P. A.: 13, 17, 404, 414
Spandau A. M. K. M.: 201, 208
Spiro M. E.: 127, 132
Stalin J.: 33
Stark W.: 87, 98
Steenkamp W. F. J.: 205, 207, 208
Stouffer S.: 405, 414
Strijdom J. G.: 58, 66
Stuckert R. P.: 129, 132
Stultz N. M.: 395
Sundkler B. G. M.: 70, 71, 85, 89, 90, 91, 98
Sussman M.: 129, 133
Szasz T.: 36, 42

Taft R.: 410, 414
Talmon Y.: 87, 98
Teunte H.: 87, 97
Theodorson G. A.: 25
Theron P. A.: 197, 199
Thion S.: 372
Thompson E.: 298, 303
Thompson J. D.: 94, 97
Thompson L. M.: 276, 278, 315, 320
Thoreau H. D.: 17
Thrupp S. L.: 86, 98
Tillich P.: 15, 17
Tiryakian E. A.: 34, 35, 41, 42
Trapido G.: 354, 355
Treurnicht A. P.: 61, 66
Tumin M.: 25
Turner H. W.: 88, 97, 98
Turner R.: 129, 133

Ulman L.: 203, 208

van den Berghe P. J.: 176, 177, 394, 395, 398, 402, 406, 408, 409, 414
van der Horst S.: 184, 187
Verster J.: 151
Verwoerd H. F.: 197, 199, 386
Vilakazi A.: 85

Viljoen H. G.: 408, 414
Viljoen M.: 65, 66
Vincent H.: 96
Vosloo A. H.: 378, 379
Voster B. J.: 59, 60, 61, 66

Wallace A.: 98
Wallerstein I.: 96, 98
Wallis R.: 383, 384
Warner L.: 305, 312
Warner L. G.: 412, 414
Warner W. L.: 274, 278
Watson G.: 275, 278
Watts H. L.: 400, 415
Weber M.: 25, 26, 35, 42, 98, 99, 100, 111, 112, 305, 312, 316, 320, 333, 339
Weber P.: 62, 66
Welbourne F. B.: 98
Welsh D.: 62, 66
Welz S. E.: 85
Werthumer M.: 415
West M.: 54, 57, 85
West M. E.: 274, 278, 394, 398
Westie F. R.: 412
Whisson M. G.: 54, 57, 85
Wiendieck G.: 384
Wilensky H. L.: 48, 57
Williams R. M.: 412, 413
Williamson R. C.: 415
Wilmott P.: 129, 133
Wilson B. R.: 98
Wilson D. F.: 365, 372
Wilson F.: 183, 187, 302
Wilson F. W.: 225, 229
Wilson M.: 148, 150, 151, 276, 278, 396, 398, 415
Wirth L.: 390, 398
Wirth M.: 129, 133
Wittgenstein L.: 40, 42
Wolpe H.: 354, 355
Wolpe M.: 277, 278
Worsley P.: 98
Wright H. M.: 273, 278
Wrong D. H.: 8, 9

Yinger J. M.: 406, 407, 414
Young M.: 129, 133
Yudelman D.: 320

Zalba S. R.: 131, 133
Zeitlin I. M.: 14, 17, 273, 278
Znaniecki F.: 398